THE ORCHESTRA FROM BEETHOVEN TO BERLIOZ

INTERIOR OF LA SCALA AT MILAN

The Orchestra

FROM BEETHOVEN TO BERLIOZ

A history of the Orchestra in the first half of the
19th century, and of the development of
orchestral baton-conducting,

by

ADAM CARSE

Fellow of the Royal Academy of Music

CAMBRIDGE
W. HEFFER & SONS LTD.

First published 1948

Printed in Great Britain at the Works of
W. HEFFER & SONS LTD., CAMBRIDGE, ENGLAND

Preface

THE present volume is intended to form a continuation of the author's *The Orchestra in the 18th Century* (1940), and carries on the history from the end of that century up to the middle of last century. But the clear lines of demarcation in the calendar of time cannot be applied to musical history; an entirely fresh start can never be made at any particular moment or stage of the story. The end of the year 1799 did not mark the conclusion of a period in the evolution of the orchestra, nor did a fresh period begin in January, 1800; therefore, in order to make it self-contained and to render the story intelligible and continuous, it has been necessary to recapitulate in the present volume a certain amount of the matter already more fully treated in the earlier work.

Following the same plan, the present history, after surveying the constitution and development of orchestras in general, goes on to set forth in more detail the history of particular orchestras. The greater length of these separate histories is due not only to the facts that orchestras in the 19th century were more numerous, larger, and took a more influential part in the development of musical art than those of the previous century, but also because so much more of the information concerning musical activity in the 19th century has been preserved and is recoverable. The preservation of these records is largely due to a great increase in the number of musical periodicals during the early 19th century.

An orchestra is treated only too often as a corporate body in which only the conductor and the leader have names of their own. The nameless players that form the main body are too readily taken for granted, or may be identified only by the name of the instrument on which they play. This throws a disproportionately strong light on two individuals who by themselves can do nothing, and covers up with an obscuring veil of anonymity the real human material of which an orchestra is made. Neither conductor nor leader, nor both together, constitute the main structure of an orchestra, nor can they rightly be regarded as the backbone or framework around which the whole is built up. Each player, for better or for worse, contributes something to the whole, each player has a name and individuality, and it is only the combination of so many individuals that makes possible the existence of the corporate body. In these pages, therefore, an orchestra will not be regarded as if it were the human equivalent of a flock of sheep.

The decision to adopt the same policy as before of naming, at any rate, the principal players in each orchestra when they can be recovered, has been taken only after due consideration, and as the only possible way of making the subject live. To refer to the first flute or the first clarinet player in any particular orchestra is as good as saying nothing; both are indispensable units of the whole, and it is giving no information merely to say that they existed. It is only when these players can be named, or when something can be told about their individuality, that they come to life again and begin to breathe as human beings rather than as anonymous units of a dead community who might as well have been identified, like convicts, by a number. But when it can be said, for example, that Charles Nicholson was the first flute, and that Thomas Willman was the first clarinet player in the orchestra at the King's Theatre in London, that Baumann the bassoon player looked like Napoleon III, that André the serpent player eventually kept a public house at Gloucester, or that the Leipzig trombone player Queisser married the proprietress of a prosperous beer garden near that city, it is only then that we get into touch with the human elements of a community which is made up of separate beings, and who can be identified only by their names.

The wind players in an orchestra, each entrusted with a part of his own, the principals of which play important solo parts in practically every piece that is performed, are just as essential and vital parts of an orchestra as are the conductor and the leader; the rank and file of the string players contribute what neither conductor nor principals can supply; all share alike in weaving together the fabric that is made up of separate strands, and each strand is an individual with an instrument, and each individual has a name. In these pages will be found the names and sometimes the individual characteristics of hundreds of players, many of whom were the first to translate into sound the great orchestral works written from the time when Beethoven produced his first symphony up to the time when Berlioz laid down his pen.

It is obvious that complete lists of all the orchestras (amounting to several hundred) that played during a period of fifty years could not possibly be assembled in one book, even if they were all obtainable; but in order to give a more complete picture than could be provided by mentioning a number of selected names, some lists of orchestras, complete from conductor to triangle player or librarian, are supplied in an Appendix.

Next in importance to the actual material (the human beings and their musical instruments) of which an orchestra is made, is the method of control by which it is enabled to operate as one composite instrument. The orchestral baton-conductor was the product of the first half of last century. The advent of this new influence and most radical change in the history of orchestral performance has been treated at some length in a chapter devoted to that subject, and is followed by an attempt to reconstruct and characterise the methods of those who were pioneers in this new branch of executive musical art.

Wagner could not have made his scores what they are had he been obliged to write for none other than the wind instruments that were known to Beethoven as a young man. The enormous strides that were made in developing the mechanics and acoustics of wind instruments during the first half of last century, together with the influence which these new devices exercised on orchestral performance and on the art of orchestration, justifies a chapter devoted mainly to the progress achieved by the makers engaged in this particular craft.

Few of those who listen to an orchestra ever give a thought to the important and laborious process of writing, copying, engraving and diffusing the scores and parts of the music without which an orchestra would be a useless thing. Scores and parts are not merely incidental to orchestra playing; they are the prerequisites of every performance, and the supply of these initial necessities must therefore be important and influential. A chapter in which they are given undivided attention will throw some light on an aspect of orchestral history which is generally overlooked or taken for granted, but on which the development of orchestras has always largely depended.

The aim has been to present in these pages as much as possible of the available information in the form of plain and substantiated historical facts rather than to fashion them into an interesting and readable story, and also to avoid the useless speculation and vague æstheticism which are so often offered as history.

Orchestral history being the sole purpose of this book, much of the general musical history, which would have hopelessly overloaded these pages and can easily be found in plenty of standard books of reference and other historical works, has been omitted. Among these omissions are the dates of the birth and death of all musicians that can be found without difficulty in Grove's *Dictionary*, also much well-known biographical and other matter that is easily accessible in even the smallest of musical libraries. In selecting the illustrations, portraits of the great composers of the period and other pictorial matter which must already be familiar to all readers of musical literature, have likewise been rejected in favour of more relevant pictures that are not so easily accessible to the general reader. Most of these appear for the first time since their original publication.

No apology is offered for the ample number of foot-note references to be found in these pages. They are indispensable in a work which must necessarily be based entirely on the contemporary evidence of one hundred or more years ago, and which is the first in any language to be devoted exclusively to the orchestral history of the prescribed period. In order to save the frequent repetition of some lengthy titles, books are usually identified in the foot-notes by means of the author's names, or if necessary, by abbreviated titles. The full titles will be found in the Bibliography.

Grateful acknowledgment for valuable assistance or for the loan of essential material is due to the following: the late E. Alexander, Esq., Augener, Ltd., W. F. H. Blandford, Esq., the late G. R. Crawford, Esq., A. W. Coates, Esq., Prof. O. E. Deutsch, Barry Duncan, Esq., Paul Hirsch, Esq., Cecil Hopkinson, Esq., Dr. A. Loewenberg, Ernest Newman, Esq., Novello & Co., Ltd., C. B. Oldman, Esq., F. G. Rendall, Esq., Dr. Percy A. Scholes, and to Lyndesay G. Langwill, Esq., for valuable help in proof-reading.

Gt. Missenden, 1946.   ADAM CARSE.

Contents

	PAGE
PREFACE	v
LIST OF ILLUSTRATIONS..	xi

CHAPTER I. Introduction: The Setting 1

Composers—Output—Contemporary music—Revival of J. S. Bach's music—Tardy appreciation of Schubert's music—Domination of opera—Lack of concert halls—Programmes—Patronage—Decline of court musical establishments—Opera houses—Political influences—Schools of music.

CHAPTER II. Constitution and Strength 18

Increase in the size of orchestras—The string orchestra—Proportionate strength of parts—More basses than 'cellos in Italian orchestras—The wood-wind group—Standard group of eight—Extra wood-wind parts—Piccolo—Cor Anglais parts—Bass clarinet parts—Basset-horn—Double-bassoon—The brass group—Four horns—Trombones—Serpent-Ophicleide-Tuba—Stage bands—Harp and percussion instruments—Tables showing strength of orchestras—Festival orchestras.

CHAPTER III. Orchestras in France 67

The royal orchestra—Opera-houses in Paris—The Opéra orchestra—Théâtre Italien—Opéra comique—Concert orchestras—The rue de Cléry concerts—The Société des Concerts or Conservatoire concerts—Other orchestral concerts in Paris—Dance and entertainment orchestras—Musard's promenade concerts—Orchestras in French provincial towns.

CHAPTER IV. Orchestras in Germany.. 107

Decentralisation of music in Germany—Berlin, the court opera—The Königstädter theatre—Dresden—Munich—The Gewandhaus orchestra at Leipzig—Orchestras at Stuttgart, Frankfort, Darmstadt, Brunswick, Hanover, Cassel, Weimar, Karlsruhe, Mannheim, Gotha, Dessau, Hechingen, Hamburg, Düsseldorf, Breslau, and other towns.

CONTENTS ix

CHAPTER V. Orchestras in England 160
London opera-houses and concert rooms—The orchestra at the King's theatre—Covent Garden theatre—Drury Lane theatre—Concert orchestras—The Ancient and the Vocal concert—The Sacred Harmonic Society—The Philharmonic orchestra—Societa Armonica—Other London orchestras—The pleasure gardens—Promenade concerts—Musard's concerts—Jullien's concerts—Provincial orchestras—Festival orchestras.

CHAPTER VI. Orchestras in Vienna, in Italy and in other Countries 249
Vienna opera-houses and concert societies—The Hofkapelle—Theater-an-der-Wien—Hofburg and Kärntnerthor theatres—The Leopoldstädter and Josephstädter theatres—Concert orchestras—The Philharmonic orchestra—Orchestras in Prague and Budapesth—Orchestras in Italy—La Scala at Milan—San Carlo at Naples—Orchestras in Russia, Scandinavia, the Netherlands, Spain, Portugal and America.

CHAPTER VII. Conducting 289
Composer and conductor—Dual control by keyboard-conductor and violinist-leader in the 18th century—Development of baton-conductor in Germany, Vienna, France, Italy and England—Divided responsibility in England—Implements used for conducting—Noisy conducting—Qualifications for a conductor.

CHAPTER VIII. Conductors 341
Spohr — Weber — Mendelssohn — Wagner — Guhr, Lindpaintner and other German conductors—Beethoven and conductors at Vienna—Nicolai—Habeneck—Berlioz—Other French conductors—Musard—Jullien—Costa and the London conductors.

CHAPTER IX. The Instruments 391
Bowed string instruments — The double-bass — Sub-basses—Simplifying d-bass parts—Harp—Wind instruments and makers—The wood-wind at the end of the 18th century—Improved key-systems in the early 19th century—Saxophones—Brass instruments—Stopping, slides and keys—Hand horn—Trumpets—Keyed bugle—Ophicleide—The valve—Slow introduction of valved instruments into the orchestra—Cornet with valves—Tubas, saxhorns and other valved bugles.

PAGE

CHAPTER X. SCORE AND PARTS. ARRANGEMENTS   424
  Diffusion of scores and parts—Opera and oratorio scores—
  Symphonies, overtures and concertos—Beethoven's symphonies—
  Haydn's symphonies—Cianchettini's scores—Mozart's symphonies
  —German scores of Beethoven's symphonies—Text-books on
  orchestration—Conductor's parts—Copyright—Composer's pay-
  ment—Arrangements and adaptations—Adapted operas in London
  —Additional accompaniments.

CHAPTER XI. REHEARSAL. PITCH. ARRANGEMENT OF ORCHES-
  TRAS. CONCLUSION   466
  Rehearsal of opera and concert orchestras—Variable pitch—
  Arrangement of orchestras and choirs—Conclusion—Protests
  against growing volume of sound and complexity.

APPENDIX   487

BIBLIOGRAPHY   495

INDEX   500

List of Illustrations

COLOURED PLATES

Interior of La Scala at Milan	FRONTISPIECE	
New Covent Garden Theatre, 1809–56	FACING PAGE	192
San Carlo Opera House at Naples	,,	272

PLATES

1. Jean Mengal, leading horn at the Opéra in 1835 .. ,, 76
2. Théâtre Italien (Salle Favart), Paris, 1829 .. .. ,, 82
3. Habeneck .. .. ,, 94
4. The old Opernhaus at Berlin (1742–1843) .. .. ,, 114
   The new Schauspielhaus at Berlin, built in 1821 .. ,, 114
5. The old Court Theatre at Dresden in Weber's time. Burnt in 1849 during the May Revolution .. .. ,, 115
6. Interior of the old Gewandhaus at Leipzig in Mendelssohn's time .. .. ,, 140
   Ferdinand David, Leader at the Gewandhaus under Mendelssohn .. .. ,, 140
7. A rehearsal at the Gewandhaus under Julius Rietz, c. 1850 .. .. ,, 141
8. New English Opera House (Lyceum Theatre) in 1821 ,, 162
   Theatre Royal, Haymarket, 1824 .. .. .. ,, 162
9. The King's Theatre, Haymarket, after reconstruction in 1819 .. .. ,, 163
10. Charles Nicholson, Flautist .. .. .. ,, 174
    Apollon Marie Rose Barret (Barré) .. .. .. ,, 174
11. Thomas Lindsay Willman .. .. ,, 175
12. Tom Cooke, Leader and Singer at Drury Lane .. ,, 200
13. Drury Lane Theatre in 1821 .. .. ,, 201
14. L'Analyse, Souvenir of the Musical Union, 1853 .. ,, 228
15. The Hall in the Augarten .. .. ,, 252
    Theater-an-der-Wien, Vienna, c. 1830 .. .. .. ,, 252
16. Kärntnerthor Theater at Vienna, c. 1825 .. .. ,, 253
17. La Scala at Milan .. .. ,, 270
18. Concert Room of the Musical Society Félix Meritis at Amsterdam, c. 1810 .. .. ,, 271
19. Charles Hanssens, Brussels Opera, 1840 .. .. ,, 314
20. Caricature of Elderly Conductor with Roll of Paper .. ,, 340
21. Weber Conducting at a Concert in Covent Garden Theatre in 1826 .. .. ,, 341
22. Adolphe Sax .. .. ,, 408
23. Theobald Boehm .. .. ,, 409

ILLUSTRATIONS IN THE TEXT   PAGE

A French church serpent player.. 34
The Grand Opera House in the Rue le Peletier (1821–73) 70
The Odéon at Paris 71
The new Opéra in the Rue le Peletier 79
Salle Ventadour, Paris, in 1850 (Conductor with violin bow) .. 85
George Hainl 104
The old Gewandhaus at Leipzig 131
The Hanover Square Rooms in 1843 161
Her Majesty's Theatre (late King's Theatre) in 1843 170
Lindley and Dragonetti 172
Henry Lazarus in 1843 176
Friedrich Baumann, bassoon player 177
Thomas Harper (Senior) and Clara Novello, 1836 180
Caricature of Tolbecque, Balfe's leader at Her Majesty's Theatre .. 188
Covent Garden Theatre in 1804.. 191
New Covent Garden Theatre as rebuilt after the fire in 1808 .. 194
Bottesini, famous double-bass player 196
Drury Lane Theatre before the fire in 1809 198
Exeter Hall in 1840 208
The Argyll Rooms in 1825 211
Caricature of Dragonetti, the great double-bass player 214
An Orchestra in the Hanover Square Rooms, 1843 221
The Colosseum in Regent's Park 229
Jullien's Orchestra at a Promenade Concert in Covent Garden Theatre, 1846 232
Koenig, cornet soloist at Jullien's Concerts 234
Prospère, with his giant ophicleide 235
Collinet, virtuoso on the French flageolet 236
Joseph Richardson, solo flautist at Jullien's Concerts 237
Jullien's Orchestra and the French Corps de Tambours at Drury Lane, 1850 238
The Philharmonic Hall at Liverpool, 1849 244
Worcester Musical Festival in 1848 246
The New Park Theatre, New York, the first Italian opera house, 1825 286
Neithardt conducting the Royal Berlin Choir, 1850 305
Danton's caricature of Habeneck 314
G. F. Anderson, Master of the Queen's Musick, conducting at Buckingham Palace, 1848 333
Jewelled baton presented to Jullien in 1853 335
Jullien in 1843 378
Caricature of Costa (1842) 383
Costa as an elderly man 384
Costa conducting Semiramide on the opening night of the Royal Italian Opera at Covent Garden, April 6, 1847 386
Balfe 389
Vuillaume's octobase, 1849 396
Figure 1. Diagrams 402
Figure 2. ,, ... 403

PAGE

Figure 3. Diagrams 404

Figure 4. ,, ... 405

Figure 5. The "Spectacle" or Brille (clarinet) 406

Saxophone exhibited at the National Exposition in Paris in 1849 .. 408

Scale for the stopped trumpet 412

Keyed bugle from Purday's Tutor 413

Nine-keyed ophicleide 415

The Distin Family in 1848, with the saxhorns supplied to them by
Ad. Sax in 1844. Originally a quintet, one of the sons, George,
died in 1848 421

Monster bass gong-drum made by Henry Distin 422

The first edition of the full score of Haydn's Symphony in D (No. 104),
published in 1802–3 by Pleyel at Paris 433

Cianchettini's full score of Mozart's Jupiter Symphony, published in
London, 1807–09 437

Steiner's first lithographed score of Beethoven's Seventh Symphony,
published in 1816 439

Examples from Beethoven's Eroica Symphony 440

The Philharmonic Orchestra in 1846, as arranged by Costa 479

I

Introduction
The Setting

FOR a setting in which to view the development of the orchestra during the first half of the 19th century, probably the most convenient and serviceable background is that provided by the composers of the period. This must embrace not only the comparatively few whose music has endured and provides a very considerable proportion of the orchestral music now in use, but also many who, even though their names are quite well remembered, count for very little in the music-making of the present time.

All but the earliest works of Beethoven and the last few works of Berlioz were written between 1800 and 1850. These two composers, then, will supply convenient boundaries for the purpose of this survey. The same limits could be expressed in many different ways, as, for example, from the end of Haydn to the beginning of Wagner, or, from *The Seasons* (1801) to *Lohengrin* (1850), or, indeed, in any other way which will define the period between the end of the 18th century and the middle of last century.

Within these limits falls either the whole or the greater part of the output of a number of influential composers who are most easily grouped according to their nationality. Of the German composers' work (for the present purpose Austrian, Bohemian and Hungarian composers can be regarded as German) the period will cover, in addition to the work of Beethoven, practically the whole output of Spohr, Weber, Schubert, Mendelssohn, most of Schumann and Meyerbeer, the earlier works of Wagner, and barely the beginning of Liszt's work as far as it concerns the orchestra. As well as most of Berlioz's music, the French contribution includes the later works of Méhul and Boieldieu, and almost all of Auber and Halévy. Italy provides the later works of Cherubini, most of Spontini, practically the entire output of Rossini, Bellini and Donizetti, and just the beginning of Verdi. From Russia came a new current, with Glinka's *A Life for the Czar* (1836) as an important landmark; but this was one which, although it was destined to become powerful, did not begin to make its influence felt until well after the middle of the century. If a British list were to be compiled it would have to be headed by such names as Bishop, Barnett or Balfe, and from other countries the contribution would be equally or even more negligible.

These were, of course, only the most prominent, influential, and still are the best remembered of the composers who made the music of their half-century. But although their names are familiar enough, it cannot be said

1

that in each case their music means much to either the musician or the music-lover of the present day.   To us, in a country where opera-going is not a national habit, some of them are just the composers of overtures to operas which we never hear, or of a few arias which occasionally crop up in concert programmes.   It is probably no exaggeration to say that many today would find it easier to name the best works of some of these composers than to quote a bar from their music.   Many regular concert-goers, and many musicians too, would probably find it difficult to whistle a tune from Spontini, Méhul or Halévy, and many would fail in a similar test with the music of Cherubini or Boieldieu.   But even if they are now more often read about than their music is heard, it is important to remember that they were all strong musical forces in their own time, and for some time after; and where there is regular opera, a few of their best works are still retained in the repertoire, or are occasionally revived.[1]

Nevertheless, it will probably be granted that the enduring strength of the musical output of the half-century lay largely in the work of the German symphonists, and in that of Berlioz, whom Nature, perhaps rather capriciously, decided to make a Frenchman.   Beethoven, Schubert, Mendelssohn, Schumann and Berlioz have left a number of symphonic works which have so far weathered all temporary changes in taste and fashion, and now provide the solid core around which so many of the orchestral programmes of today are built up.   Of operas, a picked selection by Beethoven, Weber, Rossini, Bellini, Donizetti, Meyerbeer, certain of the earlier operas by Wagner and Verdi, and a few by some lesser composers, still provide a substantial backbone for the repertoires of regular opera-producing theatres.   These, together with the 18th century composers, Bach, Handel, Haydn and Mozart, still provide the greater part of all the music in which an orchestra takes any part that is heard today.

What we owe to the first half of last century will be fully appreciated if we take the programmes of almost any series of orchestral concerts and delete all the works written between 1800 and 1850.   Serious gaps would be torn in most, and many programmes would be completely wrecked. The loss of the Beethoven symphonies alone would spoil almost any scheme that was not designed to cover some special period or nationality.   These works have been the prop and stay of orchestral concerts almost from the time when they were written; although worn by constant repetition, they have survived the hard ordeal of becoming hackneyed and over-familiar. Even wireless transmission and gramophones, by making them cheap and easily accessible, have not killed off these hardy perennials; they go on and on, if anything, gaining by ever widening publicity, and providing fresh enjoyment for each succeeding generation.

In addition to those already named, there were many composers of the half-century who cannot be placed in the front rank, yet whose music has

[1] It will be understood that this is written without taking into account the abnormal conditions which have prevailed since 1939.

the great merit that the best of it has managed, after a hundred or more years of constant repetition, to retain some of its vitality even to this day. It is generally in the form of opera that such music manages to keep alive. It seems that second-quality music may sometimes survive in opera, but not in symphony. A few operas by Marschner, Lortzing, Flotow, C. Kreutzer, Nicolai, Hérold, Adolphe Adam, Balfe and Wallace, for example, are more alive to-day than many a pretentious work by their more ambitious contemporaries. Although threadbare, they are still serviceable; while who knows how many symphonies and oratorios of the same period have not a breath of life left in them. Marschner's *Hans Heiling* (1833), Lortzing's *Czaar und Zimmermann* (1837), Nicolai's *Merry Wives* (1849), Kreutzer's *Nachtlager in Granada* (1834), Flotow's *Martha* (1847), Adam's *Postillon de Longjumeau* (1836), to name only a few at random, are typical works which pleased greatly in their time, and continued to please succeeding generations, and can still please to-day. Even if not always used as operas, we still use their overtures, and music drawn from them still provides material for the repertoires of countless military and brass bands all the world over.

Those who know music only from what they hear in the concert-room or theatre might well imagine that the first half of last century gave us some half-dozen first-class composers and about a couple of dozen who "also ran." Only a search of contemporary musical literature, musical dictionaries, old programmes, records, periodicals, reviews, catalogues and advertisements can give any idea of how many composers it takes to make one good one. Nature's way is apparently to produce a vast number of composers in the hope that one or two may turn out well. It seems a wasteful method, but it is evidently the only one that works. It appears that there must be mass-production if posterity is to be assured of getting some music that it likes. The cream of composers can only be skimmed off from a larger quantity of milk, but, as there is a use for skimmed milk, there is also a use for composers from which the best have been skimmed off. If they do nothing else, the second and third-rate composers do good service in supplying, so to speak, the bulk or quantity which is necessary, and from which the real essence may be distilled.

The records of the past show clearly enough that composers have always been as plentiful as flies in summer-time. It is a mistake to suppose that the ability to compose music is a rare gift, one which when discovered should be carefully nurtured, treasured, and be given every possible encouragement. It is a very common gift, and can be found in abundance in every civilised community. At any given time, hundreds of musicians can always be found who can compose, and who appear to be doing their job quite well; but, unfortunately, there seems to be no reliable method of finding out at the time which are, so to speak, worth keeping, and which should be thrown away. If we destroy the lot, we may be destroying just the one we ought to have kept. So we have to put up with a lot of dross, and must leave it to Time to make the selection which will eventually give us the few prizes in the lottery.

The picture of the great composer who is shamefully neglected during his lifetime, who is starved and eventually buried in a pauper's grave, is one that the sentimentalist loves to dwell on.   Yet such cases are extremely rare.   On the other hand, we can always find plenty of cases in which a composer enjoyed considerable success during his lifetime, after which his music completely disappeared, leaving no traces in the concert-room or theatre, and only some dry bones in libraries and catalogues.   There were plenty such in the first half of last century.   If we can point to Schubert and Berlioz as instances in which composers were undervalued while they lived, we can also point to a few dozen who were greatly overvalued. There are few now who care or know anything about the music of such as Paër, Mayr, Winter, Lesueur, Weigl, Hummel, Reicha, Onslow, Gyrowetz, or a dozen or two others of the same calibre.   Yet these all loomed large in the musical world of their day; they were uncommonly successful, and their work was much appreciated; they were influential and popular; they were important in the eyes of their contemporaries, but turned out to be of no particular importance in the long run, and they are now little more than names in history books.   But they were, in their day, representatives of a type of which there always has been, and still is, a plentiful supply.   There is never any lack of composers who can produce any quantity of music written in the current style of their period.   Their music appears to have every desirable quality, yet it lacks just that one quality that makes music durable.   When such music is new and its style is still current, it seems to be almost impossible to distinguish with any certainty between the first-class and the inferior article, between the durable and the perishable.   On the whole, it would appear that, contrary to the popular belief, the chance that a composer's music will be appreciated during his lifetime and forgotten afterwards, is much greater than the chance that it will go unrecognised. while he is living and be appreciated at some future period.

It is always easy to be wise a hundred or more years after the event, but it is difficult to pick out the winners while the race is being run.   When we read that "the operas of Mozart, Cimarosa, Winter, Paër, Guglielmi and Ferrari carry the art and science to its greatest possible height,"[1] we may agree as to Mozart's share, and may not withhold some credit from Cimarosa, but we wonder why the others should have been included in the list.   We probably read with some surprise that Winter's overture to *Tamerlane* "is full of sublime effects, and is of itself sufficient to transmit his name to posterity."[2]   We find it difficult now to understand why in 1838 Kalliwoda was counted "one of the first writers of symphonies now living,"[3] why Schindler put Salieri on a level with Haydn, Mozart and Beethoven, or Feska, Hummel, Onslow, Reicha, Ries and the two Rombergs in the same

[1] *Encyclopædia Londinensis*, 1818, Vol. XVI, p. 311.
[2] *The Harmonicon*, June, 1824, p. 122.   [3] *Musical World*, Feb. 23, 1838, p. 119.

INTRODUCTION: THE SETTING 5

class as Weber and Spohr.[1] Even if we did know the work in question, we should probably not be able to share the confidence of the critic who wrote of Dr. Crotch's oratorio: "We affirm without fear of contradiction, that no real critic could hear *Palestine* without ranking its author among the great composers of Europe,"[2] nor would we readily subscribe to the opinion that this oratorio was "one of the great productions of the age."[3] We now wonder why Schumann, who was no inferior critic, should have called Marschner, Schneider, Kalliwoda, Lachner and Löwe "the most distinguished German composers of the present day,"[4] and feel rather inclined to amend his description so as to make it read "the second-rate German composers of their day."

This general tendency of music to slump badly after its own day is emphasised in order to show that many more than a few outstanding composers are necessary to make the music of any one period. The "great" composers could not have accomplished their vital work if they had stood solitary and alone, any more than a few generals could win a war without a rank and file army. The number of once distinguished, but now undistinguished, composers who filled the ranks of the musical army during the period from Beethoven to Berlioz did their share in making the music of the first half of last century in a way which was just as essential to the final outcome as the work of the elect few whose music has outlived its own day. They provided the milk, and only a few rose to the top to give us the cream.

Of second- and third-rate German composers there has always been an abundant supply. Such as Romberg, Reissiger, Lachner, Rietz, Aiblinger, Lindpaintner, Hiller, and many others, used the same musical material as Weber, Mendelssohn and Schumann, but they couldn't make it outlast their own generation. Many of those in this category were opera-conductors in more or less influential positions, and it was their work which gave rise to the expression "*Kapellmeistermusik.*"

In France and Italy, too, there were always plenty of industrious music-makers, most of them opera-composers whose works, even if they were well received at first, expired after drawing a few breaths. The list of operas and ballets produced between 1800 and 1850 at the Paris *Opéra* alone will provide such names in plenty. There were, for example, Isouard (composer of 50 operas), Jadin (40), Gaveaux (35), Blangini (30), Daussoigne, Carafa (35), Sor, Chelard, Gide, Pugni (10 operas and 300 ballets), and a score of others who gained a hearing for many of their works at the famous institution which by no means opened its doors to anyone who knocked.

In Italy the flow of composers was even more voluminous. The numerous theatres there provided opportunities such as were to be found in no other country, and the public was always clamouring for more new operas. Mendelssohn wrote to Hiller, of the music in Italy: "where

[1] *Life of Beethoven*, trans. by Moscheles, I, p. 66, and XX.
[2] *The Harm.*, Sept., 1829, p. 220.   [3] *Ibid.*, March, 1828, p. 93.
[4] *Music and Musicians*, I, p. 393.

people have new music every year, and must also have a new opinion every year,—if only the music and the opinions were a little better."[1]   The Italians wanted to be entertained at the opera in their own way, and their composers gave them what they wanted.   It would be tedious to attempt to name all the Italian opera composers of the period, even if that could be done; a batch of samples must suffice: Portagello (40 operas), Zingarelli (34), Nicolini (48), Orlandi (18), Puccita (30), Mosca (44), Fioravanti (50), Lavigna, Federici, Gnecco, Trento (30), Pavesi (60), Generali (45), Farinelli (58), Coccia (40), Pacini (90), Mercadante (60), Raimondi (62), Vaccai, Cordella, and so forth.   These composers wrote quickly, their operas were quickly staged, and soon forgotten.   The earlier of them were unable to stand up to the Rossini craze which raged during the second and third decades of last century, and the later of them made the most of that craze by imitating Rossini's manner as closely as they could.

Composers who wrote almost entirely for one instrument, such as Chopin and Paganini, hardly come into the story of the orchestra; but yet another type of instrumentalist-composer, now remembered only by some of their works for a single instrument, in their day contributed a quite substantial quota of music which required an orchestra for its performance. Although their music is no longer heard in the concert-room or theatre, there is still a use for the piano music of such as Clementi, Pleyel, Cramer, Diabelli, Czerny and Moscheles.   The piano teacher knows their studies and sonatinas, but nobody now cares or knows much about the operas or ballets, the oratorios or masses, the symphonies, overtures and concertos written by these same composers.   Similarly, the violinist of to-day knows the studies and concertos of Viotti, Kreutzer, Rode and Alard, but it is not in the concert-room that he makes use of them; they are kept alive and still serve their useful purpose in the teaching room.   Yet it is odd to reflect that Czerny must have spent a lot of time writing Masses, symphonies, overtures and concertos, and that Rud. Kreutzer should have fancied himself as a composer of operas and ballets.

A few pages might be filled with the names of many others who composed music during the period Beethoven-to-Berlioz.   It would make a dull catalogue which few would have the patience to read through, although it might serve to correct the impression that the music of the period was entirely in the hands of a well-remembered few who were able to sum up in their works the best of the music of their time, and to add to it something which preserved it against the assaults of progress, time, changes of taste and fashion, and all the destructive forces which eventually kill all but a small selection from the art-product of any period.

Although, compared with the previous century, the first half of the 19th century showed no reduction in the flow of composers, there was a considerable reduction in the number of works turned out by each.   This does not imply any lessening of industry or lack of facility; it implies that more time

[1] Hiller, *Letters and Recoll.*, p. 125.

had to be expended on each piece. The music which flowed from the earlier composers like water from a tap involved less labour and less thought; but a more complex texture, a more elaborate harmonic scheme, a fuller lay-out, more detail, and more finish, made the 19th century full score a thing which required more time and effort. So, instead of turning out his symphonies or concertos in batches of six at a time, as did his predecessors, the 19th century composer was content to write one symphony or one concerto at a time, and he had to put more work into that one piece than the earlier composer put into his half-dozen. Telemann's 600 overtures, Quantz's 300 concertos, Graun's 96 symphonies, Haydn's 104, and Mozart's 40 or so, could not be matched by any 19th century composer; there were few who achieved more than ten symphonies and as many concertos. The French or German opera-composer in the 19th century did well if he produced from 20 to 25 stage works, whereas his 18th century predecessor might generally reckon up his opera-output at between 50 and 100. The Italians, it is true, were more prolific. Donizetti's 63, or Rossini's 50 or more, were almost up to the old standard, but even they, who could string together an opera in two or three weeks, could not match such as Piccini's 139 or Hasse's 100 operas.

From all the mass of music produced during the period 1800 to 1850 (disregarding that in which an orchestra had no part), it may be estimated that some 30 operas, about a dozen oratorios, cantatas or Masses, about two dozen symphonies, a dozen concertos, and perhaps 40 or 50 overtures have survived, and now form a very substantial part of the repertoires of the opera-houses and concert-giving institutions of the present day. That is only a minute proportion of the total output of the period, yet it compares well with the surviving output of any other similar period. Any half-century that can produce so much durable music does very well.

If we slightly change the view-point from that of the music written to that of the music actually in use during the same half-century, and make a comparison with the situation at the present time, we will find at least one striking difference.

For our operas and orchestral music generally, we now rely mainly on the past. The lion's share of the music we now hear belongs to the 19th century; the 18th century contributes a very fair share, but 20th century music takes only a rather small part in our opera and concert schemes. That was not so one hundred years back. By far the greater part of the music heard during the first half of last century was written during that period; it was contemporary music that occupied them, and, moreover, it was contemporary music that was wanted. By about 1830 only a handful of 18th century operas (by Gluck, Mozart, and one by Cimarosa) still remained in service. A few of Handel's oratorios, and two of Haydn's, still held their own; only a limited selection from the symphonies, overtures and concertos by Haydn and Mozart were heard. The bulk of the music enjoyed in 1830 had been composed after 1799. The numerous opera-houses in Italy and Germany, and the more centralised theatres in Paris, Vienna and London, were all busy producing new operas and ballets, nearly all of them written by living composers.   The instrumental music was likewise mainly that which had been written since the beginning of the century, as the following statistics show:

	18th Century Works	19th Century Works
Paris, Conservatoire Concerts, 1830–1839		
Symphonies	17	95
Overtures	12	48
Concertos	0	15
Total	29	158
Leipzig, Gewandhaus Concerts, 1830–1839		
Symphonies	51	154
Overtures	21	258
Concertos	6	148
Total	78	560
London, Philharmonic Society, 1830–1839		
Symphonies	64	91
Overtures	6	145
Concertos	9	65
Total	79	301

If these figures are averaged, they will show that only between one-fifth and one-sixth of the music in the three specified categories played by these three representative societies during the ten years 1830 to 1839 belonged to the previous century.   By that time the great mass of 18th century music had been discarded, and of 17th century music they knew next to nothing. The music that occupied their time and attention was the music of their own time.

That the choral and orchestral works of J. S. Bach were so rarely performed was not due to any inability to appreciate their quality; it was just because they were unknown and unheard.   Music which is not heard cannot be appreciated, and as long as the surviving MSS. of Bach's music lay hidden away in libraries, their very existence known to only a few, there could be no general appreciation of their value.   However, a start was made when Mendelssohn produced the *St. Matthew Passion* in 1829, and when that and other works of Bach were subsequently revived and repeated, they were recognised as music which towered above the passage of time and change of style, and steps were then taken to disclose what remained of them, and to make them available for performance. That was a big task, and it necessarily took a long time to accomplish. But it was not indifference, bad taste or inability to appreciate a good thing when they heard it that kept the works of this great composer from the musical public of the early 19th century; it was only lack of opportunity to hear them.

Some 20 symphonies by Haydn and half a dozen by Mozart were constantly played, and their merits were fully recognised. The others were unheard and unknown; most musicians were hardly aware that they existed. It should be remembered that in those days there were no handy *Complete Editions*, nicely printed in score and parts, available at reasonable prices, and ready for anyone to play who chose to buy the music. The student and scholar had hardly any reprints of old music to hand, and miniature full scores were quite unknown. The spoon-fed musician of the present day enjoys many advantages and facilities for study and performance which were denied to his predecessors a century ago.

The music of Beethoven, Mendelssohn and Meyerbeer met with plenty of appreciation in its own day, and, except in a few cases when an inadequate first production or a weak libretto delayed the proper appreciation of the music for some time, the works of Weber and the best of the French and Italian opera-composers won immediate acceptance and success.

That the merit of Schubert's music was not recognised during his lifetime was due to circumstances which were not at all extraordinary, and might equally well occur at the present or any other time. Schubert died at the early age of 31, with little more than a local reputation in Vienna and neighbourhood. He had not been particularly successful with his stage works, his six earlier symphonies had not the strength of Beethoven's and had made little headway in Vienna, and none outside of it. When he did write two great symphonies, neither came to a hearing until long after his death. The circumstances were as follows: Schubert sent the score of his Unfinished Symphony (1822) to a friend (Anselm Hüttenbrenner), a member of a Musical Society in a provincial town (Graz), as a presentation to the society in appreciation of his having been made an honorary member. The symphony was not performed by the society, and apparently no effort was made either by the composer or anyone else to get a hearing for it. Even if the friend did hand it over to the society (and it is by no means certain that he did), it is always easy to find reasons for not performing a work. The symphony may have been too difficult for the local orchestra of a smallish town[1]; the full orchestra for which it was scored may have been more than their resources could provide; the cost of copying the parts may have been an obstacle; it was, as far as we know, only *half* a symphony;

[1] Schubert's *Alfonso und Estrella* was found to be too difficult for the theatre orchestra at Graz. Hysel, the conductor, said that "it was technically impossible to play what Schubert wanted." (Kreissle von Hellborn, *Life of Schubert*, I, p. 252.)

the arrangements for the season may already have been completed[1]; playing symphonies may not have been part of the policy of the society; someone in the society may have disliked Schubert, or his friend; the friend (himself a composer!) may not have tried to get the symphony performed—and so on, and so forth.   These circumstances and many similar obstacles to a performance might equally well occur in any place, at any time, past, present or future, and there would be nothing unusual or remarkable about them. Such things have happened over and over again; but in this particular case it was unfortunate that it should have happened when a masterpiece was concerned.

Schubert presented the score of his great C Major Symphony (1828) to the *Gesellschaft der Musikfreunde* in Vienna, an influential society of musical amateurs which functioned not only as a performing body. It is generally said that the work was found to be too long and too difficult[2]; so it was not performed.   It cannot be denied that it is long; it plays for nearly an hour or more if all the repeats are made, and the usual length of a symphony was then not more than half-an-hour.[3]   It certainly is difficult; only the best of orchestras today can play it adequately, and any scratch orchestra (including many amateur strings) that the *Gesellschaft* could raise would certainly be quite unable to do it justice.   The symphony was shelved, and remained unknown to the public until 1839, when it was first played at Leipzig under Mendelssohn. Again, there is nothing unusual or astounding in those circumstances; many a long and difficult work has failed to get a hearing under similar conditions.   The same thing could easily happen now.   If a young composer in London, with little more than a local reputation as a song-writer, and with no friends at court, were to submit a long and difficult symphony to the Royal Philharmonic Society or the B.B.C. at the present time, that work would stand just as little chance of being played as did Schubert's symphony when he sent it to the Vienna *Gesellschaft* in 1828.   And it should never be taken for granted that the worth of a new work will be correctly assessed after a mere examination of the score by some conductor or official of a society or other body.   In most cases no great loss is incurred when a work is rejected, but, again, in this particular case the work happened to be a rare masterpiece.

Whether a large new work gets a hearing or not depends not so much on its musical worth as on the composer's reputation.   That held good a century ago, just as it does now.   It may also depend on whether the composer holds any influential position or not, on his presence in a particular

[1] This hoary excuse for rejecting a work has been employed on countless occasions.
[2] The C Major Symphony "was rejected by the orchestral players of the Society at that time as being impracticable." (von Hellborn, II, p. 79.)
[3] Those of Beethoven's symphonies which played for over half-an-hour (especially Nos. 3, 6, 7 and 9) were considered much too long when they were first produced. We can read in contemporary journals about the "interminable length" of the *Eroica*, of the *Pastoral* being "always too long," of No. 7 being "tediously long," and of the Choral Symphony being "at least twice as long as it should be."   The average time of most Haydn and Mozart symphonies is under 30 minutes.

place, on his personality, pertinacity, or importunity. Looking through the records of the performances of the past century, one can as often as not connect a performance with the composer's position, or his presence at the place where the work was played. It was not a mere accident that the names of Kreutzer or Persius, for example, occur so often as composers of works produced at the Paris *Opéra* while these musicians were employed as conductors at that theatre. It was because they were there, on the spot; and when they ceased to be there, their works were no longer played. It was no mere coincidence that the name of Ferdinand Ries should appear thirty-two times as the composer of pieces played at the London Philharmonic Concerts during the ten years that Ries was resident in London, and a member of the society. When, between 1815 and 1830, the symphonies of Franz Krommer were played by the Vienna *Gesellschaft der Musikfreunde* more often than those of Haydn, it was not because Krommer's symphonies were better than Haydn's, or that they were more in demand; it was because Krommer was alive and in Vienna at that time, whereas Haydn was dead. There is no lack of similar examples; one can find them in almost any series of old programmes.

One respect in which the musical situation in the first half of last century differed greatly from that of our own times was the extent to which opera dominated everything. Nearly all orchestras were, in the first place, opera-orchestras; it was from these that the concert-orchestras drew their personnel. Wagner remarked on this: "We owe our permanent orchestras to the various theatres"; and again: "Conductors are indebted to the theatres for their posts, and even for the existence of their orchestra."[1] Almost every composer wrote operas, and even those whose natural bent was not in that line generally tried their hand at it (Schumann), or if they didn't, were always longing to do so (Mendelssohn). Practically all singers were opera-singers, and when they sang at concerts their contributions were operatic arias.

In Italy the domination of opera over all other forms of music was the most complete. The Italians were completely at one in their universal love of opera. They knew little of the German symphonies, their concert-societies were few, and then only private affairs on a small scale. They had no concert-rooms, and visiting artists had to give their concerts in theatres or in private houses. To the Italian, music was opera or church music, and their church music was operatic in style; it was sung by opera singers and played by opera orchestras.

Again, in France it was the opera-theatres that provided the singers and players for the concerts. Their symphonies were mostly imported, indeed, the orchestral concert-institutions of Paris would probably never have existed had it not been for the symphonies of Haydn and Beethoven. The *Société des Concerts* (Conservatoire Concerts) was built up on the performance of Beethoven's symphonies; but the daily work of the conductors and

[1] *On Conducting*, pp. 5 and 10.

players was in the theatre. The court orchestra and chapel were in the hands of composers, conductors, and players who were or had been in the service of the theatres of Paris.

In Germany almost every orchestra was primarily an opera-orchestra, under whatever name it might appear at concerts. There were, however, a few exceptions to the general rule in Germany. The most outstanding exception was at Leipzig, where the orchestra of the *Gewandhaus* was maintained fundamentally as a concert-orchestra, and from which the small and less important theatre of the town drew its players. Some of the older and smaller court orchestras in Germany were independent of any theatrical establishment, but they were few, and not many of them were left by the middle of the century.

In Vienna there was no professional concert-orchestra before 1842, and then it was only the court opera-orchestra, with its conductor, under another name. In this country no concert-society could entirely maintain an orchestra; the theatres had to provide most of the players and keep them in permanent employment.

This dependence on opera was reflected in the almost complete lack of concert-halls, even in some of the most important musical centres. While there were theatres everywhere, concert-halls were few and far between. Paris had no such place,[1] if we except the *Salle* of the Conservatoire (1806), which was as much a theatre as it was a concert-room, and was not to be had on hire by anybody who wanted it. According to Fétis, the room at the *Rue de Cléry* was too small and scarcely provided room for an orchestra; the *Salle* at the Conservatoire was "by no means well adapted for concerts," and was "constructed upon bad acoustical principles."[2] Large concerts had to be held in theatres or ball-rooms. For concerts in Vienna they used either the theatres or had to fall back on ball-rooms, a riding-school, a university hall or hotel rooms. In Germany the position was not much better. The *Gewandhaus* at Leipzig and the *Odeon* at Munich (opened 1828) were notable exceptions to the general rule, and there was a small concert-room in the building of the Berlin opera-house. But Spohr complained in 1819 that there was no large and suitable hall for concerts in Berlin, and at Cassel he was obliged to hold his orchestral concerts in the theatre; at Dresden the orchestral concerts were held in the old opera-house, and Wagner's proposal to build a suitable concert hall (1846) was turned down. London was really better off for concert-rooms than any other capital, for it had the Argyll Rooms and the Hanover Square Rooms, but even these were small for orchestral and choral concerts, and were designed as entertainment centres rather than as concert-rooms.

But opera was not to retain its commanding position in music throughout the half-century, and by the mid-century some progress had been made towards establishing the claim of concert-music to a greater share of

---

[1] Berlioz, Castil-Blaze and Fétis deplored the lack of concert-halls in Paris.

[2] *Curiosités*, p. 184.

attention.   Concert societies increased greatly in number between 1800 and
1850, and some of the largest and most influential of these made the
performance of symphonies, overtures and concertos the main object of
their existence.   The London Philharmonic (1813), the Paris *Société des
Concerts* (1828), the Munich *Odeon Concerte* (1828), the Vienna *Philharmonischen
Concerte* (1842), and many similar if less influential societies in Germany,
together with the old-established *Gewandhaus Concerte* at Leipzig, were
mainly instrumental in character, although few of them could afford entirely
to abandon the position which placed vocal and choral music very high in
the range of musical activity.   Of these societies, the London and Vienna
Philharmonics were the most purely orchestral, but the programmes of
these and of all concert institutions were still of the very miscellaneous type
such as is hardly known at the present time.

The programmes show how chamber, orchestral, choral and solo music
were commonly mixed up in the same concert.   Single movements from
symphonies were frequently played, or other pieces were interspersed
between the movements; this occurs in programmes at Vienna, even at
Beethoven's own concerts, and at Paris and Berlin.[1]   At Berlin in 1824
movements from Haydn's, Mozart's and Beethoven's first two symphonies
were used as entracte-music at the *Schauspielhaus*.[2]   As well as being very
mixed in quality, the programmes were very often too long.   Moscheles
voiced a complaint (1830) that the London Philharmonic programmes were
much too long: "It is a mistake to give at every Philharmonic concert two
symphonies and two overtures, besides two grand instrumental and four
vocal pieces.   I never can enjoy more than half."[3]   Of their mixed quality,
Moscheles wrote in 1832: "Grand orchestral works and quartet music are
played at one and the same concert; third-rate singers are engaged; the
antiquated trio by Corelli is to be heard year after year."[4]   Similar complaints
in Germany were voiced by Lobe in 1860: "Above all, most concerts are
much too long; they give too much, and too much variety; pieces of all
sorts are mixed up together."[5]   Lobe also condemned the encore nuisance,
which he called "the absurd and childish Da-Capo-shouting."

The solo singer or instrumentalist was always given the best position in
the programme, although their contributions were only too often of very
slight musical value.   At that time the soloist was expected to show off his
executive skill rather than his interpretative power or musicianship.   The
soloist who did not make a great display of mere execution was not ranked
very high, and this led to the use of much music at concerts which was
designed only with a view to exhibiting the performer's virtuosity.   Large
quantities of trivial variations, fantasias and similar media for display were
performed by soloists who very often composed their own pieces, and in
such a way as to exhibit the devices in which they particularly excelled.

Soloists almost invariably appeared with an orchestra; the piano was not

---

[1] Marx, *Musikzeitung*, 1824.   [2] Kalkbrenner, p. 17.   [3] Moscheles, *Life*, I, p. 244.
[4] *Ibid.*, I, p. 261.   [5] Lobe, *Mus. Briefe*, p. 141.

commonly used for accompanying at public concerts. The solo recital, although a start had been made by such as Thalberg and Liszt, was not yet the usual medium through which an artist introduced himself to his public. The sonata and song were not considered the correct things for public performance; these were meant for use in the home circle or at the private musical meeting, but in public it was the concerto, fantasia, variations, or aria, accompanied by an orchestra, in which the solo artist chose to exhibit his skill.

The concerts of the period, however, were public only in the sense that they were held in large or public buildings. Most concerts were organised on a subscription basis, indeed, going to a concert generally implied membership of a society. Tickets could not be bought by anybody; the general public was not usually admitted by payment at the door.

But the democratisation of concert-music was in progress; it was passing gradually during the first half of last century from the hands of royalty and aristocracy or wealth into those of a music-loving upper middle-class, and it was just that class that was responsible for the institution of almost all the many concert-societies that came into being during the half-century. The difficulties they encountered were largely financial, for, whereas opera was often subsidised by the court, the state or the municipality, there were few or no subsidies for the concerts.

Although the high prices charged for admission to most concerts still kept them very largely out of reach of the lower middle and working classes, not only a beginning, but quite substantial progress was made in providing concerts at prices within the reach of all but the very poorest people. The Promenade Concerts of Musard and Jullien in Paris and London were notable and successful efforts to cater for a public which had hitherto been almost untapped. If their approach to this public was through the medium of dance music, it was almost certainly the only way by which they could have succeeded in attracting audiences that otherwise never entered a concert-room. The guinea and half-guinea concert ticket in London had always been exclusive, but during the early 'thirties and the 'forties large and comprehensive shilling and half-a-crown audiences were created.

Although it cannot be said that the maintenance of musical art by the patronage of royalty and nobility had come to an end by the middle of last century, the position by then had fundamentally changed since the middle of the 18th century. Political changes had very drastically reduced the number of states in Europe, and towards the end of the 18th and in the early years of the 19th century, many courts which once had supported musical establishments disappeared completely and finally.[1] Revolution and wars had wiped out some and had impoverished others; the sovereign, the prince, archduke or archbishop who cultivated music for his own personal pleasure and for the entertainment of his court, had to give up his pleasure or share it with his subjects.

[1] 120 small states in Germany were suppressed in 1803 (Fisher, p. 855).

The larger German states which remained after the Napoleonic wars still had their court musical establishments, but not in such an exclusive or personal sense as in the 18th century. The old court music was the sovereign's own private affair, and the musicians were his household servants. The general trend during the first half of the 19th century was for the court music to become the state music, and the musicians the employees of the state rather than the servants of the court. The public was admitted to the court theatres on payment, and began to have some say in the selection of the operas. Concerts held in the private chamber of the sovereign gave way to concerts organised and maintained by the music-loving public for its own enjoyment. Haydn belonged to the old period of court patronage; Beethoven, after he had left Bonn, held no court appointment, but still relied partly on patronage; Mendelssohn, although at times he held public or state offices, was the servant of the public and independent of royal patronage.

The system of patronage had served musical art well enough in its day, but that day was passing, and the art was coming more and more into the province of the middle and the uneducated classes.

In Germany many of the opera-houses were state-owned, and were subsidised and run by the court or state through an appointed *Intendant* or general manager; although more or less subject to court influence, the policy of the management had to be shaped so as to cater for the taste and wishes of a public which grew more and more insistent and powerful. Some theatres in Germany were the affairs of the town, others were owned by companies or societies, and some of these were occasionally let to impresarios. Small towns in Germany had often to rely on the periodic visits of travelling companies to occupy their small theatres.

The theatres in Italy were owned either by states, towns, syndicates, private individuals or families, and were generally let to impresarios. In Paris the main opera-house was state-supported and managed by an appointed official; the other theatres were either state-supported or privately owned,[1] and even in the former case were sometimes let to speculating managers. The court theatres in Vienna were generally managed or superintended by a court official or by a group of aristocrats, but even so they were sometimes put into the hands of impresarios.[2] Smaller theatres in Vienna were unsubsidised and let to speculating managers. In London the opera-theatres, although licensed by the state, were privately owned, and were let to any impresario who was ready to ruin himself over operatic speculation.

Although the wars and political upheavals which disturbed the peace of Europe before and during the early years of the 19th century were bound to react to some extent on the musical life of the time, the effect was never

---

[1] In 1846 the *Opéra, Théâtre Francais, Opéra Comique* and *Odéon* were supported or aided by the state (Hervey, p. 2).

[2] The great impresario Barbaja was at one time lessee of *La Scala* at Milan, *San Carlo* at Naples, the *Kärntnerthor* and *An-der-Wien* theatres in Vienna, and several other Italian theatres.

so shattering as might have been expected.   When an enemy force occupied a capital, it did not necessarily paralyse and bring to a standstill the musical life of the city.   On the contrary, the opera might go on as gaily as ever and provide pleasant entertainment for the officers of the occupying army.[1]

Three revolutions did not paralyse the musical life of Paris, or bring irretrievable disaster to its musical institutions.   The *Opéra*, although its title was changed often enough to suit the political situation, was always active, whether the state which ruled it was a Republic, a Directory, a Consulate, an Empire or a Monarchy; and if a political assassination did bring about the demolition of its main opera-house,[2] another and a better one was immediately built in its place.   Musicians in France did not allow politics seriously to disturb their professional work, and were quite accommodating in becoming Republicans, Imperialists or Monarchists, as circumstances demanded.

Although the map of Europe was being dotted with battlefields, and states were being handed out to new owners by Napoleon, imperishable symphonies were being written and played in Vienna, and German national opera was steadily finding its feet in Berlin, Dresden and Munich.   In the Italian states, whether under the heel of Austria or of Napoleon, opera-houses took as their motto "business as usual"; however divided the Italians might be politically, they were all united in one vast brotherhood of amity on the subject of opera.

At that time war was a thing for soldiers, politics was for statesmen, but music was for those who enjoyed it, and the one didn't seriously encroach on the preserves of the other.   There were, of course, temporary interruptions when politics and art came into conflict, and the latter might suffer some inconvenience.   If an occupying army would use the main opera-house as a food store,[3] or if a concert-room was transformed into a hospital for wounded soldiers,[4] music had to retire into the background for the time being.   Travelling artists might find their tours disarranged because armies were fighting on their route[5]; blockade might interfere with the traffic in music or instruments; conscription might hamper the work of the musical student, and the political censorship of opera librettos might quite well be a nuisance; but these things did not greatly interfere with the output and performance of musical works.   A full quota of great symphonies, concertos, overtures, operas, oratorios and Masses was forthcoming; great singers and instrumentalists went about triumphantly from one country to another; orchestras gained steadily both in size and in quality; instrumental technique advanced by leaps and bounds, and wind instruments acquired more improvements in these fifty years than they had in the previous two centuries.   Judging by results, war and social upheavals did no great harm to music in the first half of last century.

[1] Dresden, 1806, 1813; Vienna, 1805, 1809.
[2] In 1820; the assassination of the Duc de Berry.
[3] Berlin, 1806.   [4] *Gewandhaus* at Leipzig, 1813–14.
[5] Spohr, in 1812, on the road from Prague to Dresden.

The establishment of conservatoires or professional schools of music during the same period was influential in helping to provide ordered training for many instrumentalists who had hitherto had to rely on private tuition, apprenticeship, or chance experience for the qualifications which enabled them to take their places in the orchestras. The position and power of the old Venetian and Neapolitan *conservatori* (originally founded as hospitals or orphanages) was declining at the end of the 18th century, and new schools which were no longer benevolent or charitable institutions began to spring up and take their places.[1] The most outstanding of the new institutions were the Paris Conservatoire (1795), and the similar but less influential institutions at Milan (1808), Naples (1808), Prague (1811), Vienna (*Gesellschaft der Musikfreunde*, 1817), London (Royal Academy of Music, 1822), Brussels (1832), Leipzig (1843) and Munich (1846). Of these, the most powerful in its own domain, and the one which most successfully fulfilled the purpose for which it was designed, was the Paris Conservatoire. Completely centralised in its capital, the music of France was the music of Paris, and there the power and influence of the Conservatoire was paramount.

That it fully deserved to wield its almost unlimited power in France is proved by the fact that in this brilliant period of French musical history practically all the native composers, instrumentalists and singers were conservatoire-trained. The finest orchestra in Europe, and therefore in the world, was that of the Paris *Société des Concerts*, and almost without exception the players and conductors owed their training to that one institution. Such a result from a state monopoly of musical education was achieved nowhere else but in France, and in spite of a few ups and downs during the first fifty years of its existence, the Conservatoire made and ruled the music of France with complete success.

*   *   *

The foregoing is intended to form only a background or setting against which to trace the changing picture of the orchestra in the course of its development during the prescribed period. The history which follows will be traced along several tracks which, although they can only be followed separately, together combine to tell the story of this very complex and corporate instrument.

[1] The old Neapolitan *Conservatori* were suppressed early in the 19th century when Italy came under French domination.

II

Constitution and Strength

ANY statements that are made regarding the growth in the size of orchestras must always be understood to be subject to the general principle that, at all times, the size of an orchestra must be suited to the size of the room in which it plays.

The small body of instrumentalists which sufficed for the performance of Haydn's operas in the Prince's private theatre at Esterház would not have been sufficient to fill the large auditorium of the Paris *Opéra*, nor for the spacious *La Scala* at Milan or the *San Carlo* at Naples. Haydn required only about twenty instrumentalists,[1] but contemporaneous performances in the large Paris opera-house, at Milan or Naples, demanded orchestras of seventy or more players. Dittersdorf's concerts in the private apartment of the Prince-Bishop at Johannisburg were carried out with an orchestra of seventeen performers; but in the more spacious *Gewandhaus* at Leipzig or the Hanover Square Rooms in London the number of players was at least twice as great, and at the Paris *Concert Spirituel* more than three times as great as Dittersdorf's little party.

Nevertheless, apart from the necessary adjustment to suit the size of the room, there had been a general and progressive increase in the strength of orchestras during the course of the 18th century, and especially during the last two or three decades of that century. This had come about partly as the result of the addition of more wind instruments, and partly from the increase in the number of players for each string part.

A similar increase in the number of players, arising from the same causes, continued during the first half of the 19th century, but most of this increase was due to the growth in the power of each string part. While the addition of wind and percussion parts during the period 1800 to 1850 could account for not more than from eight to ten additional players, by the mid-century the average strength of the string orchestra was approximately doubled.

This addition of string-tone to the orchestra was mainly the result of the addition of wind-tone. The older 18th century composers, who were generally content to write three or four wind parts, had no difficulty in obtaining a good balance of tone between the two types with a string orchestra of no more than fourteen or fifteen players. They regarded all the parts in the score as being approximately of equal power, as indeed they

---

[1] A contemporary picture (1775) shows the interior of the Prince's Theatre, with an orchestra consisting of one *cembalo*, sixteen strings and three wood-wind (Haas, *Aufführungspraxis*).

were, and it is improbable that they ever thought about or were faced with any problems of balancing the tone-quantity. When, by the beginning of the 19th century, it had become an established custom to write for four pairs of wood-wind, a pair each of horns and trumpets, and drums, the string orchestra of fourteen or fifteen players was not powerful enough to balance the sound-quantity that was produced by twelve or thirteen wind instruments, more especially as most of the essence of the music lay in the string parts, and because the four brass instruments and the drums contributed a weight of sound that was proportionately much greater than that of any five stringed instruments, or even of fifteen or twenty of them.

The stabilisation of the wind band in a group of twelve instruments, plus the drums, called for a string orchestra of from twenty to thirty or even more players, for the addition of one brass instrument can never be balanced by the addition of one stringed instrument. Had the additions been only of wood-wind tone, a proportionate increase in the number of strings might almost have sufficed, and the problem of balance would never have become so urgent. But brass instrument tone is a much weightier matter; in any competition between brass and string-tone it is always the brass that wins, and even a tenfold increase of man-power in the string orchestra will hardly equalise the addition of one brass player.

When, during the course of the first half of last century, the weight of brass-tone in the orchestra was further increased by the addition of another pair of horns, three trombones, an ophicleide or tuba, and it became customary to employ a group of noisy percussion instruments, not only were the wood-wind placed in a position in which their sounds could be completely obliterated, but the call for adequate string-tone became what was practically an insatiable demand. Where it could be met, and that for various reasons was not in every orchestra, the strings were increased to a strength of forty, fifty or even more players. Even then, as now, the strings had a hard battle to fight in order to make their tone-weight stand up to anything approaching an equality with the overwhelming might of brass and percussion-tone when at its loudest.

The problem of brass versus string-tone in an orchestra has never been satisfactorily settled, and it is doubtful whether it ever can be. The nature of brass-tone at its full power is such that its ability to penetrate through or crush virtually any amount of string-tone is always assured. Thus, in spite of large string orchestras and every care in performance, we can now hear almost every day instances of string-tone in the orchestra being swamped or obliterated by the all-powerful brass voices, with (only too often) a *coup de grace* administered by the percussion instruments. It is strange now to read how nearly a hundred years ago the Berlin critic Rellstab wrote about the effect to the ear of the main theme of Weber's *Euryanthe* overture: "If we did not know what notes the master had written, what fiery triplet passages he had given to the violins, we would never hear them, so completely are they

c

swamped by the heavy hammer-blows of the rhythm allotted to the wind instruments."[1]   One might say the same of any performance of that overture to-day, or of dozens of other works in which this same problem of balance has never been satisfactorily overcome.

That the largest orchestras and those with the most string players in the 18th century were on the whole those employed in opera-houses rather than those used for concerts, was simply due to the fact that while there were many large theatres, there were few or no large concert-rooms.   Only very exceptionally were concerts given in fairly large halls with a suitably large orchestra, as they were, for example, at the *Concert Spirituel* in Paris.   The concert-orchestras were therefore on a more modest scale than those in the opera-houses.   The public concert hardly existed, and those given by court orchestras were held in private in the chamber of the sovereign or prince for the enjoyment of his court.   Concert-music, therefore, which was mainly the symphony, concerto and overture, was usually performed by small orchestras suited to the size of the room in which they played.   Indeed, a symphony was regarded as, and treated as, "chamber music," an expression that we now associate only with music in which each part is performed by one person, but which in the 18th century meant music played in a room or chamber before a limited and select audience.   The orchestral player permanently employed in a German court orchestra was a *Kammermusiker* or chamber musician.   The close and intimate surroundings of the "chamber" required no large volume of sound, and consequently few players. So it is not surprising to read that C. F. Cramer in his *Magazin der Musik* (1783)[2] recommended that symphonies should never be played by more than seventeen performers, and when we observe that the old sets of orchestral parts of symphonies and overtures now reposing in our libraries rarely include more than two first violin, two second violin parts, and only one each for the lower string instruments.   Presuming that the players sat two at each desk, this would mean a string orchestra of fourteen players.   Many of these sets, indeed, contain only one first and one second violin part, and were obviously played by ten or a dozen performers.

Towards the end of the 18th century concert performances, hitherto held largely in private, began to emerge from the "chamber," and in the early years of the 19th century an ever-growing number of concert-societies, which were independent of royal or noble patronage, were established for the purpose of performing to larger audiences of subscribers in larger rooms or halls.   They were what one might call semi-public concerts.   The orchestras had therefore to be enlarged, and the increase in the number of players was at a rate considerably greater than could be accounted for by the addition of a few wind-instruments to the standard combination.   The strings of concert-giving orchestras in the early part of the 19th century might be almost anything from about eighteen to thirty players, and by the mid-century concert orchestras of from fifty to sixty players were by no

---

[1] *Neue Ber. Mus. Zeit.*, 1850, p. 348.   [2] 1783, I, p. 743.

means uncommon. Cramer's maximum of seventeen players, when compared with Beethoven's wish that his symphonies should be played by an orchestra of sixty, shows the number of wind instruments just about trebled and the strings rather more than doubled in about forty years.

When orchestral concert-giving was further expanded during the second quarter of the 19th century, and the general public were being admitted by payment, still larger halls and consequently larger orchestras were necessary. The wind and percussion could then hardly number less than from eighteen to twenty, and the strings from forty to fifty players. So it seems that although the increase in the size of string orchestras was largely the outcome of the growing power of the wind band, a contributing factor to the growth in size of concert orchestras was also in some measure due to the development of concert performances before larger audiences in larger halls.

That many opera and concert orchestras in the first half of last century fell short of the proportionate strength which has just been outlined, was due mainly to financial considerations, and possibly to a lack of space in some smaller theatres and concert rooms. Many small opera-houses could not afford, or could not accommodate even the standard number of wind instruments specified in opera scores, and their strings were for the same reasons only meagrely represented. Others that were able to provide the players for every part written in the full scores had to make do with much smaller string orchestras than would have given even a reasonably good balance between strings and wind, and concert orchestras were sometimes starved or ill-balanced for similar reasons. But these conditions were not peculiar to the period now being considered. Financial stringency is liable at any period to limit the size of orchestras, and often does so at the present time. The economic axe always falls on the neck of the string orchestra; the complaint is made often enough that the strings of an orchestra are too few, but has anyone ever heard it objected that the strings are too many?

Fétis remarked in 1828 on the rather common want of proper balance between string and wind-tone. The basis of an orchestra, he wrote, will always be the strings, but "as their number has not yet been augmented in the theatres of the chief towns of Europe, the consequence is that the stringed instruments are overpowered by flutes, oboes, clarinets, bassoons, horns, trumpets, trombones, ophicleides, timpani, drums and cymbals. At the *Opéra* at Paris, where the violins and basses are very numerous, this defect is not so striking; but it is already perceptible at the *Théâtre Italien*; in the provincial theatres it is worse. In a word, in increasing the masses of sound it is not always possible to preserve a just proportion; the scarcity of artists, and the want of space, present important obstacles."[1] Fétis made a mistake if he supposed that flutes, oboes, clarinets or bassoons were ever in a position to overwhelm the stringed instruments, and he overlooked

[1] *On the revolution of the orchestra*, by M. Fétis, in *The Harmonicon*, Sept., 1828, p. 196.

the fact that it was not so much lack of artists or space that kept the string orchestras in some places too small, but lack of money. Both Berlioz and Wagner commented on the lack of string power in all but the largest European opera orchestras, and the same complaint has constantly recurred ever since their time.

Even in orchestras in which the string tone is not proportionately strong enough, the group weakest in tone-quantity will always be the wood-wind, and the strongest the brass group, aided, as it usually is, by the percussion. Fundamentally, the composer (or orchestrator) of a score is the only one who can adjust the balance of the sound from these dissimilar bodies so as to ensure that the listener hears each in its right proportion. In this respect, composers towards the middle of last century had a much harder task than their predecessors of the previous half-century. It was never very difficult to preserve a good balance between a small string orchestra, a wood-wind group, and two pairs of brass instruments on which only a limited number of open notes could be played, and which were necessarily able to contribute fewer and fewer sounds as the key of the music wandered further and further away from its home-key. So we rarely find Haydn or Mozart failing to secure a good balance, unless, as sometimes happens, their works are played by orchestras with many more stringed instruments than these composers ever counted on. Beethoven and Schubert had more difficulty in preserving an equilibrium between the stationary wood-wind group and the growing string and brass power in the orchestras of their day, and neither was able entirely to avoid the pitfalls that await composers who were apt to regard every stave in the full score as representing the same weight of tone and penetrating power. Berlioz and Wagner faced the problems of balance with the consciousness that they *were* problems, that they could not be ignored, and being aware of the dangers in their path were generally able to guard against them. But the composer who is absolutely proof against all the tricks and uncertainties that arise in handling the complexities of orchestral balance has not yet been born, and never will be. However careful or however experienced, there will always be some surprises in store for him.

The String Orchestra

The constitution of the string orchestra became stabilised towards the end of the 17th century. It has never changed since then, and no attempt has been made to alter or improve it, presumably for the good reason that experience has shown that it cannot be bettered.

The balance and blend of a well-found string orchestra seem to be well nigh as perfect as anything in music can be. Its homogeneous tone has none of that mixed quality, nor any of the uncertainty and trickiness that characterises nearly all combinations of wind instruments, and the parts coalesce quite as well or even better than the best choir of human voices. At the same time, while combining to make such a perfect communal blend, the different voices of the string orchestra possess colour

enough to endow each part with unmistakable individuality,[1] and it
was the 19th century composers who were to exploit these colour-
characteristics to an extent quite unknown to their forebears in the 18th
century.

Thus, while composers in the first half of last century made no attempt
to improve on the constitution of this perfect instrument, they demanded
from it more power, more variety and more colour. The first of these
demands was met by giving them more players to each part; the others they
themselves supplied by extending the upward range of each part, by
exploiting new and more varied textures, and they gained fresh tone-
colours by sub-dividing the parts into distinctive groups, each of which
had some special tone-character of its own.

When Beethoven silenced his violins and left the lower strings to play
alone; when Weber, Mendelssohn or Wagner silenced the lower strings and
created small ethereal choirs of violins alone; when Rossini asked for a
harmonic group of nothing but 'cellos and basses, and when Berlioz made
his violas act as a self-contained group or divided his double basses into
four parts, these composers were not demanding a new or differently
constituted string orchestra; they asked for no new part or new instrument,
and were content with the first and second violin, viola, 'cello and bass
parts that had served Haydn and Mozart; but they were asking for more
power in each part and for players enough to make it possible to sub-divide
each part into so many new colour-groups within the general framework of
the string orchestra. Haydn had not 'cellos enough to make five parts of
them, even if he had wanted to, and Dittersdorf could not have written
four double bass parts for his one player on that instrument, even if it had
ever occurred to him to do so.

To the 19th century composers the string orchestra remained just what it
had been for over a century, but they wanted it to be enlarged so that they
could have the medium for devising new ways of using it. For every one
effect that Haydn could get from his strings, Wagner could get half-a-dozen,
but he could not have got them without many more string players than
were to be found in Haydn's orchestra.

Being just as it had been, and just as it was destined to remain, there is
therefore nothing fresh that can be said about the constitution of the string
orchestra in the first half of last century. Of its strength, all there is to
record is the increase in the power of each part by the addition of more

---

[1] Unless the parts are not properly balanced, or unless the second violins are inferior
players (a circumstance by no means uncommon in early 19th century orchestras), there
can be, of course, no difference between the colour of a first and a second violin part.
Composers of all periods have been apt to imagine that there is a difference, and have often
miscalculated effects by counting on this supposed difference. The advent of music by
wireless transmission has quite obliterated any difference that may be caused in a concert-
room by the sound of first and second violin parts coming each from a different part of
the orchestra, and points of *imitation* between the two parts often suffer in wireless performances by becoming mere *repetition* instead of imitation. On the other hand, the difference
between violin, viola, 'cello and double-bass tone is always quite distinctive.

players, also some adjustments that were made in order to improve the balance of parts, and a few local peculiarities.

The balance and strength of the string orchestra in Germany at the beginning of last century is set forth in Koch's *Lexikon*, published in 1802.[1] While remarking that the size of an orchestra should always be graduated according to the size of the room, it is laid down as a general principle that for eight violins (four firsts and four seconds) there should be two violas, two 'cellos, and two double-basses, and that for ten violins the number of the lower instruments should be, respectively, three, three, and two. For the performance of symphonies and concert-music in general, Koch asked for not less than six firsts, six second violins, and the lower instruments in proportion,[2] making a total of about twenty-one string players. The balance that satisfied him was therefore just about half as many players for each of the viola, 'cello and bass parts as for each of the violin groups. These were the numbers required to play with the wind instruments usually employed at that time for concert-music, namely, four pairs of wood-wind, two horns, two trumpets, and drums. In a subsequently revised edition of the same *Lexikon* published sixty-three years later,[3] the figures for the strings are approximately doubled. For the same wind, with the addition of another pair of horns and three trombones, the new editor demands twelve first violins, ten seconds, six violas, eight 'cellos, and from four to six double-basses, that is, a string orchestra of forty or more players instead of twenty. With two more second violins, two more violas and six (but not four) double-basses, this would form a very well-balanced string orchestra practically in accordance with the modern practice. Both the old and the revised *Lexikon* recommend that the best violinists should not all be in the first violins, that older and younger players should be judiciously distributed so that one part is not played only by older men and another by their juniors, and that the viola players should not be worn-out violinists; all of which is good sound common sense.

Another specification for a well-balanced string orchestra according to German standards is that given by Gassner in his *Partiturkenntniss* in 1838,[4] that is, thirty-six years after Koch; the figures in this case are: 6–6–4–3–2 or 3. This shows a stronger viola part than in Koch's plan, and is better balanced. Gassner's figures in 1844,[5] however, indicate that the strength of the strings in good German opera-houses at that time was usually 8–8–4–4–4. Here the violas are none too many, and the equal number of 'cellos and basses is noteworthy.

Beethoven's request for not less than 4–4–?–2–2 string instruments to play one of his symphonies at Vienna in 1811[6] is very modest and probably represents what he considered a minimum number, but for the first performance of the Choral Symphony in 1824 he required 24 violins, 10 violas, and 12 each of 'cellos and basses.[7] This is unusually strong in the lower string

---

[1] Art. *Besetzung.*   [2] Art. *Kapelle.*   [3] Koch-Dommer, 1865.   [4] I, p. 7.
[5] *Dirigent und Ripienist.*   [6] Nohl, II, p. 54.   [7] Thayer, III, p. 161.

parts, especially if it is taken into account that about half of the violin players were amateurs, as was usual in all concert performances in Vienna at that time. The string orchestra at the court opera-house in Vienna[1] during the 'forties appears to have been balanced in much the same way as in the larger German theatres, with rather few violas and an equal number of 'cellos and basses. For the first performance of his second symphony (1847), Schumann asked for not less than eight first, eight second violins, four or five violas, nine 'cellos and three basses,[2] an oddly balanced plan which is rather weak in violas and basses, and abnormally strong in 'cellos.

According to Schreiber,[3] Wagner balanced the strings at Dresden as follows:

$$8-\ 8-5-4-3$$
$$10-10-6-5-4$$
$$12-12-8-7-5$$

In his report on the Dresden orchestra in 1846,[4] Wagner reported that the strength of the strings was then 22 violins, 8 violas, 7 'cellos and 6 basses. He recommended that two more violins should be added, and said that there were several weak players among the second violins, also that there were too many old players in the orchestra who should have been pensioned off some time ago.

From the French side we have Kastner's plans for two string orchestras, dated 1839.[5] The smaller of the two requires six first, four or five second violins, two or three violas, two or three 'cellos, and two basses; this probably represents the strength of the strings in the smaller Paris theatres and in the best of the provincial theatres in France. The larger is that of the Opéra orchestra, with twelve players for each of the violin parts, eight violas, ten 'cellos and eight basses. The latter orchestra and that of the Société des Concerts were the two finest and largest orchestras in Paris; both were well balanced in the middle and lower parts, but no such orchestras were to be found anywhere else in France.

Berlioz's specification for an ideal concert-orchestra is on a more generous scale. His demand was for 21 first violins, 20 seconds, 18 violas, 15 'cellos, and 10 basses.[6] This is unusually strong in the viola part, stronger, in fact, than has ever been considered necessary, but may be explained by Berlioz's complaint that viola players were generally inefficient violinists.

An English specification in 1836[7] requires 30 violins, 8 violas, 8 'cellos and 6 basses. This was said to represent the strength of the strings in the Philharmonic orchestra at that time. If it is correct, it shows that the number of stringed instruments considered necessary "to give a proper effect to full symphonies and overtures" had just about doubled since the time of the Haydn-Salomon concerts in 1791 and 1794. In this plan the violas are rather weak and the basses none too many; but the balance at the

---

[1] Kralik, p. 19.   [2] Erler, II, p. 26.   [3] Schreiber, p. 127.   [4] Newman, I, p. 436.
[5] Cours, p. 4.   [6] Instrumentation, p. 241.   [7] Mus. World, Sept. 9, 1836, p. 206.

Philharmonic concerts in 1842 was much better, namely, 16 first and 16 second violins, 10 violas, 8 'cellos and 7 basses.[1] The figures given at the end of this chapter, however, suggest that most London orchestras employed an equal number of 'cellos and basses, and this was confirmed by Hogarth, who wrote in 1836 that "the double-basses are generally as numerous as the violoncellos."[2] In most orchestras a 'cello and a bass player sat at the same desk, and were spread about the orchestra in pairs so that the bass part should be easily heard by all the players on the other instruments. The increasing use of the 'cellos as melodists in the tenor register eventually brought about the present custom of grouping the 'cellos and basses separately, but that arrangement was not generally adopted until after the mid-century.

Taken as a whole, in Germany and England, it would seem that most orchestras in the first half of last century employed an equal number of first and second violins, and that the violas, 'cellos, and basses were each approximately half as many as the first violins. The balance is therefore rather weak in viola-tone, and this weakness would be accentuated in view of the very common complaint that viola players were then generally indifferent or infirm violinists.

Berlioz and Wagner are amongst those who voiced their condemnation of that unhappy state of affairs. The former wrote: "It is an antique, absurd, and deplorable prejudice that has hitherto handed over the performance of the tenor part to second or third-rate violinists. Whenever a violinist is mediocre, it is said, 'He will make a capital tenor'."[3] Wagner expressed his views in these words: "The viola is commonly (with rare exceptions indeed) played by infirm violinists, or by decrepit players of wind instruments who happen to have been acquainted with a stringed instrument once upon a time; at best a competent viola player occupies the first desk, so that he may play the occasional soli for that instrument; but I have even seen this function performed by the leader of the first violins. It was pointed out to me that in a large orchestra, which contained eight violas, there was only one player who could deal with the rather difficult passages in one of my later scores!"[4] And that was written in 1869. But it was just Berlioz and Wagner who, by writing more important and exacting parts for the instrument, did so much to bring about a higher standard of viola-playing and a better status for the performers on that unjustly neglected instrument.

Only rather exceptionally was a solo part allotted to the viola, no doubt because the playing on that instrument was generally poor or indifferent; but the important and exacting *obbligato* part for viola solo in an opera so popular as *Der Freischütz*[5] must have exposed the inefficiency of many a leading viola player, and would draw attention to this weakness and urge the necessity for remedial action. An allied instrument, the *Viola d'amore*, achieved some prominence when Meyerbeer wrote an important solo for

[1] Published announcement, 1842.   [2] *Mus. World*, Aug. 6, 1836, p. 167.
[3] *Mem.*, II, p. 233.   [4] *On Conducting*, p. 4.   [5] Aennchen's *Romanze und Aria*, Act III.

it in *Les Huguenots* (1836). According to Castil-Blaze,[1] this was no innovation, for Kreutzer had already introduced and played upon this instrument in his opera *Le Paradis de Mahomet* at the *Théâtre Feydeau* in 1821.

From the rather scanty information which is available it seems that the strings in Italian orchestras were very badly balanced. The old Italian custom of employing more double-basses than 'cellos seems to have prevailed almost up to the mid-century, together with a deplorable weakness in the viola part. That the 'cello part was so poorly represented was certainly due to the way the Italian opera-composers used it. In their scores the 'cello was no more than a bass instrument; it enjoyed practically no independence, and was not yet used as a tenor melodist, as it often was in contemporary French and German orchestration. In 1770 there had been two 'cellos to six basses at Milan, and two 'cellos to five basses at Naples, and these were the two largest and most important orchestras in Italy. In 1816 Spohr described an opera at Florence where they had only one 'cello (and that not a very good one) to six or eight double-basses.[2] A plan of the orchestra at *La Scala* in Milan shows that as late as 1825 there were only six 'cellos to eight basses in the orchestra at that famous opera-house.[3] Berlioz commented cynically on this peculiarity of Italian orchestras: "Even the kind of music which the Italian orchestras play does not justify their always having fewer violoncellos than double-basses."[4] As late as 1846 William Gardiner was unable to understand why the opera-orchestra at Venice had seven basses and only two 'cellos; but what did it matter! the people were "talking so loud that we could scarcely hear the music."[5]

For similar reasons the viola part in Italian opera-orchestras was very meagrely represented during the early years of the century when the function of that instrument was not much more than to play in unison or octaves with the bass part. Composers, indeed, rarely troubled to write a viola part, and got over the ground quickly by directing the violas to play *col basso*. In some large orchestras with 30 or 40 violins there were only two violas, two or three 'cellos, and five or six double-basses, and at the Turin *Teatro Reale* in 1816 four violas had to do their best against forty-nine other stringed instruments.[6]

When Rossini and his followers set a higher standard in orchestration in the second and third decades of the century, the balance seems to have improved, and six violas were playing in *La Scala*, the *San Carlo* and the *Fenice* orchestras, with from twelve to fourteen first violins. These three, however, were the very best in Italy, and it would be misleading to quote them as typical examples of the orchestras in that land of innumerable opera-houses. Many of them played without any violas, or at best with but one or two very inefficient performers.

[1] *L'Acad. Imp.*, II, p. 351.   [2] *Autob.*, I, p. 288.   [3] *Harm.*, Aug., 1825, p. 140.
[4] *Mem.*, I, p. 235.   [5] *Sights in Italy*, p. 378.
[6] *Leip. All. Mus. Zeit.*, No. 12, p. 682.

Apart from local peculiarities, and viewing the situation as a whole, it seems that although the string orchestra had gained considerably in power by the middle of the century, it still required more careful adjustment of the balance of tone between its various parts. The first and second violins were virtually on an equality, a good general principle which can never be substantially altered without loss of balance; the violas still required to be brought up to a strength of not less than two-thirds or up to three-quarters of the number of first violins; the number of 'cellos still required some increase over that of the basses, while the latter had yet to settle down to a strength of not less than half the number of the first violins. The modern practice in first-class orchestras is approximately that of the Bayreuth proportions, which were $1-1-\frac{3}{4}-\frac{3}{4}-\frac{1}{2}$. In most orchestras of the half-century the actual strength of the string parts can hardly be correctly gauged only by means of figures. At that time the ability and quality of the players was far from as uniform as it now is in first-class orchestras; that, with the presence of some aged and some unripe probationers could easily upset any calculations as to balance which are based on mere numbers or man-power. We hear of one double-bass player who was equal to four others, or how the leader's violin was heard above all the rest; and who can doubt but that Lindley and Dragonetti in London contributed much more tone to the bass part than any other pair of performers on the 'cello and bass. An old *Stadtmusiker* who in his early youth had learned to finger a viola, and who after half a life-time's service on some other instrument had been obliged again to take up his neglected viola, would not produce the same amount of tone as the vigorous young man with a conservative training. It is more than likely that the players at the tail-end of the second violin desks in most orchestras of the half-century were not to be correctly valued by a mere counting of heads. These things would be enough to discount the value of any assessment based only on figures, and would certainly unbalance the tone of a string orchestra of which the number of players might be proportionately the most correct.

The value of one player in an orchestra of seventy may seem very small, but it may easily be much more or much less than a seventieth part of the combined value of all the players. Such considerations always bring one back to the view that however much one may regard an orchestra as a corporate institution, as a team, or as a collective body, in the final assessment it owes its collective superiority or inferiority to the qualities of individual players who cannot be measured by any gauge but that of individual merit.

THE WOOD-WIND

By the beginning of the 19th century the wood-wind section of the orchestra had just recently become stabilised. The standard group was then complete, with its pairs of flutes, oboes, clarinets and bassoons, making eight parts in all. All of these instruments had been used during the 18th century, the flutes, oboes and bassoons since the beginning, and the clarinets only since the mid-century, but the complete group of four pairs were not regularly employed until towards the end of the century, as they were in some of the later works of Haydn and Mozart. Previous to that, composers usually scored their movements for only one or two pairs of wood-wind, the most common of which was the pair of oboes.

Now, to begin the new century, composers generally wrote as a matter of course for the full group of eight wood-wind instruments, treating each as a single instrument, and not, as often in the earlier 18th century orchestration, as *ripieno* instruments. The group of eight remained standard during the first half of last century, in spite of occasional additions or substitutions of larger or smaller instruments of allied type, such as the piccolo, cor anglais, bass clarinet, basset horn or double bassoon.

The wood-wind then had to contend with a string orchestra and a brass group, both of which were still increasing in number and power, and this disturbance in the balance of the three main groups of instruments began to raise problems such as had never troubled orchestrators in the 18th century. But 19th century composers were compelled to take into consideration the comparative weakness of their wood-wind-tone against a more weighty string-tone and a still heavier brass-tone. The balancing of the parts now required more careful consideration and some skilful adjustment in order to provide that each part should sound with due prominence, and when a satisfactory balance was not achieved it was almost invariably because these composers over-estimated the weight and penetrating power of their wood-wind instruments. Several instances of such miscalculations can be found in the scores of Beethoven's and Schubert's symphonies, and some "touching-up" of these scores by conductors ever since Wagner's time has been by no means uncommon.

The addition of extra wood-wind instruments did not overcome or solve these problems, and was hardly intended to do so. The extra wood-wind parts which were occasionally embodied in the scores of the early 19th century were not so much additions to the tone-power of the group as temporary substitutions which for the time being carried the range of the standard instruments upwards or downwards; the piccolo took the voice of the flute upwards, while the cor anglais, bass clarinet and double bassoon extended the range of the oboe, clarinet and bassoon in the downward direction. By virtue of their extreme pitch, the piccolo and double bassoon did add some tone-weight and penetrating power to the wood-wind group as a whole, but the cor anglais, bass clarinet or basset horn were treated as solo instruments whose function it was to take over the duties of the ordinary oboe or clarinet for some special purpose and for a limited period.

Only very exceptionally did the advent of these extra instruments add permanent personnel to any orchestra; in the ordinary course, the existing players merely laid down their usual instrument and picked up the larger or the smaller one, as the case might be. Even in the largest establishments, where three or four players on each wood-wind instrument were available, the additional players were not there for the purpose of playing only piccolo, cor anglais, bass clarinet and double bassoon parts. Except in the case of the piccolo, there were not enough parts written for these instruments to justify such extravagance. Any orchestra which employed players exclusively for the purpose of playing cor anglais, bass clarinet or double bassoon parts in the first half of last century would have been paying them for doing next to nothing. The extra players were there to relieve the usual players on less important occasions, to double the parts on special occasions, or in some cases in order to provide a second orchestra in another theatre.

Even Berlioz, who was lavish enough in his demands, contrived that the nine parts for piccolo, two flutes, two oboes, cor anglais, two clarinets and bass clarinet (*Symphonie Fantastique* and *Benvenuto Cellini* overture) could be played by six players. It was only in the largest Paris orchestras that an additional pair of bassoonists was necessary, and this was only because French composers had formed the habit of writing for four bassoons; it was a local peculiarity, not to be found anywhere but in Paris, and then only in the largest orchestras. In other large centres, where musicians were procurable, an extra player for the piccolo was sometimes forthcoming, but in general, most orchestras could not provide more than eight players on wood-wind instruments, and between them they had to play all the parts written for that type of instrument.

Of the additional wood-wind, the piccolo was the only one that was able to secure a firm foothold in the orchestras of the half-century. It was available almost everywhere, and one of the two flautists could always be depended on to play the smaller instrument, or both players if necessary, as in Weber's *Freischütz*, in Spohr's *Jessonda*, or in Spontini's ballet music to *Danaïdes* (1817). It was the only one of the wood-wind group which came near to adding a permanent member to any orchestra, and was also the only one which could hope to make its voice heard through the din of a loud *tutti*.

The cor anglais, basset-horn, bass clarinet and double bassoon were only rare visitors to a few of the largest orchestras. To many they were complete strangers, and it was a matter of locality more than anything else which governed their use. These less common instruments were usually available only in the large musical centres, where there were plenty of players, where there were military bands to draw on, and where wind-instrument makers were congregated. Thus we find that the early parts for cor anglais and bass clarinet occur almost entirely in scores written for, or specially adapted for, the Paris theatres.

Few German orchestras could produce a cor anglais, as Berlioz discovered when he toured Germany in 1843; he was obliged to rewrite his cor anglais parts for the clarinet at Leipzig, Weimar, and other German towns. Even in Berlin in 1829, when Mendelssohn revived Bach's *St. Matthew Passion*, the parts for *oboi di caccia* were played on clarinets instead of on the more appropriate cor anglais.[1] But in Paris there were players and military bands

[1] *Ber. All. Mus. Zeit.*, 1829, No. 7, p. 98.

in plenty, and there were enterprising makers ready to make the unfamiliar instruments. Nearly all the cor anglais parts written in the first half of last century are to be found in the Paris full scores; they occur in Catel's *Alexandre chez Apelles* (1808),[1] in the same composer's *Les Bayadères* (1810), in Rossini's *La Gazza Ladra* (French adaptation, *Théâtre Italien*, 1817), and in his *Guillaume Tell* (1829); in Spontini's *Olimpie* (1819), Bellini's *Il Pirata* (*Théâtre Italien*, 1827); Halévy's *La Juive* (1835),[2] Meyerbeer's *Robert le Diable* (1831), *Les Huguenots* (1836) and *Le Prophète* (1849), in Donizetti's *La Favorita* (1840), Kastner's *La Maschera* (1841), and in several of Berlioz's concert works. Wagner wrote for the cor anglais in *Lohengrin* (1850), but that opera was written after he had spent three years in Paris, where he would hear and get to know the instrument.

To most German musicians the cor anglais was an obsolete instrument. Koch (1802) wrote that it was *"wenig mehr gebräuchlich"*; Gassner (1838) describes it as being almost out of use, and added, that when the instrument was not obtainable the part could be played on a viola.[3] In Vienna the cor anglais had long been known, but although in the 'twenties and 'thirties they had good players in Joseph Sellner and Jacob Uhlmann, the Viennese composers rarely used the instrument orchestrally. The Belgian, Andries, wrote as late as 1856: *"Le Cor Anglais n'est pas considérée comme instrument d'orchestre."* When used, it was always as a solo instrument, played by the leading oboe player.

The cor anglais was quite a rarity in this country. Referring to this instrument, it was written in 1823: "This would be a curiosity in England, where no such instrument is now in being";[4] in 1836 the *Musical World* thought it necessary to explain that "this instrument, on which Grattan Cooke accompanied Mrs. Bishop in Meyerbeer's song at the Quartet Concert on Saturday week, is a species of Oboe of extended compass. . . . The old Vox-humana was the grand-papa of the Corno Inglese."[5]

The bass clarinet was likewise more at home in Paris than anywhere else. The parts written for it in the first half of last century are so few that most text-books on orchestration found it impossible to produce more than one example, and that was the solo part in Meyerbeer's *Les Huguenots*. But there were a few more; Meyerbeer used it again in *Le Prophète*, and Donizetti wrote for it in *Dom Sébastien* (1843), in fact, he wrote for two in order to make a quartet with two ordinary clarinets.[6] Berlioz, of course, made use of the bass clarinet; Wagner put it in his scores of *Tannhäuser* and *Lohengrin*, but only after he had spent some years in Paris.

The German compilers of musical dictionaries, text-books and tutors, appear to have had little or no knowledge of the real bass clarinet pitched

---

[1] The part was played by Vogt. [2] Two parts, played by Brod and Vény.
[3] *Partiturkenntniss*, I, p. 20. [4] *Quar. Mus. Mag.*, Vol. V, No. XIX, p. 400.
[5] *Mus. World*, April 29, 1836, p. 114. Vox humana was an English name for the tenor oboe. By 1836 Grattan Cooke would find some use for his cor anglais, as the overture to *William Tell* was becoming very popular.
[6] Kastner, *Cours*, Supp., p. 7.

an octave below the normal instrument; they knew the basset-horn, and generally called it a bass clarinet.[1]   Even as late as 1850 very few German orchestras could produce a bass clarinet; in that year one had to be bought specially for Liszt's production of *Lohengrin* at the Weimar opera.   Even Gevaert, in the first edition of his book on orchestration (1863), admitted that he had no first-hand knowledge of the larger clarinets.[2]

Adolphe Sax came to Paris in 1842 and brought with him an improved bass clarinet; he played four octaves on it in the presence of Meyerbeer and several prominent musicians.[3]   Its prospects were improving round about the mid-century, but it had still to wait for some time before it could gain a permanent footing even in the larger orchestras.

In this country the bass clarinet made its appearance about the same time as in France.   A well-known London maker, George Wood, is said to have made one in 1833,[4] and in 1836 the English clarinet player Willman played an *obbligato* part on the "clarono" at a Philharmonic concert.   In 1837, J. Lebrun, a flute and clarinet maker in Brussels, sent the directors of the same society a "bass-clarone" of his own make.   The *Musical World* informed its readers in 1836 about Willman's performance on the unfamiliar instrument: "This newly invented instrument, on which Mr. Willman performed so admirably at the dinner of the Royal Society of Musicians, partakes of the corno-bassetto, the clarinet, and the bass-horn."[5]   At his own concert in the Hanover Square Rooms in that same year Willman played on his "new instrument the bass-clarone," and again at the Manchester Musical Festival. These were all solo or *obbligato* performances; there was really nothing else written for this instrument.   So little was the bass clarinet known in Germany that when von Gontershausen reviewed all the instruments he knew in 1855, the only bass clarinet he was able to describe was the basset-horn.

The basset-horn has always hung on to the fringe of the orchestra by the most slender of threads.   This instrument, which is really something between a tenor and a bass clarinet, had enjoyed some initial success in the last quarter of the 18th century, and it was then that Mozart wrote some parts for it.   Its reputation in the early 19th century rested entirely on its association with Mozart, as it does to this day, and it is only the occasional performance of certain works by that one composer that has saved the basset-horn from becoming completely obsolete and forgotten.   All writers in the first half of last century treated it as something rather remote and out-of-date; they said that the basset-horn was little known or used, and could find no examples of its use except those by Mozart.   Gevaert (1863) commented: *"Ce bel instrument affectionné par Mozart est abandonné aujourd'hui."*[6]

[1] Gassner, *Partiturkenntniss*, I, p. 24, and Backofen, Clar^t. tutor (1824), p. 42.
[2] *Traité général*, p. 219.   [3] Kastner, *Traité*, Supp., p. 25.
[4] Rendall, *Mus. Ass. Proceedings*, 1941–42, p. 66.
[5] *Mus. World*, April 1, 1836, p. 47.   [6] Gevaert, *Traité*, p. 10, f.n.

Kastner, however, revealed that the Abbé Vogler had also written for the basset-horn in church music, but added that it was now neglected. It is more than likely that parts for the basset-horn could be found in forgotten scores written contemporaneously with Mozart's later works. All the German authorities harked back to Mozart, and many of them would insist on treating the basset-horn and the bass clarinet as one and the same thing.

The performance in Germany of certain of Mozart's works, however, demanded that either the real instrument or some substitute for it must be found. So we hear of basset-horns being acquired for a performance of Mozart's *Requiem* by the Dresden orchestra in 1800, and of the elder Rothe, the leading clarinettist at Dresden, playing one of these instruments in "a masterly manner" at a performance of Mozart's *Titus* in 1815.[1] Other orchestras made do with ordinary clarinets, a procedure which necessitated awkward transpositions into the octave above whenever the parts exceeded the downward compass of the clarinet.

Nevertheless, the basset-horn was not quite out of use in the orchestra. Beethoven wrote for it in his *Prometheus* music (1801), and Kastner himself gave it a part in his Paris opera *Beatrice* (1839).[2] Berlioz regretted that the basset-horn was not taught at the Conservatoire, but in the same breath granted that the bass clarinet could do all that the basset-horn could, and better.[3]

Yet, although so rarely used in orchestras, plenty of these instruments were made during the first half of last century; they must have been made mainly for the military bands. In London, Willman and Williams were always able to produce their basset-horns when required for the Mozart parts, and occasionally the former would give his audience a real treat by playing on it a fantasia on the well-known air "Cease your funning," from the Beggar's Opera.[4] Although there were few opportunities of playing the basset-horn in an orchestra, the instrument was used fairly often in England for solos and *obbligati*, especially by Willman. The following throws light on the carelessness and indifference with which Mozart's instrumentation was treated in the early years of the century at the King's Theatre; it relates to the first performance in England of Mozart's *La Clemenza di Tito* in 1806: "So little attention was paid to the instrumental accompaniments at this period, that in the grand aria of Vitella, *Non piu di fiori*, a tinkling harp was substituted for the impressive and wailing tones of the Corno di Bassetto obbligato. A viola was subsequently promoted to the same post of honour; and it was not till many years after, at one of the City of London Amateur Concerts, that this majestic scene was heard with the genuine accompaniment of Mozart."[5]

[1] Schreiber, p. 134.
[2] Extracts quoted in his *Cours*, Supp., pp. 20 and 22.   [3] *Mem.*, II, 233.
[4] *Mus. World*, April 8, 1836, p. 60. Willman played a concerto for the basset-horn at Cambridge in November, 1827.
[5] *Harm.*, Feb., 1830, p. 71, f.n.

The situation with regard to the double bassoon was entirely different. This was not a solo instrument, and when it was used in an orchestra, it was introduced, not in order to provide a bass part for the wood-wind group in particular, but in the capacity of an additional wind-bass for the whole orchestra.

Towards the end of the 18th century and during the early part of last century composers seemed to have felt the lack of a powerful wind-bass more flexible than that which could be provided by the bass trombone. That instrument was not suitable for active bass parts; it could not manage a good *legato* in florid passages, and the tone was ponderous; moreover, at that time the instrument was not to be found everywhere; therefore, when

more power in the bass register was required for large-scale performances, composers looked about for a suitable instrument. Their choice was at first limited to either the serpent or the double bassoon, and later on the same want was supplied by the ophicleide, and still later by the tuba. It was not so much the particular tone-qualities of any of these instruments that was wanted; it was rather *quantity* of sound in the bass register that they needed, so they availed themselves of whichever instrument was to be found in their particular locality.

There had been difficulty in making and playing double bassoons during the 18th century, and these troubles were not altogether overcome during the first half of last century; except in certain localities, double bassoons were never plentiful. As far as they were available and playable, double bassoons and serpents were used to provide the much-needed bass part in military bands. When composers in the early years of last century sought for a heavier wind-bass than their orchestras provided, some made use of the serpent and others adopted the double bassoon, and their choice was governed entirely by the local supply. The serpent was native to France; therefore, in French scores it was always the serpent that was specified, but in Vienna and neighbourhood the double bassoon was available, so we find that Haydn and Beethoven included in their scores a part for that instrument when they wanted some reinforcement for their orchestral bass parts.[1]

That Haydn and Beethoven, and probably other Viennese composers,

A FRENCH CHURCH SERPENT
PLAYER

[1] In Grove's *Beethoven and his nine Symphonies* (p. 136) it is said that there was a double-bassoon in the Elector's orchestra at Bonn.

should have written parts for the double bassoon is easily understandable in view of the abundant evidence which shows that this instrument was made and used during their time in Vienna and in other Austrian and Bohemian towns. Surviving specimens show that Doke of Linz, Schuster, Kies, and Koch of Vienna, Schöllnast of Pressburg, and a little later, Horák of Prague, and Küss, Uhlmann, and Stehle of Vienna were making double bassoons near the end of the 18th and during the first half of the 19th century, and it is impossible to disassociate the appearance of parts for these instruments in the full scores written in these places from the fact that they were also being made in Austria and Bohemia.

In his *Manuel général* (1848), Kastner provided a picture of an Austrian double bassoon which he named *Basse d'harmonie (instrument Autrichien)*, but he was unable to portray a French instrument of the same type.[1] The pay-roll of the Imperial orchestra at Vienna in 1807 provided for a double bassoon player,[2] and from Kastner we learn that at a performance of Handel's *Timotheus* at Vienna in 1812 two of these instruments were employed.[3] When the grand concert was given in 1814 at which Beethoven's battle-piece *Wellington's Victory* was produced, there were two double bassoons in the orchestra,[4] and at great performances in the Riding School of *The Seasons* in 1839, and *The Creation* in 1843, no less than four of these instruments were included in the orchestra.[5] Franz Stöber's plan of the orchestra at the *Kärntnerthor Theater* in 1821 also provides a place for a double bassoon player. These players and their instruments were not maintained to play only in occasional large-scale performances or on special occasions; they came from the military bands, of which there were plenty in Vienna. Smart observed a double bassoon in a military band at Vienna in 1825, and the specifications of Austrian military bands in Kastner's *Manuel général*[6] make it quite clear that this instrument was a regular constituent of the larger Austrian infantry bands. Therein lies the explanation of the fact that the Viennese composers wrote parts for the double bassoon at a time when it was almost completely ignored in France, Italy and England.

The double bassoon was hardly known in France. Contemporary authorities wrote about it in rather a distant manner, as if they knew of it, but did not really know the instrument.[7] All agreed that it was rarely used in orchestras, and Berlioz said that few players cared to learn to play on it. It is difficult to find traces of the instrument in France, and parts for it are very rare in French scores before the 'seventies. Isouard is said to have written for it in his opera *Aladin* (1822), but in French scores it was

---

[1] Pl. XIII, No. 6. No. 9 on the same plate is incorrectly named *Contre-basson autrichien;* it is a bass-horn, an improved form of the serpent, and played with a cupped mouthpiece.

[2] Köchel, p. 32.   [3] *Cours*, p. 5.   [4] Thayer, II, p. 268.

[5] Gassner, *Dir. und Rip.*, plan of the orchestra reproduced in Schunemann's *Geschichte des Dirigierens*, p. 310.

[6] *Manuel général*, pp. 201, 202.

[7] Kastner, Berlioz, Andries, Gevaert. The earlier authorities, Francœur-Choron and Catrufo, do not appear to have had any definite knowledge of the double bassoon.

almost invariably the serpent that was called upon to reinforce the bass part
in large-scale performances before the ophicleide came and took over that
duty.   When Haydn's *Creation* was performed on a grand scale at the Paris
Opéra in 1800 there were four serpents in the orchestra[1]; they were obviously
there to play the double bassoon part.   According to Pierre,[2] Beethoven's
double bassoon parts were played on an ophicleide at the *Conservatoire*
concerts at Paris until as late as 1863; this adds confirmation to the view
that the double bassoon was unobtainable and practically unknown in
France.   Neither on the serpent nor on the ophicleide could the double
bassoon parts be played in the correct 16 ft. octave; neither instrument could
exceed the downward compass of the ordinary bassoon; all they could do
was to strengthen the bass part with their own 8 ft. tone.

Although quite a number of double bassoons are said to have been made
and used in Germany during the first half of last century, it is highly probable
that some of the instruments so described were not actually bassoons.   The
bass horn or "Russian bassoon," as it was called on the continent, was not a
reed instrument; it was sounded, like the serpent, by means of a cupped
mouthpiece, and had the same technique and fingering as the serpent, but
was, nevertheless, sometimes called a double bassoon.   Berlioz had some
difficulty in convincing a performer on the Russian bassoon at Brunswick
that his instrument was not a double bassoon.[3]   It has already been pointed
out that Kastner was capable of making the same mistake, and as Andries
also fell into the same error when he described the *Contre Basson* as an
instrument à vent et à embouchure,[4] it seems as if the use of this misnomer was
fairly widespread on the continent.

In Germany the position of the double bassoon was as follows: Koch
said that it was then (1802) used in wind-bands; Gassner (1838) associated
it with the serpent for the bass part in military bands, Koch-Dommer (1865)
stated that it was rarely used in orchestras, but commonly in military bands,
and Kastner's specifications of 1848[5] show that there were double bassoons
in some of the larger infantry bands in Prussia and Würtemberg.   These
German instruments, then, must have been made in order to supply the
military bands, and some of them would no doubt find their way into
orchestras when Haydn's or Beethoven's parts demanded their presence.

But it is quite evident that this instrument was by no means available in
every German orchestra, not even in some of the largest.   There is no trace
of it in the Berlin, Dresden and Munich orchestras before the mid-century.
According to Schreiber[6] there was no double bassoon in the performances of
Haydn's *Creation* at Berlin in 1801 and 1810, and it was not until the 'forties
that one was acquired by the *Gewandhaus* orchestra at Leipzig for the purpose
of playing the part in Mendelssohn's Reformation Symphony.   Schreiber
tells of a double bassoon ordered for the Grand Duke of Hesse's orchestra
at Mayence in 1817, and connects this with the proximity of Schott's and

---

[1] Castil-Blaze, *L'Acad. Imp.*, II, p. 372.   [2] *La Facture*, p. 30.   [3] *Mem.*, II, p. 79.
[4] *Aperçu théorique*, p. 24.   [5] *Manuel*, pp. 194, 197, 199.   [6] P. 135.

Heckel's instrument factory in that same town.[1]   From Gassner we have the statement that the Hanau Music Society possessed two double bassoons in 1841.[2]   A double bassoon was used at the Lower Elbe Musical Festival in 1827 with an orchestra of 116 players,[3] and Mendelssohn wrote a part for it in his Reformation Symphony.   Although it is most probable that it was employed at some of the German Musical Festivals, German composers did not appear to regard it as an instrument that they could count on finding even in large orchestras, and therefore rarely asked for it in their scores.

It is more than probable that Haydn's and Beethoven's double bassoon parts were either omitted in many German performances or else were played on a serpent or a bass-horn.   There is also the uneasy suspicion that the references to the double bassoon in Germany during the first half of the 19th century cannot always be trusted to refer to the real reed instrument; if a player on the bass-horn was able to suppose that his instrument was a double bassoon, it is quite likely that others were capable of making the same mistake.

In this country there had been more than one attempt during the 18th century to construct and play upon double bassoons, but according to both Burney and Parke these experiments were not wholly successful.   The instrument used at the Handel Commemoration Festivals at Westminster Abbey in 1784 and 1787, was used again at the Three Choirs Festival in 1788, and was played by John Ashley, senior.   In the first few years of the 19th century it seems to have been still in use at the Three Choirs Festivals, played by Jenkinson in 1803, but after that time nothing more is heard of the double bassoon for a long time, presumably because the serpent, and then the ophicleide, were coming into use for the same purpose in the large English choral festivals.

There is no record of what was done with the double bassoon parts in Beethoven's symphonies in English orchestras, and it is not at all improbable that the parts, if played at all, were played on a serpent or an ophicleide, as they were in France, in the 8 ft. octave.   In 1838, when Puzzi, Willman, Sedlatzek, Barret and Baumann were giving "classical concerts by wind instruments" in London, the lowest part had to be played on a string double-bass by Dragonetti; it seems that no double bassoon was available, and the suggestion was made that the part would be better played on a serpent.[4]   There is no trace of the double bassoon in the contemporary English wind-bands.   After a first performance in 1832, *Fidelio* was produced several times in London, and when Balfe conducted it at Her

---

[1] Heckel was only five years old in 1817, and did not work in Schott's factory until 1829.

[2] Schreiber supposes that these came from Haltenhof's instrument factory at Hanau. It seems, however, that Haltenhof made only brass instruments.

[3] *Harm.*, Oct., 1827, p. 213.

[4] *Mus. World*, 1838, Vol. VIII, pp. 112, 125, 145, 152, 179.   Cipriani Potter, describing orchestral instruments in 1837, dismissed the double bassoon with the remark that it "wants power."

Majesty's Theatre in 1851 an ophicleide was used in the grave-digging scene,[1] obviously to play the double bassoon part.   These facts lend support to the assumption that the latter instrument was unobtainable and practically unknown in this country during the first half of last century.

The foregoing particulars of the additional wood-wind parts that are to be found in some of the scores written during the first half of last century should not be allowed to give the impression that this group had been steadily increasing in number during that period.   Except that a piccolo part was often added, or more often substituted for one of the flute parts (and then more often in opera than in symphony) there had been no general increase in the number of wood-wind instruments usually employed in the orchestra at the same moment.   It would be no exaggeration to assert that, with the above exception, not as many as one in every hundred full scores written between 1800 and 1850 will be found to specify any but the usual four pairs of wood-wind that were required in the first four of Beethoven's symphonies, in Weber's overtures, or in Mendelssohn's and Schumann's symphonies.   That Wagner wrote for a group of twelve wood-wind instruments in *Lohengrin*, or that Berlioz or Meyerbeer sometimes asked for three instruments of one family instead of the usual pair, should not be regarded as proof that by the mid-century the wood-wind group had become substantially larger than it was at the beginning of the century.   These extra demands may rightly be regarded as portents of what was to come in the following half-century, but not as signs that the amplification of the group had already been accomplished.

Even when one or two extra wood-wind were employed, the much greater increase in the power of the strings had tended by the middle of the century to overwhelm the volume of sound from the wood-wind, and on a few occasions the latter were doubled in the effort to restore the balance. This was often done at large festivals, and Jullien did this in his concerts at Covent Garden in 1855 when he announced that he was doubling the wood-wind in order to correct "that balance of sound which has been greatly injured by the universal practice, both in England and on the continent, of making large additions to the stringed, without a corresponding increase in the (wood) wind instruments."   The same thing has often been done since that time, but it is questionable whether any doubling of the wood-wind parts ever gives them power to compete with the full volume of a large string orchestra.   Unless properly balanced in the orchestration (and that is the composer's responsibility), the wood-wind group, however large, is never able to meet the string orchestra on equal terms.

THE BRASS GROUP

In the meantime the orchestral brass group had been growing, and by the mid-century had almost doubled its size and power.

Four horns were required in most scores written for a full orchestra

---

[1] Davison, p. 117.

round about the middle of last century, although many symphonies, concertos, and smaller operas still required no more than one pair of these instruments.

In the 18th century Handel had written for four horns in his opera *Giulio Cesare*, and an engraving of the interior of a theatre at Milan shows four horns being played in the orchestra at a performance of Carcani's *Tigrane* in 1750.[1] Similar demands also occur exceptionally in a few of Haydn's and Mozart's symphonies,[2] and no doubt other such isolated instances of the use of four horns could be found; but the single pair was the standard number and sufficed for countless operas and instrumental works throughout the 18th century.

Towards the close of that century an additional pair of horns began to creep into the French opera scores. Castil-Blaze tells of an extra pair of horn players being added to the personnel of the Paris *Opéra* orchestra in 1788, although they still played in separate pairs.[3] By 1790 the *Théâtre de Monsieur*[4] had its two pairs of horn players.[5] In 1794 the four horns at the *Opéra* played together in the overture to Méhul's *Horatius Coclès*, and again in Cherubini's *Elisa*, produced later in the same year.[6] With that the ball was set rolling, and from Paris the custom of writing for four horns spread gradually until all but the smaller theatres were obliged to provide the necessary players.

As practically all concert orchestras drew their players from the opera theatres, it is logical that any additions to the orchestra employed for concerts should follow rather than precede any additions to opera orchestras. Composers would not write symphonies with four horn parts as long as orchestras provided only two of these instruments; but when theatres had found it necessary to augment their horns by another pair, there was no reason why they should not all be employed in symphonies as well as in operas. So it was that during the first two or three decades of the 19th century, in the time of Beethoven, that four horn parts began to appear more frequently in symphony scores.

The primary reason for employing an additional pair of horns was not so much in order to increase the amount of horn-tone in the orchestra, but rather in order to give a wider choice of notes than could be provided by one pair of natural horns crooked in the same key. At the time when the second pair began to be demanded the use of the hand-technique was expected only from solo-players, in parts which were specially written to show off their skill; thus, the only way to gain other than the open notes of a pair of horns in one key was to make use of another pair crooked in another key, so that the second pair could take over from the first pair when the music wandered away from the original key. But, by the time the two pairs had become generally available and the hand-technique was expected of all horn players, that is, in the early part of the 19th century, composers had got used

---

[1] Haas, *Tafel* XIV.   [2] Haydn, Nos. 13 and 31; Mozart, Nos. 25 and 32.
[3] *L'Acad. Imp.*, II, p. 347.   [4] Renamed *Théâtre de la rue Feydeau* in 1791.
[5] *Almanach*, 1791.   [6] Lavoix, p. 335.

to picking their notes from both pairs, and could thus make use of their horns when writing in keys even fairly remote from the original key of the music.

Three trombones had been used during the 18th century in many church orchestras, more particularly in Germany and Austria, for Masses and oratorios, but only very sporadically for opera. A greater demand for trombones in opera began in the last quarter of the century. The larger theatres were then obliged to find trombone players, and the supply was not everywhere equal to the demand. Some places had to make do with all-round performers who were ready to blow on almost any brass instrument,[1] or with double-handed musicians who could be employed as string players when there was no trombone part to play.

The situation seems to have varied locally. Although there had been a decline in the use of trombones in Germany towards the end of the 18th century, that country still possessed in its numerous town musicians or *Stadtmusiker* a valuable source from which its orchestras could draw their trombone players. The instrument had always occupied an important position in these civic organisations; it was on trombone that the *Abblasen*[2] from church towers was played, and although that ancient custom was dying out in the first half of the 19th century, the old corps of town musicians survived long enough to ensure a supply of players in Germany at the time when trombones were becoming regular constituents of opera and concert orchestras. In north Germany the trombone was much neglected at the end of the 18th century, and Mozart's operas were often performed without that instrument, but in south Germany, Bavaria and Austria the old civic organisations remained to ensure a good supply of players, many of whom bettered their status by becoming members of court or other opera-orchestras.[3] The quality of these players was evidently not always of the best, and the solo part in Mozart's *Requiem* was obviously too exacting a test for many of these roughly taught musicians; the bassoon was often used as a substitute for the trombone in performances of the *Requiem* during the early years of the century, and at Berlin in 1805 the trombone solo was played on a horn.[4] Nevertheless, in these rough town musicians the German orchestras had a supply of trombone players far exceeding that of any other country.

At Vienna, where there were always trombones in the Imperial Chapel, there would be no difficulty in finding players for the court opera-house, but in Paris, where the King's musical establishment was suppressed for some

---

[1] At the Paris *Opéra* in 1782 two players named Braun and Nau played either trumpet, horn or trombone parts (*Calendrier*, 1783). At the Worcester Festival in 1794 the orchestra included the two Flacks, who played horns and trombones (Lysons, p. 75).

[2] The old German custom of playing *Chorales* from the church tower or other public building in the morning, noon and evening. In earlier times the ancient *cornetto* was used as the soprano for the trombones, even in Bach's time.

[3] The famous trombonists Belcke of Berlin and Queisser of Leipzig both came from the *Stadtmusiker*.

[4] *Leip. All. Mus. Zeit.*, 1805, No. 7, p. 430.

time after the Revolution of 1789, and which when it was re-established by Napoleon contained no trombones, it was not so easy to find players. Gluck's operas at Paris in and after 1774 required trombones, and during the next twenty years parts were written for these instruments in a number of French operas by Salieri, Piccini, Sacchini, Cherubini, Méhul and a few other composers, as well as in several ballet scores. But the home of the trombone was Germany, and both instruments and players had to be brought from that country to Paris. The early trombone players at the *Opéra*, who were also required to play other instruments, all bore German-sounding names, such as Andreas Braun (d. 1806), Moser, Sieber and Nau, and in 1786 a M. Louis was commissioned to buy some German trombones for the *Opéra*.[1]

The increasing use of trombones in military bands during the early years of the 19th century[2] would no doubt ease the situation, but even then the supply was not always equal to the demand. The smaller opera orchestras in Paris employed only one trombone player,[3] and in London the starved orchestras at Drury Lane and Covent Garden Theatres had no more than one until they were obliged to provide three in or after the 'twenties. The players in London all came from the Royal Household or the military bands, and many of them bore German names.

This short supply of trombone players no doubt accounts for the absence of those instruments in some orchestras, and also for the fact that composers often treated them as *ad libitum* instruments and omitted the parts in their full scores, adding them only as supplementary parts which were not indispensable. In some 18th and early 19th century scores the trombone parts are not embodied in the full score, but appear only in an appendix at the end of the score.

By the 'twenties the supply of players seems to have improved, and from then, except in small theatres, three trombone players were regular members of all opera orchestras. The players appear to have been drawn at first almost entirely from the wind and military bands, which by that time were able to provide a fairly plentiful supply.[4] In the same way and at the same time as the additional pair of horns, the trombones began to find their way into the scores of symphonies, as in the works of Beethoven, Schubert and Spohr.

The standard brass group of the orchestra was then complete except for the addition of a wind-bass instrument which was to serve as a reinforcing voice for the bass of the orchestra as a whole. There were four horns, two trumpets, and three trombones, making nine parts in all, to which a tenth

---

[1] De Lajarte, p. 124.

[2] Farmer dates the use of trombones in military bands from the last decade of the 18th century. (*Rise of Military Music*, p. 63.)

[3] Auber, Hérold, Cherubini and other Paris composers often wrote for only one trombone in works for the *Opéra Comique*.

[4] Players from His Majesty's Household Band often played at the English Festivals in the 'twenties.

was added before the mid-century. It was the tuba which in the end supplied this want, but in the meantime, before the valved brass instruments became fairly well known, it was either the double bassoon (a reed instrument), the wooden serpent or one of its many improved successors,[1] or the ophicleide which stepped into the vacant place. These predecessors of the orchestral tuba were all instruments which for the first forty years of the 19th century supplied the bass part in military bands, from whence came also most of the players for the orchestras.

As has already been pointed out, the choice of this extra orchestral wind-bass was governed by local circumstances. Beethoven chose the double bassoon because it was available in Vienna. There can be little doubt that if the Choral Symphony had been written in Paris, it would have included a part for either a serpent or an ophideide, and none for a double bassoon.

In France the first choice (if, indeed, there was any choice) was quite naturally the serpent. Berton included it in the score of his opera *Montano et Stéphanie* in 1779, and until the ophicleide arrived on the scene, French composers used the instrument which had long been commonly played in their churches, and now gave the strongest bass voice to their military bands. In 1817 Halary produced his group of keyed brass instruments, one of which was the bass ophicleide. This proved to be a great improvement on the old wooden serpent. It provided an admirable wind-bass for a large orchestra; it was capable of considerable agility, the tone and intonation were good, and it had an excellent *legato*. To the French military bands the ophicleide was a god-send,[2] and it was not long before it appeared at the *Opéra*. In 1819 it made its first appearance in opera, but on the stage in the brass band in Spontini's *Olimpie*.[3] In 1822 the ophicleide was in the orchestra at the *Opéra* in Isouard's *Aladin*,[4] and then for many years all the large Paris orchestras, whether in opera or in concert-music, used this instrument just as the tuba is now used. Berlioz complained that there was no class for the ophicleide at the Conservatoire; there were, he said, from 100 to 150 ophicleide players in Paris, but hardly three of them were fit to play in an orchestra; M. Caussinus[5] was the only fully proficient orchestral player.[6]

In Germany the military bands in the early 19th century had only the bassoons, ordinary and double, and the serpent or various improvements on it, for the bass part. When a heavier orchestral wind-bass was required, it was generally the serpent that was called upon to supply it. But German composers on the whole did not seem to be so ready to use that instrument, or its successor the ophicleide, as were their French contemporaries. There are parts for the serpent or bass-horn in certain works by Spohr, Mendelssohn

---

[1] Bass-horn, Basson Russe, Serpent droit, Serpent basson, Serpent Forveille, Ophibariton, Basse-cor, Ophimonocleide, Chromatisches Basshorn, etc. These were largely wooden instruments, but some were and all could have been made of metal.
[2] As a young man, in 1840, Rivière played the alto ophicleide in a French military band in which there were 8 bass ophicleides. (Rivière, p. 53.)
[3] Castil-Blaze, *L'Acad. Imp.*, II, 350.   [4] Played by Pavart.
[5] Author of *Solfège-Méthode pour l'Ophicléide-basse*, c. 1840.   [6] *Mem.*, II, p. 234.

and Wagner, but it is rather unusual to find a part for any such instrument in German opera or symphony scores before the mid-century. When Mendelssohn and Wagner did specify the serpent, it should not be assumed that it was the old wooden curled variety that they were writing for; there were plenty of improved forms of the instrument which might still be called serpents, but which were really bass-horns or similar types between the old original serpent and the all-metal ophicleide.[1]

The ophicleide was never quite acclimatised in either Germany or Austria. In 1843 Berlioz wrote: "The bass tuba, which I have already named several times in my former letters, has dethroned the ophicleide in Prussia, if, indeed, it ever reigned there, which I doubt."[2] It is quite likely that Beethoven, who was no great traveller, never saw or heard one. When Rossini's *Siege of Corinth* was being rehearsed at Cassel in 1827, Moritz Hauptmann, then a violinist in the Cassel orchestra under Spohr, obviously didn't know the instrument specified in Rossini's score. From its name he guessed that it must be an improved serpent; he wondered what they had done with the ophicleide part in that same opera when it was produced at Frankfort; at Cassel they gave the part to a trombone player.[3]

Many opera orchestras in Germany never had an ophicleide; they, so to speak, by-passed it and went straight on to the tubas or bombardons which had appeared in Prussia in 1835. Already in 1838 the ophicleide part in Mendelssohn's *Midsummer Night's Dream* overture was played at Berlin on one of Wieprecht's tubas.[4] Berlioz found hardly any ophicleides in the German orchestras during his tour in 1843; but in several places they had a tuba, and when neither instrument was forthcoming his ophicleide parts had to be played on trombones. Actually, the tuba arrived on the scene in Germany before the ophicleide had had sufficient time to establish itself. In the 'forties all the large German orchestras had their tuba, and the serpents, bass-horns, and what ophicleides there were, retired into the lumber-rooms and museums.

Not long after Wieprecht's tubas had appeared in Berlin, the French makers began to make similar valved brass instruments in the bass register, among them Adolphe Sax, whose bass and contrabass saxhorns eventually served the same purpose in France as did the tubas and bombardons in Germany.

The larger opera orchestras in Italy apparently went through the same process of acquiring an additional wind bass instrument. Spohr told of a bass-horn at the Milan opera in 1816,[5] and in 1825 a serpent of some sort was in use at *La Scala* opera-house in that city.[6]

In this country the serpent or bass-horn came into the larger opera and festival orchestras during the first quarter of the century, and during the

[1] Fröhlich, in his *Vollständige . . . Musikschule* (1811) describes the serpent as being either curved or straight, of wood or of metal covered with wood.
[2] *Mem.*, II, p. 119.   [3] Hauptmann, *Briefe*, I, p. 23.
[4] *Neue Zeit. für Musik*, 1838, No. 43, p. 172.   [5] *Autob.*, I, p. 258.
[6] *Harm.*, Aug., 1825, p. 140.

'thirties the ophicleide began to dispute the ground with the older instruments.   For many years, however, all of these bass instruments were often
used together in English military bands and large festival orchestras, and
even after the mid-century elaborately keyed serpents were still being made
and used in this country.

Thus, by the middle of the 19th century all the large orchestras in Europe
had either an ophicleide or a valved bass instrument of the tuba type, and
with that the standard brass group of the orchestra was complete.

It was always the opera orchestras that had led the way in acquiring
additional instruments, and it was the composers of opera who demanded
these additions.   Where the resources were ample and the composer successful or influential, he could ask for almost any instrument in almost any
quantity.   At the Paris *Opéra*, first Rossini, and then Meyerbeer and Halévy
made constant demands for extra brass instruments, both in the orchestra
and on the stage.   A third or even a fourth trumpet was demanded[1];
melody-playing keyed bugles[2] or valved trumpets added to the resources of
their brass group, and when, during the 'thirties, the *cornet à pistons* became
popular in Paris, it was not long before the composers there began to make a
habit of writing for a pair of these accommodating instruments in addition
to the usual pair of trumpets.   This remained a peculiarity of French
instrumentation throughout the century.

After 1842, with Adolphe Sax on the spot to stimulate their appetites,
groups of saxhorns and even saxophones were sometimes tacked on to the
Paris composer's orchestral and stage paraphernalia,[3] and if every place had
been in a position to gratify this lust for more instruments, the orchestra
might have grown into such a thing as Berlioz dreamed of.   But what
could be done in Paris could not be done everywhere.   Even Dresden,
Munich, Vienna or London could not match the resources of Paris, and
with a few dozen smaller theatres in Germany and many more in Italy, they
helped to keep a check on this growing brass band that threatened to swamp
the orchestral strings and wood-wind.

The employment of independent military or brass bands on the opera
stage appears to have been originated almost simultaneously by Rossini
and Spontini.   The former introduced a stage military band into his *La
Donna del Lago* (Naples, 1819), and the latter required a stage band consisting
of 8 trumpets, 4 horns, 3 trombones and an ophicleide for his *Olimpie* at
Paris in 1819.[4]   In a ballet by Gallemberg entitled *Alfred le Grand*, produced
at the Paris *Opéra* in 1822, a complete military band appeared on the stage;
Rossini also repeated his earlier experiment in *Semiramide* (Venice, 1823).

---

[1] Four trumpets in the orchestra for Schneitzhoeffer's ballet *Mars et Venus*, 1826.
[2] In Rossini's *Semiramide*, 1823, and in Kreutzer's *Ipsiboé*, 1824; also later in Meyerbeer's
scores.
[3] Saxhorns in the overture to *Robert Bruce*, a Rossini *pastiche*, 1846; then in Meyerbeer's
Le Prophète (1849); both saxhorns and saxophones in Halévy's *Le Juif errant* (1852), (Lavoix,
pp. 425–6).
[4] Castil-Blaze, *L'Acad. Imp.*, II, p. 350.

Similar effects became fairly common a little later when Meyerbeer and Halévy wrote their spectacular operas for the large stage of the Paris *Opéra*. The idea took root very readily in the largest Italian theatres; in the 'twenties the producers were only too ready to introduce wind bands on the stage, even though there was no such thing in the composer's score. At Milan in 1826 brass bands on the stage were dragged into almost every opera, including Mozart's *Figaro*, and in Vaccai's *Giulietta e Romeo*, although "there was no situation in this opera which would allow the band to be marched on to the stage, according to modern etiquette," they managed to find an opportunity for bringing it on "behind the scenes, where it was very vigorous for some minutes."[1]

Such displays were not so common in Germany, and only in the *Opernhaus* at Berlin did they attempt to rival the lavishness of the Paris *Opéra*. Spontini had 38 brass players on the stage for his spectacular production of *Olimpia* in 1821,[2] but he was particularly favoured; the man who could get elephants in his stage processions could get anything he wanted.

Composers of symphonies and concert-works did not take any great part in the clamour for more brass-tone that was going on in Paris and in other large opera-houses; they were generally satisfied with the usual four horns, two trumpets and three trombones of the standard orchestra, and in Germany were often content to do without the additional pair of horns and the trombones. Berlioz, of course, always provides the exception to the rule; he was Paris-bred, and saw no reason why the concert orchestra should be denied the riches of the opera orchestra. But when he took his works away from Paris he generally had to cut down his demands to suit the more limited resources of the German orchestras, and makeshift devices had to be contrived when his scores asked for more instruments than could be provided.

HARP AND PERCUSSION INSTRUMENTS

Like several other instruments, the harp came into the orchestra via Paris. It was used at the *Opéra* in Gluck's *Orphée* in 1774.[3] In Lesueur's opera *Les Bardes* (1804) no less than twelve harps had been employed. This could have happened only in Paris; probably no other city could have provided so many harps and their players at one time. Napoleon had a harp in his private orchestra, and two were always available at the *Opéra*.

In Germany the harp was not much cultivated,[4] and Berlioz often missed it during his tour in 1843; at some places his parts for that instrument had to be played on a piano. In the 'forties, however, a harp was available in the opera orchestras at Berlin, Dresden (where there was no harp in Weber's time), Stuttgart, Hanover, and at Cassel where Spohr was conductor.[5]

---

[1] *Harm.*, June, 1826, p. 123.   [2] Kapp, p. 32.

[3] Played by Sieber, a horn player and music publisher (Castil-Blaze, *L'Acad. Imp.*, II, p. 349).

[4] "In Germany, where harpists in general cannot play the harp" (Berlioz, *Mem.*, II, p. 139).

[5] This may have been because Spohr's wife was a harpist.

Figures in brackets indicate probationers or extra players.

Orchestra	Date	Violin I	Violin II	Viola	'Cello	D. Bass	Flute	Oboe	Clarinet	Bassoon	Horn	Trumpet	Trombone	Various	Source
Berlin Court Opera	1811	22 (3)		5	10	5	4	4 (1)	4	4	7 (1)	2	3	Drums	Leip. All. Mus. Zeit. 1811, No. 13, p. 606
Berlin Court Opera (Spontini)	1820	12	12 } 24	8	9	7									Dorn, II, p. 126
Berlin Court Opera	1830	} 24		12	6	6	4	4	4	4	4	6	3	Total c. 70, augmented up to 100	Harm., Jan., 1830, p. 5
Berlin Court Opera	1843	14	14	8	10	8	3	2	4	4	4	4	4	Drums and percussion. Two harps	Berlioz, Mem., II, p. 92
Berlin Court Opera	1844	8	8	6	8 (2)	4 (1)	5	4	2 (2)	2 (2)	4	2 (2)	3	Drums, percussion, piccolo, tuba, 2 harps	Gassner, Dir. und Rip., Beilage, No. 9
Berlin Court Opera	1849	} 27		8	11	7	5	4	5	5	9	3	3	2 Drums	Das Orchester, 1849, p. 6
Berlin Königstadt Theatre	1825	} 12		2	4	3								Usual wind and drums	Smart, p. 172
Bremen Town Orchestra	1817	4	4	2	2	2	2	2	2	2	2	2	1	Drums	Mnemosyne (Leipzig), 1817, p. 11
Breslau Town Orchestra	1838	9	9	6	4	3	2	2	2	2	2	2		Drums	Leip. All. Mus. Zeit., No. 40, p. 389

Orchestra	Year													Drums	Reference
Brunswick Court Orchestra	1819	10		2	3	3	2	2	2	2	2	2		Drums	*Leip. All. Mus. Zeit.*, No. 21, p. 433
Brunswick Court Orchestra	1850	6 (2)	6 (2)	2 (2)	3 (1)	4	2	2	2	2	3 (1)	1 (3)	1 (2)	Drums, harp, cor anglais, tuba, percussion	*Das Orchester*, 1850, p. 43
Brussels Opera	1824				40 players										*Harm.*, Aug., 1824, p. 152
Cassel Court Opera	1825	16		4	4	4	2	2	2	2	2			Double set of wind instruments	Smart, p. 209
Cassel Court Opera	1844	8	4	5	3	2	2	2	4	4	3			Drums, percussion, harp	*Gassner, Dir. und Rip.*, Beilage, No. 8
Chemnitz Town Orchestra	1846	5	4	3	4	2	2	2	4	2	3			Drums, bass drum	*Signale f. d. Mus. Welt*, (Leipzig) 4, p. 249
Cologne Opera	1825	8		2	2	2	2							Usual wind instruments	Smart, p. 221
Darmstadt Court Opera	1823	12	12	7	5	4	3	3	3	4	2	3		Drums, percussion, basset horn	*Leip. All. Mus. Zeit.*, No. 25, p. 159
Darmstadt Court Opera	1825	12	10	8	10	6	2	2	2	4	2	3		Drums, percussion, piccolo and extra wind	Smart, p. 77
Darmstadt Court Opera	1837	10	10	6	6	4	3	3	3	6	2	3		Drums and extra instruments as required	*Kastner, Cours*, p. 4
Darmstadt Court Opera	1844	8	8	6	4	4	2	2	2	2	2	3		Drums, percussion, ophicleide	*Gassner, Dir. und Rip.*, Beilage, No. 11

Orchestra	Date	Violin I	Violin II	Viola	Cello	D. Bass	Flute	Oboe	Clarinet	Bassoon	Horn	Trumpet	Trombone	Various	Source
Darmstadt Court Opera	1850	} 17		6	5	3	3	2	2	2	4	2	3	Drums, tuba	*Das Orchester*, 1850, p. 3
Dessau Court Orchestra	1832	11	10	6	5	5	2	2	2	2	2	2		Drums	*Leip. All. Mus. Zeit.*, 1832, No. 34, p. 59
Dortmund Concert Orchestra	1830	4	4	2	2	2	4	2	5	2	5	2	3 (1)	Drums	Feldmann, 1830 (Schreiber, p. 102)
Dresden Court Music	1805	} 17		4	4	4	3	3	2	4	4			Trumpets and drums	Prölss, p. 246
Dresden Court Opera	1817	} 20		5	5	5	5	5	5	5	6	2		Drums, 4 copyists, tuners, attendants, instrument makers	Weber, II, p. 37
Dresden Court Opera	1825	5	5	2	2	2	2	2	2	2	5	2	3	Drums, piccolo	Smart, p. 140
Dresden Court Opera	1832	} 16		4	6	4	5	4	4	5	5	3		Two drummers	Prölss, p. 423
Dresden Court Opera	1842	} 16		4	4	4	4	4	4	3	5	4	3	Drums, harp	Prölss, p. 489
Dresden Court Opera	1844	8	8	4	4	4	2	2	2	2	4	4	3	Drums, percussion, tuba	*Gassner, Dir. und Rip., Beilage*, No.25
Dresden Court Opera	1850	} 18		5	5	5	4	4	4	4	5	4	3	Drums, harp	Prölss, p. 557

	Year	Total													Percussion	Source
Dresden Church Music	1835	10 | 10	6	5 (1)	5	3	3	3	3	4	2	2	2	3	Drums	Leip. All. Mus. Zeit., No. 37, p. 69
Frankfort Opera	1800	}10	3	5	3	3	2	2	2	2	4	2	2		Drums	Gollmick Autob., I, p. 67
Frankfort Opera	1810	}14	3	2	2	2	2	2	2	2	4	2	2		Drums	Leip. All. Mus. Zeit., 1810, No. 12, p. 644
Frankfort opera	1821	}13	4	3	3	2	2	2	2	2	2	2	2	1	Drums	Gollmick, Carl Gubr, p. 11
Frankfort Opera	1843	8 | 8	4	5	4	2	2	2	2	2	4	2	2	3	Drums	Berlioz, Mem., II, p. 13
Frankfort Opera	1847	9	3	3	3	2	2	2	2	2	4	2	2	3	Drums	Neue Berl. Mus. Zeit., 1847, p. 238
Göttingen Concert Orchestra	1828	}12	3	2	2	2	1	2	2	2	2	2	2		Drums	Leip. All. Mus. Zeit., 1828, No. 30, p. 266
Gotha Court Orchestra	1847	}12	3	2 (1)	2	2	2	2	2	2	4	3			Drums, percussion, harp	Leip. All. Mus. Zeit., No. 49, p. 392
The Hague Royal Orchestra	1840	}10	3	4	2	2	2	2	2	2	4	2	2	3	Drums	Leip. All. Mus. Zeit., No. 42, p. 136

Orchestra	Date	Violin I	Violin II	Viola	'Cello	D. Bass	Flute	Oboe	Clarinet	Bassoon	Horn	Trumpet	Trombone	Various	Source
Hamburg Opera	1832	6	6	3	2	2	2	2	2	2	2	2	3	Drums, percussion	Leip. All. Mus. Zeit., No. 34, p. 243
Hanover Court Orchestra	1826	4	5	2	3	2	2	2	2	2	2	2		Drums	Leip. All. Mus. Zeit., No. 28, p. 843
Hanover Court Opera	1843	7	7	3	4	3	Usual wind instruments							Drums, tuba from military band	Berlioz, Mem., II, p. 138
Hanover Court Opera	1849	8	8	3	4	3	2	2	2	2	4	2	3	Drums	Neue Zeit. für Mus., No. 37, p. 31
Hechingen Court Orchestra	1843	{8		3	2	2	2	2	2	2	2	2	1	Drums	Berlioz, Mem., II, p. 29
Karlsruhe Court Orchestra	1817	{12		3	2	2									Leip. All. Mus. Zeit., No. 19, p. 374
Koburg Court Orchestra	1841	8	7	3	3	2	3	2	2	2	4	2	3	Drums	Leip. All. Mus. Zeit., No. 43, p. 84
Königsberg Town Orchestra	1835	{8		3	2	2								Wind from military band	Neue Zeit. für Mus., 1835, No. 49, p. 199

Place	Year	V. 1	V. 2	Va.	Vc.	Cb.	Fl.	Ob.	Cl.	Hn.	Tpt.	Tbn.	Other instruments	Reference
Leipzig Gewandhaus	1802	6	6	4	3	3							Total, about 33 instrumentalists	Leip. All. Mus. Zeit., 1802, No. 3, p. 783
Leipzig Gewandhaus	1831	8	8	5	3	3	2	2	2	2	2		Drums	Dörffel, p. 78
Leipzig Gewandhaus	1839	9	8	5	5	4							Usual wind and drums	Creuzberg, p. 85
Leipzig, St. Thomas and St. Nicholas Churches	1825	10		2	2	2							Usual wind, including trumpets and drums	Smart, p. 161
Leipzig Theatre	1825	12		2	2	2							Usual wind and drums	Smart, p. 159
London, King's Theatre	1818	10	9	4	4	5	2	2	2	2	2	1	Drums	Quar. Mus. Mag., Vol. I, No. II, p. 257
London, King's Theatre	1831	16		4	4	5	2	2	2	4	2	3	Drums, percussion	Harm., Dec., 1831, p. 304
London, King's Theatre	1832	20		6	6	6	2	2	2	4	2	3	Drums	Anon., Mus. Recoll., I, p. 240
London, Her Majesty's Theatre	1839	14	14	8	8	8	2	2	2	4	3	3	Drums, percussion, ophicleide, harp	Mus. World, May 9, 1839, p. 23
London, Her Majesty's Theatre	1847	28		8	8	8							Usual wind, etc.	Mus. World, Feb. 20, 1847, p. 113
London, Her Majesty's Theatre	1849	14	14	9	8	8	2	2	2	4	2	3	Drums, percussion, ophicleide, harp	Mus. World, April 7, 1849, p. 212

E

Orchestra	Date	Violin I / II	Viola	'Cello	D. Bass	Flute	Oboe	Clarinet	Bassoon	Horn	Trumpet	Trombone	Various	Source
London, Covent Garden Theatre	1818	12	2	2	2	1	2	1	2	2	2	1	Drums, percussion. Several players were double-handed	Northcott, *Life of Bishop*, p. 44
London, Covent Garden Theatre	1825	6 or 8 / 6 or 8	2	2	3 or 4	2	2	2	2	2	1	1	Drums, keyed bugle, flageolet, copyist	Saxe Wyndham, I, p. 336
London, Royal Italian Opera, Covent Garden	1847	14 / 14	10	10	9	2	2	2	2	4	2	3	Drums, percussion, ophicleide, harp	*Mus. World*, Feb. 6, 1847, p. 78
London, R.I.O., Covent Garden	1848	16 / 15	10	10	10	2	2	2	2	4	2	3	Drums, percussion, 2 harps, ophicleide	Book of words, *Tancredi*
London, Oratorio Concerts, Covent Garden	1815	25	6	4	4	2	4	1	2	2	2	3	Drums, serpent	Programme, 1815
London Philharmonic	1837	14 / 14	8	8	6	2	2	2	2	4	2	3	Drums, piccolo, ophicleide	*Mus. World*, Mar. 3, 1837, p. 175
London Philharmonic	1839	16 / 16	10	8	6	3	2	2	2	4	2	3	Drums, piccolo	*Mus. World*, Mar. 7, 1839, p. 149
London Philharmonic	1842	16 / 16	10	8	7	2	2	2	2	4	2	3	Drums	Printed announcement
London Philharmonic	1846	15 / 14	10	9	9	2	2	2	2	4	2	3	Drums, ophicleide, harp	*I.L.N.*, March 21, 1846

	Year														Printed announcement
London Philharmonic	1858	14	14	8	9	8	2	2	2	2	4	2	3	Drums	
London Ancient Concert	1817	⎱17		6	4	4	⎱5		–	4	–	4	2	3	Drums	Q. M. Mag., Vol. I, No. 1, p. 64
London Ancient Concert	1832	⎱16		6	4	4	2	4	4	2	4	2	3	Drums	Programme, 1832
London Ancient Concert	1848	⎱17		5	5	5	3	2	2	2	4	3	3	Drums, harp, percussion	Grove, I, p. 86
London Vocal Concert	1819	⎱13		3	4	4	2	2	2	2	2	2	1	Drums	Q. M. Mag., Vol. I, No. 4, p. 464
London, R.A.M. Concerts	1826	⎱26		7	6	6	2	2	2	3	5	4	3	Drums, piccolo	Programme, March 6
London, an Orchestra	1836	⎱30		8	8	6	2	2	2	2	4	2	3	Drums, serpent or bass-horn	Mus. World, Sept. 9, 1836, p. 206
London, Cipriani Potter's Concert	1840	⎱22		8	6	5	2	2	2	2	4	2	3	Drums	Prog., June 15, 1840
London, Sub. Concerts, Hanover Sq. Rooms	1842	⎱30		9	6	6	2	2	2	2	4	2	3	Drums, serpent, ophicleide	Mus. World, Sept. 8, 1842, p. 288
London, Drury Lane, Jullien's Opera Season	1847	66 players													Mus. World, Dec. 11, 1847, p. 798

Orchestra	Date	Violin I	Violin II	Viola	Cello	D. Bass	Flute	Oboe	Clarinet	Bassoon	Horn	Trumpet	Trombone	Various	Source
London, St. James's Theatre, *Antigone*	1847	{14}		4	4	4	2	2	2	2	2	2	3	Drums, harp	*Mus. World*, Dec. 25, 1847, p. 825
London, Exeter Hall, Henry Wylde's Concert	1848	12	10	6	8	7	2	2	2	2	4	2	3	Drums	*Mus. World*, June, 1848, p. 367
Magdeburg Town Orchestra	1827	{8}		3	3	?	2	2	2	2	4	1		Drums, percussion, wind from military band	*Berlin All. Mus. Zeit.*, No. 4, p. 149
Manchester Philharmonic	1822	{8 to 10}		2	3	2	2	2	2	2	2	2	3	Drums	*Q.M. Mag*, Vol. V, No. 20, p. 472
Manchester, Liszt's Concert	1825	{12}		4	2 } 6		2	2	2	2	4	2	3	Drums	Ramaan, I, p. 114
Mannheim Court Orchestra	1824	6	6	3	2	3	3	2	2	2	2	2		Drums	*Leip. All. Mus. Zeit.*, 26, p. 506
Mayence Court Theatre	1817	{12}		4	3	2	2	2	2	2	2	2	3	Drums, double bassoon, bass-horn	*Leip. All. Mus. Zeit.*, 19, p. 720
Meiningen Court Orchestra	1811	{6}		1 (1)	1 (1)	2	1 (1)	2	(2)	2	2 (1)	2		Drums	*Leip. All. Mus. Zeit.*, 19, p. 462

Location	Year														Remarks	Reference
Milan, La Scala	1814	} 25	6	6	4	8	2	2	2	2	4	2		1	Drums, percussion	Leip. All. Mus. Zeit., 16, p. 252
Milan, La Scala	1825	14 14	6	6	6	8	2	2	2	2	4	2		3	Drums, percussion, serpent	Harm., Aug., 1825, p. 140
Moscow Opera	1827	Over seventy players														Harm., Jan., 1827, p. 15
Munich Court Music	1803	} 28 (2)	6	5	7	7	6	4		7						Mus. Monatschrift, Linz, p. 33 (Schreiber, p. 107)
Munich Court Music	1820	} 24 (1)	6	5	5	5	7	5	7			4			Drums, trumpets as required	Leip. All. Mus. Zeit., 22, p. 550
Munich Court Orchestra	1844	6 6	2	2	2	2	2	2	2	2	2	4			Drums	Gassner, Dir. und Rip., Beilage 15
Munich Court Opera	1844	10 10	8	6	6	6	2	2	2	2	4	6		3	Drums, percussion	Gassner, Beilage 1
Munich Odeon Concerts	1844	20 20	10	10	10	10	4	4	4	4	4	4		3	Drums, percussion	Gassner, Beilage 1
Naples San Carlo	1818	} 24	6	6	7	2	2	2	2	2	4	2		3	Drums, percussion	Leip. All. Mus. Zeit., 20, p. 495
Nürnberg, Grand Duke of Hesse-Cassel	1823	} 24	7	5	4	3	3	3	3	4	?			3	Drums, serpent, harp	Q. M. Mag., Vol. V, No. 19, p. 403
Oxford Music Room	1808	3 3	1	1	1	1	1	2	3	2	2	1			One bassoon player also plays drums	Mee, p. 158

Orchestra	Date	Violin I	Violin II	Viola	'Cello	D. bass	Flute	Oboe	Clarinet	Bassoon	Horn	Trumpet	Trombone	Various	Source
Paris, Royal Music	1806	6	7	4	4	4	2	3	4	4	4			Harp	Castil-Blaze, *Chap. Mus.*, p. 173
Paris, Royal Music	1830	7	7	4	6	4	2	2	2	2	3	2	1	Drums, 2 harps	Castil-Blaze, *Chap. Mus.*, p. 229
Paris, *Opéra*	1803	78 players, including conductors														Castil-Blaze, *L'Acad. Imp.*, II, p. 374
Paris, *Opéra*	1810	12	12	8	12	6	2	4	2	4	4	4	3	Drums, percussion	*Leip. All. Mus. Zeit.*, 11, p. 729
Paris, *Opéra*	1825	24 (I, II)		8	12	8	Usual wind, with 4 bassoons and 4 cornets									Smart, p. 237
Paris, *Opéra*	1830	12	11	8	10	8	2	2	2	4	4	2	?	Drums, percussion, harps, 2 cornets, ophicleide	Deldevez, p. 106
Paris, *Opéra*	1839	12	12	8	10	8	3	2	2	4	4	2	3	Drums, percussion, 2 harps, cor anglais, keyed bugle, 2 cornets, ophicleide	Kastner, *Cours*, p. 4
Paris, *Opéra*	c.1844	12	11	8	10	8	2	2	2	4	4	2	3	Drums, percussion, harps, 2 cornets, ophicleide	Berlioz, *Instrum.*, p. 241
Paris, *Opéra*	c.1845	12	12	8	9	8	3	3	3	4	6	4	3	Drums, percussion, 2 harps, cornets, ophicleide	Kastner, *Cours*, Supp., p. 2
Paris, *Opéra*	1855	11	11	8	10	8	3	3	3	4	5	4	3	Drums, percussion, 2 harps, ophicleide	Castil-Blaze, *L'Acad. Imp.*, II, p. 446

Paris, Rue de Cléry Concerts	1798-9	80 players												Elwart, p. 54
Paris, Musard's Concerts	1837	80 players												Rivière, p. 38
Paris, *Opéra Comique*	1827	}16	4	7	5	3	3	3	4	2	2		Drums, percussion, serpent, guitar	Schreiber, p. 109
Paris, *Opéra Comique*	1839	8}8	5	6	6	3	3	3	6	3	4		Drums, percussion, 2 harps, copyists, etc.	*L'Indicateur général*, p. 5
Paris, *Théâtre Italien*	1817	}13	4	4	5								Two of each wind instrument	*Q. M. Mag.*, Vol. I, No. 2, p. 260
Paris, *Théâtre Italien*	1826	8}8	4	5	6	2	2	2	4	2			Drums	*Leip. All. Mus. Zeit.*, 28, p. 344
Paris, *Société des Concerts*	1828	15}15	8	12	8	4	3	4	4	2	3		Drums, harp, ophicleide	Elwart, p. 101
Paris, *Société des Concerts*	1841	15}12	10	13	11	4	3	4	4	4	3		Drums	Schindler, p. 10[1]
Paris, *Société des Concerts*	1859	16}14	10	12	8	4	2	4	4	2	3		Drums, harp, cornet, ophicleide	Elwart, p. 106[2]
Prague Opera	1796	3}4	2	1	2	2	2	2	2	2			Drums	Ambros-Branberger, p. 14
Prague Opera	1813–16	4}4	3	2	2	2	2	2	2 to 4	2	3		Drums, harp, guitar	Haas, p. 256
Prague Opera	1820	4}4	3	2	2	2	2	2	2	2			Drums	Schreiber, p. 109
Prague Opera	1825	}8	2	2	4								Usual wind instruments	Smart, p. 133

[1] These figures include probationers and external members. The trumpets include cornets.
[2] Including probationers and external members.

Orchestra	Date	Violin I	Violin II	Viola	'Cello	D. Bass	Flute	Oboe	Clarinet	Bassoon	Horn	Trumpet	Trombone	Various	Source
Rudolstadt Court Orchestra	1838	6	5	3	3	2	2	2	2	2	4	2	3	Drums, percussion	Leip. All. Mus. Zeit., 40, p. 526
Strassburg Theatre	1814	4	4	2	2	2	2	1 (1)	2	2	2	1		Drums	Leip. All. Mus. Zeit., 16, p. 534
Stuttgart Court Orchestra	1823	{15}		4	4	3	3	4	4	3	3	2		Drums	Leip. All. Mus. Zeit., 25, p. 57
Stuttgart Court Opera	1837	8	8	4	5	4	4	4	4	4	6	2	3	Drums and extras	Kastner, Cours, p. 4
Stuttgart Court Opera	1843	8	8	4	4	4						2	3	Usual wind instruments	Berlioz, Mem., II, p. 21
Venice, La Fenice	1819	{24}		6	6	6	4							Piccolo, percussion	Schreiber, p. 111
Vienna, Imperial Orchestra	1807	{10}		2	2	2	2	2	2	2	1?		2	Drums, trumpets and double bassoon available	Köchel, p. 32
Vienna, Imperial Orchestra	1844	6	6	2	3	3	2	2	{7}			2	2	Drums	Gassner, Dir. and Rép., Beilage 12
Vienna, The Creation	1808	{12}		{3}			{7}				2	4	2	Drums	Haas, p. 266

Place	Year												Notes	Reference
Vienna, Beethoven Concert in Redouten Saal	1814	18	18	14	12	17							Two double bassoons	Thayer, II, p. 268
Vienna, first performance of Choral Symphony	1824	24		10	12	12								Thayer, III, p. 161
Vienna Court Opera	1821	6	6	4	4	4	2	2	2	4	2	3	Drums, piccolo, harp, double bassoon	Stöber's plan
Vienna Court Opera	1842	9	9	4	5	5	3	3	3	6	4	4	Drums, percussion	Kralik, p. 19
Vienna Court Opera	1844	8	8	4	4	4	2	2	2	4	3	3	Drums, percussion	Gassner, *Dir. und Rip.*, Beilage 1
Vienna Concert Spirituel	1844	10	10	10	6	4	2	2	2	4	2	3	Drums	Gassner, *Dir. und Rip.*, Beilage 1
Warnsdorf (Bohemia), first complete performance of Beethoven's Mass in D	1830	8	10	4	3	3	2	2	2	4	2	3	Drums. (Choir 9–10–9–8)	Haas, p. 254
Weimar Court Opera	1814	4	4	2	2	2	2	2	2	2	2		Drums	*Leip. All. Mus. Zeit.*, 16, p. 296
Weimar Court Opera	1825	5	5	2	2	2	2	2	2	2	2		Drums	*Leip. All. Mus. Zeit.*, 28, p. 446
Weimar Court Opera (Liszt)	1851	5	6	3	4	3	2	2	2	4	2	1	Drums	Raabe, I, p. 104

FESTIVAL AND SPECIAL ORCHESTRAS

Place	Date	Violin I	Violin II	Viola	'Cello	D. Bass	Flute	Oboe	Clarinet	Bassoon	Horn	Trumpet	Trombone	Various	Choir	Source
Amiens Cathedral Coronation of Charles X	1825	36		15	30		8	8	8	28				Eight drums, etc.	20-20-28-28	Castil-Blaze, *Chap. Mus.*, p. 240
Berlin, Righini's *Te Deum*	1810	36	36	12	22	10	4	4	4	6	12	4	3	Two drums, piccolo		*L.A.M.Z.*, 12, p. 425
Birmingham Festival	1820	28		12	6	4	4	4	4	4	4	4	4*	Drums, harp, 2 serpents	40-30-30-34	*Q. Mus. Mag.*, Vol. III, No. 9, p. 123
Birmingham Festival	1834	50		24	16	10	4	4	4	4	8	6	8	Drums, harp, piccolo, serpent, ophicleide, contra ophicleide, basset horn	Semi-chorus 34 Chorus 182	Programme
Breslau, *Messiah*	1819	48		16	15	10	4	4	4	5	4	6	4	Drums	46-38-44-42	*L.A.M.Z.*, 21, p. 799
Brighton Festival	1828	10	9	4	4	4	3	2	3	2	4	2	3	Drums, serpent	c. 100	Programme
Chester Festival	1829	100 players													130	*Harm.*, Oct., 1829, p. 256
Cologne Lower Rhine Festival	1821	33	35	23	18	12	4	4	5	6	6	5	5	Drums, serpent	56-57-61-60	*L.A.M.Z.*, 23, p. 632

Festival	Date	Total													Instruments	Proportion	Book of words
Cologne Lower Rhine Festival	1835	} 91	33	26	17	5	5	4	5	5	5	6	5	Drums, bass-horn	118-101-120-137	Book of words
Düsseldorf Lower Rhine Festival	1818	24 { 15	9	10	6	4	4	4	4	4	4	4	3	Drums, double bassoon	30-25-20-25	Schreiber, p. 113
Düsseldorf Lower Rhine Festival	1836	} 73	24	24	12	6	6	4	6	4	5	4	1	Drums, double bassoon, bass clarinet, serpent, bass drum	106-60-90-108	L.A.M.Z., 38, p. 410
Edinburgh Festival	1825	} 21	6	6	5							16 wind and drums					Harm., Jan., 1825, p. 20
Florence, The Creation	1839	} 70	20	16	18	8	4	6	10	14	14	8	9		60-40-90-120	L.A.M.Z., 41, p. 857
Frankenhausen Festival	1810	} 42	12	11	9	4	4	4	4	4						L.A.M.Z., 1810, p. 747
Gloucester Festival	1823	8 { 8	4	4	4	2	2	2	2	2	2	2	2	Drums, harp	21-17-17-19	Q. Mus. Mag., Vol. V, No. 20, p. 504
Leicester Festival	1827	} 53	14	7	7	3	3	5	4	4	3	3		Drums, flageolet	53-32-47-56	Programme
Liverpool Festival	1823	14 { 12	8	6	4	2	2	4	4	3	4	5*		Drums, 2 serpents	20-16-18-20	Q. Mus. Mag., Vol. V, No. 20, p. 530
London, Handel Festival	1834	} 80	32	18	18	10	12	8	8	12	10	8	8	Three drummers, 2 serpents, 2 ophicleides	145-74-70-103	Moscheles, Life, I, p. 307

* From His Majesty's Household Band.

Place	Date	Violin I	Violin II	Viola	'Cello	D. Bass	Flute	Oboe	Clarinet	Bassoon	Horn	Trumpet	Trombone	Various	Choir	Source
London, Festival at Exeter Hall	1836	\}80		38	18	18	6	8	6	8	6	4	5	Two drummers, serpent, ophicleide	104-93-86-100	Programme
Manchester Festival	1836	\}36		16	10	10	4	4	4	4	6	4	4	Drums, ophicleide	400	*Mus. World*, 1836
Newcastle Festival	1825	\}16		4	5	4								17 wind and drums	17-8-12-18	*Harm.*, Jan., 1825, p. 20
Norwich Festival	1827	\}41		18	11	10	4	6	4	4	6	6	5	Drums, 2 serpents	71-39-54-55	Programme
Norwich Festival	1830	\}40		16	11	10	5	4	6	6	6	6	7	Drums, 2 serpents, harp	70-38-61-65	Programme
Norwich Festival	1833	\}41		17	10	10	6	4	6	6	6	4	8	Two drummers, 2 serpents	81-45-62-63	Programme
Paris Opera, Haydn's *Creation*	1800	24	24	20	22	20	2	6	6	8	12	6	3	Drums, 4 serpents	150	Castil-Blaze, *L'Acad. Imp.*, II, p. 372
Paris Opera, Haydn's *Creation*	1844	40	40	40	36	30	8	6	6	8	12	6	6	Drums, 2 ophicleides	250	Castil-Blaze, *L'Acad. Imp.*, II, p. 372
Three Choirs Festival	1811	\}16		6	4	4	1	2	1	2	2	2	1	Drums		Lysons, p. 89, f.n.

Vienna, Handel's *Timotheus*	1812	60	60	37	33	21	12	12	12	12	12	9	Four drummers, b. drum, 2 double bassoons	280	Kastner, *Cours*, p. 5
Vienna, Handel's *Alexander's Feast*	1841	60	60	48	48	25	12	12	12	12	8	9	Four drummers, b. drum, 2 double bassoons, 3 ophicleides	250-170-170-200	*Mus. Postillon*, Augsburg, 1931, p. 29 (Schreiber, p. 117)
Vienna, Haydn's *Creation*	1843	59	59	40	41	25	13	12	12	12	8	9	Four drummers, percussion, 4 double bassoons, 1 ophicleide	200-150-150-160	Gassner, *Dir. and Rip., Beilag* 1
Wakefield Festival	1825	{24		10	8	8	35 wind and drums							24-18-20-24	*Harm.*, Jan., 1825, p. 19
York Festival	1823	{62		20	20	16	8	6	8	8	6	8	Two drummers, 2 serpents, 2 bass-horns	60-48-60-72	*Harm.*, Oct., 1823, p. 153
York Festival	1825	{97		32	23	16	13	6	12	14	6	10	Two drummers, harp, 8 serpents and bass-horns	90-70-90-100	Programme
York Festival	1828	{93		32	23	16	13	6	12	14	6	10	Two drummers, 8 serpents and bass-horns	90-70-90-100	*Harm.*, Nov., 1828, p. 244
Zerbst Elbe Festival	1827	{45		15	12	8	4	5	6	6	4	3	Drums, double bassoon	62-38-46-47	*Harm.*, Oct., 1827, p. 213

In Italy and at Vienna they appeared to give little attention to the harp as an orchestral instrument, although one was provided at *La Scala* in Milan from 1819,[1] and there was one at the Prague opera during Weber's time as conductor there (1813–16). *The Musical World's* list of a London full orchestra in 1836 does not include a harp; yet it was much played at that time in England as a solo and drawing-room instrument[2]; but in the 'forties it had to be provided in all full orchestras.

Some other plucked string instruments occasionally figure in opera scores, on and off the stage; the guitar and mandolin were probably the most frequent.

The usual pair of timpani were sometimes increased to three or even more. Weber's *Peter Schmoll* (1801) and *Ruler of the Spirits* (1811) overtures require three, also Mendelssohn's *St. Paul* and Spohr's Historical Symphony; Meyerbeer asked for four in *Robert le Diable* (1831). Needless to state, nobody wanted as many as Berlioz; but, as Schumann and others often required three timpani, a full orchestra at the mid-century would hardly be able to manage with less than that number.

French and Italian opera scores made free demands for other percussion instruments, the most common of which were the bass drum, cymbals, side drum and triangle. These were often called Turkish Music (*Janitscharen-musik*), and from Rossini's time they were regarded as part of the essential outfit for all full opera orchestras. Some of them were occasionally included in symphony scores,[3] but these superficial effects were not taken very seriously by the more earnest German symphony composers. It was characteristic of Berlioz, to whom no orchestral detail was unimportant, that he should have complained that the cymbals in most German orchestras were cracked.

Other odd instruments and "effects" may be found in the opera scores of the half-century, generally employed to give local colour to the music, and played on or off the stage. But none of these constituted more than the trimmings that are liable to be found at any period attached to the standard orchestral combination.

*   *   *

The salient features in the development of the orchestra during the first half of the 19th century may be summed up as follows:

(*a*) A considerable increase in the power of the strings by augmenting the number of players to each part.

(*b*) The wood-wind remain unaltered except for occasional or local additions which gave more variety but very little more power.

---

[1] Cambiasi, p. 392.

[2] "It is as expensive to keep a harp as a race-horse" (*Q. M. Mag.*, 1820), because the strings so often required renewing.

[3] Beethoven's Choral symphony, Spohr's *Die Weihe der Töne*, Schumann's first symphony (triangle). The "Turkish Music" had previously been employed in Haydn's "military" symphony.

(c) The brass group greatly increased in both power and variety by the addition of more instruments.

(d) The addition of a few percussion instruments and one or more harps.

A few features of the development which may be singled out for special notice are:

(a) The lead in acquiring additional instruments was taken by opera orchestras.

(b) Almost all the additions were wind instruments.

(c) Most of the additions emanated from Paris.

(d) The additions of wind instruments depended largely on the supply of players from military bands.

The figures given in the tables on pp. 46–63 show the strength and constitution of the larger and more important orchestras of the half-century. They show the position, however, in a most favourable light; the average strength would be considerably reduced were it possible to include the figures for many of the smaller opera-houses and concert-societies in Germany, and for most of the ordinary Italian theatres.

It should be understood that in some cases the figures are those of the entire musical establishment, and therefore do not represent the number of players usually employed at each performance. This is especially so in the case of opera orchestras. Berlioz's figures for the Berlin opera in 1842–43, for example, give the full strength of the orchestra used only for "great performances," as he said. It should not be supposed that this orchestra of about 87 performers, with doubled wind instruments, took part in every opera. The figures given by Gassner in 1844, making an orchestra of about 60 players, will better represent the number usually playing, while for some of the older and lighter operas it is possible that they would be further reduced. The figures for the Dresden opera given by Weber for 1817 are those of the full establishment; all these players would certainly not be playing at the same time, especially the wind, which were far beyond the needs of the largest opera. Again, Gassner's figures of 1844 will be nearer to the actual number usually employed in playing for the ordinary opera performances.

The above remarks apply more particularly to the opera orchestras. On the other hand, the figures for concert orchestras probably do represent the actual number of players taking part in each concert.

In some cases where no violas are included, either the figure was not known, or the violas were included amongst the violins. No respectable orchestra could be entirely without violas. In a few cases where there are no figures for trombones, it is probably because the players were not on the permanent staff, but were drawn from military bands, and were engaged from time to time as was necessary.

Some particulars of a number of large orchestras organised for special occasions and for musical festivals are appended. These figures have no relation to the strength of permanent orchestras. The proportionate strength of the parts differs wildly, and was probably governed largely by local conditions. In most of these festival orchestras there were many amateurs amongst the strings. Such performances, generally of oratorios, were often given with large forces in Vienna; in Germany they increased considerably after the first festival in Frankenhausen in 1810, and were fairly numerous in Mendelssohn's time. The festivals in the provincial towns of this country were very many, and flourished greatly during the first half of the century; they owed their being and success very largely to performances of oratorios by Handel, Haydn and Mendelssohn.

While it is possible that some of the figures given by the various authorities in the tables on pp. 46—63 are not altogether accurate, they are certainly near enough to give a correct view of the size of the best orchestras during the period under survey.

III

Orchestras in France

THE ROYAL ORCHESTRA

THE Revolution of 1789, followed by the fall of Louis XVI, brought about a temporary dispersal of the musicians who had formed the long-established *Chapelle-Musique* of the French royal house. For a period of about eleven years there was no court musical establishment in France. Then, during the first years of the Consulate, Napoleon began to entertain his court with concerts at the Tuileries, and this led him to re-establish the *Chapelle* under the superintendence of his favourite composer, Paisiello, in 1802. A small body consisting of 27 instrumentalists and 8 singers was set up,[1] and hardly had it got to work when Paisiello begged to be allowed to return to Naples, whence he had come, on account of his wife's ill-health. Lesueur was appointed his successor in 1804, and Napoleon, now become Emperor, built on the site of the *Salle de la Convention* in the Tuileries a new chapel to replace the one destroyed during the Revolution, and a new *Salle de Spectacle*. The chapel was opened with a Solemn Mass on 22nd February, 1806, by which time the musical personnel had increased to a strength of 55 vocalists and 43 instrumentalists.

In 1807 Napoleon brought Paër, whom he had carried off with his wife from Dresden in 1806, via Poland, to Paris, and there installed him as his *Maître de Chapelle*.

The Imperial orchestra included many of the finest players in Paris. Jean Baptiste Rey was *Maître de Musique*,[2] the first violins were headed by Rudolphe Kreutzer, who had joined in 1802 and became leader in 1806, and the seconds were led by Pierre Baillot. Jean Louis Tulou was then second flute, and Gustav Vogt was the leading oboist; both of these young players, destined to great renown, were products of the recently founded famous Conservatoire (1795). Among the four clarinets were Charles Duvernoy (1766–1845) and Jean Xavier Lefèvre, and the four bassoons were led by Étienne Ozi (1754–1813), author of the old standard tutor for that instrument.

Napoleon's quartet of horns was headed by two distinguished players, Frédéric Duvernoy and Heinrich Domnich (1760–1844). No noisy

---

[1] Castil-Blaze, *Chap. Mus.*, p. 166.
[2] The nearest French equivalent of the German *Kapellmeister* or conductor who nominally directed while seated at the piano or keyboard. The actual control of the orchestra was in the hands of the violinist-leader, then called *Chef d'orchestre*.

F

instruments were allowed, so there were no trumpets, trombones or drums, and the list winds up with the name of Martin Pierre Dalvimare (D'Alvimare), a harpist and teacher of the Empress Josephine. (For list of orchestra see Appendix, p. 492).

The duties of this orchestra were to play in the Imperial Chapel, at the concerts and theatricals of the court, and for the Imperial dances. For waltzes and *contredanses* another orchestra was provided.[1] However, as Napoleon was often away winning or losing an Empire, it may be surmised that the duties of this select orchestra were not very arduous; in fact, most of the players were also engaged in one or other of the three most important opera-theatres in Paris, and all of those mentioned were, or became, professors at the Conservatoire.

Like all private court orchestras at that time, Napoleon's musicians wore a court uniform or livery. Wilhelm Speyer described it in 1812 as being resplendent in green, red and yellow, and the ensemble was completed by powdered hair and a sword.[2]

The Emperor's musical taste was conservative, and, according to Castil-Blaze, the repertoire of the *Chapelle-Musique* consisted almost entirely of music by Paisiello, Zingarelli, Haydn, Martini and Lesueur. Moreover, this warlike and battle-seasoned Emperor would have no noisy music; it had to be, as Speyer described it, "*Alles dolce und pianissimo.*"

When the Monarchy was restored in 1814–15, Lesueur continued at the head of the Royal Music under Louis XVIII and Charles X, but had to share his responsibilities with Cherubini. These two musicians were *Surintendans et compositeurs de la Chapelle du Roi*; they took no active part in the performance, and merely presided "in their court uniforms at the head of the vocal personnel."[3] They assumed office alternately for a period of three months each. Under the Monarchy the two *Maîtres de Musique* were Charles Henri Plantade and Rudolphe Kreutzer, the latter being succeeded by Henri Valentino. Plantade being a vocal specialist, was in charge of the choir, while the violinists Kreutzer and Valentino successively took charge of the instrumentalists, and were the real directors of the orchestral performance. At the Restoration many members of the orchestra, among them Tulou and Vogt, were dismissed owing to their republican sympathies; but they were soon replaced, and under the Bourbon king the *Chapelle-Musique* settled down under comparatively peaceful conditions which were to continue until the revolution in 1830.

The list of the orchestra in 1830, numbering 44 instrumentalists, includes some of the old names of 1806. Baillot was now leader, and none of the original first violins remained, but a new name, one which was to become very prominent in the history of French orchestras, had taken a place in the list— that of Habeneck. Of the second violins, only three had seen service in 1806, and of these one, Auguste Kreutzer, a brother of Rudolphe, had been

[1] Castil-Blaze, *Chap. Mus.*, p. 176.   [2] Speyer, p. 9.
[3] Spohr, *Autob.*, II, p. 124.

promoted to the first desk. Tilmant and Habeneck's brother, Joseph, were among the second violins. The violas then included Tariot as leader, and François Amédée (1784–1833), who later became principal viola at the Conservatoire Concerts. Charles Nicolas Baudiot (1773–1849) led the 'cellos, which also included the two prominent players, Louis Norblin (1781–1854) and Vaslin.

The flautist Tulou had evidently been forgiven (or had changed his political views) and was back again, this time as first flute. Vogt was also reinstated as leading oboe, now seconded by his pupil Henri Brod. Charles Duvernoy still remained as first clarinet, of which there were now only two in the orchestra, with Isaac Franco Dacosta (1778–1866) as his colleague. The bassoons were likewise reduced to two players, namely, François René Gebauer (1773–1844), who had been fourth bassoon in 1806, and one Henri or Henry. Frédéric Duvernoy was still solo horn, now assisted by Jean Mengal (b. 1796) and Louis François Dauprat. Two trumpets and drums, absent in the list of 1806, figure in that of 1830, the former instruments being in the hands of Joseph David Buhl and François G. A. Dauverné (1800–1874), while the two Nadermanns, probably the famous François Joseph and his brother Henri, appear as harpists. (For full list, see Appendix, p. 493.)

Spohr heard some music in the royal chapel in 1820, and remarked that "the orchestra is composed of the first artists in Paris, the chorus is powerful and good."[1] At that time Kreutzer was still leader of the orchestra. Moscheles described the *Chapelle-musique* as "magnificent and far-famed" in 1821,[2] and Berlioz thought[3] that it was at its best in 1828 and 1829,[3] that is, when Valentino was at the head of it with Baillot as principal first violin.

The royal musicians performed at Saint Cloud on 25th July, 1830, and two days later a revolution again dispersed the French King's musical establishment.

During the reign of Louis Phillipe an orchestra was organised, and concerts were given in the Tuileries under the direction of Habeneck, while the dance music was in the hands of Jean Baptiste Tolbecque.[4] Eventually, for the third time, the orchestra was broken up by the revolution of 1848. The vocal music of the Royal Chapel, which came to an end in 1830, was not re-established until Napoleon III became Emperor (1852); Auber was then made *Maître de Chapelle* and Tilmant was appointed *Chef d'orchestre*.[5] But it is not in the story of the royal *Chapelle-musique* that the history of musical and orchestral development in France will be found. These private affairs were relics of the luxurious past of a monarchy which was steadily disintegrating and was soon to vanish for ever. The real story must be sought in the history of the opera and concert orchestras of Paris, and in the work of its instrumentalists, conductors and composers.

[1] Spohr, II, p. 124. [2] Moscheles, *Life*, I, p. 47. [3] *Mem.*, II, p. 193.
[4] Rivière, p. 35. [5] Lasalle et Thoinan, p. 208.

Paris Opera Orchestras

In Paris, as in London, it was the opera-producing theatres that maintained the orchestras from which the concert-giving institutions drew their players. The orchestra at the *Opéra* and that of the *Société des Concerts* (Conservatoire concerts) could not have played as separate bodies at the same moment, any more than could the London Philharmonic and the orchestra of the King's Theatre.

In Paris, as in London, the three principal theatres in which opera was given shared between them the best of the instrumentalists, many of whom

THE GRAND OPERA HOUSE IN THE RUE LE PELETIER (1821–1873)

could be found also at the concerts, in the Royal orchestra, at the open-air summer concerts in the *Champs Élysées*, or teaching on the staff of the Conservatoire.

Of some fifty theatres in Paris near the end of the 18th century,[1] all of them employed orchestras of some sort; but it is mainly in those of the *Opéra*, the *Opéra Comique*, the *Théâtre Italien* and the *Société des Concerts* that the material on which to base the story of orchestral progress in France during the first half of last century will be found.

The parallel with London's three musical theatres, however, does not go farther than their number. Continuity in the story of the English opera-theatres is largely maintained by the fact that each was located in a succession of buildings occupying the same sites. The Paris opera-theatres had not

[1] Matthews, p. 154.

that connecting thread. They should be regarded rather as three separate institutions, each producing a different type of opera, but having no permanent anchorage to a particular site. Thus, the Grand *Opéra*, or *Académie royale de Musique*,[1] was located in the *rue de Richelieu* from 1794, in the *Salle Favart* for a short time in 1820-21, then in the handsome building in the *rue le Peletier* from 1821 to 1873, and from 1875 in the present building. Altogether, since its beginning in 1659, the *Opéra* has been located in thirteen different buildings.[2] The *Opéra Comique* likewise wandered about Paris, finding a home in the *Théâtre Feydeau* in 1797, in the *Favart* 1804, again in

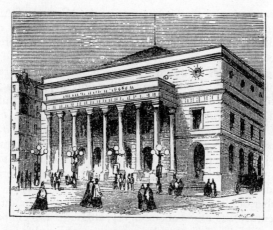

THE ODÉON AT PARIS

the *Feydeau* 1805, the *Ventadour* from 1820 to 1832, the *Théâtre des Nouveautés* until 1840, and then again in the *Favart*.[3] The Italian opera (*Théâtre Italien*) was just as restless; it found temporary lodging in the *Favart* from 1802 till 1804, then in the *Louvois*, the *Odéon* (1808), the *Favart* (1815-18), the *Louvois* (1819), the *Favart* (1825), the *Odéon* (1838), and the *Ventadour* in 1841.[4]

THE OPÉRA ORCHESTRA

The *Opéra*, with its long history reaching back through the periods of Gluck, Rameau and Lully to the 17th century, was the home of French national opera, not necessarily written by native composers, but always conceived and carried out on an imposing scale, with spectacular effect, with an essential ballet, but without spoken dialogue. The subjects, originally classical, heroic or pastoral, but veering round towards the romantic during the first half of last century, were treated in accordance

[1] After the Revolution of 1789 the official title of the *Opéra* changed with each change in the form of the French government.
[2] Lasalle, *Les treize Salles de l'Opéra*.   [3] Malliot, p. 140.
[4] Soubies, *Théâtre Italien*. Lasalle, p. 231.

with a certain traditional grandeur of style by composers such as Lesueur, Catel, Berton, Kreutzer, Boieldieu, Hérold, Auber and Halévy amongst the natives, or by Cherubini, Spontini, Rossini and Meyerbeer amongst the foreign-born composers. A few popular German operas, adapted to suit the French stage and taste, were occasionally added to the repertoire.

Being a state affair, the *Opéra* was intimately associated with the Conservatoire, and a *lauréat* or first prize-winner at the latter institution could generally count on being given employment at the *Opéra* when a vacancy occurred,[1] and could look forward to a pension when his working days were over.

The administration of the *Opéra* began at the Ministry of Arts, working its way down to a directorate, and thence to the executive musical staff which included a first and a second *chef d'orchestre* who were directly in charge of the orchestra.

According to Charles de Boigne,[2] the orchestra at the *Opéra* constituted "a state within a state"; a body recognising only its own law, and giving allegiance only to its own chief. The general manager could not even choose his *chef d'orchestre*; the Conservatoire held the reins: *La nomination appartient à la grande jésuitière musicale qu'on appelle le Conservatoire; elle choisit; le directeur accepte, est forcé d'accepter.* A regulation which came into force in 1778 had given the members of the orchestra the power to select new members by vote after hearing them play,[3] and was said (Gerber) to have been initiated by Francœur the younger.

The number of players in the permanent *Opéra* orchestra during the first half of last century was round about eighty, although it does not follow that the full strength of the whole establishment was employed for every performance, nor that it might not be augmented as occasion required. The figures given by Castil-Blaze are: 68 in 1777, 78 in 1803, 85 in 1847, and 84 in 1855, including two or three conductors.[4] The number of double-basses had grown from 3 in 1776, 5 in 1778, 6 in 1803, to 8 in 1820. It was the increase in the number of violas and double-basses, and the permanent addition of a second pair of horns, three trombones, an ophicleide, cornets, and a few percussion instruments that accounted for the increase in the total strength of the orchestra since the last decades of the 18th century. Otherwise, the number of violins and 'cellos had remained practically stationary, and the wood-wind instruments had undergone little change except for a reduction in the number of bassoons.[5]

At the beginning of the 19th century the first *chef d'orchestre* was J. B. Rey, who had been associated with the *Opéra* since 1776, and had become first *chef* in 1781 when Francœur (the younger) retired. Rey was probably the last of the old-style French *Maîtres de musique* or *Batteurs de mesure* who even

[1] "The orchestras throughout Paris are supplied from this Academy (Conservatoire), and the number of fine performers is almost incredible" (Busby, *Anecdotes*, II, p. 203).
[2] *Petits Mémoirs*, p. 296.
[3] Castil-Blaze, *L'Acad. Imp.*, II, p. 358.   [4] *Ibid.*, p. 374.
[5] As many as 8 bassoons had been employed at one time in the 18th century.

after the middle of the 18th century used to hammer out the beat
for the choruses and dances audibly on the floor, a table, or a music
desk.[1]

Rey's successor, from 1810 to 1817, was Luis Loc Loiseau de Persius,
a violinist in the orchestra since 1793. From that time the *Opéra* orchestra,
and, indeed, all French orchestras, remained for a long time entirely in the
hands of violinist-conductors who led the performance with violin in hand,
and gradually developed into time-beating conductors who used a violin-bow
instead of a baton.

Rudolphe Kreutzer, so well-known to all violinists all the world over by
his famous 42 Studies, became second *Chef* in 1815, and was first *Chef* from
1817 to 1824. From then until 1831 François Antoine Habeneck and Henri
Valentino shared the duties of first *Chef*, and from 1831 to 1846 Habeneck
remained alone in supreme command. Habeneck was succeeded in nearly
all his appointments, including that at the *Opéra*, by Narcisse Girard (1797–
1860), another violinist and pupil of Baillot. Girard died in harness while
conducting a performance of *Les Huguenots* in 1860.

Both Kreutzer and Valentino had been second *Chef* for a few years
before being promoted to first *Chef*. Habeneck had as his assistant (1846)
a violinist named Pantaléon Battu (1799–1870), who was still second *Chef*
in 1855. Charles de Boigne described Battu as: "*homme modeste, qui n'est
pas sans mérite, mais qui a surtout le mérite de s'effacer et de regarder comme son
bâton de maréchal son bâtonnet de second chef d'orchestre.*"[2] Clearly, Battu was
no show-conductor.

Another exalted position in the *Opéra* orchestra was that of solo violinist.
His duty was to play all the solos, especially in the ballet, and he was excused
all ordinary routine work. Castil-Blaze[3] tells how all the corps of soloists
(*virtuoses d'élite*) were absolved from ordinary orchestral duty in 1797, and
were allowed to reserve themselves for their special solo-work. The soloists
mentioned by Castil-Blaze were: Rode (violin), Levasseur ('cello), Hugot
(flute), Sallantin (oboe), Lefèvre (clarinet), Duvernoy (horn), and Ozi
(bassoon). Kreutzer was solo-violin from 1801; Habeneck, who first
joined the orchestra in 1805, occupied the same position from 1815, and
subsequent soloists were Baillot (1821), Launer, Urhan and Leudet.[4] When
the post of solo-violin was abolished, and the *chef d'orchestre* no longer played
the violin, the principal first violin was called *chef d'attaque*.

With very few exceptions all these leading violinists were either professors
or past-students of the Conservatoire, and trained in the same school of
violin-playing, the school of Viotti-Rode-Kreutzer. The rank and file, too,
were nearly all Conservatoire-trained; most of them were pupils of Kreutzer,
Baillot or Habeneck, and to that fact the Paris *Opéra* orchestra certainly
owed that unity of style amongst the strings which was so often observed
and commented on by visitors from other countries.

[1] Carse, *The Orchestra in the* 18*th Century*, p. 102.
[2] *Petits Mémoires*, p. 299.   [3] *L'Acad. Imp.*, II, p. 352.   [4] Elwart, p. 162.

Of the violin and viola players, Chrétien Urhan deserves mention even if only because it was said of him that during thirty-four years of service in the *Opéra* orchestra he had always kept his eyes glued to his part and never once looked at the stage. Sir Charles Hallé met this singular man at Paris in 1844, and described him as "a remarkable viola player, the best I have ever heard. . . . He was of an extremely religious turn of mind, and accepted the position of principal viola at the Grand Opera, which he held for a long term of years, only on the condition that his seat was to be so arranged that he might turn his back upon the stage and avoid witnessing the abominations of the ballet."[1] Ch. de Boigne called Urhan *"le trappiste de l'orchestre,"* and stated that he became leading second violin.[2] According to Castil-Blaze, Urhan entered the orchestra at the age of 26 in 1816, and eventually became solo-violinist. His claim to be remembered is strengthened by the fact that he was the first to play the solo part for *viole d'amour* in Meyerbeer's *Les Huguenots*.[3] Chorley, the well-known English critic, wrote of Urhan that he was "possibly the finest player on the viola in Europe."[4] Prominent among the leading 'cellists at the *Opéra* were Pierre François Levasseur (1753–1815) who played from 1785 until 1815; his brother Jean Henri, from 1789 to 1823; Auguste Joseph Franchomme who played for only one year in 1827; Louis Pierre Martin Norblin (1781–1854) who was playing from 1811 until 1841, and Desmarets, the leading 'cellist about the middle of the century.

Two leading double-bass players, successively professors of their instrument at the Conservatoire, were Marie Pierre Chénié (1773–1832) and one Lamy or Lami. The former played at the *Opéra* from 1785 till 1820, and it was of him that Berlioz wrote: "That fat, red fellow yonder is the double-bass, Father Chénié. He is a robust old fellow, in spite of his years; a host in himself, and worth four of the others. You may be sure his part will be played as the author (composer) wrote it; he does not belong to the school of simplifiers."[5] With all its good bass players, however, Paris was not able to produce the equal of Dragonetti in London, as both Fétis and Berlioz admitted. Fétis had something to say about the Paris bass players.[6] He divided them into two classes; the first, which comprised such men as Sorne, Chénié, Gélinek[7] and Lamy, were keen and devoted to their work, ever striving to overcome the difficulties of playing on their huge instruments; the other class (and he mentioned no names), took less pains, and played only the main notes written in the part. They obviously belonged to the "school of simplifiers," as Berlioz called it.

In the wind department too, the *Opéra* orchestra got the pick of the French players. Castil-Blaze wrote: *Les plus habiles musiciens de Paris forment aujourd'hui l'orchestre de l'Académie.*

[1] Hallé, p. 85.   [2] *Petits Mém.*, p. 146.   [3] Elwart, p. 138.
[4] *Athenæum*, Nov. 15, 1845.   [5] *Mem.*, I, p. 71.   [6] *Curiosités*, p. 191.
[7] Or Gelineck, G., a player in the *Chapelle-Musique* who wrote about the double-bass in the *Revue Musicale* in 1829; this was translated and appeared in the *Harmonicon* in Dec., 1829, p. 297.

The leading flautist at the beginning of the century was Johann Georg Wunderlich (1755–1819), whose period of service extended from 1787 to 1813. His successor was the widely-known Tulou, who after playing from 1813 to 1822, left the *Opéra* for a few years, and then returned to it in 1827.[1] During Tulou's absence the second flautist Joseph Guillou (1787–1853) took the leading part. This musician, of whom Berlioz remarked that he needed watching because he was apt to add embellishments of his own to the written flute parts,[2] was evidently a showy player; an English musical journal described his bravura playing as "overwhelming," but with "little foundation."[3] From 1834 the first flute was Vincent Joseph Dorus (1812–1896), a name well remembered by flautists in connection with an ingenious G-sharp key, known as the "Dorus key." Dorus, with Coche and Camus, were the first of the Paris flautists to adopt the Boehm flute. The second flute with Dorus was Joseph Henri Altès (1826–1895), and the third was Leplus, a son-in-law of Habeneck.

The oboe players at the *Opéra* included some who were closely associated with the improvements to that instrument which gave the French oboe its leading position, and whose style provided the basis of modern oboe-playing. Of the 18th century oboists, Antoine Sallantin (1754–1813) still played at the *Opéra* in the early years of the 19th century, having served since 1773. With him was François Joseph Garnier (1759–1825), son of an older Garnier who had also played in the same orchestra. These were followed by that most distinguished pair, Vogt and Brod. Vogt played from 1812 until 1824, and Brod from 1819 to 1839, each taking the first part in turn.[4] Charles Louis Triébert, brother of the well-known maker Frédéric Triébert, played from 1834 to 1839, and again in 1849–50. Stanilaus Verroust (1814–1868) was appointed in 1839, to be succeeded by a player named Cras, who was leading oboist in 1855. Of the earlier clarinet players still at the *Opéra* at the beginning of the century the most prominent were Chelard (father of the composer) and Lefèvre. The latter had been first clarinet since 1791 and remained in the orchestra until 1817; he was succeeded by his pupil Dacosta, who is said to have been the first to play the well-known solo part for bass clarinet in *Les Huguenots* in 1836.[5] Rather later the leading clarinet was Buteux, a pupil of Duvernoy, who also played at the *Société des Concerts*. About the middle of the century the clarinet pair at the *Opéra* were Adolphe Leroy (d. 1880) and Cyrille Rose (1830–1903).

In accordance with the French custom there were never less than four bassoon players in the *Opéra* orchestra. Ozi played from 1798 to 1806,[6] and Theodor Delcambre (1766–1828) until about 1825. The succession included Gebauer, who came in 1801 and remained until 1826, Charles Dominque Joseph Barizel (1788–1858) who made a short stay in 1814–15,

---

[1] On Sept. 5, 1827. *Harm.*, Oct., 1827, p. 214.
[2] *Mem.*, I, p. 71.   [3] *Harm.*, July, 1827, p. 141.   [4] Bechler and Rahm, p. 48.
[5] Pierre, *Les Facteurs*, p. 403. According to Pillaut (*Cat. Cons. Mus.*, Supp., 1894, p. 32) the part was first played by Buteux on a bass clarinet made by Lefèvre.
[6] *Ibid.*, *Le Magasin*, p. 100.

and Dossion (1779–c. 1841) who was playing until 1829. Adolphe
Reichmans (1795–c. 1849) was there from 1822 to 1833, when he went to
the opera at Bordeaux, and Jean François Barthélemy Cokken (1802–1875),
a pupil of Delcambre, was at the *Opéra* until 1862. Adolphe Joseph Divior
(1803–1881) played the bassoon from 1833 to 1868, and Jean Baptiste Willent
(1809–c. 1872) was at the *Opéra* for a few years round about 1848, but was
gone before 1855, by which time André Charles Joseph Verroust (1826–
1887) and Villaufret had joined Cokken and Divoir to make up the quartet.
Verroust had joined in 1845. A name closely associated with the final
development of the French bassoon was that of Louis Marie Eugène
Jancourt (1815–1901), the favourite pupil of Gebauer, who played in
the *Opéra* orchestra for only eleven months. Most of these wood-
wind players had been first prize winners or were Professors at the
Conservatoire.

The earlier of the horn players at the *Opéra*, whose service reached back
into the 18th century, were Domnich, author of an important horn tutor,
P. Kenn, who played from 1783 to 1808, and Othon Joseph Vandenbioeck
(1759–1832), who was at the *Opéra* from 1795 to 1816. Frédéric Duvernoy
was a very distinguished member of the orchestra from 1797 (solo horn
1801) until he was pensioned in 1816. A younger generation gave the
Opéra some more fine horn players, notably Louis François Dauprat, who
played from 1808 to 1831 and was the author of a tutor which remained
standard long after his time. Dauprat was followed by Jean Mengal, a
pupil of Domnich, and another in the succession of outstanding horn
players that emerged from the famous Conservatoire.

Belonging to a still later generation of distinguished horn players at the
Opéra were J. F. Rousselot (1803–1880), a *lauréat* and pupil of Duvernoy,
and Mohr, a pupil of Gallay. All of these were exponents of the hand-horn
technique which was then highly cultivated in Paris, and which still formed
the basis of the French school of horn-playing long after the introduction of
the valved instrument. Probably the first to play on a valved horn at the
Opéra was Joseph Émile Meifred (1791–1867). Joining the orchestra in
1822, he was largely concerned, with the makers Halary and Labbaye, in
introducing the valve-mechanism to the Paris players. Jules Léon Antoine
Halary (b. 1827), son of the brass instrument maker of the same name, was
also early in the field with the valved instrument at the *Opéra*.[1] The two
parts for valved horns in Halévy's *La Juive* (1835) were played, according to
Castil-Blaze,[2] by Meifred and Duvernoy. The latter was probably the
second son of Charles Duvernoy, and, according to Fétis,[3] was a horn player
at the *Opéra* from 1830. At that time the valved horn was not regarded in
Paris as a substitute for the hand horn, nor as an improvement on the old
horn, but rather as a new or additional instrument which had its uses but
was not competent to replace the old instrument. The horns in 1855 were

---

[1] Pierre, *Les Facteurs*, p. 336.   [2] *L'Acad. Imp.*, II, p. 347.
[3] *Biog. Univ.*

PLATE 1

JEAN MENGAL, LEADING HORN AT THE OPÉRA IN 1835

Mohr, Rousselot, Duvernoy, Urbin and Halary.[1] David Buhl played the leading trumpet part at the *Opéra* from 1816 until 1825, and was followed by Dauverné, who joined the orchestra about 1820 and remained for some thirty years. His brother played second trumpet for about the same period. There are also traces of a virtuoso trumpeter named Legros from 1826 to 1832, and later on, another pair of trumpeting brothers named Dubois made their appearance and were still playing in 1855. The popular cornet player Joseph Forestier (b. 1815) came to the *Opéra* at the time (from c. 1830) when French composers began to write for a pair of these instruments in addition to the usual pair of trumpets. The cornet was not regarded as, or treated as, a substitute for the trumpet, but as an additional instrument for which a particular style of part should be written. Like most of the earlier French cornet players Forestier was originally a horn player.

Of the trombone players at the *Opéra* we hear of one Bénard who played from 1816 to 1834, and then of the great man Dieppo, a Swede, whom Rivière considered "the greatest trombone player that ever lived."[2] Dieppo's colleagues round about the mid-century were Antoine Jean Simon, who played from 1843 to 1873, and Dantonnet, another trombonist who gained some success as a soloist. All of these, indeed, came into prominence as soloists at the popular concerts of Musard, Jullien and Rivière, which added so greatly to the gaiety of the French capital from the 'thirties to the 'fifties. It would be unkind to omit from the list the name of one Lahou, who played the ophicleide at the *Opéra* round about the middle of the century.

Jean Madeleine Schneitzhoeffer (1785–1850), who had ambitions as a composer, and who was quite content to be called "Bertrand" by those who found his name too long or too difficult to pronounce, was timpanist at the *Opéra* from 1815 to 1823. The "excellent Poussard,"[3] and another named Prévost, were later drummers in this brilliant orchestra. (For full list in 1855, see Appendix, p. 494.)

The foregoing are the names of some of the men *who made the great Paris orchestra what it was* during a period when that institution shone as a large and bright star amongst even the most brilliant of European opera-houses. The composers who, like Rossini, Donizetti, Bellini, Halévy, Auber and Meyerbeer enjoyed such resounding successes, and gave to the world a new standard of richness and brilliance in orchestration, could not, and would not, have created their dazzling effects without the skill, artistry, musicianship, enterprise and industry of the Paris *Opéra* orchestral players. Their names are worth recording, worth reading, and worth remembering.

After remarking that the players in the *Opéra* orchestra were in general

---

[1] Castil-Blaze, *L'Acad. Imp.*, II, p. 446.
[2] Rivière, p. 81. Dieppo has sometimes been described as a Dane. He played a trombone solo at Berlioz's great Festival performance in 1844 (*Mem.*, II, p. 164).
[3] Berlioz, *Mem.*, II, pp. 96, 234.

critical and inclined to be obstinate, Ch. de Boigne characterised them rather oddly as follows:

En particulier, les *violins* sont pédants;
Les *contre-basses*, mécontents;
Les *trombones* sont des viveurs;
Les *flûtes*, des hommes à bonnes fortunes;
Les *altos* (violas), des rêveurs, etc.[1]

There was certainly no opera orchestra in Europe in which fewer second-rate players were to be found, and the direction by Kreutzer, Habeneck and Girard was, at any rate, as good as any in the contemporary opera-houses in Germany and Italy.   When on their mettle and doing their best under favourable conditions, the Paris *Opéra* orchestra was certainly equal to the best and probably better than most in Germany.   But no orchestra in a theatre which is producing opera regularly can constantly maintain the same level of excellence.   The routine work of playing familiar operas in the regular repertoire, especially when under assistant conductors, is sure to engender some slackness in performance from time to time, and it cannot be supposed that the Paris orchestra was always up to the best of its form.

Reichardt, who had been in charge of the orchestra at Berlin at the end of Frederick the Great's time, visited the *Opéra* several times during his stay at Paris in 1802–3.   He heard the French mutilated version of Mozart's *Zauberflöte*,[2] and, if he found little to admire in French singing, he thoroughly admired the performance of the orchestra: "It plays with all its old strength and is rich in solo instruments.   Kreutzer, that excellent and energetic violinist, leads it splendidly."[3]   In Gluck's *Alceste* the orchestra was good as ever, and well rehearsed: "The glorious overture was played with magnificent power."[4]   When a new opera by Jadin was produced, "the orchestra surpassed itself."   On another occasion Reichardt remarked on the "excellent execution" and the "glorious ensemble of the orchestra," which gave him the greatest pleasure of the evening.

It is impossible to reconcile that account of the *Opéra* orchestra with that of Sir George Smart, who as a young man also visited Paris in 1802: "They admit that all the players in their orchestra are approved performers.   The number of our orchestra (King's Theatre) is fifty, one quarter of which are good for nothing, and yet we produce double the effect.   Their wind instruments are shocking."[5]   Spohr found much to admire in the *Opéra* orchestra during his stay in Paris in 1820–21.[6]   If his praise was tempered by a little fault-finding, it was probably because he did not hear the orchestra at its best in the *Salle Favart*, where the *Opéra* was then temporarily accommodated, and where there was not room enough for the full orchestra.   His qualified praise was no doubt also due to the fact that Spohr was not sympathetic to

[1] *Petits Mém.*, p. 299.
[2] "*Les Mystères d'Isis*, pastiche, musique de Mozart Haydn, etc., Morel, Lachnith, pâtissiers, 23 aout, 1801."
[3] Reichardt, *Briefe* (Paris), I, p. 163.   [4]*Ibid.*, I, p. 179.
[5] *Journals*, p. 28.   [6] *Autob.*, II, pp. 107–112.

French music and the French style of violin-playing; he missed his "earnest German music," and was ill at ease in the gay musical salons of Paris. Nevertheless, he fully appreciated the quality of the individual players, amongst whom were "the most celebrated and distinguished artists." Vogt the oboist and Tulou the flautist were singled out for special praise, and Spohr remarked on the playing of the orchestra in Kreutzer's ballet "with the greatest precision." Spohr also heard the mutilated *Zauberflöte*

THE NEW OPÉRA IN THE RUE LE PELETIER

which Reichardt had heard nearly twenty years earlier, but found that to him, "as a German" the performance was not wholly satisfactory; "Even the overture was not executed so well as it should have been by so excellent a union of first-rate musicians."

In its new home in the *rue le Peletier*[1] (1821) the *Opéra* orchestra would be better able to display its quality.

This "sumptuous" building was described by Busby in his *Concert Room and Orchestra Anecdotes* (1825); the orchestra was said to be "immense," and was not "exceeded by that of any theatre in Europe."[2] In 1826 Weber was in

[1] The *Opéra* remained in this building from Aug., 1821, to Oct., 1873. According to Matthews (pp. 26, 51) the auditorium seated 1,783 persons; according to Hervey (p. 23) there were places for 1,937 persons, and the stage measured 42 ft. in width and 82 ft. in depth.
[2] II, p. 201.

Paris for a short time when on his way to London, and heard a grand performance of Spontini's *Olimpie;* of this he wrote to his wife: "I have never heard anything to compare with the power and the ardour of the orchestra."[1]

When Rossini's later operas *Le Siége de Corinth* (1826), *Le Comte Ory* (1828), *Guillaume Tell* (1829), and Auber's *La Muette de Portici* (1828) were produced, followed by such as Meyerbeer's *Robert le Diable* (1831), *Les Huguenots* (1836) and other spectacular operas, the orchestra was able to take full advantage of its opportunities, and rose to its greatest height. These were great and eventful years in the annals of the Paris *Opéra*, and it fell to the lot of Habeneck to pilot the orchestra through many a memorable first performance. An English critic wrote of the *Opéra* orchestra in 1830: "The orchestra is the first and finest feature in the whole establishment. It would not be difficult to procure abler vocalists, but it would not be easy to organise a band so near perfection. With execution nearly faultless, and a precision and delicacy rivalling the best German orchestras, the music of an indifferent author is played almost into excellence, while that of a great master has every possible justice done to it; and, what is of very rare occurrence, the performance satisfies even the author himself." The only complaint this writer had to make was that the drums and cymbals were almost constantly in action. But that was the composer's rather than the orchestra's responsibility, and the above was written in the days of Rossini in Paris.[2]

H. F. Chorley, the English critic, eulogised the *Opéra* orchestra in 1836 in these words: "What brilliancy is there in its violins, . . . What a clearness and body of support, and pertinence of answer, and sensitiveness of expression in the violoncellos! Nor are the wind instruments inferior, though perhaps less dazzling in their peculiarity: if their tone be not of the highest quality, and partake somewhat of the thin shrillness which seems generic to all wind tones (the human voice included) in France, they are still admirable for their certainty, for their freedom from grossness, and for the subdued but not subordinate part they take in the dialogue of the score. When matters are pushed to an extremity, they can speak loudly enough, and still not too loudly. Indeed, the double drums allowed for—and these, of late, have seemed to my ear less wooden and overweening than formerly—I think the charge of noise brought against the French orchestra is a popular fallacy. Powerful it is, but the foundation of stringed instruments is so substantially clear and firm, that the tissue (to speak fancifully) never loses its coherence by the ornaments and embroideries assuming an undue prominence. Then there is an uniform but well-proportioned care in finish, and consent of execution—an understanding with the chorus—an understanding with the singers—a sensitiveness as to every nicest gradation of tone, slackened or hastened, never displayed by our most sensitive English orchestras—which carry on the enchantment; it is a machine, in short, in

[1] Ad. Jullien, p. 36.   [2] *Harm.*, Nov., 6.1830, p. 45

perfect order, and under the guidance of experience and intellect;—for these, as regards French music, are thoroughly personified in M. Habeneck."[1]

John Ella was likewise laudatory when he wrote of the *Opéra* orchestra in 1837: "The orchestra comprises about ninety of the best disciplined musicians in Paris, and although the band of the Conservatoire Concerts takes precedence in point of numbers, yet for the execution of intricate music of the modern opera, Rossini and Meyerbeer tell me there is not its rival in any theatre in Europe."[2] Although in some respects the *Opéra* orchestra might possibly have been equalled by that of the Berlin opera round about the middle of last century, it was certainly not surpassed by it. Berlioz admitted in 1843 that the German double-basses were more powerful than those at Paris, but the rest of the German strings could not come up to the high level of the "unrivalled violins, altos, and 'cellos of our Conservatoire."[3]

No doubt the style of the Paris orchestra was more dashing and alert, the tone more alive, and the individual players more brilliant, while the well-disciplined Berliners may have excelled in steadiness and breadth of tone. No doubt the Germans played their own operas with closer understanding than the French players could, but when the tables were turned, and the Germans essayed a French opera, it would be the turn of the Paris players to claim superiority. Chorley had no doubt about this when he wrote: "The German orchestras have no sympathy with the music (French opera). However correct and careful they be, I have never failed to find them falling short of the smart and stimulating piquancy which belongs to French blood, and to French blood alone."[4] The different temperament of the German and the Frenchman alone would be sufficient to account for any differences in their playing, and we cannot doubt that their national characteristics would reveal themselves in the playing of their orchestras one hundred years ago, just as they do at the present time.

When Habeneck retired in 1846 it could hardly be expected that the loss of such an outstanding conductor would not be reflected to some extent in the playing of the orchestra. Already in 1847 an English critic recorded a little deterioration when making a comparison between the larger opera orchestras of Paris and London: "The *Opéra* orchestra not up to its reputation, may be due to the absence of Habeneck or changes in personnel. Strings not as good as at Covent Garden, horns very little better, trombones, with one exception, not so good. Others all that could be desired, and balance of tone is admirable. Girard said to be uneasy; gives way to singers too much, and can't be compared with Habeneck."[5] It would indeed be hard for any conductor to follow Habeneck, and also to bear comparison with Costa at his best with his picked players at Covent Garden

[1] Chorley, *Music and Manners*, I, p. 17.
[2] Ella, *Mus. Sketches*, MS., *Mus. World*, Jan. 26, 1838, p. 52.
[3] *Mem.*, II, p. 97. Also—"our most astounding violins, violas, and 'cellos of the Conservatoire" (*Evenings in the Orchestra*, p. 321).
[4] *Music and Manners*, II, p. 150.   [5] *Mus. World*, Oct. 23, 1847, p. 668.

in 1847. But when Wagner came to Paris in 1861 to superintend the production of *Tannhäuser* at the *Opéra*, he was immensely pleased with the orchestra; from it, he wrote, one could "ask anything: it is the best in the world."[1]

THÉÂTRE ITALIEN

At this theatre the general musical management was in the hands of a musical director, but the playing of the orchestra was controlled by a violinist-leader. Berton occupied the first of these positions from 1807, and was followed by Spontini in 1810. In 1812 Paër succeeded, and retained his position until 1827, except for a period in 1824–26 when Rossini held the reins[2] and Paër was obliged to take second place. From 1820 to 1827, which includes the period when Rossini was general director, Hérold was *maestro al piano* at the *Théâtre Italien*, but his position was not that of a conductor in charge of the orchestra, it was rather that of an accompanist, vocal coach and chorus-master.[3] In no French theatre at that time was a pianist in charge of the orchestra.

The violinist Jean Jacques Grasset was master of the orchestra from about 1801 until 1829, and it was of his method of direction that Spohr, who was in Paris in 1820, wrote in his Autobiography: "I became confirmed but the more strongly in my opinion, that a theatrical orchestra, however excellent it may be, on account of the great distance of the extreme ends, should not be conducted otherwise than by a continual beating of the time, and, that to mark the time constantly by motions of the body and the violin, like M. Grasset does, is of no use."[4] Grasset was obviously a violin-playing conductor of the old school who played with his orchestra, and beat the time with his bow only when the ensemble was getting out of hand. Castil-Blaze told how Grasset stationed himself at the *end* of the orchestra, with his left side towards the stage; in that position he could overlook the whole orchestra without turning his head.[5]

Girard succeeded in 1830 when a new general manager (Robert) decided that it was time he got rid of Grasset. Tilmant, who became second *Chef* in 1834, was promoted to first *Chef* in 1837 when Girard left to go to the *Opéra Comique*. Ella wrote of Tilmant: "In an orchestra he is matchless; always sure of his points, which he attacks with vigour and aplomb."[6]

The orchestra at the *Théâtre Italien* was never so large as that of the *Opéra*, the strings, as Fétis remarked, being rather too few for the full complement of wind instruments.[7] But the players seem to have been of the same first-class quality, and it was not unusual for a musician to pass from one orchestra to the other.

---

[1] Wagner, *Letters* to Mathilde Wesendonk, p. 253.
[2] Rossini's title was: *Directeur de la Musique et de la scéne* (Soubies, p. 32).
[3] Ad. Adam designated him *Accompagnateur*.   [4] *Autob.*, II, p. 119.
[5] *L'Acad. Imp.*, II, p. 361.   [6] *Musical Sketches*, MS., *Mus. World*, Jan. 5, 1838, p. 2.
[7] *Curiosités*, p. 285.

PLATE 2

THÉÂTRE ITALIEN (SALLE FAVART), PARIS, 1829

In 1790 the total strength of the orchestra at the *Théâtre Italien* was forty players,[1] and it is improbable that it rose above fifty during the first half of the 19th century. An English "musical tourist" who visited Paris in 1830 said that the orchestra in that year numbered forty-six players, and added that it "is everything that could be wished, as regards precision, delicacy and power."[2]

The string section always included in its ranks some players who rose to distinction; such names as J. B. Tolbecque, Franchomme, Chevillard and Tilmant jun. occur in the lists at various times, and the great bass player Chénié served for some years before going to the *Opéra*.

In the wind department there were many players who either came from or went to the *Opéra*. Tulou was first flute at the *Théâtre Italien* from 1804 to 1813, and Paul Hippolyte Camus (b. 1796) occupied the same position for several years after he joined in 1836. Vogt in 1801, Henri Noel Gilles (b. 1779) from 1803 to 1814, Charles Triébert and Verroust were among the leading oboists, and Antoine J. Lavigne was said to be playing at the *Théâtre Italien* for several years before he finally came to England in 1847. The clarinet players included Dacosta (who eventually succeeded Lefèvre at the *Opéra*) from 1807, Jean Baptiste Gambaro (1785–1828) from 1816 to 1823, and his more famous successor Frédéric Berr (1794–1838). It was said that Ivan Müller "has succeeded to Berr's appointments" in 1839.[3]

Notable among the bassoon players were: Guillaume Fougas (1780–1854) who came early in the century and remained for thirty years, Cokken, c. 1820, Divoir, Willent, c. 1830, A. Marzoli, Jean Nicolas Savary (1786–c. 1850) whose name was so closely associated with the development of the French type of bassoon, and Jancourt.

Among the names of the horn players we find Mengal, Meifred, Gallay, Schlottman (one of several French horn players who became cornet players) and—name which meant so much to horn-players—Marcel Auguste Raoux (b. 1795), who, according to Fétis,[4] played at the *Théâtre Italien* from 1822. According to the same authority, David Buhl was leading trumpeter at both the *Opéra* and the *Théâtre Italien* from 1816 to 1825.

Most of these names, which may seem to be quite unimportant to the casual reader, are nevertheless those of players who were important and influential in the history of French orchestras, and many of them have left their mark not only on the instrumental style of that and other countries, but also on the development of the instruments on which they played. Indeed, it would be no exaggeration to assert that their work has been more far-reaching and beneficial to orchestral progress in the long run than that of some of the conductors who officiated at the *Théâtre Italien* during the first half of last century.

According to Spohr,[5] the Parisians ranked the orchestra of the *Théâtre Italien* above that of the *Opéra*, in fact, "the first in the world." All the

[1] *Calendrier*, 1791.　　　　[2] *Harm.*, Nov., 1830, p. 456.
[3] *Mus. World*, Jan. 17, 1839, p. 44.　　　[4] *Biog. Univ.*　　　[5] *Autob.*, II, p. 118.

same, Spohr could not refrain from picking holes in their playing; twice, he wrote, the wind instruments were obviously at fault, and they "wavered several times so much that the conductor was obliged to beat the time for them." But, "in other respects this orchestra is justly famed for the discretion with which it accompanies the singers, and in that might serve as a model for the other Parisian as well as many German orchestras." And that must be counted high praise from one who was indisposed to scatter compliments about when French music or playing was concerned. Smart, who was very sparing with praise for French orchestras, said that it numbered about 45 players, and was "good, and large for the size of the house," but the wind players were "nothing extraordinary, except some very excellent horns."[1] If English reports are to be believed, the repute of the orchestra at the *Théâtre Italien* declined considerably just before the mid-century. The playing was said to be "poor" in 1847, and a little later it was "execrable."[2]

OPÉRA COMIQUE

At the *Opéra Comique* a type of French opera rather lighter, less spectacular and pretentious than at the *Opéra*, was produced, with spoken dialogue, but by no means of the very light and humorous variety which we in this country associate with the term "comic opera." These works, generally designed for the resources of the company and theatre, included many by Boieldieu, Méhul, Cherubini, Ad. Adam, Hérold, Auber, and others who excelled in this particular *genre* of French opera.

The orchestra was controlled, in the same way as at the *Opéra*, by a violinist-leader who was called the *chef d'orchestre*, and who played on his violin or beat time with his bow. The *chef* at the beginning of the century was Lahoussaye, the same violinist who had directed the first performance of Mozart's "Paris" symphony at the *Concert Spirituel* in 1778. From 1802 to 1816 Mathieu Frédéric Blasius acted in the same capacity, and the succession included Frédéric Kreubé from 1816 to 1828, Crémont till 1831, Valentino from 1831 to 1836, Girard from 1837, Théodore Labarre (1805–1870), a harpist described as a mediocre conductor, from 1847 to 1849, and Tilmant from 1849 to 1868.

The orchestra, numbering 40 players in 1790, increased a little during the early 19th century, but never grew to the size of the *Opéra* orchestra. In 1830 it was said to consist of 45 or 46 performers, and it played "with admirable precision and delicacy." The same writer commented on the playing of the first horn: "It would be invidious to distinguish one performer more than another, yet I cannot help remarking, that the first horn-player has an exquisite tone, and as much command of his instrument as Puzzi himself; can praise go higher?"[3]

[1] *Journals*, pp. 227–8.
[2] *Mus. World*, 1847, pp. 662 and 669. "The orchestra has sadly retrograded" (*Illus. Lond. News*, 1847).
[3] *Harm.*, Nov., 1830, p. 455.

The players were of the same excellent quality as those at the *Théâtre Italien*, mostly Conservatoire-trained, and several passed from the *Opéra Comique* to the *Opéra* orchestra. Habeneck himself gained his early experience at the *Opéra Comique* in 1804, the year in which he won the first violin prize at the Conservatoire; his brother Joseph played in the same orchestra,

SALLE VENTADOUR, PARIS, IN 1850 (CONDUCTOR WITH VIOLIN BOW)

and from 1819 until 1837 was leader and assistant conductor. The Conservatoire first prize-winner (1834) Louis M. C. Javault (b. 1816) was solo violinist for several years. Among the celebrities who in their earlier careers were obliged to do routine orchestral duty at the *Opéra Comique* were Offenbach, the famous composer of operettas, who played the 'cello from 1834 to 1837, and H. Prosper Seligmann (1817–1882) a 'cellist who later on became a considerable virtuoso player, and who joined the orchestra at the same time as Offenbach. The most notable flautists were: Étienne F.

Gebauer from 1801 to 1822; A. Becquié (1800–1825) from 1821 until his death; Henri Besozzi, one of the last of a family famous in the 18th century as oboists, from about 1825; Jean Rémusat (1815–1880), another skilled flautist who eventually went to London to play in Jullien's orchestra; Leplus, Habeneck's son-in-law, and Camus.

Of the oboists there were Vogt, c. 1803, Frédéric Chalon who retired in 1819, Roméden, Barré (Barret) from 1827 until he settled in London in 1829, Chas. Triébert from 1830 to 1834, and one Léonard who was there in 1839. The clarinet players included Étienne Solére (1753–1817) who played from 1790 to 1810, Chas. Duvernoy until 1821, Jacques Jules Boufil (b. 1783) who joined as second clarinet in 1807 and succeeded Duvernoy as first in 1821, César Janssen (b. 1781) who came c. 1814 as second clarinet and retired as first in 1835, and one Hugot, probably a descendant of the old flautist of that name. The bassoons included Henri, Cokken, Blaise and Jancourt; Charles Petit (b. 1783), a pupil of Domnich, became the leading horn player in 1809 and remained until 1826; his successor was evidently Baneux (1795–1854), a pupil of Dauprat, who came in 1825 and was promoted to *cor solo* in 1837. His son Mathieu Gustav Baneux (b. 1825), also a pupil of Dauprat, played the same instrument from about 1840 to 1849 and then left to travel abroad, but eventually returned to succeed his father as *cor solo*. One of the trombone players at the *Opéra Comique* was Victor Cornette, who played from 1827 to 1831, and was the author of tutors for almost every wind instrument that is blown. It is said that Hérold, the composer, was at one time timpanist at the *Opéra Comique*. (For full list in 1839, see Appendix, p. 493.)

Smart pronounced this orchestra "excellent" in 1802, and said that there were about forty players. Spohr's verdict in 1821 was: "the orchestra played well, and was particularly remarkable for a delicate *piano*."[1] Although both Spohr and Mendelssohn were antipathetic to the music and the playing of French musicians, they could not withhold praise from the opera-orchestras of Paris. A correspondent of the London *Harmonicon* eulogised the orchestra at the *Opéra Comique* in these words; it was "filled by first-rate talent, and is one of the first in the capital"; it played "with a vigour and precision most remarkable and worthy of the highest praise."[2] John Ella said that at the performance of Méhul's *Joseph* in 1829 the orchestra was "perfection."

By 1839, when they were playing in the *Théâtre des Nouveautés*, the total strength of the orchestra had risen to sixty-two players in addition to Girard and his two assistant-conductors, Huny and Merlé. Of these, thirty-three were string players, and extra to the usual complement of wind instruments there were special solo players for each instrument who were excused the ordinary routine duty and reserved themselves for solo playing. At that time Javault and Dancla *aîné* were the leading violinists, Merlé was leading viola as well as third conductor, Mercadier was solo 'cellist, and Toutain

[1] *Autob.*, II, p. 132.   [2] *Harm.*, Dec., 1825, p. 234.

led the double-basses.   There were then three of the Dancla family in the orchestra, and two of the Labro family, both playing double-basses.[1]

There can be no doubt about it, that just as the *Opéra* orchestra in Paris was superior to that of the King's Theatre in London, so were those at the *Théâtre Italien* and the *Opéra Comique* on a much higher level than the orchestras at Covent Garden and Drury Lane Theatres.

In 1840 it was said that there were about seventy players at the *Opéra Comique*, and the Paris correspondent of the *Morning Post* said that, "taking it altogether, the band is infinitely beyond any one in the English theatres, except of course, the Italian Opera-house band, which, under Costa's baton, is upon the whole unrivalled."   But, although it contained some excellent solo players, it was said to be "susceptible of improvement," and the writer guessed that if "Habeneck of the *Académie* was director, in three months this very same band would exhibit a much improved *ensemble*."[2]   Nevertheless, the orchestra at the *Opéra Comique* appears to have maintained its excellent reputation during the 'forties.   An English critic described it as being "perfect" in 1845 when under the direction of Girard, but some deterioration was noticed in 1847 when Labarre, the harpist, became conductor: "The orchestra, although not so good as when it was formerly conducted by Girard, is still the best in Paris, always excepting, of course, Habeneck's Conservatoire phalanx."[3]

*   *   *

According to Pontécoulant's statistics,[4] there were 25 theatres in Paris in 1848, employing among them 636 players.   Of these the five largest theatres employed altogether 267 players, 113 provided the orchestras in five theatres of second rank, and 256 were employed in fifteen theatres of the lowest category.   A similar statement in the *Musical World* of 1852 gives the total of 639 players in 25 theatres.[5]

CONCERT ORCHESTRAS

The development of orchestral concerts in Paris during the first half of last century must be considered in connection with the older concerts of the 18th century, namely, the *Concert Spirituel* (1725), the *Concert des Amateurs*, and the *Concert de la Loge olympique* (1780).   Through the medium of these concerts Paris had acquired a certain taste for symphonies on the German model.   This had been initiated by the works of the Mannheim composers, particularly those of Stamitz, Toeschi, and others of the same school and period; it had been kept alive by the work of their successors, such as Van Maldere, Vanhal, J. C. Bach, and many others of their generation.   This taste

[1] *L'Indicateur général*, pp. 5–7.
[2] *Mus. World*, May 21, 1840, p. 316.   [3] *Illus. Lon. News*, Oct. 30, 1847.
[4] *Essai* (1857), p. 181.   According to Hervey (p. 1) there were 22 theatres in 1846.
[5] 1852, p. 581.

was greatly stimulated by the earlier symphonies of Haydn, which were first heard at Paris in 1779,[1] and which led to a commission offered to Haydn by the *Concert de la Loge olympique* to compose some symphonies specially for these concerts. The outcome of this was the group of works generally known as Haydn's "Paris symphonies" (1784–6).[2]

The Revolution in 1789 brought the *Concert de la Loge olympique* to an end, and for some time Paris was without any regularly organised orchestral concerts. Under the Republic, however, a new venture was started just before the close of the century[3] under the name *Concerts de la rue de Cléry*. There was no proper concert hall in Paris at that time, and after a few years of activity in a very unsuitable room, these concerts expired, probably for no other reason than that no adequate place for such performances could be found.

For the *rue de Cléry* concerts many of the foremost instrumentalists in Paris provided an orchestra of 80 players, including the violinists Kreutzer, Rode and Lafont, the 'cellist Duport, the oboist Sallantin, the clarinettist Lefèvre, the horn player Duvernoy, and the harpist Dalvimare. The orchestra was directed by Grasset, the violinist who later became *chef d'orchestre* at the *Théâtre Italien*, and a choir was under the direction of Plantade *père*.

Haydn's symphonies formed the mainstay of the programmes at these concerts, and, according to Elwart,[4] they were played to perfection by the very competent orchestra. Fétis asserted that the concerts at the *rue de Cléry* were only feeble imitations of the earlier concerts of the *Loge olympique*, but he granted that the orchestra was good, and that the concerts enjoyed some considerable success until about 1802.[5]

Reichardt heard two of Haydn's symphonies played at the *rue de Cléry* in 1802, and was more than satisfied with the rendering; he wished that Haydn would come to Paris to hear them; nowhere else would he hear them so well played.[6] Of another concert, Reichardt again expressed his satisfaction with the excellent performance of two Haydn symphonies, but was greatly annoyed because a Turkish band (*Janitscharenmusik*) consisting of cymbals, triangles, drums, trumpets and a large bass drum was employed in one of these works. Whenever the Turkish band began to play, he said, the ladies of the audience jumped up, shouting for joy and clapping their hands.[7] Presumably the work in question was the Military Symphony (B. and H. No. 100), in which Haydn did write parts for these noisy instruments. But Reichardt did not make it clear whether he was annoyed because of the way these instruments were used, or because of the behaviour of the ladies, or because he imagined that the Turkish band was a Parisian

---

[1] Fétis, *Curiosités*, p. 333.

[2] The parts were published in Paris under the title *Répertoire de la Loge olympique*.

[3] In the VIIth year of the Republic (Elwart, p. 54). That is between Sept., 1798, and Sept., 1799.

[4] Elwart, p. 54.   [5] Fétis, *Curiosités*, p. 335.   [6] *Briefe* (Paris), I, p. 492.

[7] *Ibid.*, II, p. 32.

addition to Haydn's score. Reichardt went on to say that although the playing of Haydn at the *Cléry* concerts was excellent, and that the orchestra included the best instrumentalists in Paris as well as a few very accomplished amateurs, he found the playing deficient in only one respect. The Parisian orchestra could produce the most brilliant *fortissimo*, or the most delicate *pianissimo*, but it lacked the intermediate shades between these two extremes. He missed the quiet grandeur of the tone of the best German orchestras, which, on the other hand, he said, were unable to play with so much energy and brilliance as the Parisians. Reichardt concluded that the different temperament of a German and a Frenchman must be held accountable for the difference in their style of performance, and in that he was probably not far wrong.[1]

On a third occasion Reichardt was again delighted with the instrumental playing at the *rue de Cléry* concerts, but, like all foreigners, he had not a good word to say for French singing. He would never have imagined that so little good singing could be heard in a city so great as Paris; they could not produce one good choir.[2] On a fourth occasion the German *Kapellmeister* found the *Cléry* concert so full that even the subscribers could hardly get in; the hall was unsuitable and uncomfortable, nevertheless, again he heard a Haydn symphony, the "parade-piece" of these concerts, splendidly played. A noble *Adagio*, played with such power, touched his soul deeply.[3]

These concerts, short-lived though they were, certainly kept alive the taste for symphonic music in Paris, and helped to bridge the gap between the last of the 18th century concerts and what proved to be the beginning of the famous *Société des Concerts* or Conservatoire concerts.

So, at the beginning of last century in Paris, Haydn provided the nourishment on which the symphony was to thrive; Mozart was rather forgotten, and Beethoven in Vienna was just beginning to write his series of nine immortal symphonies. As the immense superiority of the three great Viennese masters' works began to be realised, the symphonies of the many 18th century composers, which had enjoyed considerable popularity towards the close of that century, were being steadily consigned to a retirement from which they have never emerged.

Of all the Paris concert orchestras, the greatest glory belongs to that of the *Société des Concerts*, founded in 1828, generally known as the Conservatoire concerts.[4]

Not long after the establishment of the Conservatoire in 1795, public practice concerts by the students were inaugurated; these were known as *les Exercices des élèves du Conservatoire*,[5] and they were held in the small hall of the Conservatoire. It was customary that the first prize-winner of the violin class of each year should take charge of the students' orchestra on

[1] *Briefe* (Paris), II, pp. 32–34.   [2] *Ibid.*, II, p. 223.   [3] *Ibid.*, III, p. 87.
[4] As in the case of the *Opéra*, the title of the Conservatoire was altered with each change in the form of the French government. At the time of the foundation of the *Société*, the official title was *l'École royale de Musique et de declamation lyrique*.
[5] Fétis, *Curiosités*, p. 335.

these occasions. Reichardt was present at one of these performances in 1802, and said that the orchestra was composed entirely of students, and was directed by a student; a Haydn symphony and a difficult overture by Cherubini were played in a manner which surpassed all his expectations.[1] When Habeneck became the *lauréat* in 1804, and duly took his turn as violinist-leader, the marked ability which he showed in that capacity resulted in his being appointed regular conductor of the students' orchestra. Habeneck held that position from 1806 until 1815,[2] when the Conservatoire was suppressed and closed its doors for a while. During the same period some concerts, known as the *Concerts Français*, organised and managed by the students themselves, were also given in the Conservatoire hall. These eventually came to grief, as Elwart said, owing to an excusable lack of administrative experience on the part of those young people. The violin prize-winners Gasse and Duret took turns in directing the orchestra.

At the students' concerts some symphonies by Haydn and Mozart were played, and in 1807 Beethoven's first symphony was heard for the first time in Paris, played by these keen young students under the guidance of Habeneck. The second symphony and the *Eroica* followed in 1811.[3] According to Fétis,[4] the Conservatoire students' concerts, modestly called *Exercices*, became well-known throughout Europe; the classical symphonies were rendered with a precision and fire hitherto unknown. Of these performances it was written in an English periodical: "The exercises of its pupils are the most brilliant concerts of Paris."[5] Thus was planted the seed from which the *Société* eventually grew, in spite of the interruption when the Conservatoire was closed in 1815.

This official school of music was re-opened in 1816, this time as the *École royale de Musique*, but on a much reduced scale. It was a rather shabby affair[6] compared with the grand institution which had flourished so successfully for twenty years, and the students' practices were not resumed. This bad state of affairs lasted until 1822, when Cherubini was made director, and a more prosperous era was inaugurated.

In the meantime there had been other efforts to provide Paris with orchestral and vocal concerts after the collapse of the *rue de Cléry* concerts. One of these was an attempted revival of concerts on the lines of the old *Concert spirituel* at the *Théâtre Italien* in 1805,[7] and subsequently at other theatres, and finally, after the Restoration, at the *Opéra*. A too limited repertoire, consisting of well-worn symphonies and oft-repeated choral works, and the fact that the stage of a theatre was unsuitable for such concerts, combined to operate against the success of these efforts, and when

---

[1] *Briefe* (Paris), I, p. 157.   [2] Elwart, p. 324.   [3] *Le Conservatoire National*, p. 138.
[4] *Curiosités*, p. 130.   [5] *Quar. Mus. Mag.*, Vol. II, No. VI, p. 193.
[6] During the first year no funds were provided for heating the building, and the inspector-general was obliged to use old furniture and old pianos as fuel (Fétis, *Curiosités*, p. 140).
[7] Fétis, p. 336. In 1815, according to Lasalle and Thoinan, p. 183.

Habeneck was put in charge of the *Concert spirituel* at the *Opéra* in 1818,[1] he failed to arouse that appreciation of the works of Beethoven for which he was ever striving. He did manage to produce Beethoven's second symphony, but so strong was the objection to the *Andante* that, in order to save the rest of the symphony, he was obliged to substitute the popular *Andante* from the seventh symphony. Habeneck, judging that the time was not yet ripe for disclosing the beauties which lay hidden in the works of the great Viennese master, was in no hurry to force them on an unwilling public, and waited patiently for the moment and the opportunity when he could embark on the plan which he had so much at heart. Schindler's account of the introduction of Beethoven's symphonies in Paris does not altogether tally with the above, which is largely based on the accounts of Elwart and Fétis; but although they differ in many details, the general trend is the same. According to Schindler, Habeneck got the parts of the first two symphonies (recently published in Vienna) soon after 1803, and tried them over with a small orchestra. Little more was done until 1815, when the parts of the *Eroica* were procured and laid before Habeneck. After some delay this symphony was tried, but it was not understood, and not appreciated. Habeneck was rather discouraged, and for some time nothing more was done. But backed up by Urhan, Stockhausen, Sina and Tulou, Habeneck persevered, and when Urhan and Sina drew his attention to the fifth symphony, that work was tried and was much liked.[2]

Elwart, who was a student of the Conservatoire at that time, tells the story of the birth of the *Société des Concerts* as follows.[3] On St. Cecilia's Day, 22 November, 1826, Habeneck invited a number of his colleagues to lunch; most of them belonged to the *Opéra* orchestra, and they were asked to bring their instruments with them. Several accepted this invitation,[4] and on their arrival Habeneck put before them the parts of Beethoven's *Eroica* symphony. This work was practised, and so intently that it was not until after 4 o'clock that the guests were able to sit down to the meal provided by Mad. Habeneck. At first the symphony merely astonished the select group of instrumentalists, but after some further meetings had been held, astonishment gave way to intense admiration. The practices were continued during 1827, and in 1828 Habeneck approached Cherubini, then head of the Conservatoire, and suggested that he should seek the permission of the Ministry of Arts for this band of enthusiasts to give concerts in the large hall of the Conservatoire, for which they were prepared to pay all incidental expenses. Cherubini welcomed the idea and obtained from the Ministry not only permission to use the hall, but also a grant of 2,000 francs towards the expenses. An agreement dated 5 February, 1828, was signed

---

[1] Dandelot, p. 4.   [2] Schindler, *B. in Paris*, pp. 1–8.   [3] Elwart, p. 61.
[4] Guillou, Tulou (flutes); Vogt, Brod (oboes); Dacosta, Buteux (clarinets); Dauverné, Buhl (trumpets); Dauprat, Blangy, Meifred, Mengal (horns); Dossion, Henri, Barizel (bassoons); Tilmant, Battu, Tolbecque, Saint-Laurent, Claudel, Guérin, Urhan (violins); Amédée, Seuriot (violas); Norblin, Vaslin, Chaft ('cellos); and several others (Elwart, p. 61, f.n.).

by the Minister and some fifty past students of the Conservatoire, embodying the lines on which a society, constituted on a co-operative basis, should be formed, and at a general meeting held on 24 March, the 52 Articles of the *Société des Concerts* were drawn up, and an administrative committee was elected.

In the meantime an orchestra of 86 players and a choir of 79 voices had been formed; the choir was trained by M. Kuhn, and the whole was placed under the direction of Habeneck.   Already on 9 March, 1828, at two o'clock in the afternoon, the first concert took place in the large hall[1] of the Conservatoire, just a year after Beethoven's death.

The orchestra contained most of the best of the younger instrumentalists of Paris, all trained in the same school, and imbued by an *esprit de corps* and a youthful enthusiasm rarely to be found in established orchestras.   This was a young orchestra; most of the players were between the ages of 20 and 40 at the time when the *Société* was formed.

Among the first violins were Tilmant, Girard, Battu, Seghers (all destined to become conductors in Paris), Sauzay, Urhan, and Aug. Tolbecque who later became leader at the opera in London.   Amédée was at the head of the violas, which also included Jean Baptiste Tolbecque, a favourite Parisian conductor of light music.   The 'cellos included Norblin, Vaslin, Franchomme and Chevillard, and old Chénié led the eight double-basses. In the wood-wind section were Tulou and Guillou (flutes), Vogt and Brod (oboes), Dacosta and Buteux (clarinets), with Henri, Dossion, Barizel and Reickmanns for the bassoons.   Dauprat, Blangy, Mengal and Meifred made up the horn quartet; the trumpeters were Dauverné and Legros; Barbier, Bénard, and Devise formed the trio of trombones, and Pavart blew the ophicleide; Schneitzhoeffer, from the *Opéra*, beat the drums.   (For full list in 1828, see Appendix, p. 493.)

Six regular concerts were given in each season, and one or two extra events generally brought the season's work up to eight or nine performances. Beethoven's *Eroica* symphony appropriately opened the first concert, the piece which Habeneck and his faithful followers had studied from the day when they met at Habeneck's house in 1826.   By general request the same symphony was repeated at the second concert.   The C Minor Symphony was given three performances in the first year, and two of Mozart's symphonies were played.   The programmes always included one symphony, occasionally two, an overture, one or two vocal solos or duets, a concerto or other instrumental solo, and one or two choral items.

An analysis of the symphonies and overtures played during the first ten years of the *Société des Concerts* shows the following results:

Symphonies, 1828–1837

Beethoven 68, Mozart 5, Haydn 7, Onslow 4, others 4.

Overtures, 1828–1837

Beethoven 17, Mozart 3, Weber 23, Méhul 3, Cherubini 2, Berlioz 1, others 7.

[1] Erected in 1806.

The rather small number of performances of Mozart's symphonies may be accounted for by the fact only a very few were then available in print. These were the last three and the "Prague" symphony. The one in G minor was the most popular at the *Société's* concerts. The Choral Symphony was first played on 27 March, 1831. Perhaps the whole work at one sitting proved to be rather strong meat for a Parisian audience, for after that it was presented in rather smaller portions. The next time, in 1832, only the *Adagio* and *Finale* were given; in 1834 the whole work was performed at one concert, but it was divided into two halves; in 1837 the whole symphony was given without a break, and in 1838, 1839 and 1841 the whole work was performed twice in each season. Mendelssohn played Beethoven's G Major piano concerto, probably for the first time in Paris, in 1832, and in 1844 Hallé played the Emperor Concerto. Quite a number of solos on wind instruments occur in the earlier programmes; they included a solo by Meifred on the valved horn (then a novelty in Paris) in 1828, and a trombone solo by the great Dieppo in 1835. A noticeable feature of the programmes is the occurrence of movements from Beethoven's quartets played by the whole of the string orchestra. The same composer's Septet, played by all the strings with doubled wind parts was a particularly popular item, and was performed 27 times before 1858.[1]

Schindler gave a list of the orchestra in 1841, thirteen years after the foundation of the society. There were then 60 regular playing members, 21 probationers, mostly senior students of the Conservatoire, and seven outside players who were not members of the society, making a total of 88 performers. But Schindler pointed out that the number of players taking part in any one concert was not usually more than 60. Of the violinists, Girard and Aug. Tolbecque were no longer playing, and Dancla, Alard and Deldevez were newcomers. Seuriot led the violas as successor to Amédée, old Chénié's place as leader of the double-basses had been taken by Chaft, and Achille Gouffé was a probationer in that department. Dorus had joined the flutes, and Brod the oboist (d. 1839) was succeeded by Vény. The clarinettists Dacosta and Buteux had changed places, and Cokken was a newcomer to the bassoons. Dauprat, the first horn, had retired, but remained an honorary member; Jean Mengal was now first horn, and Gallay and Rousselot were newcomers; Dieppo was principal trombone, and Poussard had taken the place of Schneitzhoeffer at the timpani.

The second ten years of the society's work shows little change in the character of the programmes. Beethoven's symphonies remained the principal items at most of the concerts, as the following analysis shows:

Symphonies, 1838–1847

Beethoven 90, Haydn 23, Mozart 15, Mendelssohn 5, others 10.

[1] The septet was similarly treated in London. At Blagrove's concerts in 1838 and 1840 at the Hanover Square Rooms it was played by 12 violins, 8 violas, 6 'cellos, 4 double-basses 2 clarinets, 2 bassoons and 2 horns.

Overtures, 1838–1847

Beethoven 21, Weber 19, Méhul 6, Gluck 4, Mendelssohn 4, Mozart 2, others 5.

By 1859, when the *Société* had been in existence for 32 years, Beethoven's symphonies had been given 280 performances:

No. 1, 13 times	No. 4, 24 times	No. 7, 52 times
No. 2, 26 „	No. 5, 53 „	No. 8, 14 „
No. 3, 28 „	No. 6, 51 „	No. 9, 19 „

For the same period the figures for Haydn's and Mozart's symphonies were, respectively, 58 and 37; a few of Mendelssohn's works had been added to the repertoire, but the *Société* knew very little of Spohr and had played only two works by Berlioz, namely, *Rob Roy* overture and selections from *La Damnation de Faust*. Of Schubert's and Schumann's symphonies and overtures they knew nothing.

Habeneck conducted a concert of the *Société* for the last time on 16 April, 1848. Altogether he had conducted 186 of these concerts, and in February, 1849, he died, after having guided the destiny of this child of his creation for just over twenty years, and having made for Paris what was generally acknowledged to be the finest orchestra in the world.

Habeneck was succeeded by Girard, with Tilmant as his assistant. Although at first the players would have preferred the more easy-going Battu as their *chef*,[1] Girard soon won their loyalty and did all that was in his power to maintain the high reputation of an orchestra which by that time had passed out of its first youthful growth.

In 1859 the total strength of the orchestra was 85 players. Many of the original players were no longer there, and those that remained must have raised the average age of the players to a considerably higher figure than it had been in 1828. In the first violins six of the original members were still playing; two second violins, four violas and four 'cellos who had played in 1828 were still there, but not a single double-bass or wind player of the original orchestra remained.

Under Habeneck the orchestra of the *Société des Concerts* had gained a great and wide reputation. The quality of the individual players was no doubt of the best, but that alone would not account for playing which was so universally admired that it is difficult to find an unfavourable remark in the comments of those who heard it play in its younger and most vigorous days.

Perhaps the most interesting remarks are those of Wagner, who heard the orchestra in 1839, who was outspoken and blunt, and not at all disposed to be politely flattering, as one might suspect Mendelssohn sometimes was: "I received a good lesson at Paris in 1839, when I heard the orchestra of the Conservatoire rehearse the enigmatical Ninth Symphony. The scales fell from my eyes; I came to understand the value of *correct* execution and the

[1] Dandelot, p. 37.

PLATE 3

HABENECK

secret of a good performance. The orchestra had learnt to look for Beethoven's *melody* in every bar—that melody which the worthy Leipzig musicians had failed to discover; and the orchestra *sang* that melody. *This was the secret.* Habeneck, who solved the difficulty, and to whom the great credit for this performance is due, was not a conductor of special genius. Whilst rehearsing the symphony, during an entire winter season, he had felt it to be incomprehensible and ineffective (would German conductors have confessed as much?), but he persisted throughout a second and a third season! until Beethoven's new *melos* was understood and correctly rendered by each member of the orchestra. Habeneck was a conductor of the old stamp; *he* was the master—and everyone obeyed him. I cannot attempt to describe the beauty of this performance."[1]

Wagner went on to describe the difficulty experienced in getting a certain passage in the Ninth Symphony[2] properly played, and told how it was achieved with "such equable perfection" by the Paris orchestra: "The masterly execution of this passage by the Paris orchestra consisted in the fact that they played it *exactly* as it is written. Neither at Dresden, nor in London when, in after years, I had occasion to prepare a performance of the symphony, did I succeed in getting rid of the annoying irregularity which arises from the change of bow and change of strings."[3] Wagner continued: "I would ask how did the musicians of Paris arrive at so perfect a solution of the difficult problem? By the most conscientious diligence. They were not content with mutual admiration and congratulation (*sich gegenseitig Complimente zu machen*), nor did they assume that difficulties must disappear before them as a matter of course. French musicians in the main belong to the Italian school; its influence upon them has been beneficial in as much as they have thus been taught to approach music mainly through the medium of the human voice. The French idea of playing an instrument well is to be able to *sing* well upon it. And (as already said) that superb orchestra *sang* the symphony. The possibility of its being well sung implies that the true *tempo* had been found: and this is the second point which impressed me at the time. Old Habeneck was not the medium of any abstract-æsthetical inspiration—he was devoid of "genius": *but he found the right tempo whilst persistently fixing the attention of his orchestra upon the MELOS of the symphony.*"[4]

The French string players earned a great compliment from the exacting German composer when he wrote: "our celebrated German orchestras remained far behind those in France in the power and capacity of the violins, and particularly of the violoncellos."[5]

Schindler, Beethoven's friend and biographer, visited Paris in 1841, and recorded his opinion that nowhere in Germany were Beethoven's works better understood and better played than in Paris under Habeneck. Nothing he had ever heard in Germany equalled the rendering of the *Pastoral*

---

[1] *On Conducting* (English trans. by Dannreuther), p. 15.
[2] 1st Mov., bars 116 to 119.   [3] Wagner, *Ibid.*, p. 17.   [4] *Ibid.*, p. 18.   [5] *Ibid.*, p. 5.

symphony at the Conservatoire, in which every note and its meaning had been carefully studied; even when at their very best, the performances at the Vienna *Concerts Spirituels* could not compare with those of the Conservatoire orchestra.[1]   And it was not only in Beethoven's works that this great orchestra excelled; Schindler had never heard anything which approached the complete unity of the rendering and the perfect ensemble of this wonderful orchestra in Weber's *Euyranthe* overture.[2]   The only flaw he could find was the playing of the first clarinet (Buteux), which he described as mediocre (*mittelmässig*), and his tone as common (*gemein*).

In that same year 1839 when Wagner was in Paris, Chorley the English critic, who was to become one of Wagner's most virulent detractors, was also there.   Chorley's reaction to the playing of the Conservatoire orchestra was curious.   It was, he said, "the *soi-disant* most perfect orchestra in Europe," and when he heard it he could not but give it the highest praise: "The orchestra, be it remembered, is always under one and the same direction.   M. Habeneck has not, like our Philharmonic conductors, to give up his baton (I beg pardon, his violin bow), after his concert is over, to M. somebody else who, for illustration's sake, may be as spirited as he is phlegmatic, or as phlegmatic as he is spirited.   The ordering of the band is his alone, and you may see the phalanx of bows plying up and down on the strings with a mechanical consent and parallelism which in England can only be observed in those *fantoccini* orchestras that, under a monkey or a pair of white mice, borne by some black-eyed lank-haired Savoyard, loiter along those quiet streets where unfortunate literary men live.   Nor is this a solitary and disproportionate excellence.   The group of wind-instruments, too, at the Conservatoire has a like unity and coherence—a like family resemblance among its separate members—a like sensitive delicacy which is beyond all praise.   No unfortunate flute there chirps half a note before its time—no plethoric bassoon drops one of its thick Satyr-like tones in the midst of a pause—no horn totters on the edge of coarse and mail-coach falseness when the tug of difficulty comes !   All this results from training, since our own Philharmonic wind-instrumentalists could hardly severally have been more distinguished than they *were*.   Yet who ever heard eight of their meetings go over, and was not vexed by some such gratuitous exhibition—some such flaw in the perfect symmetry of the whole?   The orchestra in the Rue Bergère, I felt, *must* complete its labours perfectly. It is as unerring a machine as if there were a knout and Siberia outside the concert room, to punish all defaulters."[3]

But the Conservatoire orchestra owed its fame mainly to its playing of Beethoven's symphonies—of *German* music—and Chorley could not find in all its finished playing that true understanding of German music which to his mind could only be found in full perfection in that holy of holies—Leipzig and Mendelssohn: "What then,—asks the enthusiast, impatient of distinctions and qualifications, and foreseeing what is to come,—can be wanting to the

---

[1] Schindler, pp. 2, 26.   [2] *Ibid.*, p. 29.   [3] *Mus. and Manners*, III, p. 65.

orchestra of the Conservatoire? I was very nearly challenged in Paris for hinting that, with all the *nuance* imparted to the band by M. Habeneck's admirable training, there was still missing that healthy and satisfying expressiveness which those who have heard German music well rendered by Germans will ever after demand in its execution. The moving principle of French music appears to me rhythmical time;—an exquisite finish and exactness in laying note to note; a certain vivacity of temperament, which, even communicates its colour to the slowest music, and drives the quickest towards the *mouvement de galoppe*—the utmost indulgence of the propensity. Whether or not—to dissect with extreme nicety—such a disposition tends towards a superabundance, or at least a misappropriation, of accent, I leave to the 'darkly learned'; it tends, however, I cannot but think, to the discouragement of that solidity without slackness which is indispensable to the execution of the grandest music. And, slight though the difference was felt to be, in spite of everything that fineness of touch can do,—of a dazzling brilliancy in the stringed instruments,—of a promptitude and gentleness in the wind instruments, we conceive not here,—I remained cold. . . . They try to come out of themselves in Paris; they do their best to approach these mighty works, but the achievement is above them and beyond them."[1] That was the trouble—Paris was not Leipzig, and Habeneck was not Mendelssohn.

John Ella's comments are of interest, coming, as the did, from a violinist of ripe experience in the best London orchestras: "The unity of style, equality of *timbre* among the wood, and homogeneity of tone in the brass instruments, give to these performances a charm that cannot escape the admiration of every connoisseur. Thrice have I visited all the best concerts in Germany; and, after twenty-seven years' experience in the best bands of London, I am bound to award the palm to the Conservatoire orchestra.

"*Esprit de corps* incites them to do justice to the music, and to sustain the glory of the Institution, thereby securing to the *chef* any amount of study and practice. The performance of Beethoven's Choral Symphony, in 1834, so impressively grand and surpassingly beautiful, was the result of rehearsals extending over several months." Ella remarked on the democratic spirit of the orchestra: "Of the noble sentiment which animates the Paris Association, and the absence of that jealousy which, in London, so frequently declares itself as to rank, place, and position in our orchestras, one instance has been communicated to me worthy of record. After the death of the principal second violinist, Habeneck, at rehearsal, addressed the *élite* of the first violinists as follows: '*Mes enfants*, you see that a most important place is vacant; who among you will do me the honour of being my second?' Instantly Alard, the best violinist in France, and pupil of the venerable *chef*, rushed across the orchestra to the vacant desk, amidst the cheers of the whole band. He has lately retired. The band is composed entirely of native musicians; and the practical results of a systematic education

[1] *Mus. and Manners*, III, p. 67.

in the Conservatoire are most striking in the unity of style, taste, and expression of the performers."[1]   Finally, he commented on the orchestra as it was in 1868: "Although the present conductor, Hainl,[2] lacks the spirit and decision of the great Habeneck, the band has lost none of its wonted excellence in the unity of style and details of *nuances*, and other qualities which no other band in Europe possesses."[3]

Even J. C. Lobe, that most German of German critics, held up Habeneck and the Conservatoire orchestra as an example which all orchestras might well take as a model.   Habeneck "practised Beethoven's *Eroica* symphony with his orchestra for two years before he played it in public," with the result that they played it as a quartet party plays a well-studied quartet.[4] Ferdinand Hiller was another German who first learned from the Conservatoire players what could be done with a well-trained orchestra.

A comparison of the London Philharmonic with the Paris Conservatoire orchestra in 1835 by a German, Friedrich von Raumer, is quoted in an English musical periodical: "If I may venture, after one concert, to compare London with Paris, the result, on the whole, is this.   The mass of instruments may be equal; but the effect is better in the *Salle* at Paris, and the French performers on the stringed and wind instruments seem to me more thoroughly artists than the English.   In London, you hear distinctly that the music is produced by many; whereas in Paris it appears as if the whole were the work of one mind and one hand.   Like shadows and flickering lights on a landscape, so I often thought I perceived uncertainties and tremblings of tone, though the main stream flowed on its regular course. In Paris, my expectations, as to instrumental music, were exceeded; here, they are in a degree disappointed, because I had heard people assert that it is doubtful which capital has the pre-eminence."[5]

Perhaps the most curious of all were the comments on the Conservatoire orchestra made by the show-conductor Jullien in a letter (1856) to J. W. Davison, the musical critic of *The Times*: "The Conservatoire orchestra disappointed me.   For I expected to find them inferior all round, to the London orchestras, the Philharmonic, the Opera, and even my own, included.   But I perceived at once that as regards violinists, they are far above mine, and above those of London generally.   I wanted to engage some of them, but they all declined, as they had better positions in Paris, and they all said—'Paris and a crust of dry bread'."[6]   The great French orchestra disappointed Jullien, but only because he was unable to entice away any of the players !

This was clearly no ordinary good orchestra such as might be found at the large musical centres, at Berlin, Munich, Dresden, Leipzig, Vienna or London.   None of these lacked good players, and most of them had able conductors.   What was it that raised the playing of this Paris orchestra to

[1] Ella, pp. 396, 397.   [2] Hainl succeeded Tilmant in 1864.
[3] Ella, p. 398.   [4] Lobe, *Cons. und Dis.*, pp. 281, 287.
[5] *Mus. World*, April 15, 1836, p. 73.   [6] Davison, p. 206.

such a level of excellence that nobody could find anything unfavourable to say about it? The answer to this question must surely be found in the clues which the comments of Wagner, Lobe and Ella provide.

Habeneck began the study of the *Eroica* in November, 1826, and it was not performed in public until March, 1828. According to Wagner, the Conservatoire orchestra worked at the Choral symphony through one winter season, and then through another, and through yet another before they gave a performance of it. Ella wrote of "the result of rehearsals extending through several months." Lamenting the inadequate rehearsal allowed to Beethoven before the first performance of his Choral symphony in Vienna (1824), Schindler wrote: "Will it be believed in Vienna that Beethoven's symphonies were assiduously practised from twelve to sixteen months, and the Ninth Symphony, with Schiller's Ode to Joy, full two years, in the Conservatoire of Paris, before they were performed in public? This is a fact. It is also a fact that on the occasion of the first performance of this Ninth Symphony in 1824, at the Kärnthner-Thore Theatre, Beethoven could obtain no more than two rehearsals, because the orchestra was engaged in rehearsing a new ballet. Remonstrances and entreaties, on the part of Beethoven, for a third rehearsal, which he considered necessary, proved unavailing. He received for definitive answer—'Two rehearsals will be quite sufficient.' What will the professors of the Paris Conservatoire, and M. Habeneck, the leader, say to this?"[1]

The secret of the uniquely fine playing of the Conservatoire orchestra lay in the amount of preparation given to the music before it was played in public; it was not only that the players were superlatively good, it was because they were amply rehearsed. Therein lay the main difference between the Paris orchestra and the London Philharmonic—the one was adequately rehearsed, the other was not. The Conservatoire players studied a work as a soloist studies his piece before playing it at a concert, or as a string quartet work at a piece till each member knows the whole work from every angle, not only his own part, but the work as a whole. Habeneck did not put the parts of a new or unfamiliar piece before his orchestra in the morning, and then play it in public on the afternoon of the same day. He was, as Wagner said, no inspired conductor, but he knew the business of orchestral playing from start to finish, and knew that a correct rendering of every note and the observance of every mark of expression in each part was not enough. Each player had to grow into his part until he knew exactly what he was contributing to the whole, till the technical performance of his part had become second-nature to him and his whole attention could be given to the corporate rendering and the musical effect of the whole. In short, the orchestra must practise as a body just as the single musician must practise as an individual before he can be said to know a piece of music. There was no short cut. It took time; so Habeneck gave them time, and he was fortunate to be able to do so. Then—the Conservatoire orchestra

[1] Moscheles, *Life of Beethoven*, II, p. 153.

H

was not bothered with a lot of different conductors, each of whom had his own particular interpretation of the symphonies. "Old Habeneck," lacking "abstract-æsthetical inspiration," as Wagner put it, let Beethoven's music speak for itself. It was not "Habeneck's Beethoven" that he gave to his public; such things as Bülow's Beethoven, Weingartner's Beethoven, or Tom, Dick and Harry's Beethoven, were as yet unknown. Habeneck gave them Beethoven's Beethoven, and left it at that. And when his orchestra had thoroughly mastered a symphony, it was not played and then put aside; it was played again at the next concert, and then again, and again. No wonder this French orchestra played these symphonies as no other orchestra could.

*   *   *

There were several other attempts to provide orchestral concerts in Paris both before and after the start of the *Société des Concerts*. None of these appears to have made any great or lasting impression, even if some of them did enjoy success for a few years.

A new *Concert des Amateurs* was inaugurated in 1825 at the *Tivoli d'Hiver*, and later at the Paris Vauxhall near the *Chateau-d'Eau*.[1] At these concerts Maturin Auguste Barbereau (b. 1799) and Tilmant made their first appearances as conductors. Then followed a series under the title *l'Athénée musical*, founded by Chelard, and located at the *Salle Saint-Jean de l'Hôtel-de-Ville*. The conductors were successively Barbereau, Jean J. Vidal (b. 1789) and Girard, and many young musicians were given a chance of trying their wings in public. These concerts came to an end in 1832.

Another venture, started in 1834, and destined to enjoy only a short life, was that known as the *Gymnase musicale*. The orchestra was in charge of Tilmant, and at these concerts several works by Berlioz and Turbry[2] were performed.

About 1835 an elderly and wealthy amateur named Chabran built a large hall, seating about 2,000 people, in his garden in the *rue Saint-Honoré*, and financed a series of concerts given with an orchestra of nearly eighty performers. These were conducted by Valentino from 1837 until 1841, and the hall became known as the *Salle Valentino*. Many works by Beethoven were played, and Schindler commented that the orchestra contained many excellent artists, that they played well together, but that they hurried the *tempo* in every movement, played every work in exactly the same way, and generally lacked enthusiasm. The decline of these concerts, said Schindler, was mainly due to the fact that they had no Habeneck to inspire the orchestra, also because there were too many concerts, and because the programmes were too mixed in character, including, as they did, Beethoven's symphonies, Strauss waltzes and Musard's quadrilles. The *Salle Valentino* eventually became a ball-room.

---

[1] Elwart, p. 55.
[2] François Laurent Hébert Turbry (1795–1859), a wild, eccentric and unreliable musician who also composed a Symphonie fantastique, and eventually died in poverty and misery.

Other orchestral concerts in Paris were those of the *Union musicale*, started in 1847 and conducted by Manera, and the *Société de Saint-Cécile* (1848), conducted by François J. B. Seghers (1801–1881), and surviving until 1854. It was at a concert given by the latter society that a symphony by Schubert was heard for the first time in Paris, before any by that composer had been played in London. Early in 1850 a Philharmonic Society was inaugurated in Paris, organised and conducted by Berlioz, with an orchestra of 100 and a choir of 110. The concerts were held at the *Salle St. Cécile*, and managed to survive long enough to begin a second season in October of the same year. All of these concerts helped with varying success to provide the music-lovers of Paris with more orchestral concerts than the more exclusive *Société des Concerts* could give them, but none ever achieved the great reputation or the permanence of the famous society founded by Habeneck in 1828.

With its large number of resident musicians, and a steady flow of visiting artists, Paris had its "benefit" concerts during the musical season on a scale something like that of London. Lacking proper concert rooms, the theatres and other buildings not intended for music—ball-rooms, hotel rooms, etc.—were used for these performances, at which an orchestra was generally employed. All these, as well as the Masses with orchestral accompaniment often played in the churches, and the open-air concerts in summer-time, gave plenty of employment to many instrumentalists who at the same time found regular work in the many theatres in the French capital, or were engaged at private parties or in teaching in the better-class French families.

DANCE AND ENTERTAINMENT ORCHESTRAS

Another aspect of orchestral music in Paris which should not be ignored was the light and popular music played by large and efficient orchestras under a number of show-conductors, most of whom eventually found their way to London. The best remembered of these were Musard, J. B. Tolbecque, Jullien, and Rivière. Musard, a prize-winner at the Conservatoire in 1831, led off in 1832 with open-air concerts in the *Champs-Élysées*.[1] These were continued for several seasons with great success. This was soon after the *cornet-à-pistons* had made its appearance, and much of the success of this particular type of concert was due to the enormous popularity of the cornet solos played by Dufrêsne, Forestier, Arban, Koenig, and other *virtuosi* on this popular instrument.

Musard, with a good orchestra of about 80 players, was in a large marquee in the *Champs-Élysées* in 1837, and moved into the *Salle Valentino* for the winter.[2] The excellent players in his orchestra included Bellon as leader, Dancla, Lelong and Hubert Léonard amongst the violins, Pillet and Seligmann as 'cellists, Dorus the flautist, Dufrêsne and Forestier for the cornet, the famous Dieppo with Simon and Vobaron for the trombones, and Pasdeloup (who later started the Pasdeloup concerts) for the timpani.

[1] Elwart, p. 56.　　　　[2] Rivière, p. 38.

The following is a description by an English visitor to one of Musard's concerts in 1837: "Ten English pence gave me admission into this musical paradise, and the performance not having begun, afforded me an opportunity to explore the arrangements for the evening's amusements. The room was very spacious, and elegantly fitted up with looking-glasses, couches, and ottomans; at the end was a café attended by a troop of perfumed waiters ready for operation. In various parts of the room were statues, and fountains surrounded with exotics, which being refreshed by the crystal droppings of the water, emitted a delightfully cool fragrance. But the time of commencement arrived, and the orchestra, which was placed in the centre of the room, was speedily filled by about eighty performers. (Here follows the programme, which included works by Mozart, Auber, Rossini, Meyerbeer, Beethoven and Méhul, interspersed with quadrilles by Musard.) As soon as the band had taken their places, and the usual tuning dispatched, all eyes were directed towards the door, when a middle-sized gentlemanly looking man, dressed in deep black, and 'shocking-shaped hat,' entered, and mechanically took his seat in the centre of the orchestra. The most profound silence was manifested by the audience; the unknown gently raised his baton, and instantaneously Mozart's overture to the *Magic Flute* commenced. But who was the 'Gentleman in black?'—it was M. Musard himself. Then what a band! what pianos! what fortes! It consisted principally of pupils of the Conservatoire, who did not, like too many, strive to rival each other by playing the loudest, but, like one instrument, all moved together, forming a combination of sweet sounds the most perfect; working up their *fortissimos* with prodigious effect. The room was crowded by gay promenaders of all nations, and in the recesses were parties grouped together, chatting, eating, drinking, reading and—*sleeping*."[1]

Close on Musard's heels came Jullien, also a Conservatoire product, but yet more showy, eccentric and enterprising. Jullien, at the age of 24, succeeded J. B. Tolbecque at the *Jardin Turc* in the *Boulevard du Temple* in 1836. There he had a first-rate orchestra of about 60 players, including such as Rivière (violin), Rémusat (flute), Lavigne (oboe), Le Cerf (clarinet), Baumann (bassoon), Paquis (horn), Messeurer (cornet), Dantonnet (trombone), and Prospère (ophicleide), most of whom went to London with him. These concerts, for which only one franc admission was charged, made a sensational success and became "the talk of the town."[2] After a few years, owing to financial entanglements, Jullien was obliged to leave Paris, and for the next twenty years his happy hunting ground was London and the provincial towns of this country.

Round about the mid-century Jules Rivière (1819–1900) was exploiting dance music in Paris in much the same way. At the *Casino Paganini* he had an orchestra of 40, and later at the *Jardin d'Hiver* he had 80 players, many of them the best in Paris. Eventually Rivière settled down in London and

[1] *Mus. World*, June 16, 1837, p. 6.   [2] Rivière, p. 42.

conducted at the Cremorne Gardens, the Adelphi and the Alhambra theatres.

Just when Musard was at the height of his popularity, Paris was given a taste of dance music at its best by Johann Strauss (father) and his orchestra from Vienna. With a small party of 26 players, Strauss began his concerts at the *Gymnase musical* on the first of November, 1837, and at once won the hearts of the Parisians with his gay waltzes and spirited manner of playing them. The Viennese orchestra played at the Tuileries before Louis Philippe, the King of Belgium and the Duke of Orleans, and soon after joined Musard in a series of thirty concerts in which the first part was conducted by Strauss and the second by Musard. Paris delighted in distributing its favours to both musicians, and named Strauss "the Musard of the Waltz" and Musard "the Strauss of the Quadrille."[1] After visiting Rouen and Havre, Strauss returned to Paris at the end of the year and played incessantly at concerts and balls, earning high praise from no less than Meyerbeer and Berlioz, the latter expressing his characteristic enthusiasm in an article in the *Journal des Débats*. The orchestra, said Berlioz, consisted of only four first violins, four seconds, one 'cello, two basses, two flutes, one oboe, two clarinets, one bassoon, two horns, two trumpets, one cornet, one trombone, drums, harp and bass drum, but the effect was that of an orchestra nearly twice as large, because almost every player was able to take up two or three different instruments, quickly changing from one to the other. It was in this article that Berlioz bemoaned the fact that neither a real bass trombone (tenors only were used) nor a double bassoon could be found in Paris.[2]

Except for the inimitable waltzes and light music from Vienna, the dance music played by the French show-orchestras of the 'thirties and 'forties was trivial as it was ephemeral. It had little character except its persistent gaiety, but it was well orchestrated and it was well played. At that time the paths of "music" and "light music" were becoming ever more divergent. They eventually passed each into different hands, both as regards composers and executants, and each had its own audience. Light music became more and more commercialised, in fact, more an industry than an art.

Orchestras in Provincial Towns

In a country where the cultivation of the arts is largely centred in one place, musical activity in the provincial towns is so much overshadowed by that of the capital city that it is apt to be ignored and treated almost as if it didn't exist. It is true that Paris drew the best of everything to itself, and gave away only what it didn't want or could easily spare. It held the best composers and the best executants, and what went on outside of Paris could therefore be nothing but a weaker version of its own musical activity, drawing what life it had from that one central source. So we hear little about the French orchestras outside of Paris from those on whose testimony

[1] *Mus. World*, Dec. 1, 1837, p. 189. [2] Lange, pp. 110–118.

we have to rely for the musical state of France during the first half of last century.

All the large towns had their theatres, and in most of these opera was given from time to time. We hear of opera at Lyons, Toulouse, Tours, Rouen, Bordeaux, Marseilles, Strasburg, Nancy and a few other places. We hear of theatres in many smaller towns, and we know that where there

GEORGE HAINL

was a theatre there was an orchestra. But of these orchestras, their size and quality, it is difficult to glean any particulars, which, if they do exist, are probably hidden away in forgotten or inaccessible local records.

Concert-societies, vocal and instrumental, there were in plenty all over France, supported and largely dependent on amateur effort, and what orchestras they were able to raise could only have been drawn from the local theatres and amateurs. Wind players could sometimes be obtained from military bands, but no concert-society could entirely support an orchestra of its own.

Spohr turned down a proposal that he should make a tour in the southern provinces of France because of "the bad orchestras in the provincial towns, the bad taste and the unpleasant negotiations to lessen the amount to be given up to the theatre and the poor of the towns."[1] Nevertheless, it is probable that he would have found quite as good an orchestra at Lyons as in many a German town. It was there that François George Hainl, originally a Conservatoire-trained 'cellist, became conductor at the theatre in 1840, and eventually rose high enough to occupy a similar position at the Paris *Opéra* and the *Société des Concerts*. In that orchestra at Lyons, Rivière played when he was stationed there on military service, and in that orchestra there was a trumpeter named Luigini, whose eldest son Joseph became conductor at the Lyons opera, and whose youngest son Alexandre (composer of the popular *Ballet Egyptien*) eventually became conductor at the *Opéra Comique* in Paris. It seems that when they did get a good man in the provinces he would be claimed sooner or later by Paris.

Castil-Blaze painted a pitiable picture of the orchestras and theatres outside of the French capital. There is plenty of talent in the provinces, he wrote, but nevertheless, the orchestras are bad.[2] He granted, however, that Bordeaux, Lyons, Rouen, Marseilles, Strasburg and Nantes might possibly have something to say in opposition to this sweeping statement. The French musical historian gave six reasons why the music in the provincial theatres was so bad, and why it remained in that deplorable condition[3]:

1. The orchestra makes no effort to be any better because no one ever listens to it.

2. Two rehearsals have to do for an opera which requires many, so the opera only gets going by about the tenth performance.

3. Most of the players have never left their native place, and have never heard music well played.

4. The director pays his principal singer well, and, having to make the most of him, requires him to appear in every piece. The singer is therefore overworked, and this spoils his voice.

5. The pitch in the provinces is about a semitone higher than in the Paris *Opéra*.

6. The force of custom. Old habits prevail. The flautist will not add keys to his instrument to improve his intonation. The bassoon player is content to keep on imitating the bagpipes. Nothing good is expected, so mediocrity is tolerated.

This is clearly the vicious circle again; the orchestras were bad because no one listened to them, and no one listened to them because they were so bad.

Castil-Blaze told how he had seen *Paul et Virginie* performed without any orchestral parts. The conductor (violinist) and the bass-player played from the score, and a few wind instruments were played from memory or followed

---

[1] Spohr, II, p. 132.   [2] *L'Opéra en France*, II, 254.   [3] *Ibid.*, I, p. 436.

the voices in unison.[1]   He had seen three horn players jostling to read the first horn part while the second horn desk was vacant.   He had seen two flautists or two clarinettists playing the same solo together; pride prevented either playing the second part!   To his catalogue of horrors Castil-Blaze added that he had seen an orchestra deprived of its wind instruments because the wind players had quarrelled with the string players; so, for a month *Gulistan*, *Euphrosine* and *La Vestale* were played with only a string accompaniment.   But the public demanded flutes, horns and clarinets; so the wind players returned and the string players disappeared, and for some time the operas were played only by bassoons, clarinets, horns and trombones.

The attitude of provincial managers no doubt made it difficult for the conductors: "The double-bass player has just died; the first horn and the flute have enlisted!   Three cheers, our director cries, rubbing his hands; he beams with pleasure, he jumps for joy when he finds that he has in hand the salaries of these three players!   When it is pointed out to him that there must be a first horn, he says: Of course, the second can play the part; when told that a double-bass is absolutely necessary, he asks: Well, havn't we got a 'cellist? and that we can't do without a flute—Oh, the clarinet is there to take his place.   One more or less, the public will be quite satisfied; it is not so exacting."[2]

No doubt Castil-Blaze was indulging in a little exaggeration, and was making a good story of it.   The truth probably was that the music in the smaller provincial theatres in France was very poor, as it was in the small towns in Italy and in England.   But in the larger French towns it was probably merely indifferent, undistinguished, and not worthy of any particular notice.   The pride of French orchestras was in Paris; and there they could more than hold their own with the best that the rest of the world could produce.

[1] *L'Opéra en France*, II, p. 258.   [2] *Ibid.*, II, 271.

IV

Orchestras in Germany

WHILE in this country and in France musical activity was centred largely in the two capital cities, in Germany it was spread out over four large musical centres, with at least a dozen more of some importance, and many others which, if quite small, were nevertheless by no means negligible. The largest German opera-orchestras, comparable with that of the Paris *Opéra*, were at Berlin, Dresden and Munich; Leipzig had its important concert-orchestra at the *Gewandhaus*; Frankfort, Darmstadt, Stuttgart, Cassel, Brunswick, Hanover, Hamburg, Düsseldorf, Weimar and Karlsruhe could show orchestras which ranked in varying degree below those at Berlin, Dresden and Munich, and there were less pretentious establishments at Cologne, Mayence, Mannheim, Breslau, Magdeburg, Bremen, Kiel and several other towns, as well as some smaller court orchestras of the old private type, such as those at Gotha, Meiningen, Dessau, Hechingen and Rudolstadt.

As in the 18th century, many of the musicians in the court and private orchestras in Germany still wore a uniform or livery during the first quarter of the 19th century, and their social status, although they ranked above the domestic servants, was generally below that of the court officials. Even in the 'forties Wagner had to wear an official court uniform when conducting at Dresden. Most of the larger court orchestras included a number of probationers who played for little or nothing in the hope of securing permanent appointments when vacancies occurred.

Every German town, even the smallest one, had its corps of town musicians, the *Stadtpfeifer* or *Stadtmusiker*, whose duty it was to play chorales from the church tower in the morning, and to provide the music at civic festivities, processions, garden concerts, dances, weddings, funerals, or indeed for all occasions when music was required. The players in these, generally of humble birth, were taught under a system of apprenticeship in a rough and ready school by the *Stadtmusikus*, and were required to become proficient on three or four instruments, both stringed and wind. These civic musical organisations provided the source from which even the larger and more important orchestras drew many of their players before the institution of conservatoires or schools of music began to supply them with a more cultured and better educated type of musician. But there was no orchestra in Germany, up till about the middle of last century, that did not include in its ranks some players who had graduated as *Stadtmusiker*. Leipzig, Düsseldorf, and even Liszt's orchestra at Weimar in 1850, had to draw on the town band for some of their players, and in many smaller towns

107

where there was no court, such as Augsburg, Nürnberg, Halle, Jena and Göttingen, it would have been impossible to raise an orchestra of any sort without the nucleus provided by these very all-round players whose musical education had been picked up in a hard but practical school, and in an environment that was anything but the most cultured.

What with *Stadtmusiker* and probationers, German orchestras, therefore, included many musicians whose skill and qualifications were far below the best standard. It is doubtful whether it could be said of a single German orchestra in the first half of last century that the players were of first-class quality throughout, from first to last desk. There were always different grades amongst them, whose efficiency tailed off to a lower level in the last few desks of the string sections; weaker violinists were found in the second violins, and viola players were apt to be old musicians whose best days had been spent in playing other instruments.

Germany's great asset was the abundance of its orchestras rather than the quality of its musicians, and the fact that the love and practice of music extended throughout the whole social system, from the highest to the lowest.

These numerous orchestras provided much more work for conductors and players, and many more opportunities for composers, than could be found in the provincial towns of England and France. A composer could offer his work to a dozen or more places, a conductor could learn his art as chorus-master or as second or third *Kapellmeister* in one theatre and work his way up to a better position at another, and the ambitious player could always expect to find a vacancy elsewhere if the road to promotion was blocked in his own town.

Whereas in France or in England the musician had, so to speak, one target to aim at, in Germany he had a dozen or more. A miss at Berlin, Dresden or Munich was not so calamitous as a miss at Paris or London; the German could have several more shots at targets which, if a little less important, were still well worth hitting. The German musician also had chances at Vienna, Prague, Budapesth, Warsaw, Riga, Königsberg or St. Petersburg; for the British musician it was generally London or nothing.[1]

The decentralisation of music in Germany was, of course, all to the advantage of its music, its orchestras, conductors, players and composers. Music thrives where there is plenty of it, where it is widely diffused, and where there is opportunity, encouragement and employment for the musician.

BERLIN

The royal orchestra in the Prussian capital had a good tradition behind it. The two Grauns, the Benda family, Quantz, and P. E. Bach had given it lustre in Frederick the Great's time, and Reichardt had revived it when its fame was flagging in the 'seventies.

---

[1] "In this country a composer is confined to the metropolis, because no other theatre can afford him a remuneration for his work, or a competent band for an effective performance." (*Q. Mus. Mag.*, Vol. II, No. V, p. 74.)

At the end of the 18th century there were two main opera theatres in Berlin. The large *Opernhaus*, built by Frederick the Great and completed in 1742, still stood. It had been renovated and enlarged internally in 1787 soon after the accession of Frederick William II, and was to stand until it was destroyed by fire in 1843.

A new *Opernhaus* was then built on the same site, and was opened in December, 1844. The old building had been the home of Italian opera, favoured by the King and court. Both the old and the new building included a concert-room.

The other theatre was the *Schauspielhaus*. In 1786 Frederick William founded the German *Nationaltheater* on the remains of the old Döbbelin theatrical company. This was located in an old theatre in the *Gendarmenmarkt*, a building which dated back to 1774, and was large enough to seat 1,200 people.[1] This was closed in 1801, and the *Nationaltheater* then found its home in a new *Schauspielhaus* erected on a site nearby, and taken over on January 1, 1803.[2] Here opera in German was given, together with ballets and operettas. The building included an elliptical concert-room which was said to have suffered from an incurable echo. This theatre was burned down in 1817, but was immediately rebuilt. It was in this new *Schauspielhaus* that Weber's *Der Freischütz* was first produced in 1821 very soon after the new building had been completed.

There were also smaller theatres in the royal residences in and near Berlin. A small *Schlosstheater* in the Berlin palace was pulled down in 1805, and there were theatres at Charlottenburg, at Potsdam, and in the *Neuen Palais*; but for the public the two houses were the old *Opernhaus* for Italian opera, and the *Schauspielhaus* for German national opera. An independent theatre, the *Konigstädter*, was built early in the 'twenties. When Frederick William III succeeded in 1797 each of the two large theatres had its own orchestra and conductor. Righini was *Kapellmeister* for the Italian opera in the large *Opernhaus*, and Bernhard Anselm Weber was in charge of the German opera of the *Nationaltheater*. Italian opera in Berlin had been steadily declining towards the end of the 18th century; even the support of the King and court could not save it; it was played out, and during the first few years of the new century it wilted and finally came to an end. For some time the old *Opernhaus* stood empty, and when the conquering French occupied the Prussian capital in 1806, they used it as a food store. Righini's post then almost ceased to exist, but he retained his title of *Kapellmeister* until his death in 1812. Righini's colleague at the *Opernhaus* was *Kapellmeister* Himmel, Richardt's successor. Like Righini, his post was more or less a sinecure after 1806, but he also retained his title up to his death in 1814.

Three years after the disaster of 1806,[3] when the King returned to his capital, the opera was again set on its feet by amalgamating what remained of the old Italian company with the more vigorous establishment of the German national opera, and in the large *Opernhaus* and the *Schauspielhaus*

---

[1] Schneider, p. 211.   [2] Kapp, p. 26.   [3] Defeat of the Prussians at Jena.

B. Anselm Weber was *Kapellmeister* in chief of the reconstituted organisation. He retained his position almost until his death in 1821. Bernhard Romberg, the 'cellist, was *Kapellmeister* from 1815 to 1819, and Joseph Augustin Gürrlich (1761–1817), originally a double-bass player in the orchestra, after having been an assistant conductor from 1811, became full *Kapellmeister* in 1816 for a short time until his death in the following year. Then followed the period of Spontini's brilliant rule. This began in 1820 and continued until Meyerbeer was appointed *Generalmusikdirector* in 1842. Spontini's appointment was entirely the King's own choice; the *Intendant* Brühl tried hard more than once to get Weber as *Kapellmeister* at Berlin, but each time he was overruled by the King.[1] As assistants Spontini had Friedrich Ludwig Seidel, who had previously served as second conductor of the *Nationaltheater* and was full *Kapellmeister* at the opera from 1822 until he was pensioned off in 1829, and Georg Abraham Schneider, originally a horn player, who was appointed in 1820 and remained until 1838. Spontini was also assisted by his leader, Carl Möser.

Meyerbeer's rule at Berlin began in 1842 and came to an end in 1849. Like Spontini, Meyerbeer conducted only certain big operas, and left the rest of the repertoire to his subordinates. His assistants were Carl Wilhelm Henning (1784–1867), a violinist, who served from 1841 to 1848, and Carl G. Wilhelm Taubert;[2] the latter came to the opera in 1841, became full *Kapellmeister* in 1845, and remained until he retired in 1868. Mendelssohn's position at Berlin (1841), although he was given the title of *Kapellmeister*, was not that of a conductor at the opera, but Otto Nicolai was a real theatrical conductor, and his short period of service at Berlin from 1847 to his early death in 1849 was spent mainly at the opera. Heinrich Dorn was *Kapellmeister* from 1849 to 1869.

Towards the close of the 18th century the leader (*Concertmeister*) at Berlin was Pierre Vachon, and on his death in 1802 that position was filled by Carl Benda (1748–1836), the youngest son of Franz Benda and bearer of a name honourably associated with the orchestra since the beginning of Frederick the Great's reign. Carl Möser joined the orchestra in 1811 and became the chief *Concertmeister* under Spontini. C. A. Seidler (d. 1840) was another of Spontini's leaders, also Anton Bohrer, who came in 1826. Leopold Ganz (from 1826) and Hubert Ries (from 1836) were violinists who became joint-leaders in the time of Meyerbeer and Taubert. Among the violins, from 1824 to about 1838, was Wilhelm Wieprecht, the great reorganiser of Prussian military music and enthusiastic sponsor of the newly-invented valved brass instruments.

The leading 'cellists included Louis Duport (the younger) and Bernhard Romberg in the early years of the century before the unhappy events in

---

[1] Kapp, pp. 29–31.

[2] Wagner had something to say about these conductors: Henning "knew precious little about conducting an orchestra," Taubert was "devoid of talent and very conceited." (*My Life*, I, p. 318, II, p. 589.)

1806; two other distinguished players who later occupied the same position were Max Bohrer (from 1823) and Moritz Ganz who came to the Berlin orchestra in 1826.

The most noteworthy of the wood-wind players at Berlin were the following:

Flautists. August Schroeck (1779–1854), pensioned off in 1845; Johann Wilhelm Gabrielski (1791–1846), from 1816; Hermann Schmidt (1810–1845), a pupil of the latter, who joined in 1831; Julius Gabrielski (1806–1878), brother of the above, appointed in 1825.

Oboists. Theodor Czerwenka (1768–1827); Wilhelm Braun (b. 1791); Friedrich Westenholz (1782–1840); Heinrich Griebel (d. 1841).

Clarinettists. Joseph Beer, until 1808, a fine player on the old five-keyed clarinet; Franz Tausch (1762–1817), from 1789, said to have rivalled Beer and Stadler; W. Nehrlich; Gustav Garies.

Bassoonists. A. Gottlob Schwarz (1745–1804), from 1787; Georg Wenzel Ritter (1748–1808), from 1788 until his death; Christoph G. Schwarz (b. 1768), son of the above, played from 1788 to 1826; Carl Bärmann, brother of the famous clarinet player H. J. Bärmann; Wilhelm Franz Westenholz (d. 1830).

Amongst its notable horn players Berlin could count: Jean Lebrun, who followed the great pair Palsa and Türrschmiedt late in the 18th century; Heinrich Stölzel (1780–1844), whose name should ever be remembered by brass players for his share in the invention of the valve[1]; Andreas Schunke (1779–1849?), who played from 1812 to 1833; his son Carl Schunke (b. 1811) who followed in his father's footsteps.

Another brass player of some distinction was the trumpeter Carl Bargans, a leading performer on that instrument in the 'thirties and 'forties, while yet another notable player, and one who gained considerable renown outside of his native Prussia, was the trombone virtuoso Friedrich August Belcke. He was probably the first to exploit Stölzel's newly-invented valve-instruments, including the tenor-horn, as solo instruments. The Berlin correspondent of the London *Harmonicon* (1824) reported that: "Between the acts, M. Belcke gave a concerto by Neithardt on the trombone, which, with all its singularity, was managed with great judgement."[2] In 1844 Belcke, described as "*Premier Trombone du roi de Prusse*," played a concertino by David at one of the Conservatoire Concerts in Paris.[3] From a total force of about 80 players were drawn the orchestras for the large *Opernhaus* and the smaller *Schauspielhaus*, and for occasional performances at Charlottenburg. The full strength was employed only on big occasions when Spontini or Meyerbeer directed large spectacular presentations at the *Opernhaus*; for lesser operas and musical pieces, smaller sections were used, and were directed by the assistant-conductors.

---

[1] According to Wieprecht (Kalkbrenner, 89) Stölzel was appointed in 1816–17, very soon after he had come to Berlin with the new valve.

[2] *Harm.*, Sept., 1824, p. 172.   [3] Elwart, p. 216.

Such were the orchestras that Weber conducted in 1812 (*Silvana*) and again in 1821 when *Der Freischütz* was produced, that Mendelssohn heard during his boyhood in Berlin, that Anselm Weber, Spontini, Meyerbeer and Nicolai trained, that Berlioz conducted in 1843, and Wagner in 1844 (*Fliegende Holländer*) and 1847 (*Rienzi*).

Weber remarked on the "power and precision" of the Berlin orchestra under Anselm Weber in 1811,[1] and was well satisfied with their playing in *Silvana* under his own direction.   He had no fault to find with the playing when some years later he produced his *Freischütz* with such tremendous success.   On neither of these occasions did Weber have the full strength of the orchestra.

Of the Berlin orchestra in Spontini's time there are several contemporary comments.   Sir George Smart heard it in 1825.   At the *Opernhaus* he heard Spohr's *Jessonda*, and remarked that the wind instruments were "so much out of tune in the overture that the effect was ruined," that "the rest, however, was very good," and that the trombone playing was beyond all praise.[2]   This was, in fact, the production of his opera that Spohr himself rehearsed and conducted.   Describing the event to Speyer, Spohr said that on this occasion he had the full strength of the orchestra at his disposal, that he himself rehearsed it thoroughly, and the verdict was that such a finished performance had never before been heard in Berlin.[3]   At the *Schauspielhaus* Smart heard *Der Freischütz*, and remarked that "the overture was not well played, the violins were dead out in one passage," and that the "orchestra seemed to take little pains."   This was obviously a routine-performance under an assistant-conductor of an opera that had already been played about eighty times, and, according to Smart, could not be compared with those he had heard at Munich and Dresden.

But of Spontini's *Fernand Cortez* at the *Opernhaus* Smart had a very different story to tell.   The scenery and get-up were "equal to the most splendid opera in Paris, if not superior.   It was perfect.   The chorus was admirable."   More than 200 people were on the stage, and "the band was excellent and larger than I have ever yet heard here. . . . I was delighted with the whole performance, we have no opera so perfect in England."[4]   From these remarks we may conclude that when under Spontini and on its mettle, the Berlin orchestra was first-rate, but that in smaller and routine-performances it was slack and no better than plenty of others in Germany.

Edward Holmes heard the Berlin orchestra in 1828, and was struck with the "perfect accompanying of the band"[5]; this orchestra, he said, "might be the pattern of any in Europe" for the way it accompanied the voice, especially in recitative.[6]

Another English visitor, in 1829, commented equally favourably on the orchestra at the opera: "My interest was more excited by the prospect of hearing so celebrated an orchestra as that of the Berlin opera house.   And

[1] Weber, III, p. 58.   [2] *Journals*, p. 175.   [3] Speyer, p. 84.
[4] *Journals*, p. 192.   [5] *Rambles*, p. 217.   [6] *Ibid.*, p. 221.

I was not disappointed. I found a completeness and solidity, a power and precision in all its parts, which reminded one more of the Philharmonic orchestra of London than any that I ever heard. The orchestra in the opera at Munich is, I believe, the only one in Germany which fully equals it. I could not sufficiently admire the tone and delicacy of the wind instruments, which I have no hesitation in considering, with the splendid exceptions of those first-rate masters, Nicholson, Willman, Harper and Mackintosh, far superior to anything that is to be heard in Britain. The horns were delicious, and the oboes brilliant without hardness, contrasting charmingly with the mellowness of the clarionets. It struck me that the bassoons used on the continent generally have not the same roundness of tone as those of English manufacture; but they are remarkably sweet, and at the same time sufficiently powerful to maintain their relationship to the oboes and clarionets effectively. The orchestra, as I found it, consisted of 24 violins, 12 tenors, 6 basses ('cellos), 6 double-basses, 4 horns, 6 trumpets, and 3 trombones, which, with the usual complement of flutes, oboes, clarionets and drums, formed a grand total of seventy performers. This is the average number; but when Spontini chooses to bring forward an opera with more than usual magnificence, or to give one of his own, it is augmented to sometimes more than 100."[1] According to Kapp's recent history of the Berlin opera, Spontini increased the permanent personnel of the orchestra to 94 players.[2]

Carl Loewe's account of the orchestra in 1832 was enthusiastically eulogistic: "The orchestra was mighty, a seraphic round-dance (*Reigen*), powerful as thunder and lightning, and mild as the spring air."[3]

Mendelssohn heard Gluck's *Armide* performed in 1838, and wrote: "I have hardly ever, if ever, enjoyed anything so much at the opera. That great mass of thoroughly-trained musicians and singers, ably conducted by Spontini . . . made such an impression on me that I was obliged to say to myself that there was nothing to be done with small towns and small means and small circles, and that it was quite another thing here. But how often since have I had to retract that. The very day after, they gave a so-called Beethoven Memorial Festival, and played his A major Symphony so atrociously, that I soon had to beg many pardons of my small towns and my small means; the coarseness and recklessness of the playing were such as I never heard anywhere, and can only explain to myself by the whole nature of the Prussian official, which is about as well suited for music as a strait-waistcoat is for a man."[4] What Mendelssohn meant was that they could do much better at Leipzig.

Devrient also gave Spontini credit for his performances of spectacular opera, but like Mendelssohn had no good opinion of the same orchestra's playing in a symphony: "Under those conditions no intellectual progress and honourable ambition was possible to the orchestra, and thus it happened that the execution of symphonies at this period was entirely void of higher

[1] *Harm.*, Jan., 1830, p. 5. [2] Kapp, p. 37. [3] Loewe, p. 140.
[4] Hiller, *Letters and Recoll.*, p. 123.

insight or charm of reading, and produced but the most inadequate effect."[1]

But under Mendelssohn the Berlin orchestra did well in the *Midsummer Night's Dream* music: "The band played to perfection; Felix had had eleven rehearsals, and the result showed what was possible with means like these under the direction of such a conductor."[2]

Chorley's experience at Berlin in 1839 was unfortunate.   He heard only routine-performances at the *Schauspielhaus* when half of the orchestra was away at Potsdam.   In *Der Freischütz*, "not only was the tone of the band fatigued rather than crisp and mellow; its execution was characterless and slovenly," and the horns were "lazy and false"; he had heard better playing at Brunswick.   This was not one of Spontini's performances, and so little did it impress Chorley that he did not trouble to mention the name of the conductor.[3]

Wagner regretted that under Meyerbeer the last trace of the tradition of Spontini's strict discipline had gone from the Berlin players.[4]

It was Berlioz who gave the most interesting impressions of the Berlin orchestra in his letters to Louise Bertin and Habeneck.   The orchestra was "one of the best I ever heard"; the stringed instruments were "almost all first-rate."   Berlioz went on to analyse each department: "The wood-wind is also very good."   The Berlin clarinets were better than in Paris, the oboes were about the same, but the German flutes were far from equal to those in France.   The German double-basses had more power,[5] and their violins, violas and 'cellos were good, but could not be placed on the same level as those in the Conservatoire orchestra.   Berlioz thought that the Berlin brass players in general, and the trumpets in particular, were better than in Paris.   But all was not well in the percussion department: "The kettle-drummer is a good musician, but his wrists are not supple nor his rolls sufficiently firm; his kettle-drums are too small, and have too little tone, and he is only acquainted with one sort of drumstick, which occupies a middle place between the ordinary leather heads and those with sponge.   In this respect the Germans are far behind the French."   The cymbals in Germany were disgraceful; there was hardly a pair that was not cracked.   The Germans had few good harp players, and in this respect the Berlin orchestra was no exception to the rule.   Yet it was a good orchestra on the whole, even "a magnificent orchestra, famous for its precision, force and delicacy."

But the Berlin orchestra, like all others, was only good when on its mettle.   These were days "when it would seem that a tacit understanding between the artists and the public sanctions more or less carelessness in the performance.   Many empty places are then visible in the theatre, and many vacant desks in the orchestra.   On such evenings the leaders dine out, give balls, are out hunting, etc.   The musicians are asleep, though playing the *notes* of their parts; some do not even play at all, but sleep, read, draw

[1] Devrient, p. 217.   [2] Hiller, *Letters and Recoll.*, p. 213.   [3] *Mus. and Manners*, II, p. 86.
[4] *On Conducting*, p. 9.   [5] Mendelssohn also praised the double-basses at Berlin.

PLATE 4

THE OLD OPERNHAUS AT BERLIN (1742–1843)

THE NEW SCHAUSPIELHAUS AT BERLIN, BUILT IN 1821

PLATE 5

THE OLD COURT THEATRE AT DRESDEN IN WEBER'S TIME.
BURNT IN 1849 DURING THE MAY REVOLUTION

caricatures, play foolish jokes on their neighbours, and quite loudly." These were, no doubt, the days when the assistant conductors were in charge; but for a performance of *Armide* or of *Die Huguenotten*, with Meyerbeer in command, it was quite a different story: "In the great orchestra not a desk was empty—strings or double-wind; the chorus were there to the last of the one hundred and twenty, and Meyerbeer was in the conductor's seat. He acquitted himself as though he had been at it for twenty years; the orchestra is in his grasp, he does what he likes with it. . . . I cannot analyse the orchestral performance in Meyerbeer's *chef d'oeuvre* scene by scene; enough to say that the whole representation was magnificent, beautiful, perfect in *nuance* throughout, and with incomparable clearness and precision even in the most intricate passages. The *finale* of the second act, with its passages based on the series of chords of the diminished seventh, and its enharmonic modulations, was given with extreme clearness and an absolute perfection of intonation."[1]

On account of the destruction by fire of the old *Opernhaus* in 1843, the performance of his *Flying Dutchman* under Wagner's direction at Berlin in 1844 had to take place in the *Schauspielhaus*.

There was not room enough in this theatre for the full complement of string players; nevertheless, Wagner was fully satisfied with their playing: "All sang and played like Gods."[2] Wagner's performance of *Rienzi* in 1847 was in the large newly rebuilt *Opernhaus*, and of the orchestra on that occasion he wrote with complete satisfaction: "*Das Orchester macht mir grosse Freude.*"[3]

Like Mendelssohn, when Nicolai came to Berlin he found that the orchestra was not at its best in the concert-room: "The Berliners have not as yet the slightest notion of symphony performances such as those I gave with the Philharmonic in Vienna; yet they believe that they do this sort of thing better than the rest of the world!"[4]

But there can be no doubt about it, the Berlin royal orchestra was a very good one; there were many fine players in it, and they played splendidly when they chose to do so. Perhaps Meyerbeer was not just the ideal conductor for them, and it is evident that they took advantage of assistant conductors, as orchestras are apt to do. The famous discipline of Spontini was, no doubt, what these Prussians required. But they were in for some hard work when Nicolai came in 1847; unfortunately that was to be for only a short time. After Nicolai's time the story goes on into the second half of the century.

The royal theatres were not the only places where opera could be heard in Berlin during the first half of last century. From 1824 a suburban opera theatre flourished under the name *Königstädter-Theater*, and was run quite independently of any royal or state aid, but at their own risk as a private company by a local committee, and under the musical guidance of Ferdinand Stegmayer (1803–1863). Situated in the *Alexanderplatz*, the house was

[1] *Mem.*, II, pp. 92–103. [2] Kapp, p. 55. [3] *Ibid.*, p. 60. [4] Kruse, p. 208.

I

said to be neat though not handsome, and not very large; it could seat about 1,600 persons. This institution was successfully run, and for some years was a serious rival on the lighter side of opera in public favour to the royal theatres.

Stegmayer remained as conductor from 1825 to 1829; in the following year he was succeeded by Gläser from Vienna, and by 1837 Louis Schindelmeisser, a step-brother of Dorn and faithful friend of Wagner, was in charge of the orchestra. The smallish but quite efficient orchestra was led by Hubert Ries for some time about 1824, by Mühlenbruck from 1825, and from 1830 by Léon de Saint Lubin. Julius Rietz, who became conductor at the Leipzig *Gewandhaus* after Mendelssohn, played the 'cello in the *Königstädter* orchestra from 1826, when he was a youth of sixteen, and from 1826 until 1829 Ferdinand David, who was to become Mendelssohn's leader at Leipzig, played amongst the violins, also at the age of sixteen.

Smart visited this theatre in 1825. There were then 21 string players and the usual wind, with four horns only when necessary. Smart wrote of the orchestra: "The band at the Königstadt Theatre is good. The pitch was above my fork. The director is Mr. Stegmayer, a clever young man from Vienna, the leader, Mr. Mühlenbruck, who lives with Mr. Hubert Ries."[1]

DRESDEN

The court orchestra at Dresden could look back to a glorious past when, in the 'thirties and 'forties of the 18th century, it had been under the command of Hasse and Pisendel. Quantz had placed it head and shoulders above most others in Germany, and Rousseau had named it one of the two best in the world. If its glory was a little dimmed by the end of that century, there was, however, a better time coming, and again under Weber and Wagner it was to rank as one of the three best in Germany.

The old opera-house or *Hoftheater* at Dresden, which dated back to 1716, had been renovated and altered in 1750. It suffered during the Seven Years' War when for some time it was used as a military magazine, but on the conclusion of peace in 1763 it was again renovated and re-opened.[2]

This building, which seated only 814 persons, stood until 1849, when it was finally destroyed by fire during the May Revolution; but having in the meantime become old-fashioned and inadequate in its stage appliances, a new and larger opera-house had been begun on another site, and was opened in 1841.[3] This was the theatre in which Wagner worked, and which saw the first productions of *Rienzi*, *The Flying Dutchman* and *Tannhäuser*; the auditorium could seat 1,712 persons. It was burnt down in 1869, and after having been rebuilt the present opera-house was opened in 1878.

Another and smaller theatre at Dresden had been burnt down in 1748[4] and towards the end of the 18th century another rather small theatre was

---

[1] *Journals*, p. 177. [2] Fürstenau, II, pp. 261, 368. [3] Prölss, p. 502.
[4] Fürstenau, II, p. 257.

being used for German opera; this was the *Theater des Lincke'schen Bades*. In 1828 Edward Holmes described it as being "insignificant," and said that it was then used for Italian opera.[1] This theatre was rebuilt in 1845, and was finally closed in 1858.[2]

As at most of the German courts, Italian opera dominated the music in the Saxon capital at the beginning of last century. But a change was coming. German opera was on the way, and when the right man to guide it appeared, Dresden followed close on Berlin in giving home and sustenance to national opera in the German language. The star of Italian opera at Dresden began to decline during Weber's time there, from 1817 to 1826, and by the early 'thirties its day was more or less over, although opera in Italian was occasionally given up to as late as 1847.[3]

Church music also took a very prominent part in the music of the court at Dresden, indeed, it was claimed that in this particular sphere the *Kapelle* maintained its old reputation. But the complaint was made that the music used in the churches was too old-fashioned. Works by Hasse and his school, or by the *Kapellmeister* who followed in Hasse's footsteps, were constantly performed to the exclusion of the better music of Haydn, Mozart, Jommelli and the best of the old Italians. The same applied to opera; nothing by Gluck, Cherubini, or Reichardt was heard; everything was by Hasse, Naumann, Schuster, Seydelmann, Rastrelli, and other local *Kapellmeister*.[4]

In order to take charge of the opera in two theatres, for the music in the churches, and for the court concerts and functions, quite a number of *Kapellmeister* were employed. Naumann, who had been *Ober-Kapellmeister* since 1786, died in 1801, and was followed by Paër. The latter was given this important appointment for life in 1804, but the advent of Napoleon upset the King's plans, and the French ruler soon took Paër and his wife (a singer) away with him to Warsaw in 1806, and thence to Paris.

Two rather undistinguished *Kapellmeister*, by name Joseph Schuster and Franz Seydelmann (1748–1806), were both appointed in 1787, and both held their positions until they died, Seydelmann in 1806 and Schuster in 1812. Gestewitz was another *Kapellmeister* associated with the Italian opera at Dresden from 1790 until his death in 1805. Vincenzo Rastrelli (1760–1839) was *Kapellmeister* up to 1802, again from 1807 to 1813, and yet again from 1824 until he was pensioned off in 1831. His son, Joseph Rastrelli (1799–1842) became an assistant conductor in 1829, and received the full title in 1830. A tenor singer named Gregorio Babbi also served as *Kapellmeister* from 1805 to 1808. These were rather small men, composer-conductors of the old school who were there more for the purpose of writing music than for their skill in directing the performance of it, and they did nothing to add lustre to the music at the Saxon court.

More important was the appointment of Morlacchi as chief *Kapellmeister*

[1] *Rambles*, p. 199.   [2] Prölss, p. 559.   [3] *Idem*, p. 475.
[4] *Allg. Mus. Ztg.*, 1801, Prölss, p. 237.

of the Italian opera in 1810. Morlacchi was Weber's rival on the Italian side, and to some extent his opponent; he held his office in spite of frequent absences until his death in 1841.

Weber came to the Dresden opera in 1817, and there did much to set German national opera on its feet. During Weber's time a double-bass player in the orchestra named Franz Anton Schubert (1768–1824) held office as assistant-conductor from 1804 until his death, and Marschner shared some of Weber's duties at Dresden from 1823. Seeing no prospect of succeeding to Weber's post, Marschner resigned his position and went to the *Stadttheater* at Leipzig. Reissiger received the coveted post in 1827 and held it for the rest of his life. In a letter written by Moscheles in November, 1826,[1] the names of those who tried to secure Weber's post after his death were as follows: Wolfram (Teplitz), Hummel (Weimar), Seyfried (Vienna), Fried. Schneider (Dessau), Lindpaintner (Stuttgart), "and a great many others."

Wagner came to Dresden in 1842 for the production of his *Rienzi*, and early in the following year he accepted the post of *Kapellmeister* in place of Morlacchi. In 1849 Wagner's politics drove him into exile at Zurich. Carl Krebs, from Hamburg, filled the vacancy caused by Wagner's departure, and remained at Dresden until he retired from active work in 1872. August Roeckel came as *Musikdirector* or assistant to Wagner and Reissiger in 1843, and was dismissed in 1848 and subsequently imprisoned on account of his revolutionary activities.

Under this great array of conductors and their assistants there served an equally large number of leaders and assistant-leaders. The chief *Concertmeister* or leader at Dresden at the beginning of the century was Christofero Babbi (1748–1814), a brother of the Gregorio Babbi already mentioned; he was appointed in that capacity in 1781, and held his position until his death. His successor, Polledro, remained at Dresden until 1824, when he accepted a similar appointment at Turin. Polledro was the principal leader under Morlacchi and Weber. His successor was Antonio Rolla, son of the violinist of that name at Milan. Rolla served from 1823 until his death in 1837,[2] and was followed by Lipinski, who came to the Dresden orchestra in 1839 and remained until 1860. Lipinski was Wagner's leader, and was of great service to Berlioz when that composer conducted two concerts at Dresden in 1843. Wagner maintained that although Lipinski was an ardent musician and skilled violinist, he was not a good leader; he literally led the orchestra by always playing ahead of it, and the sound of his violin could always be heard above or before the rest of the violins. Wagner said that Lipinski was vain and self-important, and the relations between conductor and leader were by no means happy or smooth.[3] Franz Schubert, *not* the Viennese composer, but a son of the Franz Anton S. mentioned above, was assistant-leader from 1837, became second *Concertmeister* in 1847, and after

[1] *Harm.*, Dec., 1826, p. 237.   [2] Rolla was leader of the Italian opera.
[3] Wagner, *My Life*, I, p. 304.

sharing the duty with Lipinski for some time, eventually succeeded him at the first desk of the violins. Franz Anton Morgenroth (1780–1847) was among the violinists who played under Weber in 1817, and became *vice-Concertmeister* in 1828. Another of the first violins, Ludwig Tietz, became *vice-Concertmeister* in 1818; he was leader of the German opera in Weber's time, and was probably the father of C. Tietz, a double-bass player at Dresden, who in 1857 dunned Wagner for money lent him about twenty years earlier. Moritz Hauptmann, the eminent theorist and future *Cantor* at Leipzig, was one of the violinists at Dresden (1812) before he joined Spohr's orchestra at Cassel in 1822. Theodor Uhlig came as a violinist in 1841, and is remembered as a staunch friend and correspondent of Wagner's, and as the first arranger of the piano score of *Lohengrin*.

Franz Pohland (b. 1773) was playing the viola at the beginning of the century; by 1832 he was leader of his section, and as a veteran of 69 he was still playing in 1843 when Wagner and Berlioz were at Dresden. No doubt he was one of the somewhat elderly viola players who were startled and shocked by Spontini's disturbing remark in 1844: "Are the violas dying?"

Several distinguished 'cellists served in the Dresden orchestra. In the early years of the century it could boast of Jean Balthasar Trickler, who joined in 1783, of Heinrich Megelin, whose service began in 1774 and who reached the leading desk before he died in 1806, and of Johannes Eisert (b. 1775). Later well-known 'cello players who served under both Weber and Wagner included Dotzauer, who led his section from 1821 until 1852, and Friedrich August Kummer, who played from 1817 till 1864, when he was able to celebrate the jubilee of his first entry into the orchestra. Moritz Hauptmann told how Kummer got his first appointment in the orchestra in 1814. There was no vacancy amongst the 'cellos just then, but there *was* a vacancy for an oboist. So young Kummer set to work, quickly learned to play the oboe, and succeeded well enough to be engaged as second oboe. He then had to wait until 1817 before there was a vacant place in the 'cellos.[1]

As in most other German court establishments, employment in the Dresden orchestra was kept "in the family" as much as possible, and sons often succeeded fathers. In addition to the two Schuberts already mentioned, there was a Joseph Schubert (1757–1812) playing the viola, and another, Anton (b. 1766), who played the double-bass. Burney (1772)[2] mentioned a violinist named Hunt; forty-five years later his son Carl Hunt (b. 1766) was playing the same instrument in the same orchestra. The Besozzi family, famous in the annals of Dresden music far back in the days of Hasse, and, indeed, renowned as oboe and bassoon players all over Europe in the 18th century, still had its representatives in the Dresden orchestra during the early years of last century. Franz Besozzi (1766–1810), a son of Carlo, was playing the oboe in 1805, and Joseph Besozzi played the

[1] *Briefe*, II, p. 188.
[2] *Present State* (Germany), II, pp. 44, 46; probably Franz or Nicolaus Hunt.

double-bass under Weber in 1817. The latter was still in the list of 1842, when Wagner came to Dresden. Carl Haudeck was born in 1721 and played the horn beside Hampel in 1756[1]; the same name appears under the horns in the lists of 1805 and 1817. Marpurg named Franc. Joseph Götzel as a flautist at Dresden in 1756[2]; one Friedrich Götzel was playing the same instrument in the same orchestra in 1817.

Beside Götzel, Johann Friedrich Prinz (1755–1812)[3] played the flute; his name occurs in Forkel's list of 1784,[4] and it figures in the Dresden list of 1817 as the highest-paid of the flautists. Most renowned of the later Dresden flautists was Anton Bernhard Fürstenau, who played from 1820 until his death in 1852. This was the Fürstenau who accompanied Weber to London in 1826 and was the last man to see him alive. His son Moritz played beside his father from 1842, and became the historian of Dresden's court music.

In the early years of the century the oboists were Franz Besozzi, Fried. Aug. Kummer (father of the 'cellist), and Carl Gustav Dietze. The latter was still playing in 1832; another son of the elder Kummer, Carl Gotthelf, had joined the oboes by 1817 and was still there in 1850. All of these played under Weber. Johann Gottlieb Kretzschmar (b. 1809) joined the orchestra in 1836, and with Edel, Hiebendhal,[5] and the younger Kummer, played the oboe during Wagner's time at Dresden. In 1817 there were five of the Kummer family in the orchestra.

The clarinet players at the beginning of the century were the brothers Johann Traugott Rothe (b. 1768) and Gottlob Rothe (b. 1774), both of whom were still playing under Weber in 1817. At that time Johann Gottlob Kotte (or Cotta) (b. 1797) was a young clarinet player (receiving only a quarter of the salary paid to the elder Rothe) who rose to some distinction as a solo player. His concert in 1824 was described as being one of the most effective and best attended of that year in Dresden. On that occasion Kotte played "a new concerto for the clarinet, composed by C. M. v. Weber, and Variations by Bärmann, both in a pleasing and masterly style."[6] Kotte was accompanied on the piano by "M. Benedikt," i.e. Julius Benedict. Kotte's name still appeared in the list of 1850, but long before then the brothers Rothe had been followed by another pair of brothers named Lauterbach, and at the mid-century the leading clarinet player was F. A. Dominick.

Four or even five bassoon players were available in the Dresden orchestra. Franz Schmied (b. 1766) became the leading player in Weber's time, and was still playing in 1832. Carl Eisner (b. 1796) came from St. Petersburg to the

---

[1] Marpurg, *Beyträge*, 1756, II, p. 476.   [2] Also Burney, II, pp. 44, 47.
[3] The date of his death, from Gassner's *Lexikon*, is probably incorrect.
[4] *Almanach*, (1784), p. 147.
[5] One of the unfortunates who lent money to Wagner, and who incurred Berlioz's displeasure by adding gratuitous ornaments of his own to the written part.
[6] *Harm.*, Sept., 1824., p. 173.

Dresden orchestra in 1836. Three of the Kummer family played this instrument at various times between 1800 and 1840,[1] and Gottlob Peschel was playing before 1817. On the same occasion when Kotte played the clarinet in 1824, Peschel "gave with great effect Variations for the Bassoon, also by v. Weber, on a Hungarian air, full of spirit." Kabasius and Suchanek were the bassoonists during Wagner's time.

After Carl Haudeck, the principal horn players were August Haase (b. 1792), who was appointed in 1813, and his brother Ludwig Haase (b. 1799), who joined in 1817 and played under both Weber and Wagner; Ludwig H. was said to be the finer player of the two.[2] A later horn player of note was Joseph Rudolph Lewy (1802–1881), brother of the Viennese horn player. Joseph came to Dresden in 1837 and was Wagner's leading horn.[3] Both Joseph and Ed. Lewy were early among those who adopted the valved horn. The trumpeters at Dresden under Weber were Johann Georg Klemm and Carl Friedrich Grimmer. Somewhat later the *Stadtmusikus* Zillmann[4] joined the orchestra as trumpeter, and under Wagner the trumpeters included one Kunze and Friedrich Benjamin Queisser (1817–1893), the latter a brother of the famous trombone player at Leipzig. Weber's trombone players are not named in the list of 1817; under Wagner they were Karl Gottschalk[5] (1802–1882), Adolf Julius Rühlmann[6] (1816–1877), who joined in 1841, and Johann Gottlieb Queisser (b. 1808), another brother of the Leipzig player.

The orchestra at Dresden was well provided with personnel. In Weber's time about 65 orchestral instrumentalists were maintained, but these rarely played all together. Two theatres had to be supplied with players, and only in the large church performances was the full force united. The German opera was allowed only about 35 players in Weber's time. In addition to the regular staff there were 15 probationers in 1850, several bearing names which suggest that they were sons of the serving members. There were also a piano tuner, an organ tuner, an instrument maker, four copyists, two organ blowers, and an attendant. It was no doubt the latter who handed Wagner a baton wrapped in "clean white paper" at each rehearsal.[7] (For full lists, see Appendix, pp. 487, 488.)

[1] Carl Salomon Kummer (b. 1766), Heinrich Auguste K., and Gotthelf Heinrich K. The latter, although over 60 years of age in 1840, was described by Schumann as being "still an admirable master" of the bassoon.

[2] Gassner, *Lexikon*.

[3] Haase was the senior player in Wagner's time, but in his scheme for the reorganisation of the Dresden orchestra, written in 1846 (Newman, I, Chap. XIX), Wagner said that Haase and Kretschmer were too old to be of any further service. Jos. Lewy became a "spy" for the *Intendant* in the opera orchestra, and reported to him all that was said at the orchestral players' meetings (Newman, II, p. 51).

[4] Zillmann used to conduct the afternoon concerts in the *Grosser Garten* at Dresden, to which the young boy Richard Wagner was an eager listener (*My Life*, I, p. 35).

[5] Gottschalk was a fine copyist, and made the fair copies of Schumann's works when that composer settled at Dresden in 1844.

[6] Rühlmann became a teacher of Musical History at the Dresden Conservatoire, and wrote several historical articles for the *Neue Zeitschrift für Musik*.

[7] Wagner, *Prose Works*, III, p. 129.

Little can be said of the playing of the Dresden orchestra before 1816. According to the *Allg. Mus. Zeitung* in 1801 it was then "one of the best," but was inclined to rest on its laurels, and was content to keep to a well-trodden path; although still enjoying a good reputation, when compared to what was going on elsewhere, the orchestra was not all that it might have been. But the early years of the 19th century were a rather disturbed period in the history of the Saxon capital. Napoleon was in possession of the city in 1806, although that did not prevent the opera from carrying on its usual work. Some years later Dresden became the centre of military operations by the allies against Napoleon. In 1813 the Russians were in occupation, and again the opera carried on as usual. After Waterloo things were more settled, and the King was back in his capital. Moscheles gave his impressions of the opera orchestra in 1816; they were none too favourable. He said that "the director is called Polledro," which indicates that the orchestra was then controlled by the violinist-leader, and not by the *Kapellmeister*. Moscheles was "irritated with their constant *ritardandos* at the finish of each melodious phrase, and the halts and draggings of the band." Then—"the orchestra, of which I had formed such great expectations, left much to be desired, notably the first horn-player. One passage in the *Andante* of the overture (*La Vestale*) could not be recognised."[1] It was evidently an off-night for Carl Haudeck. In 1824 Moscheles was again in Dresden. This was in Weber's time, and Rolla was then leader. This time the orchestra was "admirable."[2]

Weber also found "much to be desired" when he came to Dresden as *Kapellmeister* of the German opera in 1817. He at once began to stir things up; he got busy reorganising, planning and systematising the rehearsals, and met with plenty of opposition in so doing; nor was Morlacchi at all inclined to be helpful. The German opera organisation was poor; the Italians got the best of everything. This did not suit Weber at all. He put all his energy into the work of building up an effective organisation for performing German opera, and in so doing sapped his scanty stock of physical strength. By 1824 he was clearly failing; Moscheles said: "I am sorry to see him in a state of debility and suffering, and dread the exertions which London will cost him."[3]

In his account of his visit to Dresden in 1825 Sir George Smart gave some glimpses of the orchestra after Weber had been there for eight years. He heard *Der Freischütz* performed under the composer's direction with only five firsts, five second violins, two violas, two 'cellos, and two double-basses; all the necessary wind were there, the two flautists had to play the piccolo parts in the drinking song. The beginning of the overture was unfortunate, for the "horns cracked horribly"; but apart from that misfortune, "the band, particularly the oboe, was good, but not strong. More strength of string is required. . . . Still the performance was very perfect," and the wind instruments were "very good."

---

[1] Moscheles, *Life*, I, p. 33.   [2] *Ibid.*, I, p. 93.   [3] *Ibid.*, I, p. 94.

At a rehearsal of *Euryanthe* Smart was impressed with the perfect order that was maintained. The overture was "well played, particularly the slow part for eight violins and two viole," and again he remarked on the excellent playing of the wind instruments. At a less important opera Marschner was conducting, seated at a square pianoforte, on which he played the accompaniment for the recitative; on this occasion "the orchestra went extremely well."[1] So, it seems that, except for the unfortunate cracking of the horns in *Der Freischütz*, the standard of performance was excellent. But it is evident that Weber did not get the best of everything at Dresden.

After Weber's death the orchestra would have an easier time, for Reissiger was no martinet, and Morlacchi was not the man to inspire and stimulate an orchestra that was quite ready to sit back and take things easily. Chorley's impression of the Dresden orchestra in 1839 was that, although brilliant and powerful, and carefully directed by Reissiger, he was puzzled by the effect of languor which seemed to surround the whole performance. He decided that this must have been due to the low pitch at which they played; it was "nearly half a tone lower than any I have ever heard." Perhaps it was the combination of Reissiger and the low pitch that made the Dresden orchestra sound languid and "mawkish" to Chorley.[2]

But if it was languid during the 'thirties, it is quite certain that when Wagner came early in 1843 a fresh breeze would begin to stir and disturb the placidity of the calm waters through which the Dresden orchestra was quietly sailing. What Wagner expected of an orchestra we know from his scores, and from his book *On Conducting*. We know his views on German theatres, orchestras and conductors: "The Directors of court theatres took good care to engage none but demure and subservient persons."[3] There was nothing demure or subservient about Wagner, and the leader Lipinski was a man of energy and authority. When *Tannhäuser* was produced in 1845 at Dresden the violinists had great difficulty in playing the passages that Wagner had written for the instrument: "It was noised abroad that passages had been written for the first violins which were unplayable, and the audience listened expectantly for the 'scramble.' No doubt there were violin passages as difficult as original, but the heart of the leader, Lipinski, was in his work, and he set himself so earnestly to teach individually each violinist difficult phrases, even carefully noting the fingering, that the performance was any but a scramble."[4]

Lipinski had been at Dresden since 1839, and Wagner had handled the orchestra as guest-conductor for the production of *Rienzi* in 1842. Early in 1843 the latter was installed as permanent conductor, and at once began to disturb the complacency which had prevailed under Reissiger and Morlacchi. He re-arranged the seating of the orchestra, "but oh! the hubbub it has produced is dreadful." To change what had satisfied Morlacchi and Reissiger was sheer impertinence, and he was charged with lack of reverence for

[1] *Journals*, pp. 139, 140, 145, 148.   [2] *Music and Manners*, III, pp. 140, 177.
[3] *On Conducting*, p. 5.   [4] Praeger, p. 138.

tradition, and with taking delight in upsetting the established order of things.[1]

Just at that time Berlioz came to Dresden and gave two concerts. We can gather from his disjointed comments that the orchestra had already been whipped into better shape by Wagner and Lipinski: "And now to speak of Dresden, where I was engaged for two concerts, and found a chorus, orchestra, wind band, and also a famous tenor. Such treasures as these I had not found since I first came to Germany. Moreover, at Dresden I was destined to meet with a devoted, energetic, enthusiastic friend, Charles Lipinski, whom I had formerly known in Paris. I cannot describe, my dear Ernst, the ardour with which this excellent man seconded me. His position of first *Maître de concert*, and the general esteem in which both his office and talent are held, gave him great authority over the members of the band, and good use he made of it." There was clearly no taking things easily now: "Lipinski so excited the self-love of the musicians, that their ambition to succeed, and especially to surpass the Leipzig performance (there is a kind of hidden rivalry between the two towns), made us work tremendously hard. Four long rehearsals seemed scarcely sufficient, and the band itself would willingly have asked for a fifth if there had been time. The result, accordingly, was a first-rate performance."

Wagner willingly lent his aid and authority: "The Dresden band, formerly directed by Morlacchi, the Italian, and by the illustrious composer of *Der Freischütz*, is now conducted by Reissiger and Richard Wagner. In Paris, we know scarcely anything of Reissiger, except his slow melancholy waltz, known as *Dernière Pensée de Weber*. As for the young *Kapellmeister* Richard Wagner, . . . his authority was exercised for the first time in assisting me with my rehearsals, which he did with both zeal and good-will." Berlioz remarked on some of the individual players; he picked out Dotzauer the 'cellist, and the first oboe, who had a fine tone, "but an old-fashioned style, and an irritating mania for trills and mordents."[2] Lewy, the horn player, came in for special praise: "The most remarkable of the horn players is M. Lewy, who enjoys a great reputation in Saxony. He and his colleagues use the cylinder (rotary valve) horn, to which the Leipzig band, unlike all others in the north of Germany, has hitherto refused admission."[3]

Under Wagner the orchestra at Dresden again held a high position, and could once more rank at least equally with those at Berlin and Munich. Wagner himself described it as being "the most costly and accomplished in Germany."[4]

But Wagner, while he was at Dresden, allowed the orchestra no time to rest upon its laurels. It was a period of ever growing strain, with opposition both from above and below, and with friction which threatened to produce flame long before the political events in 1849 put an end to an almost intolerable state of affairs. Wagner would have no stereotyped routine-performances; every opera had to be carefully studied and presented with

---

[1] Praeger, p. 132.   [2] Hiebendahl.   [3] *Mem.*, II, pp. 63–71.   [4] Chamberlain, p. 48.

artistic thoroughness, and no amount of tradition was to stand in the way of what his conscience and insight told him was musically and dramatically true. This meant more and harder work for the orchestra. Some of the more enlightened players sympathised with his artistic aims and supported his unceasing reforms; others found the pace too hot for them and formed an opposition party whose ultimate aim it was to get rid of this disturbing bundle of energy, and to find again the peace and security that they had hitherto enjoyed under the complacent Reissiger. Amongst the malcontents was Lipinski, who in spite of all his zeal and energy found that his authority was being undermined, and was loth to give up the power and influence that had always appertained to the important position of *Concertmeister* in all German musical establishments. These players, who like all in Germany were certainly underpaid, and were now also being overworked, only helped to swell the number of the enemies that Wagner by his intense zeal and uncompromising artistic thoroughness (aided no doubt by his tactlessness) was raising about himself in the town, the higher administration of the opera, and the court. Thus, when, as the immediate outcome of his part in the Revolution, Wagner was obliged to flee from Dresden in 1849, it was as if fate was only anticipating by a short time the final crash that was impending and which in any case would have deprived the Dresden orchestra of its conductor.

While Wagner was at Dresden his duties included conducting a certain number of concerts given by the court orchestra. These were held in the old opera-house, and it was at one of these concerts in 1846 that Wagner gave a performance of Beethoven's Choral Symphony such as had never before been heard in Dresden, or indeed in any other German town. The rehearsals, so many and so exhaustive, must have opened the eyes of even the most obtuse and lethargic amongst the players, and could hardly have failed to convince them that here was a man who was an orchestral interpreter-conductor such as they had never encountered before.

When it lost Wagner in 1849 the Dresden orchestra was deprived of a great driving force, and some time was to elapse before another was found who was able to restore to it the reputation it had gained under Weber and Wagner.

Berlioz said that he was offered the post of *Kapellmeister* at the Dresden opera-house in 1854, as soon as there was a vacancy.[1] It would have been an interesting experiment to put a French conductor without routine experience of opera-conducting in charge of a large German opera organisation. However, whether the matter was ever seriously considered or not, no vacancy occurred, and Berlioz did not occupy the position.

MUNICH

The mantle of Mannheim fell upon Munich when the Elector Carl Theodor inherited Bavaria, and in 1778 transferred his court and the greater

[1] *Mem.*, II, p. 340.

part of his musical establishment to the Bavarian capital. From that time
the musical fame of Mannheim declined, and Munich rose to be one of the
most important of the musical centres of Germany.

The court theatre at Munich at the beginning of last century was the old
Theater an der Residenz (1753), originally intended only for the court and
invited guests, but now open to the public. In 1818 a larger *Hof und
Nationaltheater* was erected adjoining the old theatre, and connected with it
by a bridge[1]; this handsome building was burnt down in 1823, but was
rebuilt and reopened in January, 1825.[2]

In the meantime another theatre had been erected in front of the gate
leading to the bridge over the *Isar*. This was built in 1811, and was known
as the *Isarthor* theatre. One of the first things the new King of Bavaria
(Ludwig I) did in 1825 was to close this theatre.

At Munich, as at Berlin and Dresden, Italian and German opera were in
opposition, the court favouring the former and the people the latter. In
1819 each had a separate *Intendant* and vocal staff, and the arrangement was
to give Italian opera at the old *Residenztheater* and German opera in the larger
Nationaltheater.[3] It appears that the *Isarthor* theatre had its own orchestra,
but that the same orchestral staff was shared by the other two theatres.
The Italian opera at Munich finally declined with the accession of King
Ludwig I in 1825, and by 1826 it had no separate establishment of its own.

For these theatres and for the church music and court concerts several
Kapellmeister were employed. It is difficult, owing to a multiplicity of
official titles, to distinguish clearly between the rank and functions of these
various *Kapellmeister*, but it seems that those engaged during the first half
of last century were as follows:

The earlier of the Munich *Kapellmeister* all bore names well known in the
annals of Mannheim in its greatest days. Franz Paula von Grua bore that
title from 1784, and retained it until his death in 1833; he was still serving in
1826, at the age of 72, in the Royal chapel. Carl Cannabich succeeded his
father, and was *Kapellmeister* from 1800 to 1806. Franz Danzi, who had
played the 'cello in the Mannheim orchestra, was *Vicekapellmeister* at Munich
from 1798 to 1807. Ferdinand Fränzl, son of Ignaz the Mannheim violinist
and composer of symphonies, followed Cannabich in 1806, and held the
same office until 1824. Peter von Winter played as a boy in the Mannheim
orchestra, and was *Vicekapellmeister* at Munich from 1788, and full *Kapellmeister* from 1801 to 1825.

The old Mannheim names were dying out in the 'twenties, and in the
meantime fresh names began to appear. Joseph Hartmann Stuntz (1793–
1859) was chorus-master in 1824, and in 1826 succeeded Winter as *Kapellmeister*. Aiblinger was at Munich as *Kapellmeister* between 1819 and 1833,
and although probably associated with the church music more than with the
opera, he assisted Stuntz with the title *Vicekapellmeister* in 1826. Lindpaintner conducted at the *Isarthor* theatre from 1812 until 1819, before going

[1] Zenger, plate facing p. 272.   [2] Ursprung, p. 219.   [3] *Ibid.*, p. 214.

to Stuttgart. In 1836 Franz Lachner became *Kapellmeister* at the opera, and held that position until he retired in 1865. Ignaz Lachner was an assistant conductor with the title *Musikdirector* from 1842 to 1852; although it is likely that he may have conducted some performances, his work was really that of chorus-master and director of stage bands.[1] Two alien musicians who for brief periods were *Kapellmeister* at Munich were the Italian Blangini, in 1805, and the Frenchman Chelard in 1828. Blangini still held his position nominally in 1826, but took no active part in the work.

Of these *Kapellmeister*, the early group, who all derived from the Mannheim school, were violinist-conductors of the old school, but it is probable that Stuntz and Aiblinger were baton-conductors, as were Lindpaintner, the Lachners, and Chelard.

The Munich orchestra was always strong in string players. Joseph Moralt was *Concertmeister* from 1800 until his death in 1828. Five of the Moralt family played string instruments in the orchestra, and the name of A. Moralt turns up later as a horn player. Four of the brothers, Joseph, Johann Baptist, Georg and Philipp, formed a string quartet which was quite celebrated in its day. According to Gassner,[2] the 'cellist Philipp Moralt was appointed second *Kapellmeister* in 1829, with the title of *Musikdirector*. In that year it was stated that Moralt "has already commenced an important reform in the orchestra, into which a certain Turkish and Chinese taste had gradually made its way. His first care has been to add to the number of violins and violoncellos, at the same time making an important reduction in the drums, cymbals, triangles, ottavinas (piccolos), etc.; a measure which will entitle him to the thanks of all true lovers of the art."[3] From about 1814 to 1820 Pietro Rovelli was solo violinist at Munich, and Molique was *Concertmeister* from 1820 to 1826. Anton Bohrer and Hinterholzer played among the violins, and Peter Legrande (d. 1840) was a 'cellist in the orchestra when Weber was at Munich in 1811. Spohr thought that Legrande was "going down hill" in 1815.

Spohr's verdict was that the Munich strings were then excellent. In 1827 Edward Holmes said that there was "a greater weight and richness in the stringed instruments of the Munich orchestra, than in others in Germany; and though there are fewer violins than at Darmstadt, they are better, as well as better played upon."[4] Later on, Lobe remarked that the Munich string players bowed like one man, and if that could be done in one orchestra, he said, it could be done in others.[5]

There were also some first-rate wind players at Munich. Johann Baptist Becke (1743–1818), a veteran flautist who had been in the orchestra since 1766, was still there at the beginning of the century. Carl Theodor Metzger (b. 1774) was one of a flute-playing family associated with Mannheim and Munich, and was principal flute early in the century. Two other names of Munich flautists will probably always be remembered by players on

[1] Zenger, p. 310.   [2] *Lexikon.*   [3] *Harm.*, Jan., 1829, p. 22.
[4] *Rambles*, p. 64.   [5] *Cons. und Diss.*, p. 284.

that instrument. Johann Nepomuk Capeller, who invented a shake-key which is now to be found on all flutes, seems to have followed Metzger; but the name which means more to flautists than any other, that of Theobald Boehm, also occurs in the roll of the Munich orchestra from 1812. According to Boehm's own statement, he was appointed first flute at the "second Royal theatre in Munich" in the year 1812[1]; this was the new *Isarthor* theatre, which had just been built and was opened in that year. In 1819 Boehm was transferred to the large new Court and National theatre, and although frequently away from Munich, he retained his appointment until he was pensioned in 1848.

Of the oboists the best-remembered seems to have been Anton Fladt (b. 1775). He came into the orchestra in 1790, and was still playing in 1837[2]; Spohr remarked on his fine tone and very tasteful execution in 1815.[3] Another oboist was Wilhelm Legrande, brother of the 'cellist, who later became a bandmaster in the Bavarian army, and for some time was in charge of the stage-band at the opera.

Probably the most famous clarinet player of his time in Germany was Heinrich Joseph Bärmann. He joined the Munich orchestra in 1807, and remained for the rest of his life, although often making extensive concert tours throughout Europe. Bärmann was a friend of Weber, Mendelssohn and Meyerbeer, and Weber wrote several pieces for him. Ed. Holmes heard him play in 1827, and could pay no greater compliment than to say that he was the counterpart of the English player Willman.[4] The son, Carl Bärmann, succeeded his father about 1838, having joined the orchestra at the age of fourteen in 1825, and likewise gained a great reputation as a clarinet player and writer for that instrument. Three other good clarinet players at Munich were Joseph Teusch (1811), Jos. Faubel (1816) and Lutz (1827).

Weber, who was industrious in writing concertos for wind instruments round about 1811, wrote to Gottfried Weber in that year, and told him that since he had written a concertino for Bärmann the whole of the Munich orchestra wanted him to write concertos for them. Amongst others Weber wrote a bassoon concerto for the Munich player Georg Friedrich Brandt (b. 1773); this player came to the orchestra in 1800 and remained in it for the rest of his life.

Spohr said that the Munich wind players were good "up to the horns." By this we may suppose that he thought the horns were good, but was not prepared to say the same for the trumpets and trombones. A pair of horn players who could go back to the Mannheim days were the brothers Franz (b. 1751) and Martin Lang (b. 1755). They had been friends of Mozart, and are mentioned in several of his letters; these veterans were apparently still playing in 1811. Another pair of horn-playing brothers in the same orchestra were Ignaz (b. 1754) and Anton Böck (b. 1757). These two had

---

[1] Boehm, *An essay*, p. 11.   [2] Hanslick, p. 249, f.n.   [3] *Autob.*, I, p. 214.
[4] "in the softness of his tone, and the grace of his style, may be found the counterpart of Willman." (*Rambles*, p. 71.)

spent many years touring all over Europe as duettists with great success,
and eventually settled down at Munich in 1790, where they played until
about 1814. A younger horn player for whom Weber also wrote a concertino in 1815 was named Rauch. With such a fine array of players, it is
not surprising that many nice things were said about the Munich orchestra.
Weber said that then (1811) it was fully worthy of its famous chief (Winter),
but that, like him, it was proud, arrogant and exclusive.[1] On July 2, 1811,
he heard a performance of Cherubini's *Wasserträger* under Fränzl; this drew
from him the following eulogy: "The overture began, and at once my hopes
were raised to the highest pitch, for truly, it was played with such fire,
finish and power as only the Munich orchestra could have given it, and
gladly I joined in the rousing applause which came from the audience in the
stalls."[2] The total strength of the orchestra was then 87 players. A few
years later Spohr was at Munich and heard some of the twelve concerts that
were given by the orchestra during the winter season.[3] One piece he heard
was Beethoven's 5th symphony: "As the court orchestra of Munich still
maintains its ancient repute as one of the first in the world, my expectation
was greatly on the stretch; yet was it far exceeded by the execution of
Beethoven's Symphony in C minor, with which this first concert was opened.
It is scarcely possible that it could have been performed with more spirit,
more power, and at the same time with greater delicacy, as also, throughout,
with a closer observance of all the shades of *forte* and *piano*! It produced
therefore a greater effect, also, than I had believed it capable of, although I
had already frequently heard it, and even under the direction of the composer
himself in Vienna."[4] Spohr revealed that the symphonies were then played
under the direction of the *Concertmeister*, and not under the *Kapellmeister*:
"my symphony in E major was exceedingly well performed under the
spirited yet circumspect direction of Herr *Concertmeister* Moralt."

Sir George Smart's report on the Munich orchestra conducted by Stuntz
in 1825 was decidedly lukewarm. It was "no great things and contained
only three double-basses. The tromboni were good, but I have not yet
heard a trumpet equal to Harper." The playing was "not so superior to
England as I expected."[5]

In 1828 we get Ed. Holmes' estimate of the music at Munich. He
appears to have been highly delighted, and said that the orchestra could
hardly be rivalled at Berlin, and certainly not elsewhere in Germany.
Fränzl was *Kapellmeister* at that time. Incidentally, Holmes was charmed with
the singing of Mademoiselle Schweitzer, who "presented the phenomenon
of a graceful and attractive woman on the stage, though shorn of one
of her natural legs, and supplied with a substitute of cork." He was also
very pleased with the accompanying of the orchestra: "The complete
precision with which every note of the accompaniment was played, might

[1] Weber, I, p. 260.   [2] *Ibid.*, III, p. 36.
[3] These eventually became the *Odeon* concerts.
[4] *Autob.*, I, p. 213.   [5] *Journals*, pp. 90, 91.

have satisfied the most rigorous of judges; and I have found this delicacy and exactitude of the orchestra, in which the players show themselves in their proper sphere as the *servants* of the voice, an admirable peculiarity in their performances."[1] Of the individual players, Bärmann, Boehm, Moralt ('cello) and Rauch were singled out for special praise: "each of the most admirable in his kind." There can be no doubt about it; Holmes thoroughly enjoyed himself at Munich, and therefore had something nice to say about everybody and everything.

It was a pity that Berlioz did not visit Munich in the course of his tour in Germany in 1843. His remarks would have been of particular interest as a comparison with the Dresden orchestra of the same period. It was just at that time that an English critic wrote: "The orchestra at Munich is generally considered the best in Germany."[2]

Probably the most important landmark in the history of the Munich orchestra during the half-century would be in 1836 when Franz Lachner became conductor. This would certainly mark the end of the period in which responsibility for the performance was divided between *Kapellmeister* and *Concertmeister*. With the advent of Lachner the last of the old traditions of the Mannheim-Munich school disappeared, and the spirit of German romantic-heroic opera received an impetus which was to culminate in the great Wagner performances under Bülow in the 'sixties.

In addition to its work at the opera, the Munich orchestra began to figure as an important concert-orchestra in 1811, when a concert-society or *Musikalische Academie* was established. These concerts were directed at first by Winter, assisted by Ferd. Fränzl as *Musikdirector* and Moralt as *Concertmeister*, and were held in the *Königliche Redouten-Saal*, but when that building became inadequate a new concert hall named the Odeon was erected in 1828. This was the building that was adorned with busts of great composers which, however, were subject to slight changes from time to time in accordance with changing views as to which were really the great ones. According to the *Harmonicon*[3] the select party represented by busts in 1830 comprised Handel, Mozart, Méhul, Vogler, Winter, Weber, Gluck, Haydn, Cimarosa and Rossini. It need hardly be said that some of these were destined to drop out in the course of time. The new hall was said to be 130 feet long and 75 feet broad.

This society was reorganised and revitalised by Lachner in 1839, and these concerts, given with a large orchestra which in 1844 contained 70 string players and doubled wood-wind, began to rival the similar institutions at Leipzig, Vienna, Paris and London.

LEIPZIG

The musical situation at Leipzig was always rather different from that of most other large German towns, mainly because there was no court

[1] *Rambles*, pp. 63, 64.   [2] *Mus. World*, Jan. 6, 1842, p. 6.   [3] Nov., 1830, p. 482.

establishment on which the whole system could be based, and around which the musical life of the city could revolve.   Moreover, it was not opera that gave impetus to the music of this commercial city.   No German town of any considerable size was without its theatre, and like all the rest, Leipzig had its theatre where opera was given; but the *Stadttheater* there did not rank very high amongst the opera-houses of Germany.[1]   Its standing was not on a level with those at Stuttgart, Frankfort, or Cassel, and well below

THE OLD GEWANDHAUS AT LEIPZIG

those at Dresden and Munich.   Leipzig owed its musical reputation more to its church and concert music than to its opera.[2]   It was also the centre of the book and music publishing trade in Germany.[3]

The Society which maintained the concert-hall and orchestra of the *Gewandhaus* could trace its origin back to 1743, to the *Concert-Gesellschaft* which gave subscription concerts in the *Drei Schwanen* inn, and which carried on its work in spite of a few interruptions until 1781.   In that year the new concert-room in the *Gewandhaus* was built, and a new society was created and managed entirely by the music-loving townspeople of Leipzig.

[1] "The theatre here, which is also the opera-house, is suburban, neither very large, rich in its company, nor extensive in its band."   (Anon., *Rambles*, p. 248.)   Chorley said that it was "small and shabby" in 1840.
[2] "Concerts are the particular musical distinction of Leipzig" (*Quar. Mus. Mag.*, 1823).
[3] Breitkopf and Härtel, Kistner, Hofmeister, Peters, etc.

K

Of this society the most important part was a permanent paid orchestra, consisting of musicians who were employed at the theatre and some of the *Stadtmusiker* in civic employ.

From 1785 until 1810 the professional musical director of the *Gewandhaus* concert society was Johann Gottfried Schlicht. The control of the orchestral playing was in the hands of the *Concertmeister* or leading violinist, who at that time was Campagnoli, and whose appointment dated from 1797. Excepting the leader, none of the orchestral players were musicians of any particular distinction, in fact, they appear to have been rather of a homely type, without more than a local reputation. They were paid at a very modest rate, and their status and skill may be estimated from the fact that many of them played on several instruments, as the old German *Stadtmusiker* were required to do, and went from one to the other in a way which was no doubt very useful, but would not tend to produce a very high standard of efficiency on any of their instruments. Johann Gottlob Schäfer, for example, played the clarinet, oboe, trumpet and viola, while Gottlieb Heinrich Köhler could make himself useful on the flute, oboe and drums. The status and rather poverty-stricken condition of these musicians may be guessed from the fact that as late as 1835, the year in which Mendelssohn became their conductor, the members of the famous *Gewandhaus* orchestra were content to play during the summer season in coffee-and-cake gardens, performing symphonies and Strauss waltzes to the accompaniment of clattering coffee cups, beer mugs, and firework displays.[1] Such an orchestra could not rival the big court establishments at Berlin, Dresden or Munich; it had neither the support of a court nor the subsidy from a state; it had not the means to attract the more ambitious and brilliant player, and any young outstanding executant, if he did get into the orchestra, was sure soon to be lured away by higher pay and better prospects.

But if it did not get the pick of the players, the *Gewandhaus* orchestra gained by being a very united body. The members worked together under favourable conditions, and in a very suitable building. What they lacked in brilliance they no doubt made up in industry and conscientiousness. Spohr's comment on the orchestra in 1804 was: "These concerts are got up by a society of shopkeepers. But they are not amateur concerts; for the orchestra is alone composed of professional musicians and is both numerous and excellent. . . . The room in which these concerts are given is exceedingly handsome, and particularly favourable to the effect of the music."[2]

In 1791 there were 27 players in the orchestra, and at the time of Spohr's visit it numbered over 30 instrumentalists.

When Schlicht left in 1810 to become *Cantor* of the *Thomasschule*, Johann Philipp Christian Schulz succeeded as musical director of the society, and continued in that capacity up to his death in 1827. The next director was Pohlenz, who was to remain in charge until Mendelssohn came in 1835.

In the meantime Heinrich August Matthäi (1781–1835) had joined the

---

[1] Loewe, p. 191.   [2] Spohr, I, p. 72.

orchestra as second *Concertmeister* in 1803, and when Campagnoli outstayed his leave in 1816 the post of leader of the instrumental music fell into the hands of Matthäi. As his assistant Matthäi had Moritz Gotthold Klengel (1794–1870), who played for more than fifty years at the *Gewandhaus*, at first at the same desk as Matthäi, and eventually as leader of the second violins. It is difficult to find names of distinction among the *Gewandhaus* players during the first quarter of the century. For a short time in 1822–23 Wilhelm Wieprecht played among the violinists, but it was not in that capacity that he subsequently achieved his reputation. August Eberhard Müller was the principal flautist from 1794 to 1802, and Carl August Grenser (1794–1864), son of a well-known maker of wood-wind instruments at Dresden, came as flautist in 1814, and played until he was pensioned in 1855. Dotzauer, the 'cellist, who later became leader at Dresden, played from 1805 until 1811. One Reissiger played the violin in 1819–20, and may possibly have been the future conductor at Dresden; that Reissiger was a pupil of Schlicht at the *Thomasschule* and went to Leipzig University in 1818 is certain, but there is no information that he ever was a violinist.

On the whole, it appears to have been an orchestra of not very distinguished players, who were, nevertheless, worthy musicians and faithful in service, but neither very brilliant nor very ambitious.

The programmes in the early years of the century show the usual miscellaneous collection of symphonies, overtures, concertos, choral movements, arias and solos of all sorts. In addition to giving regular performances of a few symphonies by Haydn and Mozart, and many more by composers whose names are now barely remembered, the Leipzig orchestra made its first acquaintance with the symphonies of Beethoven. No. 1 received its first performance in the *Gewandhaus* in 1801, No. 2 in 1804, and the *Eroica* in 1807. From Röchlitz we learn that the orchestra willingly gave extra rehearsals gratis in order to master this "of all symphonies the most difficult, even if only to play the right notes."[1] But they evidently succeeded, not only in playing the right notes, but also in giving a good rendering of the symphony, for Röchlitz was satisfied that it was played as well as could be wished by anyone who had studied the score. The C minor symphony, played from MS. parts, was first heard in 1809.[2] This was a still harder nut to crack, and the first attempt, "on account of the great difficulties, was not very successful." It is strange now to read Röchlitz's comment to the effect that such a movement as the *Scherzo* of the C minor symphony could hardly be properly played by so large an orchestra. There were about 38 players in the *Gewandhaus* orchestra at that time. In the same year (1809) the *Pastoral* symphony, and in 1810 No. 4 were heard for the first time in Leipzig. No. 7 followed in 1816, No. 8 in 1818, and the Choral Symphony, played without a score from only the parts,[3] was first heard in 1826.

---

[1] Dörffel, p. 32.
[2] In that year the first engraved parts, but not the score, were published at Leipzig.
[3] On the authority of the *Berliner Musik-Zeitung*, 1826, edited by Marx.

Moscheles paid his first visit to Leipzig in 1816, and there he heard the *Gewandhaus* orchestra. His first impression was as follows: "the overture was played very steadily. I must make special note of the contrabasso player Wach,[1] because, with his force and energy, he seemed to keep the whole orchestra together." A little later Moscheles gave his own concert at the *Gewandhaus*, of which he wrote: "My overture to the ballet *Die Portraits*, was admirably performed at the first reading, but the orchestra wished to rehearse it again, and then it exceeded my expectations. I cannot sufficiently praise the horns and trombones, but beyond all the admirable violin of Matthäi, the leader." The concert-room greatly pleased Moscheles: "It is not easy to imagine a handsomer room, or one better fitted for its purpose." Moscheles went on to Dresden after leaving Leipzig, but it is evident that he didn't find everything so pleasant in the court-atmosphere of the Saxon capital as in the more homely surroundings of Leipzig. So, when he compared the two orchestras, he gave the palm to Leipzig.[2]

In 1825 the orchestra gained, but first in the capacity of viola player, the services of the famous trombone virtuoso Carl Traugott Queisser. Edward Holmes (1827) told how this resourceful man combined the career of a virtuoso with that of a restaurant keeper: "Here, in one of the suburban gardens, may be occasionally heard the famed trombonist M. Queisser, by his townsmen vaunted the greatest performer of the whole empire. He is himself the proprietor of this rural retreat, having captivated the affections and wedded the form of its female possessor, thus enticing the inhabitants to discuss his viands, and enhancing his fortune, as host, by means of his music. I have heard nothing so soft, round, and deep as the tone of this extraordinary player, who has, at the age of twenty-seven, attained the most surprising mastery. At the last music meeting at Zerbst he performed a concertino on his instrument, which will not be soon forgotten."[3] Schumann referred to Queisser as "god of the trombone";[4] in 1828 Queisser "performed a new concertino upon the trombone, a charming composition, which this performer executed with a facility and sweetness of expression, of which this instrument would scarcely seem susceptible."[5] Mendelssohn referred to Queisser as "our modern Handel," and in 1836 Sterndale Bennett found him still "master of the gardens," and reputed to be the finest trombone player in Europe.

The old bass player Wach, although he continued playing until 1827, was obliged to give up his leadership in 1819 to Johann Gottlieb Temmler (1782–1855), another doughty bass player who remained in the orchestra until the mid-century. Wagner[6] gave an amusing account of how this player, with "rather coarse and energetic language," persuaded the director

[1] Carl Gottfried Wilhelm Wach (1755–1833), became leading bass in 1783, was pensioned in 1827.
[2] Moscheles, *Life*, I, pp. 28, 30, 36.   [3] *Rambles*, p. 254.   [4] Schumann, I, p. 365.
[5] *Harm.*, May, 1828, p. 118.   [6] *My Life*, I, p. 69.

Pohlenz to abandon his futile attempt to conduct the *recitative* for basses and 'cellos in the last movement of Beethoven's Choral symphony, and how the passage "proceeded properly" as soon as it was left to the players without any interference from the conductor. At that time (c. 1830), it should be remembered, there was no conductor at the *Gewandhaus* for instrumental movements, and only when a chorus was employed did a time-beating conductor come into operation.

Perhaps Christian Gottlieb Müller (1800–1863), a violinist in the orchestra from 1826 to 1838, deserves mention even though it is only because he happened to be Wagner's first harmony teacher.[1]

Sir George Smart heard the *Gewandhaus* orchestra in 1825, ten years before Mendelssohn came to be its conductor; he heard a Mozart symphony "well played, but slower than we take it. The bassoon was shy, and there was much tuning between the movements."[2] In 1827 the orchestra played for the first time Mendelssohn's early symphony in C minor. This was its first acquaintance with the music of the man who was later to become its first and most distinguished conductor. It was about 1828 when Wagner, then fifteen years old, began to go to the *Gewandhaus* concerts, and there made his first acquaintance with Beethoven's symphonies, which, he said, were "played with the artistic perfection for which the orchestra was so justly celebrated, although there was room for improvement."[3]

In 1831 the jubilee of the society was celebrated by a special concert at the *Gewandhaus*. Only two men who had played in the first season in 1781 were still living, and only one of them, the veteran double-bass player Wach, took part in the jubilee concert. The orchestra on this occasion numbered 39 players, to which nine more were added as extras. The leaders were the following:

	Birth and death	Played from
Violin I. Heinrich August Matthäi ..	1781–1836	1803 to 1835
Violin I. Moritz Gotthold Klengel ..	1794–1870	1814 to 1868
Violin II. Carl August Lange	1789–1865	1805 to 1850
Viola. Carl Traugott Queisser[4]	1800–1846	1827 to 1846
'Cello. Fried. Wilh. Grenser, jun. ..	1806–1859	1827 to 1858
Bass. Johann Gottlieb Temmler ..	1782–1855	1813 to 1850
Flute. Carl August Grenser	1794–1864	1814 to 1855
Oboe. Carl Heinrich Rückner	1797–1835	1830 to 1835
Clart. Fried. Aug. Ferdinand Heinze ..	1793–1850	1811 to 1842[5]
Bassoon. Carl Ferdinand Schmitbach ..	1801– —	1829 to 1832
Horn. Carl Gottlob Steglich	1794–1849	1814 to 1846
Trumpet. Joh. Gottfried Zehrfeld ..	1795–1869	1825 to 1854
Drums. Fried. Aug. Grenser, med. ..	1799–1861	1831 to —

[1] *My Life*, I, p. 37.   [2] *Journals*, p. 162.   [3] Praeger, p. 36.   [4] The celebrated trombone player.
[5] First clarinet from 1829 to 1842, then second clarinet.

Matthäi died in 1835, having led and trained the orchestra since 1817. To him was largely due the credit of having made the *Gewandhaus* orchestra a fit instrument for Mendelssohn to exercise his skill upon. From Wagner we know that under Matthäi's direction the principal classical pieces were played regularly every season, and that when no particular technical difficulty intervened the playing was "smooth and precise."[1]

In 1835 began the period in which the *Gewandhaus* orchestra rose to its greatest height. The appointment of Mendelssohn was a happy choice for the society. He was just the man they needed; and he did not upset their smooth-running arrangements nor break with their traditions. He was also fortunate in finding an appointment which suited him so well. He had no troublesome reorganisation to carry out; he liked the musical environment and the atmosphere in Leipzig; he was rising on the wave of fame and found there plenty of friends and warm admirers who made life pleasant for him. Mendelssohn induced his friend David to accept the vacant post of leader, and he fitted excellently into the scheme. So everybody was happy, and no doubt there was plenty of opportunity, as Wagner put it, "*sich gegenseitig Complimente zu machen.*" A little opposition was encountered over the necessary change from control of the orchestra by a violinist-leader to control by a baton-conductor; but that was soon overcome, and everybody submitted willingly to Mendelssohn's kindly but firm rule.

When Sterndale Bennett came as a young man to Leipzig in 1836, the *Gewandhaus* orchestra had been in Mendelssohn's hands for one season. Bennett wrote of it: "The band is rather small, but quite perfect, and possesses great animation. . . . The overture to *Oberon* was not so well played as I have heard it in London. I mean as regards the style of playing it."[2]

By 1838 the number of string players had been increased to thirty-one, making, with the wind, a total strength of not far short of fifty players.[3]

Mendelssohn's work as conductor at the *Gewandhaus* was unbroken for six years. In 1841 he was called to Berlin, but he never completely severed his connection with Leipzig, and continued to conduct there whenever his duties at Berlin allowed him to do so. During the last few years of his life he was helped at the *Gewandhaus* concerts by David, Gade and Hiller. Even during the Mendelssohn regime the *Gewandhaus* orchestra was never able to attract particularly brilliant players. The old musicians of the *Stadtmusiker* type had more or less died out of the orchestra before Mendelssohn came, but their successors, although specialists, were by no means the pick of German orchestral players, and, excepting David, the names on the roll of the orchestra could not compare with the distinguished names of the Berlin, Dresden and Munich players.

The rank and file of the strings, although they were no doubt quite competent players, lacked distinction. The principals in the wind department during Mendelssohn's time were: Gottlob Wilhelm Haake (1804–1875),

---

[1] Wagner, *On Cond.*, p. 14.   [2] *Life*, p. 50.   [3] Creuzburg, p. 85.

who joined in 1831 and eventually succeeded Grenser as first flute; Johann Friedrich Diethe (b. 1810), first oboe after Rückner; Gustav Adolph Heinze (1820–1904), son of the Heinze who played at the jubilee in 1831, was first clarinet from 1842 until he went to Breslau in 1844; his successor, Johann Friedrich Bernard Wilhelm Landgraf (1816–1885), remained long enough to celebrate his 40th year of service in the orchestra; Carl Wilhelm von Inten (1808–1877), succeeded Schmitbach as first bassoon in 1832 and was pensioned in 1857; Carl Gustav Pfau (1809–1841) succeeded Steglich as first horn in 1837, and he in turn was succeeded in 1841 by Eduard Pohle from Dessau, who remained until 1853. Of the wind-players in 1839–40, Schumann specially mentioned Grenser and Haake (flutes), Diethe (oboe), Heinze (clarinet), and Pfau (horn).[1]

A player who did gain something more than a local reputation was Ernst Gotthold Benjamin Pfundt (1806–1871), the drummer. When Mendelssohn played Beethoven's *Emperor* concerto a year or two after he came to Leipzig, he found that he could not get the timpanist (Grenser) to play the solo part near the end of the concerto to his liking.[2] Grenser was evidently shy, and shunned the limelight. So Mendelssohn sought for a more enterprising and less modest drummer, and found him in the person of Pfundt, who was then a theological student at the university and chorus-master at the theatre. The new drummer joined the orchestra in 1837 and turned out to be an enthusiast who loved drums and drumming more than anything else in the world. Schumann was moved to write of him: "A separate (laurel) leaf should be awarded to the kettle-drummer, Herr Pfundt, who is swift and certain as thunder and lightning."[3] He was, as Schumann put it, "a true hero on his instrument," and his roll in the B flat symphony was a masterpiece such as could not be heard in Paris or New York. But perhaps the greatest compliment he ever earned was in 1846 when Wagner, in his proposed scheme for the reorganisation of the Dresden orchestra, recommended that Pfundt should be engaged as drummer.[4]

So, even though the *Gewandhaus* orchestra did not exactly scintillate with stars, it could show two brilliant high-lights in Queisser the trombonist and Pfundt the drummer.

During Mendelssohn's time the repertoire of the concerts was considerably enlarged. He introduced several previously unheard works by J. S. Bach (Concertos, Suite in D), by Schubert (C major symphony, 1839), by Schumann (B flat symphony, 1841), as well as a host of symphonies, concertos and overtures by contemporary composers who at that time were regarded as "promising." The first Schumann symphony caused some trouble owing to the technical awkwardness of some of the parts, and it took three special rehearsals before Mendelssohn was satisfied that it could

---

[1] *Music and Musicians*, I, p. 405.
[2] Thirty bars from the end.   [3] Schumann, I, p. 388.
[4] Pfundt was the inventor of a device for tuning timpani quickly and was the author of a School for that instrument (1849).

be played at a concert.   Nearly everybody found something to complain of
in Schumann's parts; the first two bars for the horns had to be altered, the
second violins were very much worried over a passage in the *finale* which
was particularly awkward to finger,[1] and the flautist Grenser didn't like his
cadenza in the same movement.   Only Pfundt, the drummer, was really
happy, for instead of playing on two drums, he now had to play on three !

With a body of good, but by no means outstanding players, Mendelssohn
raised the status of the *Gewandhaus* orchestra to a level which placed it far
above anything previously heard in Leipzig, and certainly in a position to
be counted amongst the best four in Germany.   Mendelssohn was in the
advantageous position of being free from the worries and routine duties of
an opera-conductor, and could therefore give the whole of his attention to
training the orchestra for concert playing.

Devrient was perhaps carried away a little by blind admiration when he
wrote: "He had brought the *Gewandhaus* concerts to a pitch of perfection
which placed them at the head of all symphonic performances in Germany,
and made them looked up to as the highest standard of excellence."[2]

Hiller's estimate was better balanced; he recognised that the *Gewandhaus*
orchestra could not compare with that of the Paris *Société des Concerts*, and
that there were "little imperfections in individual execution," which,
however, he thought were offset by the "spirit and life" of Mendelssohn's
conducting: "It was altogether a capital orchestra, though the only example
of extraordinary talent in it was Ferdinand David, who followed the conductor with his whole soul, and carried the whole of the strings along with
him.   Having for many years attended the Conservatoire Concerts in
Paris, I was naturally at first much struck by the contrast, especially in the
wind, and the general tone and effect.   At that time the Leipzig Conserva-
torium was not yet founded, and it was only afterwards that the *Gewandhaus*
orchestra gained such material and brilliant reinforcements from David's
pupils."[3]

Schumann's estimate of the Leipzig orchestra emphasises the united
family-feeling which permeated the whole organisation, and the complete
confidence in their conductor shown by all the players.   These valuable
qualities made up for the lack of distinguished players such as were found
in the larger German opera orchestras: "We have no solo-players like Brod
in Paris, or Harper in London; but even these cities can scarcely boast such
fine, united symphony playing.   And this results from the nature of circumstances.   Our musicians here form a family; they see each other and practise
together daily; they are always the same, so that they are able to play a
Beethoven symphony without notes (without the music).   Added to these a
concert-master who can conduct such scores from memory, a director who

---

[1] Bars 58 to 65.   Schumann got a violinist in the orchestra, Christoph W. Hilf, to go
through the violin parts with him before the rehearsal (Erler, I, p. 256).
[2] Devrient, p. 214.
[3] Hiller, *Letters*, p. 157.   The Leipzig Conservatoire was founded in 1843.

knows them by and reveres them at heart, and the crown is complete."[1]

Schumann also threw a little light on Mendelssohn's tendency to adopt fast *tempi* and its relation to the Leipzig players: "Then, with the orchestra, masses come into the question; rough, heavy players give to details, as to the whole, more weight and meaning; smaller, finer ones, like our Firlenzers (Leipzigers), must be helped out of their lack of resonance by hurrying the time."[2]

Perhaps it need hardly be said that Chorley was ecstatic in his praise for the *Gewandhaus* orchestra, its conductor and leader. Mendelssohn and David had been at Leipzig for four years when Chorley paid his first visit to Germany. A comparison with the playing of the Beethoven symphonies by the Paris orchestra was inevitable, and it would have been foolish to deny the Conservatoire players some merit; but what was mere brilliancy, delicacy, or mechanical perfection when weighed against the spiritual exhaltation which exuded from Mendelssohn, and against that understanding of German music which could only be found in true perfection at the place where the shrine of the Mendelssohn-worshippers was set up: "Never, indeed, did I hear the symphonies of Beethoven so intensely enjoyed as at Leipzig, and never as admirably performed. As regards those works of the Shake-speare of music, I felt, for the first time in my life, richly and thoroughly satisfied beyond reserve or question. There was a breadth and freedom in their outlines, a thorough proportion in all their parts, a poetical development of all their choice and picturesque ideas, which fully compensated for the occasional want of the hyper-brilliancy and the hyper-delicacy, on the posses-sion of which my friends in Paris boast themselves so vaingloriously. . . . Till, indeed, I heard the Leipzig orchestra, . . . I felt I had no right to say, 'Now I am indeed in the musical Germany of which I have so long dreamed.'. . . Had I not heard it, I should not have ventured to print the strictures upon that marvel of mechanical perfection, the orchestra of the Conservatoire, which are recorded in a former page of these journals." (See page 96.) Such a leader as David there had never been: "I have met with no one at the executive head of an orchestra to compare with Herr David. Spirit, delicacy, and consummate intelligence, and that power of communicating his own zeal to all going along with him, are combined in no ordinary measure, and with the crowning charm of that good-will and sympathy which only await citizens as worthy, head and heart (in the very best sense of the epithet), as he is."[3]

In 1842 Moritz Hauptmann left Cassel and settled down at Leipzig. In a letter to Spohr written in October of that year he gave his impressions of the *Gewandhaus* orchestra: "The orchestra here, in symphonies, under his (Mendelssohn's) direction is really excellent; there is a keenness and elasticity in the playing that is not easily found elsewhere. Mendelssohn is

---

[1] Schumann, I, pp. 364, 388.   [2] *Ibid.*, I, p. 38.
[3] *Music and Manners*, III, pp. 95, 103.

very pleased with it, but will not allow that the credit is due to him, for, as he says, although there are so many first-rate individual players in the Berlin orchestra, in spite of all his zeal and trouble, he can never get the same result as he can at Leipzig." In a later letter Hauptmann granted that the strength of the Leipzig orchestra did not lie in the skill of individual players: "When one hears the wind instrument solos, although some are excellent, others of them certainly leave something to be desired; but the ensemble is very satisfying, and the rhythmical impulse is as animated as one may hear in the performance of a good string quartet."[1]

Berlioz's judgement (1843) was certainly not clouded by blind admiration. The resources of Leipzig were rather strained in order to provide him with what he required for his exacting works: "The Leipzig orchestra is not larger than those at Frankfort and Stuttgart; but as there was no lack of instrumental resources in the town, I wished to increase it, and the number of violins was therefore raised to twenty-four—an innovation which, as I afterwards heard, aroused the serious indignation of two or three critics, who had made up their minds beforehand. Twenty-four violins instead of the sixteen that had hitherto sufficed for the performances of Mozart's and Beethoven's symphonies! What insolent affectation! . . . In vain did we try to procure three other instruments, marked for use, and indeed occupying rather prominent parts in several of my pieces (another dreadful crime); it was impossible to find a *cor anglais*, an ophicleide or a harp. Indeed, the *cor anglais* was so dilapidated, and so extraordinarily out of tune, that notwithstanding the talent of the artist who played it, we were obliged to substitute the first clarinet."

Hauptmann was present at Berlioz's concert, and commented on the extraordinary demands made in the French composer's score; 24 violins, 6 violas, 7 'cellos, and 5 basses were raised for the occasion, also four drummers playing on four drums; there were further demands for ophicleides, four horns and piano.[2] Berlioz recognised the value of the good training that the Leipzig players had had under Mendelssohn and David: "The orchestral arrangement in this beautiful room is so good, the relations of each performer with the conductor so simple, and the artists, besides being perfect musicians, so well trained in habits of attention by Mendelssohn and David, that two rehearsals sufficed to get up a long programme." His final words were certainly high tribute to an orchestra which was probably being put to a more severe test than it had ever before experienced: "As for the orchestra, to say that after only two rehearsals its performance was irreproachable, is to give it highest praise. All Paris musicians, and many others also, would I think be of this opinion."[3]

Unity of purpose and excellent team-work were no doubt always outstanding features in the playing of the Leipzig orchestra rather than the brilliance of individual players. Such corporate discipline may achieve

[1] Hauptmann, *Briefe*, III, pp. 5, 8.   [2] *Ibid.*, p. 11.
[3] *Mem.*, II, pp. 54–56.

PLATE 6

INTERIOR OF THE OLD GEWANDHAUS AT LEIPZIG IN MENDELSSOHN'S TIME

FERDINAND DAVID, LEADER AT THE GEWANDHAUS
UNDER MENDELSSOHN

PLATE 7

     ↑ Joachim   ↑   ↑ F. David   ↑
               Klengel   Julius Rietz

A Rehearsal at the Gewandhaus under Julius Rietz, c. 1850

better results than a combination of the very best players who are without it, and it was just in that respect that the London Philharmonic orchestra fell short and the Leipzig orchestra excelled. The *Gewandhaus* orchestra was no doubt correctly described in 1846 as "an orchestra equal in number and far superior in discipline to that of the London Philharmonic."[1]

Before 1842 the number of visitors to the *Gewandhaus* had increased considerably and more accommodation was called for. In that year another story was added to the old building, and galleries provided more room for the growing audiences. The hall was redecorated, and gas lighting was substituted for the old oil lamps.[2]

In 1848 Joseph Joachim, then aged seventeen, was an *Extrageiger* in the *Gewandhaus* orchestra, and for a short time from May in 1850 he became second *Concertmeister* beside David.[3] Joachim also relieved David of some of his arduous duties at the theatre in Leipzig; but his stay in the orchestra was short, and in October of 1850 he went as *Concertmeister* to Weimar. His successor at Leipzig was Alexander Dreyschock (1825–1869). The best double-bass player also went at the same time to Liszt's orchestra at Weimar. It was evidently not difficult to entice good players away from the Leipzig orchestra.

The violin and viola players at the *Gewandhaus* always stood when playing. It was not until ten years after Nikisch became the regular conductor that these players were seated.[4]

The *Gewandhaus* orchestra had earned its place amongst the best in Germany, and at the mid-century retained the distinction of being the only orchestra of importance in that country which existed independently of any theatrical institution. Julius Rietz was appointed conductor in 1848, and his successor, Reinecke, was able to celebrate the centenary of the society in 1881. Three years later the old building was abandoned, and a new and larger *Gewandhaus* arose, but not on the same site. The new palatial building was in the *Königsplatz*, and there under Reinecke, Nikisch, and Furtwängler were continued the concerts which had their origin so far back in the 18th century.

The rather small orchestra at the Leipzig *Stadttheater* was under the direction of Heinrich Aloys Praeger from about 1818 to 1828, and the players were drawn from the *Gewandhaus* orchestra, with Matthäi as leader. Between 1817 and 1828 the number of players rose from 27 to 33, and for special occasions the strings were augmented. There were only 18 string players in 1825, and in that year Smart wrote that it was "a good band, though the tone of the oboe is indifferent." When Spohr produced his *Berg-geist* there in the same year, he remarked that "the orchestra, although far inferior to ours (Cassel) was unusually good."[5] In 1828 Edward Holmes merely commented that the band was not extensive. Sterndale Bennett admired "some points" of the orchestra in 1836, and said that it was "more

---

[1] *Mus. World*, Dec. 12, 1846, p. 633.   [2] Creuzburg, p. 85.
[3] *Ibid.*, p. 93.   [4] *Ibid.*, p. 122.   [5] *Autob.*, II, p. 158.

musician-like than our orchestras in England, though it is far inferior in force and *spirit*."[1]

Praeger (son of the *Kapellmeister*) told how during the 'twenties it was the custom to play movements from Haydn's symphonies as entr'actes at the German theatres, and how at Leipzig they would break off suddenly at any moment when the bell was sounded for the curtain to rise.   He said that although the playing at the *Gewandhaus* was good, there was much careless playing in the theatre.[2]   Among the players was the famous trombonist Queisser, who had for his colleague in 1822–23 Wilhelm Wieprecht, the man who later became a great reformer and reorganiser of Prussian military music.[3]

Leaving the Dresden opera after Weber's death in 1826, Marschner became *Kapellmeister* at the Leipzig theatre for a few years before going to Hanover in 1831.   Wagner's friend (and later enemy) Heinrich Dorn conducted from 1829 to 1832,[4] and while he was there good-naturedly performed Wagner's first orchestral composition, an overture, of which the salient feature was a series of periodic thumps on the drum at every fifth bar.[5]

From 1833 to 1839 Stegmayer was *Kapellmeister*, and Julius Rietz occupied that position from 1847 to 1854.   Ferd. David continued to lead the orchestra at the theatre until 1851, and was sometimes relieved by the young man Joachim.   Between Stegmayer and Rietz there were several conductors; one of these (in 1839) was a man named Bach, an obscure Bach, of whom it was said that he had composed nothing.   Such a phenomenon was surely unheard of in Germany; a *Kapellmeister* who did not compose!   In 1844 the post of conductor was held for a short time by Lortzing.

It was at the Leipzig theatre in 1850 that Schumann's *Genoveva* was first produced, unsuccessfully, with the composer conducting.

A musical society called *Euterpe*, founded in 1824, functioned at Leipzig for some time as a rather feeble rival of the famous institution at the *Gewandhaus*, and admitted many amateur players into its orchestra.   It was at one of these concerts that the unfledged Wagner tried his wings in the capacity of composer and conductor, in an early overture in C.

Other German Orchestras

In a number of German towns, both large and small, and in a few quite small places where there was a court, permanent orchestras of from 40 to 50 players were maintained.   Most of these were there, in the first place, to play in the theatre, but they also supplied the players for concerts and for the church music in their respective towns and districts.

The orchestra at STUTTGART could look back to a time when it had ranked among the very best in Germany.   That was in the 'fifties and

[1] *Life*, p. 50.   [2] Praeger, p. 35.   [3] Kalkbrenner, p. 15.
[4] During these years the theatre came under the direction of the *Intendant* of the Dresden court theatre; in 1833 it reverted to the town.
[5] Chamberlain, p. 97; Wagner, *My Life*, I, p. 63; Newman, I, p. 85.

'sixties of the 18th century, when Jommelli was at the height of his fame, and as *Kapellmeister* and composer gave lustre to the musical establishment of the Duke of Würtemburg. Stuttgart never quite recovered its former musical reputation, and in the first half of last century could rank only after Dresden and Munich. At the beginning of the century Johann Rudolf Zumsteeg was *Kapellmeister* at Stuttgart. He died in 1802 and was succeeded by Johann Friedrich Kranz, who died in 1807. In that year, we are told, an obese and despotic King of Würtemburg kept up his state music, playing cards during the court concerts, and sitting in the cold theatre with his hands in a large muff.[1] Danzi, late of Munich, was *Kapellmeister* at that time.

Danzi's successor was Conradin Kreutzer, who was in charge from 1812 to 1816; then came Hummel, from 1816 to 1819, and then Lindpaintner, who remained until his death in 1856. Ignaz Lachner was also a conductor at Stuttgart for a few years, from 1831.

The *Concertmeister* were: Johann Ludwig Abeille from 1802; Franz Pechatschek was officiating in 1823, and from 1826 to 1849 Lindpaintner had a first-rate leader in Molique. Joseph Abenheim (b. 1804) assisted as deputy-leader and assistant-conductor from about 1830.

During Lindpaintner's rule the music of Stuttgart was in good hands, for he appears to have been a sound conductor who knew how to manage and train an orchestra.

Players of note who served in the orchestra at various times include the following: Nicolaus Kraft[2] the 'cellist, who played from 1814 to 1834, and another renowned 'cellist, Max Bohrer, from 1832 until his death; Carl Keller (1784–1855) a well-known flautist; Georg Reinhardt (b. 1789), reputed a very fine clarinet player, and Aloys Beerhalter (1800–1852), who also played the basset horn and stayed in the orchestra from 1828 until his death in 1852; two bassoon players, Anton Romberg, jun., and Wenzel Neukirchner (b. 1805) who in association with the Stuttgart maker Schaufler made some improvements to the German bassoon; the brothers Gottfried Schunke (1777–1840) and Michel Schunke (1780–1821), two members of a well-known horn-playing family, J. R. Lewy who later became Wagner's first horn at Dresden, and Ernst Schunke (b. 1812), son of Gottfried and his successor.

Smart wrote of the Stuttgart orchestra in 1825: "the orchestra was good, but not so good or so large as that at Darmstadt."[3]

In Berlioz's account of the Stuttgart orchestra in 1843 he said that it was "youthful, vigorous and full of fire," and that it contained a number of bold readers. The violins were "first-rate," and this Berlioz put down to the excellent training of Molique, the leader. The other strings were "very good," although not equal to the violins. The wind players were also good, but the old flautist Gottlieb Krüger (b. 1790), unfortunately used an "antique" instrument, and had an annoying habit of adding shakes of his own to the written parts by way of decoration. Neukirchner, the bassoonist,

---

[1] Spohr, I, p. 108.   [2] Son of Haydn's 'cellist at Esterhaz.   [3] Smart, *Journals*, p. 80.

was a first-rate virtuoso, but inclined to make "a parade of great difficulties." Berlioz criticised his intonation, and said that he played on a "bad" instrument; this was a cruel blow to Neukirchner, who played on a bassoon specially designed by himself and made for him by Schaufler. The first horn, Ernst Schunke, came in for only a qualified compliment, but Berlioz had a special word of praise for Gottlieb Krüger, jun. (1824–1895), the harpist, one of the very few good performers on that instrument then to be found in Germany. Perhaps the most remarkable man in the Stuttgart orchestra was Schrade the trombonist. He was "thoroughly master of his instrument," and caused general astonishment by sounding three or four notes at the same time![1] Altogether a good orchestra, if not very powerful, it gave at any rate an "intelligent, correct, and animated" rendering of Berlioz's difficult works.[2]

Very much in the same class as that at Stuttgart was the orchestra at FRANKFORT, but here there was no royal court to carry the music of the town on its shoulders, nor was there any long tradition to give it stability. At the beginning of the 19th century the theatre (*Komödienhaus*, 1782) was not yet twenty years old, and the permanent orchestra had been in existence only since 1792.[3] The theatre belonged to a local company or syndicate of townspeople who appointed a manager whose business it was to provide them with the sort of entertainment they wanted and to make the concern pay its way as far as was possible. It seems that the latter aim was not always achieved: "The theatre belongs to a society of subscribers, who study their pleasure more than the profit to be derived from it as a matter of speculation, for they have every year to pay a considerable sum beyond the receipts of the house."[4]

The first permanent *Kapellmeister* in the new theatre was Friedrich L. A. Kunzen, and he had Ferdinand Fränzl as his *Concertmeister*. A few years later Carl Cannabich was in charge, remaining until he went to Munich in 1800. From about 1802 until 1808 the violinist Joseph Schmidt (d. 1808) was in charge of the orchestra with the title of *Musikdirector*.

Spohr heard the orchestra in 1816 and pronounced it "excellent and worthy of its ancient (since 1792!) repute."[5] Notwithstanding that its repute was not so ancient as he thought, Spohr himself accepted the post of *Kapellmeister* in the following year and held it for two years.

Although quite satisfied with the orchestra, which he said was "one of the best in Germany," Spohr was not quite happy at Frankfort. His serious artistic aim did not at all fit in with the policy of a manager who was trying to make the theatre pay its way. At that time the leader was Heinrich Anton Hoffman, who had been there since 1803, so when Spohr

---

[1] There were several instances of wind players about that time who made a feature of simultaneously sounding more than one note, notably Bayr the Viennese flautist and Vivier the eccentric horn player.

[2] *Mem.*, II, pp. 20–25.   [3] Bacher, p. 90.

[4] *Harm.*, Dec., 1824, p. 229.   [5] *Autob.*, I, p. 217.

left, Hoffman was able to carry on the direction of the orchestra until 1821, when Carl Guhr was appointed *Kapellmeister*.

Little can be said of the personnel at Frankfort during Spohr's short time there. The first oboe in 1817 was Georg Christian Wilhelm Asmus Döring (1789–1833), who had a literary turn of mind and became a novelist and librettist.[1] His successor in 1818 was Friedrich Eugen Thurner (1785–1827), a fine player who already in Spohr's time showed symptoms of madness, and eventually died in a lunatic asylum. Weber's friend, A. B. Fürstenau, was flautist at Frankfort for three years before he went to the Dresden opera. Georg Reinhardt played the clarinet at Frankfort before going to Stuttgart in 1821, and from 1812 to 1815 the leading bassoon was Carl Almenräder, who was so influential in redesigning the German bassoon in conjunction with the maker Heckel.

Guhr's period at the Frankfort theatre, from 1821 to 1848, appears to have been quite successful. He was not so squeamish as Spohr, and his iron discipline apparently suited the orchestra and the conditions under which they worked.

Ed. Holmes was at Frankfort in 1827, and wrote his impressions of the orchestra in his *Rambles*. In this body of about 45 players, he said, the wind instruments, and particularly the horns and clarinets, were good, but the "string band wants weight as well as more bass; the violins seem to be always *con sordini*."[2] But the intonation was good and the ensemble "strict." Two symphonies by Wranitzky and Haydn were extremely well played and gave Holmes much pleasure.

Berlioz came to Frankfort in Guhr's time, and left an amusing account of his meeting with that stern conductor,[3] who, as Wagner said, belonged to the old German school, and was "sure of his business, strict, despotic, and by no means polite." Although Berlioz was unable to give a concert at Frankfort, he heard a performance of *Fidelio* under Guhr. As a theatre orchestra he thought it was first-rate; it was "admirable from every point of view. Not a shade escaped it; the tones melt into a harmonious and graceful whole; it never stumbles; it begins with *aplomb*, one might almost say like one instrument." Berlioz guessed that this was due to Guhr's strictness at rehearsal, as, no doubt, it was. The violins "belong to an excellent school; the basses have a great deal of tone." They had obviously improved since Holmes heard them. The wind instruments were "exquisite as a body," but Berlioz didn't like the "brassy" tone of the horns. It was clearly an efficient and a well-trained orchestra, even if all the material was not of the very best.

Soon after Berlioz, Chorley visited Frankfort in 1844, and remarked on the "brilliant orchestra" at the theatre.[4]

Guhr's successor at Frankfort in 1848 was Ludwig Schindelmeisser, and he in turn was followed by Gustav Schmidt (1816–1882) in 1851.

[1] He wrote the libretto of Spohr's *Berg-geist*. [2] *Rambles*, p. 38.
[3] *Mem.*, II, pp. 9–13. [4] *Mod. Ger. Music*, II, p. 228.

For orchestral and choral concerts there were two organisations at Frankfort. The *Museum* society, founded in 1808, catered for orchestral music, and the *Cäcilien* society, founded in 1818 by Johann Schelbe, for choral music. Both societies were conducted by Franz Messer (1811–1860) for many years before his death in 1860.

At DARMSTADT there was no question about making the opera-house pay its way; the Grand Duke had "so liberally endowed the theatre that the management has no need to study the taste of the public for the sake of receipts." On the face of it, this was an ideal state of affairs; there was no common public taste to cater for, it was art for art's sake. Of course, it was too good to be true; there must be a hidden snag somewhere. In this particular case the trouble was that the Grand Duke insisted on taking an active part in directing the rehearsals and the performances: "He takes a pleasure for instance in enacting the Director of Music, and Manager, in the opera-rehearsals; he therefore not only directs the orchestra from a desk in the theatre, but directs also every thing upon the stage. As he considers himself incapable of errors in both capacities, nor will allow either the director of the orchestra, or the stage manager to gainsay his regulations in the least, as a matter of course many mistakes occur." Under such conditions no orchestra could do itself justice, even if the material was of the best: "The orchestra is very numerous, and comprises several very good artists among its members; but there is also a good deal of ordinary talent among them. The Grand Duke may claim some credit for their *ensemble*, and particularly in the *pianissimo*; but as regards pure intonation, and clearness of expression, there is yet much to be desired. No orchestra in the world is so harassed as this is; for the whole of the members without exception, must attend every blessed evening in the theatre, from 6 to 9 or 10 o'clock."[1]

An English author has left the following quaint picture of an infatuated Grand Duke who cared more for his musical establishment than for the well-being of his Grand Duchy: "The opera is the ruling passion of the Grand Duke, but his subjects do not willingly see so much money spent on it by a prince who ranks so low among the 'German Gentles.' He has the best orchestra between Bale and Brussels, and the only fortification in his dominions is garrisoned by foreign troops. When, after long reluctance, he at length convoked a representative body under a new constitution, the first thing the representatives did was to quarrel with it as too antiquated and impotent. He trembled for the orchestra, became good-natured, yielded them more liberal terms, and, as they left his opera untouched, there have been no more squabbles."[2]

From 1807 until his death in 1814 the Abbé Vogler was nominally the *Kapellmeister* at Darmstadt, and from 1811 to 1820 the same position was held by Carl Jacob Wagner, a former horn player in the orchestra; but the

[1] Spohr, *Autob.*, I, p. 220.
[2] From *A Tour in Germany, and some of the Southern Provinces of the Austrian Empire, in the years* 1820, 1821, 1822 (London, 1824).

actual control of the orchestral playing seems to have been largely in the hands of the Mangold family, who knew quite well on which side their bread was buttered, and were content to be subservient to the vagaries of Grand Ducal interference.

In the 'twenties Georg Mangold (1767–1835) was *Kapellmeister* at Darmstadt, and in 1819 his son Wilhelm Mangold had become *Concertmeister*. The son succeeded his father in 1825, and remained until he was pensioned in 1858. Wilhelm Mangold's successor as *Concertmeister* was Louis Schloesser. The former's uncle, August Daniel Mangold, was leading 'cellist from 1814, and yet another Mangold, Carl Ludwig, played the violin in the orchestra from 1831 to 1839.

One of the celebrities in the Grand Duke's orchestra was August Müller (1810–1867), a man of colossal stature who made his four-stringed double-bass "sing out broadly and grandly"[1]; another was Johann G. Heinrich Backofen (1768–1839), a clarinet and harp player whose tutor for the former instrument was standard in Germany during the early part of last century.[2] Backofen came to Darmstadt from Gotha in 1811.

The words of Spohr already quoted refer to the year 1816. In 1824 the young embryo-statesman Disraeli paid a visit to Darmstadt, and wrote to his sister Sarah describing how the Grand Duke stood up in his military uniform at the opera, beating time for the performance. In 1825 Smart, and in 1828 Ed. Holmes, told practically the same story. Smart described how the Grand Duke sat in his box and closely followed the score of the opera, and told how he directed all the rehearsals and personally managed the whole concern. He described how the conductor, Wilhelm Mangold, "sat sideways with his little stick, and could therefore see the Grand Duke on his right and the singers on his left." The orchestra was ample and numbered 66 players, with percussion and extra instruments when necessary; all the members held their positions for life, and when they died their families would be provided for. The performance was Spontini's *Fernand Cortez*, and Smart "was delighted with the precision and complete well going of this orchestra."[3]

But the task of watching the Grand Duke in his box with one eye, and the performers on the stage with the other, and at the same time keeping the orchestra together in between the two, can have been no easy one. There can be no doubt about it; the conducting Mangolds fully earned their pay, their pensions, and the provision for their families after their decease.

Holmes's story a few years later is very similar: "At Darmstadt all is quietly and peaceably managed, probably because the grand-duke himself superintends the rehearsals. This venerable nobleman, now between seventy and eighty years of age, may on such occasions be generally seen standing at a music-desk on the stage, and directing the orchestra with the blandest and most affable demeanour. He appears to be the remnant of a tall well-built man, though his military uniform and sword show as if in

---

[1] Berlioz, *Mem.*, II, p. 142.   [2] Leipzig, 1803; 2nd Ed., 1824.   [3] *Journals*, pp. 76, 77.

L

mockery of a paralytic contraction which has bowed the wearer's head nearly to his chest." The Mangolds were obviously still subservient: "The road to promotion and court favour in this little state lies in musical skill, for an aide-de-camp of the duke's gave the time to the choruses; so that with this exalted assistance the capell-meister, M. Mangold, had nearly a sinecure." But apparently the performance was good, and one wonders if one of the Mangolds didn't do a little quiet rehearsing on the sly without the Grand Duke: "The interior of the house is roomy, and handsomely decorated; the band is the largest in Germany; the royal box is placed exactly in front of the stage, and the signs from it are most rigorously attended to during the whole performance. No beacon was ever more zealously watched in war-time than this by the capell-meister. As soon as the grand-duke and his suite were seated, the overture commenced,[1] and it was better played than I remember to have heard it even by the Philharmonic Society in London; the part in which the violins *con sordini* are accompanied by iterated notes on the violas, a very critical passage, was admirably executed; and much effect was produced by the basses leading off the little fugued point *pianissimo*, instead of the contrary, as is generally done."[2]

When Berlioz came to Darmstadt in 1842 the old Grand Duke was dead, and his successor left Berlioz to direct his own concert. They had five rehearsals, and all went well except a chorus in *Romeo and Juliet* which turned out to be "a regular vocal rout; the tenors of the second choir were nearly a semitone flat, and those of the first came in wrong at the return of the theme."[3] But the orchestra did its duty nobly; even the ophicleide was good, but of course one could hardly expect to find a good harp player in a German orchestra, and Darmstadt was no exception to the rule.

Just as the Mangolds managed to keep the appointments at Darmstadt as much as possible in the family, so the Müllers permeated the court orchestra at BRUNSWICK. Berlioz counted seven of the Müller family in the orchestra at the same time.

At the beginning of the century, when the youth Spohr was playing in it, little was heard of the orchestra at Brunswick; it was evidently small and undistinguished, and does not appear to have enjoyed much repute even amongst the second-class orchestras in Germany. In 1819, by which time he was *Kapellmeister* at Frankfort, Spohr heard it again in a performance of *Don Juan*, and remarked that it was then not so good as his own orchestra at Frankfort. In 1822 Gottlieb Wiedebein (1779–1854) became *Kapellmeister* at Brunswick, and in 1827 the theatre was renovated, the orchestra was enlarged, and some inefficient players were replaced. With Bösecke as *Concertmeister*, the reformed orchestra was evidently greatly improved. From 1832 Methfessel served as *Kapellmeister* for a period of ten years.

But it was not until a generation of Müllers, born between 1797 and 1809, grew up, and in the 'thirties began to attract attention by their remarkably good string quartet, that the orchestra at Brunswick came more to the

---

[1] *Euryanthe.*   [2] *Rambles*, pp. 46–50.   [3] *Mem.*, II, p. 142.

front, and for some time held a fairly high place amongst the second-rank German orchestras. Franz Fried. Georg Müller, second violin in the well-known quartet, was *Kapellmeister*, and as *Concertmeister* he had his elder brother Carl Friedrich, the first violin of the quartet. Both the remaining members, Theodor Heinrich (viola) and August Theodor ('cello) were leaders of their sections in the orchestra. The second *Concertmeister* was Julius Freudenthal, and other players amongst the strings were the violinist Zinkeisen, and the 'cellist and harpist Johann Adolph Leibrock (1808–1886), both of whom were picked out for special mention by Berlioz. Fried. Wilhelm Ferling (1796–1874) played the oboe from 1815 to 1859, and the clarinettist F. Tretbar, described by Schumann as an "excellent player," was playing his instrument during the 'thirties and 'forties.

It was when under Methfessel that Chorley heard the Brunswick orchestra in 1839. He found much to admire in the playing, and remarked on how neatly they managed a passage which had been found very troublesome at the King's Theatre in London.[1]

Berlioz (1843) found the Brunswick orchestra keen-spirited and ready to give unlimited time to mastering the considerable technical difficulties in his scores, and the result was an excellent performance at the concert.

The court orchestra at HANOVER seems to have ranked a step or two below that of Brunswick. In 1818 Wilhelm Sutor was appointed *Kapellmeister*; he died in 1828 and was succeeded by Heinrich Aloys Praeger (1783–1854), who served from 1829 to 1831. The orchestra probably improved when Marschner succeeded to that position in 1831, after experience at Leipzig and Dresden.

Several of the *Concertmeister* at Hanover bore distinguished names. There was Johann Wilhelm Leveque (b. 1759) in the early years of the century; Franz Pechatschek led from 1818, Ludwig Maurer from about 1825, Anton Bohrer from 1834, and Georg Hellmesberger, jun., for a short time just about the mid-century. In 1853 Hanover acquired a great leader, none other than the famous violinist Joseph Joachim, who held that position until the Prussians took possession of Hanover in 1866. A good leading 'cellist, August Christian Prell (b. 1805), came in 1826, after having played for about ten years in the theatre at Hamburg. Raphael Dressler (c. 1784–1835) was leading flautist from 1817, and August Kiel (b.ca. 1815) played the leading oboe part for many years at Hanover.

Smart had little to say about the orchestra in 1825; it was small, and although the bassoons were good, the violins were weak.[2] Berlioz (1843) was also rather lukewarm about the Hanoverian strings; there were some weak violins, he said, and there were not enough of them. But there were some good wind players. He praised the principal flautist, who would be Christian Heinemeyer[3] (1796–1872), and admired the "matchless pianissimo"

[1] *Music and Manners*, I, p. 294.   [2] *Journals*, p. 205.
[3] Heinemeyer played at the London Philharmonic in 1838.

of the oboe player Edward Rose. The first clarinet (Seemann[1]) had an "exquisite tone," and the two bassoons played in tune, which, he said, was a rare thing. One of the two thus complimented would be Schmitbach, who came to Hanover from the *Gewandhaus* orchestra at Leipzig in 1832. The trumpeter F. Sachse came in for high praise, and it was noted that he played on a valved instrument. The timpanist was only mediocre, and as for the man who beat the big drum—he was no musician!

The performance at Berlioz's concert was only "passable, but cold and somewhat feeble."[2]   Hanover clearly ranked below Stuttgart and Brunswick.

The orchestra at CASSEL appears to have had a rather fitful existence. When Jerome Bonaparte ruled Westphalia from 1807 to 1813 he certainly had an orchestra at Cassel, and Beethoven was invited to become its *Kapellmeister* in 1808. Reichardt accepted the offer which Beethoven had refused, and for some years there was an orchestra in which Feska was *Concertmeister*, Carl Keller (1784–1855) played the flute from 1806 to 1813, the unhappy Thurner was the oboist and the brothers Gottfried and Michel Schunke the horns. Reichardt did not remain long at Cassel, and already in 1809 King Jerome had made Blangini his musical director. The end of the Westphalian Kingdom put an end to the orchestra, and all the players were scattered.

In 1813 Hesse-Cassel became an Electorate, at which time the existence of an Electoral Orchestra is uncertain. By about 1820, however, it was under a rather undistinguished *Kapellmeister* named S. Benzon.

The Elector, wishing to improve his music, invited Spohr to come and be his *Kapellmeister* in 1822. Accordingly Spohr settled down at Cassel, and remained there for the rest of his life. The orchestra was then a mixed body of civilian and military musicians, all of whom were engaged for life. As Spohr could not get rid of any of them, he did his best to improve the orchestra by engaging some good civilian string and wind players, but he was obliged to keep his military musicians, uniforms and all.

Among the violinists Spohr collected at Cassel were his brother Ferdinand, Moritz Hauptmann, Friedrich Barnbeck who was his first *Concertmeister*, Adolph Wiele (b. 1794) who succeeded Barnbeck in 1836, Anton Bott (b. 1790) and his son Johann Joseph Bott (1826–1895) who became solo violin in 1846, *Concertmeister* in 1848, and second *Kapellmeister* with Spohr in 1852. The 'cellos included Hasemann, and from 1830 he had Carl Ludwig Dotzauer (son) as his leading 'cellist. Excepting Johann Conrad Bänder (b.ca. 1790), an exceptionally good clarinet player and pupil of Iwan Müller, the wind players do not seem to have been particularly distinguished.

Spohr claimed that after some preliminary training this orchestra became "one of the best in Germany."[3]   Smart heard it in 1825, and pronounced it "excellent"; he remarked on the fact that several of the players wore

[1] Saemann or Sämann. According to Gassner the best clarinet player in Germany.
[2] *Mem.*, II, pp. 138–9.   [3] *Autob.*, II, p. 144.

military uniform.[1] Moscheles said that the orchestra at Cassel was "splendid" in 1827, and in that same year Ed. Holmes recorded his opinion that Spohr had an "excellent band to write for, and one of the best clarinet players I have ever heard."[2] The compliment was undoubtedly intended for Bänder. Holmes also commented on the peculiarity that the orchestra was "half-filled with officers who fiddled in their regimental uniforms without considering it derogatory to the dignity of their profession."

Perhaps it was as well that Berlioz did not give a concert at Cassel in 1843, for he would not have got on particularly well with Spohr, who was rather suspicious of Berlioz's music, nor with Hauptmann, who called it *Barricadenmusik*.[3] Sterndale Bennett's comment in 1842 was: "I only wish our wind instruments in England would play as well in tune as they do here."[4]

There were one or two orchestras in Germany that had no very glorious past to look back upon, but which, if they had known, could have looked forward to a bright future. Such were the orchestras at WEIMAR and MEININGEN. The best days at Weimar were only to begin when Liszt became *Kapellmeister* there in 1848, and Meiningen had to wait until 1880, and for von Bülow and Steinbach, before it began to shine as a bright star among German orchestras.

The Grand Duke's musical establishment at Weimar was no very grand affair when August Eberhardt Müller came there as *Kapellmeister* in 1810. Nor did the small and peaceful Thuringian town show any signs of a brilliant musical future when Hummel succeeded to that post in 1819. The orchestra numbered only 30 players. August Riemann (1772–1826) was *Concertmeister* from 1818 until his death, when Carl Eberwein (b. 1784) took over that position. Johann Christian Lobe, who became an eminent writer and critic, was in the orchestra from 1811 till 1842, first as principal flute, and then as a viola player.

In 1826 a new theatre was built in place of the old one which had been burnt down; the opening of the new theatre served also to mark the jubilee of the Grand Duke, and a grand performance of *Semiramide* was given in Italian, a circumstance which drew forth some critical comments as to the propriety of inaugurating a German opera-house with an Italian opera.

The appointment of a Frenchman as *Kapellmeister* in a German court theatre was very exceptional, but Weimar provided an instance when Chelard came there as Hummel's successor in 1836. While Chelard was at Weimar he was assisted by a young pianist named C. Montag (b. 1817), who filled the position of assistant conductor (*Musikdirector*), and was very well spoken of by Schumann and by Gassner. Although not large, the orchestra gained in importance, and Berlioz thought it worth while visiting Weimar in 1843. At that time there were only 35 musicians on the permanent staff, but for Berlioz's performance the orchestra was specially augmented; the French composer, however, said that it was well organised, keen, and

[1] *Journals*, pp. 208, 216.   [2] *Rambles*, p. 276.   [3] *Briefe*, II, p .118.   [4] *Life*, p. 117.

sympathetic towards his music. There was, he said, an excellent first clarinet, and a good trumpeter who was E. Sachse,[1] brother of the Hanoverian trumpeter of that name; but, of course, there was no harp and no cor anglais.

Liszt had conducted some concerts at Weimar in 1842, but did not take up his permanent abode there until 1849. *Lohengrin* was produced in 1850, and in that decade the orchestra rose into greater prominence. It remained, nevertheless, rather a small orchestra, and had to make do with barely 40 players in 1850, not all of whom were of the best quality. The young Joachim became leader in 1850 and is said to have been very helpful to Liszt, who at that time was not very familiar with orchestral playing and management. Bernhard Cossmann, who had played in the leading orchestras at Paris, London and Leipzig, and was said to be the finest 'cellist in Germany, joined the Weimar orchestra about the same time, and was leader of his section. Liszt tried hard to improve the lot of his players in 1851, attempted to get rid of some who were too old, and asked for some additional players, but was told that his wishes could not be gratified. After his departure in 1858 the Weimar orchestra lost some of the prestige it had gained during the ten years when it was under Liszt and when Weimar became for a time a centre of advanced musical culture in Germany.

According to Spohr, the Grand Duke's orchestra at KARLSRUHE in 1816 was rather a second-rate affair: "the orchestra here, although latterly several distinguished artists have been engaged, is still very middling. A few good members cannot cloak the weak points of the rest."[2] At that time Danzi was *Kapellmeister* and Feska was *Concertmeister*. The latter was succeeded by Pechatschek in 1826. Karlsruhe remained rather in the background till after the middle of the century, but by the early 'sixties had an operatic establishment sufficiently good to have induced Wagner to contemplate producing his *Tristan* there.

Although the MANNHEIM orchestra could no longer rank as one of the best in Germany after the Elector had moved his court to Munich in 1778, it still retained a good reputation amongst the smaller German orchestras during the first half of last century. Although enjoying no great resources, the opera orchestra in 1824 was said to be good, and "animated with the true spirit of the art"; it was praised for its *ensemble*, and of some of the members it was said that they would "singly do honour to any orchestra."[3]

After being *Concertmeister* for some time, Peter Ritter held the post of *Kapellmeister* from 1803 till 1823. His successor was a violinist named Frey (d. 1832), who had also graduated as *Concertmeister*. The elder of the Lachners, Franz, spent two years as *Kapellmeister* at Mannheim (1834–36), and his younger brother Vincenz held the same position from 1836 until he was pensioned in 1873. The leading players at Mannheim in 1809[4] were

---

[1] The first translator of the *Memoirs* had probably confused Sachse with Sax the great Paris instrument maker.

[2] *Autob.*, I, p. 224.   [3] *Harm.*, Dec., 1824, p. 230.   [4] Weber, I, p. 179.

Keil (double-bass), Appold (flute), Christian Dickhuth[1] and Ahl (horns), and Ahl II (clarinet).

Berlioz was at Mannheim when the younger Lachner was conductor, and found there "a very intelligent little orchestra," although the trombones were "evidently incapable of playing their part."[2] But there was compensation in finding a good harpist and an oboist who played the cor anglais "passably."

A few court orchestras of the old household type still existed in Germany during the first half of last century. The duty for which they were retained was mainly to provide entertainment for the court, such as concerts in the evening, sometimes to play during meals or for dancing, or to take part in the chapel service.

At GOTHA, for example, the Duke retained a few string players and a small wind-band; these were combined to make an orchestra which was required to give a concert once a week in the palace chamber. The wind-band also played during meals, for court balls, or outdoor functions. As there was no theatre, the direction of the music was entrusted to a musician who combined the functions of *Kapellmeister* and *Concertmeister* in one person. At the beginning of the century Franz Anton Ernst[3] (1745–1805) was in charge of this little body of household musicians, and after his death Spohr discharged the same duty until he went to Vienna in 1812. Spohr gave the names of some of his players: Preissing, Bärwolf and Madame Schlick (violins); Joh. Conrad Schlick, Preissing, jun., and Rohde ('cellos); Hofmann (oboe), Johann Heinrich Walch (horn), and the well-known clarinet player Backofen, who served at Gotha in the capacity of clarinet, bassoon and harp player before he went to Darmstadt in 1811.[4] Andreas Romberg was at the head of the orchestra at Gotha from 1815, and was probably the last to occupy that position. In 1825 the court was broken up and the players were pensioned off when the Saxon Duchies of Koburg and Gotha were united in Saxe-Koburg-Gotha.

The court orchestra at RUDOLSTADT earned a good reputation during the 'thirties and 'forties for performances of Beethoven's symphonies under its conductor Friedrich Müller (1786–1871), who succeeded Eberwein in 1831, and remained at Rudolstadt until he retired with a pension in 1854. The theatre was open for only four or six weeks in the year, and all the rest of the year was spent in rehearsing and performing the classical symphonies, with the result that the playing acquired the smoothness and finish that can come only from constant practice under the same direction. Although numbering barely forty players, and not much in the public eye, this orchestra was able to earn the compliment that its performances of Beethoven's symphonies could hardly be bettered even at Leipzig.[5] Like many of the court orchestras in Germany, that at Rudolstadt was able to transform itself into a wind-band for use out-of-doors, and many of the players were necessarily

---

[1] Inventor of a slide-horn, 1812.   [2] *Mem.*, II, p. 39.   [3] Not the famous violinist.
[4] *Autob.*, I, p. 88.   [5] Loewe, p. 323.

double-handed. G. Müller, for example, a brother of the *Kapellmeister*, played the double-bass in the orchestra, and was first bassoon in the wind-band.

At DESSAU in Anhalt the Duke's orchestra, rather cut off from outside influences, was occupied mainly in the palace chapel and chamber, under the guidance of Friedrich Schneider, an organist-composer of the old school, who was greatly respected by German musicians. Schneider's position at Dessau was very much the same as that of Haydn at Esterház. The orchestra and choir were always at hand, ready to practice whenever they were summoned. The whole musical establishment was at the beck and call of the Duke, just like his household servants. There was no public to consider, no question of making anything pay, and no theatrical worries to disturb the peace and serenity of this little musical backwater.

Another of these toy orchestras was at HECHINGEN, where the Hohenzollern Prince "stood beside the kettle-drummer to count his bars for him, and make him come in in time." Thomas Täglichsbeck was *Kapellmeister* there from 1827, and "there were eight violins in all, three of them very feeble, three tenors, two 'cellos and two basses. Stern, the first violin, is a virtuoso of talent; so is Oswald, the first violoncello. The pastor and registrar at Hechingen plays the first bass in a manner to satisfy the most exacting of composers. The first flute, the first oboe, and the first clarinet are excellent, though the flute does occasionally indulge in those fanciful ornamentations with which I found fault at Stuttgart. The seconds among the wind instruments are passable. The two bassoons and the two horns are not quite all that could be desired. As for the trumpets, the trombone (there is only one) and the kettle-drums, one could have wished that they were absolutely silent—they knew nothing."[1] That is Berlioz's picture of the orchestra at Hechingen in 1843; yet they were bold enough to tackle a programme of the French composer's difficult works. But they were all quite happy, and the Prince thoroughly enjoyed himself.

When in 1849 this little state was absorbed by Prussia, the musical establishment ceased to exist; it was probably amongst the last survivors of the old household orchestras that had served as the breeding ground for German instrumental music before the general public had any share in shaping the course of the art in that country.

At Hamburg and Düsseldorf there were no courts, no princes or dukes to subsidise the music, so like Leipzig and Frankfort, these towns had to provide their own orchestras out of the pockets of their townsfolk.

HAMBURG, however, had its wealthy merchants, and to some extent they compensated for the lack of patrons of nobler birth. Spohr was pleased to commend the theatre orchestra in 1819, at which time, he said, it was superior to that of Brunswick. But there were obviously difficulties in keeping a good orchestra going without support from a court or state. The Hamburg correspondent of the *Harmonicon* commented on the situation in 1825 as

---

[1] Berlioz, *Mem.*, II, p. 29.

follows: "Music does not appear to prosper to such a degree in commercial towns such as our own, as in places graced by the presence of a court, and where the interest of the nobility is exerted in favour of art. Not that our town is wanting in warm and zealous supporters of music among the mercantile classes; all that we say is, that all is not done which even the modest friends of the art could wish. The truth is, we want an effective orchestra, and till that deficiency be made good, we can never hope to see music make that progress which its friends could wish."[1] It is clear that the orchestral resources of the large commercial town were not very imposing when the above was written, and although there was some improvement during the second quarter of the century, they never reached the grand scale of many lesser towns in Germany.

But Hamburg had its *Stadttheater* which, with the churches and concerts, kept a smallish orchestra employed. The newly-built theatre, however, gained strength when Carl Krebs came as *Kapellmeister* in 1827 and took the leading position in the secular music of Hamburg until the middle of the century. Various musicians, none of very great distinction, were occupied with the music of Hamburg towards the end of the 18th and in the first half of last century. Three generations of the Schwenke family were the leading musical spirits, but were concerned mainly with the church and choral music of the city. Methfessel, who eventually went to Brunswick, was *Musik-director* from 1822 for about ten years; Andreas Romberg was the foremost violinist until he left to go to Gotha in 1815, and in Prell they had a first-rate 'cellist up to 1826, when he was claimed by Hanover. The old bassoonist Johann Gottfried Schwenke was still playing when his son was *cantor*, and outlived him by a year. The flautist Peter Nicolas Petersen (1761–1830) spent almost the whole of his professional life in Hamburg, and was one of several who were each said to be the first to add chromatic keys to the flute during the last two decades of the 18th century.

In 1843 Berlioz found the orchestra at Hamburg rather small for his purpose, but they managed to augment it for the occasion, and he was able to report an "excellent performance," with special praise for Lindemann the leader of the violins, and for August Canthal who came to Hamburg as flautist in 1832.

DÜSSELDORF supported its orchestra in much the same way as did Hamburg, by keeping it employed at the theatre, in the churches, and at the concerts of the choral societies. The music of the town was at no very high level in 1833 when Mendelssohn came there as *Kapellmeister*. He soon gave up the irksome work at the theatre, and during the two years he spent in Düsseldorf, acted as a sort of general musical director, giving most of his attention to the concerts and church music, and acting merely as adviser to the theatre.

Mendelssohn's report on the orchestra was not at all favourable: "I assure you that at the beat, they all come in separately, not one with any

[1] *Harm.*, Nov., 1825, p. 212.

decision, and in the *pianos* the flute is always too high (sharp), and not a single Düsseldorfer can play a triplet clearly, but all play a quaver and two semiquavers instead, and every *Allegro* leaves off twice as fast as it began, and the oboe plays E natural in C minor, and they carry their fiddles under their coats when it rains, and when it is fine they don't cover them at all—and if you once heard me conduct this orchestra, not even four horses could bring you there a second time.   And yet there are one or two musicians among them, who would do credit to any orchestra, even to your Conservatoire; but that is just the misery in Germany—the trombones and the drum and the double-bass excellent, and everything else quite abominable."[1]

Julius Rietz followed Mendelssohn at Düsseldorf in 1835, and by 1847 had greatly improved the orchestra that Mendelssohn had found so hopeless. Hiller succeeded Rietz, and testified to the good work done by his predecessor: "At the end of 1847, when I came to Düsseldorf as Director, I found the music there on quite a different footing from that which Mendelssohn had described.   The twelve years' energy which Julius Rietz had devoted to it had not been in vain."[2]   Here was a case in which a lesser man, who was more patient and plodding, succeeded where a greater man had failed.   When Hiller left Düsseldorf in 1850 he handed over his post to Schumann, who was in no way fitted for such work.

At BRESLAU a rather small number of players provided the orchestra for a theatre which was run by a local company, for some concert-societies, and for occasional church performances.   Franz Tuczek was *Kapellmeister* at the theatre at the beginning of the century; he was followed by Heinrich Carl Ebell (1775–1824) in 1802, and the next to come was the young man Weber, who took the post of *Kapellmeister* at the age of nineteen in 1804, and held it for only two years.   Joseph Ignaz Schnabel, who was leader at the theatre as well as organist of the *Domkirche*, gave up his post when Weber came, and was one of several who did nothing to ease the work of the young conductor.

Gottlob Benedict Bierey followed Weber as conductor at the theatre, and remained until he retired in 1828.   Wilhelm Heinrich Heinze (b. 1790), a clarinet player who had been many years in the *Gewandhaus* orchestra at Leipzig, became *Kapellmeister* in 1839, and for his leader and solo violinist he had Johann Ferdinand Goebel (b. 1817), who succeeded Heinze in 1844. In that same year Gustav Adolph Heinze, son of the former *Kapellmeister*, became assistant-conductor.

The orchestra at Breslau was badly paid and the players were by no means of the best quality.   Those mentioned by Weber[3] were the violinists Jennizeck and Dozer, the 'cellists Hesse and Lohse (Lose), the flautist Adamy, the oboist Beskowsky, and Friedrich Wilhelm Berner, who in addition to being an organist was a useful clarinet player and an excellent timpanist.   Lincke, who was to become well-known as the 'cellist of the Rasoumowsky quartet in Vienna, followed Lohse at Breslau under Weber,

---

[1] Hiller, *Letters*, p. 46.   [2] *Ibid.*, p. 50.   [3] Weber, I, p. 91.

and remained until he went to Vienna in 1808. Weber tried hard to get rid of some useless players, and for two years he struggled with inadequate forces against opposition which became very irksome, and gave up his appointment at the end of the year 1806.

Schnabel was a strong musical influence at Breslau after Weber's departure; he was aided in his work by a violinist named Bernhard Forster (1750–1810), who led a concert-society formed in 1804 and named *Philomusische Gesellschaft*. Stölzel the horn player and valve inventor was at the Breslau theatre before he went to Berlin, and may have played in Weber's orchestra.[1]

The orchestra at Breslau never seems to have risen above the level of second-rate, if as high, and the comment by a correspondent of the *Harmonicon*[2] in 1825 that "the finish observable in the better orchestras of Germany is here wanted," was probably not unjustified.

Some other orchestras in Germany that could be classed as only third-rate were those at Cologne[3] (conducted by Weber's step-brother Edmund, and described by Smart in 1825 as "bad," and by Chorley in 1844 as "below mediocrity"), Mayence, Bremen, Nürnberg (described by Spohr as "remarkably bad"), Würzburg,[4] Koburg, Sondershausen, and a few other places. The Baltic towns Königsberg and Riga are of interest mainly because Wagner gained experience as a conductor in these places before he took his first important post at Dresden. Of the orchestra at Riga in 1826 it was said that it "can make no other than very modest pretentions";[5] these were evidently still modest in 1837 when Wagner became *Kapellmeister*, and had to manage with an orchestra of 24 all told, of which only seven were string players.

* * *

Although there were plenty of German orchestras in which the players were insufficient in number and by no means all of the best quality, the conditions under which most of them worked were more conducive to well-ordered playing than those prevailing in this country. While the English player was rushing about from one engagement to another, playing here under one conductor and there under another, rehearsing either hurriedly or not at all, the German player was generally a unit of a permanent body with a stable constitution which was under constant and continuous training, under which conditions the music could be absorbed more deliberately, more thoroughly, and thus could be built up into a performance in

[1] It was Bierey who wrote the short article about Stölzel's new valves in the *All. Mus Zeitung* in 1815, the first intimation about the new invention.
[2] *Harm.*, Jan., 1825, p. 16.
[3] Spohr's *Jessonda* was given at Cologne in 1825 with 10 violins, 1 viola, 1 'cello, 1 bass, and incomplete wind (Speyer, p. 87).
[4] An attempt to perform Beethoven's Choral symphony at Würzburg under Fröhlich in 1827 was given up as hopeless (Schreiber, p. 290).
[5] *Harm.*, March, 1826, p. 61.

which each player learned to know just what he was required to contribute to the corporate effort.   The typical German orchestra might well lack brilliance and spontaneity; the players might not be very fluent readers, and they might even lack technical skill, style and finish; but they were conscientious and painstaking, submissive to the will of their conductor, well disciplined and willing to work together for the good of the performance as a whole, with the result that the corporate playing was generally well co-ordinated and homogeneous.   The machinery of an orchestra can work well and smoothly only when each cog fits properly into its appointed place, when the controlling hand is used to running it, and when the parts are constantly lubricated by continual practice together.   These requirements were most frequently forthcoming under the German conditions of service, and to these invaluable assets the orchestras in that country have always owed their greatest merits.

But against the advantages of the German system there were, however, considerable disadvantages which kept the general level of performance below a standard which otherwise might have been very high.   The system by which players in the court orchestras generally held their positions for life was not without its drawbacks, and it tended to keep players employed when they were too old and past their best.   Berlioz and Wagner often complained that too many of the musicians in German orchestras were old and worn out; they clung to their offices only on account of the prospective pension which was to maintain them in a fairly advanced old age.   They were not only enfeebled by age, but were able to take little interest in their work.   The very security of employment that they enjoyed did not conduce to keenness and energy in the performance of their duty, but on the other hand fostered slackness and indifference.   The very general system of promotion by seniority instead of by merit did not operate in a manner favourable to the general efficiency, nor the circumstances by which permanent members of an orchestra were prone to secure employment for their sons or other relatives without due regard for their skill or suitability. Thus, security of tenure and lack of competition kept a brake on the efficiency of the old-established and court-endowed orchestras.

In many German orchestras the players were overworked owing to the theatres being kept open on every day of the week almost throughout the whole year, for, even though opera was not given every day, some of the players had always to be in attendance to play light operas, and to provide incidental and entr'acte music for the non-musical pieces.   The life, spent so much in the theatre, was unhealthy, and there was much sickness amongst the players.

The German players were almost all underpaid, and at a rate which did not take into account the steadily declining value of money during the 19th century.   Both Wagner and Meyerbeer made some effort to secure better conditions of life for the orchestral players at Dresden and Berlin, and Wagner in his proposed scheme for the betterment of the Dresden orchestra

in 1846 put his finger on most of the weaknesses of the system which made
the lot of an orchestral artist in Germany one of hard work and poverty,
and which deprived him of the wish to excel and put his heart into his work.

Thus, conditions which favoured the corporate efficiency of German
orchestras were offset to some extent by other conditions that constituted
drags on the wheels of progress, and gave these orchestras a sort of drab
homogeneity which was secured only at the cost of brilliance and energy.

Then, as now, discipline, solidity and order were the outstanding merits
of German music-making; but it takes more than these to make the perfect
orchestra.

V

Orchestras in England

THE history of London's orchestras during the first half of last century is closely wrapped up with the varying fortunes of its opera-producing theatres and concert-giving institutions; and these again have been closely associated with certain buildings which occupied particular sites in London.

Within a quarter of an hour's walk one could now visit the sites of the buildings (still occupied by theatres) wherein was enacted most of London's operatic history: the King's Theatre in the Haymarket (later Her Majesty's), the Little Theatre in the Haymarket (later Theatre Royal), Covent Garden Theatre, Drury Lane Theatre, and the English Opera House or (later) Lyceum Theatre.

A walk of little more than a few minutes would also suffice to visit the sites of the principal concert-rooms, namely, the Hanover Square Rooms, the Argyll Rooms, the concert-room in the King's Theatre, and the Pantheon. Other rooms which also enter into the story were: Willis's Rooms in King Street, St. James's Square; the Music Hall, Store Street, Bedford Square; the Albion Rooms in London Wall; the Freemason's Hall, and the Crown and Anchor tavern. During the 'thirties the new Exeter Hall in the Strand became the home of oratorio concerts given with amateur choral singers, and in 1850 John Hullah opened the St. Martin's Hall in Long Acre.

The Argyll Rooms served as a place of entertainment early in the 19th century, and in 1812 was already being used for concerts.[1] The building was originally situated in Argyll Street, but as a consequence of the new plan for laying out Nash's Regent Street, was rebuilt in 1820, and then formed the corner of Regent Street and Little Argyll Street. The new rooms were thus described in 1820: "They are noble rooms, and consist of four saloons, in one of which the refreshments are given, and in another public performances. The latter is more spacious (we believe) than any other in London, the Opera Concert Room perhaps excepted. The proportions are considered to be very fine. At one end is the platform, employed either as a stage or an orchestra; at the other, four tiers of boxes."[2] This building stood until it was destroyed by fire in 1830. Although again rebuilt, and still occasionally used for concerts, the Argyll Rooms never regained the reputation they had enjoyed as a musical centre from 1820 to 1830.

The Hanover Square Rooms, sometimes called the King's (Queen's) Concert Rooms, stood on the east side of the Square, near the south-eastern

[1] Edwards, p. 1.   [2] *Quar. Mus. Mag.*, Vol. II, No. VII, p. 385.

THE HANOVER SQUARE ROOMS IN 1843

corner, running east and west along Hanover Street, and were first adapted for entertainments in 1774 by the composer K. F. Abel in conjunction with Bach's youngest son, Johann Christian, and the dancing master Gallini. The large room was the scene of the famous Bach-Abel concerts from 1775 to 1781, of the Professional Concerts (1783), and the historic Haydn-Salomon concerts of 1791 and 1794; it provided the most suitable hall for orchestral concerts in London until St. James's Hall was opened in 1858.[1]

The following[2] will give some idea of the relative sizes of these concert rooms in comparison with the dimensions of St. James's Hall:

	Length in feet.	Width.	Height.
Hanover Square Rooms ..	90	30	—
Concert Room in King's Theatre	100	50	—
Freemason's Hall	90	43	60
Exeter Hall	133	77	52
St. Martin's Hall	121	55	40
St. James's Hall	134	60	60

According to a contemporary authority, the Argyll Room could seat not more than 800 people; the Hanover Square Room could accommodate between 800 and 900, and Willis's Room about 900 people.[3]   The platform area in the Hanover Square Room was said to be 943 square feet, in comparison with 1,271 at St. James's Hall.[4]

The Pantheon, more theatre than concert-room, stood nearby in Oxford Street.   It was destroyed by fire in 1792, but was rebuilt and remained in use as a place of entertainment until about 1814.

From a musical point of view, the most important theatres were the King's Theatre, Covent Garden, Drury Lane, and the Lyceum Theatres. Opera was also produced intermittently at the Little Theatre in the Haymarket, and on a small scale at a few other and smaller of the London theatres.   Oratorio concerts were given during the Lenten season at the three principal theatres, the most important being those at Covent Garden and Drury Lane.   According to Parke, Covent Garden was "the most musical of the two houses."[5]

London's central opera-house was the King's Theatre in the Haymarket. Vanburgh's original building, dating back to 1705, was burnt down in 1789, and the second building was opened in 1791.   Largely reconstructed in 1819, and again altered in 1825, this building included a fairly large concert-room which was known as the Great Room, King's Theatre, and which should not be confused with the King's (or Queen's) Concert Rooms, as the Hanover Square Rooms were often called.[6]   Nash's theatre stood

---

[1] "The Philharmonic Concerts are now (1869) given at St. James's Hall, and the late Hanover Square Room, the best in London for music, has been converted into a West End Club" (Ella, p. 72).
[2] *Illus. Lon. News*, Dec. 20, 1856.   [3] *Harmonicon*, Sept., 1829, p. 217.
[4] *Illus. Lon. News*, June 18, 1859.   [5] Parke, I, p. 282.
[6] The concert room at the King's Theatre was let only on the condition that artists appearing at the opera were engaged (Kuhe, p. 360).

PLATE 8

New English Opera House (Lyceum Theatre) in 1821

Theatre Royal, Haymarket, 1824

PLATE 9

THE KING'S THEATRE, HAYMARKET, AFTER RECONSTRUCTION IN 1819

until 1867, when it was burnt down. The King's Theatre was the home of Italian opera in London, and there the most famous singers and the largest and best orchestra were heard.

The first Covent Garden Theatre (1732) was burnt down in 1808, and was quickly rebuilt and re-opened in the following year. After considerable reconstruction in 1846, this theatre was re-opened as the Royal Italian Opera in 1847, and from that time began to take its place as London's central opera house, while the King's Theatre began to lose its former supremacy. Again destroyed by fire in 1856, Covent Garden Theatre was once more rebuilt and re-opened in 1858.

At the beginning of last century Drury Lane Theatre was the second building of that name to occupy the same site; this was opened in 1794. Burnt down in 1809, it was again rebuilt and re-opened in 1812.

On the site of the Lyceum Theatre there had been a building used for exhibitions of various sorts since 1765. This was converted into a place of entertainment about 1790, and in 1798 the interior was reconstructed, with the intention of using it as a theatre, by Dr. Arnold. Arnold's venture did not materialise, and after having been occupied by various speculators, the theatre was taken over by Dr. Arnold's son in 1809 for the purpose of producing English opera.

The building again underwent considerable reconstruction and enlargement in 1815–16, and stood until it was burnt down in 1830. Again rebuilt, it was re-opened in 1834. Balfe took over the management in 1841, and soon after that it ceased to be an opera house.

The Theatre Royal, Haymarket, opened under that name in 1824, stood on the site adjoining that of the original Little Theatre in the Haymarket. The old theatre dated from 1720 and was pulled down in 1820.

The following will give some idea of the size of the auditorium in the three principal London theatres[1]:

King's Theatre.　From curtain to box, 90 feet; width of pit, 62 feet.
Drury Lane.　　　,,　　,,　　,,　　,,　61　,,　;　,,　　,,　　,,　50　,,
Covent Garden.　,,　　,,　　,,　　,,　63　,,　;　,,　　,,　　,,　50　,,

Covent Garden and Drury Lane theatres were associated more particularly with a certain type of English or song-opera which followed the ballad-operas of the 18th century. In these the spoken dialogue was broken up by songs, duets, glees and choruses, introduced for their entertainment value rather than for the purpose of developing the drama. The music was generally composed, adapted, or compiled by English musicians who were on the spot and ready to use *any music* that suited their purpose. Planché, the dramatist and libretto-writer, wrote of these operas: "Ballads, duets, choruses, and glees, provided they occupied no more than the fewest number of minutes possible, were all that the play-going public of that day

---

[1] From Comparative Dimensions of the Various Theatres, by Samuel Beazley, architect.

would endure."[1]   Many of these so-called operas were the work of several composers; the celebrated tenor, Braham, often composed or provided his own songs when he sang in this particular brand of opera.   Shield, Dibdin, Hook, Horn, Reeve, Kelly and Bishop, are only a few of the musicians who provided the music for these loosely-constructed operas.   In addition to the English operas, and interspersed among the tragedies, comedies and pantomimes which alternated with the musical pieces, occasional productions of Italian opera in English were given, and from the 'twenties some German and French operas were also sung in English, freely altered or adapted to suit the English stage and taste.

In spite of persistent failure, bankruptcy, and all the financial risks and difficulties which have always attended the promotion of opera in this country, some hopeful speculator was always found who was ready to take over from another disillusioned promoter the difficult reins of opera-management in a country where opera would never thrive, yet would never die.   But whatever his prospects, the London impresario in the 19th century could always count on two things, namely, that he would have an exciting time, and that sooner or later the theatre would be burnt down. The following was said to be the answer of an "eminent professor" to an invitation to undertake the management of the Italian Opera in London for three years: "Give me such terms as will secure a provision for my family, and three months to make a tour of all the madhouses and select the one which I should prefer for my final retreat; and then I may talk with you."[2]

The contemporary writers on whose chronicles we depend for our knowledge of the story of opera in London during the first half of last century appear to have overlooked the fact that where there was opera there was also an orchestra.   They invariably treat the singers handsomely and never tire of describing their voices; the management is given a very fair share of attention, and even the composers who wrote the operas are not altogether ignored.   But that an orchestra had any share in the production is rarely hinted at or thought worth mentioning.   Owing to the lack of information, and to the fact that so many records have been destroyed in the periodical fires at the theatres, the task of reconstruction is difficult, and gaps in the sequence of events must be expected.   The story of the orchestras can be pieced together only from scraps of information found in contemporary musical journals or periodicals, mainly from the *Quarterly Musical Magazine*, the *Harmonicon*, the *Musical World*, and from such stray comments as may be found in the books of the period.

THE KING'S THEATRE

In 1817–18 there were 46 players in the orchestra,[3] but according to Ella,[4] the number had risen to 50 in 1822.   At that time it certainly included

[1] Planché, I, p. 80.   [2] *Harm.*, July, 1830, p. 286.
[3] *Quar. Mus. Mag.*, Vol. I, No. II, p. 257.   For full list, see appendix, p. 488.
[4] Ella, p. 310.

the pick of London's instrumentalists, at all events up till about 1825–26, after which some deterioration set in, ending in the dismissal or resignation of many of the best musicians just before the season of 1829. Apropos of this, Parke wrote : "it must have struck every one capable of judging, that the band of the Italian opera was vastly inferior to what it had been: it had indeed been declining for several seasons. This has proceeded, no doubt, from the salaries of the instrumental performers having been so much reduced, that musicians of superior talent would not remain in the orchestra."[1]

Already in January, 1826, it was remarked in the *Harmonicon* that "the scandalous manner in which many of the longest established and best performers in the orchestra have been treated, in order to make way for a set of boys,[2] will doubtless meet with the reproof which it so richly merits."[3] In the following July the orchestra was referred to as "the abused and comparatively ill-paid orchestra,"[4] and in the following month a member of this "ill-paid orchestra" wrote to explain the causes of the trouble. These were: "The introduction of a bevy of boys, to the exclusion of many excellent performers"; the "want of anything like system in the general management of the theatre; the multitude of directors, not one of whom seemed to have the least knowledge of his duties; and the manner in which the rehearsals have been conducted."[5]

In 1827 the fortunes of the orchestra were still falling: "The orchestra too, which boasts amongst its numbers many of the best performers in Europe, is weakened, and the balance that ought to subsist between the stringed and wind instruments is destroyed, by a reduction of the violins: reduced not only numerically, but by the dismissal of some most excellent musicians, and the introduction of inexperienced persons."[6] A little later the same writer continued in a similar strain: "Mr. Spagnoletti has labour enough on his hands to keep his orchestra together; for, weakened as he is in his violins, by a diminution of their number, and by the introduction of feeble players among those who are left, he is obliged to work with a six-fiddle power, to preserve anything like an equality among the various instruments."[7]

Early in 1828 an "intelligent correspondent, who is an able judge, and a credible witness," wrote as follows: "This department (the orchestra) was, according to public announcement, to be considerably augmented, by performers from the Philharmonic and Ancient Concerts. *Not the smallest increase has been made*; by far the greater portion of those whose names are now, for the first time, ostentatiously, and as a blind, inserted in the bills, have been in the opera band for many seasons. But why did not the

[1] Parke, II, p. 270.
[2] This no doubt refers to the engagement of a number of R.A.M. students in 1826 (*Quar. Mus. Mag.*, Vol. VIII, No. XXX, p. 148).
[3] *The Harm.*, Jan., 1826, p. 20.　　　[4] *Ibid.*, July, 1826, p. 154.
[5] *Ibid.*, Aug., 1826, p. 162.　　　[6] *Ibid.*, March, 1827, p. 58.
[7] *Ibid.*, June, 1827, p. 124.

'stage-manager and director of the music' honestly tell the subscribers that Messrs. Mori, Lyon, F. Ware, Monzani jun., four principal performers, and others, had resigned their situations in disgust. Where then is the augmentation?—Yes, there is one added; a person imported from a provincial theatre, who is to fiddle in the orchestra, and to write puffs in the newspapers, in support of his friend and patron, the 'stage-manager,' Nicholas Charles Bochsa! Something, however, is done; the leader of the band is deprived of his legitimate power, by not having been permitted to have a voice in choosing the band over which he is to preside, and for which the leader is responsible."[1]

In September of the same year, one who called himself "Dilettante" reported that "an attempt is making to still further reduce the salaries of the orchestral performers of the King's Theatre. They are already paid five-and-twenty per cent. below their value; and, it is a fact worth recording, that the *whole* of this excellent band, including persons who cannot be matched in Europe, were, during the late season, not paid, per night, one half of what Mad. Pasta, or Mdlle. Sontag, received for a single performance."[2] October brought a letter from "one of the band at the King's Theatre," bitterly complaining, not only about a reduction in pay, but also about the "tyrannical conditions" under which they were required to work, and the blame for this deplorable state of affairs was fixed on the notorious harpist Bochsa, who at that time held an influential position in the management and musical direction of the theatre.[3]

The climax came just before the beginning of the 1829 season, when it was announced that Spagnoletti, the two Lindleys, Dragonetti, Anfossi, Nicholson, Willman, Mackintosh, and many others "have, with becoming spirit, refused the conditions attempted to be imposed on them, and retired."[4] It was said that an effort was being made to import musicians from abroad to take the vacant places.

At the beginning of 1829 the principal players in the orchestra issued a pamphlet in which they complained about the terms and conditions offered them for the coming season.[5] Their grievances were set forth in *The Harmonicon*,[6] prefaced as follows: "The dispute which for some months has existed between the principal members of the Opera orchestra and M. Laporte (the manager), having ended in an open rupture, and in the resignation of nearly all the most efficient performers, the latter have published 'An Explanation of the Differences existing between the Manager of the Italian Opera and the non-conforming Members of the late Orchestra. Written amongst themselves'—a pamphlet of fifty octavo pages, very temperate in language, strong in facts, irrefragable in argument, and

---

[1] *The Harm.*, Feb., 1828, p. 48.   [2] *Ibid.*, Sept., 1828, p. 210.
[3] *Ibid.*, Oct., 1828, p. 224.   [4] *Ibid.*, Dec., 1828, p. 276.
[5] This was signed by R. Lindley, C. Nicholson, Thos. L. Willman, John Mackintosh, Henry Platt, Thos. Harper, S. P. Aufossi, F. W. Crouch, Jas. Taylor, W. Wagstaff, James Rae, Philip Powell, W. Lindley, George Anderson, George Nicks, and W. Card.
[6] *The Harm.*, Feb., 1829, p. 35.

convincing to all who are not determined to support such an alien as Bochsa against a body of most respectable musicians, of native talent that may challenge competition with the finest performers in Europe. Competition, did we say!—where are to be found the equals of such artists as Lindley, Nicholson, Willman, Mackintosh, Harper, etc., etc.?—they are not to be matched in the world; and yet an attempt is made to reduce their salaries, now too low, and to degrade them, though already too much depressed, by requiring them to sign conditions which the humblest mechanics would revolt at; and, what is worse, more insulting than all the rest, to set over them, with almost unlimited power, such a man as the notorious Bochsa!—Nay, to call upon them *now* to bind themselves to obey regulations not specified or even hinted at, but such as it may *hereafter* suit the caprice or the personal views of that man to issue."

Parke wrote of the King's Theatre in the 1829 season, that it had suffered from "the loss of several of the principal performers in the orchestra, Messrs. Lindley, Willman, Nicholson, Harper, etc., on account of the reduction of their salaries, and the importation of lots of Frenchmen from Paris to succeed them."[1] The loss to the orchestra was severe, even though Dragonetti remained as leading bass player. So we learn that "poor Spagnoletti is to be commiserated; his force of violins is reduced to sixteen, out of which not more than half a dozen are really efficient. But M. Laporte has shown great judgement in engaging the two Gambati as trumpeters; they completely drown the band, and screen all its weaknesses and failures from detection. . . . Who now fills Lindley's post as first violoncello?—Let him, whoever he may be, learn to accompany the recitatives better. Who is seated at the piano-forte? Alas! no Scappa, that excellent pianist;—not Coccia, the able, the watchful *Maestro*; but someone who undertakes—we do not assert that he fulfils—this important duty at twenty shillings a night!"[2] A Mons. Rousselot had, in fact, replaced Lindley at the first desk with Dragonetti; his playing was described as being "not ordinarily, but ridiculously bad," and it seems that Joseph Williams had taken Willman's place as first clarinet.[3]

The playing of the orchestra during the season of 1829 was harshly criticised: "Thus it will appear that the opera was upon the whole well performed *on the stage*. In the orchestra it was just as much the reverse; we never before heard so many blunders and so much bad playing in this theatre; and as to the Signori Gambati, they are a perpetual source of distraction and head-ache. Theirs are Brobdignagian penny-trumpets, the sound of which would infallibly raze the walls of the house, had these the sensibility of their ancestors, the walls of Jericho."[4] It appears that the Gambati brothers, who came to London in 1826, played upon keyed-trumpets: "Their execution is wonderful; but their instruments being furnished with keys, enable them to increase facility by means that take very

[1] Parke, II, p. 268.
[2] *Harm.*, March, 1829, p. 70.
[3] *Ibid.*, June, 1829, p. 145.
[4] *Ibid.*, May, 1829, p. 122.

much from the astonishment which they create at first hearing.   Their tone is rough and raw in comparison with Harper's."[1]   In *Don Giovanni*, "the band was, as it has always been this season, a chaos.   The few superior performers in it do rather more harm then good,—they expose the faults of the majority."[2]   Referring to the same opera, another writer pronounced it to be "a most imperfect performance upon the whole, on account of the miserable condition of the band."   It was explained that "the well-trained and established players had revolted against M. Bochsa's direction, and were superseded by a set of incompetents, who, whatever their individual talent might have been, were prevented from displaying it through the miserable ignorance of the harpist—or "harpy"—musical director, who not only could not read a score, but was totally ignorant of the smallest characteristics of his important office."[3]

The season of 1830 saw the orchestra still in a low state: "For these defects on the stage, the orchestra afforded no compensation; reduced in number, deficient in rehearsals, and sometimes without books to play from, the scenes of confusion continually witnessed in this department were unparalleled in the annals of the King's Theatre."[4]   A French critic could find nothing good to say about it just at that time: "The orchestra is far from equalling our own; no *ensemble*, no light and shade.   The musicians, individually *mediocre*, are desirous of attracting attention, to which end they blow and scrape with all their might, making such a din, that singers who have not an extraordinary power can with difficulty be heard."[5]   Perhaps the French critic was not aware that there were several "imported" Frenchmen in the orchestra just then.

But already in that same year there were signs that things were taking a turn for the better, and the reason for this improvement was said to be because "M. Bochsa is no longer director of the music; and one of the good consequences of his removal is the return to the orchestra of those unmatched performers, Lindley, Willman, and Harper."[6]   The orchestra then numbered 48 players; and under the management of Monck Mason, who had succeeded Laporte, better things were promised.   In his prospectus, the new manager promised that: "The various parts whereof the orchestra is to be composed, shall be arranged in such a manner, and made up of such materials as are most capable of conducing to the general effect.   The number of the Band will be increased, and the Director guarantees, that whatever alterations he may be induced to make, shall be only for the purpose of insuring to the Public the first *dramatic* Orchestra in Europe."[7]

The worst of the troubles of the orchestra seem to have been over by 1832. About that time the strength was raised to 58 players, excluding percussion and any extra instruments that were required.   (See Appendix, p. 488.)

---

[1] *Quar. Mus. Mag.*, Vol. VIII, No. XXX, p. 134.   [2] *Harm.*, Aug., 1829, p. 205.
[3] Anon., *Mus. Recoll.*, I, p. 173.   [4] *Harm.*, Jan., 1831, p. 1.
[5] *Ibid.*, July, 1831, p. 174.   [6] *Ibid.*, March, 1830, p. 134.
[7] *Prospectus*, Oct., 1831.

With the return of most of the former leading players, and the appointment of Costa as musical director and conductor, the story of the orchestra
at the King's Theatre is one of steady improvement during the 'thirties, and
one which was to continue almost up to the mid-century, by which time
Covent Garden Theatre had usurped its place as the home of Italian opera
in London, and the King's Theatre was losing its supremacy.

It is improbable that the orchestra at this theatre was ever conducted with
a baton until some time after Costa went there in 1830. The old custom
was to get some foreign composer, usually an Italian, to come and write
operas for the theatre and to direct the performances, perhaps for a few
seasons. For the time being this composer was the *maestro di capella* or
maestro al piano, who superintended the performances, but who left it to the
violinist-leader to control the playing of the orchestra. Such "conductors,"
as they were often called, were Bianchi, Nasolini, Winter[1] (1803–5), Scappa,
Coccia, Radicati, and others whose numerous operas disappeared for ever
when the vogue for Rossini's music set in. Rossini himself was engaged
for the season of 1824 as "director and composer to the King's Theatre."
His duty was to "preside at the pianoforte," as they called it, and to write and
produce new operas. For the next season (1825) Sig. Coccia was "composer
and conductor" to the King's Theatre. At the end of 1826 Coccia was
described as having "for some years past presided at the piano-forte of the
King's Theatre as Maestro."[2] When the composer was not present, a
permanent *maestro al cembalo* sat at the piano and guided the singers on the
stage, but was in no sense conductor of the orchestra. Among those who
at various times occupied this position before 1830 were Federici, Scappa,
and Coccia.

The office of "composer and conductor" began to die out during the
third decade of the century, and another, called the Director of the Music,
began to take shape. Ebers, who managed the theatre from 1821 to 1828,
wrote: "I have already stated my opinion, that in this country a composer of
operas is an unnecessary part of the establishment of the King's Theatre."[3]
Ebers outlined the functions of the Director of the Music as follows:
"The opera is under the guidance of the director of the music, if any is
employed. The director assists the manager in the selection of the performances; and when fixed upon, he distributes the parts to the singers, and
directs the general routine of representation, the effecting of which, in the
minute details, devolves on the stage-manager and the conductor of the
music."[4] Or course, there was no conductor; by "conductor" Ebers
meant the violinist-leader of the orchestra, who at that time was Spagnoletti.
Bishop was Director of the Music in 1816, and William Ayrton occupied
that position in 1817 and again in 1821 and 1825.[5] In 1822 the Chevalier
Petracchi from Milan was Director—"a man who, though so well

[1] "Composer to the King's Theatre" (Parke, I, p. 312).
[2] *Harm.*, Dec., 1826, p. 250.   [3] Ebers, p. 362.   [4] *Ibid.*, p. 361.
[5] Ayrton was the first editor of *The Harmonicon* (1823).

recommended, was a mere cypher as a successor to Mr. Ayrton."[1]   Ebers
evidently made an unlucky choice; he quoted an extract from a letter written
to him by someone who knew something of Petracchi: "you have bought a pig
in a poke in the bargain you have made with your Chevalier, who, I suppose,
is now on his road from Milan.   He seems well known to the musical
people here.   I have made enquiries of several, . . . all tally in the same
description, namely, that he knows nothing of music, and that he cannot
even *blow*, *scrape* or *thump* a tune upon any one instrument."

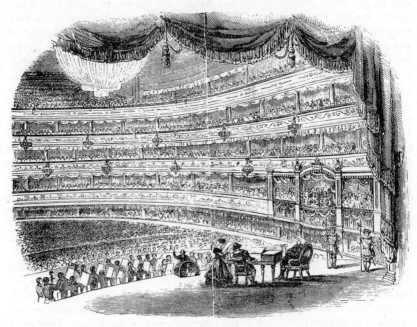

HER MAJESTY'S THEATRE (LATE KING'S THEATRE) IN 1843

In 1825 Ayrton was again Director, and in 1826, for a short time, the
singer Velluti acted in that capacity.   This was when Coccia was "composer"
to the theatre and *maestro al piano*.

The ballet, always an important feature at the King's Theatre, had its
own staff, and a composer and director of the music who was independent
of the regular opera staff.   Thus, the harpist Bochsa was composer and
director of the music for the ballet for some years during Eber's management.
This disreputable man, a refugee from French justice, having been placed
in a position of responsibility at the Royal Academy of Music, was dismissed
in 1827 in response to public attacks on his character.   In 1826 he was
attached to the King's Theatre as director of music for the ballet, and

[1] Ebers, p. 150.

although he was not actually responsible for the playing of the orchestra, he managed to secure a predominant position in the musical administration of the theatre, and was evidently the cause of all the troubles of the orchestra between 1826 and 1830. He was eventually ejected from his position at the King's Theatre after numerous defamatory letters and articles concerning him had appeared in the London papers.

Costa was made *maestro al piano* in 1830; two years later he became Director of the Music, and in 1833 his position was that of both director and conductor of the orchestra. It is probable that he began to use the baton and to exercise undivided control over both singers and orchestra early in the 'thirties, while the violinist-leader lost his power and subsided into being merely principal first violin. Costa remained in command until 1846, and in the following season he went to Covent Garden as conductor of the new Royal Italian Opera. Costa was succeeded at the King's Theatre (then Her Majesty's) by Balfe, who remained there until 1852.

Before Costa began to conduct the orchestra with a baton, it was the leader who held the most responsible position. Early in the century this post was occupied by Charles Weichsell, who came in 1802 when his sister Mrs. Billington, then at the height of her fame, was also engaged to sing.[1] Weichsell was still leading in 1818,[2] but must have retired soon after in favour of Spagnoletti, who continued playing the leading violin part almost until his death in 1834. In the meantime it appears that Nicolas Mori, who was in the orchestra from about 1810, had become leader and solo violin for the ballet, for we learn from *The Harmonicon* that in 1824 "Mori, one of the finest violin-players in Europe, and highly qualified by long experience for leading the Ballet, is displaced without any cause."[3] Nadaud, a violinist from Paris, who later became Jullien's leader at the Drury Lane promenade concerts, seems to have followed Mori as leader and solo violinist for the ballet. In Weichsell's time, Cotton Reeve (c. 1777–1845) was leader of the second violins, and Richard Ashley was principal viola.

That the leader was virtually in control of the performance is confirmed by a passage in a letter written by Mendelssohn soon after his first visit to the King's Theatre in 1829: "The orchestra very good, conducted by Spagnoletti (in December I will give you an imitation of him which will make you die of laughter)."[4] After Spagnoletti's death in 1834, Mori succeeded to his post as leader, and when the latter died in 1839 Auguste Joseph Tolbecque acted in that capacity for several years, under both Costa and Balfe.

The King's Theatre enjoyed a great asset in its leading 'cello player, Robert Lindley, who first joined as Sperati's successor in 1794 at the same time as another tower of strength, the famous double-bass player Dragonetti. Of this famous pair it was written in 1823: "Mr. Lindley has no rival, but he will have a successor in his son, if the confidence of this young

---

[1] It seems that wherever Mrs. Billington sang, Weichsell was leader.
[2] *Quar. Mus. Mag.*, Vol. I, No. II, p. 257.   [3] *Harm.*, Feb., 1824, p. 32.
[4] Hensel, I, p. 180.

professor were equal to his merit.   Dragonetti remains supreme, and uses his instrument as Jupiter his bolts—now hurling the thunder, and now glancing the innocuous lightnings of heaven—for thus only can we describe the

LINDLEY AND DRAGONETTI

alternate succession of his powerful and delicate execution."[1]   These two "the Pylades and Orestes of the orchestra," played together at the same desk in the best London orchestras for nearly fifty years, and Lindley, who was a great exponent of the art of accompanying recitative on the 'cello, lived long enough to go with Costa to Covent Garden in 1847, and finally

[1] *Quar. Mus. Mag.*, Vol. V, No. XVIII, p. 266.

retired in 1851.[1] Lindley's son William, also a 'cellist, joined the orchestra at the King's Theatre in 1819 at the age of seventeen, but never reached the same prominent position that his father had occupied in nearly all London orchestras.

A succession of excellent flautists played in the King's Theatre at a time when the flute was a favourite solo instrument and was often employed in performing elaborate obbligato parts to the prima donna's vocal solos. At the beginning of the century the leading flautist was Andrew Ashe (1759–1841),[2] successor to Teobaldo Monzani, who had turned flute-maker. Ashe was brought to London from Dublin, where he was playing at the Rotunda concerts, by Salomon in 1792 to play in the latter's famous concerts at the Hanover Square Rooms. He soon found the leading place in the King's Theatre, and remained in that position until he went to succeed Rauzzini in the direction of the concerts at Bath in 1810.

Monzani junior, one of Teobaldo's sons, probably followed Ashe,[3] and in 1818 the leading flautist was Ireland. From about 1823 until 1837 the most famous English player of the period, Charles Nicholson (1795–1837), played the first flute at the King's Theatre.

Nicholson was followed in 1838 by José Maria del Carmen Ribas (1796–1861), the flautist who so greatly pleased Mendelssohn in the *Scherzo* of the *Midsummer Night's Dream* music.[4] Ribas remained until 1843, and was succeeded for a short time by Richard Carte, who later became a partner in the firm of Rudall, Rose and Carte. John Clinton (1810–1864) joined the orchestra as first flute in 1847 after an incompetent French flautist had been tried and was dismissed.

Harrington, the leading oboist at the beginning of the century, was still playing in 1805; he was born in Sicily, was a pupil of Lebrun, and had been in the orchestra at the Haydn-Salomon concerts in 1794. His successor was a German named Friedrich Griesbach (d. 1824), a pupil of the great Fischer. Griesbach, however, was obliged for some time in 1808 to play second to the Italian Guillaume Catalani, a brother of the famous singer Angelica Catalani. Parke described the awkward situation thus: Catalini was then singing at the King's Theatre and insisted on her brother being engaged in place of Mr. Griesbach, "a German, who had for several years filled the

---

[1] *Mus. World*, March 18, 1836, p. IX. Lindley stammered badly, and told many anecdotes of the consequences of this infirmity. Going along Wardour Street one day, his attention was attracted to a very handsome grey parrot offered for sale. He stopped and said to the shopman—"C-c-c-can-h-he-sp-p-peak?" The reply was: "Yes, a precious sight better than you can, or I'd wring his blessed neck!" (Anon., *Mus. Recoll.*, I, p. 202). It was said that Lindley could "crack a nut between the tips of his fingers and the fingerboard of his 'cello." Dragonetti's left hand "was more like a claw than anything else in the world" (*Ibid.*, I, p. 340).

[2] Rockstro, p. 561; 1758–1838 according to Brown and Stratton's *Brit. Mus. Biog.*; according to Farmer (*Memoirs*, p. 39) Ashe was born in 1756.

[3] "Mr. Monzani (son) has early in life attained the highest situation of an orchestral player. He now performs, I believe, the first flute at the Italian Opera house" (James, p. 240).

[4] Rockstro, p. 626. Fitzgibbon, p. 204.

situation with great ability.   Mr. Griesbach, fortunately for Mr. Guillaume
Catalani, condescended to play the second oboe to him, and even went still
further; for when any passage occurred in the operas which Mr. Guillaume
Catalani could not execute, as was frequently the case, Mr. Griesbach kindly
played them for him.   This Mr. Guillaume Catalani, as an oboe player,
reminded me of a man I formerly knew, who, in eating asparagus, began at
the wrong end.   He was not an exotic plant, but a weed of the Italian soil."[1]
Parke wrote with some warmth on this subject because he was an oboe
player himself, and had to give up his place at Covent Garden to the Italian
"weed" when Catalani was engaged to sing there in 1809.

And this was not the only time that an Italian opera singer at the King's
Theatre brought in her trail an oboist who displaced, for the time being, one
of the regular players.   From a London weekly periodical called *The News*
(March 19, 1815) we learn that Alessandro Ferlendis (b. 1783), son of the
oboist of that name at Salzburg in Mozart's time, was engaged at the King's
Theatre while his wife was singing there during the season of 1815, and that
he was charged at a Police Court with assaulting the stage-manager because
the latter had forbidden him to come behind the scenes.   The outcome was
that Ferlendis was bound over to keep the peace on his own surety of £150.

Griesbach seems to have been still playing early in the 'twenties, and
was succeeded by either W. Ling, who was his successor at the Ancient
Concert in 1823, or by one Centroni, an Italian who was playing the oboe in
London in 1824.

In 1828 Vogt, the well-known oboe player from Paris, was engaged for
the season.   Vogt had already played in London in 1825, when, although his
execution was much admired, his tone was criticised as being too much like
the "scrannel pipe."[2]   He refused an engagement at the King's Theatre in
1826 on the ground that he would not care to "join a company in which a
character loaded with all sorts of infamy is to have any sway, though but a
nominal one."[3]   The infamous character, of course, was Bochsa.   In
March, 1828, however, Vogt took his place as principal oboe at the King's
Theatre, and during that season he played solos at many London concerts,
including the Philharmonic.   The French oboe tone did not at once please
the London critics, who were accustomed to the more robust tone of
English and German players.   This is clearly revealed in the following
extracts: "Expression and a most refined taste, combined with great power
of execution properly restrained, are the attributes of Mr. Vogt as an oboist.
His tone we did not like at first; we had been accustomed, in our youthful
days, to the elder Parke, and to F. Griesbach, whose instruments, partaking
of the nature of the clarionet, were remarkably full, rich, and less reedy than
Vogt's.   But his is the true tone of the oboe, we admit, and, by use, loses
what to many is its objectionable quality."[4]—"He performed charmingly

---

[1] Parke, II, p. 212.   Another account of the same episode appeared in *The Harmonicon*,
1830, p. 112, f.n.
[2] *Harm.*, Sept., 1825, p. 165.   [3] *Ibid.*, Jan., 1826, p. 20.   [4] *Ibid.*, April, 1828, p. 90.

PLATE 10

CHARLES NICHOLSON, FLAUTIST

APOLLON MARIE ROSE BARRET (BARRÉ)

PLATE 11

THOMAS LINDSAY WILLMAN

himself, in spite of his tone, which, though the true tone of the oboe, is not pleasing to English ears: we have been accustomed to a fuller and less reedy sound."[1]

Vogt's pupil, Apollon Marie Rose Barré (Barret), then a young man of 25 and a first prize-winner at the Conservatoire, joined the orchestra in 1829, and remained until he went with Costa to Covent Garden in 1847.

His playing was thus described in 1836: "Barret possesses a charming tone and execution; inferior, however, in quality, to old Griesbach."[2] It evidently took some time for English ears to get accustomed to the delicate tone and refined style of the French oboists.

Barret and Grattan Cooke were the two oboists in 1832, and in a contemporary list of the orchestra Cooke's name is placed first. Under Balfe the leading oboe was another pupil of Vogt, Antoine Joseph Lavigne, who eventually joined the Hallé orchestra at Manchester. Michael Sharpe, who died in 1841, had been second oboe at the King's Theatre until he retired in or about 1832.

It seems that William Mahon (1750–1816), "the eminent performer on the clarionet,"[3] played that instrument at the King's Theatre during the early years of the century, probably almost until he died in 1816. There were two brothers Mahon, both clarinet players, who were members of a musical family living at Oxford during the latter part of the 18th century. William Mahon appears to have settled in London at some time between 1776 and 1779.[4] John Mahon (1746–1834) was playing the clarinet as late as 1823, in which year his name appeared in the programme of the York Musical Festival. A "Mr. Mahon" played at the Three Choirs Festival from 1773 until 1811, or even later, and the name occurs in many programmes during the early part of the century, but the lack of any Christian name makes it impossible to distinguish between the two brothers. John Mahon died in Dublin, where he had settled down before 1830, and was in receipt of an annual allowance of sixty guineas from the Royal Society of Musicians.[5] His name occurs in the list of "Professional Subscribers" to the Society in 1818. Ella included John Mahon in his list of orchestral musicians who lived to the age of four score or more.[6]

By 1817 Thomas Lindsay Willman had joined the orchestra as leading clarinet, while John Mahon played second to him.[7]

---

[1] *Harm.*, July, 1828, p. 168. Some interesting particulars of the reeds used by well-known oboe players were given in an article "On the oboe and bassoon" by J. P., which appeared in the *Harmonicon* of 1830, p. 192. It was said that the great Fischer used a rather small reed, of a moderate length; Griesbach used a very large strong reed, almost as large as a bassoon reed, and his tone was rich, "resembling the mellowness of Willman's clarinet, to produce which required great exertion." Vogt played with a small soft reed, "which rendered his tone thin." Grattan Cooke used a reed of a size and substance between those of Griesbach and Vogt, and his tone was "very mellow and sweet."

[2] *Mus. World*, May, 1836, p. 126. [3] Lysons, p. 50. [4] Mee, p. 76.

[5] *Harm.*, Feb., 1830, p. 57, f.n. [6] Ella, p. 310.

[7] *Quar. Mus. Mag.*, Vol. I, No. II, p. 258.

Willman soon became the foremost clarinet player in this country, and continued to hold that position till he died in 1840. His playing was universally admired; the highest praise was always given him by both English and foreign critics. The following are only a few of the laudatory notices that may be found in the musical papers of his time: "Mr. Willman is the most delicate and finished clarinet player we have ever heard"—"He is, without exception, the best clarinet player we have ever heard"—"Mr.

Willman, whose clarionet certainly realizes the most poetical dream of soothing sounds."

In 1838 Henry Lazarus joined Willman at the King's Theatre, and was said to be "fully worthy to take his place by the side of Willman."[1] After the death of the latter in 1840, Lazarus became principal clarinet of the opera orchestra.

Of the bassoons, we learn from Parke that Holmes[2] was the leading player at the King's Theatre in 1806[3]; he was probably there long before that time, and had played in the Haydn-Salomon concerts in 1791 and 1794. In 1793, when he performed at the Three Choirs Festival, Holmes was said to be "the most eminent bassoon player of the present day,"[4] and in 1819 it was written of him: "At present, Holmes is the favourite."[5] Some years after his death, c. 1822, a writer

HENRY LAZARUS IN 1843.

referred to "the late Mr. Holmes, whose tone resembled the most human voice, and whose execution was as accurate as rapid."[6]

It is uncertain who succeeded Holmes, but it was most probably John Mackintosh, for we are told that in 1824 "Mackintosh, the best bassoon player in England is thrown out to make way for a stranger whose tones on the night of opening excited,—not that pleasure and admiration which this instrument has hitherto never failed to produce in the orchestra of the King's Theatre, but downright laughter."[7] It is impossible to say who it was that caused this unseemly merriment, but it was no doubt either one of the "bevy of boys" or one of the "imported Frenchmen" whose advent marked the sad decline in the playing of the orchestra in the unhappy years

[1] *Mus. World*, Feb., 1838, p. 105.
[2] James Holmes was a Professional Subscriber to the R.S.M. in 1818.
[3] Parke, II, p. 6.   [4] Lysons, p. 74.   [5] *Encyclopædia Londinensis*, Vol. XVI, p. 388.
[6] *Harm.*, May, 1830, p. 193.   [7] *Ibid.*, Feb., 1824, p. 32.

before 1830. However, it seems quite certain that Mackintosh returned to the orchestra soon after his dismissal in 1824, for his name was amongst those who resigned in 1828. According to Fétis,[1] the Paris player Willent was a bassoonist at the King's Theatre in 1827, when he was only eighteen years of age, thus coming under both categories "imported Frenchmen" and "bevy of boys." Mackintosh was often commended for his fine playing in *obbligati soli*, and was favourably compared with Holmes: "We remember Holmes' excellence on this fine instrument, and his successor, in mellowness of tone and delicacy of execution, is very little his inferior."[2]

In 1832 a Belgian player named Friedrich Baumann (c. 1801–1856) was first bassoon at the King's Theatre, and stayed long enough to go with Costa to Covent Garden in 1847. Baumann was a native of Ostend, and had been trained at the Paris Conservatoire; he was said to bear a strong resemblance to Napoleon. In 1836 his playing was compared with that of a famous foreign virtuoso and the best of the English players in these words: "Baumann is the best bassoon player we have ever heard, with

FRIEDRICH BAUMANN, BASSOON PLAYER

the possible exception of Preymeyer in the King of Sweden's band, who was over here a few seasons ago and played a concerto at the Philharmonic; but Mr. Baumann has not so pure a quality of tone as Messrs. Mackintosh or Denman; nevertheless, he is an excellent orchestral player."[3] Another scribe wrote of Baumann, "if he does not possess the full round tone of other performers on this delicious instrument, he has a greater power of delicate inflection, and a breathingness of sound that might 'create a soul under the ribs of death'."[4]

The second bassoon with both Holmes and Baumann was James Tully, a brother of the horn player of that name.

A pair of Bohemian brothers named Joseph (b. 1755) and Peter Petrides (b. 1766) were the horn players at the King's Theatre from 1802 to 1825;

[1] *Biog. univ.*   [2] *Harm.*, May, 1828, p. 115.
[3] *Mus. World*, May 6, 1836. F. C. Preumayr played at the Philharmonic in 1830, and at the Paris Conservatoire Concerts in the same year.
[4] *Illus. Lon. News*, Jan. 13, 1844.

they followed an earlier pair of brothers, the Leanders, who were said to be "excellent virtuosi" and were still living in London up to about 1805.[1] Armed with letters of introduction from the Duke of Sussex, before whom they had performed at Lisbon, the Bohemian brothers arrived at London in 1802 after having spent fifteen years in wandering as horn duettists all over Germany, France, Austria, Spain and Portugal, and meeting with many adventures, including shipwreck in the Mediterranean.   The Petrides made a successful *debut* at Salomon's benefit concert in Willis's Rooms, and were immediately engaged to play in the orchestra at the King's Theatre.   These brothers were described as "much admired performers on the horn,"[2] and also as "the quaintest beings that ever entered an orchestra, and who, in the interval of a bar or two's rest, amused themselves by kicking each other's shins, since they could not quarrel more uproariously."[3]   John Ella also gave a quaint account of these brothers: "When accused, at rehearsals, of playing a wrong note, each would answer—'was mein bruder,' and until the copyist discovered that the parts were wrong, and neither of the brothers was at fault, they would snarl and utter unkind expressions towards each other, with a menacing look.   At other times they were the most united of brothers."[4]   Ella was inaccurate when he said that the Petrides retired to their native land in 1824; they both took part in the York Musical Festival in 1825, and their names still figured in the list of professors at the Royal Academy of Music in the same year.   At the end of 1826, however, Moscheles found them in Prague, their native city, spending the remainder of their days in peace and repose.

Before the Bohemian brothers had left London, Giovanni Puzzi (d. 1876), "the fashionable horn player," was there to play the solo parts at the King's Theatre.   He was evidently a very fine player who was in the happy position of being able to reserve himself for solo-work.   Contemporary remarks on Puzzi's playing are all extremely laudatory; one described his performance as being "the most perfect that had ever been previously heard in this country"[5]; another scribe remarked that he "breathed forth some divine tones from his horn"[6]; Weber called him "the renowned Puzzi,"[7] and another critic thought that it was "impossible to conceive any thing more perfect, whether the tone, the execution, or the general expression be considered."[8]   Fétis called him "remarkably talented," and stated that he had acquired a fortune which rendered him independent of ordinary orchestral work.[9]   In 1827 Puzzi was sent abroad by Ebers, manager of the King's Theatre, to collect singers for the Italian opera in London.   One of the singers he engaged was Giacinto Toso, whom Puzzi married three months after her arrival in London.[10]   He also brought over an Italian *Opera Buffa* company to give a season of opera at the English

---

[1] *Dict. of Musicians*, 1827.   [2] Lysons, p. 85.   [3] Anon., *Mus. Recoll.*, I, p. 33.
[4] Ella, p. 337.   [5] Anon., *Mus. Recoll.*, I, p. 145.   [6] *Mus. World*, July 1, 1836, p. 44.
[7] Weber, II, p. 678.   [8] *Quar. Mus. Mag.*, Vol. V, No. XVIII, p. 266.
[9] *Curiosités*, p. 194.   [10] Ebers, pp. 312, 314, 338.

Opera House (Lyceum) in 1836. Puzzi moved in the highest society, and gave his benefit concert "at Mrs. Cox's elegant house in Grosvenor Place," and charged one guinea for each ticket. After the 'forties he appeared only rather rarely as a horn player, and occupied himself mainly in the service of Her Majesty's Theatre as "the negotiator of engagements with foreign artists, and the caterer of novelties for the theatre for many years."[1]

The horn players at the King's Theatre in the 'thirties and 'forties were Edward Platt (1793–1861) and James Rae. Platt had been as a boy in the Duke of Cumberland's private band, and subsequently served for eleven years in the band of the 2nd or Queen's Dragoons, of which his father was bandmaster. Acting on the advice of the great tenor Braham, he settled in London, and after two years in the orchestra at Drury Lane, he was engaged at the King's Theatre, it was said, owing to his having successfully deputised one night for Puzzi. Platt's playing was often harshly criticised in the musical papers: "Mr. Platt has yet to learn how to perform on his obstreperous instrument in a concert-room; there is no necessity to puff out one's cheeks, or blow until the hearer feels a sympathetic sense of pity for the performer."[2]—"Mr. Platt and his coadjutors should be taught by the conductor that there is a vast difference between sf and ff. Again and again the unwearied exertions of these rude sons of Boreas smothered every component part of the harmony save their own open notes."[3] Platt was, nevertheless, the leading horn player in London for many years, and it is only fair to mention that Costa's opinion of Platt's performance was that "in singing on the horn, it was the finest and most genuine tone he had ever heard."[4] Platt was obliged to retire in 1850, and from then the leading horn player in London was Charles Harper (1819–1893), second son of the great English trumpeter Thomas Harper.

Early in the century the leading trumpet player at the King's Theatre was John Hyde, best remembered as the sponsor of the English slide-trumpet, the instrument adopted by Harper. Hyde was described as "the most celebrated trumpet player of the last thirty years, beyond all competition for a dexterous management of the instrument."[5] He was probably succeeded by his son William, and it was no doubt the latter who figured in the orchestra list of 1817 as principal trumpet, with Johann Georg Schmidt (b. 1774) as second.[6]

In the following year Schmidt replaced Hyde as leading player, and about 1821 Thomas Harper joined the orchestra and soon became the foremost trumpeter in this country.

Harper's playing on the slide-trumpet placed him well above all competitors. Like Willman, he earned the highest praise from all native

---

[1] *Mus. World*, March 26, 1853, p. 189.   [2] *Ibid.*, March 8, 1838, p. 163.
[3] *Ibid.*, March 22, 1838, p. 199.   [4] *Illus. Lon. News*, April 20, 1850.
[5] *Encycl. Lond.*, Vol XVI, p. 390.
[6] Schmidt was leading trumpeter in the Prince Regent's band from about 1800. He was reputed the best trumpeter in Europe—"His flourish was the most terrific and appalling thing ever heard from a musical instrument" (*Mus. World*, Sept. 29, 1855, p. 625).

and foreign critics.   Yet his name was evidently not yet very well known
in 1825 when these words were written of him: "As to the trumpeter
(Harper, we believe, is his name), there may possibly have been as good,
but there never could have been a completer master of his very difficult
instrument."[1]   Harper and his colleague, Irwin, were temporarily displaced

" LET THE BRIGHT SERAPHIM."

THOMAS HARPER (SENIOR) AND CLARA NOVELLO, 1836

in 1826 and 1829 by the Italian brothers Gambati, who were in London at
that time, and played at the R.A.M. concerts in 1826.[2]

Trombones would not be required regularly at the King's Theatre at
the beginning of the century.   In 1817–18 only one player was employed,
namely, the Italian, Mariotti.   It is probable that the first trombone players
at the London theatres were drawn from either the Guards band which had
been brought over from Germany towards the close of the 18th century,[3]
or from the King's Household Band, in which the players were largely

---

[1] *Harm.*, April, 1825, p. 68.

[2] The Italian trumpeters appear to have left London soon after 1829; they were playing
keyed-trumpets at Florence in 1831, and were later heard of in New York.

[3] About 1783 or 1785.   See Parke, II, pp. 239–241; Pohl, II, p. 163; and Farmer, *Rise
of Mil. Music*, p. 69.

Germans.[1] The names of three trombone players, Flack, Swingmann and Dressler, occur in several programmes in the early years of the century, both in and out of London, and it is likely that these may have been employed at the King's Theatre on certain occasions. But, during and after the 'twenties, a group of three trombones would be required fairly often, and the players would, no doubt, be regularly engaged. The usual trio at that time seems to have been Smithies (or Smithers) for the alto, Schoengen for the tenor, and Mariotti for the bass. It is not clear, although most likely, that Smithies and Smithers were the same person; both names occur very often in concert programmes from about 1825 to 1850. Antonio Mariotti (1757–1843), whose name appeared as early as 1810 in the programmes of the Three Choirs Festival, played the bass trombone at the Philharmonic and Ancient concerts, as well as at the King's Theatre, until about 1836. He is said to have come to London in 1792.[2] According to another account,[3] Mariotti was 83 years old in 1836, and was then destitute and unable to follow his profession. He was, however, retained and paid as usual by the Ancient Concert and the Philharmonic.

Early in the 'thirties the trombones at the King's Theatre were the two Smithies (sen. and jun.) and Mariotti. When the latter retired, he was succeeded by Albrecht, who came from the Royal Household Band.

Should a serpent be required, as it might occasionally in the 'thirties, it is probable that the choice would fall upon either André or Jepp. Of the former a few particulars can be gleaned: "This surprising performer on the serpent was a member of King George IV's Household Band. He resided for some time in Cheltenham, and was connected with the formerly celebrated military band of the Montpellier Spa. He subsequently kept an inn at Gloucester, where he died."[4] André played one of Dragonetti's show-pieces, a solo by Corelli, on the serpent at Cheltenham, and was warmly commended for his skill by the great double-bass player. Jepp was another serpent player who performed at the Guildhall when Queen Victoria visited the city on Lord Mayor's day in 1837.[5]

When, a little later, an ophicleide was demanded in a score, it would surely be Ponder who was engaged. It need hardly be said that every opportunity was taken of making a pun on Ponder and his "ponderous instrument." This hardy player had the courage to play the contrabass ophicleide at the Birmingham Musical Festival in 1834. Ponder died while at the Gloucester Musical Festival in 1841; it was suggested that his death was brought about by the exertion required in playing the ophicleide; an

---

[1] The King's Household Band, known as the Prince Regent's Band before the accession of George IV, was a wind band under the direction of Christian Kramer (d. 1834) and constituted as follows: 8 clarinets, 2 oboes, 3 flutes, 4 bassoons, 1 serpent *obbligato*, 3 serpents *ripieno*, 4 trombones, 4 horns, 4 trumpets, kettle-drums (*Quar. Mus. Mag.*, Vol. I, No. II, p. 158).

[2] Mariotti was playing in Paris at the *Concert Spirituel* and the *Théâtre de Monsieur* in 1790.

[3] *Mus. World*, June 24, 1836, p. 30.   [4] Lysons, p. 126.

[5] *Mus. World*, Feb. 23, 1838, p. 125.

inquest was held, and the verdict was that Ponder "Died by the visitation of God."[1]

The drummer at the King's Theatre at the beginning of the century was Jenkinson, who appears to have been the leading performer on the timpani in London during the first quarter of the century.   He was probably the William Jenkinson who was a "professional subscriber" to the Royal Society of Musicians in 1818.   Two stories were told of Jenkinson: "It is told of the late Mr. Jenkinson, that, during a performance of the chorus in *Joshua* at a great music-meeting, he, by some inadvertency, burst in with his drums a bar too soon, and marred the sublime effect intended to be produced; on which, mortified and enraged at his own blunder, he applied the drumsticks in good earnest to his own head, and inflicted summary punishment on himself, to the astonishment of the audience."[2]   The following occurs in a notice about a performance of *The Conquering Hero* at the Ancient Concert in 1826: "By-the-bye, it is comical enough that old Jenkinson won't beat his drums when he is bid.   The voices urge him strongly, 'Sound your trumpets, beat your drums'—but no—they were mute as Lover's lute."[3] Jenkinson was still playing at the King's Theatre in 1817, but in the list of 1818 his place is taken by one Platts.   The latter's successor appears to have been the ubiquitous Mr. Thomas Paul Chipp (1793–1870), the heads of whose "valuable drums" were cut to pieces by some "mischievous fellow" in 1836.[4]

Thus, and thus only, by assembling scraps of information gleaned from many different sources, has it been possible in some measure to reconstruct the orchestra of the King's Theatre in London as it was during the first half of last century.   There remains to be added what can be told of it as a whole, and of its playing.

Early references show that however much the stage performers were criticised, the "band" was always praised, at any rate by native critics.   In 1819, when the general standard of performance at the opera was said to be poor, the playing of the orchestra was excepted: it always earned "unqualified praise."[5]   Foreign opinion, however, was not so easily satisfied, and in 1820 Spohr gave the orchestra a very poor report.   To his friend Speyer he explained how it was controlled, namely, by the leading violinist, with a puppet-conductor at the piano, and how the playing constantly wavered and threatened to break down completely at any moment.[6]

We have already seen how tragically the orchestra went down hill in the 'twenties; just at the end of that unhappy period we get some more foreign comments on its standard of performance.

Fétis severely criticised it in 1829,[7] the same year in which Mendelssohn had described it as being "very good," and it is difficult to reconcile the two

[1] *Gloucester Journal.*   [2] *Mus. World,* April 14, 1837, p. 83.
[3] *Harm.,* April, 1826, p. 82.   [4] *Mus. World,* July 1, 1836, p. 46.
[5] *Quar. Mus. Mag.,* Vol. II, No. VII, p. 376.   [6] Speyer, p. 52.   [7] *Curiosités,* p. 239.

accounts. After remarking that the chorus was quite inadequate, Fétis went on to demolish the orchestra: "As far as the orchestra is concerned, it is even worse. Not only are the players too few to produce a good effect, but they are not closely enough attached to the theatre by the inducement of a prospective pension, as are the Parisian players. The consequence of this is, that the director or conductor is unable to apply any severity in exacting good service from the players, because if he did so he would expose himself at any moment to the risk of losing them, as they could always find employment elsewhere, at concerts or by giving lessons. The rehearsals go badly, the playing is negligent; the singing, being badly accompanied, is spoiled, and the taste of the public, who never hear any really good playing, never improves. In this way the music of London is radically bad."

But we must remember that it was just in 1829 that some of the best of the English players were dismissed and were replaced by some brought from Paris.

Meyerbeer came to London in 1832 to superintend the rehearsals of *Robert le Diable* at the King's Theatre. He was delighted with the way the orchestra read through their parts, and thought that with seven or eight rehearsals all would go well. But when he discovered that there was to be only one rehearsal, and that the nuances were something quite unknown to this orchestra, he left London the same evening without waiting to hear the performance.[1]

Whether the orchestra was good, as Mendelssohn said it was, or bad, as Fétis said it was in 1829, it is quite certain that it improved greatly when it came under the guidance of Costa in the early 'thirties, and was directed with a baton instead of being "presided over" by a pianist and "led" by a violinist. Of its playing in 1836 under Costa, a critic wrote: "The band (to which we always turn, and implicitly when elsewhere dissatisfied) is, if possible, finer than ever. Between the opera and the ballet, they played in the most perfect style the overture to *Guillaume Tell,*—the most descriptive and best instrumented of Rossini's orchestral compositions."[2]

Reports in the 'thirties and early 'forties are indeed all favourable, some of them extravagantly so. Chorley of the *Athenæum* told a story of constant improvement from the moment that Costa became conductor: "The orchestra in 1830 . . . was meagre and ill-disciplined"; but of 1832 he wrote: "This was the year when (happy event for England) the Italian Opera orchestra was placed under the direction of Signor Costa." In 1840 he wrote: "Since the day when Signor Costa took up the baton its orchestra had steadily improved under his discipline, intelligence, and resolution to be contented with nothing short of the best"; and of 1843: "The orchestra of the Opera, on the other hand, had been worked up, by this time, into great beauty and European renown."[3]

Some additional personnel was added in 1838: "The opera band this year

[1] Adam, *Souvenirs,* XXIV.   [2] *Mus. World,* March 18, 1836, p. 7.
[3] *Thirty Years' Mus. Recoll.,* pp. 3, 34, 121, 146.

will be on an unprecedented scale of grandeur and efficiency. Mr. Ribas succeeds the late Mr. Nicholson as first flute; and several additional violins, a violoncello and contrabasso, have been engaged. M. Costa is, as usual, the *maestro*."[1] Altogether, a happier state of affairs seems to have prevailed at this time; and not long after the above was written there was a further increase in the number of players: "The orchestra has been enlarged by taking in one whole range of the *parterre*; and the situation of the instruments partially changed by being brought more forward, whereby a larger volume of sound is thrown into the body of the house, and less escapes to the side scenery, technically denominated the flys. The band has again been augmented by the addition of four violins, two tenors, and two basses, beyond the number of last season; so that it is now probably the most efficient and powerful orchestra in Europe. The following talented artists are among the accessions of the present season: C. Lucas, A. Griesbach, Seymour, Wagstaff, Westrop, W. Cramer, Glanville and Morris."[2]

It is evident that when Costa got the reins of the musical management into his own hands the size of the orchestra was increased to at least what it had been before the unhappy period when a reduction in the number of string players required Spagnoletti to play with "six-fiddle power," and the quality of the players was restored. Costa was not the man to put up with a mean establishment or a starved orchestra; he insisted on things being well done, and on adequate resources. An anonymous amateur, who took it upon himself to review the situation at Her Majesty's Theatre in 1838 made it very clear that there had been a great improvement in the orchestra during the season: "There is one important feature in the late season at Her Majesty's Theatre, which greatly distinguishes it from former seasons; the increased numerical strength of the orchestra, an orchestra concentrating in itself the highest talent the Metropolis can produce. In this point unmixed praise is indeed well deserved."[3] As this was unquestionably due to Costa's influence and training, he may perhaps be forgiven for having introduced an ophicleide into the score of Mozart's *Don Giovanni*: "The magnificent overture, the splendid finale of the first act, the accompaniments for the trombones and the ophicleide, imparting as they do so much additional brilliance, and so ably and judiciously added by Signor Costa, do in truth afford unmixed enjoyment. So indeed may be said of the whole opera as performed *in the orchestra*."[4] Our amateur critic saw no harm in the use of trombones to bolster up the score of Rossini's *La Cenerentola*: "Lablache as Don Magnifico, and Tamburini as Dandini, were everything that Rossini could have desired on the stage; the addition of the trombone accompaniments must have been everything he could have desired for the orchestra."[5] Only the chorus was not up to the mark: "its instrumental department is

---

[1] *Mus. World*, Feb. 23, 1838, p. 130.
[2] *Ibid.*, March 29, 1838, p. 220. These were all string players.
[3] Anon., *Her Majesty's Theatre*, p. 6.
[4] *Ibid.*, p. 8.   [5] *Ibid.*, p. 16.

excellent (the noisy and jarring drums at one end of the orchestra excepted); the choral department ought to display proportionate excellence."[1]

The chorus of praise for the King's Theatre orchestra was continued in the succeeding years, and indeed, for as long as Costa remained in command. In 1839 there was a brave array of 77 players; Mori and Cotton Reeve still led the first and second violins, and Moralt was at the head of the violas; Lindley and Dragonetti continued to give the bass part the benefit of their inimitable partnership, and all were supported by a solid phalanx of sound *ripieno* string players. Most of the players were British, and of the foreigners one was a Portuguese, four were Italians, and eight were Frenchmen. Nadaud conducted the ballets and Tolbecque played the violin solos; Mori, Lindley and Dragonetti were exempted from playing in the ballet music. The highest praise was always given to this orchestra: "The orchestra is now more numerous, more efficient in all its subordinate departments, and in a finer state of discipline than any other band in London; and, with honour and credit to Costa, be it said, there is scarcely one foreign artist in the band that could be safely replaced by native talent."[2] (For full list in 1839, see Appendix, p. 488.)

Fétis should have revisited London ten years after his visit during the unfortunate season of 1829. No doubt he would have had something better to say about the orchestra of Her Majesty's Theatre in 1839 than he had in 1829. Costa's drums and trombones would not have shocked him, for there was plenty of that in Paris, nor would he have wept much if Rossini's *tutti* were made just a little more noisy than they already were.

Her Majesty's Theatre lost most of its best orchestral players when Costa left it and started the rival establishment at Covent Garden in 1847. The events which led up to this breach began in 1845 when Costa was invited to become permanent conductor of the Philharmonic orchestra, and had to refuse the offer on account of the strong opposition of Lumley, who was then manager of Her Majesty's Theatre. But when the offer was repeated in 1846, Costa accepted it in spite of Lumley, in consequence of which he was dismissed (or resigned?) his position at the old opera-house. According to Balfe's biographer, W. A. Barrett, it was decided to offer the vacant post to either Spohr, Meyerbeer, or Balfe.[3] Without approaching either of the first two, both of whom would certainly have refused the invitation, Balfe was hurriedly brought over from Paris, and accepted the invitation to succeed Costa as conductor at Her Majesty's Theatre. The loss of his position was no great blow to Costa, for the plans to start a new Italian Opera at Covent Garden at which Costa was to be musical director and conductor had already been maturing for some time before the breach occurred.

For the season of 1846 Balfe still had Costa's old orchestra under his command: "The orchestra over which Balfe had control that year was the

---

[1] Anon., *Her Majesty's Theatre*, pp. 49, 50.   [2] *Mus. World*, May 9, 1839, p. 23.
[3] Barrett, p. 177.

same celebrated 'eighty' which his predecessor had employed all his skill and energy, over a space of many years, to bring into a perfectly homogeneous and unitedly working whole."[1]   Although he had neither the experience nor the authority of his predecessor, with such a well-trained orchestra at his disposal, Balfe appears to have been able to keep up a fairly good standard of performance.   But there evidently were shortcomings enough to show that even this well-drilled orchestra, when under less expert guidance, was not quite able to maintain fully its former excellence.   With regard to accompanying and "humouring" the singer, a critic wrote of this season at Her Majesty's: "Here lies the excellence of Signor Costa, at the Italian Opera, and which Mr. Balfe, though by no means an inexperienced conductor, has not yet acquired."[2]

The great blow to the orchestra at Her Majesty's Theatre fell in the next season (1847), when Costa engaged most of the players for the new Italian Opera at Covent Garden.   No doubt Costa picked his players carefully; no less than 53 of them accepted his engagement, leaving Balfe with Tolbecque the leader, Nadaud leader of the ballet, and 22 others who remained true to the old establishment.   Lumley admitted that the loss was severe: "Many members of the orchestra had yielded to the persuasions of their old (and it may be added, cherished) conductor, Signor Costa, and had followed their leader of many years in his new enterprise—just as a band of condottieri might in the middle ages have followed an admired captain who had taken service under a new sovereign.   Some of the instrumental artists, however, remained true to their colours."[3]   Their faithfulness, however, was questioned by the *Morning Chronicle*, which rather unkindly suggested that these players were true to the old opera-house only because they had not been offered engagements at the new one.   Besides the two leaders, Tolbecque and Nadaud, Balfe had some of the old string players left, including Deloffre, Watts, Wagstaff (violins), and the 'cellist Pillet; a few native violinists and some from abroad, including Pluys from Brussels, were engaged.   As new 'cellists Balfe was fortunate in being able to acquire Piatti from Parma as leader, and Burgoin from the Paris *Opéra*; for his double-basses he gained Anglois from Turin as principal, and as second principal, a player named Percival from Drury Lane.   But Costa had taken all the best wind players, and London was unable to provide a second complete set of leading wind instrumentalists.   The continent was scoured in hot haste, and a number of engagements were made.   A flautist named Elie came from Paris, Lavigne from Brussels was engaged as first oboe, Milan supplied a clarinettist named Dell'Uomo, and two foreign bassoon players came, Koessel from Linz and Tamplini from Palermo.   A German from Linz named Bahr was engaged as first horn; to replace Harper a trumpeter named Zeiss was imported from Brussels, and the *Opéra Comique* at Paris supplied a drummer named Ista.[4]   So, by hook or crook, and, as it turned

[1] Kenney, *Mem.*, p. 211.   [2] *Mus. World*, Oct. 31, 1846, p. 539.
[3] Lumley, p. 158.   [4] *The Pictorial Times*, Jan. 30, 1847.

out, by buying some "pigs in pokes," the strength was made up to 28 violins, 8 violas, 8 'cellos, 8 double-basses, with the usual complement of wind instruments.

Even before the performances had begun it was found that some of the foreign acquisitions were incompetent. The flautist from Paris was a bad investment, and was soon replaced by the English player Clinton; Lavigne did not arrive in time, and the first oboe part was played by the native oboist Horton; the Milanese clarinettist was unsatisfactory, but for some time no better player was available. Of the new bassoons, Tamplini[1] turned out well, and was complimented with the description "equal to any bassoon in the world," but the German horn player was not up to the mark and subsided into the position of fourth horn, his part being taken by the English player Catchpole.

So the season of 1847 began at Her Majesty's Theatre with a mixed orchestra which was said to be one third French, one third Italian, one sixth Belgian, and the rest English. Balfe had no doubt a difficult task, but it was said to his credit that he did wonderfully well; his beat was said to be getting steadier, more decided, and clearer, but that the orchestra "wants mending in several particulars," and the first clarinet was "poor." According to another account it was said that "Balfe has done wonders, . . . Attila, King of the Huns, never managed a motley multitude with more rigid discipline and perfect order than Balfe his newly-gathered orchestra." Lavigne eventually arrived and took his appointed place as first oboe; the "lovely quality and wonderful perfection of his mechanism" was remarked on, but that wretched clarinet from Milan was still "poor."

As the season progressed there were plenty of signs that Costa and his old orchestra were badly missed: "The violins want weeding out and strengthening; violas, 'cellos and double-basses want further strength. The wood-wind and brass want mending in several particulars, and the percussion want subduing."[2] It is evident that Balfe had some difficulty in controlling his mixed bag of instrumentalists, and an independent opinion was to the effect that he himself was in some measure responsible for the deterioration: "unquestionably Mr. Balfe did not prove himself equal to the new and difficult duties he was induced to undertake," and the orchestra "had fallen away from its old perfection."[3] A French critic, writing about a performance of *Robert le Diable*, said that he dared not speak of the orchestra, and Carl Loewe, the German ballad-composer and singer who was spending the season of 1847 in London, remarked rather ambiguously that the orchestra at Her Majesty's Theatre was incapable of being improved.[4]

For the season of 1848 a few changes were made in the orchestra. Tolbecque and Nadaud remained as leaders, Oury led the second violins and

[1] G. Tamplini (1817–1888) became a bandmaster, and published *The Bandsman* (1857), a series of instruction books for wind instruments.
[2] The above are all from the *Mus. World*, Feb. to May, 1847.
[3] Anon., *Mus. Recoll.*, II, pp. 173, 178.   [4] Loewe, p. 421.

Richard Hughes the violas.   One of the first violins was J. H. Mapleson, the future famous impresario.   The Paris player Jean Rémusat (1815–1880), favourite pupil of Tulou, was first flute; Lavigne and Horton remained as oboes, but the "poor" clarinet player from Milan was replaced by another Italian named Biletta, from Bologna, with the Englishman John Henry Maycock (b. 1817) as second.   The two bassoons were as before, but Tamplini was first and Koessel second.   For the first horn part one Steglich was brought over from Frankfort, and another German named Carl Kreutzer, from Mayence, played second horn. Zeiss and Maffei were the trumpet pair, Winterbottom and Martin blew the trombones, and Ista beat the drums.   The stage band was directed by Charles Boosé (1815–1869), bandmaster of the Scots Fusilier Guards, and the modest part for the triangle was played by the boy Wilhelm Ganz, whose father, Adolph Ganz, was chorus-master and viola player during that season.   In the following year Wilhelm Ganz played among the second violins.[1]

CARICATURE OF TOLBECQUE, BALFE'S LEADER AT HER MAJESTY'S THEATRE

It was written of this season (1848) that the orchestra at Her Majesty's Theatre was better, but that there was still plenty of room for improvement: "The wind were better in tune, second violins and violas were still weak, and the 'cellos and basses too obtrusive.   The first flute was not so good as last year, clarinet and horns were not quite satisfactory, and the first bassoon had a "peculiar tone."   The trumpets and trombones were noisy, but Balfe's conducting was, at any rate, "good."   At the end of the season the opinion of this critic was, that Balfe "cannot make a fine band out of a handful of excellent artists and a lot of decayed pensioners and unlearned striplings"; no doubt he was exaggerating when he said "the effect was as of a country theatre band with an emphatic leader."[2]   To the anonymous author of *Musical Recollections*, the orchestra in 1848 was "by many degrees worse than that of the previous year, being weaker in strings, coarser in the contrebassi, and noisier in its brass instruments.   The chorus was also rough and imperfect, and Mr. Balfe's beat more indecisive than ever."[3]

For the season of 1849 it was said that Balfe was making strenuous

[1] Ganz, *Memoirs*, p. 4.   [2] *Mus. World*, July 15, 1848, p. 449.
[3] *Mus. Recoll.*, II, p. 199.

efforts to get together a better orchestra. A full list of this orchestra of 76 players is available, and will be found in the Appendix (p. 489).

The orchestra of 1850 was said to be better than in the previous year, but there were still "deficiencies" in the playing, and the reason was because not all of the musicians were first-class players. Balfe's conducting came in for some praise, and, being himself a singer, it was found that "when any of the singers were *out* (and that was occasionally) Balfe sang their parts for them so well, that, except ourselves and the 'Lions,' nobody knew that anything was wanting."[1] There was evidently a certain amount of partisanship in the comparisons that were inevitably made between Costa and Balfe, as the following suggests: "Those who do not bear testimony to the nightly improvement of the orchestra under the direction of this admirable musician (Balfe), are either blind or prejudiced, and are not critics, but costermongers."[2] The last word, of course, should be understood as "Costa-mongers."

For two more years the opera at Her Majesty's Theatre struggled in rivalry with the new establishment at Covent Garden. A great support was lost in 1852 when Piatti left to join the rival orchestra; no doubt he left what he thought was a sinking ship. Piatti was replaced by Lütgen, and Jansa joined the violins in that year. But after the season of 1852 the unequal struggle between the two Italian operas in London came to an end, and from 1852 until 1856 Her Majesty's Theatre was closed. Although it was again reopened with opera in 1856 (the year in which Covent Garden Theatre was burnt down), the days of the old opera-house in the Haymarket were gradually drawing to a close, and the scene had shifted to Covent Garden.

There is a touch of sadness in the passing of the old opera-house in which so much of London's operatic history had been enacted: "The old house in the Haymarket remains closed; that once famous temple of the muses, for so many generations the centre of all the life and animation of the London fashionable season, stands deserted, desolate, and dreary. Its glory is departed, and, to all present appearance, never to return."[3] The writer of that notice then goes on to describe the opening night at Covent Garden Theatre, with its "unrivalled orchestra, in all its strength, under its able chief, Costa."

There must be many elderly Londoners now alive who, like the present writer, can just remember a part of the old arcade, the last remains of the old Her Majesty's Theatre, before the present theatre and hotel were erected on the same site.

COVENT GARDEN THEATRE

Musically, Covent Garden seems to have ranked next to, although well below, the King's Theatre. Before 1847, when the Royal Italian Opera

[1] *Mus. World*, March 16, 1850, p. 158.   [2] *Ibid.*, April 13, 1850, p. 221.
[3] *Illus. Lon. News*, April, 1854, p. 322.

was established at Covent Garden, although the auditorium was fairly large, the regular orchestra was rather small, and probably at no time numbered more than 40 players. Bishop's list of 1818–19[1] shows that only 31 musicians were regularly employed, but Dibdin's list of 1825[2] records that the number had by that time been increased to between 34 and 39 players. These numbers no doubt sufficed for the English and Italian operas that were produced from time to time, but for German operas, such as *Oberon* in 1826 and *Fidelio* in 1835, and for some of the French operas, the regular orchestra had to be augmented.

Early in the century, like other theatres in London, Covent Garden had its so-called conductor who was really the composer and musical director, but who did not actually control the playing of the orchestra.

In 1801 William Russel was composer and musical director, and in 1810 Henry Bishop began his long association with the theatre in that capacity, and remained until the end of the 1824 season, when he left to go to Drury Lane. Bishop was back at Covent Garden for some time (1839–41) during part of Madame Vestris's management. After 1824 the musical direction seems to have been for a few years more or less in the hands of Sir George Smart,[3] and it was he who was mainly responsible for bringing Weber to Covent Garden in 1826.

After Weber, the musical affairs of the theatre passed into the hands of Thomas Simpson Cooke, better known as Tom Cooke, who had for many years been leader of the orchestra and singer at Drury Lane.[4]

After a brief period in 1832 during which the theatre was under the management of Laporte, Alfred Bunn became the lessee of both Covent Garden and Drury Lane Theatres in 1833. At that time Tom Cooke seems to have combined the duties of musical director and leader of the orchestra, and when in 1835–6 the management was again changed, it was George Rodwell who became musical director. Rodwell continued in that capacity during Macready's management from 1837 to 1839, apparently with Tom Cooke as leader, and when Madame Vestris and her husband Charles Matthews took over the theatre in 1839, Bishop reappeared at Covent Garden in his old capacity of musical director.

Although it is probable that Bishop then directed the orchestra with a baton, it should be understood that previously, with the exception of Weber, and possibly of Smart, none of these musical directors were conductors of the orchestra as we now understand that expression. It was still the violinist-leader who was in charge of the orchestral playing. But it is quite certain that when Julius Benedict became musical director in 1841, he conducted the orchestra with a baton.

Between 1842 and 1847 the fortunes of Covent Garden Theatre were fluctuating and uncertain, and the theatre was often closed. When open, the orchestra was generally conducted by Benedict; for the production of

---

[1] Northcott, *Life of Bishop*, p. 44.   [2] Saxe Wyndham, *Annals*, I, p. 336.
[3] *Annals*, II, p. 37.   [4] *Ibid.*, II, p. 53.

COVENT GARDEN THEATRE IN 1804

Mendelssohn's *Antigone* in January, 1845, George Macfarren was the conductor, and for a few weeks in 1842, when a German opera company occupied the theatre, the conductor who came with the company was Vincenz Lachner.

For a few weeks at the end of 1844, 1845, and 1846, Covent Garden Theatre was the scene of Jullien's Concerts, and the immense orchestra which filled the stage on these occasions was directed by Jullien himself, a conductor who had no illusions as to the proper function of a baton-conductor.

Of the various leaders at Covent Garden, the first we hear of in the early years of the century was William Ware, who had been there since 1798. Ware appears to have left in or about 1819, and according to a pay-roll of the theatre the leading violinist was then William Henry Kearns, who was described as deputy-leader. When Ware left it was said that he took several of the players with him, and the orchestra underwent "considerable change." The next leader was apparently Cotton Reeve, and it was said that with his advent "regularity had been much promoted, and the excellence of the general performance certainly not diminished."[1]

A very good picture of the Covent Garden orchestra about this time (1818–1820) is afforded by the pay-roll, signed by Bishop, and preserved in the British Museum.[2] There were altogether twelve violins, four of which were double-handed and might be called upon to play other instruments. Kearns received 14s. a night for his services, but Thomas Brown who led the seconds was apparently worth only 8s. 4d. a night. There were two violas, two 'cellos, and two double-basses, the latter valued at only 5s. 10d. a night. The wood-wind consisted of one flute and one clarinet, but there were two oboes and two bassoons. Joseph Birch was the solitary flautist at 9s. 2d. a night; George Hopkins was alone in his glory as solo and only clarinettist, and might also have to play the violin when required; but for the production of *Oberon* in 1826, George Hopkins and his brother Edward played the clarinet parts. Probably the best remembered of that Covent Garden orchestra was William Thomas Parke, author of the well-known *Memoirs*, who was solo oboe from 1783 to 1825, and received 10s. a night. It is difficult to suggest why John Mackintosh, who was then the first bassoon, should have been paid as much as the leader for each performance, while his colleague Edmund Denman had to make do with 5s. 10d. Both of these bassoon players were to become members of the Philharmonic orchestra.

The brass instruments comprised two horns, two trumpets and one trombone, and of these Thomas Wallis, the leading trumpeter, gained 5s. extra whenever he was required to play on the keyed bugle,[3] in addition to his regular pay of 9s. 2d. a night. Samuel Pritchard carried on his shoulders the burden of the only trombone part for the modest sum of 5s. a night.

---

[1] *Quar. Mus. Mag.*, Vol. I, No. III, p. 407.   [2] Add. MS., 29365. Northcott, p. 44
[3] Bishop wrote some parts for the keyed bugle, as in *Guy Mannering*, 1816.

New Covent Garden Theatre, 1809–1856

Thomas Chipp was the drummer, but for his pay of 5s. 10d. a night he was also required to play the harp and to tune all the pianos in the theatre. The list winds up with the general-utility-man, William Goodwin, no doubt one of the old family of orchestral librarians, who for £1 a week had to play the bells, castanets, tambourine, etc., and probably do anything else that had to be done.[1]

Lack of further records makes it impossible to view the changing personnel of the Covent Garden orchestra during the 'thirties and early 'forties. Later leaders, in addition to Tom Cooke, appear to have been Evan William Thomas (1814–1892), and Hughes who was leader during Benedict's time, also J. W. Thirlwall, who led for the short time when Macfarren conducted the orchestra. William Price, who died aged thirty-one in 1844, after having played the flute at Covent Garden for twelve years, was probably Birch's successor. A veteran of long service was the double-bass player Joseph Woodham (1768–1841), who played in the orchestra for over forty years, and was for forty-five years a member of the Royal Society of Musicians.

Having spent the greater part of his professional career as oboe player in the orchestra, W. T. Parke was no doubt somewhat prejudiced when he wrote of the playing at Covent Garden in 1817: "The performance of Mozart's music by the theatrical band of that day (led by Ware) would have done honour to the Opera House."[2] When Weber heard the orchestra at Covent Garden immediately after his arrival in London, he wrote to his wife: "the orchestra was good, but not distinguished."[3] Later on he expressed himself as being satisfied with the playing at the performance of *Oberon* which he conducted not long before he died in London. The *Harmonicon* could find no more to say on the occasion of the first performance of *Oberon* than that "the orchestra did its duty well."

In 1829, when Fétis severely criticised the orchestras at Covent Garden and Drury Lane Theatres, it seems that both must have been rather second-rate affairs. But some improvement was recorded during the 'thirties, as well as an increase in the number of players: "Let us, however, do justice to the bands at each, which have been strengthened and refined in a degree more than equal to the expectations of the public, as was evinced in the superior manner in which they executed the fine and difficult overtures of the great German masters. For this improvement in the orchestras at our national theatres, we are, it must be confessed, indebted to the Philharmonic concerts."[4]

In 1833 Adolphe Adam was in London, and expressed himself quite pleased with the Covent Garden Theatre orchestra, except on one day in the week. It appears that the members of the orchestra invariably got drunk on pay-day, with the result that the performances on Saturday nights were

---

[1] For complete list, see Appendix, p. 489.
[2] Parke, II, p. 126; production of *Don Juan* in 1817.
[3] Weber, II, p. 665.　　　　[4] *Harm.*, Jan., 1831, p. 1.

nothing more or less than a riot on the part of the orchestra, while the audience looked on quite unperturbed and apparently took it all as a matter of course.   Adam described how at the start of the overture the oboe emitted a startling *couak*, only to be followed by a still more prodigious *couak* from the clarinet.   When the turn of the bassoon came, a series of most frightful snores emanated from his instrument, while in the meantime the flute continued to make unceasing *turlututus* on his instrument, as if nothing could stop him.   The trumpeter put the bell of his instrument into

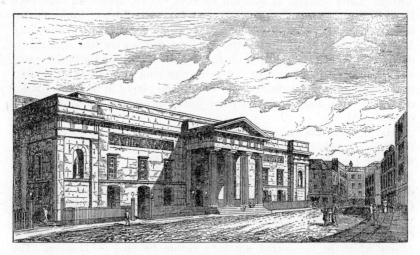

New Covent Garden Theatre as Rebuilt after the Fire in 1808

his neighbour's pocket and blew blasts of air through the clothing of his surprised colleague, and the bass drum player belaboured his instrument with diabolical ardour, as if determined not to be outdone by anything that his brother-players could produce.   Meanwhile, the conductor and the actors on the stage calmly carried on with their business as if nothing unusual was happening.[1]

Despite some improvement in the 'thirties, the orchestra seems to have remained at a level well below that of the King's Theatre under Costa, and far below the standard of the Paris opera-theatres.   When Benedict became conductor in the early 'forties there was clearly a distinct improvement in the status and the quality of the Covent Garden orchestra, and under Macfarren in 1845 the performance of the orchestra was said to be "good."

But it was not until after the reconstruction of the interior in 1846, when Costa seceded from Her Majesty's Theatre and opened Covent Garden as the Royal Italian Opera in 1847, that this theatre gained a really first-class orchestra: "Mr. Costa, who undertook the entire musical direction, presided

[1] A. Adam, *Souvenirs*, pp. 54–57.

over an orchestra of picked players, consisting of the best English and foreign professionals, and pronounced to be unquestionably the best ever assembled in England."[1]

The orchestra for the first season numbered altogether 81 players, of which 53 came from Her Majesty's Theatre. Sainton was the leader, Ella led the second violins, Moralt (1785–1847) was to have been the leading viola, but he died before the season began and his place was taken by Henry Hill; Lindley was at the head of the 'cellos, but Dragonetti's name is missing from the list; the great bass-player had died in 1846, and it was Anfossi who led the double-basses in the new orchestra. Several of the names of the string players (Blagrove, Hann, Trust) are still well remembered in orchestral circles in London. The leading wood-wind players were Ribas, Barret, Lazarus and Baumann, all principals from the old opera orchestra, Platt and Harper were the leading horn and trumpet players, and the trombones included Smithies and Cioffi; the latter was one of Jullien's soloists who was said to have gone about with a silk hat "lined with news-paper cuttings relating to his performances."[2] Prospère, another of Jullien's star performers, played the ophicleide, and Thomas Paul Chipp beat the drums in this brave orchestra, certainly the largest and undoubtedly the best opera orchestra that had ever been assembled in London. The military stage-band was from the Coldstream Guards under Charles Godfrey, and Alfred Mellon was conductor for the ballet music.[3]

No sooner was it heard than a chorus of praise greeted the new orchestra and its conductor.

For the season of 1848 another first violin, a double-bass, and a second harp were added, bringing the total strength up to 84 musicians, and a critic (Davison) was moved to write of it: "In speaking of the orchestra of the Royal Italian Opera, we take off our critical cap, and make a low obeisance, . . . It is almost unnecessary to add that it will be the finest orchestra in the world, without making any exception whatever."[4]

The chorus of praise was continued during the 1849 season: "We unhesitatingly acknowledge its vast superiority to all existing or pre-existing bodies of operatic orchestras"—"The band is beyond our eulogy"—and similar tributes were showered on the new Covent Garden orchestra.

In 1850 the orchestra lost its first horn player, Platt. He was obliged to resign, "having lost, from great and continuous pressure, the whole of his front teeth."[5] A concert for his benefit was arranged, patronised by the Queen and Prince Albert, and *Punch* hoped that "the Horn of Platt would be the Horn of Plenty." Of this season (1850) it was said that it was "impossible to speak too highly" of the orchestra.

When the season of 1852 opened, "it was at once discovered that the orchestra was richer and more brilliant than ever, having since 1851 been

[1] Anon., *Mus. Recoll.*, II, p. 188.   [2] *The British Musician*, Jan., 1894.
[3] For complete list, see Appendix, p. 489.   [4] *Mus. World*, Feb. 12, 1848, p. 98.
[5] From the advt. in the *Mus. World* of Platt's Farewell Concert, April 20, 1850, p. 252.

reinforced by the no less important additions of Signor Piatti as violoncello, and Bottesini as contra-basso *primi*, a pair of orchestral players who were expected to prove unequalled since the departure of Lindley and Dragonetti, but who failed, for some inexplicable cause, to fulfil the expectations that had been formed concerning their value and usefulness."[1]

BOTTESINI, FAMOUS DOUBLE-BASS PLAYER

The opera at Covent Garden continued to flourish in the early 'fifties, and the rival establishment closed its doors in 1852. But a calamity was to fall upon the theatre in 1856, when it was burnt down and the Royal Italian Italian Opera had to take refuge for a few years in the Lyceum Theatre. But a new and larger Covent Garden Theatre soon arose on the same site, and in 1858 the Royal Italian Opera again opened its season with Costa and his orchestra as brilliant as ever.

A few words may be added about the earlier Oratorio Concerts at Covent Garden, which were under different management from that of the theatre proper.

[1] *Mus. Recoll.*, II, p. 243.   The pair became known as "Pi and Bo."

Although complete works were sometimes performed, these so-called "Oratorio Concerts" had degenerated during the early years of the 19th century, and had become very mixed entertainments in which selections from oratorios and operas were mingled with concertos, instrumental and vocal solos of all descriptions, including such things as variations on *Rule Britannia* played on the oboe by Parke, and on *God save the King* by Drouet the famous French flautist. Henry Phillips said of these concerts, they "always terminated with a secular act of the most common and frivolous music. Habit reconciled the public to this strange *mélange*, and I suppose it answered a purpose."[1]

In 1800 these concerts at Covent Garden Theatre were under the management of John Ashley sen., while General Charles Ashley led the band, and John James Ashley was at the organ.[2] The old organ, which had been bequeathed by Handel to Rich, the original owner of the theatre, was destroyed in the fire of 1808, together with many valuable scores. The orchestra employed at the Oratorio Concerts was quite independent of the regular theatre orchestra, and included many players from the King's Theatre, and later, from the Philharmonic orchestra. Between 50 and 60 players were engaged, including three trombones and a serpent. Weichsell became leader in 1801, but in 1811 one of the Ashleys was again leader. In 1815 S. Wesley was at the organ. The orchestra then included some of the regular theatre players, as well as a number from the King's Theatre and the Philharmonic. In 1820 William Ware was the leader, and in 1825 Mori held that position. Smart was the conductor from 1813 till 1825, and in that year S. Wesley became "conductor at the organ and pianoforte."

The Oratorio Concerts at Covent Garden and Drury Lane Theatres were amalgamated during the 'twenties, and the performances were given alternately in the two houses. In 1830 J. D. Loder and Wagstaff were alternately leading, and the orchestra at that time included Lindley ('cello), Card (flute), Grattan Cooke (oboe), Willman (clarinet), Denman (bassoon), Platt (horn), Harper (trumpet), Smithers (trombone), Chipp (drums), and Ponder (serpent). Henry Phillips described the arrangement on the stage as follows: "A sort of painted theatrical front, of gothic pattern, was placed on the stage near the footlights, there were a few chairs for the principal singers, a chorus of some eighty voices, an orchestra of about fifty performers, the conductor, with his back to us, looking the orchestra full in the face, and an old organ belonging to the theatre."[3]

It was at one of these Oratorio Concerts that Weber made his first public appearance in London, conducting with a roll of paper, twelve numbers from his opera *Der Freischütz*.[4] Parke described him as standing

[1] *Mus. and Personal Recoll.*, I, p. 75. [2] *The Times*, March 28, 1800.
[3] *Mus. and Personal Recoll.*, I, p. 75. Rowlandson's aquatint (1808) shows the arrangement before the fire in that year. Saxe Wyndham, I, p. 324.
[4] Weber, II, p. 666.

"in front of the singers on the stage."   At these, as at the Ancient Concert, a professional choir was employed.   The subsequent decline of the Oratorio Concerts appears to have been co-incident with the rise and development of amateur choral societies in England.

DRURY LANE THEATRE BEFORE THE FIRE IN 1809

DRURY LANE THEATRE

Of the orchestra at Drury Lane in the early years of the century not very much information is available, but it can be assumed with tolerable certainty that it was no larger and no better than that at Covent Garden.   As at the latter theatre, there was always a "composer and musical director" at Drury Lane, whose office should never be interpreted as that of conductor of the orchestra.   Until the 'thirties, if there was any conducting, it was done by the violinist-leader of the orchestra.

Sir George Smart described the leader at Drury Lane at the beginning of the century. He was a Mr. Shaw, who "had a peculiar way of whistling through his nose rather loudly when bowing a *forte* passage. Some of the strangers who were seated close to him in the orchestra would ask if there were a dog near him which was making this noise. He never would acknowledge that it came from him."[1]

Henry Smart, Sir George's brother, was leader at Drury Lane Theatre from 1812 to 1821: "It was his peculiar pride to have formed the Drury Lane band entirely of English professors."[2] His successor seems to have been Tom Cooke, who had been associated with the orchestra at Drury Lane long before that time; but it is difficult to follow the movements of Cooke between Drury Lane and Covent Garden Theatres, and to distinguish between his functions as leader of the orchestra and musical director. In 1824 Bishop came to Drury Lane as musical director, and in the succeeding years produced many of his musical stage-works and adaptations, including *Aladdin*, which he put up in 1826 in rivalry to Weber's *Oberon* at Covent Garden.

No very good accounts of the playing of the orchestra during the 'twenties can be found. For its performance in *Der Freischütz* (1824) the Drury Lane players were thus censured: "The overture seems to lose much of its spirit in the orchestra; there is a tameness about it now that, if not corrected, will bring the efficiency of the band into question."[3] There seems to be little doubt that it was then a second-rate affair, content with rather slap-dash playing, and that it remained so until early in the 'thirties, when some improvement in its performance was recorded, as well as an increase in the number of players.

The versatility of the leader, Tom Cooke, is revealed in several contemporary accounts; there seemed to be little that this rather too all-round musician could not or did not try to do; at one of his benefit concerts he is said to have performed solos on nine different instruments,[4] and Kelly told a story of how Cooke at the same time played the first violin part and sang the solo in an aria at Dublin in 1807.[5] He was also "principal singer" at an Oratorio Concert at Covent Garden in 1816, and took the leading tenor part (Max) in the Drury Lane production of *Der Freischütz* in 1824. Fétis, who ranked the Drury Lane and Covent Garden orchestras in 1829 below those of the *Variétés* and *Théâtre de Madame* in Paris, gave the following account of Cooke's performance: "You can imagine the effect when they play *Oberon*, *La Dame blanche*, or *La Muette de Portici*. At Drury Lane M. Tom Cooke is at the same time director of the music, leader of the orchestra, and actor for the role of second tenor, when there is one in the opera. If he does not appear on the stage until the second act, he leads the orchestra during the first act, gives up his place in the orchestra to some miserable violinist during the second act, returns later enveloped in a great coat to

[1] Smart, *Journals*, p. 7. [2] *Quar. Mus. Mag.*, Vol. V, No. XX, p. 561.
[3] *Harm.*, Dec., 1824, p. 234. [4] Barrett, *Balfe*, p. 37. [5] Kelly, II, p. 232.

beat the big drum in an important part because there is no one else to do it, or assists the double-basses, which are none too many. That is how the music is treated at the English Opera."[1] Even if Fétis was exaggerating, it is obvious that there could be no finished orchestral playing at a theatre where the music was so roughly handled.

When its resources were quite inadequate for the occasion, the orchestra at Drury Lane was temporarily enlarged. Thus, for a production of *Don Giovanni* in 1833, "the orchestra, in order to do justice to such a work, was augmented by the principal instrumentalists of the King's Theatre and Philharmonic bands, Sir. H. Bishop being the conductor, and Mr. Tom Cooke the leader."[2]

Although Fétis probably heard the Drury Lane orchestra at its worst, and would have been able to give a better account of it had he heard it a few years later, it is fairly certain that it never ranked as a good orchestra, nor that it was even as good as might be found in some of the second-rate German theatres. For its share in *Fidelio* in 1836, when it was certainly better than in the 'twenties and was probably augmented for the occasion, the orchestra was thus criticised: "With somewhat more attention to the *pianos* and *fortes*, both in the chorus and the orchestral accompaniment, (which last is much too overbearing—these gentlemen should be drafted off to the French opera for a season or two) the opera is very well brought out."[3] The English orchestra certainly could not bear comparison with its opposite numbers at the *Opéra Comique* or the *Théâtre Italien* at Paris, any better than the band at the King's Theatre could compare with the orchestra at the Paris *Opéra*.

From 1832 to 1839 the theatre was under the management of Alfred Bunn, and during that period many foreign operas (adapted) as well as some native works by Barnett and Balfe were produced. In Balfe's *Maid of Artois* (1836) the *cornet-à-pistons* was a new-comer to the orchestra; it was introduced as an *obbligato* to the air "The Light of other Days is faded," and was described as "an instrument then new to the public, and producing a most charming effect."[4]

Later in the 'thirties, when Bishop was still musical director, some effort was made to increase and improve the orchestra. In 1837 Eliason was leader, and he was credited with having "vastly improved the orchestra." An important addition was the appointment of James Howell as leading double-bass in 1838; on him, it was said, had "descended the mantle of Dragonetti," and this acquisition was "equal to four double-basses." From the same source we learn that the orchestra was re-arranged, with the violins congregated *en masse*, and flanked by the trombones and drums, all the wind being on the left of the conductor. By this time the orchestra was being conducted with a baton: "Mr. Bishop was well received, and the majestic overture (*Don Juan*) of the mighty master-mind under his *bâton*

[1] *Curiosités*, p. 250.   [2] *Mus. Recoll.*, I, p. 271.
[3] *Mus. World*, May 13, 1836, p. 140.   [4] Phillips, *Mus. and Per. Recoll.*, I, p. 216.

PLATE 12

Tom Cooke, Leader and Singer at Drury Lane

PLATE 13

DRURY LANE THEATRE IN 1821

went most magnificently."[1] H. G. Blagrove and Eliason were apparently
joint-leaders in the autumn of 1838, and in January, 1839, we get the following sketch of the orchestra at Drury Lane when *Guillaume Tell* was being
played: "An orchestra, of which every individual violinist was a solo player
of strong and brilliant execution, would alone be able to do full justice to
the exaggerated rapidity of some parts of the accompaniments. The
Drury Lane band contains able players; but in the execution of these traits
of the original there wants much of the distinctness of a perfect *ensemble*.
For the full effect of these passages, as Habeneck, the able Parisian conductor
would insist upon them, we need a greater correspondence in the *coups
d'archet*. Our English orchestra is lamentably deficient in this nicety of
musical execution, without which the highest clearness and the most
decided expression are quite unattainable. It has an almost comic effect to
see the two first violins, Blagrove and Eliason, take the passages in a way the
most dissimilar that can be imagined—one bow going up the other down—
the one playing short notes with the tip, the other with the contrary extremity
of the bow; in short, the most striking opposition in the conception of the
passage, often in the comparison to the disadvantage of the English player.
This want of unity, rendered absurdly conspicuous by the position of the
two principal violins, should be remedied in every orchestra in which it
prevails, if perfection be aimed at."[2] It is easily understandable that Bishop
could not train a mixed group of violinists with the same effect that Habeneck
achieved with his Conservatoire-trained players.

Early in the 'forties Bunn again speculated with English opera at Drury
Lane Theatre, and produced several popular works by Balfe (*Bohemian
Girl*, 1843),[3] Benedict, and Wallace (*Maritana*, 1845). Another production
was Handel's *Acis and Galatea*, put on the stage in 1842 with scenery such
"as had never before been painted." The music, unfortunately, was placed
in the hands of Tom Cooke, "who played all sorts of tricks with the score,
interpolating a mass of rubbish that was wholly unsuited to the design of the
work, and totally irrelevant to its progress."[4] Henry Phillips, who took the
part of *Polyphemus*, considered this "the most perfect musical and scenic
production ever, perhaps, witnessed on any stage,"[5] but a more unbiassed
and candid observer remarked that "the orchestra was very weak and
imperfect—a result the less excusable because the music it had to play and
accompany is by no means difficult."[6]

In 1841 there were forty players in the Drury Lane orchestra, and a little
later, while Tom Cooke was still in charge, the number was increased to
45, and Thomas was the leader.

At the beginning of 1843 Benedict became conductor at Drury Lane
Theatre. The sketchy methods of Tom Cooke would certainly be abandoned

---

[1] *Mus. World*, Oct. 4, 1838, p. 69.   [2] From the *Monthly Chronicle*.
[3] An unlucky critic made a bad shot when he predicted that the *Bohemian Girl* would
"hardly outlive a day." *Mus. World*, Nov. 30, 1843, p. 394.
[4] Anon., *Mus. Recoll.*, II, p. 138.   [5] *Mus. and Per. Recoll.*, II, p. 33.
[6] Anon., *Mus. Recoll.*, II, p. 139.

at that time, and as a baton-conductor with continental experience
and a musician of some taste, Benedict would no doubt improve the
orchestra and raise the performing standard to a level much higher than
had prevailed in those dark days when Fétis saw fit to scourge the orchestras
of our two National or "Winter" theatres.

Benedict continued to conduct at Drury Lane until the end of 1844, with
Tom Cooke as leader.   Benedict was followed by Francesco Schira, who
had previously been conducting opera at the Princess's Theatre.   The
next year saw the first performance of *Maritana*, for which the orchestra was
augmented and conducted by the composer.   The leader at this time was
Hughes, and it seems that Schira continued, off and on, as the regular
conductor for some years, and was still there in 1847.

Still the orchestra appears to have been far from first-rate, and in the
following criticism it is suggested that this was due to the parsimony of
Bunn, the manager, and to shortcomings on the part of the conductor:
"The Drury Lane band requires decided amelioration.   There is a want of
quality and of tone in the leading instruments.   The violins are much too
weak for the bass strength.   We have no great confidence in the abilities of
Signor Schira as musical director.   We wish the lessee could be impressed
with the importance, in the present advanced state of musical knowledge
of making a grand orchestral improvement, and let us no longer be under
the reproach that the Drury Lane band is inferior to a tenth-rate Parisian one.
We write under the impressions of last and previous seasons.   We are
unaware that there have been any alterations of note, but if we find them we
shall be most happy to signalise them."[1]

In the summer of 1845, and again in 1846, an opera company from
Brussels was playing at Drury Lane Theatre, and was supposed to have
brought over its own orchestra of 30 players under the conductor Hanssens;
but it was found that only 17 of the players came from Brussels, and that
the rest were inferior players from Ghent, and a few others who were picked
up in London.

Late in 1846 the orchestra at Drury Lane was remodelled and enlarged;
it was said to have been brought more forward into the auditorium.   When
The Maid of Artois was revived, "the band was in excellent training.   The
overture was well played and the accompaniments generally correct."[2]
But soon after that we hear that the Drury Lane orchestra suffered, like so
many other English orchestras, from having to play under so many different
conductors: "A constant change of conductors must of necessity bother
any orchestra in the world, much more an orchestra like that of
Drury Lane, which, with all the desire to be perfect, is anything but
perfection."[3]

In the years 1847 to 1852 Drury Lane Theatre was the scene of Jullien's
concerts.   These generally lasted for a month in the mid-winter season,

---

[1] *Illus. Lon. News*, Sept. 27, 1845.   [2] *Mus. World*, Oct. 10, 1846, p. 491.
[3] *Ibid.*, Oct. 31, 1846, p. 539.

during which time the regular theatre orchestra was presumably unemployed, for Jullien occupied the stage with his own picked orchestra.

In 1847 the theatre was newly decorated, and after his usual season of concerts, Jullien speculated wildly in an attempt to run opera in English at Drury Lane on a most lavish scale. The orchestra was almost the same as that employed at Jullien's concerts, and the conductor was Berlioz. Never before had the old theatre contained so large and so fine an orchestra, nor such a distinguished conductor. The players came from Costa's orchestra at Covent Garden, from Her Majesty's Theatre, and from abroad. Among the violins were Sainton, Blagrove, Tolbecque, Nadaud, Mellon, Goffrié and Pluys; Hill, Alsept and Trust were among the violas; the 'cellos included Piatti, Rousselot, Hausmann and Lavenu, and Howell, Anglois and Casolani were among the double-basses. The leaders of the wood-wind were Richardson, Barret, Lazarus and Baumann; Platt, Charles Harper and Henry Jarrett were among the horns; Koenig played the cornet, Cioffi the trombone, and Prospère the ophicleide; altogether 66 players of a quality never before assembled in the orchestra pit at Drury Lane, and all under the command of the most energetic French conductor. Wilhelm Ganz heard some of the performances early in 1848, and wrote in his *Memories* that "the orchestra was splendid."[1] No doubt it was! but it is doubtful whether Drury Lane had ever before harboured such an unhappy conductor, for, although he had excellent material to work with, the rehearsals were too few and too hurried, and the rate of production far too hasty for such an exacting conductor as Berlioz. The ill-fated venture was soon wrecked on the rock that had brought to grief so many operatic ventures in London— finance. (For full list of players, see Appendix, p. 490.) The same orchestra played at Berlioz's own concert at Drury Lane early in February, 1848: "The band was as one instrument, upon the strings and pipes of which the conductor seemed to be playing."[2]

Early in the 'forties (1841) a German opera company were playing at Drury Lane under Adolph Ganz, and again in 1849 the theatre was occupied by a German company conducted by Carl Anschütz of Coblenz; but there is no word of the orchestra, whether it came from Germany, or was supplied by the local players.

In 1850, at one of Jullien's concerts, Drury Lane heard for the first time a new and strange instrument—the Saxophone. The Drury Lane orchestra, even if it could have competed with that of Covent Garden for the greater part of the half-century, was hopelessly outclassed when Costa assembled his opera orchestra at the latter theatre in 1847. Parke was possibly quite right when he said that Covent Garden was the more musical of the two houses.

---

[1] Ganz, *Mem.*, p. 52.

[2] *Mus. World*, Feb. 12, 1848, p. 97. At this concert Berlioz's *Harold in Italy* was performed, with Hill as viola soloist. The recitative in the "Triumphal Symphony" was played on an alto trombone by Koenig.

Several players who eventually went on to the King's Theatre began their orchestral careers at Drury Lane. Amongst these were Thomas Harper the well-known trumpeter (in 1806), John Ella (in 1821), Edward Platt the horn-player, and Joseph Calkin (1781–1846) who after ten years' service (1798 to 1807) became a viola player at the King's Theatre, the Ancient Concert, the Vocal Concert, and in the Philharmonic orchestra, in which for a long time he also acted as librarian. As a youth, fresh from Dublin, Balfe played the violin in the Drury Lane orchestra from 1823 to 1825, and sometimes took Tom Cooke's place as leader.

At Drury Lane Theatre, in addition to the non-musical plays, were produced the same sort of English song-operas and adaptations or mutilations of popular foreign operas as at Covent Garden and other London theatres. In 1824 *Der Freischütz* was served up in at least three London theatres in as many different versions. There was no limit to the mania for adaptation and the bad taste exhibited in dishing up music of different styles and periods in our "national" theatres during the first half of last century, and Drury Lane took its full share in harbouring these inartistic monstrosities.

Concert Orchestras in London

The concert-giving societies in London were unable to maintain orchestras for their own exclusive use. The players were largely those who were more regularly employed in the three largest theatres, augmented by a few who made their living as solo players and teachers. Thus, the King's Theatre and the Philharmonic Society could hardly have given performances at the same time, for between them they shared the best of London's instrumentalists; but, as opera was given on only two nights a week during a season of four or five months, it was quite possible for a player to belong to both orchestras, and also to take engagements in the summer at Vauxhall Gardens, at Jullien's concerts, at the provincial festivals, and at solo artists' or "benefit" concerts.

The most influential concert-societies were: The Concert of Ancient Music (1776–1848), the Vocal Concert (1792), the Philharmonic Society (1813), the Societa Armonica (1827), and the Sacred Harmonic Society (1832–1880).

Although the Ancient Concert was primarily vocal in character, an orchestra, which grew from about 40 players to 55, was always employed. In 1817 this orchestra numbered 45 performers; during the 'thirties and 'forties it varied between 45 and 55, excluding about 10 R.A.M. students who were allowed to participate during the last ten years of the society's existence. There was a paid choir of from 60 to 70 voices, all the altos being men, but during the 'thirties a semi-chorus of 12 voices was added, while the main choir was reduced to rather less than sixty voices.

Choral and solo works formed the basis of all the programmes, but symphonies eventually became a fairly regular feature of these performances.

Mozart's Jupiter and E flat symphonies were introduced in 1826, a few of Haydn's symphonies were added to the repertoire during the 'thirties, Beethoven's *Prometheus* overture made its first appearance in 1835, and the same composer's *Egmont* overture and second symphony were first heard at these concerts, respectively, in 1841 and 1842.[1] According to the rules of the society no music was played until at least twenty years after it was composed, but this rule was evidently relaxed when some works of Beethoven and Weber were performed during the 'thirties and early 'forties.

At the beginning of the century the concerts, twelve in each season, were held in the concert-room at the King's Theatre. Previously they had been given (since 1795) in the New Rooms, Tottenham Street. In 1804 the concerts were moved to the Hanover Square Rooms, the lease of that property having been acquired by the society. These rooms were then "fitted up in the most splendid manner for the performances," and the orchestra had been moved from the east end to the west end of the room.[2]

The conductors (at the organ)[3] were Thomas Greatorex from 1799 to 1831, William Knyvett from 1832 to 1839, and various conductors from then until 1843, when Sir Henry Bishop was appointed. John Ella suggested that the decline and demise of the Ancient Concert was largely due to the unenterprising direction of Bishop: "Had the directors nominated Costa, instead of the late Sir Henry Bishop, to the conductorship of these concerts, he would have reorganised the choral and orchestral forces, and infused vitality into the venerable institution."[4] The *Musical World* commented on the decline of these concerts as follows: "It is with regret that we contemplate the decay of these concerts, which used to be so exquisitely select with regard to the *matériel* of assistants. The Ancient Concert room *was* a theatre for the most accomplished professors, not (what it has been made of late years) a school-exhibition for students."[5]

The leaders of the orchestra were: William Cramer until 1804, when he was succeeded by his son François Cramer; J. D. Loder from 1844, and Tom Cooke from 1846 until the society's dissolution in 1848. The other names in the orchestral lists were largely those of well-known players who also belonged to the Philharmonic and the orchestra at the King's Theatre. Of 53 instrumentalists at the Ancient Concert in 1841, 37 were also in the Philharmonic orchestra. A peculiarity in the constitution of the former was the employment of four oboes and four bassoons until early in the 'thirties, no doubt a tradition which reached back to the 18th century when it was customary to use these instruments in larger numbers as *ripieno* players.[6] The regular use of clarinets, four horns and three trombones for music

[1] *Mus. Ass. Proceedings*, Feb., 1907, and programmes.
[2] Cocks, p. 7.
[3] "Till 1841 he occupied the organ-stool, a position most unfavourable for making his influence felt." (*Mus. Ass. Pro.*, 1907, p. 69.)
[4] Ella, p. 71.
[5] *Mus. World*, March 18, 1836, p. 6. This refers to the R.A.M. students.
[6] For full list in 1839, see Appendix, p. 491.

which up to the 'thirties was almost exclusively by 17th and 18th century composers, raises more than a mere suspicion that "additional accompaniments" were largely used, and that the Secretary and Librarian, Mr. W. Greatorex, an incorrigible arranger and adder of accompaniments, was kept fairly busy gilding lilies.   And when an ophicleide, harp, cymbals and triangle were included in the later orchestras to play music which could hardly have been written for any of these instruments, it becomes obvious that the Royal and Noble directors of the Ancient Concert did not disapprove of the practice of bringing the orchestration of the old masters up to date.

The Vocal Concert was a middle-class offshoot of the aristocratic Ancient Concert, and was started in 1792 by Harrison and Knyvett at Willis's Rooms. Most of the singers were the same as at the Ancient Concert.   This was essentially a vocal society; only a piano and a string quartet, led by Cramer, provided the instrumental accompaniment in the first year, but in 1793 a pair of horns were added, played by the Leander brothers.[1]   In 1794 these concerts were abandoned, probably owing to the strong rivalry of the Haydn-Salomon concerts and the Professional Concerts, but in 1801 the Vocal Concert was re-established under Harrison, Knyvett, Bartleman and Greatorex, with a "considerable band," the latter, no doubt, being a concession to the growing taste for instrumental music.   At the beginning of the century the concerts were still held in Willis's Rooms, but like the Ancient Concert, they were moved to the Hanover Square Rooms in 1804.

For some time the Vocal Concert flourished.   In 1817 it was again discontinued, but it seems to have been revived in the following season by Greatorex, with Weichsell as leader of the orchestra.   In 1819 an orchestra of 38 players was employed, under the leadership of F. Cramer.   Nearly all the instrumentalists were those whose names figured in the programmes of the Ancient and the Philharmonic concerts.   It was written in 1820 that the Vocal Concert was "composed as nearly as possible of the same musical elements" as the Ancient Concert.[2]

In 1821, by which time the concerts had been reduced from nine to six in the season, the Vocal Society again expired, only to be once more re-established in 1822 by Greatorex and Knyvett for the purpose of rescuing "our national music from perishing in the vast vortex of Italian Opera." The *Harmonicon* tells of the Vocal Concert again coming to an end in 1822, and of its revival at the Argyll Rooms in 1823 under Smart, Attwood, and Bishop, with Mori as leader of the orchestra.

The existence of these concerts after 1823 appears to have been fitful. It was said in 1825 that there were only two regular subscription concerts that season,[3] thereby implying that the Vocal Concert was not then in operation.   But in 1833 a Vocal Society came to life in the Hanover Square

---

[1] "A duet, in which they imitated the effect of a double and triple echo, continued for many seasons to be a standing favourite at concerts and music meetings." (*Harm.*, Aug., 1831, p. 187.)

[2] *Quar. Mus. Mag.*, Vol. II, No. VII, p. 378.   [3] *Harm.*, Sept., 1825, p. 163.

Rooms, directed "at the organ and pianoforte," by Turle, Goss and Horn-castle, with Tom Cooke as orchestral leader. According to the *Musical World*, the Vocal Concert still existed in 1836, and in 1838 it seems to have been again reconstituted with Lucas as conductor and Dando as leader.[1]

For their concerts both the Ancient and the Vocal societies engaged professional players according to their necessities, and such names as Cramer, Lindley, Griesbach, Dragonetti, Nicholson, Mackintosh, Hyde and Harper in their programmes suggest that they employed the best of the London players. But, as orchestras, these bodies cannot be said to have had any separate existence; they were composed entirely of players drawn from a common pool. The *Harmonicon*, although constantly criticising the programmes and general policy of the Ancient Concert, was always pleased with the orchestra: "The instrumental band of these concerts is in perfect order"[2]—"We cannot take leave of this fine instrumental band without expressing our deep regret for the loss of Griesbach and his unrivalled oboe." Griesbach was succeeded in 1823 by W. Ling, who some years later was recommended not to add embellishments of his own to Handel's oboe parts: "We are highly pleased with Mr. Ling's performance of the oboe solo in the overture to the Occasional Oratorio; we only recommend that in future he will play it simply as it is written; anything approaching to flourish, or even *extra* grace, completely destroys the symmetry that Handel meant should be preserved throughout the whole of this exquisite movement."[3] Nevertheless, Ling was allowed to be "very respectable, . . . and indeed, now that we have lost poor Griesbach, is decidedly the best performer on the instrument left us."[4]

While it is probable that the Ancient Concert perished partly owing to its old-fashioned policy and its very exclusive and aristocratic constitution, it is likely that its final demise, and that of the Vocal Concert, was largely caused by the rise of the Sacred Harmonic Society (1832–1880). Starting in quite a modest way, this typically English choral society flourished greatly from 1834, when it took up its abode in the new Exeter Hall, a building which had been opened in 1831 for "religious and scientific assemblies,"[5] and could accommodate between 3,000 and 4,000 people, as well as 500 on the platform.

The first conductor of the society was Joseph Surman, and the leader of the orchestra was George Perry, who still held that position in 1847 when Mendelssohn conducted the first performance in London of his revised *Elijah*. In 1848 Costa became conductor of the society, with the stipulation

---

[1] *Mus. World*, Jan. 19, 1838, p. 40. Early in 1838 Sterndale Bennet played a Mozart concerto at the Vocal Concerts, "a new musical association which employed an orchestra." (*Life of S.B.*, p. 69.)

[2] *Harm.*, July, 1823, p. 101.   [3] *Ibid.*, May, 1827, p. 99.   [4] *Ibid.*, April, 1825, p. 68.

[5] Edwards, p. 20. For two years the concerts were given in the small hall, but from 1836, in the large hall.

that he should enjoy "supreme authority,"[1] that authority having been hitherto divided between the leader of the orchestra and the conductor. Among those who played in the orchestra in 1838 were: Ella, Banister, and Blagrove (violins); Moralt (viola); Lindley ('cello); Anfossi (double-bass); Card (flute); Grattan Cooke and Keating (oboes); Lazarus (clarinet); Godfrey[2] (bassoon); Harper (trumpet); Platt (horn); the two Smithies

EXETER HALL IN 1840

(trombones); Ponder (ophicleide); Chipp (drums).[3] The orchestra, however, always included a substantial proportion of amateur players amongst the strings. When Costa took charge in 1848 a number of changes and improvements naturally followed, and by the mid-century the orchestra was large and powerful enough to require 16 double-basses, while an ophicleide was freely used to strengthen the bass parts in the Handel choruses. The total strength was then 700 singers and instrumentalists.

THE PHILHARMONIC ORCHESTRA

Much more important and far-reaching in its influence on the history of orchestral music in this country was the establishment in 1813 of the Philharmonic Society.

[1] Edwards, p. 25. When Surman was deposed he started a rival society called the London Sacred Harmonic Society.
[2] Charles Godfrey, founder of the well-known family of bandmasters.
[3] *Mus. World*, Feb. 9, 1838, p. 87.

This was essentially an instrumental institution, although vocal items were not excluded from the programmes; and it was primarily orchestral, notwithstanding the chamber music which remained a regular feature of the concerts for many years. But while at the Ancient and Vocal concerts the instrumental music was introduced only in order to provide relief from the sound of voices, at the Philharmonic it was the vocal element that was admitted by way of imparting variety to programmes which were mainly instrumental in character.

From the beginning until 1846, when a permanent conductor was appointed, the policy of the society was to change the direction with each concert; thus, the director of the orchestra "at the piano" was appointed for only one concert, and he was generally selected from among the members of the society. There was "no distinction of rank"[1] in the orchestra. Only good players were admitted, and any of the violinists might be called upon to act as leader for any one concert. So, for the first ten years of the society's history, the concerts were directed "at the piano" by Clementi, J. B. Cramer, Sir George Smart, Attwood, Dr. Crotch, Sir Henry Bishop, Vincent Novello and a few others. The violinist-leaders were similarly varied from concert to concert, and the changes were rung between such as Salomon, F. Cramer, Spagnoletti, Viotti, Kiesewetter, Weichsell, Mori, Loder, and a few others. Visiting composers and violinists were not excluded, and the society welcomed Cherubini in 1815 and Spohr in 1820, and certain concerts were led by Baillot from Paris, or by Spohr or Mazas. The violins in the orchestra included most of the best players in London. The violas included W. Sherrington, Viccari, W. Griesbach, Richard Ashley and John Mountain, while Lindley, Charles Ashley and F. W. N. Crouch gave backbone to the 'cellos. Henry Hill sen. was the leading double-bass player during the first two seasons, but in 1816 that department of the orchestra gained strength by the acquisition of Dragonetti.

Members and Associates of the society received "no emolument from the funds" for their services,[2] and, as there were few wind players amongst them, most of the players on these instruments had to be engaged and paid a fee. Andrew Ashe (flute) was an original member, and the first list of Associates included Christian Kramer (clarinet); these, presumably, blew their parts for the love of it, but the remaining wind players had to be paid in hard cash. Parke explained the situation as follows: "At its foundation it was so arranged, that all members, however high their professional rank, should, when not appointed to play quartets, quintets, etc. (for concertos were interdicted), descend from their stilts, and play *ripieno* parts, thereby

---

[1] "There shall not be any distinction of rank in the orchestra, and therefore the station of every performer shall be absolutely determined by the leader of the night." (*Rules of the Society*, Hogarth, p. 6).

[2] "No Member or Associate shall receive any emolument from the funds, all money received being appropriated only to the public purposes of the Society; nor shall any Member or Associate receive any pecuniary recompense for assisting at the concerts." (From the *Rules of the Society*, Hogarth, p. 6.)

forming a combination of excellence such as no other concert (since the dissolution of the Professional Concert) could boast. The French horns, bassoons, trumpets, and oboes were not admitted as members, but were engaged by the season; but for what reason that distinction was made I cannot divine, unless it proceeded from the idea, that in paying their foundation subscriptions, the professors of these flatulent instruments might be too long-winded!"[1] It seems, however, that the arrangement under which Members and Associates received no payment for performing at the concerts did not last very long: "On this plan the society flourished for three years, and as the expenses were small and the receipts large, a considerable sum was accumulated. Nevertheless, at the end of the season of 1815, personal differences broke out among the members, and an opposition concert, under the name of *The Professional*, was carried on for one year by the schismatics. But the attempt proved as abortive as it had been ill judged, and the deserters were glad in the following season to again flock to the standard they had abandoned. This temporary alienation of some of the performing members made it imperative on the directors to engage other assistance, upon the usual professional terms, which, as a matter of course, led to the payment of all who formed part of the orchestra."[2]

The following occur amongst the names of the wind players employed during the first ten years of the society's concerts: Flute—Andrew Ashe, Nicholson (from 1816 to 1836), and Ireland (from 1814 to 1821); Oboe—F. Griesbach and M. Sharp; clarinet—Mahon, Oliver, Kramer and Willman (from 1817 to 1839); bassoon—Holmes, James Tully and Mackintosh (from 1815 to 1835); horn—Leander, the brothers Petrides, Puzzi (1817), C. Tully and Arnull; trumpet—Harper.

The Philharmonic concerts were held in the Argyll Rooms until that building was burnt down in 1830, then for a few years in the concert-room at the King's Theatre, and from 1833 in the Hanover Square Rooms. The change was signalised in a periodical called *The New Anti-Jacobin* as "a blessed escape from the filthy hole in which they have assembled for some years past."

It was in 1833 that the platform in the Hanover Square Rooms was extended further into the room and was lowered to four feet at the front, making it much more suitable for an orchestra: "The great and beneficial effect of this alteration was universally admitted, and the rooms acknowledged to be the worst in London for music, are now confessedly become the best."[3] The concerts were continued in Hanover Square until 1869, in which year they were moved to St. James's Hall. The property in Hanover Square had passed into the hands of Cocks[4] the music publisher in 1845. In 1862 the old rooms were renovated and redecorated, and the organ was

---

[1] Parke, II, p. 160.

[2] Extract from a letter in *The Harmonicon*, Oct., 1828, p. 217, written by one who signed himself "Common Sense."

[3] *Harm.*, April, 1833, p. 81.   [4] For £12,820, according to *The Times*.

removed.   But its day was then over; renovation did not restore to the old
concert-room its former glory: "What concert-goer does not remember the
dingy, dirty, ugly room in Hanover Square?   He would hardly know it
again, now that it has been under the renovating hands of Mr. Dyke, to
whom Mr. Cocks, the well-known music publisher, had entrusted the task
of rendering the appearance of the large room worthy of its reputation."[1]

The earlier programmes of the Philharmonic Society generally contained
nine or ten items, usually two symphonies, two overtures, two or three

W. Read.

THE ARGYLL ROOMS IN 1825

vocal pieces, two quartets or other concerted pieces, and one or two
miscellaneous pieces, fantasias, etc.

An analysis of the programmes during the first ten years of the society's
existence shows the symphonies performed as follows:

Beethoven (Nos. 1 to 7)	32
Haydn	49
Mozart	37
Spohr	3
Other composers	28
Total	149

Such was the beginning of the famous society which gave to London its
best orchestral concerts since the memorable seasons of Salomon in 1791
and 1794, when Haydn gave to the world his last and best symphonies.
Successfully launched and favourably sponsored, the society's concerts soon

[1] *The Queen*, Feb. 16, 1862. The rooms were used for the last time for a concert of the
R.A.M. on Dec. 19, 1874 (*Illus. Lon. News*, Dec. 26, 1874).

P

became the focal point of orchestral activity in this country, and the magnet which drew so many composers and performing artists from abroad.

No doubt the playing of the large and well-constituted orchestra was something of a revelation to the London music-lovers of that time: "This performance, we will venture to pronounce, has never been surpassed in this, or any other country; and probably has never been equalled. The band consists of persons who are all at the head of their respective departments, and certainly no orchestra ever before exhibited so many celebrated leaders playing the subordinate parts. Such however was the case on this occasion, as well as in every subsequent performance; and the effect was adequate to the means. The violins in particular produced a sound so simultaneous, that it seemed to proceed from one extraordinary instrument, struck by some equally extraordinary hand. It was not only the power and unity of the band that was remarkable, but also the consummate taste and judgement of every individual composing it."[1] That was written of the first concert of the Philharmonic Society in the Argyll Rooms on March 8, 1813, when Clementi was "at the pianoforte" and the orchestra was led by Salomon, when Cherubini's *Anacreon* overture opened the proceedings, and when a symphony by Beethoven and one by Haydn (neither of which is identifiable) were performed, together with sundry items by Mozart, Sacchini and Boccherini.

Of the season of 1816, Parke wrote: "There were not any concerts this year but the three established ones, the *Ancient*, the *Vocal*, and the *Philharmonic*. The latter from its excellence had become popular."[2] Firmly established and strongly supported by the musical profession, the Philharmonic concerts easily withstood any opposition by rival offshoots: "Public estimation has increased at every succeeding season, with the exception of a very short and ineffectual opposition, which about four years since arose out of some slight dissensions, and which gave occasion to a concert (called THE PROFESSIONAL CONCERT) that was soon abandoned. Few of the members had withdrawn their names, and therefore the Philharmonic Society suffered no diminution worth notice."[3]

There can be no doubt as to the excellent quality of the players in the Philharmonic orchestra; "The band engaged for these concerts is the best that can be procured."[4] They needed only a competent and more enlightened method of direction to bring them up to the level of the best of the continental orchestras. Spohr remarked on the "numerous and particularly excellent stringed instruments of the orchestra" in 1820, and added: "In fact, as regards the stringed instruments, I have never since heard that symphony given with so much effect as on that evening."[5] The ensemble, however, under the old method of direction, was not quite satisfactory: "So numerous an orchestra, standing so far apart from each other as that of the Philharmonic, could not possibly go exactly together, and in spite of

---

[1] Burgh, III, p. 454.   [2] Parke, II, p. 116.   [3] *Quar. Mus. Mag.*, Vol. I, No. III, p. 344.
[4] *Harm.*, March, 1823, p. 41.   [5] Spohr, II, p. 84.

the excellence of the individual members, the ensemble was much worse than we are accustomed to in Germany."[1] It was then that the historic event took place in which the London players are said to have been given their first experience of being controlled with a baton.[2]

Moscheles was rather lukewarm about the Philharmonic orchestra when he first heard it a year later: "Beethoven's *Pastoral* symphony was very fairly executed under Kiesewetter's direction at the Philharmonic Society's Concert, the drums too noisy."[3] On that occasion Kiesewetter was the violinist-leader, and Sir George Smart the conductor; it is significant that Moscheles should have said that the symphony was played under the direction of Kiesewetter, and not under Smart. But if the orchestra was sometimes criticised by visitors from abroad, it seems to have given every satisfaction to local critics. One of these thought that it could not be equalled elsewhere: "The symphonies and overtures were given in the usual superior manner, unequalled anywhere else."[4]

From 1823 to 1846 the society's concerts continued on much the same lines as before, with slight changes in the style of programme, and not without some ups and downs. Many of the same directors took charge of the performances, and, although the term "at the piano" had been changed to "conductor" in the programmes after Spohr's visit in 1820, it is incorrect to assume that the orchestra was then controlled by a baton-conductor.[5] Amongst these so-called conductors some of the old names had dropped out, and some new names had appeared; the newcomers were Charles Neate, Tom Cooke, Moscheles, Lucas and Sterndale-Bennett. More or less the same leaders continued to function in turn, but with the addition of the versatile Tom Cooke. Weichsell retired in 1838, and F. Cramer in 1844. Some changes were recorded among the strings in 1838: Willy, Thomas, Marshall and Guymeyer joined the violins; Dando, J. Banister, Alsept and Pensam were new to the violas, and H. J. Banister replaced Rousselot the "imported" French 'cellist of the King's Theatre.[6] During the 'thirties and 'forties the violas included Moralt as leader, Henry Hill jun. (d. 1856) and William Sherrington (1783–1845) who had been playing since 1813. Lindley and Dragonetti remained pillars of strength in the bass department; the former retired in 1846[7] and was succeeded by Charles Lucas, and Dragonetti's successor was James Howell.

After the death of Nicholson in 1837 Ribas became principal flautist, and remained until 1851, to be succeeded in the following season by R. S. Pratten. William Card (1788–1861) for many years played the second flute and piccolo. Griesbach's successor as first oboe was Centroni in 1824, and soon afterwards Grattan Cooke was the leading oboist.[8] The latter was

---

[1] Spohr, II, p. 81.   [2] See page 319.   [3] Moscheles, I, p. 56.
[4] *Harm.*, May, 1823, p. 72.   [5] See page 321.   [6] *Mus. World*, March 3, 1838, p. 161.
[7] Lindley's last appearance as a soloist at the Philharmonic was on May 20, 1850.
[8] Grattan Cooke was the player who was once "seen struggling up the concert-room with a long ladder. He had resented the introduction of a very high note for his oboe in a new composition, and had gone for assistance to enable him to reach it" (Sterndale-Bennett, p. 111).

dismissed in 1850, much to his indignation, and his place was taken by Alfred Nicholson. Willman's successor at the Philharmonic was Joseph Williams (1795–1875), a native of Hereford. Apropos of this player and the Hereford Musical Festival in 1828, a correspondent of a musical paper wrote: "We see no reason why the good folks of Hereford are to be deprived of the best performer on the clarionet (Willman) merely because a native

of the town happens to play the same instrument. We do not deny that Mr. Williams has talent, but it is not of the first order."[1] Philip Powell (d. 1847) had played second clarinet with Willman for many years, and went to America 1837; his place in the Philharmonic orchestra was filled by Henry Lazarus. Mackintosh's successor as first bassoon in 1835 was James Denman, in 1839 Baumann occupied that position, with James Tully still playing second bassoon.

After the brothers Petrides had left London in 1825 the horn players were Schunke, Platt, Rae, Charles Tully and A. Kielbach, while Puzzi continued to appear as a soloist until about 1840. Regarding the first of these, it is uncertain which of the large Schunke family it was who then came to London. There were seven

CARICATURE OF DRAGONETTI, THE
GREAT DOUBLE-BASS PLAYER

German horn players of that name, five brothers and two sons; of these, Gotthilf and Christoph Schunke had visited London in 1814. The particular Schunke who came to London in 1825 and played in the Philharmonic and other orchestras was said to be "a good horn player, but not equal to Puzzi."[2] Later it was written of him in the same paper: "the new horn, M. Schunke, is a man of high talent." Schunke's name appeared in the programmes of the R.A.M. concerts in 1826 and 1827, and of the Birmingham Festival in 1826. After Schunke, the leading horn player was Platt, and Henry Jarrett[3] appeared a few times in the 'forties. Charles

[1] *Harm.*, Oct., 1828, p. 221.   [2] *Ibid.*, March, 1825, p. 69.
[3] Henry Jarrett became Jullien's first horn, and also his secretary and organiser of his orchestras. Later on he went to New York and made a fortune as an impresario (Rivière, p. 102). He acted as agent for Christina Nilsson, Sarah Bernhardt, and other famous artists (Hueffer, p. 127).

Harper eventually followed Platt as first horn when the latter was obliged to resign in 1850 for the same reason that caused him to leave the Covent Garden orchestra.

The elder Harper continued as first trumpet, with J. B. Irwin as his colleague, and was succeeded by his son, also called Thomas, in 1848. In the 'thirties the two Smithies (father and son) played the alto and tenor trombone, but Mariotti's place as bass trombone had been taken by Albrecht. Mr. Chipp continued to beat the drums, and his name still figured in the list of the orchestra until 1860.[1]

The programmes during this period (1823–1846) show the chamber music growing less and less towards 1840. The solos for wind instruments also became fewer about that time, while piano and violin concertos appeared more frequently. The society remained true to the symphonies of Haydn, Mozart and Beethoven; some by Spohr and Mendelssohn were added to the repertoire, while overtures by Weber and Mendelssohn began to take the place of the hitherto popular overtures of Cherubini. Notable visits by foreign composers were those of Weber in 1826, Mendelssohn in 1829, 1832, 1833, 1842, 1844 and 1847, and of Spohr in 1843. Outstanding events were the first performance of Beethoven's Choral symphony in 1825,[2] Mendelssohn's Italian symphony in 1833, and a first taste of Berlioz's music in 1841. Hueffer wrote of the latter event: "In the same year Berlioz's overture to *Benvenuto Cellini* was hissed at the second concert given by the Philharmonic Society."[3]

During the second decade of the society's existence (1823–1832) the orchestra gathered fresh laurels, and appears to have satisfied the native critics that it could not be equalled anywhere else. The following, written of the first concert in 1824, in addition to eulogising the personnel of the orchestra as a whole, also comments on the acquisition of a new oboe player to succeed Griesbach, and, incidentally, shows how the *Eroica* symphony struck a critic in 1824:

"He (F. Cramer) led the band with that enthusiasm which has led him to the summit of the art of which he is so great an ornament. At his side Kiesewetter, Mori and Spagnoletti played; perhaps no orchestra in Europe ever boasted such an assemblage of talent in this particular department. The rest of the band, it is well known, includes the most celebrated instrumentalists that can be assembled. The only novelty, however, was the introduction of Centroni, who occupied the place of Griesbach. This artist has recently come to England, and is certainly a performer of considerable merit, and possessing a great command over his instrument, the

---

[1] Thomas Paul Chipp was born in 1793, and was a chorister of Westminster Abbey before he became the foremost drummer in London. He retired in 1866 and died in 1870.
[2] According to the *Mus. World* (1837) the symphony was "mercilessly butchered" in 1825; the same performance was also described as a "caricature."
[3] Hueffer, p. 134. This was described in the *Athenæum* as an "extreme proceeding," and the *Mus. World* said that the overture was "unmitigated, veritable rubbish, beyond the redemption of any second hearing, or hundredth hearing."

hautbois.   His tone is not so rich and mellow as that of his predecessor, for even the most strenuous supporters of foreign talent are seldom found to deny that instrumentalists arrive at a higher perfection of tone after hearing the London orchestras, where this peculiar excellence is most highly cultivated.   At present, Signor Centroni's best quality may also be said to be in a degree his worst, for the facility of execution which he possesses is apt to seduce him into the practice of more ornament that sound taste would dictate in performing the compositions of the great masters.   These exuberances, however, time and good example will hardly fail to correct. In Beethoven's splendid Symphonia Eroica there are parts of such exquisite beauty and effect as to make ample compensation for the many strange and unconnected thoughts in which he has but too frequently indulged.   The length of the piece is greater than would be patiently tolerated in any composer who has not so completely pre-occupied the public judgement as Beethoven, full three-quarters of an hour being employed in its performance. In truth, the audience seemed to wish it shorter."[1]

After Weber had conducted the Philharmonic orchestra in 1826 he wrote to his wife that it was "really a very excellent institution.   A magnificent orchestra.   It delighted me."[2]   The critic of a London paper went so far as to say that Weber had "pronounced the Philharmonic to be beyond dispute the finest band in Europe."[3]

The English critic, Edward Holmes, who wandered about Germany in 1827 just as Burney had done fifty years before, and who dedicated his anonymous book to the Members of the Philharmonic Society, prefaced his story by saying: "that though one may find no band (in Germany) equal to that of the Philharmonic Society, fifty may be found only inferior to it. . . . In their singers and wind instrument players (always excepting certain individuals) they are decidedly our superiors; but in their violin school they appear to me inferior both to England and France."[4]   The *Harmonicon* commented not only on the excellent quality of the orchestra, but on the effect of the Philharmonic concerts in fostering greater appreciation of orchestral music in this country: "The present is the 15th season of the Philharmonic Concerts.   The improved state of the taste in England for music of the instrumental kind, may be attributed to these performances, which have not only snatched the orchestral compositions of the great masters from the oblivion with which they were threatened in England, but restored them with so much care, and in a style of such unusual grandeur, that it may be doubted whether, upon the whole, the authors themselves ever heard them under more favourable circumstances."[5]   In 1836 the *Musical World* held that the Philharmonic Society "ranks second to none in Europe, for the splendour of its orchestral performances."[6]

Perhaps it may be advisable to make some little allowance for local pride

[1] *Quar. Mus. Mag.*, Vol. VI, No. XXI, p. 68.   [2] Weber, II, p. 676.
[3] *Quar. Mus. Mag.*, Vol. VIII, No. XXX, p. 164, f.n.   [4] *Rambles*, IX.
[5] *Harm.*, March, 1827, p. 57.   [6] *Mus. World*, April 15, 1836, p. 80.

and loyalty when assessing the value of such panegyrics by native musicians and critics. Foreign opinions may be more outspoken, and if their judgements are more severe, it is because their standards of comparison were based on the playing of only the very best of the orchestras in France and Germany.

Mendelssohn, who got on very well with most orchestras, and who was so uniformly successful that he could well afford to scatter compliments around, was very pleased with the Philharmonic players when he first made their acquaintance in 1829[1]; but his praise savours a little of one who was anxious to be polite and pleasant to a body from which he might expect to derive some benefit in the form of engagements and further performances of his works. A much more candid judgement was that of Fétis, who spent the season of 1829 in London for the purpose of studying the state of music in England, and, even if he was a little disgruntled with his reception in this country, had no particular axe to grind.[2] When he first heard a symphony played at the Philharmonic concert, Fétis was struck by the ensemble and energy of the orchestra, and he granted that the playing was such as would elsewhere be considered excellent. But, he said, to one who has just heard the *Conservatoire* orchestra in Paris, a comparison of the first musical establishments of Paris and London was not to the advantage of the latter. The same ensemble and energy was also found in the French orchestra, but there they combined these qualities with a more youthful spirit, more delicacy, and a firmness of purpose for which one looked in vain in the London orchestra. The most delicate nuances were given only in a small degree by the Philharmonic players, and only rarely did they show any real warmth of feeling. Their accuracy was irreproachable, but their sensibility was mediocre. Fétis was careful to insist, however, that it was only when compared with the *Conservatoire* orchestra that the Philharmonic fell short. Anyone who had not heard the French orchestra would be quite satisfied with the English one. Fétis remarked that he was able to detect the same view in the judgements of some other visitors to London who were qualified to form an opinion, and mentioned particularly Mendelssohn, whom he met in London during that same season of 1829. This throws some doubt on Mendelssohn's sincerity when he so highly praised the London players. Nevertheless, Fétis greatly admired the London double-basses, who played, he said, with such precision, distinctness, delicacy and force as was not known in France. These good qualities he attributed to the excellence of the school based on the playing of Dragonetti.

Regarding the English and French wind players Fétis had some interesting comparisons to make. Nicholson's flute-playing was marked by a clean execution which left nothing to be desired, but it lacked the poetical feeling of Tulou's playing. For Willman the clarinettist he had nothing but praise: "never has a doubtful note come from his instrument," but of the

---

[1] Hensel, I, p. 184.   [2] *Curiosités*, pp. 186–195.

English oboe players he thought less than nothing.[1] It was impossible to imagine anything worse! The Philharmonic would not engage Barret (who was then playing at the King's Theatre) for fear of having no oboe at all in the event of his leaving London. Fétis strongly recommended the directors to get a French oboe player to settle in London. As a matter of fact, Barret did remain in London, and Lavigne was soon to come. The English bassoons, said Fétis, were very good, but too strong.

The French critic had little that was favourable to say about the Philharmonic horn players. The Italian Puzzi was remarkably talented, but he was a solo player, and was in a position to refuse to do ordinary orchestral work. Platt was not up to the mark—uncertain, and apt to spoil the best effects. But to Harper, the trumpeter, Fétis paid the greatest compliment by saying that Paris might well envy London its foremost trumpet player. The timpani sticks used in London were stouter than those used by the Paris drummers, and made a very good effect, especially in the storm in the *Pastoral* symphony. This was a compliment to Mr. Chipp. Fétis was going to take a pair of English drum sticks back with him to Paris.

Fétis wound up his remarks as follows: "As you see from my letter, the playing at the Philharmonic is a mixture of good and bad; but, in general, it is very satisfactory, and one might say that in a country where the music has reached such a standard they should attain to greater perfection in a short time."

Another carefully considered judgement was that of Ferdinand David, Mendelssohn's leader at the *Gewandhaus* at Leipzig. David's opinion, given in 1839, was that the London Philharmonic orchestra would be equal to the best in the world if only, instead of half a dozen conductors, they had someone like Mendelssohn, someone who would be respected by the musicians, and would drill them thoroughly for a couple of years. As it is, he wrote, the orchestra sounds like a wonderful organ played by a dull and tasteless player. "The tone (*klang*) is beautiful, but there is no shading; they attack all difficulties as if they were paid extra for them; the *sforzandos* are like elephantine footsteps, and they don't know how to play either *pianissimo* or *fortissimo*." David said that the English double-basses sounded splendid, but that the high pitch used at these concerts was "a great evil."[2]

In 1841 David wrote to Mendelssohn about the playing by the Philharmonic orchestra of his *Melusine* overture: "But it was so insipid, without either light or shade, and it made me quite angry."[3]

Both Fétis's and David's criticisms were probably nearer the truth than either Weber's or Mendelssohn's more flattering remarks. Undoubtedly, what the orchestra required was a good conductor and good training. The material was there, but the man to handle it was lacking. No doubt Smart, Attwood, Crotch, Bishop, and the like, were sound and worthy musicians,

---

[1] It was probably Grattan Cooke that Fétis heard. [2] Eckardt, pp. 102–3.
[3] *Ibid.*, p. 124.

each competent enough in his own sphere; but it can well be imagined that they had not exactly the right outlook, and neither the experience nor the gift that was required to inspire and control a large orchestra of about seventy players at the time when Meyerbeer and Berlioz were beginning to make their weight felt, and when Wagner and Liszt were beginning to show on the musical horizon.

There seems to be little doubt that in the later 'thirties, and up to the time (1846) when Costa became conductor, the orchestra of the Philharmonic Society had settled down to a standard of performance which could only be described as second-rate. There were at that time several old players who should have retired earlier, but that alone was not the cause of the decline. Dual control by the leader and conductor, an evil which was not eradicated until Costa finally put an end to it, and the choice of complacent conductors who had no special gift for orchestral conducting, being content to let the playing go on in the humdrum way that had satisfied auditors who had little or no knowledge of the higher standard that had been reached in the best continental orchestras—both of these were undoubtedly causes which contributed more to the decline in the orchestral playing than the presence of a few players who were past their best.

The comments of the anonymous author[1] of the *Musical Recollections* on the Philharmonic orchestra in 1835 point very clearly to an unsatisfactory state of affairs which was due to the direction of the orchestra rather than to the quality of the players: "The seventh Philharmonic Concert, May 25, was one of the most unequal that it ever was the misfortune of the subscribers to listen to; for the two Symphonies—Spohr's in E flat and Beethoven's in D—the latter of which threw the former wholly into the shade—Mendelssohn's *Midsummer Night's Dream* and Beethoven's *Fidelio*, were so slovenly played under Mori's leading, that it was suggested 'there was a fine opening just then for a new leader in London, as it was impossible that he, who by no means satisfied the critics in this capacity, could bear the weight of everything upon his shoulders, especially as other veteran performers were retiring, or should do so'."[2] It is remarkable that as late as 1835, fifteen years after Spohr was supposed to have reformed the method of direction, the responsibility for the playing should have been placed upon the leader of the orchestra, and not upon the conductor, who on this particular occasion was Henry R. Bishop.

Just before the opening of the 1841 season a crisis arose which seemed to threaten the very existence of the orchestra. The rehearsals had always been held on the Saturday morning for the concert on Monday, and up to that time there had been no opera rehearsal on Saturdays; but now Laporte at the Opera insisted that his orchestra must be at his beck and call, and that if necessary he would call rehearsals on Saturday mornings. As the Opera

---

[1] Rev. John Edmund Cox (1812–1890).

[2] *Mus. Recoll.*, I, p. 339. The last passage is quoted from the *Athenæum*. According to the *Hist. of the Phil. Soc.* (p. 135), Weichsell was the leader at this concert.

and the Philharmonic shared more than 35 of the same players, it was clearly impossible for the two orchestras to rehearse or play independently at the same time, and the opera engagement being the more lucrative of the two, some players were ready to give up their engagements at the Philharmonic rather than lose the whole season's work at the Opera.   The Philharmonic directors would not entertain the idea of changing the time of their rehearsal, nor would they consider altering the traditional day of the week on which their concerts had always taken place.   For a short time there was a dead-lock, and neither party would give way, but reason seems to have prevailed, and some arrangement was concluded by which the Philharmonic could have its rehearsal and concert at the traditional times without having to lose the services of its best players.[1]

About the same time (1841) there were certain changes in the orchestra, some occasioned by death or retirement, and others by the voluntary secession of members, it was said, "in consequence of the general reduction of terms."[2]   Newcomers to the violins were Eliason, Payton, Hope and Thirlwall; W. L. Phillips joined the 'cellos, and W. Bull, Charles Severn (1805–1894) and Schroeder came to the double-basses, thus raising the total number of those instruments by two.   Among those who retired, presumably on account of the "reduction of terms," were Tolbecque and Anfossi the double-bass player.

In the early 'forties the playing of the orchestra and the policy of the directors were subjects of constant criticism.   No doubt the personnel of the orchestra and the directors of the society needed some new blood; the dual control of the orchestra by conductor and leader was unsound and antiquated, and Jullien's concerts were beginning to throw new light on what might be expected from a competent orchestra under the spirited direction of one man.   Dismal forebodings as to the future of the society were being circulated, and in May of 1842 the *Musical World* prophesied the approaching demise of the old society: "For ourselves, we will not increase the death-throes of an institution, of which, it is now probable, at the close of the present season, we shall have the melancholy duty of writing the epitaph."[3]

After Mendelssohn had conducted five consecutive concerts in 1844, to the manifest improvement of the playing, the idea of a permanent conductor was seriously entertained, and it was mooted that Costa might be selected. But there was much opposition to the appointment of a conductor who was supposed to be unfamiliar with the traditions of the German classics, and was really at home only in Italian opera.   It was cynically suggested that Jullien would be a better choice.

In 1845 the same question came up again.   A permanent conductor was obviously required—who should it be?   Costa's name was again put

---

[1] *Mus. World*, Feb. 18, 1841, p. 109.   A similar crisis arose in 1861, when the Royal Italian Opera (Costa) claimed the players on Mondays.   This time the Philharmonic stood firm and engaged new players (Sterndale Bennett, p. 296).

[2] *Ibid.*, March 1, 1841, p. 140.   [3] *Ibid.*, 1842, p. 157.

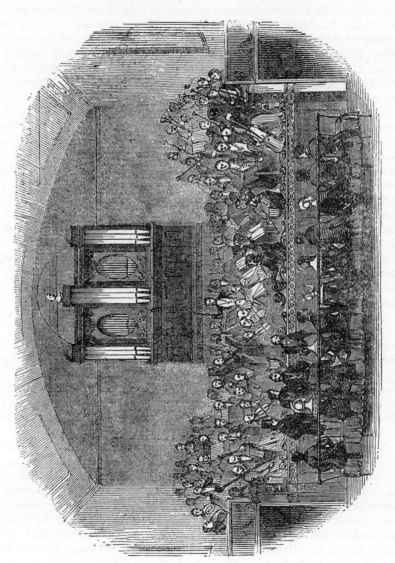

An Orchestra in the Hanover Square Rooms (1843)

forward; Davison, in the *Musical World*, said that "If M. Costa's appointment takes effect in the way intended, then adieu to the fame of the Philharmonic."[1] The Italian conductor was offered the post, but could not accept it on account of difficulties with Lumley who was then manager of the opera. When this became known Davison hailed the news "with infinite delight." Report then spoke of Habeneck as a likely conductor, and it was asked, would he conduct with a "fiddlestick or a baton?" Chorley (*The Athenæum*) had no doubt about Habeneck being a good disciplinarian, but was not at all sure that he really understood the German symphonists: "There is something more than drilling required of a conductor: sympathy with the music under his care." According to Chorley, Habeneck refined his Beethoven too much; his French taste, "if applied to the works of the great symphonists, tends to make them frivolous or affected—to chain up the flow of grand ideas—to fritter away noble proportions." Besides, Habeneck could not speak English! Of course, it was Mendelssohn that Chorley wanted, or failing him, Spohr would do, and failing Spohr, Benedict, Sterndale Bennett or Moscheles. It was the spirit of German music, and of the *Gewandhaus* in particular, that Chorley hankered for, and nothing else would really satisfy him. In the end Bishop was appointed, and as might have been expected, it soon turned out that he was not the man for the job. Bishop resigned (owing to bad health?) after the third concert, and Moscheles finished the season.

The falling repute of the performances at the Philharmonic during the early 'forties was probably mainly due to the fact that most of the conductors employed were not really orchestral conductors. Bishop, Smart, Cipriani Potter, Lucas and Moscheles were no doubt excellent musicians, but being a good musician, however distinguished, does not automatically turn a man into a first-rate orchestral conductor. None of these had the authority, nor could they enforce the discipline that was required to control a large and important orchestra in the 'forties of last century, especially when it tended towards indiscipline.

The days of dual control were not yet over at the Philharmonic, and there are plenty of signs which indicate that the orchestra lacked discipline. We can read how this orchestra rushed Bishop off his feet in the *finale* of the C minor symphony, and ended by "taking the baton (metaphorically speaking) from his hand."[2] Again in 1845, in the same symphony, when a certain *fortissimo* came, "the symphony took care of itself, and left the leader and conductor (Cooke and Bishop) to follow as well as they might."[3] In that same year the *Morning Herald* described the Philharmonic orchestra as being "intractable"; later on we read of "many rebellious subjects who fancy that they are as competent to teach the conductor as he is to instruct them," and another report speaks of the "impetuosity" of the Philharmonic players.

[1] *Mus., World*, Jan. 30, 1845, p. 50.   [2] *Ibid.*, June 8, 1843, p. 195.
[3] *Ibid.*, March, 1845, p. 183.

This orchestra, with its leader still insisting on being the centre of control, was clearly too unruly for its so-called conductors. G. F. Flowers, in the *Literary Gazette*, commenting on the state of affairs just before Costa was appointed, went so far as to say that each member of the orchestra played independently of the others: "The best players are not always the most effective in a band; second-rate performers, *under the entire subjection of the conductor*, will execute a classical work with better taste and feeling than the first-rate performers who are too proud to be led. The error of the Philharmonic band is, that every performer plays too independently of every other; each man performs too much in *solo fashion*; thus, then, the instruments will not blend together; but, on the contrary, one or more of the band *will* be heard above the rest, in order, no doubt, to show off their execution rather than the beauty of the composition."

The fact was, most probably, that Costa was the only man in London who could command the obedience of the orchestra, and it was a good thing for the society when in 1846 he was appointed sole conductor, and at the same time lost his position at Her Majesty's Theatre.

Costa stipulated that he should be given undivided control of the orchestra, and from that time the name of the leader no longer appeared in the programmes alongside that of the conductor. This was the end of dual leadership at the Philharmonic, and Costa had brought it about just as he had at the opera in 1833; it was a reform long overdue. Prosper Sainton was principal first violin under Costa, and many of the players who were to form the new Covent Garden opera orchestra were also in the Philharmonic. With that a new chapter in the history of the society's orchestra began, and under the control of a man who knew his business, the orchestra was again given the chance that it fully deserved. The critics who had been quite sure that Costa had no idea of how to render the German classics were obliged to admit, although sometimes rather grudgingly, that they had been greatly mistaken, and the playing of the orchestra under its permanent conductor was so highly praised as thoroughly to justify the new appointment and the new policy.

Already after the first concert of the season a great difference was felt: "The effect of Signor Costa's presence seemed to have magnetised the whole orchestra. A wave of his arm and the expression he required were simultaneous. The secret of conveying his own feelings to the orchestra under his control has seldom been more thoroughly exemplified by a conductor."[1]

The necessity for some changes in the personnel of the orchestra was no doubt realised by Costa from the moment that he took up the baton, but in this matter he found that the control was not entirely in his own hands. During the years that followed his first season of 1846, the new conductor managed to get rid of some inefficient players. For the season of 1848 a few old players were weeded out, and an increase in the number of string players was made; it was said that careless players were warned that their

[1] *Mus. World*, March 21, 1846, p. 131.

services might be dispensed with.[1] For this season Richard Blagrove joined the violas, and T. Harper jun. succeeded his father. A bad mishap in the *finale* of a Mendelssohn symphony was evidently the beginning of events which eventually led to the dismissal of Grattan Cooke in 1850. Piatti and Bottesini came to the Philharmonic orchestra in 1852.

What Costa was unable to do was to get sufficient rehearsal to weld the Philharmonic players into a body which could hope to rival the unity of the famous Paris Conservatoire orchestra. A comparison of the two orchestras in 1852, written by an Englishman, suggests that although man for man the Philharmonic might not fear comparison, in the matter of *ensemble* and the subservience of each player to the effect as a whole, the London orchestra had yet some way to go: "To compare the two orchestras let us begin at the bottom of the score. Their contrabassi are as superior to ours as Bottesini is to all other players—they really *play*, and don't make a fuzzy sort of sound. The 'celli show hardly so much difference, the four bassoons add much to their richness. Our tenors I think quite as good, thanks to the consummate musician and artist, Harry Hill. Our violins have more power in the fortissimo parts; like all the rest of the band in the *piano* parts, and in *tout ensemble*, they are far inferior. Their solo bassoon is richer than ours in tone, though not superior in execution. Our bassoons use too weak a reed. Of the clarinets we have already spoken.[2] Their oboes and horns are vastly superior. Our oboes never seem in tune, and our horns never seem to know their parts; how awfully they stumble about in the trio in the *Eroica*. Their flutes are not better than Ribas. Their trumpets are certainly not better than ours; while their trombones are so superior to our ear-splitting Bartlemy-Fair bulls of Bashan as can be conceived.[3] We have nothing like the pure tone of their wood-band—it is like the chords of the swell of an organ—nor have we the rich tone of their brass band; theirs is music, ours is blare. Our tympanist stands alone—none in the Conservatoire can rival Chipp. Whence, then, comes the difference? It is discipline—obedience—no one thinks of himself, nor plays for himself; every one is subservient to the whole. This is only to be got by repeated rehearsal; that is what the Philharmonic wants; and this it must have, or it will soon feel some rival at its heels."[4]

The rival appeared in that very year when the New Philharmonic Society was established at Exeter Hall with Berlioz as conductor. When, owing to differences with the directors, Costa resigned the direction of the Philharmonic concerts, his successor in 1855 was Wagner. That rather stormy season was followed by years of placidity under Sterndale Bennett.

---

[1] *Mus. World*, Jan. 22, 1848, p. 62.
[2] This was to the effect that the French clarinet players were no better than Williams and Lazarus.
[3] This brought forth an angry letter from Cioffi, first trombone of the Philharmonic, who demanded the name of the writer.
[4] *Mus. World*, Feb. 28, 1852, p. 135. The Conservatoire orchestra was then conducted by Girard.

It was rather curious that when Wagner conducted the society's concerts in 1855 he should have been able to detect so much of the Mendelssohnian tradition in the playing of the orchestra as he professed to do. Wagner wrote: "Mendelssohn had conducted the concerts during several seasons, and the tradition of his readings was carefully preserved."[1] Actually, apart from the occasion when he conducted two of his own works at one concert in 1847, Mendelssohn had conducted only five of the society's concerts, and that was in 1844. Wagner, who was not at all favourably disposed towards the Mendelssohn-Gewandhaus school of conducting, was probably annoyed when "the Directors continually referred one to what they called the Mendelssohnian traditions, but I suspect that Mendelssohn simply acquiesed in the traditional ways of the Society."[2] It was those "traditions," their own and Mendelssohn's, that roused all that was cross-grained and obstinate in Wagner's disposition. He gave the Philharmonic orchestra full credit for executive skill, but he felt that it lacked something that was difficult of supply: *"Ils jouent parfaitement, mais le feu sacré leur manque."*[3] (For full lists of the Philharmonic orchestra in 1837 and 1842, see Appendix, p. 490.)

OTHER LONDON ORCHESTRAS

An orchestral concert society of secondary importance was the Societa Armonica, which ended its existence in the concert-room of Her Majesty's Theatre in 1850 after a life of twenty-three years. This society was founded in 1827 by Henry Forbes, a pianist and organist, who conducted the performances. The leaders were Auguste Joseph Tolbecque,[4] Mori and Loder. The orchestra appears to have been made up of players drawn from the common well into which all the London concert societies dipped their hands when they wanted an orchestra. The same names occur as in the Philharmonic and opera orchestras—Lindley, Dragonetti, Nicholson, Ribas, Card, Barret, Powell, Baumann, Puzzi, Harper, and so on. The programmes were very much on the same lines as those of the Philharmonic, and were mainly instrumental, including symphonies, overtures, some chamber music, and a few solo items.

The following are extracts from a notice about the Societa Armonica which appeared in a London periodical in 1832: "This concert, held at the King's Theatre, has risen in estimation. Mori is there heard to advantage, who continues the same indefatigable professionalist, while Forbes the Conductor officiates at the Piano-Forte in the ablest manner. The band of the institution have to boast the aid of Harper, Lindley and Dragonetti, whose masterful efforts are in constant requisition. . . . This Society not being generally known, we beg leave to subjoin the plan of their concert on the 2nd of April last." The programme which followed included

[1] Wagner, *On Cond.*, p. 23. [2] Foster, *History*, p. 244. [3] Praeger, p. 238.
[4] One of a talented Belgian family of four brothers, the children of poor parents, who through the interest of Auber were admitted to the Paris Conservatoire (Rivière, p. 35).

Beethoven's fourth symphony, Hummel's Military Septet played by Forbes, Mori, Card, Powell, Harper, Lindley and Dragonetti, Weber's *Ruler of the Spirits* overture, and Rossini's overture to *William Tell*.[1] This society appears to have been the first to venture on a performance of Beethoven's Choral symphony after it had been introduced to this country for the first time at the Philharmonic in 1825. According to the *Athenæum*[2] it was "imperfectly executed" by the Societa Armonica in March, 1836. The Philharmonic Society did not revive it until the following year, under Moscheles's direction. In 1842 the orchestra of the Societa Armonica numbered 70 players, with Loder as leader, and it was still conducted by Forbes.

In addition to those of the regularly constituted societies, there were many series of "subscription concerts" organised by London artists on a speculative basis, and probably also by way of advertisement for themselves.

Quite a number of these subscription concerts came into being round about and during the 'twenties, either as (unsuccessful) rivals of the Philharmonic or with other objects in view, and later on there were many attempts to run promenade concerts on the lines that had been made popular by Musard and Jullien. All of these required orchestras, but none could produce one which was anything but a re-shuffling of the same men who played in the theatres and the established concerts.

In addition to the abortive Professional Concert (1815–16) another attempt to rival the Philharmonic was made by the promoters of the Argyll Concert in 1820. Attwood, Cramer, Crotch, Greatorex and Knyvett were the "conductors," and F. Cramer, Loder, Spagnoletti and Spohr were "leaders" of an orchestra which contained "almost every distinguished name" in the list of London's instrumentalists.

The City Amateur Concerts were started in 1818 in defiance of the principle that music could not exist without the support of the Nobility and Quality, and that concerts east of Temple Bar were wrongly situated. With Smart as conductor, Loder and Spagnoletti as leaders, and an orchestra which was "numerous and chosen with particular care principally from the members of the Philharmonic" with the addition of sixteen amateurs, these concerts at the City of London Tavern managed to keep alive for a few years, and were "suspended" in 1823. They appear, however, to have been revived in 1830.

The "British Concerts" barely lived for a season in 1822, and were designed to give much-needed encouragement to British composers, who at that time, as ever since, were constantly complaining that their music was neglected by concert-givers and unappreciated by concert-goers. This early attempt to force British music on a public that was not at all interested, perished for lack of support by the "British Nobility." By 1824 the *Quarterly Musical Magazine* had sadly to admit that "the City Amateur Concerts, the Vocal, and the British, have all ceased."[3]

[1] *The Apollonicon*, 1832, p. 2.   [2] March 26, 1836.
[3] *Quar. Mus. Mag.*, Vol. VI, No. XXI, p. 44.

Another attempt to provide artificial respiration for native music was the Society of British Musicians, founded in 1834. During the first few years of the society's existence a few orchestral concerts were given, but the public would not pay money to hear British music, and the scale of the performances was reduced to occasional chamber concerts given in a rather small way in the obscurity of Erat's harp saloon in Berners Street. This society, even in its earliest years, was dubbed "a mutual admiration society," and was said to have been carried on during the 'forties by "a mere coterie." It continued to give "chamber concerts of inferior calibre" throughout the 'fifties, and eventually expired from lack of public interest, internal strife, and the financial troubles that always pursue lost causes.

In 1825 a series of subscription concerts, to aid the funds of the Royal Academy of Music (then regarded as a sort of charity which the Nobility might be expected to support) set on foot by the committee of that institution "and governed by the noblemen and gentlemen composing that body," was inaugurated at the Hanover Square Rooms. "The instrumental band consisted of the professors of the Academy, who are indeed, generally speaking, members of the Philharmonic, with other assistance from that society—and amongst them were interspersed those of the pupils of the Academy who were able to sustain a part in an orchestra."[1] An orchestra of 67 players was employed,[2] and the programmes contained works by composers of almost every nationality except British. In January, 1828, the *Harmonicon* announced that these concerts were "discontinued."

Many resident musicians and numbers of visiting artists gave one or more "benefit" concerts in London during the season. Almost all of these required an orchestra, for the solo "recital" was not yet fashionable. No less than fifteen such benefit concerts are noticed in one issue of the *Harmonicon* in June, 1828, and of these thirteen employed an orchestra. Fétis estimated that about eighty benefit concerts were given in London during a season of two months in 1829. The *Quarterly Musical Magazine* gave a list of 39 concerts held in London during May, 1822.

There must have been plenty of work for the orchestral players of London in those days. The following extract by John Ella, who played in most orchestras from 1821 to 1848, shows how the best players were engaged during the course of a typical London season (1834): "Referring to my diary of some thirty years back, I find during the season in London that my orchestral engagements included twelve Concerts of Ancient Music on Wednesday evenings, and twelve public rehearsals on the Monday mornings previous; six concerts of the Societa Armonica, and eight concerts of the Philharmonic Society, for symphonies, overtures, solos and vocal music. At Her Majesty's Theatre the season included sixty subscription nights—Tuesdays and Saturdays—with a few extra benefit nights on Thursdays. Most of the benefit concerts, too, at the Hanover Square Rooms, were given

[1] *Quar. Mus. Mag.*, Vol. VIII, No. XXX, p. 167.
[2] For complete list, see Appendix, p. 491.

Q

with an orchestra."[1]   Under whatever name an orchestra played, it seems to have consisted largely of the same set of leading players, most of whose names have already been mentioned, and of a number of rank and file string players, many of whose names will be found in the Appendix to this volume.

Of the three largest Pleasure Gardens which had previously provided London with its summer music, only one managed to outlive the 18th century.   By the beginning of last century Marylebone Gardens had disappeared, Ranelagh was on its last legs, but Vauxhall Gardens were still fashionable.   Musically, the famous old gardens began to decline already in the 'twenties, and after dragging on for some years, went the way of Marylebone and Ranelagh and were finally closed in 1859.[2]

The orchestra had always been the central feature at Vauxhall, and in the "illuminated pagoda" were to be found some of the best musicians from the King's Theatre, the Ancient Concert, Covent Garden and Drury Lane theatre orchestras.   Up till about 1820 they numbered forty players, and, according to Parke, constituted "one of the finest bands in Europe."[3]   The leader in 1809 was named Brooks, and both of the Parkes played the oboe at various times in the Vauxhall band.   A "gilded cockle-shell sounding board over the orchestra" was added in 1824, and we are informed that the musicians at Vauxhall ceased to wear cocked hats round about 1846.[4]   Promenade concerts directed by Philippe Musard, the Paris show-conductor, were held at the gardens in 1845.

If Parke's account is correct, the decline of the orchestra began in 1821, when "with the exception of half a dozen stringed instruments," the music was "performed by the military band of the Guards, who, at the end of the acts, by doffing their coloured coats and slipping on their regimental ones, were quickly ready to perform their old duties of playing to the rope-dancing."[5]

In 1830–32 Sir Henry Bishop was musical director at Vauxhall, but its best days were then over, and a rapid deterioration in the quality of the music and entertainments gradually brought the once-fashionable gardens into the lowest repute.   A song-sheet of 1859, "The Farewell to Vauxhall," is headed by a picture showing the musicians carrying their instruments away from the old gardens for the last time.

It may be that it is possible to trace the origin of London's Promenade Concerts to the open-air orchestral playing in the pleasure gardens of the 18th century.   Even if that is so, it is certain that the stream, of which the source goes so far back into the 18th century, was joined by a powerful tributary which came from Paris in the 'thirties of the 19th century.

---

[1] Ella, p. 70.   During the "season" of 1837 there were 135 concerts in London; 79 at the Hanover Square Rooms, 33 in the room at the King's Theatre, 13 at Willis's Rooms, 6 in the London Tavern, and four in private houses.

[2] Wroth, p. 322.   [3] Parke, I, p. 284.   [4] Wroth, pp. 319, 323.

[5] Parke, II, p. 175.

PLATE 14

L'ANALYSE. SOUVENIR OF THE MUSICAL UNION, 1853

Left to right: Bazzini, H. Blagrove, Goffrié, J. Blumenthal, Vieuxtemps, Lazarus, S. Pratten, Garrett, F. Hiller, Barret, Baumann, Lindpaintner, Spohr, Molique, Berlioz, Ella.

Musard had been giving orchestral concerts on popular lines in Paris as early as 1833.   Early in 1838 a similar enterprise was announced in London: "The success of Musard's concerts in Paris, and the increasing taste for music in England, has induced Mr. Pilati to undertake the establishment of a series of instrumental concerts for the performance of overtures, quadrilles, waltzes and galops, so arranged as to offer a promenade between the acts.   This new arrangement will open at the Colosseum on Friday evening, the 12th of January."[1]

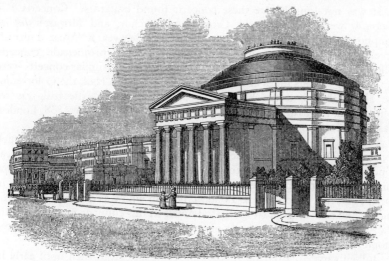

THE COLOSSEUM IN REGENT'S PARK

The Colosseum was a circular building in Regent's Park in which a panorama of London was displayed.[2]   Begun in 1824, it served as an entertainment centre until it was pulled down in 1876.   At one time it was in the hands of the great English tenor, Braham, who lost heavily over his speculation.

A few weeks after the announcement had been made it was duly reported that "Mr. Pilati commenced his exertions (after the manner of Musard in Paris) on Tuesday evening.   Many overtures, waltzes and Spanish Quadrilles were performed, and the company provided with suitable luxuries and conveniences for their enjoyment.   M. Becquire de Peyreville led the band which consisted of about sixty performers."[3]

Shortly before the end of 1838 it was announced that concerts à la Musard were to be given at the Lyceum Theatre with an orchestra of sixty players, including Harper, Platt, Grattan Cooke, Richardson, Hatton, Willy, Baumann and C. Laurent from Paris; the conductor was to be Signor Negri,

[1] *Mus. World*, Jan. 5, 1838, p. 13.   [2] Knight, VI, p. 284.
[3] *Mus. World*, Feb. 2, 1838, p. 74.

who was described as being a professor at the Royal Academy of Music. Before the end of the year the concerts had begun and were quickly becoming popular: "Overtures of the first class are executed in a masterly manner, by a most excellent band of sixty performers, and some very effective quadrilles played in a style that defies competition." Grattan Cooke "echoes his own oboe notes, by a clever management of the forte and piano," and Laurent and Harper jun. played a favourite duet on two cornopeans. The leader was John Thomas Willy, and Negri conducted."[1]

It was not long before these concerts found imitators. Concerts à la Valentino were started at the Crown and Anchor, and Mozart's *Jupiter* symphony was included in the programme. In that year a "Musard mania" developed in London, and a superabundance of promenade concerts followed. In addition to those at the Lyceum Theatre, similar concerts were exploited at various times at the Adelphi, the Egyptian Hall, the Colosseum, the Haymarket, and the Hanover Square Rooms. So the ball was set rolling, and, for many years after the start had been made in 1838, London was never for long without its promenade concerts.

Musard himself came to London as the conductor of a series of such concerts in Drury Lane Theatre in October, 1840,[2] and in the following year conducted a similar series at the Lyceum Theatre. In the meantime some summer concerts which were started by Eliason at Drury Lane Theatre in June, 1840, had introduced to London the man who was destined to become the life and soul of popular orchestral music in this country, and to do more than any other to bring the best of orchestral music within the reach of the people. This man was Louis Jullien.[3]

Jullien came to England in 1839 or 1840, and from then until early in 1859 he gave periodical seasons of promenade concerts in London and in all the larger provincial towns, except during some ten months in 1853–54, when he was touring in America. These concerts generally took place in either Drury Lane or Covent Garden theatres, or when neither was available, in the Lyceum or Her Majesty's Theatre. The usual winter season lasted for about a month in November or December, and occasionally a summer season was held at one of the theatres or (from 1845) at the Royal Surrey

[1] *Mus. World*, Jan. 17, 1839, p. 46.

[2] It appears that in London Musard was often confused with Mozart: "Do you know Mozart's Requiem? is asked, and the reply is—Oh! I did not know that Musard composed Requiems, I thought he only made galopades." (*Mus. World*, March 22, 1838, p. 195.)

[3] If the *Life of Jullien* which appeared in the *Mus. World* in 1853 is to be believed, the popular conductor could boast of not less than 35 christian names. They were the names of the members of the Philharmonic Society of Sisteron in the French Alps, where Jullien was born in 1812. Each member of the society insisted on being the child's godfather, with the result that he was christened: Louis, George, Maurice, Adolphe, Roch, Albert, Abel, Antonio, Alexandre, Noé, Jean, Lucien, Daniel, Eugene, Joseph-le-brun, Joseph-Barême, Thomas, Thomas-Thomas, Pierre, Carbon, Pierre-Maurel, Barthelemi, Artus, Alphonse, Bertrand, Dieudonné, Emanuel, Josué, Vincent, Luc, Michel, Jules-de-la-plane, Jules Bazin, Julio, César, JULLIEN. Some of Jullien's music was published under combinations of names selected from this list; in England he made use of the combination Rochalbert, and in France Noéjean.

Gardens.   After each period in London Jullien generally took his band on
tour in the provinces for about six weeks.

Jullien's aim appears to have been to attract a large audience by means of
popular dance music, to give them plenty of entertainment and amusement,
and then to introduce to them by small but increasing doses the best music
of the greatest composers.   His detractors regarded him as a mere showman
and a charlatan, and his upholders saw in him a man whose mission it was
to educate and improve the musical taste of the masses who never went to
good concerts and never heard good music.   Jullien's popularity was
unbounded, and his influence on popular taste was wider and more potent
than that of any other conductor in this country.

In 1854 Davison, the *Times* critic, who was a friend and admirer of
Jullien and a firm believer in the genuineness of his aims, wrote that "Jullien
has created a new taste for music among the middle classes, and they listen
to Beethoven and Mendelssohn because they really love and partly appreciate
their works."[1]   Again the same writer tells us that "while delighting, he was
instructing; and while he induced his auditors to listen, he was gradually
infusing into their minds a taste and liking for the best music."[2]

The attitude of many of the professional musicians was that Jullien's
music-making was something fit only for the uncultured masses, something
rather vulgar and at the same time rather childish, with which they would
not care to associate themselves.   Moscheles regarded Jullien's concerts as
a Christmas treat for his children, much on the same level as a pantomime or
a firework display, where he would take them to enjoy themselves.[3]

Joachim refused a good offer to play at Jullien's concerts at the Royal
Surrey Gardens on the ground that he did not care to associate himself
with "an undisguised charlatan," and asked: "what relations can remain
sacred to me in life if I cheapen my art by active association with a mountebank."   He would gladly accept engagements for the Beethoven and
Mendelssohn concerts "if only that confounded Jullien were not conducting
them."   He called Jullien the "chief of snobs," never guessing that there
was something rather snobbish in his own attitude, and wondered why the
directors of the Surrey Gardens did not appoint another conductor, without
stopping to think that if Jullien had not been conducting there would have
been no engagement to offer him.   Joachim felt that it was *inevitable* that
Jullien would introduce his charlatanism into the works of Mozart and
Beethoven—"a jackdaw cannot help stealing, and Jullien could not leave
off being a humbug, even if he intended to do so."[4]

But there were plenty who could not afford to ride on the high horse,
and were quite glad to accept engagements at Jullien's concerts.   It is certain
that the orchestral playing there was quite as good or even better than at
the high-class concerts, and certainly very much cheaper: "but M. Jullien
has taught the crowd that they can hear, for a shilling or half-a-crown,

[1] *Mus. World*, Dec. 2, 1854, p. 791.   [2] *Ibid.*, 1854, p. 820.
[3] Moscheles, *Life*, II, p. 114.   [4] Joachim, *Letters*, pp. 140, 141.

several times during the winter season, performances quite as good as those for which the Philharmonic directors charge one guinea."[1]   In the early 'forties, when the Philharmonic orchestra under Bishop, Smart and Moscheles was at its worst, the rather curious situation seems to have

JULLIEN'S ORCHESTRA AT A PROMENADE CONCERT IN COVENT GARDEN THEATRE, 1846

prevailed that whereas good music was indifferently played at the Philharmonic, poor music was very well played at Jullien's concerts.

Jullien liked to give his concerts in surroundings that were made as pleasant, bright and comfortable as possible for his audience.   He wanted them to enjoy themselves, as he certainly did himself.   The theatres were made to look gay and bright; floral decorations abounded, planned, it was said, by Madame Jullien, who had been a florist; there were refreshment rooms, reading rooms, and everything that conduced to the comfort and

[1] *Mus. World*, July 14, 1855, p. 457.

pleasure of the audience. They came to see as well as to hear, and the procedure and platform management were carefully planned and rehearsed with a view to providing attractive sights as well as attractive sounds. Such attractions as a crystal curtain, panoramic backgrounds, illuminations, coloured lights, fireworks and military uniforms, all combined to make the scene as brilliant and pleasure-giving as possible, but the central point on which the greatest interest was always focussed was "that essence and concentration of all—Jullien himself." The programmes at first consisted largely of gay quadrilles and other dances, selections from popular operas, topical display-pieces, showy solos by brilliant executants, and always one or two good overtures and a movement or two from some well-known symphony. This type of programme was maintained throughout the whole of Jullien's period, but as he grew more sure of his ground he began to introduce special programmes devoted one half to classical composers, including complete symphonies and concertos, and the other half to light popular music. So there were Beethoven, Mozart, Mendelssohn and Weber nights, and towards the end of each season Jullien often arranged what he called Beethoven, Mozart or Mendelssohn festivals at which the best works of these and a few other composers occupied the whole evening. Music by Wagner and Berlioz was heard at some of the later concerts, and each season terminated with a grand Bal Masqué, with an orchestra of 120 performers.

It need hardly be said that Jullien's orchestras were on an ample or even on a lavish scale. It was not in his nature to have anything to do with small or meagre resources, to stint expense or effort, or to put up with anything of second-rate quality when the best was obtainable. He gloried in big things, in big effects, in always going one better than before, in piling climax upon climax, in monster orchestras, monster concerts, and monster instruments. It was not part of his policy to make use of the classics while at the same time debasing them by presenting them through an inadequate medium or in an unworthy style; the great classics were well played by a large and efficient orchestra, and that same large and efficient orchestra played equally well the trivial pieces that served as a bait to draw his musically illiterate audiences within his reach.

Jullien's orchestras at Drury Lane and Covent Garden generally numbered from 80 to 90 performers, but in the smaller Lyceum Theatre and for the provincial tours he had to reduce the number to about sixty players. For his monster concerts in the Royal Surrey Gardens, and for such special efforts as the *Congrès Musicale* in the Exeter Hall (1849), these numbers were largely exceeded and might reach as many as three or four hundred instrumentalists. When the large Music Hall[1] was erected in the Royal Surrey Gardens in 1856, Jullien employed a choir and orchestra of a thousand persons to give grand performances of popular oratorios.

[1] Said to have accommodated 6,500 persons in the body of the hall and 3,500 in the galleries.

Jullien's players were selected from the best available in London, from the Philharmonic and the opera orchestras, from Paris and Brussels, from Germany and Italy, in fact from any place where outstanding players were to be found. Almost every one of the prominent instrumentalists already mentioned in these pages who were active between 1840 and 1860 appeared at some time or other in Jullien's orchestra.

He made a special feature of solo performances by the leading members of his orchestra. The most famous of the star soloists who were associated with him during almost the whole of his time in this country were Koenig the cornet player, Prospère the ophicleide player, Joseph Richardson the flautist, and the little Frenchman Collinet who played so marvellously on the French flageolet.

KOENIG, CORNET SOLOIST AT
JULLIEN'S CONCERTS

Koenig and Jullien were said to be as the sun and moon towards one another, and his detractors loved to imply that Jullien would have been nothing at all without Koenig. The cornet player's popularity was almost indescribable and the scribes in the papers could hardly find words to express their admiration: "But, oh, the delightful, spirit-stirring, expressive music of Herr Koenig's *cornet à piston*—played with such delicacy, and yet with such power—such sweetness, and yet such force—such *crescendos*, *diminuendos*, and, above all, such feeling! 'Twas, indeed, an exquisite treat; and when Jullien comes again to Bath, we hope he will make it a point of conscience to bring with him the handsome and practical Koenig."[1]

Koenig, who was a capable violinist as well as a trumpet and cornet player, came from the celebrated Belgian Guides Band, and it was in 1844 that he introduced at Jullien's Concerts for the first time that classic, beloved of all seaside orchestras to this day, the famous Post Horn Galop.

Prospère, whose real name was Jean Prospère Guivier, one of the five sons of a French soldier who was taken prisoner by the Russians during the disastrous retreat from Moscow in 1812, was born at Wilna in 1814. At an early age he joined a French military band and was present at the battle of Navarino,[2] and subsequently became a student at the Paris *Conservatoire*, his instrument at that time being the French horn. Having adopted the

[1] *Bath and Cheltenham Chronicle*, 1845.
[2] Jullien also claimed to have fought at that battle when he was in the French Navy.

ophicleide, he soon became known as a soloist at the Paris Promenade concerts during the 'thirties, and eventually came to this country in 1840 or 1841 where he quickly won tremendous popularity. Those (and there are many) who imagine that the ophicleide was capable of producing nothing but loud and coarse noises should note that in 1842, when Prospère was playing at Jullien's concerts in the English Opera House, his performance was thus described: "And last, but not least, M. Prospère on the giant instrument the Ophicleide, which is as gentle and as docile in his hands as *Hamlet* would have the recorder to be. Truly this gentleman's execution and power of subduing this usually obstreperous instrument passes all understanding, amongst those who have heard him; how vain would it be then to attempt a description to those who have not."[1] It was also written that Prospère "has subdued his giant instrument, the ophicleide, to every shade of softness," and that he could make it "coo" as gently as any dove.

PROSPÈRE, WITH HIS GIANT
OPHICLEIDE

Prospère created some stir when he appeared at the Hanover Square Rooms in 1843 with an enormous out-size giant ophicleide said to have been made expressly for use in the Birmingham Music Hall.

Then there was Collinet, who twittered so gaily on his little flageolet, but who was afraid to cross an ice-bound river during the American tour, and had to be taken by main force and be strapped on to a 'cello case while he was hauled across, shrieking and protesting, by a party of yelling niggers.

This little Frenchman, born in Paris c. 1797, was the son of a well-known player on the flageolet, a diminutive high-pitched whistle-pipe which was at that time indispensable in French dance bands.

Another popular soloist was Joseph Richardson the flautist, called "the English Drouet," who was said to have practised all day long and most of the night, who played in Queen Victoria's Private Band, and succeeded Nicholson as professor at the Royal Academy of Music.

[1] *Illus. Lon. News*, Dec. 10, 1842.

These, and many others like them, were *orchestral* soloists; but Jullien engaged also a number of solo virtuoso players, violinists such as Ernst, Sivori, Molique and Wieniawski, pianists such as Hallé and Arabella Godard, and many well-known singers. The orchestral soloists, however, took their part in the ordinary work of the orchestra, emerging each from his place to play a solo, and returning to his desk when it was over.

The following are the most important of many who figured as soloists in Jullien's orchestra:

1840–1859

Violin: Blagrove, Deloffre, Tolbecque, Sainton, Nadaud, J. Collins, A. Mellon, Willy, Ketenus, Goffrié, T. Baker, Thirlwall jun.

Viola: H. Hill, Vogel. *Viola d'amour*: Schreuss.

'Cello: Pillet, Hancock, Crouch, Hausmann, Lavenu, Piatti, G. Collins, De Munck, Lütgen, H. Chipp, Pacque.

Double-bass: Howell, Casolani, Rowland, Anglois, A. Winterbottom, White.

Octo-bass: (1850) A. Winterbottom.

French Flageolet: Collinet, Jullien.

Flute or *Piccolo*: Richardson, Bauller, De Folly, Pratten, Reichert, Rémusat, Jullien.

Oboe: Delabarre, Jennings, Lavigne, Barret, De Prins.

Clarinet: Lazarus, Itjen, Sonnenberg, Wuille, Maycock.

Basset horn: Maycock.

COLLINET, VIRTUOSO
ON THE
FRENCH FLAGEOLET

Bassoon: Jancourt, Chas. Keating, Baumann, John Winterbottom, Hardy.

Saxophone: Souallé, Demange.

Horn: Platt, C. Harper, Jarrett, Vivier, Steneberger, Hughes.

Valve horn: Adolph Koenig.

Trumpet: T. Harper, Müller, Duhême.

Cornet: Koenig, Laurent jun., Holt, Arban, Duhême, Leloup.

Post horn and *Alpine horn*: Koenig.

Saxhorns: The Distin family (1844).

Trombone: Dantonnet, Smithies, Cioffi, William Winterbottom, Nabich.

Ophicleide: Prospère, Handley, S. Hughes,[1] Colosanti, Lerey, Dortu.[2]

Serpentcleide: Prospère.

Bombardon, Sommerophone: Sommers.

---

[1] Samuel Hughes, a noted ophicleide player, who came from a Welsh brass band.

[2] According to Rivière (p. 116), Dortu was the only man who could play on a gigantic Bombardon (Trombotonare) made by Besson in Paris for Rivière's concerts at the Jardin d'Hiver. A facsimile of this huge instrument was for many years displayed outside Besson's premises in Euston Road, where until fairly recently it was a familiar landmark.

Clavicor: Jullien.
Guitar: Ciebras.
Harmonica: Baldicci.
Drums: Chipp, F. Hughes.

Concertina: Case.
Harp: Streather, Trust, Ellis Roberts.
Timbrel: Engelke.

Not content with the sound produced by a large orchestra, Jullien often sought to heighten the effect by introducing extra instrumental forces at moments of climax and excitement. So in 1843, in the last figure of the English Quadrilles, ten pipes, played by Baumann, Barret, Lazarus, Schmidt, Rowe, Meartine, Keating, McDonald, Richardson, and Jullien himself, joined in the happy *mêlée* and earned a nightly encore. For the enormously popular British Army Quadrilles (1846) he brought in no less than four Guards military bands in succession; at his *Concert Monstre* in the Royal Surrey Gardens in 1845 a selection from *I Puritani* was played with the aid of 20 trumpets, 20 cornets, 20 trombones, 20 ophicleides and 20 serpents, and a cannon shot marked each bar of the National Anthem. Again, at the Surrey Gardens in 1849 a party playing on 20 Roman trumpets, said to be each three yards long, joined in the performance of a Roman March composed by the Belgian Bender. In 1850 a great success was scored by introducing a

JOSEPH RICHARDSON, SOLO FLAUTIST
AT JULLIEN'S CONCERTS

French corps of drummers from the 2nd Legion of the *Garde Nationale* of Paris, headed by their mighty drum-major, M. Barbier.

After the Crimean war Jullien brought over a military band of Zouaves, and in 1856 a troupe of Zouave trumpeters "dashed into M. Jullien's orchestra at the Surrey Gardens, whose trumpetings excited the most riotous applause."[1]

New and strange instruments were always welcomed by Jullien as attractions which amused and pleased his patrons. In 1846 there were solos on the serpentcleide,[2] and Koenig played on the wooden alpine horn

[1] *Athenæum*, Aug. 9, 1856.
[2] An improved and keyed serpent, devised by Huggett, a London serpent maker.

in the Swiss Quadrilles; Sommers played solos on the Bombardon, Euphonium or Sommerophone; Jullien himself played on the Clavicor, and in 1850 the Saxophone (under the curious name *corno-musa*) was heard, no doubt for the first time in this country, played by M. Souallé.

Out-size instruments made a particularly strong appeal to Jullien, and we hear of a monster double-bass which required two performers to manage

JULLIEN'S ORCHESTRA AND THE FRENCH CORPS DE TAMBOURS AT
DRURY LANE, 1850

it, of Vuillaume's colossal Octo-bass brought over from Paris in 1850, of a monster bass drum made by Henry Distin, of a monster ophicleide, a double-bass saxophone, and of "four glorious gongs," and we may be sure that the greater the hullabaloo made by these instruments the more pleased were Jullien's patrons.

But beside all this bombast and claptrap there was always efficient orchestral playing, and the symphonies of the great masters were played to enormous audiences who had never been inside the Hanover Square Rooms, and who would no doubt have been rather bored if they had heard the same works played at the Philharmonic under Potter, Smart, Bishop or Moscheles. There was something to be said for an incongruous mixture if it was the means of reaching a new, untaught, and wider public: "we incline to think that the system of M. Jullien will do more to familiarise the general ear with good music than those societies which, while they profess to be liberal, at the same time exhibit a narrow-mindedness (particularly in regard to national improvement) which in some instances has been disgusting."[1]   Referring to

[1] *Illus. Lon. News*, Dec. 30, 1843.

a performance by Jullien of Mozart's *Jupiter* and E flat symphonies in 1855, it was written in the same paper: "Nothing could be more striking than the profound silence and earnest attention with which these long, elaborate, and refined instrumental pieces were listened to by a vast promiscuous assemblage, who, a very few years ago, would not have had the patience to give them a hearing."[1] Again, in 1858, it was written: "The Lyceum has been crowded to the doors, and the denizens of the promenade have not only been perfectly quiet but have listened to the music—even those portions of it which a few years ago would have been deemed unsuitable to a popular assemblage—with serious and discriminating attention."[2]

Not only was good music being more widely diffused, but it was also being well played by Jullien and his orchestra: "We have not heard the performance (two Mozart symphonies) surpassed by any orchestra, and seldom indeed equalled."[3] Tributes to the quality of Jullien's performances of the classics are to be found in many contemporary periodicals; the following are typical: "The Italian symphony was admirably executed by Jullien's magnificent orchestra"—"Jullien's orchestra is magnificent, it contains the *élite* of our London performers, and there is not a man amongst them who is not master of his instrument."—"The two orchestral pieces (Beethoven's *Pastoral* symphony and Mendelssohn's violin concerto) were superbly played, and fully displayed the admirable qualities of the band."[4]

If there was abundant praise, there was also some censure of Jullien's method of mixing the good and the bad, of his flamboyant style, his garishness, and no end of fun was levelled at him, sometimes malevolently, and sometimes tolerantly and in no unkind spirit. But the great show-conductor was thick-skinned enough to withstand plenty of pin-pricks, ridicule and satire, and it is more than likely that he welcomed publicity in any form even though it was not flattering.

There can be little doubt that the balance of Jullien's work in this country was largely to the good in respect of the diffusion of good orchestral music, and overwhelmingly to the good in respect of orchestral performance. While the other conductors and orchestras eddied in comparatively small circles, "Jullien and his band," like his "expansive" shirt-front, was far-reaching and all-embracing. He had plenty of imitators and many would-be rivals, but there was only one Jullien. The following tribute to Jullien's work was written soon after his death: "The late M. Jullien was a very extraordinary person. Possessed of great musical attainments, he was a man of genius, united to a degree of energy and perseverance, without which he could not have surmounted the obstacles which he had to encounter. For a time he was misunderstood and misjudged, treated as a charlatan, and exposed to the incessant ridicule of the popular satirists of the day; but, while they amused their readers by making game of his personal peculiarities of costume and manner, the public flocked to his concerts—

[1] *Illus. Lon. News*, Jan. 27, 1855. [2] *Ibid.*, Nov. 28, 1858.
[3] *Mus. World*, 1855, p. 58. [4] *Illus. London News*, 1857–58.

many, no doubt, to enjoy a laugh, but the majority to enjoy a brilliant and animated kind of music which they found very pleasing to their ears. Gradually he succeeded in gaining the object he had at heart from the beginning—an object which at first, probably, was not perceived by anybody. That object was to improve and *educate*, as it were, the popular taste; and, in setting about its improvement, he began by seeming entirely to concede to it. His earliest concerts were not what they afterwards became. They consisted almost wholly of showy and brilliant dance-music, quadrilles, waltzes, polkas, etc., things calculated to catch the most uncultivated ear. But he began to mingle this familiar music with things of a higher order: movements (short at first) from the symphonies of Haydn, Mozart or Beethoven, and a few vocal pieces from the finest Italian or German operas. But these innovations, cautiously as they were made, were not immediately successful. They were often received by the denizens of the promenade, not merely with impatient attention, but with loud (and sometimes riotous) disapprobation.[1]   But still Jullien went on, gradually increasing the whole-some doses, till his treatment of his patient (the public) at length prevailed; and he has left behind him a name which will live in our musical annals as the name of a distinguished man, who has done as much as ever has been done by any single individual in promoting the progress of his art in this country."[2]

That was written by a professional critic; the following is the tribute of an amateur who lived through the period of Jullien's popularity and by no means lacked understanding of what is best in music: "At the beginning of the year 1844, M. Jullien, who had inaugurated a series of Promenade Concerts at the English Opera-house, now the Lyceum, removed to Covent Garden, and began that strange mixture of good, bad, and indifferent selections, which took hold of the public immediately, and served, in the first direction, to improve the taste and enlarge the knowledge of the rising generation, who were influenced by musical aspirations. In spite of an enormous amount of charlatanry in this energetic Frenchman's proceedings, he became a universal favourite, and might have prospered to the end of his extraordinary career, as he did at first, could he have borne the success with which his efforts were rewarded. In the progress of English musical instruction his name must always deservedly occupy a prominent position; for at his concerts some of the greatest orchestral works that were ever written were performed with a precision and a completeness which not only interested but elevated the tone of mind of his overflowing audiences. A man who did so much and so well as M. Jullien accomplished within the

[1] "How does it happen that the opening night of M. Jullien's concerts is always marked by a disgraceful disturbance? . . . Yet it is at M. Jullien's concerts, and his alone, that the occasionally well-behaved British public becomes converted into a mob of British blackguards (that is the word), and pursues the conduct usually attributed to the frequenters of bear-gardens. . . . We believe that the *habitués* of M. Jullien's concerts expect a riot on the opening night, just as they expect 'God Save the Queen,' and either a new polka or a new waltz" (*Illus. Times*, Nov. 6, 1858).
[2] *Illus. London News*, Oct. 31, 1863.

few years that he was before the public deserved a better fate than befell him; and gladly would I pay his memory a tribute of more than passing recognition, because the advantages he initiated have become not only permanent, but are still increasing."[1]

London had a somewhat novel experience in April, 1838, when Johann Strauss and his orchestra from Vienna gave the first of a series of concerts in the Hanover Square Rooms. This was probably the first time that a foreign show-band was heard in this country, and the time coincided curiously with the first popular concerts of Pilati and Musard. The following extract shows how this novel orchestra and its playing impressed a London critic: "His strength lies in an ingenuity of detail, a striking brilliancy, strong colouring, and extreme contrasts. In the place of the elegant solo on the violin, the gentle remonstrance of the oboe, the full tide of affection from the clarinet, the tale of passion from the upper string of the violoncello—features which so distinguish the orchestra in the ballet of Her Majesty's Theatre—we have a spirit-stirring combination of horns, trumpets, trombones, ophicleides, and other instruments of a loud and sonorous character. In fact, the score is an amalgamation of brass instruments, occasionally relieved by the stringed and wind bands. But they are well put together; and if their frequent use takes away the feeling of repose and refinement, it excites an energy and vividness of sensation which is perhaps no less agreeable and enchanting. In his melodies he displays much clearness of design, and great boldness of outline. The disposition of his brass band is generally novel, frequently clever, and always claims attention. Of the wood band we cannot say so much; and the stringed band appears scarcely powerful enough to make its way through the other instruments. The performance of his music is most remarkable for precision and unanimity of sentiment; and the contrasts come out in an extraordinary manner. In these respects the band of M. Strauss is assuredly unequalled. The trumpet and ophicleide performers distinguished themselves by the power and beauty of the tone they brought from their respective instruments; and in M. Frisch, the flute player, we met with a concerto performer who, we presume, has few rivals."[2]

No doubt the *ensemble* and *élan* of the Viennese players under their violin-playing conductor gave the London players something to think about: "We can boast of professors who can do all that M. Strauss has done with the waltz, but we have no band which is so completely under the sway and subjection of the conductor—no small orchestra which can produce so vivid and exciting an impression. M. Strauss has taught the public the real power of the ophicleide, the legitimate use of the trombones, and the extraordinary perfection to which the flute can be brought. We trust his journey to England may prove of benefit to our professors, and of profit to himself."[3] During their stay in this country Strauss and his orchestra

[1] *Mus. Recoll.*, II, p. 157.   [2] *Mus. World*, April 19, 1838, p. 264.
[3] *Ibid.*, April 26, 1838, p. 284.

played in London at 38 public concerts, at 8 for Queen Victoria, 6 at Almacks, at 20 balls and parties in private houses, as well as giving numerous performances in all the large towns and watering places in England, Scotland and Ireland.[1] On May 23, 1838, they took part in a performance of Beethoven's Choral Symphony at one of Moscheles's concerts. Wherever they went they met with enormous success.

It was Jullien and his would-be imitators and rivals who, in the period 1840 to 1860, broke down the barrier which had confined the enjoyment of orchestral music in London to the limited audiences who could afford to pay half a guinea or more for their seats. If their approach to a wider and less affluent public was through the medium of dance music, and if it involved some display of childish clap-trap and unashamed showmanship, it will be granted that they used what was almost certainly the only method by which this unlimited class of potential music-lovers could be reached. The reason why so many of the promoters and conductors of popular orchestral concerts at that time were unable to stay the course for so long or so successfully as Jullien was probably because none of them could produce a personality so outstanding and compelling, and in his own particular way, so completely competent as this energetic and fascinating Frenchman.

Among many other schemes of which the aim was the same and the method only slightly different from that of Jullien, were the Wednesday Concerts at the Exeter Hall from 1848 until a few years after the mid-century. Here there was no promenade, but the prices of seats ranged from as low as one shilling up to seven shillings. Various conductors were employed, such as Anschütz, Benedict and Meyer Lutz; a large competent orchestra and first-rate soloists were in themselves strong attractions, but the central luminous star was missing—they had no Jullien to serve as the focal point around which the whole affair revolved; and no doubt the interior of the Exeter Hall was rather damping to the spirits. Another enterprise, said to be "an awkward *cross* betwixt the Wednesday Concerts and M. Jullien's performances, in some respects inferior to both,"[2] was the Grand National Concerts at Her Majesty's Theatre in 1850. Here the promenade was only one shilling, and the best seats cost only four shillings. The large orchestra of about ninety players was of the best,[3] and some of Jullien's star soloists were engaged. Military bands joined in to make the quadrilles more exhilarating; popular symphonies, overtures and concertos were played; one Labitzky was brought in to compose, arrange and conduct the dance music, and the conductor-in-chief was Balfe. But again the vital spark of an outstanding personality was lacking, and Jullien continued his concerts unperturbed and unrivalled.

All the orchestras hitherto mentioned in this chapter were largely made up of the same players shuffled up in a hundred different ways. By about the mid-century the idea that an orchestra would function better if it was

[1] Lange, pp. 118–124.   [2] *Athenæum*, Oct. 19, 1850.
[3] For full list, see Appendix, p. 492.

always composed of the same personnel had evidently taken root, and two attempts were made to organise players who were used to working together, and could be engaged as a body instead of individually. The first of these was the *Orchestral Union* (c. 1852), with Alfred Mellon as conductor. Close on its heels came the *London Orchestra* (1854), with forty players under the direction of Frank Mori. Both of these gave concerts of their own, and could be engaged *en bloc*, with or without their conductors. But, as in so many co-operative concerns designed for the mutual benefit of all members, internal dissensions soon broke out and eventually wrecked both orchestras, and the old method (by which the devil takes the hindmost) was left to rule the engagement of orchestral players in London almost up to the end of the century.

Of orchestral history in this country outside of London not very much can or need be told. A few towns, such as Bath and Dublin, maintained something of their former musical traditions, and there was plenty of fresh effort in the quickly developing industrial towns which, however, found its outlet mainly in choral singing.

There is no sign that the provincial orchestras were anything but smaller and very inferior replicas of those in London. In all the larger provincial towns there were theatres, and each of these had an orchestra of some sort from which the players were drawn to help in local concerts. A traveller in Belgium in 1849, writing of the theatre orchestras at Brussels, Antwerp, Liége and Ghent, asserted that they were all better than those at the secondary theatres in London, and added his view that the orchestras in the provincial theatres in England were the "worst of all."

Contemporary accounts of the provincial orchestras and their playing are not at all flattering. Moscheles went about the country playing concertos in the larger towns, but always complained about the inferior orchestras he encountered. At Liverpool in 1825 the orchestra was "wretched"; Mori, who came with him, did all that could possibly be done, "but what was to be made out of a band consisting of a double quartet and four halting wind instruments."[1] At Manchester the orchestra was certainly better, and they were aided by some "clever German amateurs." The Lancashire town had its old-established Gentlemen's Concerts (1774),[2] and it had its Philharmonic Concerts (c. 1798) with an orchestra which in 1823 numbered 33 players; but a contemporary comment—"of the performers individually it would be perhaps improper to speak, as my object is not to extol mediocre talent"—suggest a rather poor standard of performance.[3] Hallé first heard the orchestra at the Gentlemen's Concerts in 1848, and his comment was: "but the orchestra! oh, the orchestra! I was fresh from the 'Concerts du Conservatoire,' from Hector Berlioz's orchestra, and I seriously thought of

[1] Moscheles, *Life*, I, p. 112.
[2] The orchestra originally consisted of 26 amateurs, all of whom played the flute! (Hallé, p. 111).
[3] *Quar. Mus. Mag.*, Vol. V, No. 20, p. 473.

packing up and leaving Manchester, so that I might not have to endure a
second of these wretched performances."[1]

But some improvement was to come to the music of both Liverpool and
Manchester round about the mid-century.   The former town established its
Philharmonic Society in 1840, and in 1849 was able to open its fine concert

THE PHILHARMONIC HALL AT LIVERPOOL, 1849

hall; but the report that the fault of the orchestra in 1849 was "that each one
seems determined to play as loud as he can"[2] suggests that the northern
players had still much to learn about their functions in corporate
performances.

At Manchester the music began to improve rapidly as soon as a good
conductor came to give the necessary help, and with Hallé in command, and
Charles Seymour (1810–1875) as leader, it was said in 1854 that the orchestra
"is now, by many degrees, the best in the provinces."[3]

At Dublin in 1826 Moscheles suffered "martyrdom at the rehearsal,
chiefly from the wind instruments."   In 1828 he played at Brighton, and
again the orchestra was "wretched," while at York in 1833 they had "some
miserable overtures in which the flute was the sole support of the
harmonies."[4]

[1] Hallé, p. 111.   [2] Mus. World, 1849, p. 701.
[3] Ibid., Feb. 18, 1854, p. 109.   [4] Moscheles, Life, I, pp. 119, 282.

An account of a performance of Mendelssohn's *St. Paul* at the Professional Society's Concerts at Edinburgh in 1838 includes the following chapter of accidents: "The trombones missed fire in the introduction; and the basses at the third bar from the last took the F at the beginning, instead of the middle of it, thus causing an unprepared discord, and spoiling the beautiful tenor note E. Then the grand crashes for the brass instruments in the *Allegro* were frequently found wanting."[1]

Many such tales of woe can be found in the accounts of concerts sent by local correspondents to the London periodicals, and all go to show that, unless backed up by good players from London, the provincial towns were unable to provide anything approaching a first-class orchestra. The fact was that they simply had not the resources necessary to retain good resident players and maintain permanent orchestras, or if they had, they did not choose to spend their money in that way. London players had to be engaged when any special effort was made; Parke tells of visits to such places as York, Oxford, Bath and Margate in company with other players in order to stiffen up the local orchestras, and the names of well-known London orchestral instrumentalists constantly occur in the programmes of concerts advertised in the provincial papers. Harper, Lindley, Nicholson, Willman and others must have spent much of their time travelling to and from provisional towns in order to fulfil these engagements. The musical strength of the provincial towns lay rather in their choral societies, which increased greatly in number during the first half of last century. What orchestras there were, were got together mainly for the purpose of playing the instrumental parts in the oratorios and other choral works which formed the greater part of their programmes.

Although the musical festivals held at Worcester, Gloucester, Hereford, Manchester, Birmingham, York, Norwich and many other places shifted the centre of musical activity for a few days in each year, it was only by temporarily transferring a good contingent of London players to those towns that the orchestras on such occasions acquired the necessary strength and skill. The lists almost invariably show the names of the same group of foremost players that provided the keystones of the opera and Philharmonic orchestras in London; it was always Lindley, Dragonetti, Nicholson, Willman, Harper and others bearing well-known names that supplied the essential framework of the festival orchestras. The rank and file were recruited largely from amongst local players, both professional and amateur, and from any military band that happened to be stationed within reach. The following sums up the situation as it usually was: "though there were some weak hands amongst the provincial professors, yet all the principal parts were well filled by staunch London performers."[2] These festivals were usually conducted by native choral conductors and composers, or by local organists, but some of them owed much of their distinction to the visits of such as Spohr and Mendelssohn, and to the conducting of Costa.

---

[1] *Mus. World*, Feb. 16, 1838, p. 106.   [2] *Harm.*, Nov., 1827, p. 223 (Norwich Festival).

WORCESTER MUSICAL FESTIVAL IN 1848

It will be seen that the foregoing history, although headed "Orchestras in England," has resolved itself into a history of the London orchestras during the first half of last century. This centralisation was only to be broken up to a limited extent when in the next half-century the foundation of the Hallé orchestra at Manchester (1857), the Scottish orchestra at Glasgow (1893), and the Bournemouth Municipal orchestra (1893), created separate and independent centres that did not have to look to London for support and sustenance. To this day these three centres, with the addition of those at Birmingham and Liverpool, still provide the only orchestras in this country outside of London that can be said to have any permanent and independent existence.

Another feature that seems to emerge from the story that has been told is, that when a large number of players are concentrated in one large centre, however many orchestras there may exist in name, they become in fact little more than the same orchestra arranged in just so many different ways. Orchestras organised on these lines tend to lack individuality, the more so when they are not subjected to continuous training under permanent conductors. Some of the orchestras in German towns (as, for example, at Frankfort under Guhr, and at Leipzig under Mendelssohn), where the same group of players remained for a long time under the same training, appear to have acquired more distinct individuality than did the London orchestras in which there were better players, but which suffered from an ever-changing personnel and too many conductors. Strong individuality has never been a marked characteristic of English orchestras. Amongst the comparatively few instances in which any English orchestra ever acquired a distinct individuality, the cases of the Crystal Palace orchestra under Manns and the Bournemouth orchestra under Godfrey stand out as notable and rather rare exceptions.

The best London orchestras in the first half of last century did not lack players of the best quality. It is true, they were of rather mixed nationalities, and their assorted styles could never have been expected to coalesce with the same complete unity that was to be found in the contemporary Paris orchestras, where the style of performance was distinctly national and the personnel was largely Conservatoire-trained. But man for man, it seems that London could provide just as good a company of picked players as was to be found in either Paris, Berlin or Vienna. There remain only two reasons why the London orchestras were on the whole unable to rank with the very best in the world, and these were: too few rehearsals, and too many conductors.

That an orchestra carefully selected from the rather mixed company of players which was to be found in London a hundred years ago could achieve a level of performance not very far short of the very best continental standard is proved by the fact that, whereas in the early 'forties the orchestra at Her Majesty's Theatre, regularly rehearsed under one competent conductor, reached a high level of excellence, the orchestra of the Philharmonic Society, although the players were largely the same, played only indifferently under the direction of half a dozen conductors who were not specialists and were further handicapped by insufficient time for rehearsal: "We have heard foreign musicians of the highest eminence ascribe the fault of the, in many respects, admirable Philharmonic orchestra—its frequent unsteadiness, its deficiency in smoothness and softness, its neglect of minute and delicate designs of the composer, and its want of *subduedness* in accompanying vocal music, to its not having the advantage of being under the constant and uniform discipline of one permanent and highly qualified conductor.   The Philharmonic and the Opera orchestra are composed of nearly the same performers, yet the difference between them in uniform precision, nice attention to light and shade, and vocal accompaniment, is very apparent, and the cause is as evident as the effect."[1]   These words were written after Costa had been for eight years in sole command of the Opera orchestra, and six years before he became permanent conductor of the Philharmonic orchestra.

Even now, after a hundred years have passed, we have not yet got rid of these two obstacles to first-class orchestral playing.   These two spectres, *too few rehearsals and too many conductors*, still haunt many of the orchestras in this country, in which the individual players are fully the equals of the best that any other country can produce.

[1] *Mus. World*, Feb. 27, 1840, p. 122.

VI

Orchestras in Vienna, in Italy
and other Countries

PERHAPS the most surprising feature in the story of the Viennese orchestras is the fact that in this city of the symphony, which harboured Haydn, Mozart, Beethoven and Schubert, there was no organised concert-orchestra, no first-rate body of players that could compare with those at Paris, Leipzig, or even London, until the 'forties of the 19th century.

This does not imply that there was any lack of good players nor any want of musical activity or enterprise, for the Austrian capital was seething with musicians and bubbling over with music. Vienna ranked with Paris as one of the foremost musical centres in Europe; it had theatres in plenty and concerts in abundance; it had an Imperial court musical establishment, a music-loving aristocracy, several musical societies, and a vast number of keen amateur musicians. Yet the people of this hospitable and pleasure-loving city waited until all their great composers were dead, and until a North German (Nicolai) came amongst them before any attempt was made to organise an orchestra fit to play the great symphonies that had been written in their midst, and were already being more worthily performed in Berlin, Dresden, Munich, Leipzig and Paris.

At the beginning of the century Mozart had been dead for nearly ten years, and the Viennese people were just beginning to realise what they had lost; Haydn was still with them, fully appreciated and highly honoured; Beethoven was just beginning to throw out the first of his succession of great symphonies, concertos, and overtures; Schubert was a small child not yet old enough to go to the choir-school; Salieri was the respected official figurehead of the musical profession, and there were composers, *Kapell-meister*, players and singers of all sorts and grades, enough and to spare.

The original court opera-house in Vienna was the *Hofburg* or *Burgtheater*. Opened in 1742, this theatre was part of the Imperial premises, and was the scene of Gluck's activity as composer and *Kapellmeister*. It continued to be used for opera, ballet and plays until 1810, after which time opera was given only at the other court theatre, namely, that adjoining the *Kärntnerthor*, built in 1764 to replace an earlier *Stadttheater* which had been burnt down in 1761.[1] Originally privately owned, it was taken over as a court theatre in 1785, and remained the principal opera-house in Vienna until it was finally

---

[1] Kobald, p. 26.

249

demolished in 1870. These two buildings were centrally situated. A third and outlying opera-house was the *Theater-an-der-Wien*, the successor of Schikaneder's old *Theater auf der Wieden* in which Mozart's *Zauberflöte* was first heard in 1791. The large new theatre built nearby was opened in 1801, and, although frequently altered and renovated, still stands. It came under the control of the court *Intendant*, von Braun, in 1804, and thus became for some time virtually a third court theatre.

At the beginning of the 19th century the *Burg* and the *Kärntnerthor* theatres shared the same orchestra and chorus, while the *Theater-an-der-Wien* had its own separate musical staff. From after 1814, when opera was no longer being given at the *Burgtheater*, the *Kärntnerthor* and the *Theater-an-der-Wien* shared for some years the same orchestra, chorus, and repertoire.

All these theatres were managed either by an *Intendant* or by a group of court-appointed directors, or they were sometimes leased to an independent impresario. From 1821 both the *Kärntnerthor* and the *An-der-Wien* were for some years in the hands of the famous Italian impresario Domenico Barbaja, and in 1828 it was announced that the *Kärntnerthor* had been leased to Count Gallenberg for ten years with an annual subsidy of 50,000 florins from the Emperor.

Two suburban houses, where lighter operas were given, were the *Leopoldstädter Theater*, opened in 1781, but rebuilt and re-named the *Carl Theater* in 1847, and the *Josephstädter Theater* which originally dated from 1776 but was subsequently rebuilt, first in 1788 and then again in 1822.

The *An-der-Wien* theatre at the beginning of the century was said to accommodate an audience of 700 persons seated and as many standing.[1]

Vienna had no large hall built as a concert room. Concerts were held either in the theatres or in the large or small ball-rooms (*Redoutensäle*), the riding-school (*Winterreitschule*), the University hall, the *Landständische Saal*, in various hotel-rooms such as *Zum römischen Kaiser* or *Zur Mehlgrube*, in a hall in the Liechtenstein summer palace at Rossau, and in summer in the *Augarten*, the *Belvederegarten*,[2] or other garden resorts. In 1831 the *Gesellschaft der Musikfreunde* opened a small concert-room in which 400 persons could be seated in the body of the hall and 200 in the gallery.

The *Tonkünstler-Societät* was a benevolent society founded in 1771 in order to provide for the widows and orphans of professional musicians. This society gave performances at Easter and Christmas, generally of oratorios, in which the professional members of the society took part. In the early part of last century they relied largely on the popularity of Haydn's *Seasons* and *The Creation* to swell the funds of the society.

The *Gesellschaft der Musikfreunde*, founded in 1814, was an association of music-loving amateurs established for the purpose of furthering the cause of musical art in all its branches by giving concerts, by setting up a school of

---

[1] Biberhofer, p. 12.
[2] Where Haydn's "Paris" symphonies were heard for the first time in Vienna (Kobald, p. 50).

music, a library, a musical periodical, and by generally supporting musical effort and talent in every way. The concerts of the *Gesellschaft* were usually a large-scale annual oratorio performance and four smaller miscellaneous concerts given under amateur direction, and as far as possible by amateur singers and instrumentalists.

A short-lived *Gesellschaft der Liebhaber-Concerte* (1807), was an attempt to unite and co-ordinate the very wide-spread musical activities of the aristocracy and the upper middle-classes.

Summer orchestral concerts were given in a hall in the Augarten, under Schuppanzigh up till about 1812, and then intermittently under other direction until about 1824, by a mixed orchestra of professionals and amateurs.

The *Spirituel-Concerte* were initiated by Gebauer in 1819 for the performance of good orchestral and choral music, and lasted until 1848. These concerts were carried out largely by amateurs stiffened by professional musicians, and were given without rehearsal.

The *Philharmonische Concerte*, started in 1842 by Otto Nicolai, were the first organised orchestral concerts in Vienna to be given by a wholly professional and properly rehearsed orchestra. To the organised music-making in Vienna must be added a vast number of concerts given by composers (Beethoven amongst others) and by many native and visiting artists. In this respect Vienna was like Paris and London; everybody wanted to be heard there. The *Wiener Musikzeitung* in 1819 reckoned that about 100 such concerts were given in Vienna every year.[1]

There were professional players enough in Vienna to provide permanent orchestras for at least two fairly large and two smaller theatres. These same players provided the professional stiffening, the wind, the double-basses and the leaders for all the concerts, most of which required an orchestra; but amateur musicians supplied a substantial proportion of the string players. Some of the best of the professional players were also in the *Hof-Musikkapelle*, a small orchestra and choir retained to provide the music in the Imperial chapel, and for court concerts. This should not be confused with the orchestra of the court theatres, although several of the players were the same.

There was also in Vienna much music-making in the private houses of both the nobility and the townspeople. Small orchestras, professional, amateur or semi-amateur, were often formed to play for the pleasure of those taking part and for the enjoyment of a few invited guests. Such, for example, were the one assembled by Prince Lobkowitz in 1804 to play over the *Eroica* symphony, the little orchestra that grew out of the Schubert family quartet, and the musicians who met at Dr. Sonnleithner's house at the Gundelberg. Their performances might equally well have been described as either concerts or rehearsals.

Then there were the orchestras, large and small, playing in the many dance-resorts in Vienna, those of the Lanner and Strauss families, and the

[1] Hanslick, p. 270.

music in restaurants and gardens, or the military bands in the open air. In the early part of the century many large concerts were given for charitable, political and patriotic purposes, and there were frequent renderings of choral and orchestral Masses on appropriate occasions in the churches.

It will be seen that Vienna was simply throbbing with music, and that the amateur and professional element in all this music-making was more intermingled than in any other large centre of music in Europe.

HOFKAPELLE

The number of players in the Imperial court orchestra hardly changed during the first half of the 19th century.[1] There were rarely more than 27 musicians, excluding conductors or any extra players who might be introduced for special purposes, or any of the corps of Imperial trumpeters and drummers who were drawn upon when these instruments were required. At the head of the whole establishment stood Salieri, who retired with a pension in 1824. His successor was Eybler, and he again was followed by Assmayer in 1846. Eybler had been *Vicekapellmeister* since 1804, and on his promotion that post was occupied by Joseph Weigl in 1827, and by Assmayer in 1839.

Several well-known violinists played in this select orchestra. Joseph Mayseder was a member from 1816, Joseph Böhm from 1821, Leopold Jansa from 1825, Schuppanzigh from 1827, Georg Hellmesberger from 1831, and Jacob Dont from 1841. Notable among the 'cellists were Joseph Weigl sen. and Joseph Merk. Weigl, father of the *Kapellmeister*, had played in Haydn's orchestra at Eisenstadt for some years, and joined the Imperial orchestra at Vienna in 1792. Merk came in 1827; he was the 'cellist whom Edward Holmes ranked next only to Lindley.

Curiously enough, no flautist's name appears in the records of the *Hofkapelle* until 1857, but there were several outstanding oboists. Among them were Franz Joseph Czerwenka (1759–1835) from 1801, Joseph Khayll (1781–1829) from 1813, Ernst Krähmer (1795–1837) from 1828, Joseph Sellner (1787–1843) from 1835, and Jacob Uhlmann[2] (1803–1850) from 1843. Sellner became widely known by his *Method* (1825) for the oboe, and Uhlmann was the son and successor of Tobias Uhlmann, a prominent maker of wood-wind instruments in Vienna.

Of the clarinet players, the names which stand out are those of Johann Stadler (1756–1804) and Joseph Friedlowsky (1777–1859). The brothers Johann and Anton Stadler were, in fact, the first clarinet players to be employed in the Imperial orchestra, these instruments having been first introduced in 1787. They were friends of Mozart, and are credited with having made some improvements to the clarinet and bassethorn. Friedlowsky was the player from whom Beethoven acquired his knowledge of the technique of the clarinet.

---

[1] Full particulars in Köchel, pp. 91–101. [2] Sometimes written Ullmann.

PLATE 15

THE HALL IN THE AUGARTEN

THEATER-AN-DER-WIEN, VIENNA, c. 1830

PLATE 16

KÄRNTNERTHOR THEATER AT VIENNA, c. 1825

Of the bassoon players, the following were the most prominent: Matthaius Sedlaczek (1765–1816) from 1801, Wenzel Mattuschek (1760–1824) from 1807, Franz Höllmayer (1777–1840) from 1816, and Theobald Hürth (1793–1858) from 1840.

The Imperial horn-players included Willibald Lotter (1762–1844) from 1808, and Friedrich Hradetzky (1769–1846) from 1816. A well-known player, Eduard Constantin Lewy (1796–1846), died about two months after being appointed in 1846, and was succeeded by his son Richard Lewy (1827–1883).

The *Hofkapelle* occupied a position in Vienna very similar to that of the King's *Chapelle-Musique* in Paris. Like the French Royal orchestra, it contained many of the best musicians in the capital, and nearly all the members held their appointments for the rest of their lives. Smart heard this orchestra accompany a Mass in 1825, and described the performance by the strings and two oboes as the best he had ever heard in Vienna. Edward Holmes heard a service in the Imperial Chapel under Eybler in 1827, and pronounced it "the most delicate and finished service to be heard in Vienna. Sinfonias and full instrumental pieces are sometimes executed there in those parts of the service in which a voluntary on the organ is used among us."[1] Berlioz's verdict was that "the Imperial band, composed of picked instrumentalists and singers, is of course first rate. . . . The orchestra is not large, but it is exquisite. The band recalled to my mind that of the Tuileries in 1828 and 1829, when it was at its prime."[2]

THEATER-AN-DER-WIEN

The orchestra at this handsome theatre, from its opening in 1801 until about the middle of 1814, can be identified as a body quite distinct from that which served the two court theatres, the *Hofburg* and the *Kärntnerthor*, even though at various times between 1804 and 1825 all three theatres came under the same management. From 1815, and for some years, the *An-der-Wien* had evidently no orchestra of its own; the position in the early 'twenties is rather obscure, but it is quite certain that in the 'thirties and 'forties the two main theatres each had an independent orchestra, and were, as Berlioz said, rival institutions.

Johann Henneberg, who conducted the *Zauberflöte* in 1791, and Ignaz Seyfried had both been *Kapellmeister* in Schikaneder's old theatre, and both continued as such in the new building. The former left Vienna soon after, while Seyfried remained there until 1826. Franz Röser was another *Kapellmeister* who was employed in the early years at the new theatre, but appears to have been settled elsewhere by 1809. Philipp Riotte and Franz Gläser were also *Kapellmeister* at the *An-der-Wien*, the former from 1818 for about ten years, and the latter from 1827 to 1830. Adolf Müller (1801–1886) conducted from 1828, off and on, for about fifty years, Suppé was another who officiated from about 1845 when the theatre was in the hands

---

[1] *Rambles*, p. 161.　　　　[2] *Mem.*, II, p. 193.

of Pokorny, and in 1846–47 Lortzing was *Kapellmeister* for a short period.

The orchestra at the new theatre was said to number forty players in 1801.[1] The leaders were then Gebler and Clement. The latter, the violinist for whom Beethoven wrote his violin concerto, was leader or *Orchester-Direktor*[2] from 1802 to 1812, and again from 1818 to 1821. Spohr occupied the same position for about two years from 1812. His brother Ferdinand and Molique were among the violins about that time.[3] Spohr's duty was "to play in all grand Operas, to undertake the Violin Soli's in Operas and Ballets, and as Conductor, to lead from the score when the other leader (Seyfried) should be prevented doing so." From the same source we learn that Spohr "soon succeeded in procuring the services of the most talented young artistes, and to establish an *ensemble* that made my Orchestra not only the best in Vienna, but raised it to one of the best in Germany."[4] It was evidently Spohr's habit to regard the orchestra with which he was associated as one of the best in Germany, for he said the same thing about those at Frankfort and Cassel. Two outstanding 'cellists played in the *Theater-an-der-Wien*; they were Leopold Böhm (b. 1806) who was there until 1828, and Joseph Lincke, Beethoven's friend and a member of the Rasoumowsky quartet, who played from 1818 to 1831. Not the least remarkable of the string players was Johann Hindle (b. 1792), a virtuoso double-bass player who had a peculiar way of tuning his instrument, and was credited by Kastner with having a compass of $5\frac{1}{2}$ octaves.

Of the wind players one of the most conspicuous was the flautist Georg Bayr (1773–1833). This remarkable man could play two notes on the flute at the same time: Fétis said that he could play two parts at once,[5] and an English correspondent wrote in 1826: "The celebrated virtuoso, Professor Bayr, has at length so well succeeded in his newly discovered method of producing double tones on the flute, as to be able to effect the same thing through all the scales. Hence, on a common instrument, he can, in accompanying, produce very clear, full, and distinct thirds, fourths, fifths and sixths."[6] The clarinet player Joseph Friedlowsky was in the same orchestra, also the oboist Franz Rosenkranz (1761–1807) from 1802 to 1807; the bassoon player Valentin Czeyka (b. 1769) played from 1802 for about twenty years, also Michael Herbst (1778–1843) the horn player who became professor of his instrument at the Vienna Conservatoire. Herbst was picked out for special mention by Reichardt when the latter visited Vienna

---

[1] Biberhofer, p. 16.
[2] A position equivalent to *Concertmeister*, that is, leader and deputy-conductor.
[3] According to Spohr, Moritz Hauptmann was one of the violinists he engaged for the theatre orchestra in 1812, but in a letter to Jahn (June 6, 1860) Hauptmann made it quite clear that he was never engaged at the *An-der-Wien*. Hauptmann said that when Spohr wrote his Autobiography (c. 1860) his memory for events that had occurred so long ago was very unreliable, and that many of the details recorded in that book were incorrect (*Briefe*, III, p. 111).
[4] *Autob.*, I, p. 169.　　　　　[5] *Biog. univ.*
[6] *Harm.*, Feb., 1826, p. 38.

in 1808–9; his playing, said Reichardt, reminded him of Thürrschmidt, the celebrated horn player at Berlin.[1]

It was at the *Theater-an-der-Wien* that *Fidelio* was first produced in 1805 with Seyfried in charge of the orchestra, and it was there that Beethoven gave his unfortunate concert on December 22, 1808, with a monster programme which included the first performances of the C minor and the *Pastoral* symphonies, as well as the G major piano concerto, the *Choral Fantasia* and sundry other compositions of his own. Smart in 1825 described the orchestra as being "large," but said that it had no opportunity to display its skill in a rather light piece. The theatre was closed for some time in 1826–27; Holmes evidently did not hear the orchestra during his visit to Vienna in 1827.

Berlioz (1845) placed the orchestra rather below that of its rival at the *Kärntnerthor* theatre: "The orchestra, which I had heard much abused from the moment of my arrival, cannot certainly be put on a level with that of the Kärntnerthor Theatre, of which I shall speak presently; but it does very well notwithstanding, and the young artists composing it are full of that ardour and goodwill which occasionally works miracles."[2]

In 1847, when Lortzing was the conductor, the musicians at the *An-der-Wien* were said to be only of second rank, who did their best in competition with those at the *Kärntnerthor*, but were unable to rival the performances at the central theatre.[3]

The verdict, therefore, must be that the orchestra at this theatre, although it included some outstanding players in the early years of the century, and some keen young players in its later days, could at its best take only the second place among the opera orchestras in Vienna.

HOFBURG AND KÄRNTNERTHOR THEATRES

The following were conductors during the half-century 1800 to 1850, mostly engaged at the *Kärntnerthor* theatre after the *Hofburg* ceased to be used for opera performances:

Joseph Weigl (son), composer of the popular *Schweitzerfamilie*, from 1790.

Adalbert Gyrowetz, from 1804 to 1831.

Paul Wranitsky, c. 1785–1808.

Michael Umlauf, first as assistant to Weigl, and then his successor, from 1810 to 1825.

Conradin Kreutzer, from 1822 to 1827, also from 1829 to 1832, 1837 to 1840, and again from 1846 to 1849.

Wilhelm Würfel (1791–1852), from 1826.

Franz Lachner, assistant from 1826 and chief *Kapellmeister* from 1828 to 1834.

Julius Benedict, assistant from 1823 to 1825.

Carl Krebs, third *Kapellmeister* in 1826–27.

---

[1] *Vertraute Briefe (Wien)*, I, p. 165.   [2] *Mem.*, II, p. 180.   [3] Speyer, p. 290.

Otto Nicolai, from 1841 to 1847.
Heinrich Proch (1809–1878), from 1840 to 1870, leader and *Kapellmeister*.
Ludwig Wilhelm Reuling (1802–1879), c. 1847.
Heinrich Esser, from 1847 to 1869.

The leading *Concertmeister* and violinists were: Mayseder, solo violin from 1820; Schuppanzigh, from 1824, and leader from 1828; Mathias Strebinger (b. 1807), deputy-soloist with Mayseder; Georg Hellmesberger (father), leader from 1829 until he retired in 1867; Franz Seraph Grutsch (1801–1867), deputy-leader from about 1831.   Other prominent string players were Mathias Durst (b. 1815), viola player and member of the well-known Viennese string quartet,[1] joined the orchestra in 1841; the leading 'cellists were Joseph Valentin Dont (1776–1833), from 1804 to 1828; Nicolaus Kraft, from 1809 until he went to Stuttgart in 1814; Merk, leader and soloist from 1818; Lincke, who came from the *An-der-Wien* in 1831; Aegidius Borzaga (1801–1858) was solo 'cello alternately with Merk from about 1840.   Anton Slama (b. 1804) was leading double-bass from 1829.

The leading flautists were: Alois Khayll (1791–1867), one of a family of three wind-players, all in the same orchestra; Raphael Dressler (1784–1835) played from 1809 until he went to Hanover in 1817; Johann Sedlatzek (1789–1866), from c. 1810 to 1826; Franz Botgorschek (1812–1882), from about 1840.   The oboist Czerwenka, after playing in the Esterhazy orchestra at Eisenstadt, came to Vienna in 1794, and played at the *Kärntnerthor* theatre until he was pensioned in 1829; Joseph Khayll (1781–1829) was a military bandmaster before joining the opera orchestra as oboist; Krähmer, from c. 1815; Sellner became leading oboist in 1817; his successors were Jacob Uhlmann, from 1823 to 1825, and again in 1828; another of Sellner's pupils, Michael Alexander Petschacher (1808–1867), came in 1843.

The brothers Johann and Anton Stadler (1753–1812) were still playing the clarinet in the opera orchestra at the beginning of the century.   Anton Friedlowsky (b. 1804), said to be the equal of his father Joseph, was leading clarinet in the 'forties.   Anton Romberg, from 1809 to 1815, and Theobald Hürth were the most prominent of the bassoon players.   Friedrich Hradetzky (b. 1776) played the horn up to 1820, and Ed. Con. Lewy came at the invitation of Conradin Kreutzer during the period when Barbaja was lessee of the theatre (1821–25).   His son, Richard Lewy succeeded on his father's death in 1846.   Anton Weidinger, sponsor of the Viennese keyed-trumpet, was playing that instrument at the beginning of the century, and was followed by his son Joseph (d. 1832); Anton Khayll (1787–1834) also played the trumpet up to the time of his death.

There was clearly plenty of good material in this orchestra, yet there is no reason to suppose that the playing was at all remarkable during the first quarter of the century—that is to say, in Beethoven's time.

---

[1] Prince Czartoryski's quartet: Mayseder, Strebinger, Durst and Borzaga.

Reichardt heard one of Gluck's operas at the *Kärntnerthor* theatre in 1808, and the performance did not come up to his expectation: "The choruses were again too weak, and did not by any means realize Gluck's ideas; nor was the orchestra much better."[1] Reichardt said that the *Burg*, the *Kärntnerthor* and the *An-der-Wien* theatres all gave opera performances, but at none of them was the playing very good. He thought there were enough good players to make one first-class orchestra, but not enough to make three. No doubt the conductors of the old school, such as Weigl and Gyrowetz, were easy-going and inclined to let the orchestra go through the routine operas without any great exertion. The Viennese players, although skilled enough, had not the spirit and discipline of the North Germans, and it was probably just that energy and force that Reichardt missed. He explained that the orchestras at the court theatres had been allowed to decline while they were under the administration of the *Intendant* Baron Braun (1804). But, with the advent of Prince Lobkowitz in 1806, certain improvements had been made; some twelve young wind players had been brought in, and steps were being taken to improve the strings as well. Reichardt thought that there were plenty of good young players in Austria, Bohemia and Hungary, and that if these were all brought together, a first-class orchestra could be assembled.

In 1821 the orchestra in the *Kärntnerthor* theatre was reorganised and rearranged; the piano was abolished, and the new arrangement was shown in a sketch by Franz Stöber, the costumier at the theatre.

The orchestra at that time numbered about 46 players, and included when necessary a harp, piccolo, double bassoon, trombones, four horns and a bass drum, in addition to the usual instruments.

The theatre was evidently not open when Smart was in Vienna in 1825. He made no mention of it, and only described without any great enthusiasm a performance by part of the orchestra at the *Hofburg*: "The violins are weak, but the performance on the whole went well. The bassoons were good."[2] In 1826 the *Kärntnerthor* theatre appears to have been renovated and elaborately redecorated. In the words of a correspondent of the *Harmonicon*: "the old theatre has all the appearance of a Parisian interior in the latest taste; and has not unaptly been compared to a homely German dame, suddenly renovated by magic art, and transformed into a buxom lass of eighteen, rife with the newest fashions of the *Boulevard Italien*."[3]

When Edward Holmes arrived at Vienna in 1827 the people of this gay city were Rossini-mad, and not only mad for Rossini, but also for his imitators. Had Vienna forgotten its Gluck, its Mozart and its *Fidelio*? it was all ears for Rossini and Pacini. Compared with Munich, whence he had just come, Holmes thought the band and chorus "far inferior." Weigl was conducting: "this composer takes his place in the orchestra in so plain a costume, that his jean coat appears as though it had been doing good service

---

[1] *Vertraute Briefe*, I, p. 185. [2] Smart, *Journals*, p. 128.
[3] *Harm.*, Dec., 1826, p. 246.

in his study five minutes before."[1]   The *recitative* did not please him: "The plain recitative at the opera in Vienna is not so well accompanied, and I heartily wish the performer could hear the fanciful and exquisite manner in which Lindley does this at our Italian opera-house.[2]   The chords are indeed struck upon the violoncello (without that *arpeggio* and brilliancy, the unique excellence of Robert Lindley), but their effect is tame."[3]   Holmes ranked this opera orchestra below that at Darmstadt: "Weber's overture to *Euryanthe* was not so well played as at Darmstadt; the opera orchestra at Vienna has correctness, but less of tone than others in Germany."[4]   Altogether, rather a poor report.

The *Kärntnerthor* theatre was apparently closed for some time in 1826, and again in 1828[5]; and on its reopening in 1829 Franz Lachner was chief *Kapellmeister*.   From this time, no doubt, dates an improvement in the playing by the orchestra, and one which acquired further impulse when Nicolai came in 1841.   Chorley heard a performance at the *Kärntnerthor* in 1844, and his verdict was: "The orchestra was a fine one, and played with due intelligence, but slackly."[6]   The apparent slackness was evidently the result of overwork, for Guhr, the Frankfort *Kapellmeister*, who was at Vienna in that same year, said that although the opera orchestra was excellent and contained so many first-rate players, and was well directed by Nicolai and his assistants, the players were obviously overworked and at the same time underpaid.[7]   At that time all the attention of the Viennese public was given to Italian opera.

Berlioz, however, said nothing about slackness or fatigue in his report on the orchestra in the following year: "I have not yet told you of the orchestra or chorus of the Kärntnerthor Theatre.   Both are first-class; the orchestra especially, selected, drilled, and led by Nicolai, may be equalled but cannot be surpassed.   Besides its *aplomb*, *verve*, and great mechanical (technical) skill, this orchestra has an exquisite sonorousness, owing doubtless to the accurate way in which the instruments play together, as much as to the perfect manner in which they play in tune.   No one knows how rare this is, nor what disasters may be produced in even the best orchestra by any imperfection of time.   The *Kärntnerthor* band can accompany a singer in any style, can lead when it has the principal part, its *forte* is never noisy unless the composer has intended it to be so.   In the opera, it is perfect; in the symphony, triumphant; and, finally, to conclude my panegyric, it contains none of those conceited artists who resent just criticism, regard a comparison between themselves and foreign virtuosi as an insult, and believe themselves to be doing an honour to Beethoven when they condescend to play him."[8]   On another occasion the orchestra was engaged for a concert: "Just as the rehearsal was beginning, one of the first violins, who spoke French, whispered: 'You will see the difference between us and those

[1] *Rambles*, p. 121.   [2] King's Theatre, London.   [3] *Rambles*, p. 129.
[4] *Ibid.*, p. 158.   [5] Gassner, *Lex.*, Art. Dont.   [6] *Mod. German Music*, II, p. 135.
[7] Speyer, p. 270.   [8] *Mem.*, II, p. 185.

little wretches at the Wien theatre' (where I used to give my concerts). Certainly he was not wrong. Never was the work performed with such fire, precision, spirit, and well-ordered turbulence. And what sonority! what harmonious harmony!"[1]

Heinrich Esser, who after having been first *Concertmeister* and then *Kapellmeister* at Mannheim, became one of the conductors at the *Kärntnerthor* in 1847, gave his impressions of the orchestra at that theatre in a letter to Wilhelm Speyer written in September, 1847. He granted that the players were splendid and could hardly be bettered anywhere else, but complained that they were always overworked and tired. A long Italian season was followed by a long German season, and the same players were kept at it every day, rehearsing and playing, with the inevitable result that there was some indifferent and careless playing.[2]

Even allowing for Berlioz's tendency to exaggerate, it seems certain that by that time the orchestra at the *Kärntnerthor* theatre had come near to or possibly equal to the standard of those at Berlin, Dresden and Munich. Some difference in style must also be allowed for, and might possibly account to some extent for the slackness in their playing that was observed by critics from Northern Germany. An English correspondent described it in 1846 as "magnificent," and later on (1864) Wagner said of it: "certainly one of the finest orchestras in existence."[3] If it pleased two such exacting critics as Berlioz and Wagner there cannot have been much amiss with it.

* * *

Of the smaller orchestras at the *Leopoldstädter* and *Josephstädter* theatres in the outlying suburbs of Vienna not very much can be told. These theatres produced operettas, comedies and musical plays in endless succession, most of them as ephemeral as the fame of their composers.

Ed. Holmes (1828) said that at these theatres "nothing in a musical way is produced worth notice, though a capell-meister is there employed to beat the time to songs which are in the regular Astley and Sadler's Wells style"; and he was rather shocked by the way the beauty chorus was dressed, in a manner "calculated to delineate the form with excessive accuracy."[4]

The *Josephstädter* theatre is perhaps best remembered because it was for the re-opening in 1822 that Beethoven was commissioned to write the overture *Die Weihe des Hauses*.

Amongst the many *Kapellmeister* at these two theatres were: at the *Leopoldstädter*, Tuczek in 1802, Wenzel Müller (composer of some 200 operettas) from about 1813 intermittently almost until his death in 1835, Joseph Stadler (b. 1796) from 1819 to 1831, Gläser in 1817, Franz Volkert (1767–1845) from 1821, and Drechsler from 1822 to 1830; at the *Josephstädter*:

---

[1] *Mem.*, II, p. 286. [2] Speyer p. 289.
[3] *On Cond.*, p. 50. In 1848 Wagner contemplated an engagement at the *Kärntnerthor* theatre when the situation at Dresden was getting rather strained.
[4] *Rambles*, pp. 136–7.

Gläser in 1822, Conradin Kreutzer from 1833 to 1837, and Heinrich Proch from 1837. Later conductors at the latter theatre were Karl Binder and Franz von Suppé the composer of *Poet and Peasant*,[1] who began his career there in 1840. Schindler, Beethoven's friend and biographer, was a violinist in the orchestra at the *Josephstädter* theatre in the early 'twenties.

Smart said that the orchestra at the *Leopoldstädter* in 1825 was "large," but "the music they played gave no opportunity for the display of skill, if they had any." At the *Josephstädter*, where he heard *Der Freischütz*, the orchestra "was only tolerable. The violins were weak."[2]

ORCHESTRAS FOR CONCERTS

For concerts in Vienna during Beethoven's time, and, in fact, until the Philharmonic concerts were established early in the 'forties, the orchestras were collected from among the musicians engaged at the theatres, supplemented by amateur string players. The constitution of the orchestra for one of the *Liebhaber-Concerte* in 1808 was thus described in the *Wiener Vaterländische Blätter*: "An orchestra was organised, whose members were chosen from the best of the local music-lovers (*dilettante*). A few wind instruments only—French horns, trumpets, etc., were drafted from the Vienna theatres."[3] For Beethoven's concert at the *Theater-an-der-Wien* in the same year the orchestra was also got together from various sources: "Singers and orchestra were composed of the most heterogeneous elements, and it had been found impossible to get a single full rehearsal for all the pieces to be performed, all of them full of the greatest difficulties. You would be amazed at the quantity of music by this fruitful genius and tireless worker played during these four hours."[4] The result was a bad performance and a breakdown in the Choral Fantasia, as described by Reichardt, Czerny, Schindler and Ries.

This way of mixing professional and amateur players in their concert orchestras had been customary in Vienna long before the beginning of the 19th century, as Mozart's letter regarding the concerts at the *Augarten* in 1782 reveals: "The orchestra consists entirely of amateurs, with the exception of the bassoon-players, the trumpeters and the drummers."[5] The orchestra at the *Augarten* under Schuppanzigh appears to have been made up of similar "*heterogenen Teilen*," as Reichardt put it; and for the concerts of the *Gesellschaft der Musikfreunde*, the conductors and the rank and file of the strings were amateur players; only the double-basses and the wind instruments were in the hands of professional musicians.

If Reichardt's account is correct, the orchestral players of Vienna were in a rather depressed and listless condition in 1808. He explained the

---

[1] The very popular overture to this operetta had already served as the overture to two unsuccessful operettas at the *Josephstädter* theatre before it was made to serve as the overture to Elmar's *Dichter und Bauer*. Suppé sold it to a Munich music publisher for 8 thaler (Keller, p. 145).

[2] *Journals*, pp. 99, 100.   [3] Thayer, II, p. 112.
[4] Reichardt, *Ver. Briefe*, I, p. 206.   [5] Mozart, *Letters*, III, p. 1,200.

situation as follows: "Music here suffers because of the inertia and dejected condition of most of the musicians. It seems to me as if they hardly ever bring the zeal and goodwill to bear on their work in the orchestra without which a clean and powerful ensemble can never be attained. They generally complain about the low pay, which in most cases remains the same as it was in past times when living was incredibly cheap, but which, now that the paper money has declined to about half of its nominal value, does not provide for the bare necessities of life. So one cannot be surprised to find only dejection and disgust prevailing in most of the orchestras. A considerable number of the players are feeble old men who should have been pensioned off long ago, but who remain in service in order to earn enough money to make both ends meet. For a long time the renewal and strengthening of the personnel in the orchestras has been neglected, a matter which is all the more urgent because of the increasing difficulties in the instrumental parts of operas. When one compares an opera by Gluck with one by Mozart, and then one by Mozart with one by Cherubini, it would seem as if an ever-increasing executive skill had given these composers the courage to demand more and more from the orchestra. Nevertheless, in the same proportion as the difficulties have increased, so have the orchestras become weaker."[1]

The growing difficulty of orchestral parts tested the skill even of the professional players. The second overture to *Fidelio*, used at the first performance of that opera in 1805 "was too difficult in the part of the wind instruments, which always executed their task to the great vexation of the composer. In the third overture which was substituted for the two former, too hard a task was imposed upon the string instruments, so that these also were found deficient in the requisite precision."[2]

If the professional players in the theatres found Beethoven's parts difficult, the amateur strings in the concert-orchestras must have found them much more so. At a concert in the large *Redoutensaal* in 1814, when Beethoven directed his seventh and eighth symphonies and Wellington's Victory at Vittoria, only seven of the 18 first violins, and six of the seconds were paid professionals.[3] At the first performance of the Choral Symphony at the *Kärntnerthor* theatre in 1824, the chorus and orchestra were augmented by amateurs of the *Gesellschaft der Musikfreunde*. It is hardly possible to imagine the sort of performance that would be given of this most exacting work with such a mixed orchestra playing it for the first time from MS. parts after only two rehearsals, and under the divided direction of Beethoven himself, with Umlauf beating time, Schuppanzigh leading with his violin, and Conradin Kreutzer at the piano.

At the *Spirituel-Concerte*, where complete symphonies and choral works were performed, an orchestra of about 50 was employed, of which only ten or twelve wind players were paid professionals. Originally there were

[1] *Ver. Briefe*, II, p. 132.   [2] Moscheles, *Life of Beethoven* (Schindler), I, pp. 93–94.
[3] Thayer, II, p. 268.

no rehearsals for these concerts, or at most a short one in the case of a particularly difficult work.[1]   The first conductor was Gebauer, choirmaster at the *Augustiner Kirche* and originator of these concerts.   After his death in 1822 the direction was in the hands of the amateurs Piringer (1823), Geissler and Lannoy.   Many symphonies of Haydn, Mozart and Beethoven were played, including the Choral Symphony in 1827, and one by Schubert in 1829, as well as several by composers of less enduring fame.[2]   After 1830 the conductors were the amateurs Lannoy, Holz and Ludwig Titze (1798–1850), the latter a singer in the Hofkapelle.   In 1835 an effort was made to put new life into these concerts; some of them were conducted by Seyfried, and a prize of 50 ducats offered for the best symphony was won by Franz Lachner.   The repertoire was enlarged, and several new works by Spohr were added.   In the 'forties works by Weber, Mendelssohn and J. S. Bach began to appear in the programmes, and in 1846 a concert was conducted by Liszt.

But by about 1840 the time was past when under-rehearsed and mixed amateur and professional orchestras could do justice to works which were becoming ever technically more difficult.   In this respect Vienna was behind the other capitals and the larger German towns, and complaints were being heard about the quality of these concert performances.   In 1841 the *Theaterzeitung* complained that the playing of Beethoven's 8th symphony at one of the *Gesellschaft* concerts was unsatisfactory, but admitted that nothing better could be expected from such an unhomogeneous orchestra.   "As good as can be expected from an orchestra consisting largely of amateurs," and similar comments, show how the *Gesellschaft* and the *Spirituel* concerts were rated by the Vienna critics.   One said: "too few rehearsals and too many unreliable violinists"; another remarked "too little rehearsing and too many amateurs."[3]   Lachner told Hanslick that in the 'twenties the playing at the *Spirituel-Concerte* was so poor that Schubert left the hall during a performance of one of his own works.   Hanslick himself had attended these concerts during their last few years, and had found nothing to admire except the good intentions of the worthy old amateur conductors, and the wonderfully pious admiration of the listeners.

The time was thus fully ripe for the establishment of first-class orchestral concerts in Vienna when Nicolai came to conduct the opera at the *Kärtnerthor* theatre in 1841.   When he inaugurated the Philharmonic concerts in the following year, the *Spirituel-Concerte* had the first warning of their impending dissolution.   It was the Revolution of 1848 that finally put an end to these concerts; but in any case they were doomed.   Vienna had had a taste of good orchestral playing, and it was not going to be satisfied any longer with second or third-rate performances of its great symphonies.

When Franz Lachner was *Kapellmeister* in Vienna he started some

---

[1] Hanslick, p. 186.

[2] Krommer, Hummel, Schneider, Spohr, Feska, Romberg, Ries, Leidesdorf and Pixis (Hanslick, p. 189).

[3] Hanslick, p. 312.

subscription concerts at the *Kärtnerthor* theatre in 1833, under the title *Künstler Verein*, making use of the opera chorus and orchestra. These performances quite put into the shade the amateur efforts to which Vienna had previously been accustomed. Works by Beethoven, Mozart, Weber, Cherubini, and some of Lachner's own compositions were played, and everyone concurred in the opinion that these performances excelled all previous efforts as far as the orchestral playing was concerned. Unfortunately this good beginning was not continued when Lachner left in 1834 to go as *Kapellmeister* to Mannheim. From then until 1841 nothing further was done towards establishing a series of first-class orchestral concerts, probably because they had not got the right man in Vienna to do it. When Nicolai arrived in 1841, that man had come, and in the following year the new concerts were established, and the first *Philharmonische Academie* took place in the large *Redoutensaal* on March 28, 1842.

The concerts were organised on a co-operative basis very similar to that of the Paris *Société des Concerts*. Each member of the orchestra received an equal share of the proceeds; members of the managing committee were each given an extra share, the leader, Georg Hellmesberger, received two extra shares, and the conductor got four shares. Six concerts were given during each season, and the orchestra was that of the *Kärntnerthor* theatre with the strings augmented by the addition of outside professional players to 16 first violins, and the other parts in proportion. No amateurs were admitted, and the wind players were those of the regular opera orchestra.[1]

The programme of the first concert included Beethoven's 7th symphony, the Leonora overture No. 3 and the overture in C, Op. 124, with a few vocal solos by way of relief. The future programmes were based largely on the works of Beethoven and a few symphonies by Haydn and Mozart, overtures by Weber, Mendelssohn and Meyerbeer, and arias by Cherubini, Spohr, and a few others. No trivial music or virtuoso pieces were admitted. On March 19, 1843, the people of Vienna were able to hear the Choral Symphony worthily performed for the first time, after careful preparation by Nicolai in thirteen rehearsals. Nicolai wrote in his diary that although Hellmesberger was a good musician, he was "a bit too quiet for me"; he would have preferred the deputy-leader Grutsch to lead the orchestra.

Before Nicolai left Vienna he had undoubtedly raised the standard of orchestral playing in the Austrian capital to a level which was worthy of its reputation as one of the most important musical centres in Europe. The Philharmonic orchestra under Nicolai (described as a "dry composer," but "first-rate conductor") was ranked in 1846 as "one of the first in all Europe,"[2] and there is no reason to suppose that this great compliment was undeserved.

The concerts were continued with growing success until Nicolai left to take up his appointment at Berlin in 1847. Unfortunately there was no worthy successor to Nicolai in Vienna. Hellmesberger, the leader, and the two opera conductors, Wilhelm Reuling and Heinrich Proch, conducted

---

[1] Kralik, p. 19.   [2] *Mus. World*, March 28, 1846, p. 144.

264 THE ORCHESTRA FROM BEETHOVEN TO BERLIOZ

some concerts in 1847–48, and then came the Revolution. The Philharmonic concerts were broken up and discontinued for a few years, and it is difficult to say whether this temporary dissolution was due to the loss of Nicolai or to the politically disturbed state of the Austrian capital at that time. After the revolutionary period the concerts were newly established in 1854 with Carl Eckert as conductor, and from then the Vienna Philharmonic orchestra went from strength to strength, and earned for itself a worthy place among the finest orchestras in Europe.

ORCHESTRAS IN PRAGUE AND BUDAPESTH

Few, if any, of the many private orchestras maintained by the Bohemian and Hungarian nobility survived the 18th century. Although their patronage of music was not entirely withheld in the early part of last century, it was on a somewhat reduced scale, and the public in the towns had to share with them the cost of providing orchestras in the theatres.

The *Landständischen-Theater* at Prague was opened in 1784. It was owned by a group of Bohemian noblemen who appointed an *Intendant* to manage it. This theatre was the scene of the first performance of Mozart's *Don Giovanni* in 1787, when there were only three first violins, three seconds, and two each of the lower strings in the orchestra.[1] About 1796 the number of string players was still the same, and the total strength of the orchestra was only twenty-five, of which thirteen were wind instruments.[2]

Reichardt described the orchestra in 1809 as being small and good, but not distinguished.[3] The *Kapellmeister* from 1808 to 1813 was Wenzel Müller, the Viennese operetta composer. He was followed by Weber in 1813, who was charged with the task of reorganising the musical arrangements at the theatre and of improving a standard of performance which had fallen rather low during Wenzel Müller's time. Weber did his best to improve the rather small orchestra, and got Clement to come from Vienna to act as leader. He also induced Sellner the oboist to come to Prague, and he had a good flautist in Michael Jannusch, professor of the flute at the Conservatoire. Weber left Prague in 1816, and was succeeded by Methfessel from Rudolstadt. Friedrich Wilhelm Pixis, who had been leader since 1806, seems to have been the next *Kapellmeister*; he died in 1842, and when Berlioz came in 1845 one of two brothers named Scraub apparently occupied that position, with Moritz Mildner (1812–1865) as his *Concertmeister*.

The Conservatoire at Prague, a good practical school for instrumentalists under the direction of Dionys Weber, provided some good players not only for the local orchestra, but for many further afield. This institution had been founded in 1810 by eight Bohemian noblemen, because it was found to be difficult to get together a complete orchestra in Prague.[4] According to Holmes, it was serving its purpose admirably: "The Conservatoire of

[1] Jahn, II, p. 300.
[2] Ambros-Branberger, p. 14 (*Das Konservatorium für Musik in Prag.*).
[3] *Ver. Briefe*. I, p. 88. [4] Hanslick, p. 46.

Prague furnishes Germany, Russia and France with some of the best of their singers and players, and it is the principal assistance to the cultivation of good music in the city. Every year the numbers of pupils are thinned—the elder young men are drafted off to different orchestras, the young women to different operatic establishments." Among the professors at the Conservatoire who also played in the opera orchestra were: Pixis for the violin, Johann B. Hüttner (b. 1793) for the 'cello, Anton Eiser (b. 1800) for the flute, Johann Friedrich Bauer (b.c. 1785) for the oboe, Thaddäus Blatt (b. 1793) for the clarinet, and Johann Janatka (b. 1800) for the horn. The following note from the The *Quarterly Musical Magazine* in 1823 shows how efficiently the Prague Conservatoire was working at that time: "This conservatory has produced an immense number of professors who enjoy eminence in the various Courts of Europe and in the various orchestras. At the Vienna opera, Bettlach and J. Nowak (bassoon), Malik (oboe), Paur (clarinet), Keil and Janatka (horn), Weidl (violoncello), F. Nowak (double-bass).

"At the theatre at Leopoldstadt, Joseph Zelenka (horn). At the theatre at Pesth, Taborsky (violin), Zwrczek (horn), Wesetsky (bassoon). Also in the Military Chapels (bands) in Hungary, F. Zelenka (clarinettist and master of the Chapel (band) to the Hesse Homburg Hussars), Hochmann (trumpet), Klepsch (hautboy), Böhm (clarinet).

"At the theatre at Gratz, Kallusch (double-bass), Eiser and Müller (flute), Chwoy, Duk, Frinta and Machaczek (violin), Kopitus (viola), Hofner and Klindera (horn).

"At the Music Society at Iglaw, Loffelmann (teacher of the violin). At the theatre at Hanover, Stowiczek (violin), Matys (violoncello). At the Landgrave's Chapel at Donaueschingen, Kalliwoda, a foreigner (violin), Marcziczek (horn), Koch (clarionet), at Naples; and Gellert (violin) at St. Petersburg."[1]

From Carl Loewe's account of a performance by the Conservatoire orchestra at Prague, it would appear that Dionys Weber's method of training was to make the students play as loudly and as fast as possible; he was not satisfied unless they played Mozart's *Figaro* overture in $3\frac{1}{8}$ minutes, and the noise nearly deafened Loewe.[2]

Although he said that it was not large enough for the theatre, Smart's report on the opera orchestra at Prague in 1825, when it was in charge of Pixis, was very favourable. Some of the players must have been past their best at that time, for seven of them, including the leading 'cello, bass, second violin and clarinet, had played under Mozart in 1787. Nevertheless, he said, "the power of the band is extraordinary," and there were only sixteen string players; but it was "perfect, and the effect wonderful considering there were so few violins."[3] Edward Holmes was also very pleased with the Prague orchestra in 1827. He described the theatre as "long, narrow, and dark," but the band as "admirable," and he confirmed that even then

[1] *Quar. Mus. Mag.*, Vol. V, No. XX, p. 487. [2] Loewe, p. 314. [3] *Journals*, pp. 132, 134.

some of the members still serving had played in *Don Giovanni* under Mozart.[1] One of these was the old bass player Wenzel Swoboda, who was evidently still playing during the 'thirties when Wilhelm Kuhe was a boy at Prague.[2]

Spohr was quite satisfied with the orchestra when he came to Prague in 1837 to direct a performance of his *Berg-geist*. Some years later (1843) he was offered the post of *Kapellmeister* at Prague, but did not care to leave Cassel, where he had been for over twenty years.

The theatre in 1845 appeared to Berlioz as "dark, small, dirty, and very bad for sound." The orchestra matched the small dimensions of the theatre, and seemed "rather to reproach the manager with parsimony. With so small a number of performers, it really is not permissible to attempt any masterpieces in a high style, and yet this is just what the Prague Theatre occasionally does."[3]   Berlioz placed the Conservatoire, then under the direction of Johann Friedrich Kittl (1809–1868), second only to that of Paris.

Prague had to wait until 1862 for a larger National Theatre, and for Smetana and Dvořák before Bohemia could free itself from the domination of German music.

There is not much that can be told of the orchestras at Budapesth.   That city was rather off the track for touring musicians, and many did not go out of their way to visit it; Moser described it in 1839 as the *"vom Weltverkehr abgelegenen Pest."*   There was a National Hungarian theatre and a German theatre; it was no doubt for the opening of the latter in 1812 that Beethoven wrote his music for *King Stephen* and *The Ruins of Athens*, and it was in the same theatre, where his first teacher Stanislaus Serwaczynski (1791–1862) was leader, that the small boy Joseph Joachim heard an orchestra playing for the first time in his life.

But Budapesth was not too far out of the way for Berlioz in 1846, when he found that the two theatres would never under any circumstances unite their rather small orchestras in order to form one big one.   Berlioz chose the National Theatre orchestra, which, he said, was "so small that it was impossible to think of getting up my symphonies with its little band of violins only."[4]   However, the members of the local Philharmonic Society came to the rescue and provided him with a dozen excellent violinists, led by one Treichlinger, and they "acquitted themselves marvellously."   This was when Berlioz wrote his famous Hungarian March, which he afterwards revised and amplified.

The very able conductor at the National Theatre since 1838 was Franz Erkel, who is said to have brought the opera orchestra to a high state of efficiency, and Berlioz mentioned one Kohne as *Concertmeister*, a "man of great talent."

Some of the smaller towns in Austria, Bohemia and Hungary possessed theatres at which opera was given from time to time by transferring an opera company from one place to another.   By this means such places as

[1] *Rambles*, p. 182.   [2] Kuhe, p. 6.   [3] *Mem.*, II, p. 219.   [4] *Ibid.*, II, p. 204.

Pressburg, for example, might enjoy a brief season of opera by taking over a company from Graz. But nothing is known about their orchestras, nor is there any reason to suppose that such places were able to maintain permanent orchestras except on a very modest scale.

ORCHESTRAS IN ITALY

The opera-houses in Italy[1] during the first half of last century were very many. It would hardly be possible now to identify them all; but in order to give an idea of how many opera orchestras there were in that country, an attempt must be made to name some of these theatres and places.

In all the large towns there were several theatres which, although they did not necessarily produce opera all the year round, gave performances at certain seasons, making their strongest effort during carnival time. The following were the most important theatres in the larger towns:

MILAN. Teatro della Scala, T. Canobbiana, T. Carcano, T. Re.

NAPLES. San Carlo, Fondo, Nuovo, Fiorentini, Re, Ferdinando.

VENICE. Fenice, San Benedetto, San Mose, San Luca, Giovanni Crisostomo, San Samuel.

FLORENCE. Pergola, Cocomero, Borgognissanti, Goldini, Alfieri.

ROME. Valle, Argentina, Apollo, Tordinona, Re, Alberti.

GENOA. San Agostina, Falcone, Carlo Felice.

TURIN. Regio, Sutero, Carignano, d'Argennes.

BOLOGNA. Gran Teatro, Communale, Marsigli Rossi, Corso.

TRIESTE. Grande, Moroner.

In each of the following towns there was at least one theatre:

Ancona	Este	Perugia
Alessandria	Fermo	Piacenza
Arezzo	Ferrara	Pisa
Bassano	Imola	Prato
Belluno	Intra	Reggio
Bergamo	Leghorn	Rimini
Bra	Lugo	Rovigo
Brescia	Lucca	Sienna
Cagliari (Sardinia)	Lodi	Sinigaglia
Casalmagiore	Mantua	Sondrio
Castel S. Pietro	Messina	Treviso
Carpi	Modena	Trieste
Cesena	Novarra	Varesi
Codogno	Padua	Vercelli
Como	Palermo	Verona
Crema	Parma	Vicenza
Cremona	Pavia	Udine

[1] By Italy, must be understood Austrian and Napoleonic Italy, the kingdoms of Sardinia and Sicily, and the Papal States.

The above list is by no means complete, and it would probably be no exaggeration to estimate that there were between 150 and 200 theatres in Italy, most of them capable of producing opera.

An Italian authority estimated that in 1825 there were in Italy: 230 *prime donne*, 250 *seconde donne*, 140 *primo tenori*, 130 *secondi tenori*, 240 *buffi comici* and *buffi cantati*, many *secondi buffi* and *terze donne*, nearly 200 theatres, more than 50 living opera composers, and 30 opera poets.[1]

The orchestra at each of these many theatres was there as a necessary part of the apparatus for producing opera and ballet. It might be called upon occasionally to play in a church or at an artists' concert in the theatre, but it would not have occurred to any Italian at that time either to give or to go to a concert at which the performance of the orchestra itself was the only or the main attraction.   The Italians were not interested in symphonies, and knew little about them; instrumental music, unless produced by a soloist, was to them something fit for little more than to act as an introduction and an accompaniment to a vocal performance or a ballet, and as long as it served its purpose in that capacity, no more was expected of it. Not only did the Italians maintain their orchestras primarily in order to produce opera, but they also demanded that the opera should be written according to their own formula, even though it was the work of a German composer; and it had to be sung in their own language.

To understand the position of Italian orchestras at that time, it is necessary to take into consideration the music they played, for therein lay much of the difference between an Italian and a French or a German orchestra.

The operas produced at the Italian theatres up to about 1815 were nearly all by native composers of the pre-Rossinian period. Excepting a few by Mozart which were then beginning to find their way into the Italian repertoires, these scores made very small demands on the skill and intelligence of their orchestral players.   The texture of the music was bald and simple, and the orchestration was conventional and elementary; these composers kept the statue well on the stage, and the pedestal in the orchestra. The music was not the sort that could give the orchestras any opportunity or any chance of improvement, and the orchestration was often referred to contemptuously by German and French musicians. Spohr wrote of Italian orchestration in 1816: "The instrumentation, however, as compared with ours, first introduced by Mozart, is still very meagre, and the Italians in that still cling too much to the old. The viols (violas) and bassoons almost always go through the whole opera *col Basso*, and the clarinets and hautboys in *Unisono* . . . they are far behind the Germans in the knowledge of how to get the best effect from the wind instruments."[2] Weber ridiculed Italian orchestration thus: "Oboi col Flauti, Clarinetti col Oboi, Flauti col Violini, Fagotti col Basso, Viol 2do col Primo, Viola col Basso, Voce ad Libitum, Violini colla parte."[3] Berlioz, of course, exaggerated wildly in his skit on Italian orchestras: "In all the theatres there is in front of the stage

---

[1] *Harm.*, Oct., 1825, p. 193.   [2] *Autob.*, I, p. 288.   [3] Weber, III, p. 302.

a black hollow filled with wretches blowing and scraping, as indifferent to what is being shouted on the stage as to what is being buzzed in the boxes and parterre, and possessed of but one thought, that of earning their supper. The assemblage of these poor creatures constitutes what is called an orchestra, and this is how an orchestra is generally composed: there are usually two first and two second violins, very rarely a viola and a 'cello, almost always two or three double-basses."[1]

When the Rossini craze had got a firm hold on all the Italian opera-houses during the 'twenties, nearly all the composers who had hitherto held the field faded into permanent obscurity, and a new group began to supplant them. These were the Rossini imitators, who aped not only his music but also his manner of orchestrating.

With the increasing popularity of Rossini's more mature operas, Italian orchestras could not but benefit from the more exacting technique which these scores demanded, and from the greater finish required for their effective rendering. Between 1820 and 1840, in addition to the works of Rossini and a host of lesser lights, the Italian theatres began to be occupied with the operas of Bellini, Donizetti, and the early works of Verdi, and with occasional productions by Mozart, Meyerbeer, Spontini, and even here and there an opera by Hérold and Auber. The scores of these composers demanded, and, no doubt, received better playing than had sufficed for the pre-Rossinians. Yet there is no reason to suppose that even the best of the Italian opera-orchestras ever approached in finish and refinement the standard of the best French and German orchestras in the 'thirties and 'forties of last century. The following was written in 1837: "It is a fact perhaps not generally known that Italian orchestras are incapable of getting through even the notes of such operas as *Der Freischütz*, *Robert le Diable*, etc., not only from the difficulty of the keys in which they are written, but on account of the precision required in the performance of concerted music; to Italians any other music than that of their own country and time, is an unknown tongue."[2]

Writing in 1830, Fétis said that on the whole Italian orchestras accompanied well enough, and that their wind players were good, but he rather spoiled the compliment when he added that many of the best performers on these instruments were Germans.[3]

Information regarding the size and personnel of Italian orchestras is difficult to unearth. No doubt such information, when it exists, will be found in local records which are at present unpublished and inaccessible. But we may be quite sure that the size of the orchestras in all these Italian theatres varied according to the size of the auditorium and the financial resources of the establishment.

The very largest theatres had some 80 or more players, as at *La Scala* in Milan and the *San Carlo* in Naples.

[1] Berlioz, *Evenings*, p. 258.   [2] *Mus. World*, Aug. 4, 1837, p. 127.
[3] *Curiosités*, p. 51.

The *Teatro alla Scala* was opened in 1778, and replaced an older *Regio Ducale Teatro* which was burnt down in 1776. It was originally the property of box-owners who provided the funds for erecting the building, but later became the property of the municipality. There was seating accommodation for over 3,000 people.[1] Towards the close of the 18th century the orchestra numbered 80 players, and contained, as was usual in Italian orchestras, more double-basses than 'cellos.[2]

Following the usual custom, the *Maestro al Cembalo* presided over the musical side of the production, but the orchestral playing was controlled by the leading violinist, called *Primo Violino* or *Capo d'orchestra*. Seated on either side of the *Maestro* at the piano were the leading 'cello and double-bass players, distinguished from the rank and file of these instruments as *Primo violoncello al Cembalo* and *Primo basso al Cembalo*. That central group was responsible for accompanying the recitatives, with which the main body of the orchestra had no concern.

Vincenzo Lavigna (1777–1837), a composer and singing teacher, served as *Maestro al Cembalo* at *La Scala* from 1802 until he was succeeded in 1834 by Giacomo Panizza (1804–1860). These were concerned with the vocal side of the performance, and the status of these *Maestri* may be judged from the fact that although every solo singer and dancer was named, the name of the *Maestro* (unless he had composed the music) did not appear on the playbills. Their position was nearer that of an accompanist and vocal coach than that of an orchestral conductor.

The violinist-leader (and virtually conductor of the orchestra) with Lavigna, from 1803 to 1834, was Allesandro Rolla, and Eugenio Cavallini served in the same capacity with Panizza. Rolla gained a considerable reputation as a violinist, and in 1830 Fétis ranked him as the best in Italy. The leading double-bass, Giuseppe Andreoli, seems to have acquired more than a local reputation; according to Gassner he was one of the best performers on that instrument that had ever lived. Of the wind players, *La Scala* could boast of Giuseppe Rabboni, a flautist of some renown, and another notable performer on the same instrument, Giulio Briccialdi (1818–1881), who joined the orchestra just about the mid-century and is well remembered on account of his B flat lever key; Rockstro said that he was "one of the finest performers that I ever heard on any instrument," and that was indeed high praise. There was also a celebrated clarinettist named Ernesto Cavallini, who played with "prodigious facility of execution and marvellous volubility" on a six-keyed clarinet,[3] and Luigi Belloli (1770–1817), a great horn player in his day, who was succeeded by his son Agostino in 1816. The elder Belloli had "a very beautiful tone, much skill and a cultivated taste."[4] This orchestra proudly possessed a drummer named Carlo Antonio Boracchi who took his art seriously, for not only did he

---

[1] Cambiasi, XX.   [2] Gyrowetz, p. 44.
[3] Fétis, *Biog. Univ.* Sometimes called "the Paganini of the clarinet."
[4] Spohr, I, p. 260.

PLATE 17

LA SCALA AT MILAN

PLATE 18

CONCERT ROOM OF THE MUSICAL SOCIETY FÉLIX MERITIS AT AMSTERDAM, c. 1810

invent a device for tuning timpani at one operation in about a second, but he was also the author of a *Manuale del Timpanista* published at Milan in 1842.

Before going to Italy, Spohr was warned that the orchestras in that country were worse than in the provincial towns of France, and accordingly wrote some solos with particularly easy accompaniments for his Italian tour. The performance of the orchestra at *La Scala*, however, was much better than he had been led to expect; "it was pure, vigorous, precise, and withal very calm," but Spohr complained that the audience made so much noise that one could scarcely hear the music. At his own concert in *La Scala* the orchestra accompanied with great interest and attention. They played his overture to *Alruna* with great power, but not without mistakes: "The orchestra is accustomed to too many rehearsals to be able to execute anything free from fault after one rehearsal only." So they were not good readers, although they were careful accompanists.

The *Teatro della Canobbiana* at Milan, opened in 1779, served as an auxiliary to *La Scala* for smaller productions, and both shared the same musical staff. This was the theatre where Berlioz heard *L'Elisir d'Amore* in 1832, or rather, where he didn't hear it because the theatre was "full of people talking at the top of their voices, with their backs to the stage; the singers all the time gesticulating and shouting in eager rivalry."[1] The same complaint about the noisy audiences in Italy had been made by Burney in 1770,[2] by Gyrowetz in 1788,[3] and by Spohr in 1816.

The great rival theatre at Naples, the *San Carlo*, was originally built in 1737; destroyed by fire in 1816, it was quickly rebuilt and re-opened in the following year.

The large auditorium in this theatre demanded an orchestra much on the same scale as at *La Scala*. In 1818 there were nearly 70 musicians in the orchestra, of which 43 were string players. The full complement of wind included four horns and three trombones, and to the usual drums was added the "Turkish music" (percussion) which at that time was becoming very popular in Italian opera.[4]

The eccentric violinist, Giuseppe Puppo was *Capo d'orchestra* at the *San Carlo* from 1811 to 1817, and from then until 1839 another violinist, Giuseppe Maria Festa (1771–1839) was in charge of the orchestra. For some years, from 1825, Julius Benedict was *Maestro al Cembalo* when the theatre was under the management of Barbaja.

The only wind players with more than a local reputation appear to have been the flautist Negri and the clarinet player Ferdinando Sebastiani (b. 1800) who was described as "the first performer on this instrument in Europe" when he visited Paris in 1828.[5] A French critic wrote of Sebastiani: "He sings well on his instrument, overcomes difficulties

---

[1] *Mem.*, I, p. 254.

[2] "the noise during the performance was abominable" (*Present State*, Italy).

[3] *Selbstbiographie*, p. 44, reprint.   [4] *All. Mus. Zeit.*, July 15, 1818.

[5] *Harm.*, Jan., 1828, p. 23.

without labour, and has much vigour.   His manner does not resemble that of Bärmann, nor the German school; but in his style he is effective."[1]

Spohr heard a performance at the *San Carlo* in 1817, just after the opening of the new building, and said that the orchestra, "under the correct and spirited but somewhat too loud direction of Signor Festa," had studied the piece well, but was "somewhat wanting in *nuances* of *piano* and *forte*"; also that the wind instruments were "always too loud in the *piano*."[2]

Nevertheless, the orchestra at the *San Carlo* earned some praise from foreign visitors.   From a French critic (1828) we learn that it was "an excellent orchestra" which merited "honourable mention."   Kandler (1829) placed the orchestra at the *San Carlo* well above all others in Naples: "Among the orchestras at Naples, that of *San Carlo* is the most distinguished. It is under the direction of Signor Festa, who, besides his talents as a practical musician, is said to be a good scholar.   Years, however, begin to sit heavy on him, and the orchestra would gain by the vigour and activity of a younger artist; but where shall we find one with the talents of the veteran director?"

Mendelssohn could find nothing that was good to say of any Italian performance.   His verdict on the orchestra at Naples in 1831 was very crushing: "The orchestra is composed of wind instruments out of tune and screaming fiddles, and does not go together.   I swear to you that the opera at Wittenberg (whether there is one or not) is better than the *San Carlo* at Naples."[3]   Berlioz was not so unkind, and gave the orchestra qualified praise: "In comparison with the orchestras I had heard (in Italy), this one seemed to me excellent.   There is nothing to fear from the wind instruments; the violins play fairly well, and the violoncellos are harmonious, though too few."   Berlioz was annoyed by the noise the violin-conductor made by tapping his bow on the desk, but was assured that this was necessary in order to keep the players together.   He indulgently concluded his remarks with: "after all, one must not expect much from an orchestra where instrumental music is almost unknown as one would in Berlin, Dresden, or Paris."[4]   William Gardiner (1846) also drew attention to the leader's annoying habit of tapping with his violin bow: "The violins, as usual, were too weak, and indifferently played, partly in consequence of cramming four performers upon one bench, not giving them elbow-room for the free use of the bow. . . . I was much annoyed by the leader tapping a tin candlestick all night with his bow, to beat the time, when he had better have been playing."[5]

Next in rank, after *La Scala* and the *San Carlo*, came the *Fenice* at Venice, but of the orchestra at that theatre no information is available.   At the *San Benedetto* the orchestra earned no better compliment in 1846 than the remark that it was "bearable," and the writer commented on the "paucity of violoncellos" which even then remained a peculiarity of Italian orchestras.[6]   At Turin also, under Polledro, who had been leader at Dresden up to 1824, the

---

[1] *Harm.*, June, 1828, p. 141.   [2] *Autob.*, II, p. 13.   [3] Devrient, p. 118.
[4] *Mem.*, I, p. 235.   [5] *Sights in Italy*, p. 45.   [6] *Mus. World*, 1846, p. 167.

SAN CARLO OPERA HOUSE AT NAPLES

orchestra appears to have ranked fairly high amongst those of Italy.   What little can be told of other opera orchestras in Italy is much on the same lines as the preceding.

The smaller towns could not maintain anything approaching first-class professional orchestras.   A French musician travelling in Italy in 1828, writing of the opera at Lucca, said: "The orchestra was in great measure composed of amateurs, a thing usual in Italian towns of the second order, and tolerably good."[1]

It seems to have been reserved for Rome to produce the very worst of Italian orchestras.   Nobody had a good word to say about them; Spohr gave a concert at Rome with a scratch orchestra: "The orchestra, composed of the best musicians of Rome, was nevertheless the worst of all that had yet accompanied me in Italy.   The ignorance, want of taste, and stupid arrogance of these people beggars all description.   Of *nuances* in *piano* and *forte* they know absolutely nothing.   One might let that pass, but each individual makes just what ornamentation comes into his head and double strokes with almost every tone, so that the *ensemble* resembles more the noise of an orchestra tuning up than harmonious music."   The wretched Roman players could not even read: "the musicians have so little musical taste, and are so unskilled in note-reading, that we nearly broke down twice."[2] Of an opera by one of the Rossini-imitators performed at the *Valle* theatre Spohr wrote: "The orchestra, composed for the most part of professors (!) who had played at my concert, played crudely, incorrectly, and without any sort of difference between piano and forte."   At the *Argentino* theatre things were no better: "the orchestra was worse than in the smallest provincial town in Germany, and in a word, it is an assemblage of folks such as had all Italy been ransacked for the purpose, it would have been difficult to find worse.   God help the composer whose work falls into such hands!" At the great church of St. Peter "the orchestral accompaniment was, as is usual in Rome, very bad."[3]   At the *Valle* theatre in 1816 the orchestra was said to be composed mainly of "workmen and petty shopkeepers engaged during the day in pursuit of their trade.   The first clarinet was a barber, who habitually shaved Rossini."[4]   There was something peculiarly crushing in the succinct report of a correspondent in 1848 that "there are two operas (in Rome) at the Apollo and at the Valle theatres; the former is the worst."[5]

In his survey of the state of music at Rome in 1828, Kandler, a German long resident in that city, made the following remarks about the orchestras: "The orchestras, also, are evidently on the decline.   Since the new order of things, the churches have become impoverished, and no longer possess the means to encourage music as formerly.   The productions for the theatre are rare, and frequently imperfect; and, generally speaking, the art no longer finds the same protection among the great as formerly.   Hence

[1] *Harm.*, March, 1829, p. 52.   [2] *Autob.*, I, pp. 308–9.   [3] *Ibid.*, I, pp. 315, 319; II, p. 38.
[4] Sutherland Edwards, *Life of Rossini*, p. 115.   [5] *Illus. Lon. News*, Feb. 12, 1848.

fathers of families have neither an inducement nor a desire to give their children a musical impulse, and bring them up to the exercise of the art. The middle classes of society supply a considerable number of instrumental performers, but the greater part are content to remain in a state of mediocrity." The best orchestral leader in Rome was then Pellicia, and two others, Landoni and Stobilini, "notwithstanding the reputation they have acquired, by no means deserve the praise lavished on them." Rotta was said to be the best 'cello player. Fétis said that Italian composers admitted that the Roman orchestras were not even mediocre.[1] Hauptmann thought that the arrangement of the players and the method of direction were unsatisfactory; no score was used, and the leading violinist conducted from a part written on two staves.[2] When Berlioz wished to describe an orchestra at Bonn as being just midway between the very worst and the very best, he said: "It occupied a position between a Roman or Florentine orchestra and that of the *Société des Concerts* of Paris."[3]

Even Genoa could do better than Rome: "The orchestra was tolerable; the violins played in tune, and the wind kept good time."[4] But there is a lack of enthusiasm in the report that at Genoa "the orchestra possesses several artists of merit, and did its best to merit the favour of the public."[5]

No doubt the Italian orchestras varied locally according to their financial resources; where the means to employ better players were forthcoming a higher standard would be reached. At Modena, for example, where the Duke and Duchess liberally supported the opera, some of the best Italian players were engaged. In 1826 the *Maestro* at Modena was Antonio Gandini (1786–1842), and at the head of the orchestra was Prosperus Silva, said to be a "well-informed and spirited leader." Tadolini on the 'cello, Angiolini on the oboe, Curoni on the clarinet, Andrei on the bassoon, and Galeotti on the horn were also described as being "extraordinary men in their several departments."[6] Gandini was succeeded by his son Allessandro (1807–1871), who wrote a history of the theatre at Modena.[7]

Even allowing for some degree of prejudice and a total lack of sympathy for Italian music in the cases of Spohr and Mendelssohn, and for some exaggeration in the case of Berlioz, it is clear that there was no orchestra in Italy during the first half of last century that could be ranked with the best in France or Germany. Nor is it at all likely that finished or sensitive playing would be heard where audiences scarcely listened to the orchestra, where they talked through the overture, played cards during the opera, and only gave any attention to the music when it took the form of a vocal solo or duet. The Italian orchestras during the 'twenties and 'thirties were playing music which was far removed from that which occupied the contemporary French and German orchestras; they were not playing the symphonies of Beethoven or Mendelssohn; they knew not *Fidelio, Jessonda*

---

[1] *Curiosités*, p. 52.   [2] *Briefe*, I, p. 67.   [3] *Evenings*, p. 320.
[4] *Mem.*, I, p. 180.   [5] *Harm.*, Feb., 1825, p. 37.   [6] *Ibid.*, June, 1826, p. 125.
[7] Amplified by Valdrighi and published in 1873: *Cronistoria dei teatro di Modena*.

or *Der Freischütz*,[1] and they were not faced with problems like the Choral Symphony or the *Symphonie Fantastique*. If they could rattle briskly through a Rossini overture, and if they discreetly handled the conventional accompanying figure in an aria, they were doing all that was required of them.

Following Rossini's lead, great use was made in the larger Italian theatres of bands on the stage. The French critic, already quoted, remarked on this: "The abuse of means employed by Rossini, and especially that of heightening the effect by *la banda sul palco* (the band on the stage), has become general (1828); you have the noise of the great drum, of cymbals, octave flutes, and, above all, of trumpets, the performers on which appear to make a merit of drowning the whole orchestra."[2]

ORCHESTRAS IN RUSSIA, SCANDINAVIA, THE NETHERLANDS, SPAIN AND PORTUGAL, AND AMERICA

There is not very much that can be told of orchestras in countries other than those already considered. In all large towns there were theatres, many of them able to produce opera, and all had orchestras. From St. Petersburg, Moscow, Warsaw and the Scandinavian capitals in the north, to Madrid, Barcelona, Cadiz, Seville, Oporto, Lisbon, Athens, Corfu, Odessa, Smyrna, Constantinople, and Algiers in the south, in Switzerland, and in Amsterdam, Rotterdam, Brussels and Antwerp, orchestras were maintained mainly by the theatres, also in some places by royal courts, but never entirely by concert-giving institutions, all of which were obliged to draw the bulk of their professional players from the theatres.

At the beginning of last century, in all these places and countries, it was Italian opera, largely sung by Italian artists, that reigned supreme on the operatic stage. Before 1830 this conventionalised form of music drama had crossed the wide ocean and had established itself in the New World, at New York in the north and at Rio de Janiero in the south. Wherever there was opera, the Rossini craze had to take its course, but some of the most popular French and German operas had begun to undermine the monopoly of the Italians before the mid-century was reached. Except that a beginning had been made in Russia by Glinka and Dargomijsky, native opera hardly existed in any of these countries; all had to be fed from Italy, France and Germany, not only with operas, but also with singers and players to perform them.

Russian native music at the beginning of last century was almost entirely confined to that of its church choirs, its folk music, and its peculiar horn bands. The operatic and concert music, and practically all who took any part in performing it, came from abroad. The nationalism in Russian music which was presently to burst into flame, was at that time only smouldering beneath the surface. An Italian named Catterino Cavos had gone to Russia with an Italian opera company just before the end of the 18th century, and

[1] Weber's opera was not played at *La Scala* until 1872.
[2] *Harm.*, March, 1829, p. 53.

T

remained to be a composer and conductor to the Italian, French and Russian theatres at St. Petersburg until his death in 1840.

In his *Autobiography* Spohr gave a few glimpses of the music in St. Petersburg as it was when he went there with his teacher Franz Eck in 1802. He told of an Imperial orchestra, of a court and an Italian theatre, of court and private concerts, and the musicians he named appear to have been of almost every nationality except Russian. Orchestras for concerts were evidently on a large scale, for Spohr told of one with 36 violins and 20 basses, of another with 70 violins and 30 basses, and both with doubled wind instruments.

According to Gassner,[1] there were German, French, Italian and Russian theatres in St. Petersburg in 1827, occupied largely by alien musical staffs. From the same source we hear that the Italian opera organisation ceased to exist in 1830, and that the orchestra was then turned over to the German theatre. We hear of Cavos and Sapienza, both designated *Kapellmeister*, making operas on Russian themes in the Italian style. The Ballet had already become an important element in Russian theatres early in the century. Boieldieu was musical director at the French theatre from 1803 till 1810, when he was followed by Steibelt, who remained until his death in 1823. Of their orchestras there is hardly any information; the *Harmonicon* informs us that in 1824 the orchestra in the Russian theatre was inferior to those in the French and German theatres, "particularly with regard to an exact attention to time, and to shades of expression in *piano* and *forte*."[2]

In 1830 most of the operas were given at the Great (Imperial) Theatre, and it was said that the orchestra was "bad and incomplete." During Lent all the theatres were closed, and concerts were given in the Philharmonic rooms, at which many distinguished artists performed, but "never a Russian name is found among them." At these concerts the orchestra was "not numerous; it performs with tolerable precision, but without expression; and it would, probably, be much embarrassed if required to execute one of Beethoven's symphonies in its true character."[3]

The year 1836 brought to light Glinka's opera *A Life for the Tsar*, and with it the initial chapter in the story of Russian national opera. A report on the theatre orchestras at St. Petersburg in 1837 states that the best was to be found at the Russian (Imperial) theatre, where Cavos was director and Böhm the leader. At the German theatre, where the *Kapellmeister* was Keller and the leader Romberg, the orchestra was equal in power but inferior in quality; most of the players were said to be "old men or raw lads." At the French theatre, under L. Maurer, the orchestra consisted of those who had retired from the other orchestras on account of age or infirmity. There were altogether from 160 to 180 players in the three orchestras.[4] Adolphe Adam wrote to *La France Musicale* about the theatre music at St. Petersburg in 1840; it was the "least flourishing" of any, and

[1] *Lex.*, Art. *Russische Musik.*   [2] *Harm.*, 1824, p. 161.
[3] *Ibid.*, July, 1830, p. 281.   [4] *Mus. World*, Vol. VII, p. 220.

he found it difficult to understand why the opera orchestra should be so feeble.

Berlioz wrote about the Italian and German theatres at St. Petersburg in 1847, and of the "large and well-trained" orchestra and choir that were got together for his concerts. Maurer and Heinrich Romberg were named as conductors at that time, and Berlioz was well satisfied with the performances of his difficult works.

The violinist Maurer came to St. Petersburg about 1820, and became leader at the French theatre in 1835.[1] A German violinist named Böhm (b. 1800), a younger brother of the Böhm at Vienna, also settled there and became a leading player and teacher.

Notable amongst the wind-players at St. Petersburg were: Joseph (b.c. 1770) and Heinrich (b.c. 1780) Gugel, Heinrich Soussmann (1796–1848) the flautist, Heinrich Luft (1813–1868) who became solo oboist in 1839, and Carl Eisner (b. 1796) the horn player. The brothers Gugel were said to be (Gassner *Lexikon*) amongst the finest of the German horn players in the early years of the century; they spent the best part of their working lives at St. Petersburg, and the younger of the pair, Heinrich, was the author of some very difficult exercises for the horn which were published at Mayence in 1826. Pearsall, who called him Guzel, related a curious story about this player. About 1823 he left St. Petersburg and went to Paris, intent on establishing himself there as a concerto-player: "As he was about to execute this project, his lips, which up to that time had been remarkably *flat* (and this he said was the great secret of his success), took another shape. They bulged, probably from age. He was much distressed as he now lost some of his highest notes. One morning he came to me, saying, that he was sure he should recover his powers, if he could get a skilled surgeon to pare his lips down flat as before. Unable to prevail on any surgeon to undertake such an operation he performed it himself with a razor! This ruined him. In 1830, I accidentally met him at Paris in a state of great destitution."[2]

At Moscow, we hear of Italian opera from 1821, performed by an Italian company. In 1824 the leaders were Morini and Spring, the leading clarinet was Fanari, and "the remainder of the orchestra is composed of Russians, and, though as a whole, it cannot be compared with those of cities where establishments of this kind have been long instituted, yet it does honour to the founders."[3] In 1828 the Italian opera at Moscow was directed by Morini, and one Scholz (d. 1831) was said to be leader of the Imperial orchestra.

Berlioz wrote about "third-rate musicians" and "fabulous choristers" when he gave a concert at Moscow in 1847. A performance of Glinka's opera was so "imperfect" that he could hardly "make out" the "highly original airs in the work."[4] Vertovsky was director at the Imperial theatre at that time, and had occupied that position since 1824.

[1] Newmarch, p. 66.
[2] *Mus. World*, July 26, 1838, p. 216.
[3] *Harm.*, Aug., 1824, p. 161.
[4] *Mem.*, II, pp. 268, 279.

At Warsaw the orchestra at the National Theatre was in the charge of Elsner (Chopin's teacher) from 1799, Carl Kurpinski (1785–1857) from 1825 to 1841, and Thomas Nidezki (1800–1852) from 1841.   Both the personnel and the operas performed were largely of either Italian, German or French origin, but already in 1821 a Conservatoire was opened which aimed at replacing the foreign musicians by those of native birth, and but for the political disturbances in 1830 which closed this institution, would probably have succeeded in its object.   The orchestra at the theatre was said to be "very good" in 1836.[1]

In the south, at Odessa, there was an Italian theatre, and we get just a glimpse at its orchestra in 1831 from the communication of a foreign correspondent: "The orchestra is composed, in great part, of Italians, Ronzoni being director, Dugnazzi and Casati first violins, Lavelli principal viola, Strinasacchi first violoncello, and Ghirardini first oboe; the first trombone is a Frenchman of considerable talent, named Demin."[2]   At that time there had been an Italian opera at Corfu for many years, in the autumn and during the carnival, and, as we are told that only "obscure singers" were engaged, it is reasonable to suppose that they were accompanied by equally obscure instrumentalists.

Of the Scandinavian orchestras only a few disconnected scraps of information can be gleaned.

Probably the best orchestra outside of the inner European ring was that at Copenhagen.   The opera in the Danish capital dated back to about the middle of the 18th century, and in the earlier part of last century was warmly supported by a music-loving King (Frederick VI) and his Queen.

Friedrich Kunzen was in charge of the court and opera orchestra at Copenhagen at the beginning of the century, assisted by Claus Schall (1757–1835) as violinist-leader; the latter had been leader since 1792, and became conductor in 1817.   Gläser from Vienna was conductor from 1842. Among the noted players were Kuhlau, who was first flute early in the century, Christian Samuel Barth (d. 1809) and his son Philipp Barth (b. 1773), both oboists at the beginning of the century, Carl Anton Philipp Braun (b. 1788), who became first oboist in 1807, Funke the 'cellist, and Wexall the violinist, both active in the 'twenties and 'thirties.   Of the horn-playing brothers Andersen, Moscheles said in 1830 that their "style is so much approved as to form the Danish school for that instrument."

Weber was at Copenhagen in 1820, and was delighted with the Danish orchestra; it was "splendid," and he heard the overture to *Così fan Tutte* played better than he had ever heard it.[3]   That was high praise from one who knew the orchestra at Berlin and Dresden so well.   It was at Copenhagen, beginning in the 'forties, that Lumbye's orchestra flourished at the Tivoli, and by its performance of dance music written and played much in

[1] *Mus. World*, June 24, 1836, p. 29.   [2] *Harm.*, Nov., 1831, p. 284.
[3] Weber, II, p. 262.

the same manner as that of Strauss in Vienna, earned for that conductor-composer the title "Northern Strauss."

In the Swedish capital the King and court supported the musical establishment. There had been opera at Stockholm since 1773, and a large new opera-house was built in 1782. The Abbé Vogler was in charge of it from 1786 to 1799, and his successor was Johann Christian Häffner, who remained until 1808. Jean Baptiste Edouard Du Puy or Dupuy (1773–1822), a violinist and singer who had been second *Concertmeister* at Stockholm at the end of the 18th century, was *Kapellmeister* from 1812 until his death, and after that the leading spirit of the Royal orchestra appears to have been the Swedish violinist Johann Friedrich Berwald, whose appointment dated from 1834.

Gassner counted the Stockholm establishment among the "better" orchestras of Europe, but stated that the personnel was largely German. Of the players who travelled abroad and gained much more than a local reputation there was Henrik Bernhard Crusell (1775–1838), a noted clarinet player,[1] the bassoon player Fran. Ch. Preumayr, who played concertos in London and Paris in 1830, Carl Widemann (b. 1790), another successful performer on the same instrument, Hirschfeld (b. 1775) the Swedish horn-player whom Spohr met at St. Petersburg in 1802, Wilhelm Braun (b. 1791), one of the well-known oboe-playing family, and Gotthilf Schunke (b. 1799) a member of the large German family of horn players.

There was apparently no opera in the Norwegian capital in 1826: "This country does not yet possess any public theatres; but in all the towns there are a few amateurs who play comedies and comic operas during the winter."[2] Gassner (1849) stated that the music in Norway was much the same as in Sweden, and that the art was cultivated only at Christiania and Bergen, the two largest seaport towns which were the most subject to foreign influence.

In the Netherlands musical activity was much overshadowed and influenced by the music and musicians of Germany and France. There were theatres giving opera at Brussels, Liége, Antwerp, Ghent and Mons, also at Amsterdam, Rotterdam and the Hague. Concert societies of mixed amateur and professional players and singers were being formed in nearly all the towns, and a strong force was the cultivation of wind-band playing that developed a competitive spirit early in the century and which found its outlet in festival meetings with prize competitions.

Opera was heard at Brussels mainly in the *Théâtre de la Monnaie*, the second of three buildings which have occupied the same site. In 1816 Bishop was in the Belgian capital, and said of the orchestra that it was "large, considering the size of the theatre, but did not produce much effect."[3] In the 'twenties an orchestra of about 40 players was said to contain "some distinguished

---

[1] A Trio for clarinet, horn, and bassoon by Crusell was played at the London Philharmonic in 1826 by Willman, Platt and Mercke.
[2] *Harm.*, Oct., 1826, p. 208.   [3] Northcott, *Life of Bishop*, p. 31.

talents far above the common rank."[1] According to Smart, the orchestra at the Brussels opera in 1825 was "no great affair" and its playing was only "tolerable."

It is probable that this orchestra was not baton-conducted during the first part of the century, but was placed in charge of a violin-playing leader who controlled the playing in the same way as was done in the opera theatres at Paris. An earlier leader named Gensse was succeeded in 1813 or 1814 by Joseph François Snel (1793–1861). From 1825 until 1831 Charles Louis Joseph Hanssens (aîné),[2] also a violin-conductor who came from the theatre at Ghent, was in charge of the orchestra, after which time Snel again held the reins until 1835. Hanssens was back again from that year until 1838, and, after two more years absence, again resumed control in 1840. Sometime before the mid-century (1848?) Hanssens was succeeded by his nephew, also called Charles Louis, who had already served in the Brussels opera as 'cellist and as sub-conductor, and had had similar experience in Paris, the Hague and at Ghent. A Dutch violinist named Lambert Joseph Meerts is said to have been leader and solo violinist from 1832 to 1835, and his successor appears to have been Jean Baptiste Singelée (b. 1812), who remained until about 1852. Charles Bosselet, a harmony professor at the Conservatoire, was said to be second chef at the opera from 1835.

The principal wind players at the Brussels opera were:

Flute. Jean François Joseph Lahou (b. 1798), from 1822 to 1837. Jules Antoine Demeur (b. 1814), from 1838, the first to adopt the Boehm flute. Egide Aerts, from 1847 to 1853.

Oboe. Louis Albert Delabarre (b. 1809), a pupil of Vogt, c. 1840 and still there in 1860.

Clarinet. Georg Christian Bachmann (b. 1804), until his death in 1842. Arnold Joseph Blaes (1814–1892), a distinguished solo player who succeeded Bachmann and was said to have "no living rival" in 1845.

Horn. Maurice Artôt (1772–1829), father of the famous violinist. Jean Désiré Artôt (1803–1887), son and successor of the above.

Trumpet. Zeiss, fairly early in the century. Hippolyte Jean Duhême (b. 1828), c. 1845, pupil and successor of Zeiss.

These were artists of some distinction, and most of them made their appearance in London as soloists at Jullien's promenade concerts from about 1849 until these concerts ceased in 1858.

It is certain that this orchestra was better than merely "tolerable," as Smart had said, in the second quarter of the century, when good artists were visiting and settling at Brussels and were also emerging from the reconstituted Conservatoire.

[1] *Harm.*, Aug., 1824, p. 152.
[2] There were three musicians of this name: (a) Joseph Hanssens, violinist and *chef* at Amsterdam who died in 1822; (b) Chas. L. J. Hanssens, violinist and *chef* at Brussels and elsewhere; and (c) his nephew Chas. L. Hanssens (b. 1802), a 'cellist who also became *chef* at Brussels and was still there in 1861.

The Brussels Conservatoire (1832) gave to the Belgian orchestras the same sort of advantages as were enjoyed by those of Paris, and Conservatoire Concerts were instituted on lines similar to those which governed the *Société des Concerts* in the French capital.   Indeed, musically, Brussels became a small-scale Paris.   The credit for these concerts and for the excellence attained by the orchestra was due to Fétis, who came to Brussels in 1833 as director of the Conservatoire and was the conductor at these concerts.   The orchestra consisted of professors, advanced students, and players from the opera.

In 1838 the *Musical World* said of these concerts: "The seventh of Beethoven's symphonies, the overture to *Fidelio*, and the finale of the first part of Haydn's *Creation* were the principal pieces of the concert; and were given with a truth and delicate discrimination of light and shade beyond all praise.   The execution of these masterpieces has discovered to the public the existence of an orchestra which rivals that of the Conservatoire at Paris. A remarkable change has taken place in public opinion during the last five years.   The sublime compositions of Beethoven were then known only by name, and listened to with coldness and *ennui*, and these very compositions are now everywhere received with bursts of admiration."[1]

The great advantage of training under one conductor, so long enjoyed by the Brussels Conservatoire orchestra, was stressed in a notice by an English correspondent who made the inevitable comparison with the playing of the London Philharmonic orchestra under its many conductors prior to 1846: "The orchestra of the Conservatoire is first-rate.   It has not the impetuosity of the London Philharmonic, but in precision, finish and equality of effect (every performer being proficient) it is far superior.   Then the conducting by Fétis by long custom has become familiar, and the good effects of the system of one conductor, which ought to be adopted in every theatre as well as in every concert-room, are too palpable to admit a doubt of its efficacy.   The fact is that no orchestra in the world can do itself justice under the direction of several conductors."[2]

Very little can be told about the orchestras at Liége, Antwerp, Ghent or Mons.   In 1824 Liége was said to possess "an orchestra known for its taste and science"[3] which migrated to Spa for the summer months.   Both of the Hanssens were conductors of the orchestra at Ghent at various times, and in 1845 Jules Bovery (1808–1868) succeeded to that position.   In 1828 Ed. Holmes found the music at Antwerp centred mainly in the Cathedral, the wind-bands, and the amateur musical society.   The brothers Jacob Bender (1798–1844) and Valentin Bender (1801–1873), who became directors of military bands at Antwerp, gained some reputation for their skill as clarinet players.   The younger Bender became bandmaster of the Belgian Guides, a band of over fifty players that Jullien brought to London to play at the Royal Surrey Gardens in 1857.   Most of the players had been trained

[1] *Mus. World*, April 12, 1838, p. 251.   [2] *Ibid.*, Dec. 19, 1846, p. 653.
[3] *Harm.*, Aug., 1824, p. 152.

at the Brussels Conservatoire, which institution served as an excellent nursery for wind players. Martin Joseph Mengal (1784–1851), elder brother of the well-known Paris horn player, conducted the theatre orchestras at Ghent, Antwerp and the Hague at various times between 1825 and 1830; in fact, he and the two Hanssens between them seem to have provided most of the conductors at the Belgian theatres from about 1820 till the mid-century.

A report on the Belgian theatre orchestras in 1849 by an English corre-spondent placed the Antwerp orchestra only second to those at Liége and Ghent, and far below that of Brussels, yet all were said to be better than the orchestras in the secondary theatres in London.[1]

The principal Belgian centres were to gain a higher status for their instrumental music in the second half of the century when branches of the Conservatoire were set up in several towns.

According to Gassner, the best orchestras in Holland were to be found at Amsterdam, Rotterdam and the Hague. Of these towns Amsterdam appears to have been the most musically inclined and the most active; it could boast of a French theatre, a German theatre, and a National (Dutch) theatre, all capable of producing opera intermittently, and it supported more than one concert society in which professional and amateur effort were combined. The French theatre, a small building able to accommodate barely 900 people, was the fashionable resort. Early in the century the orchestra was directed by one Kleine, and in the 'twenties by the Dutch violinist van Bree. The orchestra no doubt matched the size of the theatre and was probably a small affair without any distinction, but it was said to have deserved "honourable mention" in 1836 when it was under the direction of its leader Molineuf, then an old man of seventy-five. This was no doubt the orchestra in which the younger Hanssens played the 'cello at the age of ten in 1812, and of which he became second conductor in 1822 before going to occupy a similar position at Brussels in 1824.

In the same year (1836) it was said that the orchestra at the German theatre, "although weak, compensates, as far as practicable, by its skill for want of strength"; the leader at that time was one Werner.[2] It was this theatre that had been described as being in a "languishing state" in 1826 when Hieronymus Payer (1787–1845) was conductor, and greatly displeased his audience by beating time with a baton.

A concert society named the *Harmonic* was established at Amsterdam in 1822 with young Hanssens as conductor. But more important were the winter concerts of an institution named *Félix Meritis*, one of the few concert-societies in Europe that possessed a concert-room of its own, and which was directed first by Anton Fodor (1759–1849), and from 1829 by the violinist van Bree.

This society made its appeal, no doubt very wisely, not only to the musical tastes of its patrons, but also to their taste for social intercourse,

---

[1] *Mus. World*, 1849, p. 722. [2] *Ibid.*, Nov. 11, 1836, p. 136.

and seems to have combined eating and drinking, not to mention smoking, with musical enjoyment in a way which suggests that the former attractions may have been considered quite as important as the latter.

In 1835 Moscheles was playing at Amsterdam, and his wife gave the following account of the proceedings at one of the concerts of the society: "At the subscription concerts, the first part is scarcely finished when all the gentlemen vanish. Where are they? My olefactory nerves soon answer the question, as the tobacco fumes issue from the adjoining room. The ladies meanwhile drink chocolate and lemonade, and I, in my solitude, found time for studying the bareness of the four whitewashed walls of the concert room." Moscheles, here as elsewhere, complained of the bad orchestra: "The Directors take every imaginable pains. I myself seldom sit at the piano when I rehearse a concerto, but run about between the leading violin and the double drums, up and down, whispering the note into the ears of every player; after all my trouble, the music will not 'go'."[1] But if they couldn't make the music go, they probably made the refreshments go. The Dutch people seem to have enjoyed themselves at these concerts, and we hear of their pride in their local players: "The clarinet players, Mess. Kleine and Christiani, delighted the audience in Krommer's duet in E sharp (*sic*); M. Lahou also played a difficult flute concerto, and M. Mann, on the bassoon, gratified the audience by the beauty of his tone and rapidity of execution. M. Potdevin, in his concerto on the horn, was rapturously applauded, as was the young violoncello player, M. Jacobson."[2]

The Dutch flautist Jan van Boom was for a long time a prominent member of this society. It was at Amsterdam that the mad oboist Thurner took his last engagement about 1818. He died there in a mad-house in 1827.

At Rotterdam there were a French and a Dutch theatre. At the former operas were given in the winter by a company from the Hague, but at the Dutch theatre, "there is but little vocal music, and the symphonies and overtures performed between the acts are wretched attempts." This was in 1822. The concerts were more important: "The orchestra is made up both of amateurs and professors (the latter are very poorly paid); it is strong rather than finished, but upon the whole, very good." Mr. Bonn was leader of the orchestra, and "Messrs. S. Gang, E. Dattmar, Boimi and Hutschenruyer jun. have severally displayed great ability on the violoncello, flute, bassoon and French horn. The ripieno parts of the orchestra are very respectably supported."[3] The veteran horn player at the theatre in Rotterdam, Wouter Hutschenruijter, died in 1878 at the age of 82. He had directed several musical societies in and near Rotterdam, including the *Eruditio Musica* from 1826, and was in charge of the band of the *Bürgergarde* from 1821. His son Wilhelm (b. 1828) was said also to be an excellent horn player.

---

[1] Moscheles, *Life*, I, p. 332.   [2] *Quar. Mus. Mag.*, Vol. V, No. XX, p. 490.
[3] *Ibid.*, p. 492.

The leading spirit of the music at The Hague, the seat of the court, appears to have been a violinist named Johann Heinrich Lübeck (1799–1865), who had settled there in 1823, became director of the newly-founded Conservatoire in 1827, director of the court music in 1829, and conductor of a musical society called *Diligentia*.

Although Brussels was no doubt well on the way towards possessing a first-class orchestra by the mid-century, it is evident that there were none in the Netherlands which could compare with the best of those in Germany or France. The future, however, was to bring renown to a great Dutch orchestra at Amsterdam, but that was not until 1883, when the famous Concertgebouw orchestra was started.

None of the towns in Switzerland was able to support a permanent orchestra. There were theatres at Lucerne, Zurich, Basel, Berne and Freiburg, to which small opera companies came for short seasons. What they did for orchestras can only be guessed from the fact that there were not sufficient competent professional players resident in any of these places to make up an orchestra even of second-rate quality. What music there was in the Swiss found its outlet mainly in choral singing. Largely owing to the efforts of Nägeli and Pestalozzi, choral societies were established in most of the towns and districts early in the century, and some of these combined to make annual musical festivals, held at the larger centres. The instrumental parts in the oratorios they performed had to be undertaken by amateur players and a few teachers of music. Spohr gave hair-raising accounts of the orchestras of this sort that he encountered at Basel, Zurich and Freiburg in 1816; each was worse than the other, and yet the audiences seemed to be quite satisfied.[1]

Switzerland had no court establishments to support its music and provide backbone for its orchestras, and there was no ordered musical training for instrumentalists; neither French nor German musicians of any standing found it worth while settling down in the Swiss towns; and the federation of districts called Switzerland was disturbed and restless before they acquired a settled constitution in 1848. Thus, the story of Swiss music remained almost a blank until after the middle of the 19th century.

In Spain there were theatres producing opera intermittently at Madrid (*Teatro della Croce* and *Teatro Principe*), Barcelona, Cadiz, Seville, Zaragoza and Valentia, and in Portugal at Lisbon (*San Carlo*) and Oporto. The quite lavish establishments at Madrid and Barcelona were given up almost exclusively to Italian opera, played by Italian artists and directed by Italian *Maestri*. Quite an exception to the general rule was made when the native composer Ramon Carnicer was made director of the opera at Barcelona in 1820, and in 1828 succeeded Mercadante at the Madrid opera-house. In 1827 it was said that "the orchestra (at Barcelona) is one of the most complete in Spain; indeed, by many competent judges, it is considered as superior to that of Madrid."[2]

---

[1] *Autob.*, I, pp. 234–249.   [2] *Harm.*, Dec., 1828, p. 279.

At Lisbon exactly the same state of affairs prevailed, and there is no reason to believe that the opera orchestras in these two countries were any better than those of the better theatres in Italy. Little interest was taken in purely instrumental music, and what there was found its outlet in semi-private concert-societies on a small scale. A Philharmonic Society was formed at Lisbon in 1821 by J. D. Bontempo (1781–1847), and at these concerts symphonies and concertos were performed. Of the orchestra we are told that "one professor takes the principal stand in each department, and the rest are filled by amateurs, who are all subscribers."[1]

The following estimate of the quality of Spanish orchestras round about the mid-century is given in an English periodical: "Spanish orchestras are beneath the standard of excellence, being composed partly of renegade French artists expelled from that more classic proscenium, and of wretched native musicians."[2]

The first impulse to form orchestras in North America appears to have arisen from the need for instrumental accompaniments to the oratorios and similar works performed by the earlier choral societies. Some of these societies were in existence already in the 18th century, and their number and scope was considerably increased during the first quarter of last century.

An American correspondent of the *Harmonicon* wrote to that paper in 1824 and told of the establishment of two societies in New York, *The New York Choral Society* for "classical sacred music," and *The Philharmonic Society of New York* for "secular music generally." The same writer mentioned *The Handel and Haydn Society* at Boston, and at Philadelphia *The Musical Society Fund* which was said to possess "the best instrumental band in this country." The first performance of the *N.Y. Choral Society* was held in a church, and it was written of it in an American periodical that a favourite overture by Jommelli was "executed in very good style," and that Handel's aria *Comfort ye my people* was sung "with great taste and expression by Mr. J. Petrie, a professional musician and singer (*sic*) recently arrived in this city." Of a chorus from Beethoven's *Mount of Olives* the American critic wrote: "the effect was indeed grand, and was heightened by the trumpet of Mr. J. Petrie, and the excellent drums owned by *the Handel and Haydn Society*," which instruments were "politely loaned for the occasion." There was a choir of about fifty voices, and the orchestra numbered twenty-five players.[3] Of the personnel of this orchestra nothing was said, but it may be safely assumed that it was composed largely of amateur musicians. That a principal vocalist had to play the trumpet, and that the drums had to be borrowed from Boston, does not point to any great orchestral resources in New York.

The lack of competent orchestral players was evidently keenly felt in 1825 when "Mr. Price, the active and respectable manager of the theatre at New York," brought over from Europe a few Italians and the Spanish

[1] *Quar. Mus. Mag.*, Vol. V, No. XIX, p. 399.
[2] *Tallis's Dramatic Magazine*, March, 1851, p. 145.   [3] *Harm.*, Dec., 1824, pp. 222–3.

Garcia family for the purpose of producing opera.   From that time New York had its Italian opera more or less intermittently, but the difficulty of providing an orchestra was obviously acute.   In 1828 the opera company was still in New York, and we learn that "for some time the orchestra of the opera of New York was sadly deficient in the necessary instruments, and the manager was obliged to supply their absence by an additional number of trombones.   The great *Maestro* himself (Rossini), passionately

THE NEW PARK THEATRE, NEW YORK, THE FIRST
ITALIAN OPERA HOUSE, 1825

fond as he is of this instrument, would have shrunk from the overwhelming crash that deafened the ears of the astonished natives.   At present, several of the orchestras of Europe would be unable to keep the field against that of New York."[1]

In 1829 we get the following account of the orchestral situation: "There are four theatres in New York—Park, Bowry, La Fayette, and Shottam. Here are given comedies and tragedies, grand spectacles, parts of operas, and minor pieces; but no great operas, for the orchestras are extremely bad and incomplete.   There are seldom two clarinets, and generally no bassoon. Oboes, trumpets and drums are never to be met with.   Oboes are almost unknown in this country; in the whole of North America there is only one player, who lives at Baltimore.   Notwithstanding the imperfection of their orchestras, they play the sinfonias of Haydn; and although the want of instruments often brings them to a stand-still, they treat the silence as if it were a pause, and play on.   In every orchestra there is a trombone, which never plays its part, but generally that of the violoncello; and if the

---

[1] *Harm.*, Feb., 1828, p. 31.

performer is skilful enough, he sometimes plays that of the violin. Trombones and double basses are best paid; they receive sixteen or seventeen dollars a week; the others have but ten or twelve; the best clarionet has fifteen dollars. They play every day, except Sunday, commencing at half-past eight, and ending about one o'clock in the morning."[1]

A letter describing the State of Music in America, written from New York in 1829, tells how the original Italian opera company had incredible trouble in collecting a tolerable band, but that more musicians were now beginning to arrive at New York: "Among the instrumental performers I have only remarked two who have arrived at excellence on their several instruments—Norton, late second trumpet to Harper at the Ancient Concert and Italian Opera of London—and Chiossi, whose management of the alto-trombone would do him credit in Europe—the band however at the Park Theatre play well together."[2] In 1831 *The New York Musical Fund* gave a concert which opened "with *part of a* symphony by Beethoven," and closed with a glee by Webbe. On this occasion "the orchestra is said to have been weak, and, in spite of all the efforts of the leader, a Mr. Hill,[3] to have been frequently out of tune and out of time."[4]

In 1833 the orchestra at the Richmond Hill Theatre in New York comprised 26 musicians; "and we do not hesitate to state, that it is now as good a band as was ever heard in America; and, if another double bass and violoncello are added, as we hear is in contemplation, it would be a fair orchestra in any part of Europe."[5]

From the foregoing rather scattered accounts it becomes quite clear that there were few competent orchestral players in New York, and that by the 'thirties, although some better musicians were then beginning to settle in America, much still remained to be done before an orchestra could be assembled that could compare with even the second-rate European orchestras.

The most important and far-reaching step towards forming an efficient orchestra in New York was taken in 1842, when a Philharmonic Society was established on lines very similar to those of the London society and the Paris *Société*. This was an orchestral organisation of professional musicians, and was started by a combination which included the aforementioned Hill, a Bohemian named Heinrich, C. E. Horn, Vincent Wallace, Alfred Boucher, Dr. Hodges, two Germans named H. C. Timm and W. Scharfenberg, George Loder, and a French musician named Étienne. As in the London Philharmonic, the policy for many years was to employ various members of the society as conductors, and the programmes included symphonies, overtures, concertos, chamber music and vocal solos. By 1846 the society had advanced so far as to be able to perform Beethoven's Choral Symphony, and soon after the mid-century the foundations of the now famous New York Philharmonic Orchestra appear to have been securely established.

[1] *Harm.*, Aug., 1829, p. 192.   [2] *Ibid.*, Feb., 1830, p. 68.
[3] No doubt Mr. Ureli Corelli Hill.   [4] *Harm.*, Aug., 1831, p. 205.
[5] *Ibid.*, May, 1833, p. 113.

Orchestras in North America, even in their earliest days, have always been characterised by a strongly cosmopolitan make-up. That of the Grand Opera of New York in 1850 was said to be composed of 27 Bohemians, 12 Germans, 9 Frenchmen, 8 Englishmen, 7 Italians, 4 Spaniards, 2 Hungarians, one Pole, one Portuguese, and one African negro "who beats the big drum. There is not a single American in the whole number."[1]

In Central America Italian opera was given intermittently by the Garcia company in Mexico, and in South America there were theatres at Rio de Janiero, Pernambuco and Bahia. At Rio de Janiero Italian opera was heard already in the 'twenties, sung by Italians, with French dancers for the ballet, while the chorus, presumably native, was said to have made "the most odious compound of villainous noises that ever assailed the ears of man."[2] Of the orchestras at these places nothing is known, but there is no reason to suppose that any important contribution to the history has been lost owing to this lack of information. What these theatres could offer was probably not sufficiently enticing to induce good instrumentalists to wander so far afield in order to find employment, and it is likely that only the dregs of the European orchestral musicians, or those that were obliged to leave their country for some discreditable reason, found their way into the theatre orchestras of South America. At that time there was no proper training for musicians in any part of the American continent, and the local product could be only either self-taught or inadequately trained.

[1] *Tallis's Dram. Mag.*, Jan., 1851, p. 95.   [2] *Harm.*, Dec., 1829, p. 313.

VII

Conducting

In the year 1800 it would have been difficult, or even impossible, to find any orchestra in which the playing was controlled by a musician who did nothing but beat the time and indicate by gestures how the music should be interpreted. By 1850 it would have been equally difficult to find any but small orchestras in which the playing was controlled by any other means than by a time-beating conductor. The rise and development of orchestral baton-conducting falls almost entirely within the first half of last century, but in order to appreciate how and why the new method of control evolved, it will be necessary to examine the position as it was during the previous century, and to follow the course of the development which led to the situation that prevailed at the beginning of last century.

Before the 19th century the musical conductor was the man who was employed to compose the music for a chapel, church, theatre or other musical establishment, and was also charged with the responsibility of seeing that it was properly performed. He was the master of the establishment, and was accordingly called the *kapellmeister, maestro di capella, maître de musique*, or other such term. He acquired his title of "chapel-master" because the earliest musical establishments were chapels or churches. This is how Marpurg explained its origin: "The chapel-master got his title from the church music; he was put in charge of the singers, because already in the temples of old, and later in the churches of the Christians, music was sung to the glory of God; and, after the time of Constantine the Great, when for their own convenience in worshipping God, the great lords built churches within their castles, which to this day are called chapels, and in which the service is opened and closed with both vocal and instrumental music, the man who was made responsible for the music was called a chapel-master."[1]

The chapel-master retained his title even when his charge was no longer only a chapel, but also when it was a theatre, concert-society, orchestra, band, choir, or indeed almost any sort of musical establishment in which corporate vocal or instrumental music was cultivated.

The inseparability of composer and chapel-master or musical director goes back to the origin of the term. Throughout the 18th century the main qualification for the position was ability to compose music for the establishment. The musician in charge could not then stock his repertoire by sending an order to a music-seller; the music had to be made there, on

[1] Marpurg, *Beyträge* (1756), II, p. 124.

the spot, and by himself, and that was what he was paid to do.   Hundreds of musicians in the 18th century who occupied the positions of *Kapellmeister* or *Cantor* were composers first and musical directors second.   This situation, even though it began to be modified towards the end of the 18th century, still prevailed very largely during the first half of last century.   In Germany the *Kapellmeister* and composer were almost invariably combined in one person, and he held his position mainly by virtue of his standing as a composer.   The following was written of Germany as late as 1838: "There, no one hears of a *Kapellmeister* who has not been previously reckoned a *Ton-meister*, a writer of symphonies, operas, Motets, and Masses."[1]   It was not so much his merits as a conductor, but the fact that he was the composer of the opera *Rienzi* that gained for Wagner his appointment as *Kapellmeister* at Dresden; Liszt had neither reputation nor the necessary experience as an opera conductor when he was made *Kapellmeister* of the opera-house at Weimar; Schumann (notoriously inefficient as a conductor) certainly did not owe his appointment at Düsseldorf to his reputation as a conductor, and it can hardly have been a mere coincidence when Chelard was made *Kapellmeister* at Munich immediately after he had produced his opera *Macbeth* in that city.   All these, and hundreds of others, ascended the conductor's rostrum with the passport of a composer or a player on some instrument.

But by the middle of last century, although composer and conductor were still far from being completely divorced, some progress had been made towards separating and isolating the two functions.   Whereas in 1800 all conductors were composers, by 1850 not every composer was a conductor.   During the 18th century it had been held that whoever composed the music was the one best fitted to superintend the performance of it; for "conducting" a musical piece at that time implied nothing more than superintending the performance.   But during the first half of last century the conductor was being asked to do more than look after the performance of his own music; he was being asked to take charge of the music of other composers as well, and by the mid-century he was beginning to be valued as a conductor according to his ability to do so.   Yet the composer and conductor, and often the player too, were still very often combined in the same person.   It was still largely held that a musician who neither composed nor played nor sang could not possibly be competent to direct the playing or singing of others.

When orchestral baton-conducting was developing during the first half of last century, it was found that gifts for composing and conducting were sometimes combined in the same person, as they were in Spontini, Spohr, Weber and Mendelssohn.   The last three also included in their equipment a high standard of virtuosity on their own particular instrument; Liszt was a rather later example of this union of player, composer and conductor.   Others, it was found, did the composing better than the

[1] *Mus. World*, Jan. 19, 1838, p. 34.

conducting, as in the cases of Beethoven and Schumann; on the other hand, although both were excellent conductors according to the standard of their time, Berlioz and Wagner were amongst those who composed even better than they conducted; but their standard as composers was very high, and they would have required supreme gifts as conductors to have equalled their composing.   Others again were better conductors than they were composers; such were Habeneck and Costa, although it would probably have been difficult to convince them that such was the case.[1]   Yet the two functions would not part company completely until the second half of the century, when the specialist-conductor, who had no ambitions as either composer or player, began to develop.   But even then all conductors began their careers as composers or players.   It was left to the present century to produce those who started from scratch as conductors and nothing else.

Nearly all the conductors in the first half of last century were also instrumentalists, although not necessarily of virtuoso standard.   Most were either pianists or violinists, a few were organists, 'cellists or performers on other orchestral instruments, and there were one or two who were singers, such as, for example, Balfe and Lortzing.   The great and solitary exception was Berlioz, whose only instruments were the flageolet, flute and guitar, and who, according to his own showing, was not very good on any of these.[2] But Berlioz stood alone in so many ways; it is useless to attempt to classify him.

The qualities required for a baton-conductor were not always to be found in the composer or player, however skilled he might be, and if a lack of these essential qualities was not so damaging to success as long as 18th century methods of control were in force, the advent of the time-beating and interpretative methods in the following century tended more and more to separate the requirements of the conductor's function from those of the composer and player, and to begin the creation of another type of musician whose essential gifts were not only musical, but who required also such qualities as leadership, assertiveness, authority, organising ability and personality, in addition to his artistic gift.   So, provided other non-musical qualities were present, it became quite possible for a musician to be a good conductor even though he did not possess any particularly strong musical gift.[3]   The writer of a letter to the *Musical World* in 1839 appears to have discovered the fact that musical knowledge alone would not make a good conductor: "I need not remark to you, that we have many sound musicians who are most incompetent conductors, and we have ordinary musicians (as theorists) who possess considerable skill in keeping a band together."

[1] Rossini said in 1856: "Ce bon Costa m'a envoyé une partition d'oratorio et un fromage de Stilton.   Le fromage était très bon." (Davison, p. 109.)

[2] *Mem.*, II, p. 271.   Berlioz had some difficulty in convincing the grand marshal at the Russian court that he could possibly give a concert without playing or singing himself: "a composer . . . a man who could not play anything . . . a mere incapable!" (p. 272).

[3] There are many excellent conductors to-day who are endowed with no more inborn musical gift than is possessed by most of the players in their orchestras.

V

In the 18th century the composer and musical director in charge of a performance in which an orchestra took part generally sat at a keyboard-instrument, it might be a harpsichord or an organ, or later, a piano, and with either the score or a bass part in front of him, played the harmonies of the *basso continuo*, and generally watched over the whole performance, more especially the vocal parts, when there were any. The leader of the violins collaborated by leading, guiding and superintending the performance of the instrumentalists. It was a form of divided control which apparently satisfied the requirements of the time, but which would now be difficult to reconstruct.

There is plenty of evidence to show that in the early 19th century this two-fold authority was being found unsatisfactory and unworkable. Edward Holmes described a German baton-conductor in 1828 who, "placed on an elevation in the front of the orchestra, gives the cue to all, very properly setting aside the offices of leader, chorus director, etc., which in England frequently causes the band and singers to be wandering in opposite directions."[1] Even though there was no choir, the orchestra might be divided in trying to follow two leaders: "Mr. Loder led the *Andante* of Haydn, No. 1, too fast; indeed, both he and Mr. Moscheles, the conductor, appeared to be at times at variance."[2] Nevertheless, in spite of the obvious unsoundness of the method, that was the way in which opera performances, and, indeed, almost all sorts of musical performances were directed in Italy, in Germany, and in this country during the 18th and the early years of the 19th century.

Purely instrumental music, such as symphonies, concertos and overtures, were generally controlled in the same way, except that the actual leadership was then more in the hands of the violinist-leader, even though it remained nominally with the director at the keyboard. In some places, where an orchestra was kept to play only instrumental music, a violinist-leader was often placed in supreme control, and a keyboard player occupied a sub-ordinate position as accompanist.

In Germany the director at the keyboard was called the *Kapellmeister*, in Italy he was the *Maestro di Capella* or *Maestro al Cembalo*, and in England he was called the Conductor. The violinist-leader was the *Concertmeister* or *Aufführer* in Germany, the *Capo d'orchestra* or *Direttore d'orchestra* in Italy, and the Leader in this country. The nearest corresponding titles in France were, respectively, *Maître de Musique* and *Chef d'orchestre*.

The keyboard-director began to lose his power over the orchestral playing when composers began to incorporate the harmony of the music in the written orchestral parts, and no longer relied on the playing of the *basso continuo* to give the music the necessary harmonic backing. This was roughly during the last thirty years of the 18th century. By the beginning of the 19th century, although it had been turned out of a few orchestras, the keyboard-instrument was generally retained, even if only for the purpose

---

[1] *Rambles*, p. 38.   [2] *Mus. World*, April 15, 1836, p. 77.

of accompanying the recitatives in Italian opera when no other than a bass part was written. In many theatre orchestras a piano was still kept throughout the first half of last century, or even later, and sometimes the baton-conductor continued to sit in front of it, using it mainly as a music-desk for the full score to rest on. The status of the piano in the orchestra was thus described by H. Sutherland Edwards, writing in 1869: "The piano, employed in France until the time of Gluck, in Italy until that of Rossini, for accompanying recitative, is now banished generally from the orchestra, though it occasionally figures as a sort of non-combatant at the conductor's desk, where it may serve at need to bring back an erring vocalist to the sense of musical propriety."[1]

Near the end of the 18th century the actual control of the orchestra varied somewhat in different localities and according to different views. Some insisted that the keyboard-director, having the score in front of him, was alone in a position to direct the performance, while others held that as he could exercise so little control over the playing, it was better to leave it entirely in the hands of the violinist-leader, even though he had no score in front of him. As far as the orchestra was concerned, the control at that time was actually passing into the hands of the violinist-leader, and his power over it increased as the influence of the keyboard-director declined. Yet the latter died hard, and was still to be found during the first thirty or forty years of last century nominally at the head of the orchestra, especially in Italy and in this country.

In some places it was the keyboard-director who eventually became the baton-conductor; in others he just disappeared, and it was the violinist-leader who acquired the baton.

In France the situation was rather different; not only in the method employed, but also because music in France was so completely centralised in Paris, and largely in that very powerful institution, the *Opéra*.

The keyboard-director had never flourished in France so much as in other countries, neither in opera nor in concert-music. As long as it was essential in the orchestra, the keyboard-instrument was used in French orchestras, but the player on it did not occupy the influential position in the orchestra that he did in Germany or in Italy; his position in France was rather that of an accompanist subordinate to the actual controller. In Paris it was the violinist-leader who exercised full control over the playing of the orchestra, but when a chorus or ballet were concerned, a time-beater (*batteur de mesure*) was employed to beat time audibly with a stick or baton. How they actually managed at the *Opéra* near the end of the 18th century is rather obscured by a lack of unequivocal contemporary information, but it is quite certain that during the early part of the 19th century it was the violinist-leader who gained control over the performance, and it was he who developed into the baton-conductor in France.

But the time-beater was not a French invention. In some form or other,

[1] *Life of Rossini*, p. 158.

time-beating is as old as music itself. From the later Middle Ages at least, and certainly in the 18th century, it was not an uncommon practice to employ someone to beat the time for choral music in churches, especially when the choir was large or widely spread out. The choral time-beater, as distinguished from the orchestral conductor, survived well into the 19th century. At the Leipzig *Gewandhaus* and in Vienna, a time-beater, who had up till then been inoperative, came into action when the last movement of Beethoven's Choral Symphony was performed, and in this country the same sort of guidance was often given to large choral bodies: "I remember that in the time of Dr. Boyce it was customary to mark the measure to the orchestra[1] with a roll of parchment, or paper, in hand, and this usage is yet continued at St. Paul's Cathedral, at the musical performances for the Sons of the Clergy."[2]

But it was not the skilled professional instrumentalist who was given such guidance; choral singers and choir boys might have to be kept in step by a visible or an audible beat, but the experienced orchestral player was quite well able to play in time without having the beat hammered out for him.[3]

Although orchestras in the 18th century were controlled by a playing pianist or violinist, it should not be supposed that a visible or audible time-beat did not to some extent enter into their methods of control. The chords and accents of the keyboard-conductor, the movements of his arms and head, the movements of the violinist's bow-arm, of his head and body, and also of his feet, all supplied a time-beat that could be either seen or heard. The keyboard-conductor had beside him the leading 'cello and bass player, one on each side, playing from his own copy; from their accents and physical movements the beat was conveyed to others in the orchestra. Even in the first half of last century the playing of the leading bass player was counted an important element in keeping the *ensemble* intact, and Dragonetti was sometimes credited with the power of leading or misleading an orchestra: "Although he has been accused of leading the orchestra, or, in the estimation of some leaders, of mis-leading (for no man in that situation approves of public correction), yet it must be acknowledged that he has upon various occasions, by his promptitude and decision, brought back a whole band who 'like sheep had gone astray'."[4] Finally, the music of the 18th century itself supplied a steady beat which helped to keep the players together. Musicianly players could get the beat from the music, even if it was not made visible by any sort of physical movement.

There is evidence that, towards the end of the 18th century, the keyboard-conductor and the violinist-leader sometimes ceased to play on their instruments, and made use of a visible time-beat in order to steady playing

---

[1] At that time "orchestra" in England meant the whole performing body, including soloists and choir, and not only the instrumentalists, who were generally called "the band."
[2] From a lecture by Sam. Wesley, in 1827.
[3] Anon., *Wahrheiten die Musik betreffend* (1779) p. 48. See also Rellstab, *Über die Bemerkungen* (1789), p. 38.
[4] *Mus. World*, May 12, 1837, p. 131.

which was getting out of hand. Hanslick[1] quotes an extract from the *Jahrbuch der Tonkunst für 1796* which shows how the former might use his hands: "The *Concertmeister* is in the position, as it were, of the front-rank man (*Flügelmann*) to whom the whole orchestra looks for guidance. But the *Kapellmeister* at the piano must sometimes stop playing in order to cut the air with both hands. It would surely be much better if the *Kapellmeister* left the conducting entirely to the *Concertmeister*, and occupied himself only with supervising the performance as a whole, and with seeing that the singers made their entries correctly. It would be a good thing if they studied the piece together and came to some agreement about the *tempo*. How easily things go wrong when two persons direct the performance, one at the piano and the other with the violin. Some of the musicians look to the *Kapellmeister* for guidance, and others follow the *Concertmeister*. Suppose (as is quite possible) that each adopts a different *tempo*, and think what the result will be." The expression "cut the air with both hands" (*mit beiden händen die Luft zu durchsäbeln*) clearly indicates a time-beat. The above also shows that the disadvantages of dual control were beginning to be felt.

Then, at a later period, we see the violinist-leader also beginning to adopt a time-beat when the ensemble is getting shaky. Spohr wrote of the orchestra at the *Théâtre Italien* in Paris in 1820: "they wavered several times so much that the conductor (Grasset) was obliged to beat the time for them."[2]

The need for a time-beating interpretative conductor began when orchestras grew larger and could not be so compactly grouped; when the players had to be spread out over wider spaces and could not all see or hear one another or their leader; when the sound had to travel further, and when it grew in volume; when the steady pulse of the music was not so constant and unbroken; when the time and *tempo* changed more frequently, and pauses, *rallentandos* and *accelerandos* broke up the uniformity and regularity of the beat; when the structure and texture of the music became less transparent, and the rhythm was more irregular; when the orchestration and lay-out became more complex and the entries of the instruments were not so obvious; when the dynamics changed more often, and the light and shade required more sensitive adjustment; when the execution of the parts became more exacting and more precision was demanded; when, in consequence of all these things, a good ensemble was more difficult to attain.

The methods of control which sufficed to hold together a small orchestra playing a symphony by Haydn or Mozart would not keep together an orchestra two or three times as large in a symphony by Berlioz or Schumann. The thin light score of an 18th century Italian opera might almost be left to be played without any controlling force, but the heavier stuff of Meyerbeer or Wagner must have a firmer guiding hand. All this had begun to emerge even before the close of the 18th century, and it became ever more pressing

[1] *Concertwesen*, p. 94.   [2] *Autob.*, II, p. 118.

during the early years of the following century.   Old methods were inadequate, so something more efficacious must grow out of them.

Very little was written about orchestral baton-conducting in the first half of last century.   The story of how it began and how it developed can be pieced together only from scattered scraps of information found in contemporary books, in the musical dictionaries, histories, text-books, biographies, memoirs, letters, commentaries and articles in periodicals written by those who lived during the period, or by those who followed so soon after that they were able to retrieve the facts from those who saw them happen.   Contemporary pictures sometimes throw more light on the subject than a score of books, but from the full scores and the programmes we can learn nothing; the latter, indeed, owing to the various meanings attached to the word "conductor," are sometimes more misleading than helpful.   There are, therefore, obscurities and gaps in the sequence of events which only leave us deploring the fact that while there were so many who could have told us all about it, there were so few who troubled to do so.

The greatest difficulty in reconstructing the story arises from the way in which the word *Conductor* (or any of its foreign equivalents) was used by contemporary writers.   When we now use the word *Conductor* in a musical sense, the picture of a musician facing his orchestra or choir with a score in front of him and a baton in his hand quite naturally presents itself. But that picture would be entirely wrong if we apply it to any period before the 19th century, and it may be quite incorrect and misleading if applied to the first thirty years or so of last century; it may even be uncertain or equivocal during the 'thirties, but it will probably be quite correct if applied to the 'forties or any later period.

The "conductor," during the period of uncertainty, may mean so many different things.   It may mean the man who arranged a concert even though he took no part in the performance of the music; it may mean the man who directed a performance from a piano or an organ; it may mean the man who led the playing with his violin or bow; and it may mean a man who beat the time with a baton or with any other implement.   "Conductor" may also mean the accompanist on the piano at a performance in which there was no orchestra or choir.   When we read about anyone "conducting" an orchestra between about 1800 and 1830, we must be prepared to understand that his method of direction or his function may have been any of these, and unless it is specifically described it may be unsafe to come to any conclusion as to the method he employed.

When we read of Beethoven conducting his symphonies in Vienna, we must not place a baton in his hand, for there is no evidence that he ever handled such a thing.   By *"Kapellmeister"* we must be prepared to understand "the composer who is appointed to write the music ordered by a court, to select and procure the rest of the music, and to take charge of the performance of all the music" (1802).[1]   In the English "conductor" we

[1] Koch, *Lex.*, Art. *Kapellmeister*.

may have to recognise "the person who arranges, orders, and directs the necessary preparations for a concert,"[1] (1813). But we must not take for granted that either of these used a baton, or that he beat the time, or even controlled the performance. The London musical periodicals up to nearly as late as 1840 constantly tell us of conductors "presiding at the pianoforte," or "at the organ," or sitting "at the piano as conductor." We can read that Mr. Bochsa placed "himself at the pianoforte as the conductor of the performances" (1829), or that "Messrs. F. Cramer and Spagnoletti led each an act, and Sir George Smart sat at the pianoforte," (1829). At a Classical Chamber Concert in 1836, where there was neither orchestra nor choir, Mr. Potter was the "conductor."[2] The same paper informed its readers that the "Quartet concerts . . . will be resumed this winter under the same able conductors."[3] Each of the chamber concerts given by the Vienna *Gesellschaft der Musikfreunde* in 1825 had its *Dirigent*. But we must not suppose that these quartet parties played to a time-beating conductor.

Always bearing in mind that a conductor at the beginning of the 19th century was almost certainly carrying out his function according to 18th century methods, an approach to the development of baton-conducting can best be made by following the course of events as far as is possible in each country separately.

GERMANY

It may be that it would be possible to trace the beginning of orchestral baton-conducting in Germany as far back as 1776, when Reichardt was appointed *Kapellmeister* at the court opera in Berlin. Reichardt at once rearranged the orchestra, abolished the piano, and directed the performance from a separate desk placed almost in the centre of the orchestra close to the footlights.[4] Exactly how he conducted remains uncertain, but we know that Reichardt was a composer and violinist, and that he did not use the piano in the orchestra.

Traces of time-beating conductors in north German theatres begin to appear soon after Reichardt's time. A certain Guillaume Alexis Paris (b. 1756) is said to have directed performances of French opera at Hamburg with a foot-long baton as early as 1794,[5] and from the Leipzig *Allgemeine Musikalische Zeitung* we learn that Righini at the Berlin opera was beating time audibly with a thick roll of paper in 1800. From the same source we learn that Bernard Anselm Weber, who came to Berlin as *Kapellmeister* of the *Nationaltheater*, and eventually became chief conductor of both the German and the Italian opera in the large court *Opernhaus*, used to beat time with a roll of strong leather stuffed with calf's hair, and that he pounded the score so vigorously that the hairs flew around. Gassner[6] described his conducting as being often too noisy (*ein oft zu geräuschvolles Taktiren*), but

[1] Busby, *Dict.*, Art. *Conductor*.   [2] *Mus. World*, April 22, 1836, p. 94.
[3] *Ibid.*, Nov. 25, 1836, p. 174.   [4] Anon. (1788), *Bemerkungen* p. 57.
[5] Schreiber p. 252.   [6] *Lex.*, art. B. A. Weber.

allowed that Weber distinguished himself by the way he handled the orchestra. These things, happening round about the turn of the century, even if they point to only a rather rudimentary form of baton-conducting, at any rate show which way the wind was blowing, and suggest that the old method of control was being found defective, and that some better means of control was becoming necessary.

Anselm Weber remained at Berlin until about 1818, and by that time the idea of directing musical performances by means of a time-beat had clearly gained some ground in Germany. Already in 1807[1] the theorist Gottfried Weber discussed the question as follows: "I know of nothing more futile than a dispute about which instrument is best suited for the direction of a big musical work. Surely, none other than the baton (*Taktirstab*). There must be one whose will is supreme, . . . and who will be blindly followed. When all follow one leader, the whole chorus and orchestra will keep together just as easily as do the two hands or the ten fingers of a pianist. Whoever likes to hear an audible time-beat, whoever can endure foot-stamping, or tapping on the desk with a violin bow, let him entrust the direction to a violinist-leader. But who would gladly see this disorder abolished, let him place one man at the head of everything, one who is not concerned with any particular part, one who can give his undivided attention to the whole, one who only beats time, not by hammering on the music desk, but only by means of visible signs." It mattered not whether the conductor was pianist or violinist, but Gott. Weber thought it best that he should have a violin handy in order to help out the singers; but his main concern must be for the whole performing body, and not only for any particular part.

Even if Gott. Weber was only theorising, his remarks show clearly enough the general trend of events. He describes the function of the baton-conductor quite clearly; his remarks indicate a retreat in the status of the keyboard-director, a protest against the usual methods of the violinist-leader, and they also reveal that noisy time-beating was not uncommon. But he could not have written thus without some practical background to his ideas. Time-beating was clearly in the air, and was beginning to take a more important part in the German methods of orchestral control.

In 1805 Spohr succeeded the violinist Ernst as musical director of the court orchestra at Gotha. This was an old-fashioned court, and there was no opera. The concerts were directed by Spohr, then already a distinguished violinist, and his method was no doubt that of the violinist-leader of old who played with his orchestra and beat time with his bow only when it was necessary to pull things together. In 1810 a musical festival was organised at Frankenhausen, the first of a series of German festivals, and Spohr was appointed director. Gerber tells how Spohr conducted with a roll of paper, and without the least noise.[2] An oratorio and several instrumental works, including a symphony and an overture, were performed. As

---

[1] *Allg. Mus. Ztg.*, 1807, p. 805.   [2] Spohr, *Autob.*, I, p. 142.

regards the choruses in the oratorio, the direction with a time-beat would not necessarily be an innovation, but for the symphony and the overture it broke new ground. Later in the same notice, Gerber again describes how Spohr "raised his roll of paper" to conduct.

In 1815–17 Spohr was *Kapellmeister* at the Frankfort opera, and his own words tell how he changed the method of direction in that place: "My predecessor had led with the violin, and by the wish of the singers I began also in the same manner, indicating the time with the bow, and keeping the violin ready at hand, in order to assist with that when necessary. But I soon accustomed them to so precise a practice of their parts that such assistance as that was soon no longer necessary. I now laid the violin aside and directed in the French style, with the baton."[1] In 1820 Spohr conducted the London Philharmonic orchestra with a "directing baton."[2] When he finally settled down at Cassel in 1822, Spohr was an experienced baton-conductor.

After some experience at Breslau from 1804 to 1806, Carl Maria von Weber became *Kapellmeister* at Prague in 1813. In the meantime he had produced his *Silvana* at Berlin in 1812, and his conducting there was described as being "firm and noiseless."[3] In 1817 he was appointed to the much more important post at Dresden. Previous conductors there had always sat at the piano, directing the opera according to the old method of the Italian *Maestro al cembalo*, but Weber at once began to conduct with a baton, a proceeding which in the orchestra caused some opposition, which, however, was soon overcome. Weber himself had written in 1818, that now the time was past when a director could sit at the piano politely turning over the pages of the score for the leading bass player who sat at his side, and could leave most of the work to the leading violinist. That might still be done in Italy, he said, but not in Germany or France.[4] In 1826 Weber conducted in London with a roll of paper in his hand. An English periodical thus described his conducting at an Oratorio Concert at Covent Garden Theatre: "He took his place on the stage, facing the audience, with a *baton* in his hand, with which he gave the time to the orchestra. In this office he seemed in no way embarrassed, and showed much energy and decision; qualities which, we learn from good authority, were exhibited at the rehearsal in a still stronger manner."[5]

Spontini took up his appointment at Berlin in 1820, and made an impressive first appearance there as conductor of his opera *Fernand Cortez*. The *Vossische Zeitung* told how "with fire and genuine inspiration, and without any noise, the composer directed an excellent performance of his most exacting work."[6] Spontini used neither piano nor violin, but held in his right hand a long and thick baton which he held in the middle "and

---

[1] Spohr, II, p. 54.   [2] *Ibid.*, II, p. 81.   [3] Weber, I, p. 354.   [4] *Ibid.*, III, p. 174.

[5] *Harm.*, April, 1826, p. 85. According to a contemporary notice in the *Morning Post*, Weber directed the first performance of *Oberon* "at the pianoforte."

[6] Robert, p. 28.

manipulated it in a way to show one plainly that he looked on the baton as a marshal's staff and used it, not for beating time with, but commanding."[1]

And it was not only in large and important places that the baton was gaining ground; there are signs that time-beating had been adopted in some small centres during the early years of the century. Carl Loewe told how Daniel Türk used to beat time at the concerts in Halle as early as 1810, and how he used his baton with such energy that he sometimes struck the chandelier above his head and brought down on himself a shower of broken glass.[2]

It will be observed that these contemporary comments on the conducting of Spohr, Weber and Spontini all draw attention to the fact that it was noiseless.

By the 'twenties the visible time-beat had clearly gained ground as a means of controlling orchestral playing in Germany, and as the musicians of a later generation grew up they naturally took to the new method. Sir George Smart travelled through Germany in 1825, and in his *Journals* described the methods of conducting the orchestras at some of the most important of the places he visited. At Stuttgart the conductor stood in the centre facing the stage, beating time with his violin bow and occasionally playing the violin; at Munich, Stuntz beat time seated at a small piano which he touched once or twice; at Dresden, Weber sat at a square piano and beat time with a roll of paper; at Hanover, Sutor also beat time seated at a square piano; at Cassel, Spohr beat time with a stick, and did not use his violin; at Cologne, Weber's step-brother, Edmund von Weber, used a violin bow to beat the time, and played his violin only once.[3]   A few years later Edward Holmes found Guhr at Frankfort taking "his stand with the score before him and his baton of office."[4]

According to Devrient,[5] the boy Mendelssohn conducted the family orchestra in his father's house at Berlin with a baton (1821–24),[6] and also when later on he revived Bach's *Matthew Passion* at the *Singacademie* in 1829. On his first visit to London in that same year Mendelssohn, in his own words, "mounted the orchestra and pulled out my white stick"[7] to conduct the Philharmonic orchestra in the Argyll Rooms. Of this occasion it was written in the *Morning Post*[8]: "Mr. Mendelssohn conducted his Sinfonia with a baton, as is customary in Germany, France, etc., where the *discipline* of bands is considered of more importance than in England." Again in 1832 Mendelssohn conducted with a baton at the London Philharmonic concerts. Further experience at Düsseldorf (1833) fitted him for the more influential post at the *Gewandhaus* in Leipzig in 1835.

At Leipzig they were slow to adopt the visible time-beat in the orchestra. At the *Gewandhaus* all the instrumental works had hitherto been played under

[1] Wagner, *Prose Works*, III, p. 130.   [2] Loewe, p. 29.
[3] Smart, *Journals*, pp. 80, 90, 140, 205, 212, 216, 221.   [4] *Rambles*, p. 38.
[5] Devrient, pp. 6–7.   [6] According to Dorn (*Recollections*) Mendelssohn sat at the piano.
[7] Hensel, I, p. 184.   [8] May 27, 1829; probably written by John Ella.

the guidance of the violinist-leader Matthäi, who from his place at the first desk of the violins controlled the performance by playing with the orchestra, or by beating the time with his bow only if he found it necessary to pull the ensemble together.[1] Wagner described the procedure as follows: "In the days of my youth, orchestral pieces at the celebrated Leipzig *Gewandhaus* concerts were not conducted at all; they were simply played through under the leadership of *Concertmeister* Matthäi, like overtures and entr'actes at a theatre. At least there was no 'disturbing individuality' in the shape of a conductor! The principal classical pieces which presented no particular technical difficulties were regularly given each winter; the execution was smooth and precise; and the members of the orchestra evidently enjoyed the annual recurrence of their familiar favourites."[2]

Mendelssohn's advent in 1835 put an end to the old method of violin-direction at Leipzig; he controlled the performances entirely by means of a time-beat given with a baton. The innovation at the first concert he conducted was thus commented on by the *Allgemeine Musikalische Zeitung*[3]: "In the second part we had Beethoven's fourth symphony, and seldom have we heard it so excellently played. As a new and desirable plan, the musical director conducted the symphony; for when the leader, who must play first fiddle, does this, he greatly interferes with his own performance in looking after the time of the others." Thereafter the baton always ruled at the *Gewandhaus* performances, except for a period in 1841–42, when Mendelssohn was called to Berlin, and the Leipzig orchestra was left in charge of its leader, Ferdinand David.

In a letter to Mendelssohn, David described the difficulty of combining the functions of conductor and leader: "But it is embarrassing to have to conduct and lead at the same time. The more modern pieces, and quite new works, demand conducting throughout, and by one who is himself not required to play. At the most critical moments I find that I must always beat the time, and these are just the moments when it is most important that I should be playing. Nevertheless, I am quite glad to have the opportunity of gaining experience in this capacity, and when you come back again I shall be all the better violinist for it."[4] Actually, what David did was just to return to the old method of direction which had prevailed before Mendelssohn came to the *Gewandhaus*, when Matthäi used to play and occasionally beat time with his bow; but it is noteworthy that David should have remarked that a time-beat was all the more essential when the more modern pieces were being performed.

At that time the technique of orchestral conducting was still in an undeveloped state, and there is no reason to suppose that it went very much farther beyond its original purpose than that of giving a visible time-beat which was intended mainly to keep the *ensemble* intact. There are signs that it was still regarded as a means of pulling things together when the *ensemble*

[1] Dörffel, p. 83.   [2] *On Conducting*, p. 14.   [3] Oct. 14, 1835.
[4] Eckardt, p. 149.

was in danger. When satisfied that all was going well, conductors some-times let the orchestra play on without a time-beat, as Weber did at Dresden: "Weber had trained it so well that he would sometimes beat the first four bars in the *allegro* of the *Freischütz* overture, and then allow the orchestra to go on alone up to the pauses near the end. Musicians may well be proud when they see their chief fold his arms on such occasions."[1] Schumann also told how Mendelssohn often did the same thing at the *Gewandhaus*: "But often enough, in the course of the performance, he would lay down his baton on the desk and leave it there for some time, while the orchestra played on without any further guidance."[2]

Devrient also stressed the use of the time-beat only to remedy unsteadi-ness: "The continued beating throughout a movement, that must neces-sarily become mechanical, vexed me, and does so still. Compositions are really whipped through sometimes by this process. It always appeared to me that the conductor ought to beat time only when the difficulty of certain passages, or unsteadiness of the performers, rendered it necessary. Surely the aim of every conductor should be to influence without obtruding himself."[3] This suggests that the original purpose of a time-beat still underlay the new conception of orchestral conducting, and that the interpretative side of it was as yet comparatively undeveloped. Wagner's remark about the "disturbing individuality in the shape of the conductor" was not written until 1869, by which time the rendering or "reading" of musical works according to the temperament or individuality of the conductor had become part and parcel of his outfit.

By early in the 'forties, baton-conductors ruled in all the larger and more important orchestras in Germany. After his tour in 1843, Berlioz reviewed the German conductors in these words: "First, the composer himself, who almost always conducts his own rehearsals and performances, without in the least wounding the conductor's self-love; next, the *Kapellmeister*, usually an able composer, who conducts the principal operas and all important musical works of which the authors (composers) are either absent or dead; and the leader, who directs the small operas and ballets, and also acts as first violin when not conducting, in which case he conveys the *Kapellmeister's* remarks and directions to the further end of the orchestra, superintends the material details of the studies, sees that nothing is wanting either in the way of music or instruments, and sometimes points out the bowing or phrasing of a passage—a task forbidden to the *Kapellmeister*, who always conducts with a baton."[4]

The German conductors at that time were mostly contemporaries of Weber or of Mendelssohn, although most of them outlived these two more famous musicians. Such were Aiblinger of Munich, Guhr (1787–1848) of

---

[1] Berlioz, *Mem.*, II, p. 71.   [2] Dörffel, p. 85.

[3] *Recoll.*, p. 60. The last sentence might well be taken to heart by many conductors of to-day.

[4] *Mem.*, II, p. 3.

Frankfort, Lindpaintner of Stuttgart, Marschner of Hanover, Reissiger of Dresden, the three Lachners, Hiller and Rietz. These were just the type that Wagner could not get on with. Being a fluent and voluminous writer, he missed no opportunity of having a dig at them, and he didn't trouble to cover up his remarks with any veneer of politeness: "The general public is so ready to take the excellence of their doings for granted, and to accept it as a matter of course, that the middle-class musical people are not troubled with the slightest doubt as to who is to beat time at their musical festivals, or on any other great occasion when the nation desires to hear some music. No one but Herr Hiller, Herr Rietz, or Herr Lachner, is thought fit for this. It would be simply impossible to celebrate the hundredth anniversary of Beethoven's birth if these three gentlemen should happen suddenly to sprain their wrists. On the other hand, I am sorry to say, I know of no one to whom I would confidently entrust a single *tempo* in one of my operas; certainly to no member of the staff of our army of time-beaters."[1]

It is not difficult to fill in the names thatWagner did not mention when he wrote this: "German *Kapellmeisters* are unfortunately chosen from a class of musicians who have gained a specific musical training entirely aloof from the theatre, people who can read their scores, play the piano a little and give the orchestra its beat, and are therefore competent to render excellent service in ecclesiastical institutes, singing-academies, musical unions and such like,—but havn't the remotest idea of music's application to a dramatic representation."[2] That the function of the composer and the conductor were still far from being differentiated in Germany by the mid-century underlies the following remark by Wagner: "Nowadays every *Kapellmeister* or Music-director, instead of being simply chosen for his ability to conduct correct performances of true musical art-works, must at least be also held by a few intimate acquaintances for a considerable composer."[3] Wagner himself, of course, joined the ranks of the German court opera-conductors in 1843, and was as much a composer-conductor as any of the others, but with the difference that his ability in both capacities was almost immeasurably far above theirs.

Lobe named Mendelssohn as the conductor who brought orchestral playing to its highest degree of perfection. He coupled Mendelssohn's name with that of Habeneck, and then asked: "but how many Habenecks or Mendelssohns have we?" The conductor must study the work that he is to conduct so long and so thoroughly, said Lobe, that he completely absorbs its spirit and makes it as much his own as if he were the composer. Many conductors could not do that; others who could, would not or did not do it—because it entailed too much trouble.[4]

It need hardly be said that the advent of the baton in Germany, as elsewhere, did not at once meet with universal approval. Many who had long

[1] *On Conducting*, p. 102.   [2] *Prose Works*, III, p. 373.
[3] *Ibid.*, IV, p. 263. See also *On Conducting*, pp. 1 to 12.
[4] *Cons. und Diss.*, pp. 281-2.

been accustomed to the older methods found it disturbing and tyrannous; it made the performance stiff; it hampered the freedom and flexibility of the playing. Objections to the rule of the baton were raised even after that method of control had become firmly established and any return to the old method was hardly likely to be entertained.   In 1836 it was propounded in the *Neue Zeitschrift für Musik*[1] that the less an orchestra was conducted, the better would it play.   One of those who voiced his objection to the tyranny of the baton was Moritz Hauptmann, who played for so long in Spohr's orchestra at Cassel: "The cursed little white stick always did annoy me, and when I see it domineering over the whole orchestra, music departs from me; it is as if the whole opera exists merely for the sake of beating time to it . . . and when I think of *Matrimonio Segreto*, with the *Maestro* sitting quietly at the *cembalo* accompanying the *Recitativo secco*, when everything goes of its own accord, I am in quite another world, far away from this barbarous present time stripped of all sweetness and dignity—I can't tell you how disagreeable and disappointing this German art is to me."[2] Hauptmann was no lover of the time-beat; he refused the conductorship of an important choral society[3] because he could neither sing nor play the piano, and would therefore be obliged to beat time.   In all societies, said Hauptmann, where everything went smoothly, there was no time-beating; Schelbe, Zelter, Dreyssig and Schneider didn't beat time; here in Cassel they did beat time, and everything went badly.[4] From Carl Loewe's description, however, it would appear that Zelter's method at the Berlin *Sing-Academie* in 1832 was to mark the time with one finger; he quoted Zelter as saying: "They are only charlatans who fight and use their arms like the sails of a windmill; I lead my Academie with my right forefinger."[5]

That the time-beat and baton were not immediately welcomed as an improvement on the older method of control is also indicated in the following account of Hieronymus Payer (1787–1845) directing an opera in the German theatre at Amsterdam in 1826: "His mode of leading the orchestra is also novel, but certainly not commendable.   He takes his seat by the side of a piano, of which he makes but little use, and has revived the Gothic practice of beating the time with a baton.   Nothing could be more unseemly, or better calculated to destroy the quiet and pleasurable feelings of an audience.   We have been accustomed to see the leader in an elevated position, from whence he could command the whole orchestra at a glance, and in directing music, there is no assistance so certain as that of the violin."[6] So much, in fact, did the Amsterdam opera-public object to Payer's innovation that they very soon got rid of this offending stick-wagger.

Somewhat similar was the comment of a correspondent who described the conducting at the musical festival at Lausanne in 1824: "His (Taillez of

[1] No. 13, p. 130.   [2] *Briefe*, I, p. 196.
[3] The *Cäcilien-Verein* at Frankfort in 1839 (Speyer, p. 210).   [4] *Briefe*, I, p. 255.
[5] Loewe, p. 124.   [6] *Harm.*, Feb., 1826, p. 40.

Strassburg) manner of beating time is too violent and *outré*, and his furious
stamping and vigorous exercise of his musical baton might well have been
dispensed with."[1]

No doubt there was plenty of poor and ineffective conducting at a time
when it was still taken for granted that whoever had composed an opera
was the one best fitted to direct its performance. The *Neue Zeitschrift für
Musik*[2] painted the picture of a composer-conductor at one of the smaller
German theatres trying to conduct a performance of his opera: he takes his
stand at the conductor's desk "and beats time with aching arms, and quite

NEITHARDT CONDUCTING THE ROYAL BERLIN CHOIR, 1850

unnecessarily too, for the opera would go on like clockwork quite as well
under the guidance of the prompter without any time-beating. The fine
Herr Kapellmeister is nothing but an ornament, and we have sometimes
observed that when the orchestra is getting into difficulties he quietly lays
down his baton, blows his nose, and then waits until the *Concertmeister* has
rescued it from its perilous situation by the vigorous use of his violin.
Then, as if nothing had happened, he gracefully resumes his time-beating."

Schumann did not take kindly to the baton when Mendelssohn began to
direct the *Gewandhaus* orchestra by means of a time-beat in 1835: "For my
part, I disliked the conductor's stick in the overture as in the symphony.
I sounded Florestan, who remarked that the orchestra should stand like a
republic in a symphony, refusing to acknowledge a superior."[3]

No doubt the old 18th century method served well enough for such as
Cimarosa's slight opera performed with a small orchestra in intimate surroundings, and no doubt a conductor at the piano did well enough for small
German choral societies directed by respectable old organists, and also for
the complacent orchestra and audience at the *Gewandhaus* before Mendelssohn
came to Leipzig; but these methods would not do for the grandiose operas
of Meyerbeer and Wagner, or for Berlioz's or Schumann's works, nor for

[1] *Harm.*, Feb., 1824, p. 31.   [2] 1841, No. 38, p. 153.   [3] Schumann, I, p. 37.

large-scale performances of Mendelssohn's or Spohr's oratorios. The baton had come to German orchestras and choirs, and it had come to stay. By the mid-century the orchestras and choirs in Germany were all baton-controlled.

VIENNA

The *Kapellmeister* at the piano and the *Concertmeister*[1] with his violin between them controlled the performance of opera in Vienna at the beginning of the 19th century, just as they did in Germany and in Italy. At the piano Mozart had directed the performance of his *Zauberflöte* at Schickaneder's old theatre in 1791, and in the same way Beethoven directed his *Fidelio* at the *Theater-an-der-Wien* in 1805. Thayer quoted a passage from the *Edinburgh Review* (1805) written by one who was present at the first performance: "Beethoven sat at the piano and conducted the performance."[2]

The older *Kapellmeister* at the Vienna theatres almost certainly used the same old-established method, although the necessity for actually playing on the piano had largely disappeared. Gyrowetz (b. 1763), Weigl (b. 1766), and Seyfried (b. 1776) were composer-conductors of the old school and brought up to 18th century methods; although they lived long enough to see the baton come into use, they were probably then too old to want to change their methods. Gyrowetz was a *Kapellmeister* at the *Kärnthnerthor* theatre from 1804 until 1831, and in the whole of his autobiography there is not to be found the slightest hint that he ever beat time or used a baton; his work at the opera was to compose and to superintend rehearsals and performances. In 1831 Seyfried wrote in the Mayence *Cäcilia* opposing the use of a baton, from which we may safely conclude that he did not use it himself.[3] Umlauf was a violinist-composer who certainly made some use of a time-beat, but there is no evidence to show that he ever used a baton. Conradin Kreutzer and Gläser most probably used a baton, and the two Lachners and Nicolai certainly did.

Symphonies, overtures, and concertos were often controlled in Vienna entirely by the violinist-leader of the orchestra. Schuppanzigh and Clement were *Concertmeister* who were in complete charge of their orchestras when not playing in opera under the *Kapellmeister* at the piano. The former, described by Seyfried as a "natural-born and really energetic leader of the orchestra,"[4] took full charge of the orchestra at his concerts in the *Augarten* for many years previous to his departure for Russia in 1816. These were essentially orchestral concerts, and this form of direction, that is, playing with the orchestra and occasionally beating the time with the bow when some steadying was required, was one which remained a characteristic of the dance orchestras of Vienna (Lanner and the Strauss families) long after baton-conducting had become the established method of controlling orchestral performances.

---

[1] Sometimes called *Orchesterdirektor* in Vienna.   [2] Thayer, II, p. 52, f.n.
[3] Schunemann, p. 260.   [4] Thayer, I, p. 238.

Although Beethoven had played the viola as a young man in the Elector's orchestra at Bonn, he was probably not violinist enough to direct an orchestra with a violin in the manner of Schuppanzigh and Clement. So, for performances of his orchestral works he sat at the piano with the score in front of him, and generally supervised the performance without actually exercising much control over the orchestra. Ries[1] related that at a concert in the *Augarten* (1804) where he (Ries) played the C minor concerto, "Beethoven himself conducted, but he only turned the pages, and never, perhaps, was a concerto more beautifully accompanied." This "conducting" was obviously only a sort of general supervision; the actual control of the orchestra would then be in the hands of the violinist-leader, and that is how we must understand the accounts of Beethoven "conducting" his works in Vienna during the early years of the century.

In the small orchestra at the City seminary (Stadtkonvict), Schubert led the playing with a violin,[2] in the manner of Schuppanzigh and Clement.

As in other places, the violinist-leaders in Vienna made some use of their feet to mark the time when less forcible means failed to keep the playing together. Reichardt, who was in Vienna in 1808–9, said that he rarely heard a *forte* or a *fortissimo* without a good deal of foot-stamping by the leader.

It is noteworthy that nearly all the *Kapellmeister* in Vienna were pianist-composers. None of the violinist-leaders (Clement, Schuppanzigh, Spohr, Mayseder, Hellmesberger) became full conductors in Vienna.

Performances of oratorios or other large choral and orchestral works were often given in Vienna, and when on a fairly large scale, a time-beater for the choruses came into operation in addition to the usual piano and violin leaders. Such was the case at the oratorio performances given by the *Tonkünstler Societät*, where Umlauf was director at the piano, Hofmann led with the violin, and Salieri gave the beat for the choruses with his hand or with a roll of paper.[3] For the performance of Spohr's *Last Judgement* in 1812 Umlauf was at the piano, Spohr led the orchestra with his violin, and Salieri was in charge of the whole. For the first performance of the Choral Symphony in 1824, Schuppanzigh and Kletrinski were leaders of the orchestra, Conradin Kreutzer was at the piano, Umlauf was director of the whole, and it was announced that "Beethoven will himself participate in the general direction." According to Thalberg, "Umlauf told the choir and orchestra to pay no attention whatever to Beethoven's beating of the time, but all to watch him."[4] By that time Beethoven had become very deaf, and his contribution to the direction of the performance apparently did more harm than good.

At the opening of the *Josephstädter* theatre in 1822, when Beethoven's *Weihe des Hauses* overture was played, "Beethoven had reserved the direction for himself and sat at the pianoforte, the greater part of the orchestra within

Biog. Notizen, p. 113.   [2] Hanslick, p. 142.   [3] *Idem*, p. 93.
[4] Thayer, III, pp. 164–166.

W

view, his left ear towards the stage . . .Chapelmaster Gläser stood at his right, and Schindler, who had recently abandoned the law, led the first violins . . . The rehearsal and performance demonstrated plainly, Schindler says, that under no circumstances was Beethoven able longer to conduct large bodies of performers."[1]

The above extracts serve to illustrate how divided was the responsibility, and also how long the piano retained its place in the Vienna performances. It is difficult to understand, for example, why it was necessary to have a piano for the performance of the Choral Symphony.

Although it is evident that there was some time-beating in Vienna during the first two decades of last century, it is difficult to find any evidence that a baton was used. Hanslick relates that Sonnleithner and other old musicians in Vienna had told him that quite a sensation was caused when Mosel beat time with a baton (stäbchen) at a performance of Handel's Timotheus in 1812. But this was, without doubt, only for the choruses, and for such a purpose the visible time-beat was no innovation, either at Vienna or elsewhere.

Nevertheless, a visible time-beat was obviously becoming the main controlling force in the Viennese orchestras during the course of the 'twenties. Smart described the conductor, Wenzel Müller, at the Leopold-städter theatre in 1825 as sitting at a "queer-toned long pianoforte" and beating time with a roll of paper. At the Josephstädter theatre also, "the conductor beat time at a desk in the centre even with the violins,"[2] and Holmes told how in 1828 a conductor was employed to beat the time at both of these theatres.

It is impossible to say exactly when the baton came into general use for directing the orchestras in the central theatres at Vienna; if it was in Beethoven's time, it was certainly not till towards the end of his life. Hanslick was unable to fix the year in which the baton was adopted at the Kärntnerthor theatre, but it seems most probable that it was in the early 'twenties. When in 1821 the orchestra at that theatre was rearranged[3] there was no longer a piano in it; but it is not safe to assume that the disappearance of the piano necessarily coincided with the advent of the baton. It may be that the baton came into the opera with Conradin Kreutzer in 1822, and it is certain that Franz Lachner would conduct with a baton when he became first Kapellmeister in 1828. By the time Nicolai came in 1841, baton-conducting would be well established in Vienna. The control would then rest entirely in the hands of the conductor, while the responsibility of the Concertmeister would be similar to that of the principal first violin in the orchestras of to-day. When the piano was abolished in the Kärntnerthor theatre in 1821, the recitatives were accompanied by the leading 'cello and bass players, as Holmes described in 1828.

It seems likely that a baton or a visible time-beat of some sort also began to be employed at the Theater-an-der-Wien fairly early in the 'twenties; a

[1] Thayer, III, pp. 80–81.   [2] Smart, Journals, pp. 99, 100.   [3] Stöber's plan, 1821.

Viennese musical paper remarked on the *"feurigen Tactiren des Kapellmeister Roser"* at that theatre in 1823.[1]

FRANCE

The development of baton-conducting in France proceeded along different lines. In that country, or more correctly, in Paris, the baton, at first used in the crudest manner, gave way to the control of the violin-conductor, who turned his bow into a baton, using it without the noise and rigidity which had formerly always been associated with the time-beat given with a baton.

The word *bâton* is French, and a *Batteur de mesure* functioned as part of the regular performing apparatus at the Paris *Opéra* in the 18th century.[2] We know that even after the middle of the 18th century the choruses and dances were given an audible beat.

The testimony of Grétry points distinctly to the use of a time-beat in the *Opéra* when he wrote, i.e. towards the close of the century; but this does not necessarily imply a continuous beating of the time all through the performance. In his *Essais* (1789) Grétry writes of "the slightest movement of his stick or foot," and suggests that a *bâton de mesure* should be used only for large choruses and dances, but that in the arias the orchestra should follow the singer without the intermediation of a time-beater.[3] He paints a picture of a scene which is supposed to take place during a rehearsal at the *Opéra*:[4]

Actress on the stage. What's all this about, Sir? there seems to be a revolution in your orchestra!

Time-beater in the orchestra. A revolution, Mademoiselle? We are all here to serve the King, and we do so zealously.

Actress. I wish to serve him myself, but your orchestra puts me out and prevents me from singing.

Time-beater. But, Mademoiselle, we are playing in strict time.

Actress. In strict time! What nonsense is that? Please to follow me, Sir, and understand that your orchestra is the very humble servant of the singer who is reciting.

Time-beater. When you are reciting, Mademoiselle, I follow you, but you are singing an air with a rhythm, a well-marked rhythm.

Actress. Rubbish! stop this nonsense, and follow me.

The above clearly implies that the aria was sung to an orchestral accompaniment controlled by a time-beat.

In the same work Grétry again remarked on the situation in such a way as to lead one to suppose that it was not only the choruses and dances that were performed to a given time-beat, but that the arias were conducted in the same way: "Except in the case of large choruses, for which I think it

---

[1] *Allgem. Musikal. Zeitung, Wien*, 1823, p. 472.
[2] Rousseau, *Dict.*, Art. *Bâton de mesure* and *Battre la mesure*.
[3] *Essais*, I, pp. 53–56.   [4] *Ibid.*, I, p. 225.

necessary in the theatre, it (the baton) is a hindrance to good execution, and for this reason: every musician is obliged to keep his eye on the artist who is singing; it is the only way to accompany properly. When each bar is beaten for him, he is freed from this duty; for he cannot and should not follow two persons at the same time. Furthermore, every soloist, vocal or instrumental, takes liberties with the time for the sake of expression; woe to him who is never alive to this fault. It is therefore clear that the accompanying players become cold and indifferent, when they do not follow the actor directly. The stick that directs them humiliates them, and takes away from them the wish to excel that is natural to every man who, being able to follow his chief guide, finds himself constrained to obey the direction of a third person."[1]

To the above the editor of a later edition of the *Essais*, published in 1829, appended the following foot-note: "This well-known truth explains the superiority of orchestras conducted with a violin by a capable man; every musician is in touch with the singer. A time-beater is only too often a charlatan who fatigues himself and tires the spectator's eye, and like the fly on the wheel, thinks that everything has been done by himself. The *Académie Royale* of Paris (the *Opéra*) has given up its old prejudices, and M. Habeneck has proved that his talent can overcome the difficulties presented by an innovation that seemed impossible. The execution at the *Opéra* is perfect, conferring honour on the orchestra, and bringing joy to the singers."

In 1826 Castil-Blaze wrote on the same subject as follows:

"Rousseau, in his writings on ancient French music, has specially aimed his shafts of satire at the method of performance adopted at the *Académie Royale*. He calls the director of the orchestra a woodcutter, on account of the repeated blows he gave on the desk with a large and heavy cudgel of wood.[2] In spite of the reforms which our dramatic music has undergone, this stick still exists, but of smaller size; and the holder contents himself with flourishing it in space, to mark the first beats of the bars. As soon as the rhythm is well felt and the impulse is well established, he leaves the singers and orchestra to themselves until his help is again required to hasten or slow down the movement of the music.

"The sound of the stick hitting the desk rhythmically destroyed the illusion and annoyed the attentive music-lover. This fault in the execution was inseparable from French music in the time of Rousseau. The orchestra would drag along on the heels of the singers without keeping time, and when a number occurred which had to be played in strict time, both players and singers were so surprised to find that they had to keep in time that the director could keep them together only by marking each beat for them.

"Although the *Académie Royale* still obeys the conductor's baton as formerly, Rousseau's sarcasms are no longer applicable to it than those which he uttered against French music would be to the works of Gluck and

---

[1] *Essais*, I, p. 54.
[2] See also Grimm's *Le Petit Prophète* (1753), Chap. IV, p. 9, *Le Bucheron*.

Méhul. It is not the baton, but the manner in which it is used that merits consideration. When large numbers have to be started, when a chorus of singers has to begin behind the scenes, or a crowd of dancers is waiting in the wings for the moment when they bound on to the stage, it (the baton) must necessarily be heard. That signal, which the actors skilfully perceive, is hardly noticed by the listeners, whose attention is diverted by the scene on the stage. The orchestra generally produces a greater volume of sound and masks the disagreeable noise of the baton, and when the conductor restricts himself to simple gesticulation, it is not noticed except by those whose duty it is to see it. Is not the musician who, in the Italian manner, conducts his orchestra with the violin, also obliged from time to time to rap with his bow on his desk in order to rouse the attention of the players at the commencement of the aria or chorus which follows a *recitative* or spoken dialogue? The orchestra of the *Opéra Comique*, and those of most provincial theatres are conducted with the violin bow."[1]

From these remarks we can gather that, near the end of the 18th and in the early years of the 19th century, a time-beat was given at the *Opéra* for the choruses, dances and large *ensembles*; also, that it was sometimes made audible, but was not a continuous hammering with a heavy stick as in the days of Lulli, and at the time when Rousseau described it. We can also discern that this beat was a mere clock-like pulse intended only to keep the *ensemble* together, and that it was not concerned with the interpretation or the artistic side of the rendering; that side of the performance was the province of the violinist-leader. What we do not get from either Grétry or Castil-Blaze is a straightforward answer to the question: did they or did they not beat time with a baton throughout the whole opera, and not only when it was necessary for the handling of large bodies on the stage?

But what does seem to emerge from the uncertainty is this: that the time-beat in Paris, whether audible or not, was always directed at the stage, and not at the orchestra. It was given for the benefit of singers and dancers; the orchestra, large though it was, looked to their leader, who, violin in hand, played with them, indicating by his movements, attitudes and signs, the manner of performance, the nuances, and all that goes to make orchestral playing more than a mere correct performance of the written notes. The violinist-leader was the interpreter and the musician; the time-beater was little more than a human metronome. When necessary, the violinist-leader gave some beats with his bow, to steady the *ensemble*, to regulate *rallentandos* or *accelerandos*, or to determine the duration of pauses. For such purposes he used his bow as a baton.

Although neither Grétry nor Castil-Blaze leave us quite satisfied as to the method of direction employed at the *Opéra* towards the end of the 18th century, there seems to be no doubt that a continuous time-beat was used in the first few years of the 19th century. The clue is supplied by a passage in Smart's *Journals*. In the year 1802, at the age of 22, Smart was taken

[1] *L'Opéra en France*, I, p. 444.

to Paris by his father; his description of a performance at the *Opéra* includes the following: "The orchestra consists of ninety performers, a *maître d'orchestre*, with a small roll of wood, conducts. He stands with the score before him and answers the purpose of the prompter at our opera house, they have no other prompter."[1] The significant part of this extract lies in those words: "answers the purpose of the prompter at our opera house." This conductor was *not* the conductor of the orchestra; he was there for the guidance of the people on the stage, to give them their cues, to give them signs for their entries, to keep the singers, chorus and dancers together, and to give the time of the music for their benefit. He was, in short, nothing more or less than a survival of the old *Batteur de Mesure*, who had functioned throughout the whole of the 18th century, and was not yet extinct. But his days were numbered; he was soon to disappear altogether and give way to the violinist-leader who had always been in charge of the orchestral performance, and who then acquired the controlling power over the whole musical performing apparatus, the singers, chorus, dancers, and instrumentalists.

There is no reason to suppose that a *Batteur de mesure* functioned at any of the Paris opera theatres other than the grand *Opéra*. There is no sign of him at the *Opéra Comique* or the *Théâtre Italien*; there the violinist-leader controlled the whole of the musical performance. Smart described the direction at the *Théâtre Italien* in 1825 much as Spohr had done in 1820: "At the pianoforte, placed as at our opera-house, was Mr. Hérold. The leader was Mr. Cassé,[2] who occasionally directed with his bow when necessary; he sat in the same situation as the leader at our opera-house."[3]

Although it is certain that the violin was used by the Paris conductors in the 'twenties, a feud between upholders of the violin and the baton was evidently not quite settled by 1825, as the following suggests: "The ancient quarrel between the bâton and the violin is not yet settled at the royal academy of music (the *Opéra*). After certain observations, launched forth in some of the journals, like pilot-balloons to discover which way the wind blows, it appears that, in the orchestra, the violin is to be reinvested with the government. It seems however to us, that the leader of a numerous musical army will encounter great difficulties, if at the same time he must attend to the singers, to his own particular troops, to the score, and at the same time draw those pure sounds from an instrument which ought alone to claim all his attention. But MM. Habeneck and Valentino, whose talents are so well known, are the most proper persons to decide to which the sceptre belongs. We only wish to observe, that a general should direct his army, and rarely fight himself."[4]

---

[1] Smart, *Journals*, p. 27.

[2] This leader cannot be traced. It is highly probable that Smart had mistaken the name; it was no doubt M. Grasset, who was leader at the *Théâtre Italien* throughout the 'twenties.

[3] *Journals*, p. 227.   [4] Paris correspondent of the *Harmonicon*, June, 1825, p. 103.

In the first half of last century almost all of the regular conductors in Paris were violinists: Persius, Kreutzer, Valentino, Battu, Habeneck and Girard at the *Opéra*; Grasset and Tilmant at the *Théâtre Italien*; Lahoussaye, Blasius, Kreubé and Crémont at the *Opéra Comique*; Manera, Musard, Jullien, Seghers and Rivière were also violinists, while Hainl and Offenbach (*Comédie Française*, 1850) were 'cellists, and Labarre was a harpist. Berlioz was no violinist, and it would not be natural to him to handle the bow. Neither the flute nor the guitar were convenient things for a conductor to use, so he used a baton. But Berlioz held no regular position as a conductor; he took to conducting only in order to be able to direct performances of his own works, which the other Paris conductors neither understood nor appreciated.

Berlioz was not quite alone in upholding the use of a baton rather than a bow. Kastner, who was evidently no violinist, voted in favour of a rigid baton: "Most conductors today (1839) use a violin bow; nevertheless, it would be more rational to employ an inflexible rod, which would mark the beats of the bar with greater precision."[1] Again, Kastner held no position as a regular conductor in Paris. Notwithstanding the advice of these two non-violinists, the violin bow was used in all the Paris theatres as well as in the provincial theatres.

So the violin bow became the baton of the French conductors. And for some considerable time after the mid-century it was still used in preference to a baton, even though the violin was not used. As late as 1878, Deldevez, who became first *Chef* at the *Opéra* in 1873 and conductor of the Conservatoire concerts in 1872, preferred the bow to the baton: "*le violon est l'instrument naturel du chef d'orchestre*"; the conductor who was a violinist moved his arms in quite a different way to the non-violinist.[2] Deldevez combatted at some length[3] Berlioz's argument in favour of the baton.

The process by which a violinist-leader of the old school developed into a conductor who used a violin bow instead of a baton is not difficult to reconstruct. At first he normally played with the orchestra, and fell back on time-beating only when it was necessary; as he developed, he used his violin less and less, and beat the time with his bow more and more, until finally it was all time-beating and no violin-playing. When Habeneck first directed the *Exercices* of the orchestral class at the Conservatoire in 1804, he would do more playing than time-beating; but by the time he reached the end of his career in 1848 it is improbable that he used the violin at all during a performance. The caricature of Habeneck by Danton shows him as an oldish man conducting with a bow, but, although the violin is not visible, it is probable that he either held it in his left hand or kept it handy. A French correspondent (V. de P.) described Habeneck's method at the Conservatoire in 1840 as follows: "There is no conductor, or, rather, it may be said that the leader is the conductor, only with a fiddlestick instead of a baton; for he makes no use of his violin, which he holds downward all the time. It is the same at the Opera, and the advantage seems to be, that he has the means of taking up a point in case of need, which the conductor with a baton is wholly unable to do."[1]

DANTON'S CARICATURE OF HABENECK

A French conductor always kept his violin handy even though he didn't play upon it. It was indispensable at rehearsal. Instead of showing his orchestra what he wanted by singing a passage, as a conductor now often does, the violinist-conductor played it to them. He would demonstrate the phrasing, the accents and inflections, the nuances, the manner or style, on his violin just as naturally as another conductor might with his voice.

[1] *Mus. World*, March 26, 1840, p. 195.

PLATE 19

CHARLES HANSSENS, BRUSSELS OPERA, 1840

He liked to have his violin within reach; it was his natural mode of expression. A contemporary picture of Ch. Hanssens, conductor at the Brussels opera in 1840, shows him standing ready to conduct with a bow in his hand; his left hand is free to turn the pages of the music in front of him, and his violin lies ready to hand on a special shelf just below the desk.

The violinist-conductor in France generally had in front of him a first violin part in the case of an instrumental work, and a specially condensed version on two or three staves of an opera score. At the *Opéra* he sat in the centre of the orchestra just behind the prompter's box, the cover of which provided a convenient object for him to tap with the point of his bow.[1] Castil-Blaze remarked on the bad effect of the gas from the footlights on the health of the conductors at the *Opéra*.[2] Lahoussaye at the *Opéra Comique* and Grasset at the *Théâtre Italien* stood at the extreme end of the orchestra pit, having the stage to their left.[3] The position of the conductor in a theatre orchestra evidently remained unsettled for some time: "One of the questions debated during the year 1862 was that of deciding whether the correct place for the conductor should not be on the extreme right of the footlights, with his back to the proscenium. Time will decide it, unless custom, so powerful in France, treats the public interminably to the sight of that convulsive stick and arm, which singularly detract from the illusion of the scene."[4]

The great advantage accrueing to the violinist-conductor was his close knowledge of the orchestra. He was at home there, and had worked his way up to the top of it. He knew the business of orchestral playing from start to finish, and when he got to the top of the tree he had much less to learn than the pianist-conductor, who often started at the top.

In France, in the first half of last century, a pianist or organist was put in charge of a choir. The *Batteur de mesure* of the old French opera did not become a *chef d'orchestre*; he remained a chorus-master, an accompanist, or a vocal coach, and beat time for a chorus or dancers who were out of sight of the *chef d'orchestre* or out of hearing of the orchestra. Or he simply disappeared, leaving a mechanical contrivance to convey the beat of the conductor to the chorus at the back of the stage or behind the scenes.

The natural and logical process by which violinists became the conductors of French orchestras was certainly fully justified in Paris. By common consent the best orchestral playing was to be heard there, and even Germans had to admit that it was in Paris that they heard the best performances of Beethoven's symphonies.[5] On the very rare occasions when they did put a non-violinist in charge of a Paris orchestra, the result was most unsatisfactory. Labarre, the harpist, was not a success at the *Opéra Comique*, and when, later in the century, a composer-organist named Louis Dietsch was

---

[1] See Berlioz's amusing story, "A victim of the tack," *Evenings*, p. 123.

[2] The *Opéra* in the *rue le Peletier* was the first theatre in Paris to be lighted by gas (Matthews, p. 27).

[3] Castil-Blaze, *L'Acad. Imp.*, II, p. 361.   [4] Lasalle et Thoinan, p. 352.

[5] Schindler, Lobe, Wagner.

made conductor at the *Opéra* (1860–63), the result was an unmitigated failure.[1]

ITALY

The *Maestro* at the piano and the leading violinist of the orchestra divided between them the control of opera performances in Italy at the beginning of last century, just as they did in Germany, with the same division of responsibility which placed the singers under the guidance of the *Maestro al Cembalo* and the instrumentalists in charge of the violinist-leader.   The title given to the latter, *capo d'orchestra* or *primo violino, capo e direttore d'orchestra*, indicate clearly enough which was his province, although it can hardly be questioned that whoever guided the playing of the orchestra enjoyed the lion's share of control over the whole performance.

The state of affairs that prevailed in Italy during the course of the half-century is indicated by stray remarks dropped by visiting musicians.

Spohr gave his impression of the method of direction at *La Scala*, Milan, in 1816, as follows: "Signor Rolla . . . directed as first violin.   There is no other directing, whether at the piano, or from the desk with a baton, than this, but merely a prompter with the score before him, who gives the text to the singers, and if necessary, the time to the choruses."[2]   This remark of Spohr's should not be understood to mean that the keyboard-conductor was not present and had ceased to function, but rather that, although still there, his power to influence the performance was negligible or non-existent.   The list of the musical staff at *La Scala* throughout the half-century was always headed by a *Maestro al Cembalo*.

An English visitor to *La Scala* reported that late in the 'thirties the orchestra was "led by Cavallini," and commented—"for they have no conductors in Italy"[3]; by which he meant, of course, that the conductors there did not direct with a baton.   In 1840 it was said that the *Maestro al Cembalo* still sat at the piano and turned over the pages of the score for the leading 'cello and bass players, who sat on either side of him and played from his copy.[4]   As far as the orchestra was concerned, it is evident that the violinist-leader held the reins and practically controlled the performance in spite of the presence of a nominal conductor at the piano.

Soon after the mid-century the violinist-leader seemed to be losing his power to control the performance.   By 1859 the *Maestro al Cembalo* at *La Scala* had become the *Maestro concertatore*, and by 1869 he appears to have gained complete control over the whole, and rejoiced in the title of *Maestro concertatore e direttore delle opera*, while the former *capo d'orchestra* had subsided into the position of a mere *primo violino*.[5]

---

[1] Dietsch conducted the unfortunate production of *Tannhäuser* at the Paris *Opéra* in 1861; Wagner wrote of him: "that pitiful creature Dietsch, the most asinine, thickest-skinned, most unmusical of all the Kapellmeisters I ever came across in Germany" (Newman, III, p. 106).

[2] Spohr, I, p. 258.   [3] *Mus. World*, April 18, 1846, p. 179.
[4] *Allg. Mus. Zeit.*, No. 43, p. 102.   [5] Cambiasi, p. 393.

The method of direction at the *San Carlo* at Naples in 1829 was briefly described by Moritz Hauptmann: "The arrangement of the orchestra and the direction of it were not good; there is no full score, the leading violinist conducts from a part written on two staves."[1] A year or two later Berlioz was at the *San Carlo*, and his equally brief comment on the method of direction was: "I must protest against the disagreeable noise which the conductor makes by striking his desk with his bow."[2] Both Hauptmann and Berlioz ignored the *Maestro* at the piano, who was nevertheless certainly present and functioning in the old 18th century manner, although practically powerless to influence the playing of the orchestra. Again we see that the leader was beginning to use his bow as a baton, much in the same way as was done in France. Thus, it would seem that in the 'thirties and 'forties the violinist-leader in Italy was well on the way to becoming the sole controller of the performance, and that the keyboard-conductor was almost useless and had lost power.

These rather meagre scraps of information tend to show that in Italy the development of the baton-conductor was proceeding more slowly than in Germany, France, or even in England. It was still the violinist who controlled the playing of the orchestra; he sometimes used his bow to beat time with, but he clung to his instrument and was still a player in the orchestra; and he did not hestitate to make his beat heard as well as seen. Otto Nicolai said that in the 'thirties the leader in Italy had practically replaced the keyboard-director, and that his way of stamping his foot in order enforce the beat often made more noise than the playing of the orchestra.[3]

The future of the leader was, either to abandon his violin and become a baton-conductor, or to slip back into his position as a violin player and resign the control to one who held the baton.

As it eventually turned out, in the end it was not the violinist who generally became the conductor of opera in Italy. The position of the pianist-composer appears to have been the stronger when it came to the point of combining the control of both vocal and instrumental forces in one person. In a country where the vocal element in music was so predominant as it was in Italy, the orchestrally-trained musician could perhaps hardly have hoped to gain the foremost place in an organisation so essentially vocal as was Italian opera; thus, the Italian conductors after the mid-century were more often than not the composers of operas rather than the leaders of orchestras. Nevertheless, in time to come Italy was to find some of its greatest conductors in the ranks of the orchestra.[4]

ENGLAND

Those who have the patience to search the English musical books and periodicals written during the first thirty or forty years of last century will constantly come across statements such as the following:

[1] *Briefe*, I, p. 67.   [2] *Mem.*, I, p 235.   [3] Kruse, p. 51.   [4] Mancinelli, Toscanini.

1813. "The performances were conducted, for the first time at the organ, by Sir George Smart." (Parke.)

1823: "Mr. F. Cramer led the band, and Mr. Cramer (J. B.) sat at the pianoforte as conductor." (*Harmonicon*.)

1823. "Mori led, and Signor Coccia sat at the pianoforte as conductor." (*Harmonicon*.)

1824. "The orchestra is much improved by placing the Maestro, who presides at the pianoforte, in the centre." (*Harmonicon*.)

1825. York Festival. "Conductor, Mr. Greatorex. Dr. Camidge will preside at the organ and Mr. Greatorex at the pianoforte." (*Harmonicon*.)

1836. "The band was led by Mr. H. Farmer, and the concert conducted by Mr. Wooley, who presided at the pianoforte with his accustomed ability." (*Musical World*.)

1836. "Conductor, Sir George Smart, who will preside at the pianoforte." (*Musical World*.)

We were slow to change our methods in this country. The keyboard-director still hung on to his old-established right to be regarded as the "conductor" of a performance, and the violinist-leader clung to his right to be master of the orchestra. As we have seen, they sometimes came into conflict, and if a choir and orchestra might be "wandering in opposite directions," each following its own leader, when there was no choir the orchestra would have to choose between two leaders or become divided in itself. The conductor "at the piano" might well have given an occasional time-beat with his hand, especially when a choir was present, and almost certainly when it was a large one. There was ample precedent for this, and it was no innovation either in this country or elsewhere.

The position of a conductor "at the organ" would be most unfavourable for beating time, and it is difficult to understand why, if he wanted to beat time, he should have sat at the organ. The following only leaves one wondering exactly what Mr. Knyvett did: "Mr. W. Knyvett both conducted and presided at the organ, a plurality of appointment which is incompatible with the well-going of such an orchestra."[1]

But it would appear that this "conducting at" or "on the organ" was no conducting at all, or that, at all events, it provided no sort of visible time-beat: "justly as Mr. Greatorex is to be praised for the masterly manner of his conducting on the first of all instruments, we cannot approve of his forgetting, occasionally, that it *is* an organ, and *not* a pianoforte."[2] Leading a choir solely by means of an organ always tends to create a time-lag on the part of the singers, as the following suggests: "In the noble fugue, the chorus singers, instead of taking up the points as they occur, have a habit of *hanging fire*, and waiting to be led by the organ, instead of boldly starting off simultaneously with it."[3] When there was no choir, the position of

---

[1] *Mus. World*, May 20, 1836, p. 159   [2] *Harm.*, April, 1824, p. 75.
[3] *Ibid.*, April, 1831, p. 96.

the conductor at the piano was weaker, because orchestras were in the habit of following their own violinist-leader, and that they did follow their leader will be shown by several extracts which will be quoted later. The conductor "at the piano" had really become little more than an old custom, a mere tradition, but one to which in this country musicians clung tenaciously for more than ten years after Spohr had shown them in 1820 how to conduct an orchestra with a baton.

In a letter to Wilhelm Speyer dated April 14, 1820, Spohr described the customary procedure at the Philharmonic concerts; he is referring to the rehearsal for the concert on April 10: "The way of conducting here, both in the opera house and at concerts, is the most topsy-turvy one imaginable. They have two conductors, but neither really functions. The 'conductor,' as he is styled on the bills, sits at the piano and plays from the full score, but gives neither the beat nor the tempo. This is supposed to be done by the 'leader' or first violin; but as he has only the first-violin part in front of him he can't be of any help to the orchestra, so he contents himself with emphasising his own part and letting the orchestra keep with him as best it can. The players have long recognised the defects of this system and the impossibility, under it, of an orchestra of 50 or 60 ever attaining an ensemble; but they dare not venture to change it, because the established thing is regarded here as holy and untouchable, the English in general, in spite of their political freedom, being the most wretched slaves to etiquette. However, at the rehearsals I conducted in the old-established way from the score, and in the evening when it is *de rigueur* for the 'conductor' to be at the piano, I had it all so much by rote that I could help the orchestra even without the score. Thus my symphony was so precisely rendered, and especially nuanced, as I could never have hoped after a single fairly hasty rehearsal."[1]

So it appears that Spohr bowed to custom on that occasion, and conducted "at the piano."

In his *Autobiography*, however, Spohr gave an account of how at a rehearsal and concert of the Philharmonic, he introduced the baton. As he mentions particularly that Mr. F. Ries was the official conductor on that occasion, it must have been the concert on May 8 that he referred to; the only other concert during that season at which F. Ries was "at the piano" was on March 6, and it is highly improbable that if the introduction of the baton had occurred before he wrote to Speyer on April 14, he would not have described the event in his letter. Spohr's description of the event has often been quoted and is probably familiar, but it has almost invariably been quoted in an abbreviated form. This is the story in full, as it appears in the English translation of the *Autobiography* :

"Meanwhile my turn had come to direct one of the Philharmonic concerts, and I had created no less sensation than with my solo play. It was at that time still the custom there that when symphonies and overtures were performed, the pianist had the score before him, not exactly to conduct from

[1] Speyer, p. 51.

it, but only to read after and to play in with the orchestra at pleasure, which when it was heard, had a very bad effect.   The real conductor was the first violin, who gave the *tempi*, and now and then when the orchestra began to falter gave the beat with the bow of his violin.   So numerous an orchestra, standing so far apart from each other as that of the Philharmonic, could not possibly go exactly together, and in spite of the excellence of the individual members, the *ensemble* was much worse than we are accustomed to in Germany.   I had therefore resolved when my turn came to direct, to make an attempt to remedy this defective system.   Fortunately at the morning rehearsal on the day when I was to conduct the concert, Mr. Ries took the place at the piano, and he readily assented to give up the score to me and to remain wholly excluded from all participation in the performance.   I then took my stand with the score at a separate music desk in front of the orchestra, drew my directing baton from my coat pocket and gave the signal to begin.   Quite alarmed at such a novel procedure, some of the directors would have protested against it; but when I besought them to grant me at least one trial, they became pacified.   The symphonies and overtures that were to be rehearsed were well known to me, and in Germany I had already directed at their performance.   I therefore could not only give the tempi in a very decisive manner, but indicated also to the wind instruments and horns all their entries, which ensured to them a confidence such as hitherto they had not known there.   I also took the liberty, when the execution did not satisfy me, to stop, and in a very polite but earnest manner to remark upon the manner of execution, which remarks Mr. Ries at my request interpreted to the orchestra.   Incited thereby to more than usual attention, and conducted with certainty by the *visible* manner of giving the time, they played with a spirit and a correctness such as till then they had never been heard to play with.   Surprised and inspired by this result the orchestra immediately after the first part of the symphony, expressed aloud its collective assent to the new mode of conducting, and thereby overruled all further opposition on the part of the directors.   In the vocal pieces also, the conducting of which I assumed at the request of Mr. Ries, particularly in the recitative, the leading with the baton, after I had explained the meaning of my movements, was completely successful, and the singers repeatedly expressed to me their satisfaction for the precision with which the orchestra now followed them.

"The result in the evening was still more brilliant than I could have hoped for.   It is true, the audience were at first startled by the novelty, and were seen whispering together; but when the music began and the orchestra executed the well-known symphony with unusual power and precision, the general approbation was shewn immediately on the conclusion of the first part by a long-sustained clapping of hands.   The triumph of the baton as a time-giver was decisive, and no one was seen any more seated at the piano during the performance of symphonies and overtures."[1]

[1] Spohr, II, pp. 81–82.

The last sentence has given rise to a generally accepted belief that, after Spohr's visit, the Philharmonic orchestra was always conducted by a time-beating conductor. Further support for that belief was found in the fact that in the programmes of the Society's concerts after Spohr's visit the expression "at the pianoforte" was changed to "conductor." Both historians of the Society have stated that the piano was then removed, and that the conductor stood, as he now does, before a desk facing the orchestra.[1]

But there is conclusive evidence to prove that such was not the case. It should be remembered that Spohr was a visitor to London for only four months in 1820, and that he did not come to this country again until 1839. Hogarth, who wrote the first history of the Philharmonic Society, did not come to London until 1830, ten years after Spohr's visit; he became secretary to the Society in 1850, and his *History* was not published until 1862. M. B. Foster's statement was obviously taken from Hogarth's history.

Evidence that the concerts were still directed in the old way, by a conductor "at the piano" in conjunction with the violinist-leader, is over-whelmingly strong, and comes from witnesses who were present at the concerts between 1820 and 1830, when neither Spohr nor Hogarth was there.

The first witness is Moscheles, who first came to London in 1821, and after making several long visits during the next few years, made London his home from 1826 to 1846. He became a Director of the Philharmonic Society, and was in close touch with all that was going on in the musical life of London.   The following appears in Moscheles' *Life*,[2] under the year 1823: "Moscheles was very much astonished at the English custom of placing a famous musician at orchestral concerts in front of the band, at the piano, and on the occasion of a Philharmonic Concert we find him asking the question: What do they mean by the term 'Conductor, Mr. Clementi?' He sits there and turns over the leaves of the score, but after all he cannot, without his marshal's staff, the bâton, lead on his musical army. The leader does this, and the conductor remains a nullity."[3]   In 1830–31 Moscheles again commented on the way the Philharmonic orchestra was controlled: "In criticising the Philharmonic Concerts of this year Moscheles finds fault with the conductor still sitting at the piano, and turning over the leaves of his score; without a bâton of course he has no influence over the band, which is under the sole command of the first violin —a process leading to constant unsteadiness in the performance of large orchestral works."[4]   These remarks could not possibly refer to anything that took place before Spohr's visit in 1820 because Moscheles was never in London before 1821.

The second witness is a correspondent who criticised the playing of the Society's orchestra in a letter to *The Harmonicon* in May, 1825: "I am in the habit of seeing a gentleman at the pianoforte as *Conductor*; what his duties

[1] Hogarth, p. 26.   M. B. Foster, p. 43.   [2] By his wife, based on her diary.
[3] *Life*, I, p. 76.   [4] *Ibid.*, I, p. 249.

are, I will not presume to determine, but would strenuously recommend that he, having perhaps more leisure than the leader to peruse the score, and judge how far it may be possible to execute the various passages at a certain speed, would occasionally suggest some amendment on this point, and thereby relieve himself from the suspicion of holding a sinecure."[1]

A third witness is Fétis, who spent the season of 1829 in London, and made the following comment on the method of directing the performance of the Philharmonic orchestra: "An old custom is preserved at the Philharmonic concerts; I mean the conductor at the piano, which is the function given alternately to Sir George Smart and Dr. Crotch. We must concede that the use of the piano with a song is perhaps quite effective, because it helps the singer, especially in the Recitatives; but in symphonies, in noisy overtures, as are most of the modern works, this instrument is ineffective and may even be detrimental; for if it is possible to hear the piano amongst the other instruments, its peculiar tone-colour, which the composer did not allow for, may impair the effect."[2]

These are eye-witness accounts; they speak for themselves and show quite conclusively that the conductor "at the piano" still functioned for at least ten years after Spohr's visit in 1820.

To the above may be added the testimony of a German musical periodical in 1829, in which it was said that the old method of direction was then still in force at the London Philharmonic. The writer commented on the matter much in the same way as Fétis had done: "The piano serves well enough to support a singer in the Recitative; with the full orchestra it is either not heard at all or the sound of it, which the composer did not mean to be heard, gets mixed up with that of the orchestra greatly to the disadvantage of the effect. This arbitrary addition of the piano becomes still more unpleasing in soft passages when the chords continue to reverberate after the sound of the orchestra has ceased."[3]

A curious comment on the divided control of orchestras in England in 1830 was that of an English musician who wrote about the *undivided* control of Spontini at Berlin in these words: "While I do not entirely approve of the position in which the conductor is placed, he being too conspicuous to the whole house, and thus apt to distract its attention by the incessant waving of his wand, there can be no question of the superiority of the plan over that pursued with us. For (at Berlin) our ears are not excruciated by two distinct beats, intended to represent the same time:—one being clapped by the hands of the *conductor*, and the other being stamped, sometimes furiously, with the foot of the first violinist or leader, which, to say the least of it, is a very reprehensible *pedal* accompaniment. I am for despotism in musical governments, but I fear that the British constitution will not admit such a mode of rule in any case; we must, therefore, rest contented with things as they are."[4] This, incidentally, adds another variety of noise, the clapping

---

[1] *Harm.*, May, 1825, p. 89.   [2] Fétis, *Curiosités*, p. 188.
[3] *Berliner Allgemeine Musikzeitung*, 1829, No. 6, p. 286.   [4] *Harm.*, Jan., 1830, p. 5, f.n.

of hands, to the many which were used in order to keep orchestras together during the first half of last century.

Even as late as 1832 the "conductor" at the Philharmonic appears to have been still more or less a dummy: "Why, if one of those stuffed figures which the wardrobe of the King's Theatre could supply were to be placed in the conductor's chair, the business would go on just as well as now. There is a great deal of *humbug*, Mr. Editor, in conducting; but nowhere is it arrived at so high a pitch as at the Philharmonic concerts. . . . I have yet to learn the use of a conductor for instrumental concerts."[1]

Spohr's lesson in 1820 had obviously not been learned; the control was still in the hands of the leader, while the "conductor" at the piano was little more than an onlooker.

As a visiting conductor to the Philharmonic in 1832, Mendelssohn used a baton to conduct his own works, although the regular conductors still officiated at the piano: "The author (Mendelssohn) conducted with a baton: the intelligence of his look, gesture, and rise of the baton imparted a confidence to the band which was productive of the most beneficial results. It is almost superfluous to repeat that we have always strenuously advocated this system of conducting with a baton.   The superior execution of this new overture (the *Hebrides*) ought to carry conviction home to the Directors of its great advantages and importance; or we might adduce, as a still more striking example, the perfect execution of *Der Freischütz* at the King's Theatre with only three rehearsals, conducted by Herr Chelard."[2]

But even then the "leaders" at the Philharmonic frowned on this method of direction which threatened to deprive them of their power and status. John Ella told how Mendelssohn, with characteristic tact and politeness, was quite ready to give up the baton rather than offend the leaders, but that he was dissuaded from doing so by Costa, Meyerbeer and himself: "Mendelssohn at last pledged his word to use the baton.   I was present at the concert, and well remember the frowns of the fiddlers whose authority Mendelssohn's baton so completely usurped."[3]

It seems to have been in the 1833 season that baton-conducting became regularised at the Philharmonic: "Sir G. Smart, in the true capacity of a conductor, stood with a baton in his hand, and we never heard the band go better."—"Bishop conducted with a baton—let us hope, therefore, that the Leader's occupation's gone."[4]   So it took twelve years, after Spohr's innovation, to convince the Philharmonic Directors that baton-conducting was the best way of controlling an orchestra.   In spite of that decision, the wish that the Leader's occupation was gone was not yet to be fulfilled, and except in the case of Costa and some visiting conductors, the leaders in London for many years more still contested the conductor's right to control the playing of an orchestra.

---

[1] *Harm.*, Feb., 1831, p. 35.   Written by an Associate of the Society.
[2] *Morning Post*, 1832.   [3] Supp. to *Musical Union Record*, June 11, 1867.
[4] *Athenæum*, *re* second and third concert.

It is noteworthy that when Costa was made sole conductor of the Philharmonic concerts in 1846, he accepted the appointment only on the condition that he should have "sole and undivided control of the orchestra."[1] Costa would not make that stipulation without reason; it is evident that up to 1846 the control of the orchestra *was* divided, and that the leader still retained much of his power to dominate the performance, as Moscheles had described.

The divided control was clearly not working well during the 'thirties; the following was written in 1838: "Mr. Bishop should either conduct or allow Mr. Mori to do so for him. We cannot see the propriety of a conductor turning his back on the audience, for the sole apparent purpose of coquetting with the baton and score, and leaving the business—the work— to the leader."[2]   In the same year it was written in the *Morning Post*: "The spectacle of a conductor and leader combating for the direction of the band can no longer be tolerated."[3]   The same complaint was again made in the following year: "We felt that inconvenience we have so often been made sensible of before, arising from the foolish custom of double-leadership. The exact boundary distinguishing the provinces of 'leader' and 'conductor' being as little defined as the disputed territory in America, agressions are frequently committed by the executive under the conflicting influence of these rival powers, which nothing can prevent but the final settlement of the disputed claims.   The movements of the baton and fiddlestick till then will continue to be as simultaneous as the telegraphs of the Admiralty and Shooter's Hill."[4]

Some light is thrown on the curious method of directing the performances of concertos at the Philharmonic during the 'thirties in a long leading article in the *Musical World*.[5]   Describing how Strauss, the Viennese waltz conductor, directed a concerto at a private concert, the writer goes on: "Instead of retiring, as is the custom of some Philharmonic Directors, during the performance of a concerto, into an obscure corner, or sitting down in the face of an audience, with a happy indifference on the duties of a Conductor, Herr Strauss took his place in the centre of the orchestra, and amidst all the licences and allowed liberties of the concerto-performer, watched both his band and the music with Argus-eyed attention, the brilliant effect of which was discovered and appreciated by every musician in the room."   Again, in the same article, we read: "The present practice at the Philharmonic Concerts is for the Conductor to take his ease at the pianoforte, or to retreat to some hole or nook, throughout the execution of a concerto or song, and calmly to leave the hapless wretch, who has accepted the invitation to be victimised at a Philharmonic sacrifice, to the tender mercies of a band, which is not ashamed to use a giant's strength with a tiger's ferocity."

[1] Foster, *Hist.*, p. 193.   [2] *Mus. World*, May 24, 1838, p. 69.
[3] *Ibid.*, June 21, 1838, p. 133.   [4] *Ibid.*, April 11, 1839, p. 231.
[5] *Ibid.*, June 14, 1838, p. 109.

While it is evident that baton-conducting became the rule at the Philharmonic in 1833, it seems that some time had still to elapse before it became the universal custom at all concerts in London. It is most unlikely that any such change of method could take place suddenly. Spohr was greatly mistaken if he supposed that in one day he had changed the habits and customs of the London musicians, that he had in a moment reformed the long-established custom which gave the actual control of the orchestra to the violinist-leader, and passive general supervision to the keyboard-conductor. Moscheles, Fétis, and the critical correspondent of the *Harmonicon* were not dreaming when they described what they saw and heard at the Philharmonic concerts, when neither Spohr nor Hogarth was there to see.

That the programme gave the title "conductor" to the presiding musician, instead of designating him "at the piano," implied no radical change of method. They were only getting rid of a rather cumbrous expression which was going out of use, and were substituting one which was more compact and had already been long in use, and one which meant to them just what it meant to Busby; for during the 'twenties the "conductor" *did* arrange, order, and direct the necessary preparations for a concert, and he did superintend the performance, but in England he did not conduct it with a baton.

It seems that Spohr's use of the baton in 1820 did not really create quite such a sensation as he imagined it did. There is apparently no other record of the occurrence at the rehearsal or concert, and there were plenty present who might have left an account of it if it had struck them as an unusual and epoch-making event. The Philharmonic season of 1820 was reviewed in the *Quarterly Musical Magazine*, the only English musical periodical of that time; Spohr's symphony was noticed and full attention was given to his violin-playing, but not a word was written about his novel method of conducting, or of any sensation caused by it.[1] Hogarth (in 1862) recorded the supposed change in the manner of conducting, and he recorded Spohr's visit in 1820, but he did not connect the two. For the scene at the rehearsal we rely solely on Spohr's account. There is no reason to doubt his narrative, or to question the truth of what he said took place; but he was obviously quite mistaken when he remarked on the subsequent effect of his action, when he supposed that "no one was seen any more seated at the piano during the performance of symphonies and overtures."[2]

There is plenty of evidence that the conductors at the Philharmonic did begin to use the baton during the early 'thirties, but it is quite certain that the violinist-leader retained his power over the orchestral playing and disputed the conductor's right to control the performance until Costa

[1] *Q. M. Mag.*, Vol. II, No. VII, p. 383
[2] Spohr wrote his *Autobiography* late in life, and it is quite likely that his memory for events which had occurred about thirty years earlier may have been somewhat unreliable. Indeed, Hauptmann (*Briefe*, III, p. 111) pointed out that some of the details in the *Autobiography* were inaccurate.

finally put an end to the faulty system in 1846. This palpably unsound method was clearly giving poor results in 1840, when the following was written: "While our concert-orchestras are maintained at a greater cost than those of any other country—while their content of executive talent here is as great as abroad, . . . the performance of our bands is notoriously insecure. From the Philharmonic, downwards, all are alike open to the suspicion of uncertainty;—the playing of all is sometimes fine, sometimes directly the reverse, and commonly wavering midway between the extremes. The causes of this very unnecessary discredit to our musical *status*, are to be found, we think, in the strange customs retained in this country in the matter of orchestral discipline. . . . In every English orchestra we find a leader and a conductor; one of which offices is manifestly superfluous, and both, not infrequently, are as evidently useless. The wisdom of our ancestors has posted one man on a joint-stool to direct an orchestra, if he *can*, and another a little higher up to overturn all his arrangements if he *likes*, and thus bequeathed us an intolerable absurdity. Down goes the conductor's *baton*, ditto the heel of the leader's boot—perhaps simultaneously, perhaps not, as the case may be—'*piano!*' vociferates the conductor, 'S-s-s-sh!' responds the leader—that is, if he thinks *piano*; he may, perhaps, think *forte* and act accordingly, whereupon, as a matter of course, wind and strings follow suit. Should the conductor call a halt to discuss some knotty point of style, the leader never concerns himself—why should he? If the matter in hand be some old composition, *of course* he can play his part; if otherwise, he still needs no enlightenment from his fellow-director, and so forthwith betakes to tuning his fiddle, or some other harmless diversion, thereby telegraphing fidget and inattention to the whole orchestra. And yet this manifest folly—this childish un-reason, is constantly acted even in our best orchestras. . . . Orchestral performances, we are convinced, will never reach perfection in England until the office of leader—as generally understood—be definitely abolished, and the conductor invested with unshackled authority."[1]

At the *Societa Armonica* the same absurd state of affairs prevailed: "The remarks we have made in reference to the faulty system of conducting which obtains at the Philharmonic meetings apply with tenfold force to those of the *Societa Armonica*, which is a very ill-favoured likeness of its sister association."[2] Of the conductor at these concerts the *Morning Post* wrote: "Mr. Forbes amazes us as a conductor; we never know whether he is three bars before or behind his beat. If the things go well, it is when nobody is looking to the gyrations of his baton." A little later it was said that Forbes "is a mere cypher."[3] It is evident that the leader held the reins at the *Societa Armonica*.

At the Ancient Concert the baton was used for the direction of madrigals in 1833: "The conductor has adopted a new plan, which has succeeded well,

---

[1] *Mus. World*, March 26, 1840, p. 185.   [2] *Ibid.*, June 14, 1838, p. 112.
[3] *Ibid.*, May, 1838, pp. 22 and 50.

thus far: there is yet ample room for improvement, which we do not despair of witnessing, if he persevere in his endeavours to accomplish. Instead of sitting before the instrument and *thumping* it, by way of marking the time, he quits the chair, and standing in front of the orchestra, with *baton* in hand, gives the time in a way to be seen by every performer."[1] But the choral and orchestral performances at the Ancient Concert were still "conducted at the organ" in 1837, when a critic thought fit to advise the conservative society that the time was now ripe for a change to more up-to-date methods: "We have one other suggestion to make, and it is founded on a generally received maxim in musical matters, and universally adopted by Sir George Smart and other great concert directors, that no conductor can at the same time conduct an orchestra, direct a chorus, and play the organ. It is not so at the Vocal Society, nor is it so at the great Metropolitan Choral Societies. If Mr. Knyvett is to *pedal* his instrument continuously, which he ought to do, his sole attention must be taken with his execution. No man on earth can do that well and attend to other things also."[2]

In 1838 the man at the organ still tried to control the performance of the Ancient Concert while seated at the instrument: "Until the Noble Directors determine to appoint a genuine organist—one who by the assistance of his feet can bring into full play the powers of the instrument, and thus relieve the present Conductor from that portion of his duty, it is an abuse of terms to compliment the institution with the possession of such a functionary at all. If the music needs no direction, offices should still be called by their right names, and a hand-organist should not be elevated to the dignity of a Conductor."[3] But the old aristocratic institution was even then beginning to totter, and before the middle of the century it had perished from inanition and the competition of stronger forces.

At the Sacred Harmonic Society a time-beating conductor shared with the orchestral leader the responsibility for the performances, and this divided control evidently prevailed up to the time when Costa was made conductor in 1848. It was the same old evil as at the Philharmonic; in 1840 Surman and Perry were still contesting the right to establish the *tempo*: "In the commencement of the chorus 'The Lord gave the word,' the leader and conductor were so palpably at issue, that, for a moment, a halt and a fresh start appeared inevitable. Mr. Surman, in his accustomed fashion, was minded to bestow his tediousness on the brilliant conception that lay at his mercy, and Mr. Perry was equally resolved that it should have at least the benefit of a rational degree of speed, and, in consequence, the band presently gained a bar on the chorus."[4] The reform that Costa made immediately on taking up office was to put an end to that unsatisfactory system, as he had already done at the Opera and the Philharmonic. Henry Phillips recorded the change in these words: "To begin, there was no leader, only a first violin; so that the whole responsibility devolved on the

[1] *Harm.*, April, 1833, p. 80.
[2] *Mus. World*, March 10, 1837, p. 187.
[3] *Ibid.*, June 14, 1838, p. 113.
[4] *Ibid.*, April 16, 1840, p. 242.

conductor."[1]   It was a pity that they did not get rid once and for all of the title "leader."   It is still in use, although the leadership of the orchestra has been entirely in the hands of the conductor for over a hundred years, and the principal first violin now leads only the first violins.

The London players got used to the baton by slow degrees.   A visible time-beat was not completely strange to them before Spohr's visit, for the choruses in large-scale performances had often been held together by such means.   For symphonies and other purely instrumental works, no doubt it was new to them in 1820.   But they would get used to it under Spohr, Weber (1826), Mendelssohn (1829 and 1832), and under Chelard and Hummel in 1832 and 1833, when these two visiting conductors directed the German opera company which played at the King's Theatre during those two seasons.   After Costa had become musical director and conductor at the King's Theatre in 1832, they would no doubt soon experience some more baton-conducting, and by the 'forties they would be well used to it.   Charles Nicholson gave a clue to the situation in 1836, when he wrote the following in his *School for the Flute*,[2] published in that year: "A very great improvement has taken place *within the last few years* in the orchestras of this country, which may be mainly attributed to the introduction of *Conductors*, whose province it is to mark the time with a bâton or stick, by which the eye (so much quicker than the ear) is attracted, and the time more strictly regulated."

The stabilisation of the baton-conductor in England required many years of experience, and the traditions of the past were not easily nor quickly uprooted.   The following leading article from the *Musical World* in 1838 is quoted here in full, not only because it reveals a very good conception of the function of the conductor, but also because it shows the dwindling power of the violinist-leader, and gives us a glimpse of the last dying struggles of the old-style conductor at the piano:

"It would be an idle ceremony for us to attempt any laboured proof of the importance of the duties, and the value of the services, attached to the office of Conductor at a musical performance; or of the worse than useless eminence, to which an individual is raised, who is invested with power he is unable to wield and clothed with a dignity he only contrives to render ridiculous.

"The well-trained member of an orchestra is perfectly conscious that there can be no faithful delineation of a composer's ideas unless the closest attention is paid to each passage in detail.   He justly regards himself as a unit among many; and confining himself to the proper execution of the part assigned to him, he leaves to another the task of determining the general expression of the whole.

"This duty of right appertains to the Conductor, whose isolated position enables him, if he be qualified for his post, to produce that grand result which arises from the performance of numbers under the implicit direction of one.   He is, or ought to be, the master-spirit of the band over which he presides—an impersonation of the mind of the composer. The Conductor should evince not only the imaginative glow of the poet, but also display a thorough acquaintance with the minutest details of the work entrusted to his superintending care. By his coolness, decision, urbane, yet inflexible demeanour, he should inspire the timid, check the presumptuous, and command the respect of all. He should exhibit a warm sympathy with the intentions of the author, and a perfect familiarity with the machinery by which they are to be developed. The mere possession of a love for wahtever is striking or ennobling in the art, a faculty common, in a greater or less degree, to all who are endowed with a natural taste for the science of sweet sounds, is not a sufficient qualification for assuming the official baton. The requisites of a good Conductor, in addition to the technical knowledge which we have laid down as indispensable, should include the energy and tact which can control a fiery leader; a watchful apprehension of such passages as are apt to exercise an imperceptible influence on the performers, and to create a measure of uncertainty in point of time and expression; and the skill to humour what is technically termed 'the swing' of an orchestra. These are the points which a genuine Conductor would always keep in view, when directing the performance of a musical composition. For want of a strict, or, indeed, any attention to them, how often do we witness a Conductor, whose exertions are fully occupied in a continued struggle to catch the *time* which the band, or singers, have fallen into; too happy if he can succeed in this his primary object, to permit the *expression* to take care of itself. His utter inability to separate the component parts of the score in his mind, is shown by the wandering eye, the unsteady hand. A confused motion of his head, a tremulous grasp of his instrument of office, indicate his internal disquietude, and that last remnant of virtue, which cannot wholly exclude a sense of shame. Conscious of his imbecility, and half apprehensive that others observe it, the unhappy substitute for a Conductor flourishes his rod in mystic evolutions; in the midst of his enchantments lays it aside, resumes his seat at the piano, which he approaches with a supplicating glance, as if he expected its unconscious vibrations with his fingers, would solve his conjectures, and relieve his uncertainty.

"The engagement of an inefficient Conductor in the direction of an orchestra, however small or limited its resources, inevitably leads to a neglect of details, and a general slovenliness in the execution of the music selected for performance. An insult is thereby offered to the memory of deceased, an injury inflicted on the reputation of living composers; a very equivocal compliment is paid to the good sense and correct taste of the audience, and certain disgrace is reflected on the management, which appoints, or endures, a person of such conspicuous incompetence."[1]

Although in the 'forties all orchestras in London were directed with the baton, it seems that, except in the case of Costa, Jullien, and a few foreign visiting conductors, the leader was still disputing with the

[1] *Mus. World*, April 12, 1838, p. 241.

baton-conductor the right to control the performance. The following extracts from contemporary sources leave no doubt as to the state of affairs at the Philharmonic during the few years immediately preceding Costa's appointment in 1846:

Apropos of a piano concerto played by Sterndale Bennett and conducted by Bishop in 1843, we learn that the soloist "laboured under the exceeding disadvantage of the continual clock-work bow-waving of the leader, who had much better have minded his fiddle, instead of labouring to put Mr. Bennett out (rather than assist him) by beating time against him, as though for a wager."[1]

Of a Philharmonic concert in 1844 at which Smart was the conductor, we read the following: "There cannot be advantageously *two* guiding stars to direct the attention of the band. Either a conductor is useless, or a leader is useless." The writer then goes on to describe the plight of a soloist who "was fettered by the discordant beatings of no less than three different individuals, viz.—Sir George Smart, who wielded the baton—Mr. Loder, the leader of the evening,—and Mr. T. Cooke, *not* the leader of the evening. These gentlemen were all beating different times, and the consequence was, that the band was bewildered."[2]

In 1844 Mendelssohn conducted some of the Philharmonic concerts, and it is difficult to believe that he would allow any but his own hand to exercise any control over the playing. But Mendelssohn was, above all, tactful, and it may be that he gave way to some extent to the English custom by permitting the leader to have a fairly large finger in the pie, as is suggested in the following: "This concert, conducted by Mendelssohn, and led by T. Cooke (who, by the way, conduced to more than half the effect by his precise and steady leadership), went off beautifully."[3]

Another example of too many cooks spoiling the broth is found in Chorley's criticism of the playing at the Societa Armonica in 1836: "The orchestra is, we are sorry to say, as far from neatness and solidity as formerly: its leader and conductor do not understand each other, for some of the players look for their government to Mr. Forbes, others to Mori, and a remnant to Lindley and Dragonetti."[4] The "remnant" were perhaps far from unwise in choosing a steady bass part for their guidance in preference to a competing pair of time-givers.

Even in 1845 the same absurd pantomime was going on at the Philharmonic: "While the professed conductor calmly waved his baton to one measure, the leader as calmly moved his bow, and not seldom stamped his feet—to another."[5] In this case the contestants were Bishop and Loder, but when confronted with a leader who was thoroughly determined to be master of the situation, it seems that the complacent conductor made no attempt to dispute his claim: "Cooke seemed determined to have everything

[1] *Mus. World*, June 8, 1843, p. 195.   [2] *Ibid.*, April 25, 1844, p. 141.
[3] *Illus. Lon. News*, July 13, 1844.   [4] *Athenæum*, Jan. 4, 1836.
[5] *Mus. World*, May 1, 1845, p. 199.

his own way, and Bishop quietly followed in his wake."[1] The next year (1846) saw the necessary change when Costa was made sole conductor of the Society's orchestra and it was announced that "in future there will be no leader at these concerts. . . . The direction of the orchestra will be vested solely in the conductor, as at the Opera House."[2]

At the Sacred Harmonic Society's concerts the situation was further complicated by the presence of an organist who, with the baton-conductor and leader, were evidently each competing for the mastery in 1845, when it was asked: "who is to be attended to by the band? Is it Mr. Surman with his *bâton*, Mr. Perry with his violin bow, or Mr. Miller with his cracked organ? Here is a tripartite conductorship—most absurd. Why not abolish all this absurdity. Let us have a *real* conductor and a principal violin, or, as the French call him, a *chef d'attaque*."[3]

While it cannot be determined exactly when the baton superseded the old piano-direction at the King's Theatre, it is quite certain that the change did not take place before the early 'thirties. The old *Maestri al Cembalo* still functioned up to the appointment of Costa as conductor. In 1824 "Rossini quietly made his appearance amongst the other musicians, and made his way to the pianoforte. . . . He bowed to the audience, and immediately sat down to the instrument and prepared his copy."[4] Coccia appears to have officiated in the same way up to 1828. There was no baton-conductor in 1827 and 1829 according to the testimony of Wesley and Mendelssohn, and when Costa was first engaged in 1829 it was in the capacity of *Maestro al Cembalo*. In 1832 and 1833 Chelard and Hummel were conducting seasons of German opera at the King's Theatre, and then the baton was certainly used: "Herr Chelard, a distinguished musician and disciplinarian, conducted the band with a baton, on the principle so often advocated in our notices of the Philharmonic Concerts";[5] and the following from another source states that this method was an innovation: "The arrangement of the band was new. The conductor with his baton, instead of sitting at the pianoforte, stood on a conspicuous elevation, seeing and seen by every person in the orchestra. The Leader's place was occupied by the principal Violoncello and Double Bass, while *he* was placed in their accustomed situation."[6] Thus, the inference is that Costa began conducting the Italian opera with a baton, not before 1832, but most likely in 1833, when his position was that of Musical Director and Conductor.

The rights of the conductor had been established at the Opera, at the Philharmonic, and were soon to come in the Sacred Harmonic Society, and in each case it was Costa who had wrought the change. In 1847, even in that stronghold of conservatism, the Ancient Concert, the post of leader was abolished, and Tom Cooke had to subside into the position of principal first violin.

[1] *Illus Lon. News*, April 19, 1845.   [2] *Mus. World*, May 7, 1846, p. 112.
[3] *Ill. Lon. News*, Dec. 20, 1845.   [4] *Morning Post*, 1824.
[5] *Ibid.*, 1832.   [6] *Spectator*, 1832.

Even then the leaders in the English orchestras did not yield to the conductors without some further struggles which were prolonged until after the mid-century.   The following extracts show the leader still resisting feebly, but being steadily vanquished by the all-powerful wielder of the baton (1850): "The whole system of modern execution of works has undergone a change; the old style of a divided authority between leaders and conductors has exploded.   There must be one directing mind and poetic influence to interpret the scores of the great masters."[1]   Writing of the Leader in 1853, Davison told of "the frequently anomalous and antagonistic, but now, happily, almost obsolete office of *leader*, in a large orchestra directed by an intelligent conductor."[2]   A little later he wrote: "yet there is no doubt that many performances are marred in consequence of the reluctance of the gentleman who has the *violino primo* to take the time and general reading of a composition from the conductor."[3]   By 1856 the leader had apparently given up the struggle, and the *Daily News* finished him off in these words: "There is no 'leader' in an orchestra—the office being superseded by that of the conductor.   But there is a 'principal violin' on whom the conductor relies for strength, firmness, and precision, in taking up any point."

The baton having been firmly established in London by the mid-century, we hear no more of orchestral conductors "at the piano" or "at the organ." But the old connection between conductor and piano was not yet completely severed, and during the rest of the century the programmes frequently show the word "conductor" being used to describe the piano accompanist at concerts where there were neither choirs nor orchestras.   An English survey of the duties of a conductor in 1853 includes the following: "A good conductor must, at all times, be prepared to accompany on the pianoforte all kinds of pieces, songs, duets, violin solos, etc., etc., in all sorts of keys . . . at a moment's notice."[4]

It is true that the conductors in English and continental theatres often sat in front of a small piano which took the place of a music desk.   But these were not conductors "at the piano" in the former sense.   They did not use the piano to lead the orchestra, but it was sometimes used for accompanying recitatives, and for non-violinist conductors it was useful at rehearsals.   The "Spy" cartoon of Costa shows the great conductor seated in front of a small keyboard; the score rests on the music desk, the baton is upraised and safeguarded by a cord passed round his wrist.   But there was some use for the conductor's piano in opera; in 1855 we are told that "Costa will sit on the same stool, touch with his fingers the same narrow harpsichord (when Ronconi is in search of a note)."[5]   Yet, although Costa sat in front of the instrument, he was no "conductor at the piano"; he was probably the best and first real baton-conductor permanently resident in

[1] *Illus. Lon. News*, Sept. 21, 1850.   [2] *Mus. World*, Jan. 15, 1853, p. 31.
[3] *Ibid.*, Jan. 29, 1853, p. 67.   [4] *Ibid.*, Jan. 15, 1853, p. 30.
[5] *Ibid.*, 1855, p. 121.

this country, and the man who abolished the system of puppet-conductors that had prevailed here for so long and which worked so badly.

*   *   *

Although the particular sort of implement used for conducting is of little importance, a short review of the various objects that conductors have held in their grasp may not be out of place here.

Nearly all the earlier musical dictionaries describe a baton as a stick or roll of paper. The roll of paper often figures in early pictures as the symbol

G. F. ANDERSON, MASTER OF THE QUEEN'S MUSICK,
CONDUCTING AT BUCKINGHAM PALACE, 1848

of the time-beater's authority, and we have seen that it was sometimes adopted by the earlier orchestral conductors in the 19th century. The wooden staff or *bâton* was at home in France from the earliest days of opera in that country, and became shorter and lighter as the audible time-beat gave way to one which was intended only to be seen. There is a curious echo of the old Lullian baton in a description by Chas. de Boigne of Cherubini rehearsing his *Ali Baba* at the Paris *Opéra* in 1833: "During the rehearsals, the march of the forty thieves had completely absorbed him. He kept on beating the floor with his baton, crying—*En mesure, Messieurs— Messieurs, en mesure.*"[1] But this was not the orchestral conductor's baton, for Cherubini was not conducting the orchestra either at the rehearsal or at the performance; it was as the staff of the stage-manager or the

[1] Bellasis, p. 329.

ballet-master that he was using it, in the old French way, just as it had been used by Lulli a hundred and fifty years before.

According to Hensel, the baton that Mendelssohn gave to Berlioz in exchange for the French composer's "cudgel of lime tree with the bark on"[1] was a pretty light stick of whalebone covered with white leather. Berlioz also described this exchange of batons, and said that his was "a heavy oaken staff."[2] Mendelssohn's elegant baton makes its appearance again in 1848, when Bishop conducted at the Ancient Concert with a baton given to him by Mendelssohn: "It was a kid-covered stick with which Mendelssohn had conducted the *Elijah* at Birmingham in 1846."[3] This dainty implement would match the white kid gloves that were worn by conductors in England at that time. When on his first visit to London in 1829, Mendelssohn used a white baton which he had specially made for him by a turner who "took me for an alderman, and would insist on decorating it with a crown."[4] After Mendelssohn's death five of the batons he had used were found amongst his possessions; his widow gave one to each of his four surviving children, and the fifth was given to Joachim.[5]

In his *Instrumentation* Berlioz recommended a wooden stick about a foot long, and of light colour. A portrait shows him with a baton about 15 inches long.

The *Taktirstäbchen* which Spohr produced on the occasion when he introduced baton-conducting to the London Philharmonic orchestra must also have been fairly short, for he was able to keep it in his pocket. John Ella's mention of "those distracting white wands used at London concerts"[6] recalls the "cursed little white stick" that annoyed Moritz Hauptmann so much at Cassel. When conducting in London Weber used a roll of paper, but at the first performance of *Der Freischütz* at Berlin he is said to have used a very small stick.[7]

Wagner told how at the Leipzig *Gewandhaus* old Pohlenz took his place at the conductor's desk to beat time for the choral items, and how he used to come on to the platform with a very important-looking blue baton in his hand.[8]

A violin bow, the favourite baton of the French conductors, was a natural and handy thing for a fiddler to use, but it was easily broken: "Habeneck struck the desk in irritation, and broke his violin bow," and Berlioz only added fuel to the fire by saying: "Good heavens! if you were to break fifty bows, that would not prevent your time from being too slow by half."[9]

Anselm Weber's roll of leather stuffed with calf's hair was probably unique, and his successor at Berlin, Spontini, also had a curious taste in batons. When Spontini came to Dresden in 1844, and was invited to conduct his *Vestalin*, he asked Wagner what sort of baton they used at Dresden. Wagner indicated the length and thickness of an ordinary baton of wood such as was served out to the conductor there each day wrapped

---

[1] *Mend. Fam.*, II, p. 185.   Now in the Paris Conservatoire Museum, No. 1209.
[2] *Mem.*, II, p. 53.   [3] Northcott, p. 111.   [4] Hensel, I, p. 184.   [5] Moser, p. 65.
[6] Ella, p. 364.   [7] Kapp, p. 34.   [8] *My Life*, I, p. 69.   [9] *Mem.*, I, p. 308.

round with white paper. Spontini sighed, and asked Wagner if he thought he could get made for him by the next day a baton of black ebony of great length and thickness, with a fairly large knob of ivory at each end. Wagner promised that Spontini should have something which at any rate looked just like it by the next rehearsal, and that another should be made of the very materials that Spontini wanted in time for the performance. Wagner got the stage carpenter to make a baton according to Spontini's specification, and when this was presented to him, he said nothing, but grasped it "fairly in the middle with his whole fist."[1]

In 1852, when Berlioz was conducting the concerts of the New Philharmonic Society, Spontini's widow came to London to hear some extracts from *La Vestale*, and presented Berlioz with Spontini's baton.[2]

Jullien is said to have used a jewelled baton, and to have put on a new pair of white kid gloves whenever he conducted a piece by Beethoven.

JEWELLED BATON PRESENTED TO JULLIEN IN 1853

Costa used an ordinary wooden baton, notwithstanding some contemporary comments that describe him as "tapping thrice on the desk with an ivory baton," and on another occasion with a "gilt baton." These may have been presentation batons used on special occasions in order to honour the donors.[3] That particularly impracticable implement, the *presentation* baton, appears to have made its appearance fairly soon after the baton had come into general use. Berlioz was given a golden baton at Vienna in 1845, and a silver one at Weimar in 1852. The artists at the Vienna theatre gave Balfe a golden baton inscribed with the titles of his operas; a silver one was presented to Liszt on the occasion of the first production of *Lohengrin* at Weimar in 1850, and Spohr was another who was honoured by the gift of a presentation baton at Hanover in 1855. But all these pale before the jewelled baton given to Jullien by his English admirers prior to his departure for America in 1853.

This gorgeous bauble was 22 inches long, and was made of maple wood mounted with chased gold circlets. It was entwined with two golden serpents each with a diamond in its head; another circlet of gold was set with seven diamonds, and the whole was surmounted by a brilliant valued at sixty guineas. The cost of this glorious toy was variously said to be 200, 300 and 400 pounds, and it was presented to Jullien on July 11, 1853, at the Hanover Square Rooms, being the gift of 5,000 of his patrons.

* * *

[1] Wagner, *Prose Works*, III, pp. 129, 130.   [2] Hueffer, p. 209.
[3] In 1853 Sims Reeves presented Costa with "an elegant and costly orchestral baton, made of elaborately carved ivory, with massive gold mountings" (*Mus. World*, March, 1853).

Many references to audible time-beating during the first half of last century will have been noticed.   The frequency of these references, and the many complaints about it, indicate how common this nuisance must have been.   Stamping with the foot and striking the desk with the baton or bow were the usual forms of this disturbing noise, which, although it was universally condemned, was obviously very generally practised.

Berlioz[1] referred to "the employment of noises," and mentioned both foot-stamping and tapping the desk: "It is worse than a bad method; it is a barbarism"; but he allowed that in a theatre a conductor might possibly be obliged to give an audible beat when owing to the exigencies of stage evolutions the chorus could not see the conductor.   Deldevez (1878) also admitted that the difficulty of keeping orchestra and chorus together in a theatre might justify an occasional stamp on the floor by the conductor.[2] The amusing caricature by Hess (c. 1830) of an elderly conductor, suggests that as he is unable to make his beat heard with his paper-roll baton, he is just about to do so with his foot.[3]

A critic of the London Philharmonic orchestra in 1825 earnestly pleaded for "doing away with that perpetual and insufferable nuisance of marking the time by stamping or striking the bow on the desk."[4]   Indeed, it seems to have been quite a common thing in London for leader or conductor, or both, to emphasize the beat by making some sort of noise when the orchestra was not well synchronised.   There are many complaints in the 'thirties: "The maestro should be seen by every performer, but not heard.   We can with propriety extend this observation to the instrumental part of the orchestra, beseeching both leader and conductor to abstain from such merciless *stamping of feet* as occurred during the performance of most of the full pieces."[5]   One auditor complained that his countrymen "do not at present appear to me to have acquired that happy method of conveying their own ideas, or instructions to a large orchestra, which I have more than once seen so skillfully displayed by Moscheles, Hummel, Chevalier Neukomm and Mendelssohn.   Let any one of these gentlemen be installed maestro, and you will find the band invariably go well, unless, indeed, it be thwarted and checked by the caprice of an overbearing, arbitrary leader: there is no 'stamping of the feet' with them; but all is conducted in silence. . . . There is no ambiguity, every motion of the baton is decisive, every glance of the eye expressive, and he makes himself clearly understood by each individual performer."[6]   Another correspondent asks if the symphonies at the Philharmonic "cannot be played without the desperately annoying accompaniment, the *hushing* of the leader to the *piano* parts of the composition."[7]

The audible beat was more strongly entrenched in France than in Germany.   Hauptmann complained about Habeneck's annoying habit of

<hr />

[1] *Instrumentation*, p. 252.   [2] Deldevez, p. 137.   [3] From *Galerie Musicale*, by H. Hess.
[4] *Harm.*, May, 1825, p. 90.   [5] *Ibid.*, March, 1833, p. 55.   [6] *Ibid.*, May, 1833, p. 96.
[7] *Ibid.*, April 30, 1830, p. 156.

tapping on the prompter's box with his bow at the Paris *Opéra*, and said that such a thing could happen in Germany only at rehearsals. He thought that Spohr would have held the performance together better than Habeneck.[1] But in France the tradition reached back to the days of Lulli; it still flourished in the time of Rousseau; Grétry and Castil-Blaze granted that it was not abolished in their days; Habeneck could not get rid of it, and even Deldevez had to admit the usefulness of an occasional foot-stamp. Anything so firmly rooted was obviously difficult to eradicate, and if they did not succeed in doing so it was because the stage at the *Opéra* was large and the chorus-singers were distant from the source of the time-beat.

When Wagner was at Prague in 1832 he described how the students at the Conservatoire were compelled to practise his new symphony under "the dry and terribly noisy baton" of Dionys Weber.[2] Loewe was at the Prague Conservatoire in 1839, and said that Weber had worn a deep hole in his music stand by perpetually hammering on it with his baton.[3]

Already in the early stages of the orchestral baton-conductor there are indications that he was sometimes suspected of having the easiest job in the orchestra, and that it would be no serious loss to the performance if he were not there. A correspondent of the *Manchester Advertiser* in 1836 had the impertinence to ask whether a conductor at a musical festival was really of any use.[4] The passage, already quoted, about the conductor being "only too often a charlatan who fatigues himself and tires the spectator's eye, and like the fly on the wheel, thinks that everything has been done by himself," more than hints at this uneasy suspicion that the conductor is a fraud who takes to himself all the credit which should rightly go to the orchestra. Even in the present enlightened times the orchestral conductor has to submit to occasional outbursts of doubt as to whether he is really quite so indispensable as he is supposed to be.

The new sort of orchestral conductor that had developed during the course of the first half of last century was the result of combining in one person the functions previously carried out separately by the violinist-leader, the keyboard-director, and the choral time-beater. The great merit of the fusion was that it got rid of divided responsibility and gave the performance one centre of control. The increase in responsibility which accompanied this concentration of power in one individual was set off to some extent by the fact that the conductor was now relieved of the necessity to play on or handle any instrument while he was conducting, and was free to devote his attention to the performance as a whole.

The new conductor had to build up a technique of baton-conducting which comprised the old technique of time-beating, a new technique of gesture or signs, and a new technique of rehearsing.

The technique of time-beating would offer no difficulty, for it was old-established and easily acquired. The technique of gesture was one which

[1] Speyer, p. 237.   [2] Wagner, *My Life*, I, p. 80.   [3] Loewe, p. 314.
[4] *Mus. World*, Aug. 12, 1836, p. 143.

would create itself out of experience; it comprised such things as the effective use of the left hand, the manner of using the baton or bow, the attitude of the body, the expression on the face, and all the visible signs that enable a conductor to influence the playing of his orchestra. The technique of rehearsal would be developed out of the necessity for doing without an instrument; the conductor had to use his own voice; he had to find words to explain what he wanted; he had to accustom himself to express his meaning, and his orchestra to receiving it.

As long as conductors were all composers, a reasonably strong musical gift, a good ear, sufficient knowledge of the orchestra and ample musicianship might almost be taken for granted; but these were not enough. The new orchestral conductor required also such qualities as leadership, a certain assertiveness, a suitable temperament, organising ability, and the power to maintain his authority. These were personal qualities quite apart from musical gifts. Just how these various qualities, both musical and personal, were distributed in the same person was the factor which eventually determined who would make a good conductor and who would not. By the middle of last century the process of selection had hardly had time enough to come into full operation, so there were still plenty of composers conducting who were not good conductors, and plenty of conductors composing who were not good composers. But, although not yet in full operation, the process which was to pick out the best conductors was beginning to take effect.

Already in 1839 Kastner had perceived that the composer and conductor were not quite of the same species. He even went so far as to say that he considered the two functions to be incompatible. He wanted the conductor to be musician enough to be able to compose, but would prefer that he didn't do so, the reason being because "a conductor who also composes will have an invincible propensity for getting his own music played . . . It is very difficult for a man enjoying a certain amount of influence and conducting a musical society or in a theatre wholly to renounce the love that everyone feels for his own works."[1] He would trust the composer-conductor to give reasonably fair play to foreign or deceased composers, but not to his fellow-countrymen and contemporaries! What Kastner demanded in a conductor—apart from his musical gifts—were perspicacity, coolness, perseverance, patience and firmness. Berlioz, in his *Instrumentation*,[2] avoided the difficulty of specifying the non-musical qualities desirable in a conductor by calling them: "other almost indefinable gifts, without which an invisible link cannot establish itself between him and those he directs."[3] But in his *Memoirs* he stated what he considered to be the three qualities indispensable to a finished conductor. Unlike Kastner, Berlioz could see no objection to a conductor being a composer, in fact, one of the

---

[1] *Cours*, Supp., p. 15.
[2] The portion on conducting was not added until 1856.
[3] *Instrum.*, p. 245.

three essential qualifications he expected was that he should be a "learned composer, skilled and enthusiastic";[1] the other qualities he demanded were a strong feeling for rhythm and a perfectly clear and exact mode of beating time. Berlioz could or would not separate composer and conductor, although he pointed out the absurdity of supposing that every composer was born a ready-made conductor: "It is generally supposed that every composer is a born conductor, that is to say, that he knows the art of conducting without having learnt it."[2]

The individuality or personality of the conductor was an aspect of his art which was as yet hardly recognised by the middle of last century. The interest was still centred in the music rather in the conductor's rendering of it. The performance might be better or worse in the case of different orchestras and conductors, but that was a matter of technical proficiency. The good orchestra gave a good performance because the players were technically well equipped and the conductor knew his business, but it is difficult to find at that time anything to suggest that the conductor ever came in between the music and the listener to the extent of impressing his own personality on the rendering of the piece. Virtuosity in instrumentalists and singers was recognised and greatly appreciated, but not in conductors. The public would crowd into a building in order to hear this or that artist play or sing; they would go for the purpose of hearing this or that work performed; but they did not go to hear any particular conductor's rendering of the music.

In the middle of last century the conductor was no box-office draw, and he got no head-lines; his name did not usually appear on theatrical bills which gave in full the name of every singer and dancer, as well as the names of the scene-painter, costumier and stage-manager. The conductor's name appeared in small letters on concert announcements, and if a performance was reported and criticised, more likely than not the conductor's name was not even mentioned. Notices of hundreds of operatic performances in the first half of last century can be read without once coming across the name of the conductor, and orchestral concerts were often reported without any mention of the name of the man who shouldered the heaviest responsibility. In two columns about a Philharmonic concert in London in 1842 (*Musical World*) the conductor's name is the only one missing. When Costa was received with applause at the Royal Italian Opera in 1847 it was regarded as something rather unusual: "Never was such a fuss made about a conductor. Applauded when he comes on, applauded when he goes off."[3] Wilhelm Kuhe commented on the status of the conductor in these words: "In the old days the poor conductor, . . . was a mere harmless and necessary figure in a scheme of attractions in which his drawing capacity was not reckoned."[4]

With the exception of Jullien and a few others of his type who knew how

[1] *Mem.*, II, p. 185.
[2] *Ibid.*, p. 240.
[3] *Mus. World*, April 3, 1847, p. 213.
[4] Kuhe, p. 279.

to attract a public, the orchestral conductor of one hundred years ago didn't understand the value of advertisement and publicity; he was a mere child in the matter of taking to himself all the credit for a good orchestral performance, and was content to be treated much as the accompanist at a concert is treated nowadays. The real self-advertising, all-absorbing, limelight-loving, autobiography-writing virtuoso-conductor had not yet arrived on the scene by the middle of last century; but he was due to appear soon after.

PLATE 20

CARICATURE OF ELDERLY CONDUCTOR WITH ROLL OF PAPER

PLATE 21

WEBER CONDUCTING AT A CONCERT IN COVENT GARDEN THEATRE IN 1826

VIII
Conductors

Spohr

Spohr's lifetime covered the whole of the period which saw the beginning and the first development of orchestral conducting; it bridged the wide gap between the methods of Mozart and of Wagner, between the old type of *Kapellmeister* who sat at the piano and the modern conductor who ruled with the baton.

As *Kapellmeister* Spohr served at Gotha (1805), at Frankfort (1817), and in 1822 he settled down as conductor of the opera and the court music at Cassel, there to remain until his death in 1859. As a violin virtuoso he travelled extensively, as composer and conductor his activity was almost equally widespread; he served as *Concertmeister* at Vienna (1812), and from after 1810 he was much in demand as a conductor of Musical Festivals.[1]

In Spohr's time it was unusual in Germany for a violinist to occupy the position of *Kapellmeister*, and he himself deplored the fact that he was no pianist. He told Moritz Hauptmann that he would gladly have given a hundred *Louisd'or* to be able to play the piano.[2] Instead of using a piano for the preliminary rehearsals of an opera, Spohr made use of a string quartet, and this he found awkward and inconvenient.

The following are contemporary estimates of Spohr's conducting:

"Herr Spohr's leading with a roll of paper, without the least noise, and without the slightest contortion of countenance, might be called a *graceful Leading* if that word were sufficient to express the precision and influence impressed by his movements upon the whole mass, strange both to him and to itself. To this happy talent in Herr Spohr I ascribe in great part the excellence and precision—the imposing power, as well as the soft blending of this numerous Orchestra with the voices of the Singers in the execution of *The Creation.*" (Gerber.)[3]

"When Spohr wields the baton we at once recognise the great musician. The performance is precise, and all play together. The playing is governed more by intellect than by sentiment; there is in it more rhythmical force than either delicacy or colour." (Fétis.)[4]

"As a conductor Spohr was thoroughly capable. Not only when he stood in front of his own orchestra, but also when he was faced with strange orchestras made up of the most heterogeneous elements such as are

---

[1] Frankenhausen, Erfurt, Halberstadt, Nordhausen, Aachen, Lucerne, Brunswick, Bonn.
[2] Hauptmann, *Briefe*, I, p. 243.   [3] Spohr, *Autob.*, I, p. 142.   [4] *Biog. Univ.*

sometimes assembled for musical festivals, was he at once able to win complete confidence and secure a successful performance." (Lobe.)[1]

"It is truly delightful, wonderful in precision and firmness of beat, and at the same time accompanied by motions plainly indicative of the effect proposed." (*Spectator.*)[2]

Moritz Hauptmann said that Spohr conducted as if he were quite unconscious of himself, so completely was he wrapped up in the music.[3] According to Gassner, Spohr demanded precise, clear and uniform playing, and allowed no liberties to be taken with the written parts.[4]

If to the foregoing extracts we add what we know of Spohr by his music and by reading his Autobiography, we shall probably have a fairly correct view of him as a conductor. His performance would be steady and smooth, dignified and rather solemn, precise, and perhaps rather rigid; there would be no violent contrasts, nothing impetuous or vehement, no great display of colour, and no meretricious effect. He would certainly earn the respect of his players, and lead them firmly but gently, neither coaxing nor bullying, neither flattering nor abusing them. If we can imagine Spohr at one pole and Berlioz at the other, we shall probably have them in their right places as conductors.

WEBER

Born and brought up in a theatrical atmosphere, Weber was essentially an opera conductor. His appointments as *Kapellmeister* were at Breslau, Prague, and finally at Dresden in charge of the court German opera.

On taking up each of these appointments Weber immediately began to reform and reorganise. He tried to get rid of inefficient players and to engage new personnel, he rearranged the orchestra, instituted systematic rehearsals, and extended his activities to a general supervision of the whole performing apparatus, including the chorus, ballet, scenery, costumes and stage-management. Such a live wire was bound to meet with some obstruction, and many applecarts had to be upset before he got his teams into working order.

Weber was only eighteen when he started as *Kapellmeister* at Breslau, and he had yet to gain experience. At first he was criticised for paying too much attention to the orchestra and neglecting the singers; he was also censured for his quick *tempi*.[5] He was hard-working, and never spared himself; in three months at Prague in 1814 Weber produced no less than ten operas.[6]

When Weber directed his *Silvana* at Berlin in 1812, the unusually good performance and close attention of the choir and orchestra was ascribed to his "quiet, judicious, firm and noiseless" conducting.[7]

Brühl, the *Intendant* at Berlin, made more than one effort to secure Weber as conductor of the opera in the Prussian capital, and strongly

[1] *Cons. und Diss.*, p. 358.   [2] Norwich Festival, 1839.   [3] *Briefe*, I, p. 157.
[4] *Dir. und Rip.*, p. 53.   [5] Weber, I, p. 102.   [6] *Ibid.*, I, p. 433.   [7] *Ibid.*, I, p. 354.

recommended him to the King: "Weber has recently given unequivocal evidence of his skill as a conductor; in a short time he raised the rather mediocre orchestra at Prague to a remarkable state of efficiency. When he conducted his opera *Silvana* here, I had an opportunity of observing his great gifts as a conductor; whereas most conductors would have required six or seven rehearsals to prepare the difficult music, Weber did it in three rehearsals."[1] But Brühl's efforts were unavailing; when a vacancy occurred it was Bernhard Romberg who was engaged. Again Brühl tried to persuade the King to secure Weber after the unexpected death of Gürrlich in 1817: "not only is Weber most highly esteemed among the younger composers in Germany, but his success in training the orchestras at Prague and Dresden has brought him a reputation as one of the best conductors in this country."[2] Again Brühl's advocacy was unsuccessful; the King had his eye on Spontini, and it was he who was eventually brought to the Berlin opera.

At Dresden Weber proved himself to be a most stimulating and exacting conductor: "He had eyes and ears for everything; a wrong note from the remotest corner of the orchestra brought to the offending player a sharp glance; tirelessly he would stop the playing in order to repeat a passage; now he was in the orchestra, now on the stage putting a singer or a supernumerary right, giving directions to the scene-shifters, simultaneously doing the work of stage-manager and conductor, and giving his orders with such precision that there could be no delay in carrying them out."[3]

From a Viennese paper[4] we get a picture of Weber as a conductor when he produced his *Freischütz* there in 1822: Often he would beat only a bar or two at the beginning of a movement to fix the *tempo* and the rhythm, and would then let the orchestra go along of its own accord. His manner on the whole was quiet and undemonstrative, and no unnecessary movements were made, but when the music required it, he could become fiery and energetic. His beat was clear and precise, but in a *crescendo* his second, third and fourth beats would bring his hand as far down as for his first beat. His way of conducting in recitative was splendid, and in big ensembles his lively eyes worked like lightning, animating the players and meeting their questioning glances. Above all, it was all done in a quiet manner; there was no noise, no hammering on the desk, no shouting, no calling out for *piano*; his work as a *Kapellmeister* was all done in the most dignified manner.

There can be little doubt that as long as his frail and weakening body left him any vestige of strength, Weber's conducting was alert and masterful. From one who was in close touch with him during the rehearsals for *Oberon* we have the following: "I had seen him, whilst conducting the music, throwing his whole heart and soul into the work, imparting a stimulus to principals, band, and chorus such as they had never experienced before, and manifesting an energy that would have wearied a man in rude health."[5] Another English impression was: "Mr. Weber's mode of conducting was in

---

[1] Kapp, p. 29.   [2] *Ibid.*, p. 31.   [3] Weber, II, p. 59.
[4] *Wiener Allgemeine Musikzeitung*, 1822, p. 174.   [5] Anon., *Mus. Recoll.*, I, p. 132.

the old fashion, standing in front and giving the time with a roll of paper. The calm quiet manner in which he exercised his office—his weak and emaciated appearance might disappoint the imagination while they extorted the sympathy of the audiences that crowded to see the great German genius."[1] From Marx's *Erinnerungen* we learn that although firm and exacting, Weber was polite and considerate to his players.

That there was nothing inflexible in Weber's *tempi* or stiff in his beat may be judged from his own words written in a letter to Praeger of Leipzig, and quoted by Weingartner:[2]

"The beat (the tempo) must not be like a tyrannical hammer, impeding or urging on, but must be to the music what the pulse-beat is to the life of man.

"There is no slow tempo in which passages do not occur that demand a quicker motion, so as to obviate the impression of dragging. Conversely there is no *presto* that does not need a quiet delivery in many places, so as not to throw away the chance of expressiveness by hurrying.

"But from what I have said, for heaven's sake let no singer believe himself justified in adopting that lunatic way of phrasing that consists in the capricious distortion of isolated bars, and gives the hearer the same intolerably painful sensation as the sight of a juggler violently straining all his limbs. Neither the quickening nor the slowing of the tempo should ever give the impression of the spasmodic or the violent. The changes, to have a musical-poetic significance, must come in an orderly way in periods and phrases, conditioned by the varying warmth of the expression.

"We have in music no signs for all this. They exist only in the sentient human soul; if they are not there, then there is no help to be had from the metronome—which obviates only the grosser errors—nor from these extremely imperfect precepts of mine, which, considering the extent of the subject, I might be tempted to pursue much further, were I not warned by painful experiences how superfluous and useless they are and how liable to be misconstrued." It is evident that Weber believed in a flexible *tempo*, thus foreshadowing the principles which underlay Wagner's ideas of conducting.

SPONTINI

From Dorn, Marx, Hanemann and Wagner we can get a fairly complete picture of Spontini as conductor.

With no particular reputation as a conductor, but with a very considerable reputation as the composer of *La Vestale*, *Fernand Cortez* and *Olimpie*, Spontini came to Berlin from Paris in 1820 at the pressing invitation of Frederick William III. His appointment as *Generalmusikdirector* pleased the court, but did not altogether please the public, which would have preferred someone who was more interested in German national opera. He secured for himself a position which gave him immense power, but his

---

[1] *Quar. Mus. Mag.*, Vol. VIII, No. XXX, p. 145.   [2] *On Cond.*, p. 41.

interest was centred largely in his own operas. Apart from these, although he devoted much attention to a few operas by Mozart, Gluck and Cherubini, Spontini left the general repertoire in the hands of his assistants.

The following is a picture, shown in its best light, of Spontini as a conductor, drawn by *Kammermusiker* Moritz Hanemann:[1] "In the Spontini operas Berlin possessed a jewel such as no other place in the world could produce. It is impossible to describe how perfectly, elegantly and gloriously these operas were put on the stage. Spontini's *piano*, played by the whole mass, sounded like the *pianissimo* of a string quartet, and his *forte* surpassed the loudest thunder. Between these extremes were his inimitable *crescendo* and *decrescendo*. He bestowed the greatest care on the light and shade. By means of numerous rehearsals, sometimes as many as eighty, everyone who took part in them became completely familiar with the operas. As the result of constant rehearsal the ensemble was impeccable. To me it was a wonderful experience when I first played in one of these operas; that is to say, worked, not played.

"Like a king Spontini strode into the orchestra, and taking up his field-marshal's position, he looked all round with his piercing eyes, fixing them on the heavy artillery—that was what he called the 'cellos and basses—and then gave the signal to begin. Like a bronze statue he stood at the desk, moving only the lower part of his arm. He was the perfect model of a conductor. The orchestral players sat in wholesome fear of their master, but nevertheless played with undiminished enthusiasm from the beginning down to the last note. As he left his place at the end of the opera Spontini always said—*I thank you.*"

Dorn contributes the following description of Spontini's dynamics[2]: "*Forte* like a hurricane, *piano* like a whisper, *crescendo* that makes one unconsciously open one's eyes wider, *decrescendo* giving the effect of magical exhaustion, *sforzando* that wakes the dead."[3]

It is from Wagner that we learn how Spontini grasped his ebony and ivory-knobbed baton in the middle, "and manipulated it in a way to shew one plainly that he looked on the baton as a marshal's staff, and used it, not for beating time with, but commanding."[4] But, according to Dorn,[5] Spontini did beat the time with his baton. Anton Seidl added the information that Spontini used a large baton for choruses and processions, and a smaller one for the arias.[6] His beat was energetic and precise, the movements of his right arm were almost angular although not ungraceful, and his domineering grasp of the whole was just as if he had been a figure cast in bronze. He looked right and left without for a moment disturbing the majestic restfulness of his olympian head.[7]

[1] From *Aus der Musikerwelt*, Berlin, 1875, p. 90, as quoted in Robert's *Spontini*, p. 55.
[2] *Aus meinem Leben*, II, p. 127.
[3] This was no doubt inspired by Schubart's description of the playing of the Mannheim orchestra. See *Ideen zu einer Aesthetik der Tonkunst*, p. 84.
[4] *Prose Works*, III, p. 130.   [5] *Aus meinem Leben*, I, p. 34.
[6] *Bayreuther Blätter*, 1900, p. 300.   [7] Dorn, I, p. 2.

Spontini believed in the power of the eye: "My left eye is for the first violins, and my right for the second violins; wherefore, to work by a glance, one must not wear spectacles as bad conductors do, even if one is shortsighted. I—he admitted confidentially—can't see a step before me, and yet I use my eyes in such a way that everything goes as I wish."[1]

Spontini was a stern disciplinarian; his was no coaxing manner, he believed in commanding. Wagner, writing of Mendelssohn and Meyerbeer, bemoaned that at Berlin "the last trace of the traditions of Spontini's strict discipline have faded away."[2] When Spontini entered the orchestra with his aristocratic demeanour, dressed in a dark moss-green coat, his breast covered with orders, all the musicians sat motionless, bows ready over the strings and mouthpieces ready at the lips.[3]

Spontini's performances were always safe and sure; everything went like clockwork. Like Weber, he commanded both on the stage and in the orchestra. An English visitor to Berlin in 1829 wrote of Spontini's autocratic direction: "These two masses (i.e. chorus and orchestra) are under the sole guidance of the conductor, seated close to the stage with his back to the audience: and as he only follows the score and marks the time, there is produced that unity of effect which so much distinguishes the operatic performances on the continent."[4]

But the real secret of Spontini's success at Berlin lay in the fact that he was able to have unlimited rehearsals. His method was perfectly simple and perfectly sound; he just rehearsed and kept on rehearsing until everybody knew his job perfectly. Nothing was left to chance or to the inspiration of the moment; the apparatus was put into perfect working order and had only to be started. Spontini would not be hurried into premature performances; he never produced a work until he was satisfied that it would all go without a hitch. When everything could be depended on to work like a well-oiled machine he had only to watch over the performance, and with a hand on the lever let it run along its well-prepared track. As Dorn remarked, it was all the same to the orchestra whether he gave a down or an up beat at the beginning of the bar; he could move his mighty sceptre in any direction, or hold it quite still, the playing would go on just the same. No other orchestra could have played the recitatives under Spontini's direction unless they had been drilled by him. From the foregoing it is not difficult to reconstruct Spontini the conductor. His performances would be rigid and correct, but they would lack spontaneity; there would be plenty of colour, but little charm; the contrasts would be violent, the dynamics extreme, the lines would be boldly drawn, even harshly, but they would not be very delicately shaded; the rendering would have the advantage of great unity; it was one man's performance, and it would give no rein to the individuality of the player. Spontini's performances were like the man; he could command admiration and respect, but not affection.

[1] Wagner, *Prose Works*, III, p. 134.   [2] *On Cond.*, p. 9.   [3] Marx, I, p. 220.
[4] *Harm.*, Jan., 1830, p. 5.

Spontini feared rivalry, and did nothing to smooth the path for Weber when *Der Freischütz* was produced in Berlin not long after Spontini had begun his work there. The English visitor, already quoted, said of Spontini: "Spontini, though standing very high as a composer, is not personally a favourite: he bears himself towards every one with a hauteur and repulsiveness of manner totally unworthy of a man of genius."[1] Spontini was obviously a proud and a vain man. Clara Novello gave a clue to his character when she described a visit to his home at Berlin in 1837: "His house was a gallery of portraits of himself, alternating with sonnets in his praise, busts of himself, etc., all the way to his own sort of throne room, where he sat on a raised dais in an armchair with his portraits, busts, medals, and sonnets all round him."[2]

The reign of Spontini at Berlin was brilliant, and it brought fame to the orchestra; but its very virtues became sins when the point of view was unsympathetic. Devrient, who was a Mendelssohn-worshipper, could see no good in this brilliant "ministry of Spontini"; to him it was "a period of false splendour, ruinous to the spirit of German music, of which Spontini had not an idea. The violent contrasts in which he sought his effects, the startling shocks of his *sforzati*, in fact all his effects, calculated to tell only on the nerves and senses of his listeners, could not but demoralise his orchestra. To this was added that the perfect precision and control for which his conducting was famous, ceased when he no longer held the baton."[3]

Spontini was fortunate in being able to occupy a position so favourable for his methods and ideals. He had the support of the king and court, the musical resources at Berlin were ample, he was able to rehearse as often and as long as he liked, and was allowed to pick and choose what he would conduct. He was not overworked, and, as he grew older, knew how to take it easy: "Spontini has an easy berth of it here; he neither composes nor directs, but contents himself with sitting in his box and looking on."[4] When Frederick William III died in 1840 Spontini lost his best and last supporter; he tactlessly offended the new king, and the public showed their strong dislike of him in no uncertain way. Although he retained his title and salary, his day in Berlin was then over, and he finally left the Prussian capital in 1842, leaving few friends behind him. Already before he left, eyes had been fixed on Meyerbeer as his successor.

Spontini was an almost childishly vain man, indeed, rather a spoilt child amongst the conductors of his period; everything fell into his lap at Berlin, and it is just a question whether he would have made any mark had the conditions under which he was obliged to work been less favourable. It was a great pity that the Lord Chamberlain refused the licence sought by Alfred Bunn in 1838 to present at Drury Lane Theatre a German opera company under Spontini.[5] It would have been interesting to have seen

[1] *Harm.*, Jan., 1830, p. 7.   [2] C. Novello's *Reminiscences*, p. 70.   [3] Devrient, p. 216.
[4] *Harm.*, July, 1831, p. 180.   [5] Bunn, III, p. 91.

what he would have made of the second-rate orchestra in that theatre
brought up on the slap-dash methods of Tom Cooke, of the few players,
the scanty rehearsals, and the hurried productions that were always the rule
in London.

MENDELSSOHN

Just as Spohr and Berlioz were poles asunder, so were Spontini and
Mendelssohn. The one was distant and aloof, the other was friendly and
amiable, a lovable man who was always able to surround himself with
adoring friends.

Mendelssohn was essentially a concert and choral conductor. He was
not at home in the more troubled atmosphere of the theatre, and his brief
association with the opera at Düsseldorf was neither happy nor successful.
With his attractive personality Mendelssohn made friends just as easily as
Wagner made enemies; he was well educated and refined, polite and tactful;
he would have made an ideal conductor for an English choral society.

Of musical gift Mendelssohn had plenty and to spare. As a boy he
picked up the elements of practical conducting by experience in his own
home at Berlin, and by conducting his own works in many other places
while he was yet quite a young man. This was ripened by further experience
at Düsseldorf and at musical festivals, and by the time he went to Leipzig
in 1835 his reputation as a conductor was well established.

Mendelssohn was not the great organiser that Weber was, and it suited
him thoroughly to find the machine all ready and in working order at the
Gewandhaus, where the quiet and orderly surroundings suited him in every
way.

Already in his youth at Berlin Mendelssohn had given evidence of a
distinct flair for conducting, and in taking charge of the first revival of
Bach's *St. Matthew Passion* in 1829 he accomplished a difficult task with
considerable success. Devrient described the twenty-year-old conductor
at work: "Felix was calm and collected in his difficult post as though he had
already conducted a dozen Festivals. The quiet simple way in which he
by a look, a movement of the head or hand, reminded us of the inflections
agreed upon, and thus ruled every phrase; the confidence with which he
would drop his *bâton* during the longer movements, when he knew they were
safe, with a little nod as much as to say, 'this will go very well without me,'—
listen with radiant countenance, occasionally glancing towards me,—in all
he was as great as lovable."[1]

Most of the contemporary accounts of Mendelssohn's conducting were
written by devoted friends who were perhaps rather blinded by admiration
for their hero. In reading these panegyrics some allowance must be made
for this unbounded admiration and steadfast devotion. Hiller wrote of
Mendelssohn at Leipzig in 1840: "His eminent talent as a conductor was
especially favourable to the performance of orchestral works. Vigorous

[1] Devrient, p. 59.

leaders had managed, before his time, by the help of their fiddling, to put plenty of spirit and precision into them, but no one had ever imagined so deep a conception, or such artistic finish in the performances of the great symphonies. . . . But all the little imperfections in individual execution were thrown into the background by the spirit and life which Mendelssohn instilled into the orchestra, his complete devotion to the cause, and the delight which lit up his expressive features at every successful achievement, and acted like electricity upon the public. When I speak of his conducting thus influencing the audience, it must not be supposed that he in any way courted notice by his behaviour at the desk. His movements were short and decided, and generally hardly visible, for he turned his right side to the orchestra. A mere glance at the first fiddle, a slight look one way or other, was sufficient. It was the sympathy in the cause, which gathered strength from the sympathy brought to bear on it by so wonderful a man."[1]

Lampadius was even more enthusiastic, and could hardly find words strong enough to express his rapture: "He was as great as a conductor, as he was as virtuoso and composer. His fame as a conductor is now world-wide. When once his fine, firm hand grasped the *bâton*, the electric fire of Mendelssohn's nature seemed to stream out through it, and be felt at once by singers, orchestra and audience. . . . But Mendelssohn conducted not only with his *bâton*, but also with his body. At the outset, when he took his place at the music-stand, his countenance was wrapped in deep and almost solemn earnestness. You could see at a glance that the temple of music was a holy place to him. As soon as he had given the first beat, his face lighted up, every feature was aflame, and the play of countenance was the best commentary on the piece. Often the spectator could anticipate from his face what was to come. The *fortes* and *crescendos* he accompanied with an energetic play of features and the most forcible action; while the *decrescendos* and *pianos* he used to modulate with a motion of the hands, till they slowly sank to almost perfect silence. He glanced at the most distant performers when they should strike in, and often designated the instant when they should pause, by a characteristic movement of the hand, which will not be forgotten by those who ever saw it. He had no patience with performers who did not keep good time. His wondrously accurate ear made him detect the least deviation from the correct tone, in the very largest number of singers and players. He not only heard it, but knew whence it came. . . . To singers, his rehearsals were a constant enjoyment. His praise was always delightfully stimulating; his criticism, not chilling nor disheartening. By throwing in all kinds of bright and merry words, he knew how to rouse the most indifferent and idle to the best performance they were capable of, and to keep the weary in good humour."[2] From Moscheles we hear how Mendelssohn's personality and bearing influenced the orchestra: "his admirable conducting, speeches and observations—in fact, his general behaviour to the orchestra—fills his subordinates with affection and respect."

[1] *Letters and Recoll.*, pp. 156–7.   [2] Lampadius, p. 155.

—"His influence over the band gave it fire, tenderness, and requisite nuances."—"Mendelssohn's conducting was as admirable as ever, the band obeyed his slightest hint."[1]

To Schumann, Mendelssohn's rendering of symphonies was unequalled in Germany, and to Hauptmann his talent as a conductor was extraordinary. Although Schumann rather resented the time-beating baton when Mendelssohn first came to the *Gewandhaus*, he could not but admire his method: "And yet it was delightful to watch Meritis (Mendelssohn); in his eyes we read beforehand the mental windings of the composition, and its shadings, from the most refined to the most powerful effects; like a seer he forewarned us of what was to come.   How different from the chapel-masters who seem ever threatening to whip score, orchestra, and the public with their batons."[2]

Lobe ranked Mendelssohn only with Habeneck, and thought that his conducting was even greater than his piano-playing: "Nature, up-bringing, and study have combined to make him a model conductor. His noble figure, his fiery eye, his acute ear, his wide education, his presence of mind in an emergency, the gift of speech which he could use so impressively when necessary, his musical insight and complete knowledge of the classics, and finally his early experience in handling large forces, made it possible for him to reach what so few others ever achieved.   This was proved by his rendering of the Beethoven symphonies at Leipzig."[3]

In England as well as in Germany Mendelssohn's influence over the orchestra was the subject of eulogistic comment: "The presence of Mendelssohn infused new spirit into the band; and the music was executed with an ardour that evinced the influence he possesses, and the confidence he inspires whenever he wields the baton."[4]   The following also indicates the depth of the spell which Mendelssohn's personality cast over his English admirers: "It is a beautiful sight to see him conduct a full orchestra.   We shall never forget the impression he produced at the great Birmingham Festival, on the occasion of the production of his famous Hymn of Praise.   The magnificent band followed him as if under a spell, which his genius alone kept unbroken. With every action of his wand the sounds and harmonies seemed marshalled in a grand and solemn order, which no intrusion could disturb.   The eyes of the musicians were all, as it were, focussed within his own; he communicated with them as if by electricity—made them sympathize with his spirit, catch the impulses, and partake of the emotions of all that was to be interpreted before the thronging multitude, who were listening with blended awe, excitement, and admiration, to every feeling symbolized, and every thrill evoked."[5]

Chorley, although a blind admirer of Mendelssohn, thought he was not at his best as a conductor when away from the congenial atmosphere of the

---

[1] Moscheles, *Life*, I, p. 321; II, p. 75; II, p. 160.   [2] Schumann, I, p. 37.
[3] Lobe, *Mus. Briefe*, p. 241.   [4] Ayrton, in *The Examiner*.
[5] *Illus. Lon. News*, June 18, 1842.

Gewandhaus: "When at the head of his own Leipzig band, no one could be more successful than he; elsewhere he was fretted by want of understanding and sympathy among his forces, and fretted them accordingly. In England he obtained no great results as a conductor, save in his own compositions. In these, the effect of his presidence was magnetic."[1] From Chorley, too, we learn that Mendelssohn's gestures when conducting were not obtrusive, but that he was very exacting: "Dr. Mendelssohn's conducting, though easy in appearance, and, therefore, anything but distracting to the eye, is about the strictest in spirit of any I have ever witnessed, that of Moscheles alone excepted."[2]

Mendelssohn's great musicianship and his attractive personality undoubtedly combined to make him one of the most outstanding conductors of his time. If the adulation of his friends spoilt him a little, it also helped to give him unbounded confidence in his own powers, and helped to make him the leader and figurehead of a school of conducting which was widely accepted as authoritative in Germany and England.

Towards the end of his life, at Berlin, where the officialdom of the Prussian musical machine rather jarred against his friendly disposition, he was not at all happy. He did not get on very well with the orchestra that was used to the hard discipline of Spontini and was inclined to take advantage of Mendelssohn's easier manner. In 1841 he wrote to David the following account of his experiences at the rehearsals for *Antigone*: "At the first rehearsal the orchestra was disposed to behave badly; disorder and argument prevailed, and I could hardly believe my eyes and ears. At the second rehearsal, however, the tables were turned, and it was my turn to be rude; I punished (fined?) half a dozen of them, and now they regard me as another Spontini. Since then there has been no sulking; as soon as they see me they are attentive, and they do their best; instead of being haughty they are now obsequious, they bow and scrape, although that carries little weight with me. In the meantime they are obedient, but I knew beforehand that I could not alter them; this is only fresh evidence of it. You can have no idea of the fawning servility and arrogance of these people. These two qualities generally go together; I have not found more than four amongst all these forty people with whom I can really get on well."[3]

Leipzig always remained Mendelssohn's spiritual home; there he was happy, there he had set up the shrine at which his disciples worshipped, and there everything in the garden was lovely. But perhaps it was not all quite so lovely as it appeared to be; for in that garden there was growing up a prickly plant, and it was called Wagner.

Mendelssohn liked quick *tempi*; he liked to get over the ground quickly: *nur flott, frisch, immer vorwärts* he urged his pupils; the first[4] movement of Beethoven's Ninth Symphony at the *Gewandhaus* was too quick even for Schumann, and Wagner could not make him see that the *Tempo di Menuetto*

---

[1] *Thirty Years' Mus. Recoll.*, p. 84.
[2] *Music and Manners*, I, p. 226.
[3] Eckardt, p. 156.
[4] Bülow, *Ausg. Schriften*, II, p. 209.

in the Eighth Symphony should not be hurried into a sort of Ländler.[1] Quick *tempi* covered up imperfections in the execution and enabled him to "get away with it," and his renderings were "smooth and genial." Wagner alleged that he found traces of Mendelssohn's love of quick *tempi* in the playing of the London Philharmonic orchestra in 1855: "The music gushed forth like water from a fountain, there was no arresting it, and every *Allegro* ended as an undeniable *Presto*."[2] Mendelssohn had said to Wagner "with regard to conducting, that he thought most harm was done by taking a *tempo* too slow; and that on the contrary, he always recommended quick *tempi* as being less detrimental. Really good execution, he thought, was at all times a rare thing, but shortcomings might be disguised if care was taken that they should not appear very prominent; and the best way to do this was *to get over the ground quickly*."[3]

This way of getting over difficult places by skimming lightly over them was all very well for the "elegant" and "cultured" school of composers of which Mendelssohn was the founder and spiritual head, but to Wagner it was a weak spot, a flaw which could not be mended by a mere superficial gloss of speed. Wagner gave Mendelssohn his due, and acknowledged him to be a "master," but to Wagner the "elegant tribe of *Kapellmeisters*" who adopted the Mendelssohnian maxim *chi va presto va sano*,[4] were as a red rag to a bull.

Perhaps it would have been too much to expect to find every good quality combined in one ideal conductor. That man would have to have been a compound of Spohr, Berlioz, Weber, Spontini, Mendelssohn and Wagner, and that was clearly an impossibility.

WAGNER

Although much of Wagner's work as a composer was to come after the middle of last century, his work as a conductor comes well within the period of this survey.

Like Weber, Wagner belonged to the theatre from childhood. As a conductor he made a modest beginning as chorus-master at Würzburg in 1833; two years as *Kapellmeister* at Magdeburg (1834–6), a short term at Königsberg, and two years at Riga (1837–9) gave him the necessary experience, and after spending an interim of three years at Paris, he came to the important post at Dresden early in 1843, there to remain for over six years. His work in these places had included a certain amount of concert-conducting, but his main work was in the theatre; the last regular theatrical post he held was at Dresden, and that came to an end in 1849.

Again like Weber, Wagner extended his power from the orchestra pit on to the stage. He had the same idea as Weber, that of uniting the music and the drama in one whole; orchestra, actors, scenery, costumes, and everything pertaining to opera production were to form one complete presentation controlled by one will.

[1] A south German dance which developed into the waltz.
[2] *On Cond.*, p. 23.   [3] *Ibid.*, p. 22.   [4] *Ibid.*, p. 42.

Well equipped in the technique of conducting, Wagner's conception of performance was based on finding the right *tempo* by means of a vocal-melodic delivery of the music.   He admitted that he owed this conception largely to the singing of a fine artist, Frau Schröder-Devrient, and his application of it to orchestral playing to the performances of the Paris orchestra under Habeneck.   His faith was pinned to the use of a flexible *tempo*, varying according to the emotional character of the melody.   In Wagner's conducting, as Seidl said, it was not the time-beat that ruled; it was the phrase, the melody or the expression.   That was the key to Wagner's method of conducting, and also the cause of much trouble and misunderstanding when he stood before orchestras that were not accustomed to his method.   Praeger, son of the *Kapellmeister* at the Leipzig theatre, who became a friend and upholder of Wagner, emphasized that he did not regard the baton as an implement to be used for marking the time-beat: "Wagner does not beat in the old-fashioned automato-metronomic manner.   He leaves off beating at times—then resumes again—to lead the orchestra up to a climax, or to let them soften down to a *pianissimo*, as if a thousand invisible threads tied them to his baton."[1]   Berlioz's comment on Wagner's conducting in London (1855) was that he "conducts in free style, as Klindworth plays the piano."[2]

From the purely musical standpoint Wagner was undoubtedly a great conductor, and the inaugurator of modern conducting as it developed in the hands of such as Bülow, Levi, Richter, Schuch, Seidl and Mottl.   If he was not exactly a succesful conductor, it was because of a personality that was egoistical, impatient, and tactless.

In his book on conducting (1869) Wagner treated the subject for the first time as something apart from mere time-beating; and in it he revealed his greatness, and also his pettiness.   The spiteful remarks which he could not resist throwing at other conductors, (smaller men, no doubt, but probably not so black as he painted them) do not obscure the fact that he was musically on a plane well above his contemporaries, and that what had previously passed for conducting was now due to be transformed into something much more than the process of merely keeping an orchestra together and getting the right notes played with the correct degree of light and shade.

Weingartner wrote the following about Wagner's conducting:

"I regret that I never saw Wagner conduct.   He was described to me; the body, of no more than middle-height, with its stiff deportment, the movement of the arms not immoderately great or sweeping, but decisive and very much to the point; showing no restlessness, in spite of his vivacity; usually not needing the score at a concert; fixing his expressive glance on the players and ruling the orchestra imperially, like the Weber he used to admire as a boy.   The old flautist Fürstenau of Dresden told me that often, when Wagner conducted, the players had no sense of being led.   Each believed himself to be following freely his own feeling, yet they all worked

---

[1] Praeger, p. 235.   [2] Newman, II, p. 440.

together wonderfully. It was Wagner's mighty will that powerfully but unperceived had overborne their single wills, so that each thought himself free, while in reality he only followed the leader, whose artistic force lived and worked in him. 'Everything went so easily and beautifully that it was the height of enjoyment,' said Fürstenau; and the eyes of the old artist gleamed with joyful enthusiasm."[1]

From one who was antagonistic to Wagner we have the following: "He is an excellent conductor, full of spirit and fire. At the rehearsals he led his men with voice, hands and feet, just as a keen officer sets out to storm a fortress at the head of his company. We would not care to assert that all the cosmetics that Wagner uses in order to rejuvenate such an intrinsically youthful and perfectly healthy piece of music are really necessary; nevertheless, it was good to hear the *Freischütz* overture, usually played in the old jog-trot manner, rendered again with renewed energy and extremely fine shading. The gradual swelling and dying away of the horns in the introduction, the somewhat modified pace of the song-like theme in the *Allegro*, and the prolonged holding of the two pauses before the *Coda* (nothing is feebler than too short pauses), all combined to make a wonderful effect."[2] That was written by Hanslick in 1863.

Much more flowery is the picture presented by a staunch adherent, Anton Seidl:

"He was a man of iron energy. Although rather short, he became a giant when he stood up in front of the orchestra. The powerful head and uncommonly sharp features, lit up by wonderfully piercing eyes, every emotion, every little movement and every shade of expression reflected in his face, will always remain an unforgettable memory. There he stood, without moving his body, his eyes glowing, his fingers working nervously; every musician was inflamed by his presence; and invisible power entered into the hearts of all who were taking part in the performance, and worked them up, for none could resist the power of this wonderful man. Wagner held everyone bound to him by magic fetters; the musicians could not help it, they were spellbound.

"At first the rehearsals went badly, because the master was impatient and expected everything to be perfect at once; the strange and significant movements of his long baton bewildered the players, and put them out until they began to understand that it was not the time-beat that ruled here, but the phrase, or the melody or the expression. But his look soon chained them, the magnetic fluid engulfed them, and the master had them all in the hollow of his hand.

"Under his direction the weakest orchestra grew strong and played gloriously; their tone acquired life and expressiveness, the strictest rhythm and the most sublime expression of feeling conquered, and the whole was reflected in Wagner's face. Everybody hung on his look, he seemed to be looking at everybody at the same moment.

---

[1] Weingartner, *On Cond.*, p 11.   [2] Krebs, p. 127.

"On one occasion I sat next to a great actor who had never before seen this demonstration of the power of the eye and the facial muscles. He stared at Wagner as if transfixed, and could not take his eyes off him. Later on he told me that Wagner's face expressed more than all the world's greatest actors with all their resources could tell him."

Wagner expected ample time for rehearsal, and hard work from his players. For the performances of the Choral Symphony at Dresden in 1846, 1847 and 1848, he made tireless preparations and conducted many detailed rehearsals of every section of the performing body. He himself was an indefatigable worker and spared neither himself nor his orchestra. Preparatory to the performances he "went through all the band parts himself, marking the nuances and the tempi. As to rehearsals, he was unrelenting. For the double-basses he had special meetings, and would sing and scream the parts at them."[1]

This boundless energy and love of hard work did not, of course, always fall in exactly with the views and habits of the orchestras that Wagner conducted. When he came to Dresden in 1843 he had to stir up an orchestra that was none too fond of hard work: "He spared not his orchestra. This not unnaturally created amongst the less intelligent some amount of irritation. Custom had sanctioned a certain slovenly rendering, and they revolted at the revolutionary spirit of the new conductor." But he won over the leading players: "the intelligent members of the orchestra idolized Wagner, and never wearied under his baton." From the same source we learn that Wagner was a disciplinarian: "He held the orchestra completely in his hand. The members were so many pawns which he moved at will, responding to his slightest expressed will."[2]

Wagner's season with the London Philharmonic Society in 1855 was neither happy nor successful, partly because of the inadequate rehearsals allowed him, partly because of his manner and method, and partly because of his disregard of traditions which, he said, dated back to Mendelssohn. The latter knew exactly how to get on well with the London Society; everybody was happy and everything worked smoothly. But in Wagner they had a very different person to deal with. His disposition was not of the amiable and tactful sort that had made Mendelssohn such a favourite; he was obstinate, determined, blunt and outspoken, and he had none of the gloss of French politeness which made Berlioz so much more acceptable in London. Praeger, who knew Wagner well, said that his "natural characteristic was a plainness and directness of speech, which often took the form of abruptness"; he was "impatient of incapacity, blunt in speech, and vehement in declamation, even with bursts of occasional rudeness"; he had none of the amiability which "usually runs into insincerity."[3]

In London Wagner was also handicapped by being unable to speak English. Hence the season passed uneasily, and not without friction.

Added, no doubt, to some tactlessness on his part, and the short time

[1] Praeger, p. 141.   [2] Ibid., pp. 124–5.   [3] Ibid., p. 196.

Z

allowed for rehearsing in London, Wagner had to face the ill-will of most of the professional critics, who, led by Davison of *The Times*, were nearly all ardent Mendelssohn-worshippers, and were bitterly prejudiced against anyone who did not see perfection in everything that Mendelssohn had done. They didn't like Wagner's music, nor his theories and ideals, and they could not forgive him his expressed anti-Jewish views. Already before he came to London he was condemned as a conductor, and from start to finish of the season, Davison, Chorley, and most of the remaining critics kept firing at him a steady stream of gnat-like deprecatory remarks intended to show that he was easily the worst conductor the Society had ever engaged, and that, if continued, his engagement would bring disaster to the Society and its orchestra. Davison had told Praeger that "as long as I hold the sceptre of musical criticism, I'll not let him have any chance here." That was said before Wagner had reached London. Then, Wagner would not pay calls on the London critics, although Praeger had assured him that such was the custom. There were other things that jarred: Wagner didn't like to wear white kid gloves when conducting, as was customary at the Philharmonic, and showed his dislike of that custom quite plainly. Mendelssohn would never have done any such thing. When he was asked to conduct a symphony by Lachner, Wagner replied: "What! have I come all this way to conduct a prize symphony by Lachner? No! No!" And when one of the orchestra told him that "they had not been in the habit of taking this movement so slowly, and that, perhaps, the next had been a trifle too fast," can it be expected that the self-willed German would keep control of his temper and his tongue?[1]

After each concert the puny critics revelled in their opportunities of abusing Wagner's conducting. Even when a performance was admittedly good the *Times* critic could not bring himself to give Wagner any of the credit for it: "Haydn's Symphony No. 7 was executed with amazing spirit. Such a familiar work, however, in the hands of such a company of players, would fare well even without a conductor." When Wagner conducted the *Eroica* symphony from memory, even though his memory did not fail him, and all went well, the same critic asked his readers to imagine what would have happened "supposing" there had been a mishap: "Supposing a leading instrument, entrusted with an important passage, were to be found 'napping' (which is possible), and that Herr Wagner's memory should fail him at a pinch (which is possible—for if Homer nods, why not the author of *Lohengrin*?), what would be the consequence? A dead standstill, nothing less. Herr Wagner, however, did not 'nod' last night, but exhibited unabated energy and fire."[2]

Davison could not understand Wagner's beat: "He conducts with great vivacity, and beats 'up' and 'down' indiscriminately. At least *we* could not, with the best intentions, distinguish his 'ups' from his 'downs,' and if the members of the band are down to his 'ups' and up to his 'downs'

---

[1] Praeger, pp. 202, 217, 227, 234.   [2] Hueffer, pp. 53–4, from *The Times*.

by the end of the season, we shall be ready to present each of them with a quill tooth-pick, as a forfeit for our own lack of discernment."[1]

That a critic should fail to understand a conductor's beat is perhaps not so very distressing, but when an orchestra fails to do so, the situation becomes much more serious. After the second concert Davison had still not mastered Wagner's beat, and the "new readings" and flexible *tempi* of the German conductor were all wrong: "We may begin by saying that the band has not yet learnt to comprehend—or, at least, does not appear to be over ready and eager to follow with that undeviating attention indisputable to a good performance—the motions of Herr Wagner's *baton*. For our own parts, the more closely we observe, the less we can understand him. He seems to have no fixed basis upon which to found, no system to render intelligible, his manner of beating. Under these circumstances it was not surprising that the familiar overture to *Der Freischütz*—which, to make matters more perplexing, was full of 'new readings,' retardations and accelerations of time, etc.,—did not go with quite as much precision as was desirable."[2] All the same, the overture was encored.

The *Eroica* had been "all sixes and sevens," the first movement of the choral symphony was "all higgledy-piggledy"; it seemed like going to pieces, but only by good luck "the end was actually attained without a breakdown." The *Hebrides* overture was "zig-zag," Wagner's reading of the *Jupiter* symphony was "fantastic, old-maidish, and ultra-sentimental," and the first movement was "murdered outright." Wagner, who "is not a musician at all," made "a signal failure in this country, as a composer and as a *chef d'orchestre*." In fact, nothing would please the Mendelssohnian critic; Wagner's music and his conducting drew nothing but peevish fault-finding from a critic who was clearly determined not to be pleased: "The engagement of Herr Wagner has not proved fortunate. No foreign conductor ever came with such extraordinary pretensions and produced so unfavourable an impression. We should not quarrel with Herr Wagner's 'new readings,' although we agree with few of them, if he could render them intelligible to his orchestra. But this he has failed to do, and the result has been a series of performances unparalleled for inefficiency. The fact is that the author of *Lohengrin* knows better how to theorise fancifully than to reduce his theories to practice. His conducting shows a great lack of the requisite science as his music. . . . Herr Wagner has cut a sorry figure in this country, where plain common sense goes for something. . . . We believe him to be a very clever man, one of the most subtle and specious indeed of a race of modern German system-makers; but his works present irrefutable proof that his organisation is *not* musical, and a musician, like a poet, is born, not made. Another such set of concerts would go far to annihilate the Philharmonic Society."

Chorley thought that Wagner had entirely spoiled the Philharmonic orchestra: "his reading may be credited with a certain coarse and overstrained

[1] *Mus. World*, March 17, 1855, p. 171.   [2] *Ibid.*, March 31, 1855, p. 203.

enthusiasm. To impress this on the orchestra, that precision which the band (with all its imperfections) had been wrought during later years, has been already sacrificed. A case of more discreditable scrambling through well-known music—period and place considered—is not in our recollection." (*Athenæum*.) Chorley decided that Wagner was a complete failure: "Herr Wagner makes no way with his public as a conductor. The *sinfonia* of Mozart (No. 39 in E flat) went worse than we have ever heard it go. The violins were rarely together; the wind instruments were hardly able to hold out in the middle movement, with such caricatured slowness was that *Andante con moto* taken,—and the *finale* was degraded into a confused romp by a speed as excessive." (*Athenæum*.)

Davison and Chorley between them, aided by some of the smaller fry, seem to have thoroughly enjoyed tearing Wagner to shreds. It is very probable that the Philharmonic players did not at first understand the movements of Wagner's baton, or rather, they did not understand that he did not use it to mark the time-beat. They would no doubt find it difficult to grasp that he used it, as Praeger and Seidl said, to shape the phrase and the melody, to show the expression and the underlying temperament of the music. His flexible *tempi* and disregard of the traditional *tempi* of the orchestra's renderings of the classical symphonies would no doubt be upsetting to players of long standing who thought that they knew all that there was to know about these works. That Wagner could not talk to them in their own language, and that he had to make do with one rehearsal when two would hardly have been sufficient, would add to the difficulty of securing a good understanding between conductor and conducted. No doubt there were some anxious moments at these under-rehearsed performances, and possibly some of the "nervous trepidation" that Davison wrote about.

But if everything was painted in such dark colours by the Mendelssohn-worshippers, there was obviously another side to the picture. Hogarth of the *Daily News* found much that pleased him in Wagner's renderings. The Haydn symphony (which would have been equally well played without a conductor!) "was certainly never more delightfully played. The *Andante* was taken a little slower than usual here, and we thought that the effect of the movement was thereby enhanced." And the *Eroica*, which *might have been* such a fiasco *if* Wagner's memory had failed him, was "magnificently executed from beginning to end; we never heard the band play more evidently *con amore*, nor ever observed a better understanding or more complete sympathy between them and the conductor, and we felt as much gratified as surprised that such a result should have been effected by a single rehearsal."[1] Writing about the first concert in the *Illustrated London News*,[2] the same critic declared that Wagner was just as complete a success as Davison and Chorley had said he was a complete failure: "His appearance at the head of the Philharmonic band enabled the public to judge only of one

[1] Hueffer, p. 57.   [2] March 17, 1855.

thing—his capacity as a *chef d'orchestre*; a point which that one evening settled beyond all question. Though the whole orchestra—till the rehearsal, two days before—were utter strangers to him, yet that single rehearsal had established so thoroughly an understanding between them, that, at the concert, every piece was performed with a clearness, spirit, and delicacy which we have never heard surpassed; and this was the more remarkable, as his manner of marking the time, and his readings of many passages, differed materially from those of his predecessor. . . . So convinced were the audience of the admirable manner in which he had acquitted himself that, at the conclusion of the concert, he was saluted with repeated rounds of applause."

The critic of *The Spectator* also found a freshness in Wagner's performances of well-worn pieces that had long been ploughed through time and again during the last thirty or forty years under the joint direction of so many leaders and complacent conductors: "It is felt on all hands that the present conductor, Herr Wagner, gives a certain newness of character even to the orchestral works which are most familiar to us. This was strikingly exemplified in the case of the overture to *Der Freischütz*, which, though always heard with pleasure, *has long since ceased to create any remarkable sensation*. Now, however, a feeling of freshness was infused into it to which we had long been strangers; the audience were animated and excited by it as of old, and the sudden outburst of applause which accompanied the final chord showed how much this had been the case. A stronger testimony to the skill of the conductor could not have been given, and the effect is easily accounted for. The completeness with which the performers are 'held in hand' by the conductor has always been a marked feature in German orchestral playing. Under his baton, the largest band is as easily swayed, as flexible, as readily accelerated, retarded, or hushed to the softest whisper, as the performers of a chamber quartet under the impulse of their leader. Wagner has already obtained this control over the band; *a fact willingly admitted by the ablest of its members*; and in this *Freischütz* overture, . . . Wagner gives every passage the same dramatic reading which it has in the opera itself." (*The Spectator*.)

In the Choral Symphony, which to Davison was "all higgledy-piggledy," the critic of *The Spectator* asserted that "Wagner's ability was equally conspicuous."

Wagner's own account of his relations with the Philharmonic orchestra in London was certainly much better than Davison and Chorley would have had us believe was the case; and although he admitted that there were difficulties, and probably took little trouble with the Italian arias and the concertos that he (unwillingly) was obliged to conduct, his impression of his season in London was that it ended as a triumph for him: "At the last concert the public and the orchestra roused themselves to a demonstration against the London critics. I have always been told that my audiences were very much in my favour, and of the orchestra I could see that it was always most willing to follow my intentions as far as bad habits and want of time would allow. . . . The musicians rose solemnly, and, together with the whole thickly crowded hall, began a storm of applause so continuous that I really felt awkward.   After that the band crowded round me to shake hands, and even some ladies and gentlemen of the public held out their hands to me, which I had to press warmly.   In this manner my absurd London expedition finally took the character of a triumph for me, and I was pleased at least to observe the independence of the public which this time it showed towards the critics."[1]

Nevertheless, measured by the Mendelssohnian standard, Wagner was a failure in London.   If only his conducting could have been clothed in Mendelssohn's personality, and if his music had been something like Mendelssohn's, he would probably have been the greatest conductor that London had hitherto known.   But he was a disturbing little egoist, who would not be polite or flattering, who could not even talk English, who wanted more rehearsals than anybody else had ever asked for, and who would not give the orchestra (and the critics) a plain, straightforward, four-square time-beat such as they had been used to.

So Wagner left London never to return until, after his position had been established, he came back to give six concerts at the Royal Albert Hall in 1877.   Wilhelm Ganz said that he was then "no longer at his best, and had lost something of his great skill as a conductor."[2]   Hueffer admitted that "he scarcely did himself justice on this occasion," and added that in any case "Wagner's strength did not lie in keeping great masses together by a firm beat, or in helping an orchestra over the difficulties of making acquaintance with new and intricate music."   It was then that Richter came to the rescue.

But in spite of Wagner's undoubted influence on the development of orchestral conducting as an interpretative art, the Davisons and Chorleys of London could never forget that although he quite appropriately conformed to the Philharmonic's custom of wearing white kid gloves while conducting Mendelssohn's *Italian* Symphony,[3] he flung away these gloves as soon as the symphony was over.   This slight to the composer that they adored was quite enough to damn him in their eyes.

Although Joachim was by no means a wholesale admirer of Wagner's music, and found his personality rather going against the grain, he had to admit Wagner's ability and power as a conductor: "The fellow has a lively sense of feeling for the music he conducts, and has the conductor's gift of imparting that feeling to the players in the orchestra, of which he is the complete master.   Were he as modest as he is capable, he would be just right.   Unfortunately that is not the case."[4]   Modesty had no part in Wagner's make-up, and is a quality with which outstanding conductors are not as a rule very generously endowed.

[1] Hueffer, pp. 58, 59.   See also Wagner's *My Life*, II, p. 625.   [2] Ganz, p. 171.
[3] Davison, p. 169.   [4] Moser, p. 214.

When it came to the practical management, organisation and administration of an orchestra, Wagner was no mere visionary filled with Utopian ideas that could never be carried out in practice; his plan for improving the organisation of the Dresden orchestra (1846)[1] contains nothing but sound workable propositions, devised by one who was able to put his finger on every weak spot and shortcoming, and who was able to point out the remedy for everything which interfered with the well-being of the players and stood in the way of the artistic ideals he had set up as his ultimate object. In this respect he was much more practically-minded than Berlioz, and asked for nothing that was impossible or even unreasonable. As it happened, the hide-bound court administration at Dresden turned down the whole report, and the loss, artistically, was theirs.

OTHER GERMAN CONDUCTORS

Wagner recognised two sorts of German conductors; these were, the old type of which there were then (c. 1860) very few left, and a later generation "who came forth from the school of Mendelssohn, and flourished under his protection and recommendation."[2] The earlier type he characterised as "a formidable personage who knew how to make himself respected at his post—sure of his business, strict, despotic, and by no means polite."[3] To this class belonged Carl Wilhelm Ferdinand Guhr (1787–1848) of Frankfort. Guhr was clearly a disciplinarian; Berlioz said of him in 1842: "It is plain that he will never err through over-indulgence when at the head of his orchestra."[4] Edward Holmes saw him conduct in 1828, and observed how he took care that "the musicians attend to their parts, though there seems to be little fear that they will be omitted through carelessness and indifference."[5] Guhr seems to have been much respected by the musicians of his time, and Wagner referred to him as having been wonderfully renowned as "a conductor of genius."[6] Unlike most of the old Germans, Guhr evidently had a weakness for sensational effects. Thus, in a performance of Haydn's *Creation*, at the words *Let there be Light*, he caused several Prussian and Austrian military bands to join in the great major chord.[7] Speyer also told how on one occasion, at a performance of the same work under Guhr, at the word *Light*, all the gaslights in the theatre were suddenly turned up.[8]

Friedrich Schneider of Dessau was another of "this now extinct species" (Wagner). Holmes called him a celebrated *Kapellmeister*, and thought that his compositions for the church would leave his name an undying inheritance.

Lindpaintner of Stuttgart, Reissiger of Dresden, and Marschner of Hanover were just a little later on the scene, yet were too early to be counted as belonging to the Mendelssohnian school. The first of these appears to have been a very capable conductor. Wagner's words—"of blessed

---

[1] In Vol. XII of the Collected Literary Works; summary in Newman, I, p. 434.
[2] *On Cond.*, p. 7.　　[3] *Ibid.*, p. 2.　　[4] *Mem.*, II, p. 9.　　[5] *Rambles*, p. 38
[6] *My Life*, I, p. 133.　　[7] Hiller, *Mendelssohn Letters*, p. 125.　　[8] Speyer, p. 269.

memory"—and that Mendelssohn thought he was the best conductor in Germany, are good testimony to his ability, and Gassner added the tribute that Lindpaintner was able, as few others could, to train an orchestra, keep it together, and give good performances. Berlioz praised the playing of his orchestra at Stuttgart, but criticised Lindpaintner (together with Mendelssohn, Krebs and Guhr) for his too hurried *tempi*. Lindpaintner conducted with considerable success the concerts of the New Philharmonic Society at the Exeter Hall in London in 1853, and again in 1854.

Reissiger was Weber's successor and Wagner's colleague at Dresden. He was apparently an easy-going conductor, and for that reason was much beloved by the Dresden orchestral players. According to Wasielewski,[1] he would look at his watch during a performance, and would if necessary hurry the *tempo* in order that he should arrive home not later than he had promised his wife to be back. Praeger described Reissiger as a "phlegmatic" conductor, in contrast to Wagner who was "energetic"; he also knew how to smooth over difficulties by giving way to and thus pleasing the *Intendant* at Dresden, an art which Wagner could not or would not master. It is likely that Reissiger was one of those conductors of whom Wagner said that they were famed for their skill in bringing out an opera in a fortnight, for their clever cuts, for effective closes written to please singers, and for their interpolations in other composer's scores.[2]

Marschner, after experience at Dresden, Dantzig and Leipzig, settled down at Hanover in 1831, where he remained for twenty-eight years, doing much routine-work with a rather second-rate orchestra in spite of his considerable reputation in Germany as a very successful opera-composer.

A younger group, born a few years before Mendelssohn, included Dorn, Krebs, Franz Lachner and Georg Müller. Rietz and Hiller were a few years younger than Mendelssohn, and came into what Wagner called the "elegant and cultured" class. Most of their work was done in the larger German towns between the end of the 'thirties and the beginning of the 'seventies. They may be classed as good workmen whose attainment never fell below or rose much above the German standard which prevailed after Weber's time, and before the more exacting demands of Wagner's later operas called for conducting and playing of a higher order.

Heinrich Dorn, a bitter opponent of Wagner, followed Praeger (the elder) at the Leipzig theatre in 1829, was the successor of Krebs at Hamburg in 1832, of Wagner at Riga, and of Nicolai at Berlin. He had a keen ear, a good memory, and was precise and strict. As a conductor his bearing was quiet, the movements of his baton were short and sharp, and with slight motions of his head he would indicate their entries to the players. Spontini, whom Dorn greatly admired, bequeathed to him his baton.[3]

Franz Lachner, the best-known of the three brothers, all of whom became conductors, was *Kapellmeister* in Vienna and Mannheim before going to the court opera at Munich. Although hardly an inspired conductor, he was

[1] *Aus Siebzig Jahren*, p. 171.   [2] *On Cond.*, p. 7.   [3] Krebs, p. 98.

certainly very capable, reliable and painstaking, and it was his training and building up of the orchestra at Munich that laid the foundation which fitted it to undertake so successfully the great performances under Bülow of *Tristan* and *Die Meistersänger* during the 'sixties. It is probable that Clara Schumann summed him up very fairly when she said that Lachner was "a capable conductor, although he seems to have more understanding than poetry; but at any rate he commands great respect."[1]

Karl Krebs, first at Hamburg and then at Dresden, was said to be a "severe" conductor. He was one of those encountered by Berlioz in the course of his German tour in 1843. According to the French composer, Krebs fulfilled "his functions with a talent and strictness that is excellent in a conductor."[2]

Schumann would, no doubt, come into the class that "came forth from the school of Mendelssohn." Excepting his musical gift, which was ample, Schumann appears to have lacked all the necessary qualities of a good conductor. The following, written by one who was present, describes a rehearsal of Schumann's *Faust* under the composer's direction at Dresden in 1849: "His manner of conducting was just as peculiar as his whole nature was unorthodox. He was deeply absorbed in the score, while his baton seemed to move quite independently and mechanically. The Dresden orchestra was accustomed to play under the watchful eye and steady guidance of its conductor; Schumann, however, took it for granted that these players, whose main concern in life was the mastery of their instruments, would intuitively give to their rendering of the music the same inspired understanding that he himself was able to give to it. Inattention on the part of the players often brought about confusion or even chaos, and constant but inevitable repetition served only to increase the despair of all who were present. When, in spite of frequent trials and repetitions, an unharmonious horn-note broke in on the quiet of a placid *piano* passage, annoyance and irritation gave place to amazement when with inexhaustible patience Schumann would lay down his baton, excitedly rub his hands together, and then in a most polite and friendly manner request the orchestra to play the whole passage once again."[3] Another witness of Schumann's conducting, Robert Radecke of Berlin, testified that in 1851, when Schumann rehearsed his choral society at Düsseldorf, his soft and gentle voice was hardly ever heard, and that the direction was actually in the hands of his wife, Clara Schumann, who accompanied on the piano on these occasions.[4] Regarding a performance of his *Paradies und Peri* which Schumann conducted at Dresden, Wagner remarked that "his peculiar awkwardness in conducting on that occasion aroused my sympathy for the conscientious and energetic musician whose work made so strong an appeal to me."[5]

Yet it is curious that Schumann appears to have had no idea of his

---

[1] Joachim, *Letters*, p. 153.   [2] *Mem.*, II, p. 87.
[3] Erler, II, p. 96 From *Jugendleben*, by Ludwig Meinardus.
[4] *Ibid.*, II, p. 16.   [5] Wagner, *My Life*, I, p. 385.

shortcomings, and fancied himself as a conductor well enough to ask Sterndale Bennett if he could not arrange for him to appear in that capacity at the London Philharmonic in 1851: "I should not like to remain idle at my wife's side, but should also like to show myself as a musician, namely as a Conductor, which is my greatest desire."[1]

Julius Rietz belonged to the Mendelssohn school, but unlike most of them, he was not a pianist; his instrument was the violoncello. He succeeded Mendelssohn both at Düsseldorf and Leipzig, and followed Reissiger at Dresden. It was said that his manner, unlike Mendelssohn's, was brusque and rough, but he knew his scores intimately, and was said never to have made a mistake while conducting. His performances were precise and finished, but evidently dry and uninspired. His rendering of the *Meistersänger* at Dresden is said to have been remarkable for the way he kept the same unyielding *tempo* going thoughout the whole of the opera. It will be remembered that Rietz, with Lachner and Hiller, came under the lash of Wagner's pen.

Most of Hiller's work as a conductor lay in the second half of the century. He had some experience at Düsseldorf, Leipzig and Paris, before becoming *Kapellmeister* at Cologne. Wasielewski (*Aus Siebzig Jahren*) has left some comments on Hiller's conducting. At Paris, where he conducted Italian opera for some time, he is said to have driven the singers with too tight a rein. At a musical festival he took the *Hallelujah Chorus* so slowly that David, the leader, reckoned that they might possibly be finished in time to begin next year's festival. On another occasion, when rehearsing Beethoven's C minor symphony, as a safety measure Hiller arranged to beat two blank bars before the beginning. Unfortunately some of the players forgot all about this at the performance and started immediately, while others waited for two bars before beginning. The result was chaos and a complete breakdown. It seems, however, that conductors in those days did have some difficulty in getting a good start for the first movement of this symphony, and it throws some light on the state of the conductor's art at the time: "Habeneck and Valentino, in conducting this masterpiece in the first *Allegro*, adopt a wise method to produce an *ensemble* at the onset, by beating a bar previous to the subject; a proceeding which we recommend for adoption at the next performance of the symphony."[2] It was the amateur conductor's dodge—"one bar for nothing."

Hiller wrote an essay on conducting from memory,[3] and in it very much deprecated any display of virtuosity or obtrusion of the conductor's personality into the rendering of the music. Wagner had no great opinion of Hiller as a conductor. He was amongst those (the others being Reissiger and Mendelssohn) who seemed to be quite unable to overcome their usual habit of taking the *tempo di minuetto* in Beethoven's 8th symphony otherwise than in waltz-time, in spite of Wagner's

---

[1] S. Bennett, *Life*, p. 220.   [2] *Mus. World*, April 11, 1839, p. 232.
[3] *Mus. und Per.*, *Ueber das Auswendig-Dirigiren*.

convincing arguments that the movement was intended to be played in minuet-time.

Too hurried *tempi* appears to have been a fairly common complaint against the German conductors just before the middle of last century. Wagner blamed Mendelssohn and his school for this; Berlioz allowed that the Germans ought to know best how to play their own operas, but he condemned the "tremendous pace" at which he heard French operas performed at Stuttgart, Leipzig, Hamburg and Frankfort.[1] Even the German Gassner (1844) protested against the "tearing pace of quick movements at the present time."

In the case of opera, that habit of speeding through a work might possibly be attributed to the fact that German conductors in the course of their ordinary duty had to direct so many routine-performances of familiar operas. That in itself would be enough to bring about some lack of interest in the quality of the playing, and would inevitably engender a certain careless haste in getting over the ground. But the same excuse could hardly be offered in the case of concert-performances. There it may have been due to the common delusion that speed imparts brilliance, to the tendency of the virtuoso to "show off," to mistaken "traditions" which had grown up, to the impression that it was a conductor's duty to "whip up" an orchestra and show off its paces, or to a real lack of sympathetic understanding of the music; for it should not too readily be taken for granted that a conductor, merely because he is one, possesses that gift intuitively.

The tendency of conductors to rush through quick movements, however, was not peculiar to the Mendelssohnian period. It was still rife when Weingartner wrote his brochure *On Conducting* (1895–1905),[2] and to-day we still often hear a *Finale* galloped through, apparently for no better reason than that the orchestra can play it at that rate without missing a note.

BEETHOVEN

Beethoven should not really figure in any survey of conductors, and the only justification for including him in this instance is that the bad conducting of a great man is always more interesting than the good conducting of a small man.

Beethoven held no appointment as *Kapellmeister* either at Bonn or at Vienna. He took charge occasionally of performances of his own works, but had no qualifications as a conductor, no routine-experience as such, and he never travelled far afield to hear orchestras outside of Vienna.

Schindler explained the situation in these words: "At the time when his hearing was yet perfect, he had not often occasion to come in contact with the orchestra, and especially to acquire practice in the conducting department

[1] *Mem.*, II, p. 21.

[2] Weingartner gave an admirable precept: "No slow tempo must be so slow that the melody of the piece is *not yet* recognisable, and no fast tempo so fast that the melody is *no longer* recognisable" (p. 28).

at the theatre, which is the best school for that purpose. In the concert-room the talent most fitted for this difficult function is never fully developed, and remains one-sided and awkward. Thus we see composers of eminence incapable of conducting the orchestra in the performance of their own works, if they have not previously acquired the necessary routine, in listening to, and in superintending numerous bands."[1]

In 1808 Beethoven was invited to become *Kapellmeister* at Cassel. That he did not occupy that position was, no doubt, all for the best, whether regarded from his own point of view or from that of the music at Cassel. Beethoven had enough music in him to have made scores of conductors, but he had neither the necessary experience, the temperament, or the right personality for such work; added to which, his growing deafness would in any case have been enough to prevent him from ever becoming proficient as a conductor.

When we read of Beethoven "conducting" this or that work of his own, it should not be assumed that he took complete control of the playing of the orchestra as a conductor now does. We have already seen that he sometimes sat at the piano and supervised the performance in the manner of the 18th century keyboard-conductor, leaving the actual control to the violinist-leader. But there are also contemporary descriptions of Beethoven standing up in the orchestra and making movements with his arms which might easily be mistaken for conducting in the modern sense of the word. Descriptions by Moscheles, Seyfried, Czerny, Franz Wild, Ries, Reichardt, Spohr, Schindler and Atterbohm, all tally in that they make it quite clear that even if Beethoven did sometimes give a time-beat, his main concern was to indicate the expression, the dynamics, and the style of the performance in general by means of gesticulations.

Beethoven's method of indicating the expression appears to have been quite his own, as the following extracts will show:

"He had ears only for his composition and was ceaselessly occupied by manifold gesticulations to indicate the desired expression. He used to suggest a *diminuendo* by crouching down more and more, and at a *pianissimo* he would almost creep under the desk. When the volume of sound grew he rose up also as if out of a stage-trap, and with the entrance of the power of the band he would stand upon the tips of his toes almost as big as a giant, and waving his arms, seemed about to soar upwards to the skies. Everything about him was active, not a bit of his organism idle, and the man was comparable to a *perpetuum mobile*."[2]

"For scarcely had the music begun before its creator offered a bewildering spectacle. At the *piano* passages he sank upon his knee, at the *forte* he leaped up, so that his figure, now shrivelling to that of a dwarf, disappeared under the desk, and anon stretched up far above it like a giant, his hands and arms

---

[1] Moscheles' translation of Schindler, in *Life of Beethoven*, I, p. 112.
[2] From Seyfried's *Studien*, Thayer, II, p. 94. Another translation of the same in Moscheles' *Life of Beethoven*, II, p. 309.

working as if with the beginning of the music a thousand lives had entered every member. At first this happened without disturbance of the effect of the composition, for the disappearance and appearance of his body was synchronous with the dying away and the swelling of the music; but all at once the genius ran ahead of his orchestra and the master disappeared at the *forte* passages and appeared at the piano."[1]

"Beethoven had accustomed himself to give the signs of expression to his orchestra by all manner of extraordinary motions of his body. So often a *sforzando* occurred, he tore his arms which he had previously crossed upon his breast, with great vehemence asunder. At a *piano*, he bent himself down, and the lower, the softer he wished to have it. Then when a *crescendo* came, he raised himself again by degrees, and upon the commencement of the *forte*, sprang bolt upright. To increase the *forte* yet more, he would some-times, also, join in with a shout to the orchestra, without being aware of it."[2]

"At last he (Moscheles) amuses his hearers exceedingly by imitating Beethoven's movements as a conductor; his stooping down more and more until he almost disappeared at the 'piano' passages, the gradual rising up at the 'crescendo,' and standing tiptoe and bounding up at the 'fortissimo.' Moscheles does not forget to add: 'Inasmuch, however, as I cannot emulate the great man in his works, I abstain from copying him in his attitudes; with him it was all originality, with me it would be caricature'."[3]

"At a *pianissimo* he knelt down and stretched his arms towards the floor; at a *fortissimo*, like an arrow from the bow, he bounced up, appearing to have suddenly grown tall, and thrust his arms wide asunder; between these two extremes he was constantly swaying up and down."[4]

These are the words of eye-witnesses. Even if Beethoven thought that he was controlling the orchestra, it is fairly clear that he was not really doing so; in fact, he was hampering it, and steps had to be taken to provide some guidance which the players could understand and on which they could depend. Seyfried told us that "the orchestra had to have a care in order not to be led astray by its master,"[5] and at the revival of *Fidelio* in 1814 when "Beethoven conducted, his ardour often rushed him out of time, but Chapelmaster Umlauf, behind his back, guided everything to success with eye and hand."[6]

But it is, at any rate, open to question whether Beethoven ever thought that he was actually conducting at these performances. It is difficult to believe that he would have tolerated the presence of another active conductor if he had imagined that he was himself in control of the performance.

A translated extract from a Viennese journal which appeared in the *Harmonicon*,[7] referring to the first performance of the Choral Symphony, suggests that Beethoven's share in the performance was not that of the conductor, but rather that of one who supervised the rendering, without

[1] From Franz Wild's *Autob.*, Thayer, II, p. 262.   [2] Spohr, *Autob.*, I, p. 186.
[3] *Life of Moscheles*, II, p. 140.   [4] From Atterbohm, Hanslick, p. 276, f.n.
[5] *Studien*, Thayer, II, p. 94.   [6] *Treitschke*, Thayer, II, p. 278.   [7] Oct., 1824, p. 180.

actually controlling it: "The leaders of the music were Kapellmeister Umlauf and M. Schupanzigh, and the great Composer himself assisted on that occasion.   He took his place at the side of the principal leader (Umlauf), and, with his original score before him, indicated the different movements and determined the precise manner in which they were to be given; for, unfortunately, the state of his hearing prevented him from doing more."

There are stories of misunderstandings and breakdowns, and the more deaf Beethoven became, the more distracting were his efforts to direct and influence the performance of his works.   Throughout the whole story there is no evidence that he ever held a baton or any other implement in his hand.

The picture is rather confused, and it is certainly unique.   The tragedy of Beethoven's deafness hangs over it all and gives a sad tinge to what might otherwise appear to have been rather grotesque.   Nature has played some queer tricks, but none more capricious than giving Beethoven the power to conceive the nine great symphonies, the overtures and concertos, *Fidelio*, and the great Mass in D, and then taking away his hearing and letting him stand in the orchestra behaving like a mountebank while the leader and another conductor behind his back did their best to rescue the performance from the effects of his strange conducting.

It seems that Beethoven was also unreliable regarding the *tempi* of his own works.   He changed his mind about the metronome speeds, and Schindler told how he gave the *tempi* for the Choral Symphony to Umlauf at his house, and then altered them again at the rehearsal.

OTHER CONDUCTORS AT VIENNA

The foremost *Kapellmeister* in Vienna during Beethoven's time were Salieri, the senior member of the group and official figure-head, Gyrowetz, Weigl, Umlauf and Seyfried.   No doubt these were all sound and experienced musicians who did their work as conductors well enough according to the standard of their time, but there is no reason to suppose that their gifts in that capacity were at all outstanding.   Beyond the usual statements in musical dictionaries about their careers and their compositions, it is difficult to find anything that will characterise them as conductors.   From an English source we learn that Seyfried was quiet and efficient: "Of this great leader it may with truth be said that, although his absence from the orchestra is at once sensibly felt, yet his presence there is scarcely noticed from the unassuming manner in which he leads; his mode of directing the band is so noiseless that he may be seen, but is never heard."[1]

A rather later generation at Vienna included Gläser, Conradin Kreutzer, Franz and Ignaz Lachner, and Drechsler, all reliable routine conductors of whom the most outstanding was probably Franz Lachner, and who later on was to do good work at Munich.

[1] *Harm.*, June, 1824, p. 117.

It was not until 1841 that Vienna could boast of a conductor who could stand side by side with the best then to be found in France and Germany; this was Otto Nicolai, creator of the Vienna Philharmonic orchestra and composer of *The Merry Wives of Windsor*.

Berlioz had high praise for Nicolai: "I regard him as one of the best orchestral leaders I ever met. He is one of those men whose influence alone suffices to bestow a marked musical superiority on the town in which they live, when provided with the necessary opportunities. He possesses three qualities indispensable to a finished conductor. He is a learned composer, skilled and enthusiastic, he has a strong feeling for rhythm, and his mode of conducting is perfectly clear and exact; in short, he is an ingenious and indefatigable organiser, grudging neither time nor trouble at rehearsals; one who knows what he is doing because he only does what he knows. Hence the excellent qualities, moral and material, the confidence, devotion, patience, marvellous assurance and unity of action of the *Kärntnerthor* orchestra."[1]

Nicolai was strict and thorough, a disciplinarian, a hard worker who was careful of detail; he transformed his orchestra from a collection of individuals into one great instrument.[2] Like all good conductors, Nicolai knew the value of careful preparation; for the Choral symphony he required thirteen rehearsals. Vienna heard that great work properly played for the first time under Nicolai in 1843.

Unfortunately Vienna was not to keep its first great conductor for long. Already in 1844 an effort had been made to secure Nicolai for Berlin, but in the capacity of *Kapellmeister* at the *Domkirche*. This offer was refused on the ground that such a position would not provide sufficient scope for one who was essentially an operatic conductor, and who wished to remain such. A further offer of an engagement as third *Kapellmeister* at the opera was also refused, as well it might be, for Nicolai was conductor-in-chief at the opera in Vienna, and occupied a high position in the music of the Austrian capital; in Vienna he conducted none but the operas of Mozart, Beethoven, Gluck and Cherubini.[3] A breach with the directors of the opera at Vienna, who had declined to produce his *Merry Wives of Windsor*, eventually led him to resign his position there in 1847. After some long-drawn-out negotiations Nicolai accepted the post of *Kapellmeister* at the Berlin opera, virtually as successor to Meyerbeer, and as a colleague of Taubert. So Vienna lost its best conductor, and there was nobody there fit to step into his shoes. Neither Hellmesberger, Reuling nor Proch could carry on what Nicolai had started, and for some years Vienna was again without any outstanding conductor.

HABENECK

The very high standard of performance reached by the orchestra at the Paris *Opéra* and the Conservatoire Concerts during the second quarter of

[1] *Mem.*, II, p. 185. [2] Kralik, p. 18. [3] Kapp, p. 63.

last century cannot have been due only to the individual excellence of each of the players. A combination of the world's greatest players would not necessarily make the world's finest orchestra; failing an equally good conductor, it would always be possible that an inferior orchestra under an outstandingly good conductor would give the better performance.

In Habeneck Paris undoubtedly found the right man to take charge of a body of players which could hardly be rivalled in Berlin, Dresden, Munich, Vienna or London, and which easily surpassed that best that any other German or any Italian town could produce.

Habeneck was a first-rate violinist, but a second-rate composer. According to Wagner, he had no special "genius"; he was not an "inspired" musician who closed his eyes and allowed some God-given power to operate through the medium of his person; we do not read of Habeneck that "the temple of music was a holy place to him," or that "he held everyone bound to him by magic fetters"; we are not told that the power of his eye (he wore spectacles) at once hypnotised his players and swept away from their path all technical difficulties, nor is it suggested that his musical insight went deeper than that of a dozen other conductors. But we do read that Habeneck was master of the orchestra and that everyone obeyed him,[1] that he rehearsed "with extraordinary care,"[2] that if Beethoven's ninth symphony was at first incomprehensible he kept on rehearsing it until he and his players thoroughly understood it, and that they were able to give an intelligible rendering of that great work in Paris before Leipzig, Dresden, Vienna or London could do it justice. We know that the Germans Wagner, Lobe, Rellstab, Schindler, Mendelssohn and Hiller gave unqualified praise to the playing of the Conservatoire orchestra under Habeneck, that the Frenchmen Fétis, Kastner, Elwart and Deldevez, and the Englishman Ella, could find no fault with his performances of Beethoven's symphonies. The man that could do so much, even though he beat time with a violin bow, and had only a first violin part in front of him, even though he had no "abstract-aesthetical inspiration" to help him, was certainly an uncommonly fine conductor.

The great French conductor was evidently something of a martinet, and his rule at the *Opéra* was no doubt somewhat dictatorial. Berlioz even went so far as to say that the manager, M. Pillet, went in terror of Habeneck. Schindler too, characterised Habeneck's manner as commanding rather than ingratiating. But Elwart said of him that he hid a kind heart beneath a rough exterior, and credited him with a sympathetic attitude to the young students at the Conservatoire.[3] Kastner, after laying down what was required of a good conductor, continued: "As a model of this type, we cannot resist a desire to mention the able conductor of the *Conservatoire* and the *Académie Royale de Musique*, M. Habeneck, who in our opinion combines them all, and represents for us the ideal type of an orchestral conductor."[4]

---

[1] Wagner, *On Cond.*, p. 15.   [2] Berlioz, *Mem.*, I, p. 295.   [3] Elwart, p. 328.
[4] *Cours, Supp.*, p. 15.

Berlioz, of course, regarded the official musicians in Paris as his natural
enemies, and there was no doubt some justification on either side for this
cat-and-dog state of affairs, but his tales about Habeneck need not be
accepted at their face value any more than many of the other lurid stories
which make such entertaining reading of the *Memoirs*. Conductors at that
time did not take their responsibilities quite so seriously as they do now;
they were regarded as mere time-beaters rather than as interpreters of music,
and we hear of one who suspended his operations while he paused to blow
his nose, and of Habeneck's way of stopping to take a pinch of snuff while
the performance proceeded without any time-beat. From Sir Charles
Hallé[1] we learn that it was Habeneck's habit occasionally to lay down his
stick (bow) and take snuff, and it was just this habit that caused the unfortunate incident at the performance of Berlioz's *Requiem* in 1837.[2] It was sheer
bad luck that the snuff-taking should have occurred just as the performance
was approaching a moment when the guidance of a conductor was most
essential, and we cannot acquit Habeneck of gross carelessness; but when we
are asked to believe that the great conductor deliberately chose to make a
fool of himself in public just in order to spite Berlioz, we must bear in mind
that the author of the *Memoirs* was also the author of *Evenings in the orchestra*,
and that his fertile imagination and inimitable humour fitted him perfectly
for making a good story out of an unfortunate accident.

That Habeneck conducted the Beethoven symphonies with only a first
violin part in front of him we have on the authority of Berlioz[3] and
Deldevez.[4] The latter played under Habeneck and eventually became
chef d'orchestre at both the *Opéra* and the Conservatoire concerts. He stated
that the parts used by Habeneck, in which each of the principal instrumental
entries was marked with a red cross, were then (1878) in the Conservatoire
library. They are probably there now. It has been implied that Habeneck's
use of a first violin part denoted a lack of musicianship, an inability to read a
full score. The man who spent his life in leading and conducting the finest
orchestras in Paris, who conducted the first performances of many operas
by Rossini, Meyerbeer, Auber and Halévy, and who himself composed
concertos, operas and ballets, was no half-baked musician who would be
bewildered by the sight of a full score. Habeneck used a violin part because
as a violinist-conductor he was accustomed to hold his violin in one hand and
his bow in the other, in which case a full score is a nuisance on account of
the continual turning over of the pages. He and his orchestra knew the
Beethoven symphonies through and through; he needed no score, and his
players did not depend on a sign from the conductor every time they joined
in. In any case a score is not *read* by a conductor during a performance;
it serves merely as a reminder of what is coming, or as Weingartner put it,
as a support for his memory.[5] During a performance a conductor does not

---

[1] Hallé, p. 66.   [2] See *Mem.*, I, p. 290.   [3] *Ibid.*, II, p. 241, f.n.   [4] Deldevez, p. 141, f.n.
[5] "He should know it so thoroughly that during the performance the score is merely a
support for his memory, not a fetter on his thought" (*On Cond.*, p. 40).

and cannot read all the detail in a score; if he attempted to do so his attention would be more than fully occupied, and he would be quite unable to look after the playing of the orchestra.   Habeneck no doubt felt that he was more free to devote his whole attention to the orchestra when he was saved the distraction of constantly turning over the pages of a score which he did not require and knew perfectly well.   And who shall say that he was not quite wise in dispensing with the score?   Far from being a "barbarism" or "deplorable system,"[1] it was more likely good common-sense.   And whatever his method, the fact remains that Habeneck's performances of Beethoven's symphonies were acknowledged to be the best that could be heard during his time all the world over.   He was certainly a great conductor and was probably all the better for being without "abstract-aesthetical inspiration."

Schindler said that Habeneck's *tempi* in the Beethoven symphonies were very deliberate; he did not race through the quick movements and get over the ground quickly, as Mendelssohn recommended.   Schindler had very little fault to find with Habeneck's *tempi*, and wondered if the great French conductor had been in communication with Beethoven in his dreams when he slept with that composer's scores under his pillow![2]

Chorley, although his ideal was Mendelssohn, acknowledged that Habeneck's complete control over his orchestra was remarkable: "Nothing can exceed his perfect sway over his forces.   Though he directs with his violin bow, I have never seen him use it; and by the exquisite neatness and precision of the least important or most unmanageable instruments (the piccolo, for example), as they enter, not *scramble*, into their parts when the composition demands them, it may be seen that his presence is everywhere—that his method and meaning have pervaded the whole hundred he commands ere they are paraded before the public."[3]

The following tribute by an English critic, written just after Habeneck's death in 1849, points out that the great French conductor's influence was not confined to the playing of the Paris orchestra alone, but also served as an example and a stimulus to the German *Gewandhaus* and the English Philharmonic orchestras: "Habeneck, having had solely the organisation and direction of the Conservatoire concerts, brought the execution of the symphonies and overtures of the great masters to a pitch of unparalleled perfection. . . . The fire and energy of Habeneck's conducting, his observance of rhythmical time, and the precision and finish which he obtained from his forces, have led to the improvement of the other great orchestras in Europe; and to Habeneck's colouring may be ascribed the perfection afterwards attained by the Leipzig band, and by our own Philharmonic orchestra.   The dazzling brilliancy of the stringed instruments in the Conservatoire band, perhaps, has never been equalled—certainly never surpassed.   Habeneck had the extraordinary faculty—in which he has no

[1] Berlioz, *Mem.*, II, p. 241.   [2] Schindler, *Beethoven in Paris*, pp. 19, 44.
[3] *Mus. and Manners*, I, p. 20.

successor as yet but Costa—of communicating his own feelings to his troops, inspiring them with his zeal, encouraging the timid, rebuking the too daring, rousing the sluggish; and, by thus being identified with the executants, giving to the work under interpretation the charm, truthfulness, and intelligence, as if the spirit of the composer himself were animating the masses." The same writer said that Habeneck had brought about a "revolution in orchestral execution," and that "unity and coherence were the distinctive qualities of Habeneck's system." He added that the great French conductor was a "simple-minded, kind-hearted man."[1]

BERLIOZ

In Paris it was held that because quite two-thirds of the members of an orchestra played on bowed stringed instruments, the logical course was to place it in charge of one who himself was an expert on one of these instruments. Therefore all the regular Paris conductors were violinists, or at any rate, string players.

But Berlioz was neither violinist nor pianist; and who would have thought of putting a guitarist at the head of an orchestra? So Berlioz was never given a permanent appointment as conductor in Paris. When he conducted an orchestra he was not generally put at the head of it by authority of the official musical system in Paris—he put himself there.

Berlioz took to conducting because he found that it was the only way to secure a proper interpretation of his own works: "Since my defeat at the *Théâtre Italien*, I had such mistrust of my own skill as a conductor that I allowed Girard to direct my concerts for some time longer; but, at the fourth performance of *Harold*, he made so serious a mistake at the end of the serenade (where, if one part of the orchestra does not double its speed, the other part cannot go on, because the whole bar of the former corresponds to the half bar of the latter) that, seeing at last that there was no hope of working up the end of the *Allegro* properly, I resolved in future to conduct myself, and not allow anyone else to communicate my ideas to the performers."[2]

In the course of his career Berlioz conducted numerous concerts of his own works in France, Belgium, Germany, Austria, Bohemia, Hungary, Russia and England, and so gained considerable experience. His engagements as conductor, apart from his own works, were few; one was for Jullien's ill-fated season of opera in English at Drury Lane in 1847, and another was the first season of the New Philharmonic Society at the Exeter Hall, London, in 1852, and again in 1855.

In 1856 Berlioz added to his *Instrumentation* a chapter on conducting. There he treated the subject almost entirely as a matter of time-beating; the movements of the baton, diagrammatically described, occupy about half of the chapter, and the rest is given up to such things as metronomic devices, the arrangement of the players on the platform, and some of the common

[1] *Illus. Lon. News*, Feb. 17, 1849.   [2] *Mem.*, I, p. 282.

faults of orchestral playing. The whole essay is full of good sound, practical and common-sense advice; one misses the imagery, the exaggeration and the delightful humour of the author of the *Memoirs*. When Richard Strauss edited and amplified the *Instrumentation* in 1905, he had no amendments to make, and nothing to add to the chapter on conducting.

If Berlioz practised what he preached, he believed in maintaining an exact and steady *tempo*, without *rubato* or any of the flexibility and variability which characterised Wagner's conducting. But like Wagner, Berlioz attached great importance to finding the right *tempo*, and he believed in the usefulness of the metronome, although deprecating any mechanical rigidity of the beat: "I do not mean by this to say that it is necessary to imitate the mathematical regularity of the metronome; all music so performed would become of freezing stiffness, and I even doubt whether it would be possible to observe so flat a uniformity during a certain number of bars. But the metronome is none the less excellent to consult, in order to know the original time, and its chief alterations."[1]

But the writer of the sensible text-book and Berlioz the conductor were evidently not quite the same person. From his musical and literary works we can guess that Berlioz's conducting was no tame-cat affair; although he insisted on a clear time-beat and a steady *tempo*, the composer of the *Symphonie Fantastique* could not possibly have been a colourless time-beater.

Moscheles's comment points to something more exciting and compelling: "Berlioz's conducting inspired the orchestra with fire and enthusiasm, he carried everything as it were by storm."[2]

Seidl's description, gleaned from Cosima Wagner, also shows something much more temperamental and illustrative than the stiff arrows in the text-book: "Now he was up in the air, then under the music-desk; now he turned uneasily to the big drummer, then he was coaxing the flautist; now he was drawing out the tone from the violins, then stabbing through the air at the double-basses, or extracting a cantilena of love-yearning from the violoncellos. The musicians were rather afraid of this demoniac sarcastic face and struggled to escape from his clutches."[3]

But however demonstrative Berlioz was with his gestures and attitudes, he clung to a precise and intelligible time-beat: "The master conducted the chorus and orchestra with very exuberant movements of his arms, and with a beautiful rhythmic precision."[4] Rimsky-Korsakof also confirmed that Berlioz's beat was clear and understandable: "Berlioz's beat was simple, clear, beautiful. No vagaries in shading."[5]

When Berlioz was conducting in London at Drury Lane in 1847-8 it was said that "his beating was emphatic and intelligible, and the mass of instrumentalists followed the slightest indication of his baton, the minutest shade of expression which he desired to obtain, with marvellous accuracy."[6]

---

[1] *Instrum.*, p. 246.   [2] Moscheles, *Life*, II, p. 229.   [3] *Bayreuther Blätter* (1900), p. 305.
[4] Kling, *Le Livre d'Or du Centenaire d'Hector Berlioz*.   [5] Wotton, p. 174.
[6] *Mus. World*, Feb. 12, 1848, p. 97.

Again, at the New Philharmonic in 1852: "his manner of beating was clear, decided and emphatic."[1]

There seems to be little doubt that Berlioz, unlike Wagner, used his baton mainly as a time-giver, and that he relied on other means to secure the expression he required.

Berlioz was decidedly successful as a conductor in London, and the same critics that would not say a good word for Wagner gave him high praise. Davison wrote of his rendering of Mozart's G minor symphony at the New Philharmonic in 1855: "Mr. Berlioz, whose general conception of the symphony would have proved him, had proof been wanting, one of the greatest and most intelligent of conductors."[2] Wagner, who was conducting the old Philharmonic in London at that time, wrote of that selfsame performance: "I . . . was amazed to find a conductor, who was so energetic in the interpretation of his own compositions, sink into the commonest rut of the vulgar time-beater."[3] Wilhelm Ganz, who played under Berlioz at these same concerts in 1852, said that he was a "wonderful conductor," that his beat was "clear and precise," and that "he took endless trouble to get everything right."[4] Sir Charles Hallé, writing about Berlioz in 1837, gave him credit for being not only a perfect conductor, but also a striking figure: "And what a picture he was at the head of his orchestra, with his eagle face, his bushy hair, his air of command, and glowing with enthusiasm. He was the most perfect conductor that I ever set eyes upon, one who held absolute sway over his troops, and played upon them as a pianist upon the keyboard."[5]

We may be sure that Berlioz called for a good deal of colour from his orchestra; no one could orchestrate as he did and be satisfied with dull or colourless playing. We can guess that he would be sometimes polite and insinuating, and at other times cutting or sarcastic. His rehearsals would be no dull affairs, and there would be plenty of hard work for the orchestra.

It seems that Berlioz was by no means popular with the Paris orchestral players. When Tilmant retired from the *Société des Concerts* in 1863, and a new conductor was chosen by vote of the orchestra, there were five ballots before a final decision was reached. In the first ballot Berlioz came in third, with 10 votes out of a total of 102; in the second ballot he got no votes, and only one in the third; in the fourth and fifth ballots he received no votes.[6] Hainl, the 'cellist, was elected, followed closely in number of votes by the violinist Deldevez. The Conservatoire orchestra had clearly made up its mind that it was not going to be conducted by a guitarist.

Berlioz had twice previously angled for an appointment as a regular opera-conductor in Paris, and in both cases had failed. The first was at the *Théâtre Italien*, and the second at the *Opéra* when it was thought that Habeneck would retire and take over the direction of the Conservatoire

[1] *Mus. World*, Nov. 27, 1852, p. 203.   [2] *Ibid.*, June 16, 1855, p. 381.
[3] Wagner, *My Life*, II, p. 628.   [4] Ganz, *Mem.*, p. 61.   [5] Hallé, p. 64.
[6] Dandelot, p. 57.

from Cherubini. In the last case it was said to be the strong opposition of the members of the orchestra that decided against Berlioz.

In other countries Berlioz appears to have been much more popular with orchestral players than in Paris. The German orchestras were, on the whole, very ready to meet his demands for hard work and many rehearsals, and in London he created a very favourable impression amongst the players: "by his polished and courteous manner; no conductor that ever entered an orchestra was more affable in his demeanour, or more gentlemanly in his conduct. M. Berlioz loves and respects his orchestra."[1] The Frenchman Berlioz knew well how to ingratiate himself with the English players in a way which was quite foreign to the German Wagner. It was an odd coincidence that these two opposites should both have been conducting in London at the same time in 1855, the German at the old Philharmonic and the Frenchman at the New Philharmonic.

OTHER FRENCH CONDUCTORS

All the regular French conductors of the first half of last century were rather overshadowed by Habeneck, and there is little that can be told of them except what is found in the usual biographical notes. Those that come more or less into prominence were Persius, Kreutzer, Grasset, Valentino, Battu, Manera, Seghers, Girard, Tilmant and Hainl. Valentino at the *Opéra* and Tilmant at the *Opéra Comique* were responsible for the first performances of several successful and well-known operas, and must have been quite competent conductors. Girard stepped into Habeneck's shoes, and carried on the Conservatoire Concerts with success; he also conducted some of Berlioz's performances and is allowed to have "acquitted himself well" on one occasion, although at other times he came in for some stinging comments from the exacting composer.

We may guess that none of the above had quite the strong personality or the authority that raised Habeneck well above his contemporaries; but even if their stars shone less brilliantly than his, they could hardly have occupied the positions they held in Paris without merits which entitle them to be considered at least the equals of most of their contemporaries in Germany.

The show-conductors, Musard and Jullien, struck out on a line of their own, and on that ground may be given some attention.

Musard was the pioneer who first developed the idea of giving concerts of light music and dance music of a very popular type at low prices, but with a large and first-class orchestra.

The new element of showmanship was now introduced into the conductor's art, and was one which, as long as it was associated only with light music, did no harm, and gave pleasure and amusement to large numbers of a public who otherwise would never have gone to a concert. The appeal was now to the eye as well as to the ear. The legitimate conductor at that

[1] *Mus. World,* Feb. 12, 1848, p. 97.

time directed all his physical movements solely at the orchestra, with the object of influencing the performance of the music; but the show-conductor went further than that; while ostensibly acting in such a way as to control only the orchestra, he was also directing his movements at the audience, with a view to impressing, amusing, or entertaining them. The physical act of conducting as well as the sound of the music was, as we would now say, part of the show.

According to Rivière, Musard was an able musician who conducted in an original, not to say, eccentric manner.[1] He was a violinist and dance composer, a "lord of quadrilles and gallops" who was also possessed of "an almost diabolical business flair"; he turned all music into quadrilles and gallops, and became absurdly popular in Paris, where he was spoken of as "Napoléon Musard," or "the Great Musard." He certainly owed nothing to good looks, for he was a little man with a yellow pock-marked face, and was always dressed in black. He is said to have been always untidy, unkempt, and grotesque in appearance. But like all show-conductors he was a good actor, and embodied in his conducting all sorts of eccentricities of action and behaviour. He would throw away his baton, and (according to Rellstab) would smash the stool on which he had been sitting, or walk to the edge of the platform and fire a pistol into the air.[2]

JULLIEN

Jullien, on the other hand, was good-looking and well dressed; he was, as one journal described him, "a highly decorous and well got-up gentleman."[3] A saying in Paris was: "If you want to see a handsome man, go and eat an ice in the *Jardin Turc* at Jullien's feet."[4] Such a dandy, it need hardly be said, was "the idol of the ladies," and there can be little doubt but that he was well aware of this, that he traded on it, welcomed it, and encouraged admiration from the fair sex as part of his stock-in-trade. On several occasions he presented his portrait to every lady in the dress circle.

Jullien exploited the visual aspect of conducting to its fullest extent, and based his methods on the principle that the pleasure-seeking public wanted to satisfy more than its sense of hearing. A picture of this remarkable character, but able conductor, can be painted only with the material left by those who saw and heard him in the period of his greatest success in England, namely, between 1840 and 1859.

It may be that there was always in Jullien a touch of the madness which eventually destroyed him, and it is impossible now to say how much there was in his make-up of mere eccentricity and self-delusion, and how much of artistic sincerity. But it is certain that in his work was included an apparent seriousness of intent which, whether it was genuine or not, did add something to the effect he created, and something which had a definite entertainment value.

[1] Rivière, pp. 38–39. [2] Kracauer, pp. 29, 30, 36; from Rellstab, *Paris im Frühjahr* 1843.
[3] *The Illustrated Times*, Nov. 6, 1858. [4] Kracauer, p. 36.

Chorley credited Jullien with much innate self-delusion and pose: "Jullien was, in every sense of the word, a character; he was an adventurer, not merely by circumstance, but by temperament.—He was sanguine, self-deluding, and busy in no uncommon degree, crossed with a vein of bombast, which helped him on his way, not merely by amusing the public,

JULLIEN IN 1843

but by inspiring himself with a dream that his sublimities were real." (*Athenæum*, 1860.) But he also credited him with intelligence enough to know that his efforts must be backed up by musical efficiency and by some show of artistic sincerity: "Strong, however, as is the spice of quackery in his entertainments, his orchestra is too well composed, his solo players are too eminent, and his recurrence to classical music is too frequent, for any one who considers how mixed a thing a vast shilling audience is not to commend him as one who caters liberally—and in some measure intelligently—for a public in quest of amusement rather than of art." (*Athenæum*, 1851.)

Davison, while admitting his peculiarities, gave Jullien credit for more artistic sincerity and a genuine belief that he had a mission to bring good music into the life of the people: "Jullien was essentially and before all a man for the people. He loved to entertain the people; he loved to instruct the people; and the people were just as fond of being taught as of being amused by Jullien. His peculiarities, even his foibles, were but particles of a whole, portions of an idiosyncracy, which—combined with such geniality, moral and physical, such hearty earnestness and such intense devotion to his task, as has seldom distinguished a public character in that particular walk of life in which his energies were exhibited—made Jullien what he was." Davison gave him credit for being "a refiner of public taste," and for having "a keen and lively intellect, uncommon enthusiasm, and as warm a heart as ever beat with kindly sympathy for others."[1]

There is evidence to show that people went to *see* Jullien conduct as

[1] Davison, *From Mendelssohn to Wagner*, pp. 471, 473.

well as to hear the music: "Who would not give his half-crown to see this pet of Apollo work his enchantments upon the air" (*Cheltenham Chronicle*, 1845).—"To see Jullien and his conducting is of itself worth all the money" (*Mus. World*, 1847).—"Then we had the picturesque *conducteur*, who is a whole gallery of pictures in his own proper person" (*Mus. World*, 1841). Wilhelm Kuhe said that, to his knowledge, many people attended Jullien's concerts "more for the sake of watching his 'beat' than hearing the music."[1]

Dress and deportment entered largely into the make-up of the show-conductor: "M. Jullien, the long-haired and dark-eyed, the graceful-actioned M. Jullien," was written of him in 1841 (*Mus. World*). No doubt he owed his dark eyes to Nature, but it cannot be supposed that his hair was long because he had not the price of a hair-cut in his pocket, or that his graceful actions were not thought out and rehearsed with a view to making some impression on his audience.

In an American paper we read: "There stands Jullien, in faultless coat, irreproachable shirt-bosom, immaculate wrist-bands, unexceptionable trousers, and glistening little boots. From the curls of his head to the soles of his patent leathers, it is Jullien all over" (1853). Wilhelm Ganz has told us that "it really was a sight to see him conduct, waving his baton right and left. He always wore an embroidered shirt-front, with a white waistcoat open wide enough to show it off."[2] In another sartorial tribute we are informed that Jullien was "in full fig, white-waistcoated, accurately trousered, and neatly bewhiskered" (*Mus. World*, 1847). We read that "he might have been a hairdresser's or, still better, a tailor's dummy," that "he always wore a suit cut in the very latest fashion, a sparkling diamond tie-pin, and yellow gloves," that his hair was "so crimped and singed that it looked like a wig," and that his moustaches were "so beautiful that they almost seemed artificial."[3] George Augustus Sala described how in 1856 he travelled in a railway compartment in Germany with "a magnificent Incarnation, all ringleted, oiled, scented, dress-coated, and watered-silk faced, braided, frogged, ringed, jewelled, patent-leathered, amber-headed sticked, and straw-coloured kid-gloved," how this "magnificent creature shone like a meteor in the narrow carriage," and that, although he did not recognise him at the time, it turned out to be Jullien with whom he had travelled.[4]

Other appurtenances which appealed to the eye (so often overlooked by conductors) were not forgotten by Jullien. His music-desk and the chair he rested in between the pieces, also his manner of using the latter, were all part and parcel of his outfit: "The pedestal of Jullien stood high in the centre, . . . his golden music-stand, and his lustrous fauteuil, formed a group of objects distinct from everything else. . . . When he sank into his arm-chair, you sympathised with the charming languor that naturally supervened upon exertions something more than human. It is needless to say that he was received with a hurricane of acclamations, and that he wore a

---

[1] Kuhe, p. 88.   [2] Ganz, p. 37.   [3] Kracauer, p. 37.
[4] Sala, *A journey due North*, p. 16. See also Sala, *Life and Adventures*, p. 279.

waistcoat of unparagoned whiteness." (*Morning Herald*, 1850.) We read further about "the royal air with which he reclines in his chair" (*Mus. World*, 1844), about how "he flings himself gracefully in his gilded chair and enjoys his triumph," we hear about his "golden throne," and learn that he did not omit to take the desk and chair to America with him in 1853: "The famous desk, dressed in scarlet and supported by a pensive seraph petrified into well-chased gold," and "the gilded chair with which his dignity has been supported before the Gothamites"; these were part of Jullien's furnishings that were not overlooked by the reporter of a Cincinnati paper.

Jullien's manner of manipulating the baton were obviously calculated to take effect not only on his orchestra, but also on his audience: "There, in his pride of place, soared M. Jullien, the soul of the great Polybody, a pharos in the mystical sea of harmony; there was the wizard, with his plenitude of ringlet and whisker, his exuberance of costume, his necromatic baton, and his vigorous flourish, marshalling and supermarshalling his euphonious colleagues, in a style most productive of grand effects, and most eminently satisfactory to all beholders." (*Mus. World*, 1842.) There can be no doubt but that Jullien's movements did serve the double purpose of impressing both orchestra and audience: "He has succeeded in training a very excellent band to work with great energy and precision, and his conducting is a thing quite unique, efficient in regulating his orchestra, as well as entertaining to the eye of his spectators." (*Mus. World*, 1844.)

Tributes to Jullien's effective baton-play are very many. In 1845 the *Manchester Times* describes how "M. Jullien stood in front of his band waving his sparkling baton, and animated with the kindred spirits around him. . . . The joy which he felt he communicated by the talismanic influence of his wand, throughout the vast hall"; the *Birmingham Journal* was moved to inform its readers how "Jullien was, as usual, all energy, tempered and regulated by the most *correct grace*. He sweeps his baton through the noiseless air, and a burst of harmony follows; he moves his arm in slow and gentle undulations, and the music, obedient to his behest, rises and falls with the softest cadence, the variations of which are felt rather than heard. The slightest motion, and the most animated, are followed by their appropriate musical effect. It seems as if he alone were the performer"; the *Cheltenham Observer* thought that there must be "a mysterious virtue in Jullien's baton, akin to the secret influence of mesmerism."

It is impossible now to draw a line between Jullien's gift for showmanship and his undoubted ability as a conductor, and difficult to decide how much of his success he owed to his acting and how much to his musical gift; both qualities probably combined to make a whole which served very well his purpose of simultaneously giving his audience both good entertainment and good musical performances. The movements of his body and his attitudes were obviously vehement and illustrative of the musical effect he wished to evoke: "Not a vestige of the efflorescent pantomime of the illustrious maestro was lost; and his energies seemed fuller and more impressive than ever. His baton flew about with the restlessness of lightning, and his attitudes, while working up a climax, dallying with a diminuendo, or enunciating a staccato, were as explanatory as words, and infinitely more prompt." (*Morning Herald*, 1850.)

Some years ago the deportment of one of the most eminent of our living conductors was likened by an American critic to that of an adagio-dancer. But this was nothing new; he had obviously been forestalled by Jullien nearly one hundred years ago: "To see this Adonis conducting was a sight in itself. Now he would comport himself as daintily as a dancer interpreting music by the graceful and sinewy movements of his body"; but these effeminate movements could be changed in a moment to something more masculine and warlike, when he assumed "the ferocity of a general on parade, picking out some unfortunate member of the orchestra and glaring at him irascibly as though suspecting some fault."[1] Here, combined in one person, were the insinuating grace of the ballet dancer and the fiery tyranny of the sergeant-major.

But behind all this play-acting there must have been something more than empty showmanship. Behind the showman stood the capable musician who was able to command and to train his orchestra to play equally well not only the trivial Quadrilles, Waltzes and Polkas, but also the symphonies of Mozart, Beethoven and Mendelssohn: "Because he conducts quadrilles, waltzes and polkas better than most of his fellows, it has been rashly inferred that he is incapable of anything else. . . . M. Jullien has most of the requisites of a good conductor. He has great experience of the resources of an orchestra, indeed, as much as most men. He has a quick ear, a ready hand, and an intelligible beat—the last of these qualities is indispensable. To sum up all, he studies his author's score ere he directs its performance in public—and this was evident in both the symphonies, every point of which he took up and enforced with a precision and a readiness that would not have disgraced Costa or Habeneck." (*Mus. World*, 1846.) Kenney, Balfe's biographer, wrote of Jullien that "he had shown himself capable of conducting with the rarest knowledge, sympathy, and practical skill the immortal masterpieces of the great composers."[2]

Rivière said of Jullien: "apart from his eccentricity of manner, he was a very capable conductor."[3] Although a showman, perhaps a madman, Jullien was no mere impostor; his orchestra played both good and bad music, but whatever they played was well played, and that could not have been done for so long under an incompetent or sham conductor.

Jullien was characterised as a "solemn and charming person"; no doubt he had much of what would now be called personal magnetism. In spite of his solemn manner when before the public, he had plenty of humour, and was ready as anybody to laugh at the many humorous sallies made about him in *Punch*, in the Christmas pantomimes, and in the comic songs of the day. When his audience laughed at him he was quite pleased: "The

---

[1] Kracauer, p. 37.   [2] Kenney, *Mem.*, p. 217.   [3] Rivière, p. 107.

causes of merriment were also causes of attraction, and every titter was as acceptable as a puff of incense. . . . His eccentricities are the freaks of a man of real talent, who has felt that he possesses by them a means of rendering himself remarkable to the mixed public more than conductors in general, and of acquiring a power which he often turns to good account." (*Mus. World*, 1844.)   There was nothing mean or grasping in Jullien's character; on the contrary, he was probably rather too generous; although he made a lot of money and at one time owned a *chateau* in Belgium, he was twice made bankrupt, the first time over his season of opera in English at Drury Lane in 1847, and subsequently by his unfortunate speculation in the enormous concert-room in the Royal Surrey Gardens, but both times he emerged with untarnished honour, and with the sympathy of his friends and the public.

Jullien gave his farewell concerts in England early in 1859, prior to going to France in order to organize the greatest of all his projects, a grand tour throughout all the civilized countries of the world.   Arriving in France, he was put in prison for debt.   After his release he attempted to arrange performances of oratorios in Paris in the English style, but before the scheme materialised his mind gave way, and about a week after his admission to a lunatic asylum, he died at the age of forty-eight.

Jullien's son gave some promenade concerts at Her Majesty's Theatre in 1863 and 1864, but soon discovered that there could never be a second Jullien.   His wife was left unprovided for, and eventually occupied a humble position as "house-keeper" at Drury Lane Theatre, the scene of so many of her late husband's triumphs.

Musard died a wealthy man, and Jullien died a pauper and a lunatic. Before finally leaving London, Jullien conceived the idea of setting The Lord's Prayer to music; it would, he said, make such a grand title-page:

THE LORD'S PRAYER,

words by

JESUS CHRIST,

music by

JULLIEN.

Costa, and the London Conductors

It was a pity that the greatest English conductor in the first half of last century was no Englishman.   Of Spanish descent, but by birth and education an Italian, Costa came to this country in 1829, making his first appearance as a vocalist.   Having already had some experience in taking charge of opera performances in Italy, he was appointed *Maestro al Cembalo* at the King's Theatre in 1830, and became conductor of the orchestra in 1833. In 1847 he went to the Royal Italian Opera at Covent Garden Theatre, and from 1846 to 1854 conducted the London Philharmonic Society's concerts.

Costa's Italian musical upbringing betrays itself in the comment of a London paper on his rendering of *Don Giovanni* at the King's Theatre in 1836: "We could not avoid the feeling that Sig. Costa is not at home in the German school of music,"[1] and in Moscheles's remark: "Costa wields the baton more in Italian than in German style, but he kept the 700 performers admirably together, although the *tempi* were not always what I am used to."[2]

No doubt he had to adapt his style to the English musical taste of his time. Nothing could have been further removed from Costa's early musical environment than that of the English church and oratorio music, with its Mendelssohnian influence superimposed on a strong Handelian tradition; yet he succeeded in so thoroughly absorbing this peculiarly British trait that he eventually became a great conductor of large-scale oratorio performances, and the leading spirit at many of the large musical festivals throughout this country.

CARICATURE OF COSTA (1842)

It was Costa who first undermined and then overthrew the old system of divided responsibility in conducting which still prevailed in London even during the 'thirties and 'forties of last century. There can be no question but that he soon made himself sole master of the opera orchestra, and lifted it out of the unhappy state into which it had sunk by the end of the 'twenties. He would tolerate no divided control: "M. Costa is what a conductor ought to be—the master-spirit of the band."[3] When he was invited to become sole conductor of the Philharmonic concerts, he accepted the engagement only on the condition that he would be given complete charge of the performance.[4] His letter in reply to the invitation included the following: "Allow me to state that the stipulation I named I consider to be no more than would be required by any conductor really interested in the welfare of the Philharmonic Society, and as I am firmly convinced that no orchestra can go well unless the entire control is placed in the hands of him who is the only responsible person for the accurate performance, and if the Directors do not give me that power, I am of necessity compelled to relinquish the Engagement they offer me."

Costa had sufficient musical gift, and the right personality for a conductor.

[1] *Mus. World*, June 24, 1836, p. 22.
[3] *Mus. World*, April 5, 1838, p. 236.
[2] Moscheles, *Life*, II, p. 202.
[4] Foster, *History*, p. 193.

He was masterful but not tyrannous; he was a disciplinarian but not a slave-driver. Ella wrote of his "acts of kindly feeling towards those under his baton," and eulogised his influence on the playing of English orchestras in these words: "No musician within my recollection, foreign or native, has achieved so much in the improvement of our public musical institutions and orchestras,—no artist, vocalist, or instrumentalist has survived the vicissitudes of public opinion in his laudably ambitious career with greater credit and approbation." Absentees from rehearsals at the opera were fined when Costa first went there; but, as that had no deterrent effect, he obtained power to deal with this trouble more drastically. He announced the change to the orchestra in these words: "Gentlemen, I am happy to tell you that I have abolished fines for absentees (great applause); but, anyone absent at rehearsal without my permission, forfeits his engagement (murmurs, sotto voce)." The outcome was that "the complete band attended at all future rehearsals . . . . The six or eight rehearsals were gradually reduced to two or three, and finally the choir and band were so thoroughly well drilled, that the revival of any opera never required more than *one* patient rehearsal."[1]

COSTA AS AN ELDERLY MAN

Testimony to Costa's professional skill as a conductor of Italian opera, and to his character and bearing towards those engaged under him are expressed in the following: "In his professional capacity, Signor Costa is admirably fitted for the situation of conductor to the Italian Opera. He possesses a thorough knowledge of the modern school of Italian music. He unites great firmness and determination of purpose, without ever compromising the man of good sense and the gentleman. He has no mean and narrow prejudices, or spiteful revenges in his disposition. All under his direction, from the leader to the double drum, experience equal distinction and consideration. We have never heard but one opinion of Signor Costa, from those professionally engaged with him, and that redounded to his honour; it is therefore with real pleasure that we record this testimony to his merits."[2]

[1] Ella, pp. 246–8.
[2] *Mus. World*, Aug. 19, 1836, p. 156.

Tributes to Costa's merits as a conductor came not only from his English admirers. According to the testimony of Wilhelm Kuhe, Meyerbeer, Rossini and Mendelssohn regarded Costa as a "magnificent conductor,"[1] and Meyerbeer told the author of *Musical Recollections* on more than one occasion that he was "the greatest *chef d'orchestre* of the world." Onslow also had unbounded admiration for him, and said that he would rather entrust his works to Costa's direction than conduct himself: "His power over a band has no parallel within my recollection."[2]

Although there was some momentary doubt as to Costa's ability to shine as a concert-conductor, there was never any question about his skill with an opera orchestra. Chorley wrote: "From the first evening when Signor Costa took up the baton, a young man from a country then despised by every musical pedant, a youth who came to England without flourish, announcement, or protection, as a singer without much voice, to do what was never done in England before, it was to be felt that in him were combined the materials of a great conductor—nerve to enforce discipline, readiness to the second, and that certain influence which only a vigorous man could exercise over the disconnected folk who made up an orchestra in those days."[3]

Chorley, as well as those other English critics who had previously made up their minds that Costa could conduct only Italian opera, and that he would be a failure in German symphonic music, had to eat their words soon after the Philharmonic orchestra came permanently under his direction in 1846.[4] Chorley's notice of the first Philharmonic concert of that season shows how mistaken he was when at first he prognosticated that Costa's appointment would be "the first step towards making these concerts a dependency on the opera-house, for the sake of securing the services of the Italian singers." The eminent critic was obliged to change his opinion, and to his credit be it said that he had the courage to do so handsomely: "Without unnecessary words or exaggeration, it may be stated as past question, that the first Philharmonic Concert established Signor Costa in the foremost rank of conductors of classical music, and justified the directors in their choice. As we somewhat mistrusted the discretion of his appointment, it behoves us emphatically to say, that we have heard no Philharmonic performance to compare with Monday's (March 16). The orchestra is entirely under the control of Signor Costa's *bâton*, and the difference of such a discipline made itself felt ere Haydn's simple old Symphony in B flat, No. 9, had been played. We felt conscious of an alertness and a submissiveness, a delicacy and a spirit new to the Hanover-square Rooms; of a near approach to the highest continental style of finish, such as is produced at Leipzig under Mendelssohn, and at Paris under Habeneck."[5]

When Costa started at Covent Garden Theatre in 1847, Davison wrote of him: "Perhaps no individual in Europe is more happily endowed by nature

[1] Kuhe, p. 59.   [2] *Mus. World*, May 23, 1846, p. 246.
[3] *Thirty Years' Mus. Recoll.*, p. 84.   [4] *Athenæum*, 1844, p. 1051.   [5] *Ibid.*, 1846, p. 298.

with qualities befitting the conductor of an operatic band than Signor Costa; he has an amazingly quick ear, decision and promptitude in using the baton, and he never spares himself time nor labour."[1]

It seems that Costa, like Weber, Spontini and Wagner, ruled not only the orchestra, but also the stage; actors, machinists, scene-shifters and all subordinates came under his surveillance.   This, it was said, was a contributory cause to his disagreement with Lumley which came to a head in 1846 and ended in Costa leaving the opera at Her Majesty's Theatre.

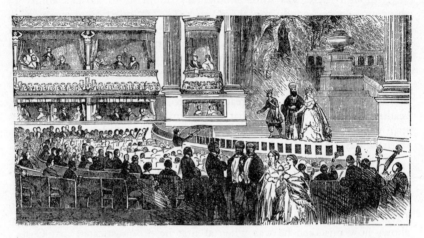

COSTA CONDUCTING SEMIRAMIDE ON THE OPENING NIGHT OF THE ROYAL
ITALIAN OPERA AT COVENT GARDEN, APRIL 6, 1847

Costa was constantly referred to by his contemporaries as, above all, a disciplinarian; he was said to be "despotic," and was often called "the autocrat of the orchestra."   This may have been because other London conductors failed to exercise sufficient control over their players, and were only too often willing to share their responsibility with the leader.   It seems that Costa was indeed the only resident conductor who could successfully impose his will on the London orchestras: "Why discipline should be strictly enforced whenever Mr. Costa is director, and utterly set at nought elsewhere, it would be difficult to explain.   But such is too evidently the case.   Our orchestral performers will not pay the proper attention to other conductors; and to this despotic monopoly of one man must be attributed nearly all the deficiencies that are observable when he is not engaged as conductor."[2] At provincial festivals, when the local organists were in command, it was said that the orchestral players "took matters entirely into their own hands." When Wagner came to conduct the Philharmonic season of 1855, he quickly sensed that Costa was the real master of the orchestra, and, rightly or

[1] *Mus. World,* 1847, p. 538.   [2] *Ibid.,* July 29, 1854, p. 504.

wrongly, judged that he was responsible for the "attitude of hostility" with which Wagner felt he was surrounded in London. He even went so far as to suppose that the players dared not give him the best of their service for fear they would lose their engagements at Covent Garden.[1] Costa certainly had supreme power over the engagement of players at the opera, and a member of the Philharmonic Society wrote in 1855 to the *Musical World* to say that the real reason why Costa resigned his conductorship of the Society's concerts after the 1854 season was because the directors would not allow him to replace players who were inefficient, and because they tolerated the deputy system.

Costa's conducting seems to have been above all firm and precise; it was probably inflexible and rather bandmaster-like. No doubt he lacked the sensitivity of Berlioz and had little of the deep musical insight of Wagner; but he would be cooler and more level-headed than either of these. He would excel in music that required bold or brilliant treatment rather than delicacy or subtlety, and he certainly had the gift of controlling large forces, which Wagner apparently lacked. There can be no doubt that he was a thoroughly practical conductor, who knew his business from start to finish; his renderings were evidently not very emotional or deeply expressive, and his *tempi* were said to be rather fast. In fact, it seems that, like Habeneck, he was not blest with over much "abstract-aesthetical inspiration." But perhaps it was discipline rather than inspiration that the London players of his time required, and he was certainly the man they needed in the 'thirties and 'forties of last century. Costa was undoubtedly the first real conductor permanently settled in this country.

Costa has often been censured for his readiness to add parts to and alter the orchestration of the scores committed to his charge. The censure may be well deserved, but he can share it with many others of his time, with Wagner, Habeneck and Mendelssohn, with many of his great successors, and with many prominent conductors of the present day.

*   *   *

Of the other conductors, native and foreign, who took charge of London's orchestras during the half century, there is not very much that can be told of either their ability or of their characteristics. Many of them could hardly be described as conductors. The custom of placing a musician in charge of a performance only because he enjoyed some distinction in the profession, or occupied some prominent position, was not well calculated to produce good orchestral conductors. If the violinist-leaders had been allowed to develop into conductors, as they were in France, it may be that an English Habeneck would have been discovered. But that was not the way in this country. The leader, however great his power in influencing the performance, was reckoned as one of the "band," even though he actually controlled the playing; a puppet-conductor was always present,

[1] Wagner, *My Life*, II, pp. 623, 625.

B 2

and was nominally his superior. The musicians occupying this superior position were almost invariably chosen from amongst those whose natural element was not the orchestra. They were composers, organists, choir-trainers, vocalists, pianists, musical directors, or indeed almost any but the men whose training, experience, and environment had best fitted them for handling an orchestra. The training ground for conductors at that time was the theatre, not the concert-room. It could hardly be expected that pianist-composers such as Clementi, J. B. Cramer, Ries, Potter or Moscheles, nor church-trained men like Attwood, Greatorex, Knyvett, Crotch, Vincent Novello, Surman or Forbes, would provide the material from which great orchestral conductors are made.

There was, perhaps, a little more promising material in Bishop, Smart, Perry, Balfe and Benedict. Bishop had wide experience as a composer of theatrical music and as musical director at several theatres; yet, although well-practised with the orchestra, there is no reason to believe that he had in him the necessary elements required to give distinction to a conductor. He was described as "the tamest of tame conductors" in 1848 when, under his conductorship, the Ancient Concert expired.[1] Another, and more stinging pen, described his conducting in these words: "Lenient to torpidity in his presidency over rehearsals; courageous to temerity in changing, adding to, and otherwise transmogrifying music committed to his care; incorrect in almost every *tempo* he takes, whether it be German or Italian music, Mozart or Handel, we have experienced enough from the Ancient Concert performances to augur doleful results from Sir H. R. Bishop's promotion to a situation in every respect so much more trying. His has always been the most stagnant Philharmonic Concert of the season, and eight similar inflictions will throw back the average intelligence, sensitiveness, and spirit of the orchestra's performances to a point even behind their old inequality."[2] And this conductor who, according to Chorley, "took every *tempo* but the right one," was selected to conduct the Philharmonic season of 1845.

Smart seems to have reached a higher level, but it was more as a choral than as an orchestral conductor that he shone. He had authority and administrative power, and was well fitted to undertake the multifarious duties that fall to the lot of a festival conductor and demand qualities that may exist quite apart from his musical gifts or abilities. For many years his was the guiding hand that steered so successfully many of these musical feasts, both in London and in the provinces, before the time when Costa became the favourite. But it may be questioned whether Smart had just the gift that was required of an orchestral conductor: "His tact was extraordinary. He seemed able, as if by intuition, to detect in an instant if anything were wrong amongst the several members of his orchestra, and at once set it right by a pleasantry which put everyone in good humour. He never wearied his forces by constant fault-finding. He acted upon the good old principle, that 'one pennyworth of oil is worth more than a whole

---

[1] *Mus. Recoll.*, II, p. 45.   [2] *Athenæum*, 1845, p. 204.

pound's-worth of vinegar,' and so smoothed difficulties, that they disappeared almost as soon as they started up."[1] These were just the qualities
that were invaluable for the conductor of a choral society; but tact and
organising power alone do not suffice to make a great orchestral conductor.

Benedict and Balfe were more practised in theatrical conducting, and
Perry was an all-round man with some ability, but without distinction; but
we look in vain for signs of
a man who could rank with
Habeneck, Costa or Nicolai.

Benedict had plenty of experience in the theatre, both in
England and on the continent.
He earned the respect that was
due to a conscientious and sound
musician whose gifts were comprehensive rather than special-
ised, but there are no indications
which point to his having
possessed just that strong personality and musical insight
which, combined with wide
experience, raise the great conductor above the respectable
level of the competent but
uninspired practitioner. A contemporary described Benedict
as "far from being an ideal
conductor. His beat was too

BALFE

uncertain, with the result that the players sometimes had the greatest
difficulty in following him."[2]

Of Balfe as a conductor it is difficult to arrive at a fair estimate. His
biographers gave him unstinted praise, and would have us believe that he
was "second to none" as a conductor. But at that time biographers were
apt to paint the portrait of their subject in the most glowing of colours,
and were only too ready to overload with indiscriminate praise a man who,
like Balfe, was evidently a good friend and a lovable character. Balfe
undoubtedly faced a very difficult task when he succeeded Costa at Her
Majesty's Theatre, and the more frank comments of contemporary critics
do not by any means accord with the lavish praise of biographers and devoted
friends. Wilhelm Ganz, however, said that Balfe was "a first-rate conductor,
and did not only beat strict time, as some conductors do, but he showed
sympathy with the singers by allowing them *tempo rubato* and also *ritardandos*
and *accellerandos* if they did not over-step the rules of music or sing out of

[1] *Mus. Recoll.*, I, p. 91.   [2] Kuhe, p. 253.

time.   Being a singer himself, he knew exactly when to give way to singers."[1]
Kuhe explained that the old operas then in vogue did not demand such
able conductors as the more modern works, and said that Balfe did well
enough at Her Majesty's Theatre, but qualified his praise by adding that
even his warmest admirers could hardly have considered him a leader of
exceptional merit.[2]

But when Balfe, perhaps rather unwisely, undertook conducting symphonies at the Grand National Concerts in Her Majesty's Theatre in 1850, it
seems that he was venturing on ground that was not his own, and one critic
declared that "there must be a protest entered against the slovenly style in
which the symphonies, many of the overtures, and the vocal accompaniments
are executed."[3]   Chorley also found Balfe's rendering of the German classics
so far deficient as to merit the cutting remark: "Mr. Balfe is so innocent of
classical knowledge, that the Eroica symphony must have proved to the
fashionables as tedious as to exercised musical ears it was all but burlesque."[4]
Perhaps it could hardly have been expected that Balfe would be at home in
or have much sympathy with a style of music that was so completely alien
in spirit to that of his own more superficial Italian-French operatic style.

[1] Ganz, *Mem.*, p. 64.   [2] Kuhe, p. 254.   [3] *Illus. Lon. News*, Nov. 16, 1850.
[4] *Athenæum*, May 18, 1850.

IX

The Instruments

OF the bowed string instruments used in orchestras during the first half of last century there is little that calls for remark except in the case of the double-bass. The violins, violas and 'cellos remained in all essentials just as they were during the previous century, and as they are to-day.

By the early years of last century certain adjustments, demanded by a changing and ever advancing technique, had been made on most of the old violins, and were being embodied in the newer instruments, which, nevertheless, were modelled after the patterns of those that had served so well in the past. The neck was lengthened, the bridge was made higher and more arched, and the angle of the fingerboard was made to conform to the raised position of the strings caused by the higher bridge, which also demanded some internal strengthening of the structure in order to resist the increased tension and pressure. The old and shorter bow, with its outward-curved stick, had already towards the end of the 18th century given place to the longer Tourte bow. This, in the case of the violin bow, was about three inches longer; it was less flexible, and the inward curve of the tapered stick offered more resistance to pressure. A stronger tone and an extension of upward compass were the main results of these adjustments, which had been brought about by the gradual development of violin-playing during the last half of the 18th century. The solo parts of violin concertos by Bach, Mozart, and Beethoven will illustrate well enough the changes in the style and the great expansion of the technical and aesthetic range of violin-playing during that period. What was expected of the solo player in one half-century was expected of the *ripieno* player in the succeeding half-century, and the progress was continued during the whole of the 19th century; indeed, it has not yet come to a standstill. Nevertheless, except for such modifications of the fittings as have been mentioned, the violin was structurally the same instrument in the year 1800 as it had been in 1700, and the same in 1900 as it was in 1800.

Similar adjustments were made on the violas and 'cellos, and they too shared the advantages of the newer type of bow. Although the viola was treated as having next to no value as a solo instrument, the technique of playing on it advanced alongside that of its smaller brother under the constant urge of the ever increasing demands made in the orchestral parts written by such as Berlioz and Wagner. The 'cello was quickly gaining ground and importance as a soloist and tenor melodist in the orchestra, and like the violin, was adding greater range to its upward compass, and penetrating power to the tone of the instrument.   Round about the middle of the 19th century greater freedom of action and power was gained by the adoption of the adjustable tail-pin by means of which the 'cello rested on the floor instead of being supported as heretofore between the player's knees.

The double-bass was the only instrument in the string orchestra of which there was no standard type.   The instruments varied in size, in number of strings and tuning, according to the taste, the habit, or the nationality of the player.   Some basses were viols, some were violins; many were converted or altered in some way, and all were subject to changes of neck, bridge and fingerboard, but in no ordered plan, and very much according to the ideas or fads of individual players.   The double-bass bow did not undergo the same change as those of the smaller stringed instruments, and was represented by many different patterns.

In Germany the bass generally used throughout the first half of last century was the four-stringed instrument tuned in fourths, viz. E–A–D–G,[1] although the lowest string was sometimes tuned down to E flat or D. A five-stringed bass tuned to F–A–D–F sharp–A, an older type with a fretted fingerboard, was still to be found in Germany, but was going out of use, and three-stringed basses were not unknown; but, according to Koch (1802),[2] the standard bass in Germany at the beginning of the century was the four-stringed instrument tuned in fourths.   Koch remarked, however, that there was no universal pattern, and that really good players were uncommon.   The process of tuning had lately been eased by the invention of the metal screw pegs, for which *Kammermusikus* Bachmann[3] of Berlin is given the credit.

But the four-stringed bass was no new thing in Germany.   Quantz had recommended it as the best orchestral bass in 1752,[4] and Leopold Mozart stated in 1756[5] that it was then the standard instrument.   In 1827 Edward Holmes observed that German basses were "frequently strung with four instead of three strings, thinner than those in use with us, and descending to E below the usual scale."[6]

According to Gassner in 1838,[7] double-basses with five strings were rarely used at that time, and although the three-stringed instrument was still often played, it was the four-stringed bass tuned in fourths that was the most common.   Gassner also remarked that different tunings were adopted by some players, and that the low E string was sometimes tuned down to D.   In the same writer's *Lexikon* of 1849 it is said that the four-stringed bass was the most useful, and was then generally used in Germany.   John Ella remarked on the advantages of the German four-stringed bass over the

---

[1] The tuning given here is in all cases counted from the lowest string, going upwards.
[2] *Lex.*, Art. *Contra-violon.*
[3] According to Gerber, Koch and Gassner, it was Carl Ludwig Bachmann who invented the screw peg, and not his father Anton Bachmann, as is stated in Grove's *Dictionary.*
[4] *Versuch*, XVII, Sec. 5.   [5] *Ibid., Einleitung*, par. 2.   [6] *Rambles*, p. 51.
[7] *Partiturkenntniss*, I, p. 13.

English bass with only three strings: "Here I cannot omit adding a few words in respect of the ponderous tones and splendid effects of the fourth string (E) of the German double-basses, four notes below the lowest note (A) of the English three-stringed instruments. The dominant pedal note (G) in the above Symphony (Beethoven's fifth) and the tonic (A flat) of the slow movement are the most prevalent intervals employed. In England we lose these impressively grand pedal basses by transposition."[1]

Castil-Blaze and Kastner also testified to the common use of the four-stringed bass in Germany, and in the Koch-Dommer *Lexikon* of 1865 it is said that although the three-stringed bass tuned in fifths (G–D–A) might still be found in South Germany and in France, the four-stringed instrument was generally used by German players.[2]

In France, at the beginning of last century, the ordinary double-bass (*contre-basse*) was provided with three strings tuned in fifths, viz. G–D–A. This is according to the testimony of Francœur-Choron (1813), to whom the four-stringed bass was apparently unknown. By the 'twenties, however, the four-stringed instrument was evidently finding its way into the Paris orchestras, and Gassner[3] gave Habeneck the credit for having first introduced it at the Conservatoire. The Paris bass-player G. Gélinek wrote in 1829: "Of the four double-basses now used in the Chapel of the Tuileries, two have been made for four strings, and similar ones are found in some of the orchestras in Paris."[4] Catrufo (1832) knew both types, the three-stringed (G–D–A) and the four-stringed (E–A–D–G). A few years later in Kastner's *Traité* (1837), it was said that the bass commonly used in France was the three-stringed instrument tuned in fifths, but Kastner recommended the four-stringed bass as being more generally useful, and hoped that it would soon be universally adopted. In the *Supplement* (1844) to his *Traité* Kastner quoted a few less common tunings for both types. He cited G–D–G and A–D–G (the English tuning) for the three-stringed bass, and F–A–D–G or G–D–G–A for the four-stringed instrument. Among the unusual tunings mentioned by Kastner were those of the well-known Viennese virtuoso Hindle,[5] who tuned his bass to A–D–F sharp–A, or B flat–E flat–G–B flat. Kastner mentions a tutor for the four-stringed bass by A. Gouffé, a player in the Conservatoire orchestra, which must therefore have been published before 1837.

[1] *Mus. Sketches*, p. 214.

[2] Similar information is found in Smart (*Journals*, 1825) and C. Potter (1837).

[3] *Lex.*, Art. Habeneck.   [4] *Remarks on the double bass*, *Harm.*, Dec., 1829, p. 297.

[5] Elwart, who said that Hindle was a pupil of Dragonetti, was probably mistaken in calling him an Englishman (Elwart, p. 208). A correspondent of the *Harmonicon* in Vienna (1824) described him as "a young professor" who had "lately excited great astonishment by his performance on the double bass, and we almost hope to possess, in him, a German Dragonetti." When Hindle played at Prague in 1828 he was said to have used the thumb on a fretted fingerboard, and it was remarked that, when playing in E flat, he tuned each string a semitone higher than usual, so as to gain the use of the open strings (*Harm.*, July, 1828, p. 170). Hindle made a successful tour of N. Germany in 1828–29, and gave a concert at the *Kärntnerthor* theatre at Vienna early in 1829. He played at the Conservatoire concerts at Paris in 1842.

From Berlioz we have similar information about the three and four-stringed basses, with a preference for the latter on account of the sounds obtainable on the lowest string, and also because of the greater facility of fingering on an instrument tuned in fourths. The advantage of tuning in fourths was also mentioned by Fétis when writing about the English bass-players in 1829, and by Gélinek in the same year. Castil-Blaze provides very similar information about the French basses, and mentioned Gouffé in 1832 as the "Montéclair of the four-stringed bass."[1]

The change from three to four strings in Paris seems to have come about between 1830 and 1850. Chénié and Lamy, the professors at the Conservatoire up to about 1835, taught the three-stringed instrument, but Schaft, who was professor from 1835 to 1852, taught his pupils to play on four-stringed basses. Of eight players at the Opéra in 1855 only one remained true to the old three-stringed bass.

Both of the Belgian authorities, Andries (1856) and Gevaert (1863), stated that basses with either three or four strings in the standard tunings in fifths and fourths respectively were used in French and Belgian orchestras, and Gevaert gave an alternative tuning for the latter, viz. E–G–D–A.

In Italy the standard double-bass (Contra basso or Violone) was the three-stringed type tuned in fifths, just as it was in France. For this we have the authority of both Kastner and Berlioz. The latter was very scathing in his comments on the Italian bass players: "the men who play them (i.e. the double-basses), for a few coins handed to them at the end of the evening, are greatly embarrassed when they have to play something in which they cannot use their three open strings, in B major, for instance, where the three natural notes G, D and A do not figure (they have retained the three-stringed double-basses tuned in fifths)."[2] The instruments used by the famous Italian virtuosi were all three-stringed instruments, but they were not all agreed as to the best method of tuning. Dragonetti tuned his strings in fifths, whereas Bottesini preferred the tuning in fourths. The latter, in his tutor for the instrument, asserted that the addition of a fourth string was detrimental to the sonority of the instrument, and laid it down that the more strings there were on a double-bass, the worse was the tone.

As we have already learned from Ella's remarks, the English bass was the three-stringed instrument tuned in fourths, viz. A–D–G. Berlioz also commented on the drawbacks of this English bass, which, he said, involved "an ungraceful and unreasonable transposition" when the part was written below A.[3] Further confirmation is found in the Encyclopædia Londinensis (1819),[4] where it is stated that the double-bass "now most commonly in use" in England was the three-stringed instrument tuned to A–D–G. In 1839, Ferdinand David, who was then in London, wrote to Mendelssohn

---

[1] Michael Montéclair (1666–1737), a famous player on the three-stringed bass at Paris early in the 18th century, and said to have been the first to play the double-bass in the Opéra orchestra (Gerber).

[2] *Evenings*, p. 258.   [3] *Instrumentation*, p. 40.   [4] Vol. XVI, p. 385.

and described how the English players transposed the well-known passage at the beginning of the *Trio* in the *Scherzo* of Beethoven's C minor symphony an octave higher because they had no G string.[1]

When August Müller, the colossal bass player from Darmstadt, came to London in 1838, he was advertised as "the only one who plays on four strings."[2]

In 1841 a certain Mr. Schroeder, who had been a member of Queen Adelaide's private band, joined the Philharmonic orchestra and played upon a four-stringed bass going down to E, it was said that "even amongst the great number who play at the Philharmonic, we could perceive the voluminous richness of these lower notes, and therefore longed, however heretical may be the desire, for the restoration in England, of this very important part of the compass of the instrument."[3]

The old-fashioned short bow seems to have been used by all players, at all events up to the time of Bottesini. According to Castil-Blaze, the bow was straight in France and curved in Italy.

It is always unsafe to assume that because a composer—even a "great" composer—wrote a certain note for a certain instrument, this note was necessarily playable on the instruments of his time. This is especially true of double-bass parts. Beethoven, like Haydn and Mozart, sometimes wrote his orchestral bass part down to low C; but that provides no reason to suppose that a double-bass with a low C string was commonly used either in Vienna or elsewhere during the early part of last century; in fact, there is not the slightest reason to suppose that such was the case. Beethoven, like his predecessors and contemporaries, wrote *bass parts*, but not *double-bass parts*. They did not concern themselves much with either the downward compass or the difficulties of fingering the instrument; they wrote the bass part they wanted, as they would for the 'cello, and left it to the players to make the best of it, to transpose into the higher octave when it became necessary, and to simplify the quick passages just as they thought fit.[4] Weber and Schubert were rather more careful not to exceed the downward range of the ordinary double-bass with four strings, but both occasionally wrote below the low E. Mendelssohn and Schumann often wrote down to E flat and D, and now and then, probably inadvertently, they let the part slip down to low C. In the cases of Berlioz and Wagner the actual compass of the instrument and its technical limitations were given more practical consideration, and we may suppose that when they wrote below E they were

---

[1] Eckardt, p. 103. This is confirmed by Cipriani Potter in the *Musical World*, 1837.

[2] "Mr. Müller's performance was respectable, and in some things remarkable, but his music, of which he did not appear to know more than his own part, was wretched drivel." Re Müller at the Philharmonic, in the *Mus. World*, June 7, 1838, p. 100.

[3] *Mus. World*, March 1, 1841, p. 140.

[4] Referring to a rapid passage in Beethoven's Choral Symphony, Berlioz wrote: "Now, it is impossible for double basses to execute a succession of notes so rapid; and no one has yet been able to explain how a man so skilful as Beethoven in the art of instrumentation could possibly forget himself so far as to write for this heavy instrument a feature of this kind" (from *A Critical Study of Beethoven's Nine Symphonies*, p. 114).

aware that the ordinary double-bass could not produce the sounds in the correct octave.

A few isolated efforts were made to construct monster basses on which the sounds below E could be played without leaping into the upper octave,

VUILLAUME'S OCTOBASSE, 1849

and which were really intended to produce a bass part sounding an octave below that of the 'cello part.   These remained little more than impracticable curiosities that did not get beyond the experimental stage.   Ad. Sax's four-stringed bass, pitched an octave below the 'cello (c. 1844),[1] and

---

[1] Kastner, *Traité*, Supp., p. 10, f.n.   This was tuned in fifths.

Vuillaume's monster three-stringed *octobasse* were among the attempts made to give the orchestra a bass part reaching down to the 32 ft. C. The latter gained a prize at Paris in 1849,[1] and was brought to London in 1850 for Jullien's concerts at Drury Lane. It was said to be 12 feet high, and was tuned C–G–C.

Almost without exception, all who wrote about the double-bass before Berlioz made it quite clear that players were not then expected to play every note in the rapid or figurated passages that occur so frequently in the bass parts of the period. In Francœur-Choron's book (1813) it is stated quite clearly that composers left it to the double-bass players to simplify the part whenever it was necessary. Similarly, we are told that in this country in 1819 the performer looks at the violoncello book, playing the same notes an octave lower, or omitting such notes as he thinks will not have a good effect."[2] Kastner said that the player claimed the right to simplify passages that were too difficult, and according to Gassner (1838),[3] in difficult passages only the main notes were to be played on the double-basses, the others (passing notes) being left to the 'cellos. This, it was said, made a better and clearer bass than when the double-bass players attempted to play every note. An example, showing how such passages may be simplified, is given in Gassner's book,[4] and is very similar to that given by Quantz in 1752.[5] Berlioz came down heavily on the "school of simplifiers," as he called them[6]; but he was, and quite rightly, just as ready to blame the composers who thoughtlessly wrote impossible or ineffective parts for the double-bass as the players who were unable to play them. Fétis also remarked on those who attempted only the main notes of the part when he criticised the Paris double-bass players and unfavourably compared them with the London players in 1829.[7] A method for the double-bass, published by Cocks and Co. of London in 1833, included "an explanation of the mode of simplifying Bass-parts, so as to adapt them to the instrument."[8]

Except for a few outstanding players here and there, it seems that the double-bass playing in orchestras, even towards the middle of last century, was by no means good. The well-known passage for 'cellos and basses alone in the *Scherzo* of Beethoven's C minor symphony no doubt provided a very good test of the players' executive skill, and there is evidence that in more than one case the result was such as to demand some compromise in order to make the passage sound well. Berlioz said that for long it was customary to omit the double-basses at the Paris Conservatoire Concerts, leaving the 'cellos to play the passage alone.[9] When Berlioz assembled a

---

[1] Museum of the Paris Conservatoire, No. 203 (1884 Cat.). Two of these instruments were made, one of which was sent to Russia. See also Berlioz's *Instrumentation*, pp. 240, 243.
[2] *Ency. Lond.*, Vol. XVI, p. 385. [3] *Partiturkenntniss*, I, p. 7.
[4] *Ibid.*, II, No. 25. [5] Quoted in *The Orchestra in the 18th Century* (Carse), p. 123.
[6] *Mem.*, I, p. 71. *Instrumentation*, p. 41. [7] *Curiosités*, p. 192.
[8] "The double-basses should take the principal notes, omitting the passing ones, which renders the effect more imposing and less confusing" (Cipriani Potter, *Mus. World*, Vol. V, p. 132).
[9] *Evenings*, p. 323.

monster orchestra for a festival in the building of the Paris Industrial Exhibition in 1844, he described the effect of the 36 basses rehearsing the same passage: "When we came to the *Scherzo* of Beethoven's Symphony in C minor, it was like the grunting of about fifty ferocious pigs. Such was the incoherence and want of precision in the performance of this passage."[1] The recitative for 'cellos and basses in the Choral Symphony was played by four 'cellos and two basses at the original performance at Vienna.[2] Eckardt tells how this same passage was played as a solo by Dragonetti, instead of by the whole body, when this symphony was performed under Moscheles at the London Philharmonic in 1841.[3] If such expedients were necessary in the case of such outstanding orchestras as the Paris *Société des Concerts* and the London Philharmonic, we may be quite sure that in the lesser orchestras they would be obliged to make similar compromises. But when Liszt conducted the C minor symphony at the Beethoven Festival at Bonn in 1845, he had the *Scherzo* played "just as Beethoven wrote it," and Berlioz was "quite surprised to find the Symphony in C minor still more beautiful when executed integrally than when corrected. I had to go to Bonn to make this discovery."[4]

Solo players generally used small three-stringed basses with thinner strings. Anglois, who played a concerto at the London Philharmonic in 1837, played on a small three-stringed bass tuned a fourth higher than the ordinary English bass, viz., D–G–C.[5]

Outstanding double-bass players in the first half of last century were: Cavaliere Antonio dall 'Occa (1763–1846) a native of Bologna; Johann Hindle, Vienna; Köhler (1783–1841), Karlsruhe; Dragonetti, London; August Müller, Darmstadt; Carl Gottfried Wilhelm Wach (1755–1833), Leipzig; Schmidt, Brunswick; Chénié, Lamy, and Gouffé, Paris.

THE HARP

The up-to-date French harp at the end of the 18th century was that known as the *single-action* harp.[6] This was provided with 41 strings tuned to the scale of E flat major, and by means of mechanism, operated by seven pedals, one for each note in the octave, the strings could be shortened to sound a semitone higher. The compass was five complete octaves and a sixth, starting on the low F and finishing on a high D. The facilities for modulating on this instrument were rather restricted, and many chromatic passages and some chords and arpeggios were quite impossible. But for diatonic music without sudden modulations to extreme keys the instrument was serviceable, and many a harpist in the first half of last century knew no other.

By 1810 Erard had perfected his *double-action* harp.   On this the compass was extended to 6½ octaves, tuned to the scale of C flat, and ranging from

---

[1] *Mem.*, II, p. 158.   [2] Smart, *Journals*, p. 123.   [3] Eckardt, p. 123.
[4] *Evenings*, p. 323.   There were 8 or 9 'cellos and a dozen double-basses, the latter led by Dragonetti.
[5] *Mus. World*, June 16, 1837, p. 11.
[6] *Harpe à simple mouvement*, or *à un seul accrochement*.

C flat to G flat.   By means of a greatly improved mechanism each string could be shortened to sound either a semitone or a tone higher.   This double pedal action greatly increased the possibilities of modulating on the harp, and some chromatic chords and some effects peculiar to the instrument were added to the resources at the disposal of the player.

The advent of the double-action harp did not mean that every harpist immediately became possessed of one of these elaborate and expensive instruments, and some time had to elapse before composers could write for it with any hope that it would be available in an orchestra.   Choron did not mention the double-action harp in his book of 1813, and although Catrufo knew of it in 1832, he still regarded the single-action harp as the standard instrument.   In 1836 Kastner advised composers to continue writing for the old harp in E flat, which was still used in most orchestras, until such time as the newer instrument became more generally available.[1] Berlioz was probably exaggerating a little when he wrote (1844) that the double-action harp "has been adopted by all harp players of the present day."[2] No doubt the best of the Paris harpists had the new instrument by that time.

In Germany, where the harp was not much in demand and the few players there were played the instrument only as a side-line, the double-action harp was rarely to be found until after the mid-century.   Gassner knew only the old instrument in 1838, and in 1843 Berlioz complained, not only about the lack of harps in German orchestras, but also about the old-fashioned instruments and the lack of skilled players.[3]   At Hanover, however, he found "a lady in the chorus" who played a double-action harp.   As late as 1846 Wagner recommended that the two old single-action harps at Dresden should be replaced by double-action instruments.   Soon after the mid-century, when Wagner and Liszt were writing more important and more exacting harp parts, the Germans were obliged to pay more attention to the instrument, and had to see that better instruments and competent players were included in their orchestras.

In London there were plenty of harps and harpists, and there would be no difficulty in finding players for the comparatively few harp parts in the scores of the period.

*   *   *

While the bowed string instruments remained practically unchanged, nearly all the vital improvements that have fallen to the lot of wind instruments were made during the first half of last century.   The wood-wind gained the key-mechanisms that have made them into the serviceable instruments they are to-day, and to the brass accrued the valve-system, the one and only revolutionary change in their whole history.   With the valve came a whole group of new instruments without which the brass band of to-day would be an impossibility.

[1] *Traité*, p. 23, f.n.   [2] *Instrum.*, p. 61.   [3] *Mem.*, II, pp. 21, 29, 34, 44, 55, 78, 97.

It was between 1800 and 1850 that the work of most of the important improvers and reformers of wind instruments was done. To such men as Boehm, Triébert, Sellner, Klosé, Buffet, Ivan Müller, Savary, Almenräder and Heckel, the wood-wind players of to-day owe the instruments on which they are able to play with such amazingly certain execution and such good intonation the exacting parts which face them at the present time; and to such as Blühmel, Stölzel, Sax, Périnet, Halary, Wieprecht, Meifred, Uhlmann and Riedl, the brass players of to-day owe the chromatic instruments which gave them resources for so long denied to the players on unmechanised natural instruments, the hunting horn, the cavalry trumpet, the bugle and the post horn.

The debt of the modern player and composer to the ingenious and persevering makers and players of wind instruments in the first half of last century is greater than is generally realised or acknowledged at the present time. Such names as Raoux, Courtois, Labbaye or Besson of Paris, Müller of Mayence, Moritz or Griessling and Schlott of Berlin, Embach of Amsterdam, Köhler or Pace of London, Pelliti of Milan, and Charles Sax of Brussels, mean little to most musicians and music-lovers of to-day. The names of Rudall and Rose, or Key of London, Godfroy of Paris, Bachmann of Brussels, Maino or Piana of Milan, Koch or Ziegler of Vienna, and Grenser or Golde of Dresden, will bring no response from many to whom the names of Stradivarius or Amati are familiar enough. Even if a few of the names still survive in the firms of the present time, the man in the street does not know them as he knows the names Bechstein or Erard, and, although he is quite familiar with the word Saxophone, may be surprised to learn that Sax was the name of a man. Those who wish to know something of the lives and work of these men will find that all except a few of them are ignored in the standard Musical Dictionaries, which are, nevertheless, full of the names of unimportant composers and singers.

Players, conductors, composers and listeners of to-day are asked at least to read through these lists of names without impatience, and to remember that the first half of last century gave us most of these men, and that they were the men who gave us the vastly improved wind instruments which we now so readily take for granted without troubling to enquire into their history.

Wind instruments in the 18th century were made in workshops by hand, with the aid of simple tools and by rule of thumb, by skilled craftsmen; by the middle of last century most of them were being made in larger factories, with the aid of machines, by more elaborate processes and according to more precisely calculated formulæ by skilled specialists. The former craftsman made either wooden or brass instruments; he worked in either wood or metal, but rarely in both. The larger works or factories of the 19th century tended to produce wind instruments of all sorts, of wood and of metal, and the instruments passed through the hands of relays of different skilled workers before they were completed.

THE WOOD-WIND

The design of wood-wind instruments in and before the 18th century was the result of a compromise between the demands of the musical scale and the limitations of the human hand. The note-holes on the comparatively simple instruments were covered and controlled by the players' finger-tips, and mechanical aid was enlisted only when a hole was situated where no finger was available, or when it lay well out of reach of the short little finger. The situations of the holes controlled by the finger-tips were therefore dictated largely by the natural spread, or distance apart, of the fingers, rather than by the requirements of the musical scale, and that a diatonic scale. Yet another limitation was the fact that the finger-tips could completely cover holes only up to a certain size; therefore, the diameter of any hole must hardly exceed about half an inch.

Thus it was that on 18th century instruments keys were provided only at one or both ends of the series of six finger-holes which gave the natural diatonic scale of the instrument. In the cases of the flute and oboe it was only at the lower end; for the clarinet the keys were necessarily not only at the lower end, but also at the upper end in order to fill up the gap between the top of the fundamental scale and the beginning of the scale of "harmonics" which were "overblown" at the twelfth; on the bassoon the keys were all at the lower end of the scale. All the keys were therefore (with the exception of the two clarinet keys at the upper end) provided for the purpose of carrying the fundamental scales downwards, below the six-finger-hole scale.

On these old instruments the finger-holes had to be placed in two groups of three each, one for each hand, and the natural spread of the fingers demanded that the holes must be practically equidistant. They had to provide for a diatonic scale, and from these same holes the player had to produce his chromatic scale, which could be done only by means of fork-fingering,[1] a device which more or less adversely affected both the intonation and the quality of the sounds so produced. These all-purpose holes could not all be placed in acoustically desirable positions even on the smaller instruments, and on the larger ones they must needs be still more badly situated.

On all these instruments, the only note of the chromatic scale which could not be "forked" was provided with a special hole controlled by a key for the righthand littlefinger; this was the lowest D sharp on the flute and oboe, and the lowest G sharp on the clarinet and bassoon. In the case of the clarinet, one thumb, and two additional holes (with keys) were needed to complete the diatonic scale, and on the bassoon both thumbs were required to cover holes.

The standard wood-wind towards the end of the 18th century were therefore equipped as follows:

[1] Lowering the pitch of a sound from an open hole by closing the hole immediately below it.

Flute—6 finger-holes and one key.   Lowest note D.
Oboe—6 finger-holes[1] and two keys.   Lowest note C.
Clarinet—7 finger-holes, one thumb-hole and 5 keys.   Lowest note E.
Bassoon—6 finger-holes, two thumb-holes and 5 or 6 keys.   Lowest note
     B flat.

Figure 1 shows the number, positions and approximate sizes of the holes
on the ordinary flutes, oboes, and clarinets near the end of the 18th century.
The contemporary bassoon is shown in Fig. 4.

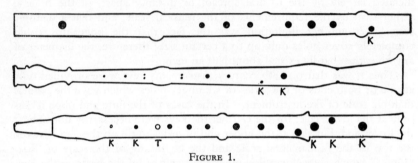

FIGURE 1.

One-keyed flute.   Two-keyed oboe.   Five-keyed clarinet.

K = hole controlled by a key.   T = Thumb-hole.   The black circles are the holes on
the top or front of the instrument; the hollow circles are those on the underside
of the clarinet.

The few necessary keys were of the most rudimentary design.   A single
lever served for the holes that were to remain closed when the key-lever was
not pressed down, and two levers, one acting on the end of the other, served
for the open-standing keys.   Each key lay in a channel cut in a raised ring
or swelling of wood left for that purpose when the instrument was turned
on the lathe; only on the bassoons were metal saddles used to support the
axles on which the keys pivoted.   A metal pin served as an axle, and a
flat spring pressed down one end of the lever.   A piece of leather stuck on
to the flat under-surface of the key kept the closed hole more or less airtight.

The rudimentary design of these instruments imposed severe handicaps
on the player's execution except when playing in a limited number of
favourite keys.   The scale, and especially the chromatic scale, was uneven
in quality, and in varying degree the intonation was faulty.   The solos for
virtuoso players, the large majority of which were composed by the players
themselves, show a very small range of keys, and in the orchestral music of
the 18th century it is unusual to find a movement written in any key with
more than three sharps or flats in the key-signature.

Although in the case of the flute the first important improvements were
initiated before the end of the 18th century, by far the greater part of the

[1] The twin-holes on the oboe was a device for lowering the sound by a semitone when
one of the two was closed.   (See Fig. 1.)

progress achieved on all instruments came about during the first quarter of last century. It was then that the oboes, clarinets and bassoons began to gain their amplified key-systems.

The most urgent improvements were firstly, acoustical, and secondly, as a consequence, mechanical. That is to say, the addition of new note-holes and the readjustment in the position and size of the old ones demanded that additional key-work be provided in order to control the holes. By about 1825 the up-to-date instruments were equipped as follows:

Flute—6 finger-holes and 8 keys. Lowest note C.
Oboe—6 finger-holes and from 8 to 12 keys. Lowest note B.
Clarinet—7 finger-holes, one thumb-hole and from 8 to 13 keys.
Bassoon—6 finger-holes, 2 thumb-holes and from 8 to 11 keys.

Figure 2 shows the lay-out of the holes on the instruments made during the 'twenties.

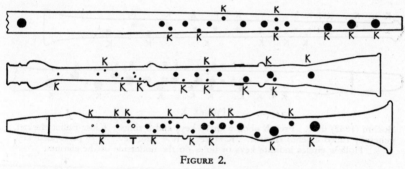

FIGURE 2.

Eight-keyed flute. Eleven-keyed oboe (Sellner type). Thirteen-keyed clarinet.

If Figures 1 and 2 are compared, it will be seen that almost every semitone in the fundamental chromatic scale now has its own note-hole; each of these additional holes had, of course, to be provided with a closed key in order to control it. There is also some improvement in the situations of the holes, and some increase in diameter, especially on the flute and clarinet, for which larger note-holes are advantageous. A few keys peculiar to each type of instrument had also been added, notably the duplicate F natural keys and foot-keys on the flute, the octave-key on the oboe, a shake key which is still found on every clarinet, a thumb-plate over the left thumb-hole and the pin-hole key on the crook of the bassoon.

The keys at that time, however, remained the simple levers that they had always been. Still mounted in wooden supports, the number of rings, swellings or blocks on the outside of the instruments had greatly increased, till the surface was littered with awkward projections. The manipulation of the many new keys was not without its difficulties; there were places where one finger had to operate two or even three adjacent keys, and the movement of the finger from key to key, or from hole to key, was often very awkward; some *legato* movements were difficult, or even impossible.

Certain improvements in the key-work, however, made for greater precision and reliability. Cupped keys holding a stuffed pad instead of the flat leather, metal linings to the note-holes and the bearings in which the keys worked, and rollers which eased the passage of a finger from key to key, were among the improvements which facilitated the fingering. The gains were: a reduction in the number of fork-fingerings, with a corresponding improvement in the intonation and quality of many sounds; some improved facility in playing in the more remote keys; two semitones added to the downward compass of the flute, and one (or even two) to the oboe;

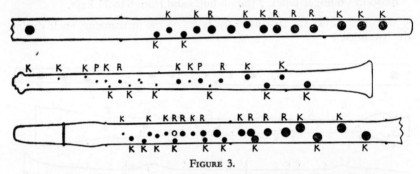

FIGURE 3.

Bochm (1832) flute. French oboe with 16 keys and 2 rings. Klosé-Buffet clarinet, generally called Boehm clarinet. K = key. R = ring-key. P = perforated key. Hollow circles indicate keys or holes on the underside of the clarinet.

an addition to the upward range of the bassoon; greater facility in certain *legato* passages from note to note, and means for playing some shakes which were formerly awkward or impossible.

But the control of the many note-holes on the instruments was still far from perfect, and the situations of some of the holes, and their sizes, remained irrational. It was within the next period of about 25 years, roughly from 1825 to 1850, that so much was done to improve the situation and size of the holes, and at the same time to provide key-work which gave the players adequate control over the ever-increasing number of holes. In this period falls the work of such as Boehm, Triébert, Klosé, Buffet, Sax, Savary jeune, Almenräder, and Adam Heckel.

The lay-out and approximate sizes of the holes of the flute, oboe and clarinet round about the middle of last century are shown in Fig. 3, and of the bassoon in Fig. 4 (right).

A comparison of Figures 1, 2 and 3 will show how the bodies of the instruments had been pierced with an ever-increasing number of holes. It will be seen that these were more rationally distributed in accordance with the requirements of the chromatic scale, and that there had been, especially on the flute and clarinet, an increase in the diameter of the holes. There were also additional holes for facilitating the sounding of harmonics, and some for the production of shakes.

The old lever-keys, although they were retained wherever they were still serviceable, had been unable to provide adequate control over the newly-distributed and more numerous holes. Some new key-mechanism was wanted, and it was forthcoming when the keys projecting from horizontal rod-axles were devised. These were first made practicable on Boehm's conical flutes of 1832 together with the ring-keys, and after a few years the same mechanical advantages began to spread to practically all other wood-wind instruments, the oboes and clarinets benefiting very considerably by the new mechanism, and the bassoons only to a smaller degree.

The finger-plates, ring-keys and key-covers projecting at right-angles from horizontal rod-axles proved to be of inestimable value in easing the fingering when playing in the more remote keys. The mechanism was light and dependable; the heavy and clumsy wooden mounts gave way to neat metal pillar-mounts[1] with steel screwed-in axles. Needle-springs[2] largely replaced the old flat springs; interlocking devices and clutches were introduced into the rod-axle mechanism, and made new key-movements possible which would have been quite impossible with the simple lever-keys. Moreover, the new key-work was made with much greater precision, and it worked more reliably.

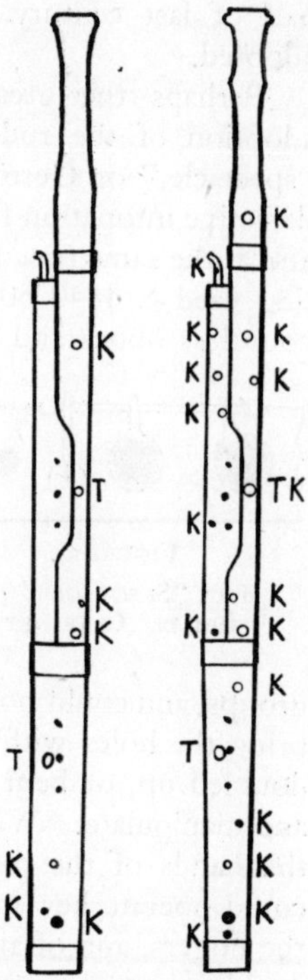

FIGURE 4.

Six-keyed bassoon, c. 1800. Bassoon (French type, c. 1850) with 17 keys. T = thumb-hole. TK = thumb-key. The black circles indicate the holes on the front, and the hollow circles the holes on the back of the bassoon.

While all these improvements were being made, there came also a more sharp division of the wood-wind instruments into national types. These were mainly German and French types, and the distinction still holds good. The Boehm flute, although devised by a German, won its success in France and in England, while German flautists remained true to the old type with improved key-work. The French and German oboes also retained each their individuality, and only fairly recently has the French oboe been welcomed in Germany. While the French players were ready to adopt the Klosé-Buffet clarinet, players in Germany refused to recognise it, and went on improving the old type quite independently of the French reformation of that instrument. The bassoon also branched out into two different types, one German and one French; both remain to this day quite distinctive.

[1] First seen on the glass flutes of Laurent in 1806.   [2] Invented by Buffet, c. 1837.

But all makers and players adopted and benefited by the general improvement of the key-work and lay-out of the holes which was going on in all
countries where wood-wind instruments were being made during the first
half of last century.   In this country the French types were generally
adopted.

Perhaps the greatest and most universal benefit accruing from the
adoption of the rod-axle and ring-key mechanism was the well-known
"spectacle," or German *Brille*. This solved the age-long problem of the
defective intonation from the hole covered by the right hand middle-finger,
and at the same time preserved the old and still useful "fork."   Since it was
first used c. 1840–50, this device has been embodied in the key-work of
countless oboes and clarinets of the so-called "simple system."

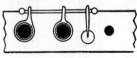

FIGURE 5.

THE "SPECTACLE" OR
BRILLE (CLARINET).

To the larger instruments of each type,
notably the cor anglais, bass clarinet and
double-bassoon, the new key-mechanism came
as a much-needed blessing. As long as the
finger-tips had to lie immediately over the
main note-holes, it had been quite impossible
to place these holes rationally on these longer
tubes; they had to remain close together in two
groups, and could not be larger than the finger-tips could cover.   In order to
bring the holes within reach of the hands, the instruments had been curved,
doubled up, or bent into curious shapes, and they were awkward to hold
and manipulate.   With the advent of keys working on horizontal rod-axles,
the hands of the player could be conveniently placed, while the fingers
could operate keys placed over holes situated at almost any distance from
the fingers, and of any size that was desirable.   In this way some awkward
problems in the construction of bass clarinets and double-bassoons were
eased, and it also brought about a straightening of the tubes of the cor
anglais and basset horn.

While the position of the holes and the key-mechanism of the wood-wind
instruments were being so greatly improved, attention was also being given
to the bore of the tubes.   Each had its own problems and requirements,
and they were dealt with by such as Boehm (flute), Triébert (oboe), Ivan
Müller and Klosé (clarinet), and Savary and Almenräder (French and
German bassoons), as well as by other persevering makers and players.

Round about the middle of the century the old boxwood instruments with
brass keys gave way to those made of hard dark woods with white-metal
keys and fittings.

Many minor improvements were to follow, but the bulk of the work had
been done and all the radical changes were accomplished during the
combined working lives of Beethoven and Berlioz.

Of any other wood-wind instruments not already mentioned, little need
be said; none of them was used, unless quite exceptionally, in orchestras
during the first half of last century.   The larger-sized flutes appear to have

been quite out of use, although Jannusch, the Prague flautist, did make an attempt to revive the alto flute (*flûte d'amour*) in 1824.[1]   The flutes pitched, respectively, a semitone and a minor third above the ordinary concert flute and piccolo, remained purely military band instruments.   A flageolet or "octave flute,"[2] actually a whistle-flute of the recorder type, was sometimes used in English orchestras in place of the piccolo.[3]   The *Oboe d'amore*, although quite well known in the 18th century, had practically disappeared, and was not due to be resuscitated until the revival of J. S. Bach's music had made further progress.   A baritone or bass oboe, made by Triébert for Vogt, appeared about 1825, and had a few successors, but these were given little encouragement.   On the whole, composers left the high clarinets to the military bands, and of the lower ones only the basset-horn and bass clarinet held a very uncertain foothold in the orchestra before 1850.   The *clarinet d'amore* languished unnoticed, and the contrabass clarinet was launched on a career which has always remained uncertain and precarious. The tenor bassoon, although a few were made from time to time, was given so little attention by composers that it could hardly claim to be regarded as an orchestral instrument.

The saxophone (patented 1846) was of too recent date to be able to establish itself even in French orchestras before the middle of the century. Sax had been working on his new instrument before he settled in Paris at the end of 1842, and soon after his arrival there he demonstrated its powers to a number of prominent musicians, including Kastner, Rossini, Meyerbeer, Halévy and Berlioz, winning their approval and considerable encouragement.

At that time only the bass instrument in B flat had been made, and Berlioz included a description of it in the first edition of his new *Grand Traité* of 1843 (p. 150), also in the subsequent German-French edition of the same book published a few years later by Schlesinger (p. 162).

The new instrument was first heard in public at a concert given in Paris (*Salle Herz*) in 1844 under the direction of Berlioz, who had written for the occasion a piece specially devised to show off the merits of Sax's various instruments, and at that concert the saxophone part was played by Sax himself on an unfinished instrument.[4]   Kastner claimed that he was the first to write a saxophone part in an orchestral score, namely, in his *Le dernier Roi de Juda*, a biblical drama composed in 1844.   In 1845 the new instruments were introduced into some French infantry bands.

The patent specification of 1846[5] shows that Sax had planned to make the

---

[1] An account of this flute appeared in *The Harmonicon*, Dec., 1824, p. 218.

[2] A scale for the "Improved Octave Flageolet" was published in London, and clearly distinguishes between the English Flageolet, the French Flageolet, and the Common Flute or Recorder.

[3] Mr. Adams played the Flageolet or Octave Flute at the Leicester Musical Festival in 1827, and at the Birmingham Festival in 1834.

[4] Comettant, p. 51.

[5] *Brevet de Adolphe Sax*, No. 3226, *du* 21 *Mars*, 1846, *pour Systèmes d'instruments à vent dits Saxophone*.

saxophones in two groups of four each, pitched an octave apart. The main or lower group was to be as follows:

No. 1.   Tenor in E flat.
No. 2.   Saxophone in C, or in B flat (the original type).
No. 3.   Contrabass in G, or in A flat.
No. 4.   Bourdon in C, or in B flat.

SAXOPHONE EXHIBITED AT THE NATIONAL EXPOSITION IN PARIS IN 1849

The higher group, numbered 5, 6, 7 and 8, were to be pitched each an octave higher than those in the lower group, the highest being No. 8, the small straight instrument in E flat. This projected scheme was apparently never carried out, and at that time only Nos. 1 and 2 were actually in being.

The group of saxophones described by Kastner in 1844[1] comprised only four instruments:

Soprano in C or B flat.
Alto or tenor in F or E flat.
Bass in C or B flat.
Contrabass in F or E flat.

In 1847[2] Kastner gave the following extended group:

High soprano in F or E flat.
Soprano in C or B flat.
Alto in E flat.
Alto-tenor in B flat.
Tenor-baritone in E flat.
Bass in C or B flat.
Contrabass in F or E flat.

Berlioz's group in 1856[3] was as follows:

High soprano in E flat.   Soprano in C or B flat.
Alto in F or E flat.   Tenor in C or B flat.
Baritone in F or E flat.   Bass in C or B flat.

In 1852 Halévy wrote parts for four saxophones in the score of his opera

[1] *Traité*, Supp., p. 39.   [2] *Manuel général*, pl. XXV.   [3] English trans., p. 233.

PLATE 22

ADOLPHE SAX

PLATE 23

THEOBALD BOEHM

Le Juif errant,[1] and in 1856 Jullien had five in his wind-band (called "zouaves") with which he toured England in that year. After that time saxophones appeared in a number of French scores, and were used in some military bands, but they never became very well known or popular until the time when they were made to take a prominent part in vulgarising the dance music of the present century.

The first sign of the saxophone in England was in 1849, when Henry Distin,[2] a member of a brass quintet known as the Distin Family, advertised that he had these instruments for sale at his depot in Cranbourne Street (Est. 1846). In that same year (1849) *The Illustrated London News*[3] gave a woodcut of the saxophone exhibited at the Paris National Exposition, and in 1850 the new instrument was heard at Jullien's concerts, and again in 1852 at both Jullien's concerts and the Musical Union, played by Souallé and Wuille, both of whom were Belgian clarinettists.

BRASS INSTRUMENTS

Before the advent of the valve system, first heard of in 1815, three different ways of partially bridging the gaps between the sounds of the natural harmonic series on brass instruments had been tried. These were: (*a*) by "stopping," i.e. inserting the hand in the bell; (*b*) by a lengthening slide; and (*c*) by keys controlling holes in the tube.

The first of these devices was most successful when it was applied to the French horn, and had been in use for solo-playing since soon after the middle of the 18th century, but in the early years of last century was being demanded more and more in ordinary orchestral parts. By partially stopping the horn with the hand in the bell, all the consecutive sounds between the sixth and the sixteenth open notes could be produced without much loss of quality, and those which were naturally out of tune could be corrected. A number of additional notes, hitherto impossible, between the third and the sixth open notes were also made available by this process; so, provided the player kept within a limited dynamical range, the horn became practically a chromatic instrument in the upper part of its compass, and also a useful melodist in the medium and best part of its scale. The effectiveness of this hand-technique considerably delayed the adoption of valves on the horn up to well after the middle of the century, especially in France and in this country.

Stopping was less effective on the trumpet, although this instrument was sometimes made in either a shortened, a curved (*demi-lune*), or a circular-coiled form, in order that the player's hand could be placed in the bell; but the choked quality of the stopped sounds destroyed the characteristic ring of the trumpet-tone, and players and composers in general remained true to the instrument in its original simple form, preferring a limited series of good notes to a more comprehensive scale of mixed quality.

[1] Lavoix, p. 426.
[2] In 1846 H. Distin became sole agent in England for all Sax's instruments.
[3] July 7, 1849.

The lengthening slide had long been known as the most essential part of the trombone; it was, in fact, so much part of it that without a slide the instrument at that time could not have been a trombone. A tentative effort had been made to apply the slide-mechanism to the horn, but nothing came of it, probably because stopping had already given as good results as the slide, and possibly because that device would have required the introduction of a considerable length of cylindrical tubing into the conical tube of the horn. These drawbacks did not stand in the way of adapting the slide to the trumpet; stopping was ineffective on that instrument, and the tube was largely cylindrical. Yet, when the slide was adapted to the trumpet, the instrument made little or no headway except in this country, and here it probably owed much of its success to the merits of a succession of outstanding players, namely, the two Hydes and the two Harpers.

The use of finger-holes or key-holes pierced in instruments sounded by means of cupped mouthpieces in order to sound a scale of consecutive notes was an old device, and had for long been employed on the old *cornetti* and the serpents. The former were obsolete before the end of the 18th century; the latter, originally a church instrument, was just coming into use towards the end of that century as a bass voice for military bands, and both were wooden instruments. The same method, but that all the holes were controlled by keys, was then applied to sundry metal instruments during the early years of the 19th century, and met with considerable success in the case of the keyed-bugle, and rather later, of the ophicleide. Keys had also been tried on horns, apparently with no success, and on trumpets with only partial success.

The brass instruments commonly used in orchestras at the beginning of the 19th century were therefore:

HORNS. The hand-horn, with a selection of crooks by means of which it could be put into any key between B flat alto (9 feet) and B flat basso (18 feet).

TRUMPETS. The natural trumpet, made or crooked in keys from 6ft. F down to 8 ft. C. Trumpets in any key higher than F were not generally used or demanded in the scores, but by combining crooks and tuning-bits the instrument could be lowered to 9 ft. B flat, or even to A or A flat, both of these last being rarely used.[1]

SLIDE TROMBONES. The Alto (E flat), the Tenor (B flat), and the Bass (F), in Germany and in this country, but in France only tenor trombones were used. Berlioz remarked: "Repeated observations at Berlin led me to think that the best way of grouping the trombones in the theatres is, after all, that adopted at the Paris *Opéra*, where three tenor trombones are employed."[2]

---

[1] The C and D crooks were combined for the key of B flat. The C, D and E crooks were combined for the key of A. The C, D and E flat crooks were combined for the key of A flat. Composers generally specified a D trumpet for a movement in the key of A, and a C trumpet for a movement in G.

[2] *Mem.*, II, p. 95.

Of the other varieties of trumpet already mentioned, none ever gained universal acceptance in all countries, and composers continued to write for the natural instrument without a slide, keys or stopping. Some particulars of the slide and keyed trumpets, however, will not be out of place at this point.

Soon after its introduction by John Hyde at the beginning of the century, the slide trumpet became the standard instrument of the English orchestral players. Although not altogether unknown in France,[1] players elsewhere ignored this very useful and effective instrument, if they ever knew it. On the English model the slide was drawn by two fingers *towards* the player, and its length provided sufficient additional tubing to lower every open note by one semitone with true intonation, the 4th, 5th and 7th open notes by a whole tone with intonation which was slightly sharp,[2] and was also used to correct the faulty intonation of the 7th, 11th, and 13th open notes. Thus, the instrument was not fully chromatic below the 6th open note, and as the lower crooks demanded increased extensions of the slide, the whole-tone shifts became less and less available as the crooks became longer.[3] Nevertheless, it was a serviceable instrument and possessed considerable advantages over the old natural trumpet. But it should be remembered that the parts played on the slide trumpet in England during the first half of last century were practically all written for natural trumpets, and that, therefore, the slide only came into use to correct the intonation of those open notes which were out of tune.[4] The instrument remained in use in England long after the appearance of the valved trumpet, and was not wholly extinct by the end of last century.

Just before the time when the slide-trumpet began to blossom in England, the keyed trumpet made its appearance in Vienna. Before the end of the 18th century (1796) Haydn wrote a concerto for this instrument,[5] and the Court trumpeter Weidinger, who is given credit for designing the keyed trumpet, began to exploit it in 1801, and displayed his skill in performing on it in many continental towns. It found little favour in Germany and made no headway in France, but it seems to have been adopted to some extent in Italy, and was evidently used by some Italian trumpeters in Rossini's time. In England the keyed trumpet was unable to face competition with the superior slide trumpet, but there are plenty of signs which show that it was by no means unknown in this country. Harper disposed of the keyed trumpet in a scathing foot-note in his tutor of 1836: "N.B. The Author is aware that there are Keyed Trumpets, but as the Trumpets written for in

---

[1] "*On avait jadis une trompette nommée trompette à coulisses*" (Kastner, *Traité*, p. 51). This probably refers to the slide trumpet devised by the Paris trumpeter Buhl, which was recommended in 1833 by the members of the *Institut de France* (*Revue Musicale*, 1833, p. 123).

[2] Harper's tutor, 1836, p. 11.

[3] In the younger Harper's tutor (c. 1875) it is said that the whole-tone shifts were not available when the instrument was crooked lower than D.

[4] For the English slide trumpet, see portrait of Harper on p. 180.

[5] Recently unearthed and now often played on the valve trumpet.

this Work are capable of accomplishing in a Superior Style, all that may be required, the Scales of those with keys are omitted."[1]   Some time during the 'thirties R. Cocks and Co. published a tutor for the keyed and valved trumpet, in which it was said that the former was "of recent invention, and now in general use."[2]   These trumpets were usually made in G or F, and could be crooked in the usual trumpet keys down to B flat.   By opening the key-holes, of which there were from four to six, in succession, a chromatic scale was obtainable from the third open note, for about two octaves.   The keys were manipulated by the left hand, but the quality of the sound deteriorated progressively as the holes became more and more distant from the bell-mouth.

In 1830 Karl Bargans, the leading trumpeter at Berlin, in an article entitled *On the trumpet, as at present employed in the orchestra*,[3] said that in Germany the keyed trumpet was then "not often used in the orchestra." The instrument in general use, he said, was the "common, or proper trumpet," that is, the old natural trumpet, but now reduced in length by being four times folded.   In this form it was possible to "stop" the bell with the hand, and Bargans gave the following scale for the instrument:

The circles indicate the open notes, described as "pure or natural." The half-circles indicate the stopped sounds, described as "artificial." The cross indicates the fully stopped sounds, which could not be "produced purely and promptly without great difficulty."

Keyed bugles made after Halliday's model (patented 1810) quickly spread over the continent of Europe, and although eagerly adopted in military and brass bands, were very sparingly used in orchestras.   They were admitted in some scores written for the Paris *Opéra*[4] under the name *Trompette à clefs*, but there is plenty of evidence to show that the instruments so called in France were not really trumpets; they were none other than the keyed bugle, variously named *Bugle à clefs*, *Trompette à clefs*, or *Cor à clefs*.[5]

In England the keyed bugle or Kent bugle quickly became popular in

[1] *Instructions for the Trumpet*, p. 13.

[2] For scale and fingering, see Carse, *Musical Wind Instruments*, p. 336.

[3] *Harm.*, Jan., 1830, p. 23.

[4] A part for keyed bugle in Kreutzer's *Ipsiboé* (1824) was played at the Paris *Opéra* by Bauman.   Parts also occur in a few operas by Rossini and Meyerbeer.

[5] Noblet's tutor (before 1834) for the *Bugle ou Trompette à clefs* makes it quite clear that this was a bugle: "*La Trompette à clefs, dite Bugle.*"   The illustrations in this tutor, also that of Halary's *Clavitube ou Trompette à clefs* (1821), leave no doubt as to the nature of the instrument.   Further evidence will be found in Catrufo (p. 22); in Kastner (Cours. Supp., p. 14); in Kastner, *Traité* (p. 52); and in the *Supplement* to the latter (p. 35), where the instrument is called *Trompette à clefs ou Bugle*.

military and brass bands, and made its appearance in a few light opera scores.[1]

There is no reason to suppose that German orchestras made use of the keyed bugle, but they employed it freely in their military bands. Some Italian scores call for a soprano keyed instrument which must have been either a keyed trumpet or a keyed bugle.

This instrument was usually made in 4 ft. C or B flat, and, fitted with from 6 to 9 keys, gave a chromatic scale from a semitone below the second open note up to the eighth open note, a range of just over two octaves.

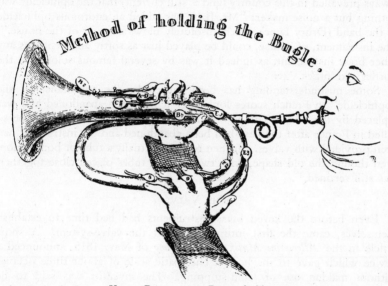

KEYED BUGLE FROM PURDAY'S TUTOR

The Regent's bugle was an improved form of Halliday's keyed bugle, devised in 1811 by J. G. Schmidt, who was then the leading trumpeter in the Prince Regent's private band and later became first trumpet at the King's Theatre.[2]

When Halary's ophicleides appeared in 1817 (patented 1821) both the alto in E flat and the bass in 8 ft. C or B flat were welcomed in military bands, and it was not long before the bass instrument began to be specified in Paris opera scores. For augmenting the bass part in large festival orchestras it was just the thing that was wanted, and so for some years the ophicleide successfully competed with the older serpent and the more recent bass-horn,

[1] Several tutors were issued in England: *Tutor for the Royal Keyed Bugle*, by a "Professor of Eminence" (Z. T. Purday, c. 1835); Logier, *A Complete Introduction to the Keyed Bugle*; Tully, *Tutor for the Kent Bugle* (R. Cocks, c. 1838); also Instructions in the elder Harper's Trumpet Tutor (1836).

[2] See Fétis, *Biog. univ.*, Art. Schmidt, and Pontécoulant, *Organographie*, p. 111.

until, in its turn, it was driven out by the valved tubas or bombardons. The ophicleide was fully keyed, and had a chromatic compass reaching from the fundamental note of its harmonic series to about three octaves above. It had a good *legato*, and was able to negotiate florid bass parts with much greater ease and much better effect than the bass trombone; moreover, the key-produced sounds were of good quality, excepting those few notes for which the last two or three keys on the narrower part of the tube were brought into use.

From the time when it was first introduced a quite mistaken idea has always prevailed in this country (and is still current) that the ophicleide was nothing but a noise-maker: "Mr. Balfe has added an enormous ophicleide to the band (Drury Lane) which absolutely blows one out of the house."[1] The instrument, of course, could be played just as softly and gently as any other brass instrument, as indeed it was by several famous soloists in the 'forties and 'fifties.

Some misunderstanding has been caused by the appearance of the "ophicleide" in French scores long after it had been abandoned and was replaced by the tuba. This is because the ophicleide continued to be so called in France after the keys had been abandoned and the instrument had been provided with valves. It then became virtually a tuba or bombardon, even though the old shape, with two parallel tubes placed close together, was still retained.[2]

THE VALVE

Even before the keyed brass instruments had had time to establish themselves, came the first intimation about the valve-system. A short article in the *Allgemeine Musikalische Zeitung* of May, 1815, announced a device which gave to the horn a chromatic scale of about three octaves without making use of hand-stopping. The inventor was said to be Heinrich Stölzel, the horn player, who proceeded to exploit the invention in Berlin, and then became associated with a Silesian bandsman named Friedrich Blühmel, who later on claimed to have invented the valve. In 1818 this contrivance was patented in Prussia for ten years, and before the expiry of the patent, valved instruments were being introduced into the bands of some Prussian cavalry Guards. By 1826 valved instruments had found their way to Paris, and by about 1830 they were just becoming known and were beginning to be made in most European countries.[3]

---

[1] G. A. Sala, *Life and Adventures*, p. 46; quoted from a contemporary critique.

[2] For evidence see: Kastner's *Méthode pour l'Ophicléide* (c. 1840), in which an *Ophicléide à 3 pistons ou Bombardon* is described; also, in Caussinus's tutor, the *Ophicléide ou Bombardon à 3 pistons* is discussed. According to Pierre (*Les Facteurs*, p. 328), Raoux exhibited a valved ophicleide in 1844. Garnier's *Méthode* for the ophicleide (c. 1845) is entirely for the valved instrument. See also pl. XVI, No. 9, in Kastner's *Manuel* (1848); Kastner's *Traité*, p. 57; and pp. 47 and 48 in the Supplement to the same.

[3] Rode, *Neue Berliner Musik-Zeitung*, 14 *Jahrgang*, No. 7. Bands of the *Jäger* Guards in Prussia acquired their first valved horns in 1825, and valved trumpets in 1828 (Kalkbrenner, p. 33). Prussian infantry bands got their first valved instruments in 1830 (*Ibid.*, p. 34).

The valve-system, as it was commonly adopted, gave the player the means of instantaneously adding to the sounding-length of his instrument any of three lengths of tubing which served to lower its pitch by a semitone, a tone, or a minor third. Thus, an instrument in C could in a moment be turned into one in either B, B flat, or A, each capable of sounding the natural harmonic series proper to its length. By adding these extra lengths of tubing either singly, in twos, or all three together, the player had under his control seven different sounding-lengths, or the equivalent of seven natural instruments, each with its series of open notes. So an instrument in C could be turned into one in either B, B flat, A, A flat, G or F sharp at will, and with the open notes of all these different lengths at his disposal the player had command of a chromatic scale ranging from an augmented 4th above the fundamental sound up to as high as he could play.

The three additional tube-lengths were added to the main tube in the form of loopways, and in order to be able to add any of them to the air-passage through the instrument, or to cut them off, some form of valve-mechanism was necessary. As far as is known, the piston valve was the first mechanism to be employed in Berlin, but before long two other devices made their appearance; these were the rotary valve and the Vienna valve.[1] Other valve-mechanisms were subsequently devised and tried, but in the end the only ones to survive were the three already mentioned. The rotary and the Vienna valves were favoured in Germany and Austria, while in France and England the piston valve was the favourite. The Vienna valve eventually went out of use, leaving the piston and the rotary valves to share the field between them, as they do to this day.

NINE-KEYED OPHICLEIDE

When they became known and were obtainable, valved instruments were readily adopted by military and brass bands all over Europe. As far as the orchestra was concerned, horns and trumpets were the instruments destined

[1] For further particulars, see Carse, *Musical Wind Instruments*, Sec. VIII.

to be most affected by the advent of the valve.   It was not until the 'thirties
that the new instruments began to find their way into orchestras, and then
some twenty or more years had to pass before they came into anything like
general use.   Germany was the first to give the valved instruments a general
welcome.   Berlioz reported that in 1843 horns and trumpets with "cylinders"
(rotary valves) were to be found in all the most important orchestras, as
well as the valved tuba or bombardon.   Schumann's symphonies (1841–
1851) mark the period of transition in Germany; that composer wrote for
both natural and valved instruments, using the latter rather timidly and
inconsistently.   Even in Wagner's early works the two types are used
together, and there is some reluctance to take full advantage of the new
mechanism; but after the mid-century the composer's confidence in the new
instruments was firmly established, and there was no more hesitation in
making use of their possibilities to the fullest extent.

In France the adoption of the valve proceeded rather more deliberately.
In spite of Meifred's and Halary's efforts, French players in general clung to
the hand-horn, and the mid-century saw that instrument still the standard
orchestral horn.   Meifred had played a solo on a valved horn at the Conservatoire Concerts as early as 1828,[1] but that was clearly a performance
intended to show off the paces of a new and untried instrument.   According
to Rivière, who was there at the time, the only valved instrument in general
use at Paris in 1839 was the cornet.[2]   Berlioz argued in favour of the German
valved horns and trumpets, and would not admit that the tone of these
instruments deteriorated when the valves were used[3]; he remarked impa-
tiently: "I am not speaking of Paris; some ten years hence we shall have them
there."[4]   Kastner (1844) also pleaded for a more general use of valved
instruments in the Paris orchestras, and could not detect any loss of quality
just because the air-passage went through a valve-tube.   The Paris makers,
however, were all busy making valved instruments in the 'thirties and
'forties, but mainly for the military bands; and once Adolphe Sax had got
hold of the idea he began to exploit it in every possible way.   Starting about
1830, composers for the *Opéra* occasionally introduced parts for valved
instruments into their works, notably Bellini, Donizetti, Halévy and Meyerbeer, and, although slowly, the new instruments began to usurp the positions
of the hand-horn, the natural trumpet, and the keyed ophicleide, their
conquest was by no means complete in France by the middle of the century.

The brothers Lewy were playing duets on valved horns in Vienna as
early as 1827,[5] but there, again, they were being introduced as novelties,
and such performances provide no evidence that the valves were then in
general use.   There is evidence, however, that the Viennese makers Riedl
and Uhlmann were both making valved instruments before 1830,[6] and there,
no doubt, as in other large musical centres, the gradual infiltration of the new

---

[1] Elwart, p. 131.   [2] Rivière, p. 52.   [3] *Mem.*, II, pp. 92, 93.   [4] *Ibid.*, II, p. 23.
[5] *Harm.*, March, 1827, p. 56; the instruments were described as "newly-invented."
[6] Nemetz, *Posaun-Schule*, p. 20.

instruments into the orchestras would be going on during the 'thirties and 'forties.

Of the progress of the valve in Italy there is little precise information. Some surviving instruments by Pelitti of Milan belonging to the period before the mid-century suggest that the valve had reached Italy soon after 1830, that they had been copied, and were gradually coming into use both in military bands and in orchestras.

In this country valved trumpets seem to have come about 1830 by a rather circuitous route via Russia.[1] Even if that is so, it is difficult to believe that the valved cornet did not come to England direct from France, where it was first made. It is quite certain, however, that valved instruments were being sold in London (even if they were not made there) in 1830, and that they came direct from either Germany or France. A writer in *The Harmonicon*[2] in 1830 described an instrument which he saw at Percival's manufactory in St. James's Street; it was a Chromatic Bass, folded like a bugle-horn, and provided with "three moveable stops." This was certainly a valved instrument, probably of the tuba type. The same writer in the same year mentions French horns with two valves which had been added by Pace of Westminster and by Percival.[3]

In his slide trumpet Tutor, written in 1836,[4] the elder Harper included some instructions for playing the valved trumpet and the cornet. The former he called "The Russian Valve or Stop Trumpet," and to the latter he gave the names *Cornet à Pistons*, small Stop Trumpet, Stop horn, Post horn or Cornopean. The last name was very commonly used in this country for many years. The London makers Pace, Köhler, Garrett, Percival and Keat, were making valved instruments during the 'thirties and 'forties, mostly trumpets and cornets, but there is no reason to suppose that the London horn and trumpet players used these instruments in the orchestras much before the mid-century.

In 1837 a Mr. Percy played a solo on a valved horn at a concert in the Mary-le-bone Literary and Scientific Institution[5]; this was hailed as a complete novelty, and it is obvious that the horn with valves was then quite unfamiliar to most players in London.

That the valve should have required some thirty or forty years to establish itself in orchestras is not at all surprising when all the circumstances are taken into consideration. For some ten years after it was first brought out in Berlin, the supply of instruments with valves must have been very limited. The demands of the Prussian military bands would easily absorb all the instruments made by probably not more than two makers.[6] After 1825, when the valved instruments were just beginning to find their way

---

[1] Farmer, *The Rise of Military Music*, p. 103; *Memoirs of the R.A. Band*, p. 69.

[2] *Harm.*, July, 1830, p. 281.   [3] *Ibid.*, Aug., 1830, p. 320.

[4] "he has been much occupied of late, in preparing a complete preceptor for the trumpet, and other brass instruments." (*Mus. World*, June 17, 1836, p. xi.)

[5] *Mus. World*, March 17, 1837, p. 8.   [6] Moritz, and Griessling and Schlott.

into other countries, some years must have elapsed before the makers of brass instruments could acquire the tools and machinery, also the skill and experience required for making a mechanism so much more complicated than anything they had previously made.   When a fair supply became available in the 'thirties, it could hardly be expected that every player would immediately abandon the instrument he knew so well, and had spent a great part of his life in mastering, for one which was strange to him, and had yet to prove its worth.   There is also evidence that many players and composers were at first prejudiced against the new device, and this may easily have been quite well justified in the earlier years of valve-making, before the makers had acquired the experience and precision which could be gained only by experiment and by gradually improving on the design and working of the original device.   Musicians in Germany regarded the valve as an unnecessary artificiality,[1] and distrusted the introduction of mechanism into the instruments which they regarded as being in a natural and pure state.   It is also easily understandable that composers should have hesitated for some time to write for instruments which they knew were not forthcoming in most orchestras.

The situation in the military bands was quite different.   Both military and brass bands in the early years of the 19th century were crying out for brass instruments with a capacity for melody-playing, more especially in the soprano register.   No natural brass instrument could fulfil the function of melodist in the same way as could the orchestral strings.   In the orchestra the call for melodic brass instruments was not so urgent.   When the keyed brass instruments offered to supply the want of the purely wind-bands, even though imperfectly, it was no wonder that the military and brass bands eagerly welcomed them, while the orchestra hesitated; and when the valves finally gave an easily manageable chromatic scale to all brass instruments, can it be wondered that these more recent organisations, the purely wind combinations, should have welcomed the innovation with open arms, while the orchestra with its older traditions and a constitution built up round a body of stringed instruments, was less enthusiastic.

As soon as the makers had learned how to make valves, they began to apply the system to a number of brass instruments other than the horn and trumpet.   In this way some instruments which had not hitherto been used in orchestras became useful in a new way, and some eventually found their way into orchestral scores.   Their advent was in the period from 1825 to 1850.   They came singly and in groups, under a bewildering variety of names, and in all registers from high soprano to contrabass.   They all had this in common, that their useful range lay between the second and the eighth open notes of their harmonic series, but, unlike the old trumpets and horns, did not freely ascend into the fourth octave of the series.   This made them easier to play than the horn and trumpet, and no doubt accounts for the quick popularity which some of these instruments achieved in a short

[1] "*Verkünstelung,*" Kalkbrenner, p. 19.

time. The type, in general, was the bugle, with its widish conical bore, and its adaptability to any size or pitch.

Among the first of these newcomers was the *cornet à pistons*. This appeared in Paris soon after 1826, and was the result of adding the valve-system to a small circular horn hitherto known in France as *Le cornet* or *Cornet de Poste*, an instrument in all essentials very similar to the German circular *Posthorn*.[1] This little instrument was really a high soprano horn in 4 ft. C; it had a conical bore and was played with a horn-like mouthpiece. At that high pitch the *Cornet* lost the mellow tone-quality of the French horn, yet had not the metallic ring of the old trumpet-tone. As used in French military bands before it became valved, the *Cornet* was usually provided with crooks for B, B flat, A and A flat, or even G, thus beginning just where the old trumpet left off, and for that reason sometimes called *Petite trompette aigue*. Subsequently, in order to distinguish it from the *cornet à pistons*, this valveless cornet was sometimes called *Cornet simple*[2] or *Cornet ordinaire*. From this modest little instrument, now almost entirely forgotten, the most popular of all brass instruments developed.[3]

With valves added to it, the cornet soon became very popular in France. Before long it reached other countries, and took its place in light orchestras, dance orchestras, in military and brass bands, and as a solo instrument at popular concerts. In France composers began to write for a pair of cornets in addition to the usual pair of trumpets, as Berlioz did already in the 'thirties, and this remained a characteristic of French scores for full orchestra. In Germany the valved cornet did not gain ground so quickly, probably owing to competition with the valved *Flügelhorn* which had made its appearance about the same time, and there it was never admitted into high-class orchestras.[4] In other countries, however, cornets were often used instead of the usual trumpets.

As it was first made in France, the *cornet à pistons* was in 4 ft. C, with shanks and crooks for B flat, A, A flat, G, F, E, E flat and D,[5] and it was played at first with a conical mouthpiece more like that of a horn than of a trumpet, and by horn players.

The cornet made its appearance in this country early in the 'thirties. It is said to have been introduced by George Macfarlane, a performer on the keyed bugle, and to have been at once adopted in the band of the Coldstream Guards. From the same source we hear that by the end of 1837 "military

---

[1] The Paris maker Halary is often given credit for having been the first to add a valve-system to the *Cornet*.

[2] Berlioz included some particulars of the *Cornet simple* in the earlier editions of his *Grand Traité*, but omitted them in the *Traité* of 1856.

[3] Contemporary particulars of the cornet without valves will be found in the following: Kastner, *Traité*, p. 50; Caussinus, p. 10; Andries, p. 29; Gevaert, p. 83. Illustrations in Carse, *Musical Wind Instruments*, p. 245, and Kastner, *Manuel*, pl XV, No. 1.

[4] The instrument called *Kornett* in Germany during the 'thirties and 'forties should not be confused with the French *cornet à pistons*; the *Kornetten* were valved bugles, the equivalents of the *flügelhorn*, *althorn* or *tenorhorn*.

[5] The English cornet (cornopean) was provided with crooks down to F.

bands are now considered incomplete without it."[1] It is probable that the first time a cornet was used in an orchestra in England was for the *obbligato* part of *The Light of other days* in Balfe's *Maid of Artois* in1836. In that same year Harper included some instructions for playing the cornet in his new trumpet tutor, and in 1837 appeared the first published book of airs arranged for the "cornopean" and piano by Macfarlane.

Almost simultaneously with the cornet came the valved bugle or *Flügelhorn*, successor to the keyed bugle, followed by the tuba or bombardon,[2] and then in quick succession all the large and small valved instruments of the bugle and cornet types, the altos, tenors, baritones, basses and contrabasses, the groups of saxhorns and others, under a multitude of different names, the instruments which to-day provide the basis of the brass band, and are now known in this country as the soprano or sopranino cornet, flugelhorn, tenorhorn, baritone, euphonium, bass and contrabass tubas or bombardons.

Although the Saxhorns were not patented until 1845, Adolphe Sax had already made a few of these instruments in Paris before that year,[3] and in the summer of 1844, Jean Arban (1825–1889), the "incomparable cornet player," performed upon a saxhorn at a concert in Paris at which six of Sax's new or improved instruments were introduced in a piece specially written for them by Berlioz.[4]

The saxhorns were first heard in this country on October 14, 1844, in the Royal Adelaide Gallery (Strand), where Sax himself, accompanied by Arban and Dubois, took part in a performance by a "Sax horn Band" conducted by Laurent jun. The entertainments for which Sax and his companions were engaged by a London manager, however, were not very successful and did not attract much attention, and the Frenchmen hurried away from London before they had completed their engagement.[5] A few weeks later, on December 3, the Distin Family, a quintet of English brass players consisting of a father (John Distin) and four sons, successfully introduced the saxhorns to a wider audience at one of Jullien's promenade concerts at Covent Garden Theatre,[6] playing on a set of these instruments specially made for them in Paris by Sax a few months earlier. For several years after that the Distins played on these saxhorns at innumerable concerts all over the United Kingdom, and also in France, Germany and the United States.

These and many other instruments of the same type, which differed largely in name but very little in construction, all settled down to the keys of B flat and E flat for use in wind bands, and only one of them, namely,

---

[1] *Mus. World*, Dec. 29, 1837, p. 254.

[2] Devised by Wieprecht and the maker Moritz in Berlin, 1835.

[3] According to a letter written by Henry Distin (*Mus. Opinion*, July, 1896, p. 673), Sax had as yet made only three saxhorns when the Distin family visited him in Paris in the summer of 1844, namely, the high E flat, the soprano in B flat, and the alto in E flat.

[4] Comettant, p. 51.

[5] *Illus. Lon. News*, Oct. 19, 1844, p. 243. See also Comettant, pp. 119, 135, and *Mus. World*, Feb. 13, 1845, p. 76.

[6] *Illus. Lon. News*, Dec. 7, 1844, p. 365.

the tuba, at first in E flat or B flat but subsequently in F, took a permanent place in the orchestra as successor to the keyed ophicleide.[1]   Some of these instruments may be said to have joined the orchestra in the sense that they were occasionally employed to enlarge the brass section, or as auxiliary military or brass bands both on and off the stage, in the large operas produced at the Paris *Opéra*, or at Berlin or Milan, or wherever resources for large-scale spectacular productions were forthcoming.

THE DISTIN FAMILY IN 1848, WITH THE SAXHORNS SUPPLIED TO THEM
BY AD. SAX IN 1844.
Originally a quintet, one of the sons, George, died in 1848

About 1830 valves began to be applied to the trombones in place of the usual slide, but except in some military bands, and especially in cavalry bands, the valve trombone never supplanted the old and characteristic slide instrument.

By giving the instruments chromatic scales entirely of open notes, the valve-system largely revolutionised the playing and the way of laying out the parts written for all the brass instruments of the orchestra except the trombones.   The valve also brought about a considerable reorganisation of all military bands, and it virtually created the purely brass band as we know it to-day.   And all this sprang from the device so inconspicuously introduced to the musical world by the short paragraph in the *Allgemeine Musikalische Zeitung* of May, 1815.   The inventor, or inventors, of the valve-system died poor and unnoticed,[2] and as they were dying the brass tone of the orchestra was growing ever richer and richer, and ever more flexible.

[1] The tuba or bombardon in F was known for some time in France, i.e. from c. 1840, as the *Ophicléide Monstre*.
[2] Stölzel (1780–1844) left a widow and children unprovided for; Blühmel must have died before 1845.   Neither is given an article in Grove's *Dictionary*, nor in many other standard musical books of reference.

It is hardly surprising that a half-century so fertile in mechanical invention should not have failed to produce several attempts to devise a mechanism which would quicken the process by which drums were tuned. Such inventions, indeed, there were in plenty. They came from Germany as early as 1812, from France, Italy and from this country; and if none of

MONSTER BASS GONG-DRUM MADE BY HENRY DISTIN

tnem ever succeeded in supplanting the old universal method of tuning by hand screws, some of them evidently served their purpose for, at any rate, as long as their respective inventors were there to look after them and see that nothing went wrong with the works. At least two English devices are recorded; one by Cornelius Ward was patented in 1837, and another about the same period was sponsored by the London timpanist Thomas Chipp. It was a compliment to English drum-makers when Wagner recommended in 1846 that new timpani for the Dresden orchestra should be bought in London. The timpani were often referred to as "double drums" in English programmes. Another expression, "long drum," is often met with in English orchestra lists. This referred to the bass drum which at that time was made with a shell considerably deeper (longer) than the diameter of the head.[1]

One or two monster gong-drums were made round about the mid-century in England, for Jullien's concerts and for some large-scale performances in the Crystal Palace.

The one illustrated here was said to measure seven feet in diameter, and the whole erection stood over ten feet from the ground. Such drums were used at Handel Festivals, brass band festivals, and on similar occasions.

[1] See picture of Jullien's concert on page 232.

X

Score and parts. Arrangements

PROVIDING and disseminating the music required for the performance of orchestral works, or any work in which an orchestra takes part, is necessarily a much more cumbrous process than for music written for only one or a few instruments, and the more elaborate means which have to be employed have not been without their influence on the history of orchestras and of their playing. Whereas the performance of a solo piece requires only one copy of the music, the orchestral piece demands that a score must be written, and then, before it can be played, each of the individual parts must be copied out. It is hardly possible to write orchestral music, except of the simplest nature, without first making a score, and it is quite impossible to play it without the separate parts. The music must therefore exist in these two forms, and in addition, the parts for the stringed instruments must be duplicated in accordance with the number of string players employed, generally at the rate of one part for each pair of players. It is also just worth noting that orchestral music can be played without using a full score, and that this was often done in the early years of last century.

Whether the necessary music exists in print or only in manuscript is a circumstance that has considerable effect on the diffusion of orchestral music. The piece of which the score and parts are available in print can be disseminated more quickly and more widely than the piece which remains in manuscript, and the number of performances given to a printed work will generally, other conditions being equal, greatly exceed that of the work which depends on the circulation of manuscript copies. When the programmes of orchestral concerts round about the beginning of the 19th century are examined, it will be found that the symphonies of Haydn and Mozart played at that time, when they can be identified, were almost invariably those of which the parts (but not the scores) had been printed and published during the last quarter of the 18th century. These comprised only a small proportion of the total number of symphonies written by these two composers; their unpublished symphonies were hardly ever played, indeed, their existence was unknown except to the few who had in their possession either the autograph scores or MS. copies of them. The parts of all Beethoven's symphonies were printed within a few years of their first performances, and these works were soon being played almost everywhere where there were orchestras to play them. On the other hand, Schubert's orchestral works remained in MS.; they were hardly ever played, and were never widely performed until they began to appear in print about the middle of the century. Bach's works also had to wait for printed copies before they could meet with the appreciation and wide recognition which they so fully merited and eventually received.

In order to look into the situation at the end of the 18th century, it will be most convenient to divide the works into two classes, because the procedure was not generally the same for all types of orchestral music. One class will comprise works which also included vocal parts, most of them operas, oratorios or cantatas; the other class comprises all purely instrumental works, the large majority of which were symphonies, overtures and concertos.

OPERAS, ORATORIOS, ETC.

In the case of the first class, in which operas were the most numerous, the usual procedure was for the composer to deliver his full score, or a MS. copy of it, to the theatre or other institution where it was first to be produced. The copyist at that place then copied out the parts, and both score and parts remained permanently in the theatre's library. When the work was to be produced at another place, the copyist at the first theatre made another copy of the score, and this was sent to the place where the new production was to take place, where the local copyist made a new set of parts. In that way each theatre accumulated its own library. By this process of multiplication vast quantities of MS. scores and parts came into existence; many of these have perished in the flames which destroyed most theatres in the past, and it is probable that the orchestral parts of numerous dead operas have been deliberately destroyed just in order to get rid of useless and bulky matter. The surviving scores now repose in numerous libraries. Towards the end of the 18th century an increasing number of full scores of operas and a few oratorios by some of the most prominent composers were being engraved and published, mostly in Paris. By the beginning of the 19th century a number of scores by Gossec, Gluck, Grétry, Piccini, Sacchini, Dalayrac, Kreutzer, Paisiello, Cherubini, and a few others, were available in print from the Paris publishers, the parts usually remaining in MS., while Leipzig, Vienna and London each added a rather smaller quota to swell the number of printed full scores.

These scores were printed, not so much in order to provide conductors with a clear copy of the score, as to facilitate the ready transference of the works to many centres at the same time, where the parts would be copied afresh. It was not, especially in the case of opera, that there was any hope of making a profit from the sale of printed full scores. The scores were printed rather with the idea of controlling the right of performance and of accelerating the rate of distribution. The value of an opera lay in its power of attracting the public into a theatre, rather than in the right to sell the music.[1] One or two hundred copies of the full score would suffice for even the most successful opera, but unless the right to produce it went with it,

---

[1] The sale of pianoforte arrangements or extracts from a popular opera might, on the other hand, be of considerable value, but not the sale of the full score.

publication of the full score would always entail a loss.   Some publishers
would not sell the scores to anybody who offered to buy them; they retained
the copies solely for performance, and by this means were able to guard
against unauthorised productions.   In this way Ricordi of Milan was able
to keep control over the performances of Bellini's and Verdi's operas, of
which the full scores were not sold.

During the early part of the 19th century the issue of engraved full
scores of operas, and of some oratorios, Masses and other church works
was steadily increasing, and by the mid-century a substantial number of such
publications had accumulated.   In this activity the Paris firms, notably
Sieber, Imbault, Gaveaux, Pleyel, Richault, the Conservatoire,[1] Leduc,
Lemoine, Frey, Troupenas, Brandus, and Schlesinger, were the most
productive; Breitkopf and Härtel, Hoffmeister and Kühnel, and Peters of
Leipzig; Schlesinger of Berlin; Schott of Mayence; Simrock of Bonn;
André of Offenbach; Artaria, Steiner, Haslinger,[2] Mollo, and Diabelli of
Vienna; Clementi, Cramer, Addison and Beale, and Novello in London, all
contributed some important as well as some unimportant additions to the
gradually expanding library of printed full scores.

A detailed survey of all the operas, oratorios and kindred works published
in full score during the first half of last century cannot be undertaken here,
but a general survey will suffice to show the progress that was being made
in rendering the scores more freely accessible for the use of theatres and other
performing institutions.

From the Paris publishers there flowed a good stream of new operas,
and occasionally a Mass or other church work.   Among these were a few
operas by Cherubini, including *Les deux Journées* (1800), *Anacreon* (1803) and
several of his Masses; also several operas by Méhul and a number of similar
works by Berton, Carafa, Winter and Isouard.   In their turn came some
full scores of Boieldieu (including *La Dame blanche*, 1825), several by Hérold,
by Auber (including *La Muette* and *Fra Diavolo*), and some of Halévy's
operas (*La Juive* and five others).   Some of the alien composers who wrote
operas for the Paris theatres also found publishers there for their full scores;
amongst these were Spontini's *Julie* (pub. 1805), *La Vestale* (1807), *Fernand
Cortez* (1809), *Olimpie* (1826); Rossini's *Le Barbier de Séville* (pub. 1821),[3]
Guillaume Tell (Troupenas) and five others; Meyerbeer's *Robert le Diable*,
Les Huguenots (both by Schlesinger), *Le Prophète* (Brandus) and *Streuensee* by
the Berlin Schlesinger about 1846; also a few opera scores by Adam, Bellini
and Donizetti.

[1] A *Magasin de Musique* was established in connection with the Paris Conservatoire in
1794.   See Pierre, *Le Magasin de Musique à l'usage des Fêtes Nationales et du Conservatoire.*
Paris, 1895.

[2] S. A. Steiner was established at Vienna in 1812; Tobias Haslinger was first an assistant,
then a partner with Steiner, and finally his successor in 1826.   Hoffmeister and Kühnel
became C. F. Peters of Leipzig in 1814.

[3] Castil-Blaze's adaptation.   A lithographed score of the Italian opera was made at
Rome about 1830.

Berlioz's first version of his *Faust* music (*Huit scènes*) appeared in score as early as 1829, but he held back most of his larger works until he was quite satisfied that he had given them their final touches, and it was not until after the mid-century that the printed full scores appeared in their first editions with the imprints of Brandus, Richault, and the Paris Schlesinger. *Benvenuto Cellini* did not appear until the 'eighties (Choudens) although the overture had already been published by Schlesinger in 1839.

Some of Beethoven's works which included choral parts appeared in printed full score fairly early in the century. *Christus am Oelberge* led the way in 1811, followed by the Mass in C during the following year, both by Breitkopf and Härtel at Leipzig; *Wellington's Victory* came out as a litho-graphed score in 1816 by Steiner of Vienna; the Choral Symphony appeared in print (score, parts and vocal parts) in 1826, and the great Mass in D in 1827, both at Schott's of Mayence.

Farrenc at Paris was the first to produce a printed full score of *Fidelio* in 1826, but no German version appeared until about 1847, when it was supplied by Simrock, who had hitherto been Farrenc's agent in Germany.

Those of Schubert's stage works, Masses and other church music which were not lost did not appear in printed score until long after the middle of the century, and Weber, in spite of the great popularity of *Der Freischütz*, saw very few of his full scores in print.   A Mass of his was published by Haslinger at Vienna in 1836, but *Der Freischütz* had to wait until 1849, when the first full score was published by Schlesinger at Berlin.[1] *Euryanthe*, *Preciosa*, and *Oberon* followed after the mid-century, *Euryanthe* in 1866 and *Oberon* in 1872, both by Schlesinger.   Mendelssohn's choral works soon appeared in score as their popularity grew; both full score and parts of *St. Paul* were published by Novello in 1838, also by Simrock of Bonn, followed by *Elijah* in 1848 (Simrock) and other choral works in their turn. A number of scores by other German composers were printed from time to time, mostly by B. and H. at Leipzig; amongst these were Spohr's *Fall of Babylon* (1842), Schneider's *Das Weltgericht*, and Romberg's *Das Lied von der Glocke* (Simrock of Bonn, and Ewer of London, 1838).

Wagner multiplied the full scores of his earlier operas, not by means of engraved, but by lithographed copies which he produced at his own expense. The lithographic process required the music to be written on specially prepared paper, from which it was transferred to stone, and thence to paper, in facsimile.   In this way 25 copies each of *Rienzi* and *Der Fliegende Holländer* were made in 1844-5 at Dresden, the music having been written out by a copyist.   For *Tannhäuser*, Wagner himself did the copying on the prepared paper, and 100 copies of the full score were made before the production of the opera at Dresden in 1845.   Moritz Hauptmann remarked in 1848 that the score was clear and distinct, but commented, that to issue an opera score before its production on the stage showed unusual self-confidence, because such works were always much altered after the experience gained

[1] A score of the overture appeared in 1843.

by a first production.[1]   The full score of *Lohengrin* was written out by a copyist, and 60 lithographed copies were made in 1852.[2]   It was not until 1860 that the full score of *Tannhäuser* was engraved by B. and H. at Leipzig; *Lohengrin* had to wait until 1887, and *Rienzi* and the *Holländer* until 1897.

Nevertheless, many quite successful opera full scores remained in MS. during the composer's lifetime, and for some time after.   None of the full scores of works by Lortzing, C. Kreutzer, Flotow or Nicolai were printed until a long time after they had earned great popularity.   The score of Nicolai's *Lustige Weiber* did not appear in print until 1882, and Marschner's *Hans Heiling* had to wait until 1892; both were published by Peters.   English publishers could hardly be induced to engrave the full scores of even the most popular of operas by native composers.   Even the successful *Bohemian Girl* and *Maritana* remained in MS., although three of Balfe's less successful operas had appeared in full score in Paris.[3]

In addition to those of contemporary composers, some progress was made in the first half of last century in providing printed full scores of such 18th century works as had outlived their respective composers.   These were mainly the works of Handel, Haydn and Mozart.   At the same time some of the choral and orchestral works of J. S. Bach, which had remained hidden away and almost forgotten ever since his death, were being unearthed and made available for performance.

In this country certain of Handel's oratorios had never lost their hold on public taste, but in Germany and Austria these works were by no means familiar until after they had been revived in Vienna, first with Mozart's additional accompaniments in 1788–89, and then in similar arrangements by Mosel in 1812–16.   These revivals fostered an increased taste for Handel's oratorios which gradually spread over Germany, and brought about a demand for more easily accessible scores with German words.   By the 'thirties quite a number of Handel's scores had been published in Germany, including *Messiah, Judas Maccabœus, Saul, Athalia, Deborah, Alexander's Feast, Belshazzar* and *Jephtha*,[4] some with Mozart's and others with Mosel's accompaniments.

In this country either the old scores of Walsh or the later edition of Arnold (1787–97) were in use at the beginning of the century,[5] and a few of the most popular oratorios were subsequently freshly engraved in London. But changed performing conditions had brought about a demand for fuller accompaniments.   Those added to *Messiah* by Mozart reached London in 1805,[6] and the precedent thus established set going an epidemic of re-arranging and adding to the instrumental parts of the oratorios, a process in which

---

[1] *Briefe*, II, p. 80; also p. 61.   [2] *Philobiblion*, 8 *Jahrgang*, Heft 8 (1935).
[3] Barret, *Life of Balfe*, p. 164.
[4] The last two were Mosel's arrangements, pub. by Haslinger, Vienna.
[5] "Walsh's scores are become very scarce, and Dr. Arnold's are not easily to be obtained." (*Q.M.M.*, 1826.)
[6] Saxe Wyndham, *Annals*, I, 309.

many English musicians took a hand. The *Dettingen Te Deum* appeared about 1820 (D'Almaine), *Samson* in 1826, *Messiah* with Mozart's parts was engraved in full score by Goulding and D'Almaine in 1828. Others followed, and then in 1843 the London Handel Society was formed, and more of the oratorios were printed, more or less drastically edited or arranged by Smart, Mendelssohn, Moscheles, Rimbault, Mudie and Sterndale-Bennett. It was not until the German *Händel Gesellschaft* was started in 1856 that the systematic collection and publication of all Handel's music in its original form was begun.

Of Bach's works, the scores of a few Cantatas and Motets were published by B. and H. during the first three decades of the 19th century. A doubtful Mass in G (Breitkopf, 1805) and the Mass in A (Simrock, Bonn, 1818) also appeared in score during that period, and the larger works followed soon after. Schlesinger of Berlin provided a full score of the *St. Matthew Passion* in 1830, Trautwein of Berlin contributed the *St. John Passion* in 1831, and the B minor Mass came from the firms of Nägeli at Zurich[1] (1833), André at Offenbach (1838), and Simrock at Bonn. The systematic publication of all Bach's surviving works by the *Bach Gesellschaft* (1850–1900) occupied the second half of the century.

The full scores of several of Haydn's Masses and a *Stabat Mater* came from Breitkopf at Leipzig during the first few years of last century, also *The Creation* (Vienna, 1800), *The Seasons* (Leipzig, 1801), and *The Seven words from the Cross* (Leipzig, 1801).

Of Mozart's operas, the full score of *Don Giovanni* was first published by Breitkopf in 1801–2, followed in 1810 by a French edition from Frey at Paris; *Die Zauberflöte* and *Figaro* appeared, respectively in 1814 and 1819, both at Simrock of Bonn, and both subsequently appeared in Frey's **Paris** edition[2]; *Idomeneo* and *Die Entführung* were also Simrock's publications, **the** latter in 1813, but both *Così fan tutte* and *La Clemenza di Tito* came from Breitkopf at Leipzig, the former in 1810. The scores of some of Mozart's Masses and a few other church works appeared early in the century at Leipzig, and the *Requiem* with some other Masses came rather later from André at Offenbach.

The publication of these scores not only widened the field over which the works could be disseminated, but it also accelerated the rate at which copies could be distributed. A given number of printed copies could be sent simultaneously to as many different places, there to be copied into parts and rehearsed; the slow and laborious process of copying by hand and then of handing on the score from one copyist to another could easily be spread over some years, whereas printed copies could reach every musical centre in Europe in the course of a week or two. As soon as the full score of Haydn's *Creation* was published in Vienna, a courier brought a copy to London within a few days, where a staff of copyists was waiting for it;

---

[1] The *Kyrie* and *Gloria* only; the rest was not published until 1845.

[2] By 1823 four of Mozart's operas in full score had been published in Paris.

six days after its arrival on March 22, 1800, the work was performed at Covent Garden Theatre on March 28.[1]

Of course, it was not every composer who could get his scores printed. The process was always expensive, and even in the case of a successful work the number of buyers could never be very many.   Schumann's comment in 1839 was: "orchestral scores are such costly and dangerous goods, that publishers will scarcely accept them as a present."[2]   Ed. Holmes wrote in 1828: "It is a general complaint among the composers of Germany, particularly those who put forth voluminous and classical works, that the publication of their scores is rendered impracticable on account of the scanty number of purchasers; hence that more than half their design remains locked up in the original."[3]   In spite of the growing number of printed full scores, they formed only a small proportion of the total number of works written and performed.   The MS. score and parts still bulked large (in every sense of these words) in the theatres, concert-rooms and churches during the first half of last century.

Although London publishers did not find it worth while publishing many full scores, they began to supply the printed orchestral parts of certain choral works for which there was a growing demand in the first two or three decades of the century, and which was caused by an increasing number of amateur choral societies then being established in the provincial towns. Novello, in particular, took the lead in this direction by supplying printed orchestral parts of a considerable number of Masses by Haydn and Mozart, as well as of a few other choral works that were becoming popular.

SYMPHONIES, OVERTURES AND CONCERTOS

When symphonies or other instrumental works were published towards the close of the 18th century, it was always the orchestral parts that were printed, but not the score.   Since the middle of that century not merely dozens, but hundreds of such works had been published in the form of separate instrumental parts, most of them in Paris, Amsterdam and London. The names of most of the composers who wrote these pieces are now hardly remembered; many are completely forgotten, and only two of them figure regularly in the programmes of to-day, namely, Haydn and Mozart.   The best remembered of the remainder are such as Dittersdorf, Boccherini, Abel, J. C. Bach, Vanhal, Stamitz, and a few more of the Mannheim group.[4]

[1] Saxe Wyndham, *Annals*, I, p. 275.   The *Musical World* (Feb. 9, 1838, p. 92) adds to the story the excitement of a race across Europe: "THE CREATION.   On the first publication of this oratorio, Salomon was exceedingly anxious to have the honour of introducing it to the British public.   Mr. Ashley, who was at the time of publication conducting the oratorios at Covent Garden, was no less ambitious.   Salomon directed the composer to send his copy per post from Vienna the very day of its first appearance, whilst Ashley entrusted his wish to the sagacity of a courier.   The score for Salomon arrived; but the postage amounting to thirty pounds sixteen shillings, Salomon declined taking it in.   Mr. Ashley received his copy a day earlier, at the trifling expense of two guineas and a half, and it was rehearsed within forty-eight hours from the time it reached London."   A slightly different version of the same story was given in *The Harmonicon*, Feb., 1830, p. 46, f.n.
[2] Schumann, II, p. 40.   [3] *Rambles*, p. 244.
[4] See *Early Classical Symphonies* by Adam Carse, *Mus. Ass. Proceedings*, 1935–36, p. 39.

At that time instrumental pieces were commonly played under the direction of a violinist-leader, who had only the first violin part in front of him, and who did not require nor use a full score.   In actual practice there would be no difficulty in directing a performance of a typical 18th century symphony or overture without a score.   Those works were very simple in structure, texture and orchestration, and in any case a score was useless, for a violin-playing leader could not be constantly turning the pages of a score.   Hence the custom of supplying only the parts of these works.

At the beginning of the 19th century the later instrumental works of Haydn and Mozart were quickly driving those of their contemporaries into obscurity, and Beethoven had just come to administer the final blow which deprived them of whatever vitality they had ever possessed. Yet when Beethoven's orchestral works were published in the early years of last century, it was still only the separate parts that were printed, but no full score.   In this way the first six of Beethoven's symphonies appeared in print not long after they were written.

For the first twenty years of the century these symphonies must have been performed without making use of a score, under the direction of the violinist-leader, just as was customary in the 18th century.   But the baton-conductor was just then beginning to come into the picture, the time-beating conductor who could use and required a score. Moreover, the new symphonies were much more complex than the older works, and some means of knowing what was going on in the orchestra and how the matter was distributed amongst the instruments became more and more desirable. So, early in the 'twenties, the publication of the full scores of Beethoven's six symphonies was begun in Germany. In the meantime an Italian firm of music importers in London named Cianchettini and Sperati had stolen a march on the German publishers, and had engraved the full scores of the first three of Beethoven's symphonies, thus anticipating the Germans by about twelve years.   The following shows the course of events:

Symphony	First performed	Parts published	Publishers	Score published in Germany	Publishers	Score published in England by Cianchettini[1]
No. 1	1800	1801	Hoffmeister and Kühnel, Leipzig	1822	Simrock, Bonn	1807–9
,, 2	1803	1804	Kunst und Industrie Comptoir, Vienna	1822	Simrock, Bonn	1807–9
,, 3	1805	1806	ditto.	1823	ditto.	1807–9
,, 4	1807	1808	ditto.	1824	ditto.	
,, 5	1808	1809	B. & H., Leipzig	1826	B. & H., Leipzig	
,, 6	1808	1809	ditto.	1826	ditto.	

[1] Grove mentions this edition, but did not know the date. See *Beethoven and his Nine Symphonies*, p. 66, f.n.

The last three of Beethoven's symphonies appeared simultaneously in score and parts, Nos. 7 and 8 by Steiner of Vienna in 1816, and the Choral symphony by Schott of Mayence in 1826. Although the appearance of these printed full scores coincided with the rise of baton-conducting, it would be unsafe to assume that their advent was in response to the demands of conductors who had begun to use the baton. In fact, the first symphony scores to be printed preceded the orchestral baton-conductor. At no place were orchestral pieces directed with a baton as early as 1801, yet it was in that year that Leduc of Paris began to publish the full scores of some of Haydn's symphonies, and by 1806 twenty-seven of them were ready. These were probably the first full scores of symphonies ever printed, and the demand for them could hardly have been caused by anticipating that the conductors during the next twenty or thirty years were going to adopt the baton.

Leduc's series of Haydn's scores comprised five of the "Paris" and three of the "London" symphonies, seventeen of the earlier symphonies written between 1770 and 1782, only one of the earliest (*Le Matin*, 1761), and the overture to *Armida*.

These scores were clearly engraved, generally with two sets of staves on each folio page, and without that economy of space which mars so many of the early editions. There is the usual sprinkling of engraver's errors that is found in nearly all the printed music of that time, also the sparse marks of expression and inconsistency in the slurs and dots which indicate the bowing for the stringed instruments and the articulation for the wind. The brass and drum parts, if any, are placed at the top of the score, the wood-wind in the middle, and the four string parts are at the bottom, the 'cellos and basses sharing the same stave. In order to save engraving, free use was made of the conventional abbreviation signs which are now no longer used in printed music; thus, the viola part is often represented only by the abbreviation sign and *Col Basso*, but it is not always made quite clear whether the violas are to play an octave higher or in unison with the 'cellos. In a few cases the music is not that which now appears in the *Gesamtausgabe*; the symphony known as *L'Impériale*, for example, has no menuet in Leduc's edition, and an entirely different *Finale*. The Leduc scores, however, compare very favourably with other early editions of contemporary orchestral music, although the accuracy and careful editing of the modern editions of the classics is not to be found in these or in any other scores of that period.

Hardly had the Leduc scores begun to appear when Ignaz Pleyel, himself an industrious composer of symphonies and Haydn's rival in London in 1792, who had recently established himself as a music publisher in Paris, issued in 1802–3 the first full scores of four of Haydn's "London" symphonies, namely: Nos. 99, 102, 103 and 104 (B. and H.). These were neatly engraved by Richomme on a small page no larger than that of a modern miniature score, and included the usual assortment of engraver's

THE FIRST EDITION OF THE FULL SCORE OF HAYDN'S SYMPHONY IN D
(No. 104), PUBLISHED IN 1802–3 BY PLEYEL AT PARIS

errors, the same careless and inconsistent slurring, and a few curious discrepancies in the text, of which perhaps the most remarkable are the absence of the telling oboe solo in bar 16 of the slow introduction to No. 104, and the inversion in the flute parts (6ths instead of 3rds) of a characteristic wood-wind figure in the last movement of No. 102.   The drum and brass parts were placed at the top of these scores, all of which were subsequently re-issued by Richault of Paris.

In the same year (1806) that Leduc's series came to an end, Breitkopf and Härtel started publishing a short series of scores of Haydn's symphonies, of which six had appeared by 1808 when the series came to an end.   All of these were "London" symphonies, but three of them had already appeared in score in Pleyel's edition (Nos. 99, 103, 104) and one (No. 93) in Leduc's edition; the other two, Nos. 94 and 101, appeared for the first time.   These scores were in folio, with the staves packed closely together in order to get as much as possible on each page; twenty-one pages sufficed for a symphony which in the later Peters' Edition occupied fifty pages.   This compression makes the scores awkward to read; the flutes and oboes often have to share a stave; horns and trumpets sometimes have to make do with one stave between them, and occasionally the drum part is squeezed in as well, so that two clefs are employed simultaneously on the same stave.   The bassoon parts appear at any odd place in the score where a stave happens to be vacant, or they are just directed to play *Col Basso*.   The repeat sign is used, even if only for a single bar, just to save an inch or two of space.   This excessive economy sometimes makes it difficult to follow the course of a particular part, and there are places where it is quite impossible to do so.   Wrong notes, scanty marks of expression and inconsistent or careless marks of articulation all add to the inaccuracy and general inefficiency of these rough and ready scores.   In this edition the wood-wind were placed at the top of the score, as is now customary.

Before the B. and H. scores were completed, Cianchettini and Sperati of London had embarked on a scheme to publish "a compleat Collection of Haydn, Mozart and Beethoven's symphonies in score."   Francesco Cianchettini was an Italian musician who had married Dussek's sister and was living in London at the close of the 18th century; their son Pio[1] became well known in England as a pianist during the 'twenties and 'thirties.   The intention was to publish all the symphonies, also the quintets and quartets by the three great masters, in score, but later on Cianchettini complained that his project had received little support from "British Professors," that he obtained only 62 subscriptions for his series, that he had been a considerable loser by it, and was therefore obliged to abandon the undertaking in an unfinished state.[2]

This series of full scores made its appearance in 1807–1809 and comprised

---

[1] It was the father, Francesco C., who was the publisher, not the son Pio, as is stated in *Grove*.

[2] *Harm.*, July, 1827, p. 139.

eighteen of Haydn's works, six of Mozart's, and the three Beethoven symphonies already referred to. Cianchettini was Leduc's London agent, and as most of his Haydn scores were laid out page for page and bar for bar exactly as in Leduc's edition, it is obvious that he relied largely on Leduc's scores for copy. Cianchettini, or his engravers, Tilley and T. C. Bates, corrected some of Leduc's misprints, added some fresh ones, and made a few unimportant editorial emendations. Sometimes an extra set of staves is squeezed into the quarto page, and some textual divergencies include the addition of a menuet to the *Impériale*, and the substitution of another *finale*, both of which now appear in the *Gesamtausgabe*.

There are no trumpet or drum parts in Cianchettini's scores of Haydn's symphonies. It is true that many of the earlier symphonies were written for a small orchestra without trumpets or drums, but the later works such as, for example, the Oxford Symphony, certainly included parts for these instruments; nevertheless, Cianchettini's score of this symphony shows no trumpet or drum parts. But even if the parts were not written by the composer, they were sometimes supplied by arrangers or conductors; Tom Cooke, for example, added trumpet and drum parts to Haydn's symphony in C (No. 90) for a performance under Dr. Crotch at a London Philharmonic concert in 1829. The order of the parts in these English scores is very much the same as in Leduc's edition, with the brass parts at the top, but in some of the symphonies Cianchettini placed the bassoon parts between those of the violas and the 'cellos.

Among them, the four editions of Leduc, Pleyel, B. and H., and Cianchettini provided 55 scores of Haydn's symphonies,[1] but if the duplication be taken into account, this number is reduced to 33 different works from the four publishers. And this was accomplished in under ten years—it set the ball rolling and created a demand for orchestral scores which was quite unknown in the 18th century and was to grow to considerable proportions during the 19th century. The Haydn symphony scores, which by 1810 were to be found in print, are shown on page 436.

Between 1850 and 1900 several German publishers issued full scores of selected symphonies by Haydn, each numbering the works as they published them; thus, in addition to the "Paris" and "London" numbers, there have been at least ten different ways of numbering these symphonies.

Although the last four of Mozart's symphonies were constantly being played in the early years of last century, it was not until 1807 that the first engraved full score appeared. In that year Breitkopf and Härtel published a folio score of the *Prague* symphony, and the others followed at long intervals, the G minor in 1811, the E flat in 1814, and the *Jupiter* in 1828. In the meantime Cianchettini and Sperati had included the same four works in their "Compleat Edition," as well as the overtures to *Figaro* and *The Magic Flute*. These scores were uniform with those of Haydn in the same series, but that the trumpet and drum parts were included in the case of Mozart's

---

[1] This number includes the two scores of the overture to *Armida*.

works.   In the score of the *Jupiter* symphony Cianchettini's engraver saved himself some work and some space on the plate by engraving the drum part on a stave of only three lines, which sufficed for the two notes C and G. (See p. 437.)

Cianchettini's version of the G minor symphony (no doubt taken from the original printed parts) is in the original scoring, without the clarinet

B. and H. Gesamtausgabe	Leduc 1801–6	Pleyel 1802–3	B. and H. folio 1806–8	Cianchettini 1807–9
No. 6 Le Matin	No. 20	—	—	—
„ 41	„ 17	—	—	No. 5
„ 44 Trauer	„ 2	—	—	„ 10
„ 45 Farewell	„ 9	—	—	„ 8
„ 48 Maria Theresa	„ 15	—	—	—
„ 51	„ 4	—	—	No. 12
„ 53 Impériale	„ 7	—	—	„ 15
„ 57	„ 1	—	—	„ 11
„ 61	„ 26	—	—	—
„ 63 Roxolane	„ 23	—	—	—
„ 64	„ 21	—	—	No. 16
„ 66	„ 5	—	—	„ 9
„ 67	„ 24	—	—	—
„ 69 Laudon	„ 6	—	—	No. 2
„ 70	„ 16	—	—	„ 7
„ 71	„ 22	—	—	„ 17
„ 74	„ 27	—	—	—
„ 75	„ 25	—	—	No. 18
„ 83 La Poule	„ 3	—	—	„ 4
„ 85 La Reine	„ 8	—	—	„ 6
„ 90 (Paris No. 9)	„ 10	—	—	„ 13
„ 91 (Paris No. 11)	„ 12	—	—	„ 1
„ 92 Oxford	„ 11	—	—	„ 3
„ 93 (London No. 2)	„ 13	—	No. 5	—
„ 94 Surprise (London No. 3)	—	—	„ 6	—
„ 95 (London No. 5)	No. 18	—	—	—
„ 98 (London No. 4)	„ 19	—	—	—
„ 99 (London No. 10)	—	Tome 4	No. 3	—
„ 101 Clock (London No. 11)	—	—	„ 4	—
„ 102 (London No. 9)	—	Tome 3	—	—
„ 103 Drum roll (London No. 8)	—	„ 1	No. 1	—
„ 104 (London No. 7)	—	„ 2	„ 2	—
Overture, Armida	No. 14	—	—	No. 14

THE HAYDN SYMPHONY SCORES

parts which Mozart added to his first score.   Apart from a few engraver's errors, this score shows a curious divergence from the version now in use; in the slow movement there are two groups of four bars each which do not appear in later editions of the score.[1]   These superfluous bars appeared in the original parts and in all the earlier editions of the score, including that

---

[1] Between bars 28 and 29, and between bars 99 and 100

of B. and H. in 1811 and their later octavo edition.   Jahn (II, p. 207, f.n.)
explained that these extra bars got into the movement as the result of a
copyist's mistake.   Mozart had reorchestrated both groups of four bars on
a separate sheet, and both the old and the new versions were inadvertently
copied, one after the other, thus making two orchestrations of the same
music follow each other.   Schumann noticed the superfluous bars, and

CIANCHETTINI'S FULL SCORE OF MOZART'S JUPITER SYMPHONY,
PUBLISHED IN LONDON, 1807–1809

drew attention to them in an article entitled: *On certain probably corrupted
readings of passages in the works of Bach, Mozart, and Beethoven* (1837).[1]   It
appears that at that time the movement was generally played according to
the incorrect scores and parts, but Schumann mentioned that both Habeneck
at Paris and Mendelssohn at Leipzig always cut out the superfluous bars
when they played the movement.   At the London Philharmonic the
incorrect version was still being played as late as 1841, according to a leading
article in the *Musical World* (Sept. 23, 1841, p. 193).

As Cianchettini's scores of Beethoven's first three symphonies were
published probably without the composer's knowledge, and certainly without his supervision, even though they are first editions of the scores, they

[1] *Music and Musicians*, I, p. 26.

cannot be regarded as authoritative, more especially so as we know that a liberty had been taken in altering the notes of a famous passage in the *Eroica* symphony.

The well-known two bars,[1] just before the recapitulation in the first movement, where the second horn plays the first two bars of the main theme against the B flat and A flat of the violins, is altered in Cianchettini's score so as to abolish the dissonance between the horn and the violin parts. This was done by changing the A flat of the second violins to G. The responsibility for this alteration must have rested with either the editor or the engraver, who no doubt concluded that the A flat was an engraver's or a copyist's error. It is not altogether surprising that for a long time this alteration was accepted as correct in this country, where the English scores were used, but it is surprising to learn that the same alteration was sometimes made in Germany, where the correct scores and parts were used. In Moscheles' translation of Schindler's *Life of Beethoven*[2] the passage in question is quoted in music type, accompanied by these words: "This passage has puzzled many a leader and conductor, and many have altered it thus: (the passage is quoted with G in the second violin), whilst in the score it is written: (the passage is quoted with A flat in the second violin)." Further evidence that G was sometimes played instead of A flat occurs in Ambros's *Bunte Blätter*,[3] where the author states that he was present at a performance of the *Eroica* at Prague in 1842 under Dionys Weber, and heard the passage played with G in the second violin part. Still more amazing is his statement that Wagner made the same alteration when conducting the symphony at Vienna in 1872, at which performance Ambros was also present.[4] Wagner conducted the London Philharmonic concerts in 1855, and the *Eroica* was played under his direction on March 12; no doubt the English score was used on that occasion, and it may be that, seeing the G in the second violins in the printed score, he concluded that it was correct, and that the A flat in the parts was an engraver's error.

It is probable that the first German scores of Simrock, B. and H., Steiner and Schott represent the Beethoven symphonies as nearly as possible as he intended them to be. In some respects Beethoven was very particular about the accuracy of his printed music, as his many letters to publishers reveal; he was very annoyed when mistakes were allowed to pass.[5] Simrock of Bonn had been a horn player in the Elector's orchestra at Bonn when Beethoven was employed there before he settled in Vienna, and there can be little doubt that when Simrock turned music-publisher and started publishing the scores of the symphonies, it was done with the composer's approval and under his supervision. We also know that Beethoven was

---

[1] Bars 398 and 399 in the first movement.   [2] II, p. 287, f.n.

[3] II, pp. 105–8. *Musikalische Uebermalungen und Retouchen.*

[4] Ambros also quoted the passage in music-type; curiously enough, both he and Moscheles quoted the horn part (actual sounds) an octave too high.

[5] Nohl, *Neue Briefe*, pp. 51, 262. See also Beethoven's letter to Steiner in *Beethoven and his Nine Symphonies* (Grove), p. 267.

often in touch with both B. and H. and Schott by correspondence, and that
he was in personal touch with Steiner and Haslinger at Vienna.

In the German scores of the first six symphonies the drum and brass

STEINER'S FIRST LITHOGRAPHED SCORE OF BEETHOVEN'S
SEVENTH SYMPHONY, PUBLISHED IN 1816

parts are placed at the top of the score, but in the 7th symphony (Steiner's
lithographed score) the wood-wind are at the top.   The old lithographed
scores of the 7th and 8th symphonies were superseded by engraved folio

scores published by Haslinger (Steiner's successor) in 1827, and in these the brass and drums resume their old place at the top of the score.

Disregarding Cianchettini's unauthorised versions of the first three, the first printed German scores of Beethoven's symphonies are reasonably accurate.   There were, however, serious mistakes in the *Scherzo* of the C minor symphony (two redundant bars) and in the first movement of the *Pastoral* symphony (first violin part omitted for three bars), in both the printed scores and the parts.   Both were played according to the faulty scores and parts at the London Philharmonic during the early 'forties.[1]   It was not until 1856 that the redundant bars in the C minor symphony were omitted at the Philharmonic.[2]   But, on the whole, there are not many wrong notes, incorrect note-values or faulty accidentals, and the dynamics are shown amply and clearly enough to leave little doubt as to the composer's intentions.   But the slurs and dots which indicate the articulation or phrasing are often inconsistent and confusing.   In this respect Beethoven seems to have been either careless or indifferent.   The same passages are often articulated in quite different ways in various places in the scores in a manner so inconsistent as to suggest that either the composer was not very particular, or that he often changed his mind, or, still more likely, that he forgot how he had previously written them.   Parts played together in unison or in octaves may be found slurred in two or even three different ways, without any apparent reason, in a most haphazard manner:

EXAMPLES FROM BEETHOVEN'S EROICA SYMPHONY

[1] *Mus. World*, Sept. 23, 1841, p. 193.   [2] *Ibid.*, 1856, p. 314

During the 'thirties and early 'forties Paris publishers (Troupenas, Farrenc, Marquerie Frères) were issuing new full scores of the Beethoven symphonies. These were no doubt the scores that roused Berlioz to such fury when he saw the proposed editorial alterations suggested by Fétis.[1]

Later editors have had a difficult task in sorting out and co-ordinating the inconsistencies found in the early editions of Beethoven's scores, and, as there is often some ambiguity, one cannot be surprised that they did not always arrive at exactly the same solution. Purists who want their Beethoven symphonies played exactly as he wrote them may be disappointed to learn that all the scores and parts of these works now in use by our orchestras have had to be edited, and not without good reason.

Of other contemporary symphonies besides those of Beethoven, although hundreds were written, very few were published. One by Weber appeared in printed parts only, and Spohr's third (Schlesinger, Berlin), fourth (Haslinger, Vienna) and sixth were important enough to bring about their appearance in print during the composer's lifetime.

More important and more durable were the Mendelssohn symphonies, which came later than Spohr's, and still later, those of Schumann. Mendelssohn's first symphony was published in lithographed score and parts by Schlesinger of Berlin in 1834, seven years after its first performance at Leipzig. The final version of the *Hymn of Praise* appeared in parts (orchestral and choral) in 1840, and the full score was ready by September, 1841. B. and H. were the first publishers of this, as well as of the Scottish and Italian symphonies. Of these two, the score and parts of the former were published in 1843, and of the latter, which was first played in London in 1843 and was subsequently revised, the score and parts did not appear in print until March, 1851. The Reformation symphony had to wait until 1868, when both score and parts were brought out by Simrock of Bonn.

Schumann's orchestral works appeared in print fairly soon after their respective first performances, that is, during the period extending from 1841 to 1853. In this respect Schumann was rather fortunately situated; he lived (until 1844) at Leipzig in the very centre of the music-publishing trade, was in touch with all the important publishers, and in his capacity as editor of a musical periodical was not without influence. The four symphonies, also some overtures and choral works, appeared in printed scores and parts during the period named above, but even then the old tendency of providing printed parts without a printed score still prevailed to some extent. Thus, the parts of the first symphony in B flat were published late in 1841, but the engraving of the full score was delayed until 1853.[2] The second symphony also made its first appearance in parts (1847), followed a few years later by the full score.

In 1850 the publication of Schubert's orchestral works was begun; in that year B. and H. issued the first score and parts of the great C major

[1] *Mem.*, I, p. 268.   [2] Erler, I, p. 276.

symphony.[1] The Unfinished Symphony was not published until 1867 (Spina, Vienna), and the first six symphonies, which were seen in Vienna by Schumann in 1838, and then again by Grove and Sullivan in 1868, remained in MS. until the Complete Edition of Schubert's works was undertaken by B. and H. Two of the *Rosamunde* entr'actes were published by Spina (Diabelli's successor) in 1866.

A few other symphonies written during the first half of last century, although they enjoyed all the advantages of print, were nevertheless unable to keep their places in the permanent repertoires. They include works by Lachner, Rietz, Kalliwoda, Kittl, Preyer, and a few other composers whose names have long since vanished from orchestral programmes.

The published overtures and concertos in the early years of last century, like the symphonies, always appeared first in the form of separate instrumental parts, without a score; if the latter was wanted, a MS. copy had to be made.

In accordance with this custom the parts of all the earlier overtures of Beethoven (*Prometheus, Corolian, Egmont*) were published at Leipzig or Vienna not long after their first performances, while the scores remained in MS. until the 'twenties or 'thirties. Of the later overtures (*King Stephen, Namensfeier, Die Weihe des Hauses*) both the scores and the parts simultaneously made their appearance in print, most of them during the 'twenties and 'thirties, with the imprints of Steiner, Haslinger, B. and H., or Schott. Two of the *Leonora* overtures and that of *Fidelio* were made available in score and parts during the 'thirties.

The same course was taken with Beethoven's concertos, all of which were composed before 1810. Mollo of Vienna published the parts of the first piano concerto in 1801, and all of them, including the violin concerto, were available in the same form by 1811. It was, no doubt, in response to a demand for full scores of these concertos that Richault of Paris and Dunst of Frankfort began to publish them, but it was not until the 'thirties that this want began to be supplied.

Mozart's piano concertos were treated in just the same way. André of Offenbach published the parts of six of them in 1800, and during the next five years twenty concertos were similarly issued by B. and H., but not until the 'fifties or later could they be procured in the scores engraved by Richault and André.

Although the revival of J. S. Bach's music began with his keyboard and choral works, the instrumental works also began to be valued as soon as they became available in print. This appreciation came rather later in the case of the instrumental works, and began with the publication of several concertos in score by C. F. Peters at Leipzig in the 'forties and early 'fifties. The orchestral Suites were first published early in the 'fifties by Peters at

---

[1] Schumann (*Music and Musicians*) stated that the parts were published before the full score.

Leipzig under the editorship of Dehn,[1] and the Brandenburg concertos followed soon after. Even as late as Mendelssohn's time orchestral works were often published at first without a full score. The overture to *A Midsummer Night's Dream* made its first appearance in a set of parts published by B. and H. in 1832, and only three years later was a printed score available. The rest of the incidental music to Shakespeare's play was not printed until 1848.

As almost every concert-programme in the first half of last century included one, and often two overtures, the very considerable demand for such works brought about the publication in score and parts of many popular opera overtures. Even in the case of quite successful operas, the overture was often the only part of the work which ever appeared in printed score. Brandus of Paris and Schlesinger of Berlin were the publishers of many of these overtures in octavo score, and in this way the best of the French overtures and some popular overtures by Weber and a few other German composers were freely circulated and were being constantly played at concerts long before the mid-century was reached.

The orchestral parts, both printed and MS., used during the first few decades of last century were by no means models of accuracy. Beethoven complained to B. and H. about the mistakes in the printed parts of his C minor symphony and the Emperor Concerto, and asked why they never published a work of his without many mistakes, and before he had sent them a corrected proof.[2] Wagner wrote about "serious mistakes in the orchestral parts of *Figaro*, from which the opera had been played with special unction—heaven knows how often—under the solemn conductorship of a celebrity."[3] Busby wrote sarcastically in 1825: "Out of a dozen rehearsals, *twelve* are attended with delays and inconveniences, owing to mistakes in some of the principal or subordinate parts," and went on to suggest that composers should number every twenty bars of their scores and parts in order to save time at rehearsals when a mistake was discovered, "instead of beginning the whole movement a second time."[4] This foreshadows the later custom of lettering scores and parts for convenience at rehearsals, a device of which Spohr was also given the credit of having been the inventor.[5]

The order in which the instrumental parts were placed in the full scores, both MS. and printed, during the first half of last century, cannot be reduced to any standardised plan; indeed, the plans were so many that it would be useless to attempt to describe or classify them all. The best that can be done is to group them in three general classes, each of which may be only very roughly identified with the habit of Italian, German and French composers, and even then are subject to endless exceptions:

---

[1] Librarian at the Royal Library in Berlin.
[2] Nohl, *Neue Briefe*, p. 51. [3] *On Cond.*, p. 103.
[4] *Anecdotes*, II, p. 134. [5] Gassner, *Dir. und Rip.*, p. 46.

A.   The first plan roughly follows this arrangement:
(From the top) Violins, followed by Violas.
> Wood-wind in the usual order.
> Horns, trumpets, trombones, drums.
> 'Cellos and basses.

This method was adopted by many Italian composers, and also by some as diverse as Mozart and Meyerbeer.

B.   An arrangement often found in German scores:
> Drums, followed by the brass parts.
> Wood-wind in the usual order.
> Strings in the usual order.

This plan was often varied by separating the trombone parts from the rest of the brass group, placing them immediately above the strings.

C.   A third scheme, generally used by French composers, is approximately that of the present day:
> Wood-wind in the usual order.
> Horns, trumpets, trombones, ophicleide.
> Drums, etc.
> Strings.

The grouping was often varied by placing the bassoons below the horns. Vocal parts were almost invariably placed just above the 'cello and bass parts, thus dividing the parts for the string orchestra into two portions. This arrangement, a relic of the days when the conductor at the keyboard instrument played the *basso continuo*, still persists in many full scores of the present time.

*   *   *

Although far from exhaustive, the foregoing is comprehensive enough to show how the volume of printed orchestral material increased during the first half of last century.

It is not unreasonable to suspect that, without this considerable output of printed music, most of these works would not only have taken a much longer time to get known, but also that, if they had depended entirely on MS. copies, some of them might have remained unknown except in certain localities, or might have been altogether lost. It cannot be regarded as merely coincidental that the works of Haydn, Mozart and Beethoven which figured in the concert programmes of the period were almost entirely those of which either the parts or the scores, or both, were then available in printed copies. More than that, it is not illogical to suggest that the facilities afforded by the circulation of printed scores or parts provided at any rate some of the impulse which brought into being some of the many concert-societies and orchestras which blossomed and flourished during the half-century. Habeneck's famous Conservatoire concerts owed their

start to voluntary gatherings of orchestral players assembled for the purpose
of practising Beethoven's *Eroica* symphony, and it may well be questioned
whether these gatherings would ever have taken place if Habeneck had not
been in possession of the printed parts of the symphony.

The first performance of many a work at many a place where an
orchestra was available often coincided closely with the first appearance of
the music in print, and it is hardly possible to disassociate the two events,
or to suppose that the same result would have been brought about, and so
quickly, had the works been circulated only by means of MS. copies.   The
parts of Beethoven's 5th and 6th symphonies, for example, were first
published in 1809; in that same year both symphonies were given their first
performance at the Leipzig *Gewandhaus*.   The 7th symphony appeared in
print in 1816; in that year the symphony was played for the first time at the
Gewandhaus, and in the following year it was given for the first time at the
London Philharmonic concerts.   Printed scores also provided conductors
with greater facilities for studying and becoming familiar with the works
they were to conduct, and composers and students with better means of
learning how to orchestrate.   Mendelssohn commented on this in a letter
in which he criticised Auber's orchestration: "But a grey-haired man, a
pupil of Cherubini's, and the darling of the public, ought at least to be able
to orchestrate, in our times especially, when the publication of the scores of
Haydn, Mozart and Beethoven has made that task so easy."[1]

At this point it will be appropriate to mention the books on orchestration
which appeared between 1800 and 1850.   With the possible exception of
Francœur's *Diapason général des instruments à vent* (1772), no such text-books
had been written in the 18th century; the books dealing with musical
instruments had hitherto always been designed as instruction books for
those who wanted to play the instruments, but the new 19th century type
was intended primarily for composers and arrangers who required to learn
how to write for orchestral instruments, rather than to play on them.
Berlioz is often regarded as the pioneer who was the first to write specifically
on orchestration, but there were several before him, as the following list
shows[2]:

Vandenbroeck.   *Traité général de tous les instruments à vent* (c. 1800).

Fröhlich.   *Vollständige theoretisch-praktische Musiklehre für alle beym
    Orchester gebräuchlichen wichtigen Instrumente* (1810–11).

Francœur—Choron.   *Traité général des voix et des instruments d'orchestre*
    (1813); an amplification of Francœur's *Diapason*.

Sundelin.   *Die Instrumentierung für das Orchester* (1828).

Catrufo.   *Traité des voix et des instruments à cordes, à vent, et à percussion*
    (1822).

Swoboda.   *Instrumentierungslehre* (1832).

[1] Hensel, *The Mendelssohn Family*, I, p. 126.   The letter was written in 1825.
[2] For fuller particulars see *Music and Letters*, Vol. XXII, No. I, Jan., 1941, *Text-books
on Orchestration before Berlioz*, by Adam Carse.

Kastner.   *Traité général d'instrumentation* (1837, *Supplément* 1844).

Kastner.   *Cours d'instrumentation considéré sous les rapports poetiques et philosophiques de l'art* (1837, and *Supplément*).

Gassner.   *Partiturkenntniss* (1838).

Berlioz.   *De l'instrumentation* (1841–42).[1]

Sundelin and Catrufo were the first to give any attention to the new valved brass instruments, and Kastner was the first to give copious examples in score from the works of prominent composers.   His *Cours* of 1837 includes about 65 folio pages of score, selected from the works of Gluck, Haydn, Mozart, Beethoven, Méhul, Weber, Meyerbeer, Berlioz and others, as well as some examples of military band scoring.   Kastner's books were approved by the French Academy of Fine Arts, and were adopted by the Conservatoire.   Meyerbeer gave the *Traité général* a puff which concluded with these words: "The work will be of immense utility to young composers who may consult it.   Thus, having before their eyes all the resources of the modern orchestra, they will learn without trouble what in general is only acquired by long experience, and after many unsatisfactory essays."

These books must have been a great boon to French and German students at that time, when, it should be remembered, there were no complete and cheap editions of the classics, and no handy miniature scores.   For the benefit of German students, Gassner devoted the whole of the second volume (157 pages) of his *Partiturkenntnis* to musical examples, ranging from Haydn to Meyerbeer.

Reference has already been made in the previous chapters on conducting and conductors to the violinist-leaders and conductors who had only a first violin part in front of them, and directed the playing of an orchestra without a full score.   This practice led to the use of a version of the music which was neither a part nor a score, and was largely employed, especially for opera, in France and Italy during the first half of last century.

Referring to a conductor, Berlioz asked: "should he conduct, reading from a full score, or from a first violin part (leader's copy), as is customary in some theatres?"[2]   He also referred to "He who employs a *simplified score*, or a simple first violin part, as is often done in our day, more especially in France," and called it "a deplorable system."[3]   Kastner likewise referred to the French violin-conductors, especially in provincial theatres, who did not have a score in front of them, and Castil-Blaze (1826) described a sort of reduced score in these words: "Sometimes one combines the principal

[1] Berlioz's well known work appeared first in a series of 16 articles, without musical examples, in *La Gazette Musicale* at intervals between Nov., 1841, and July, 1842.   These were first published in book-form in French at Paris by Schonenberger late in 1843.   An edition with a few additions was issued in German and French (parallel columns) by Schlesinger a few years later.   An article on new instruments appeared in the *Débats* in Oct., 1847, and another on conducting in *La Gazette Musicale* in 1856, and both of these were embodied in a *nouvelle édition* of the *Grand Traité* published at Paris in 1856.   The English translation was issued by Novello, Ewer & Co. in 1858.   There have been several subsequent translations and modernisations.

[2] *Instrumentation*, p. 254.   [3] *Mem.*, II, p. 241.

parts with that of the leading violin, and this is called a *Partition d'intelligence*. It suffices to show him the general design, and to mark the entries and effects. But he should remember that the various parts are there only for his eye, and that his bow should not follow the voice or the bassoon, the flute or the oboe in their solos."[1]

Deldevez, writing as late as 1878, devoted a special chapter to the question: "From what part should the conductor conduct?"[2]   He referred to engraved scores "which are generally published to be read, and not for the use of the conductor," and described how, "at a period not far distant," the conductor in a theatre used a "mere first violin part, with the voice part cued in the recitatives."   Such a part, it appears, was used for the production at the *Opéra* of Rossini's *Le Comte Ory* in 1828.   Deldevez then describes what he called a principal violin part, or *violon conducteur*, specially arranged for the use of the conductor of an opera: 1st, an upper stave is given to the first violin part, written out in full; 2nd, a lower stave contains the bass part in full; 3rd, between these two, two more staves are given up to a reduction of the orchestral parts; and 4th, a stave which contains the chief entries of the vocal parts, the recitatives, airs, concerted numbers, choruses, etc.   This sort of arrangement, Deldevez said, called for considerable work, extreme care, and some skill, from the copyist who made it. De Lajarte, a later librarian at the Paris *Opéra*, recalled how he used to see Le Borne, the chief copyist from 1820 to 1865, compiling these *conducteur* scores on four or five staves for use at the performances by the *chef d' orchestre*.[3]

While insisting that a full score was indispensable at rehearsals, Deldevez, himself conductor at the *Opéra* and Conservatoire concerts, had much to say in favour of a score reduced in this manner.   The continual turning over of the pages, especially in quick movements, he said, was apt to occupy too much of the conductor's attention, and there was always a chance that he might lose touch with what was going on, or with what was about to occur, owing to a belated or too-early turn-over.

Although reduced scores on two or three staves are now used only for light music which is not generally to be had in full score, there is something to be said for this method of condensing the music into less space on paper than is possible when every part in a work for a large orchestra is laid out in full, one above the other, on the same page.   During a performance the conductor can, in any case, give only an occasional glance at a full score which presents him with a mass of detail that he cannot take in, and the content of the music and the orchestration can be seen and grasped much more quickly when it is thus condensed than when it is sprawled over a whole page.   But for the purpose of rehearsal a full score is essential, and that is probably the reason why condensed scores of serious music have so rarely been printed.

[1] *L'Opéra en France*, I, p. 435.
[2] *L'Art du Chef d'orchestre*, Chap. VIII, p. 139.   [3] De Lajarte, p. 17.

The dissemination of the great mass of MS. and printed music used during the first half of last century was in the hands of a rapidly expanding music-trade and an army of copyists. The publishing was nearly all done in Germany, Paris, Vienna and London, while in Italy the traffic in music was almost entirely in the hands of copyists. Burney remarked in 1772 on the lack of printed music in Italy: "there is no such thing as a music-shop throughout Italy, that I was able to discover"; fifty years later a traveller told exactly the same story: "From Naples to Milan, I believe there is no such artist as an Engraver of Music, and you never see a Music-shop. You must therefore go without it or employ a Copier, whose trade is regulated by the most approved cheating rules."[1]   Before the mid-century, however, Giovanni Ricordi had laid the foundation of a music-publishing house which expanded greatly and eventually controlled not only the sale of a large proportion of Italian opera-music, but also the only means of performing it.

All the most important publishers of orchestral music before the mid-century have already been named. In addition to these there were countless music-sellers, agents and importers of music in all the large centres. According to Busby,[2] there were no less than 150 music-sellers in London alone in 1825. The advent of the steam railway and the steamboat greatly facilitated and accelerated the traffic in music and instruments, and improving postal arrangements contributed to the considerable quickening pace of inter-communication and exchange between one country and another.

But, side by side with a more active and better organised music-trade, copyright laws still remained in a very ill-defined and chaotic state.

A full account of the state of copyright during the first half of last century cannot be undertaken here, but the situation may be briefly summarised by saying that whereas most European states gave their authors and composers some sort of protection, it might be by law or only by custom, there was no international agreement by which a composer's rights were protected in other countries.[3]   Thus, a musical work owned in one country could be freely performed or published in any other country without any hindrance or payment; all that need be done was to get hold of a copy of the work, and this could generally be done without much difficulty, either by the simple process of importing a printed copy or of getting a MS. copy made by a copyist.[4]   A British copyright act in 1838 did not clear up the very unsatisfactory position of foreign copyright in this country, and nobody seems to have known whether they really had any exclusive right in a foreign work even when they had bought and paid for it: "the whole system of English copyright in foreign music seems to be a vague lottery, in which all may speculate who will."[5]   There was frequent litigation, and apparently no secure rights for a composer except in his own country.

[1] Matthew's *Diary of an Invalid, Harm.*, Feb., 1823, p. 22.   [2] *Anecdotes*, III, p. 198.
[3] International Copyright was not instituted until 1885–6.
[4] English publishers told Moscheles that they preferred to wait until a composition had been published on the continent before publishing it in this country; it was so much cheaper! (Speyer, pp. 281, 443).   [5] *Mus. World*, June 17, 1841, p. 385.

Under such conditions, it is not at all surprising that composers sometimes offered their works to several publishers, each in a different country, at the same time, as Beethoven is known to have done. In so doing they were not only acting well within their rights, but were trying to guard against their work being appropriated by foreign publishers for their own profit, without making any payment to the composer.

Composers of music are generally discontented people, and confirmed grumblers; even now, when they are given the protection of international copyright, and when they benefit by performing and broadcasting fees, they are rarely satisfied that they are getting the just reward for their labours. But in the first half of the 19th century it seems as if they really *had* something to grumble about. They seem to have been regarded as fair game by opera-managers and publishers, and if some of the more spirited of the species did occasionally retaliate and employ methods that were not altogether straightforward, they were only seeking to defend themselves with weapons which matched those by which they were being attacked and exploited.

Although the sale of printed orchestral scores and parts was probably not profitable enough to invite any extensive piracy, a considerable foreign traffic in MS. opera scores, and especially in the case of successful works, was carried on openly by opera-managers and copyists, who evidently regarded this as their perquisite, who put the proceeds in their own pockets, and from which the composers gained no pecuniary benefit. The managers who bought the scores were equally shameless in thus acquiring operas for their theatres without in any way recompensing the composers. It is true, there were managers who were honest enough to insist on dealing directly with the composers, but many complaints show only too clearly that it was very difficult for a composer to keep any control over the use of his operas, especially in countries other than his own.

Treitschke, who revised the libretto of *Fidelio* for the revival of that opera at Vienna in 1814, wrote apropos the score of the new version: "others preferred to get it in a cheaper way by hiring cunning copyists who, as is still the custom, stole the text and music and sacrificed them for a few florins." Beethoven betrayed the same fear when he wrote to Treitschke: "We must talk about sending out the opera so that you may receive your quarter, and that it is not sent out in stolen copies all over the world."[1] A notice appeared in the *Wiener Zeitung* (June 28, 1814) to the effect that correct copies of the score of *Fidelio* were to be had *only* from the composer or the librettist.

Spohr wrote similarly in "an address to the German Composers," in which he appealed to the directors of theatres to "purchase works of no one but the composer himself," and to "remunerate his talent justly and properly," adding significantly: "This latter stipulation will doubtless appear quite extraordinary to the managers of theatres, as heretofore the

[1] Thayer, II, pp. 283, 284.

whole requisites of an Italian or French opera were to be obtained at merely the price of the copyists' labour."[1]

Weber complained in the same strain; he taxed Castil-Blaze, the adapter of *Der Freischütz* for the Paris *Odéon* (*Robin des Bois*), with having procured the score by underhand means: "You procure an adaptation from a source altogether illegitimate (would it appear legitimate to you?), for my work being neither engraved nor published, no theatre or music-seller had a right to dispose of it." And it was not only against the way in which Castil-Blaze had acquired the score that Weber protested in vain, but he also complained that the former had published his adaptation: "I, however, have this moment heard that you have just published the adaptation of the *Freischütz*—Ah, Sir, what will become of all that is sacred amongst us!— and without even having acquired it by legitimate means." In a letter to Castil-Blaze written in January, 1826, Weber wrote: "It has been communicated to me, that a piece is about to be produced at the *Odéon* in which there are extracts from the *Euryanthe*. It is my intention to bring this Opera out at Paris myself. I have not sold my interest in it, and nobody has it in France. It is perhaps from an engraved adaptation for the piano that you have copied those parts of it which you wish to appropriate. You have no right to mutilate my music by introducing into it passages, the accompaniments of which are of your own composition."[2] Previous to his departure for London, Weber endeavoured to prevent his *Oberon* being appropriated free of charge by addressing a circular letter to opera-directors in Germany, Denmark and Sweden, requesting them to apply to him only for correct copies of the score, should they wish to produce the opera.[3]

It was not only the score of an opera that might be filched without permission or payment, but publishers freely helped themselves to any choice tunes that appealed to the popular taste, and arranged and published them entirely for their own profit. In Spohr's *Address*, referred to above, the German composer bemoaned that "scarcely has an opera appeared, when the traffickers in petty larceny fall foul of the score, which no precautions on the part of the author, or any protests in the public journals, can prevent. Thus they steal all the choicer parts of the composition, and defraud the author of what he has so dearly earned by the laborious efforts of his genius."

Even if an opera-manager had legitimately bought the score and the right to produce an opera, he could not be sure that a rival manager would not forestall him by some underhand means. After the great initial success of Meyerbeer's *Robert le Diable* at Paris in 1831, the composer sold the score for a handsome sum to Mason, the manager at the King's Theatre, London, where it was intended to produce the opera. In the meantime the managers at Drury Lane and Covent Garden theatres had each procured copies of the pianoforte arrangement, then just published, and had the music orchestrated

---

[1] *Harm.*, Nov., 1823, p. 160.   [2] *Ibid.*, Feb., 1826, pp. 41 and 42.
[3] *Ibid.*, April, 1826, p. 80.

by their own musicians; both produced garbled versions of the opera at their respective theatres[1] before it could be brought out at the King's Theatre.[2] When a full score could not be procured, London managers just handed a piano arrangement to their musical director or some other musician to be orchestrated. No score of Donizetti's *Betly* was available for the production of that opera at the Lyceum Theatre under Balfe in 1841; so the whole opera was orchestrated from the piano copy by C. J. Loder.

The recompense a composer could get for his work depended largely on what he could make out of it when it was new, before anyone else had an opportunity of appropriating it. Copyists were evidently not trusted, and were often required to do their work under supervision, in the composer's house or on the premises in a theatre, in order to ensure that they did not make copies for anyone else. Thus, when Beethoven sent a score to the Archduke Rudolf in 1811, he begged that it should be copied in the Archduke's palace, as this was the only way to make sure that it would not be stolen.[3] Once a work was published and the copies circulated, there was little chance of the composer getting any more out of it, so he naturally made as good a bargain as he could, before the work could be exploited by others. The usual course was to sell the work for an agreed sum; there is no sign that the royalty system was employed.

The financial arrangements a composer could make for an opera were very much the same all over Europe, although customs varied a little in some countries. In Italy the customary arrangement was for the composer and manager to make an agreement under which the composer undertook to complete the work by a given date, to supervise the rehearsals and take charge of the first three performances "at the piano," for an inclusive fee; the opera then belonged for two years to the theatre at which it was produced. The composer generally came to the place where the production was to take place, a few weeks before the stipulated date, and wrote his music there and then, sometimes working in conjunction with the librettist. Under such conditions Rossini and many other Italian composers turned out opera after opera in the early years of the century. In that way Rossini's *Barber of Seville* was written in a short time in the Argentina theatre at Rome in 1816: "In the room where the two inventors (Rossini and Sterbini) were at work a number of copyists were employed, to whom the sheets of music were thrown one by one as they were finished."[4] The right to publish the music of an opera was of no value in Italy, because they didn't publish music there; but a successful opera soon found its way to France, Germany and England, and publishers in these countries quickly appropriated the

---

[1] As *The Demon* at Drury Lane on Feb. 20, 1832; and as *The Fiend Father* at Covent Garden on the following day.

[2] *Life of Moscheles*, I, p. 264; Hogarth, *Memoirs*, II, p. 350.

[3] "Sie brauchen nur gnädigst zum Schlemmer um einen tauglichen Kopisten zu schicken, der das trio jedoch nur in Ihrem Palaste kopiren müsste, weil man sonst nie sicher vorm Stehlen ist" (Nohl, *Briefe*, p. 75).

[4] Sutherland Edwards, *Life of Rossini*, p. 136.

music without permission or payment, and often gained substantial profits from the sales of the arias or piano arrangements.

When an Italian opera scored a success the composer's market price, so to speak, went up, and he was able to ask a higher price for his next work. And when the composer left his native Italy, and went abroad to trade on his success, he was in a position to extract a much higher price for a new opera from the managers in France, Germany or England. In this way composers hired themselves out to produce new operas just wherever a good price could be obtained. Rossini made good bargains with managers in Paris, Vienna and London, and Weber was induced to write and produce his *Oberon* in London at much better terms than he could get for a new opera in Germany.[1] But it had to be a new work, to which nobody else had access; any opera which had already achieved popularity could be had for the price of a full score from a copyist or a manager. Rossini's *Barber* was played and published all over Europe, making money for managers and publishers, but not for Rossini. In the same way Weber's *Der Freischütz* was earning money for anybody who chose to exploit it, but not for the composer.

In France a more equitable system was in force. There the composer received a fixed proportion of the receipts from the performances of his opera, and a successful work would produce a handsome return. But it was almost necessary for the composer to be on the spot to look after his interests, otherwise an arranger or adapter might step in and pocket the fees. Rossini was able to feather his nest very comfortably by the receipts from the operas he wrote while in Paris, and he was cunning enough to dish up his old Italian operas under new names, and gained the fees for the performances just as if they had been new works. He was also able to dispose of the publishing rights in Paris. Troupenas gave 6,000 francs for the right to publish *Le Siége de Corinthe*, the first of Rossini's operas of which the publishing right was sold by the composer. But Weber was not able to benefit from the adaptation of *Der Freischütz* in Paris, and no doubt Castil-Blaze collected the fees.

In Germany an inclusive initial fee was generally paid to the composer for a new opera, and he was at liberty to sell the music to a publisher; but he was quite unable to prevent his opera being produced or published free of charge in France or England, where the managers and publishers were in the advantageous position of being able to pick out only the successes, while leaving the failures alone.

The fees paid for operas by the German theatres, however, were lamentably meagre, and in the case of small theatres or travelling companies, ridiculously small. Most of the theatres paid only one small initial fee to the composer for the score of his opera, and were then at liberty to play it

---

[1] Weber received £500 for the copyright of *Oberon* in England, £125 for conducting at the Oratorio Concerts, and £250 for conducting *Oberon* at Covent Garden Theatre. (Smart, *Journals*, p. 240.)

as often as they liked; a successful opera might be played over and over again without the slightest benefit to the composer. At Berlin they paid for each performance—on a very moderate scale—but that equitable system was the exception rather than the rule in Germany. Nicolai and Lortzing complained bitterly about the small sums offered them by the German theatres for the right to produce their operas in perpetuity, and the latter throughout his hard life, in spite of several pronounced successes, was hardly able to keep his large family above starvation limit.

Good terms were given in London for a new opera, and many a composer went there for no other reason than that a better price might be obtained for his work than in his native country. But if the work was not new, and not exclusively purchased, the London managers, especially at Drury Lane, Covent Garden and the English Opera House, were only too ready to stage any opera that had been successful on the continent without going through the formality of applying to the composer or of paying anything more than a copyist's fee for the score.

ARRANGEMENTS AND ADAPTATIONS

Quite apart from the financial aspect, opera-managers all over Europe always considered themselves at liberty to alter, arrange or adapt any operatic works they had acquired, to suit their own particular theatre or audience. The amount of adaptation that went on, especially in France and England, makes strange reading in these days when composers enjoy the protection of copyright laws, and when their intentions are respected—at any rate, in moderation. And, it should be remembered, it was not only the works of deceased composers that were attacked and butchered; those of living composers were treated in just the same way. The contemporary music of the time was fair game for the arranger and adapter of the early 19th century, equally with the legacy of the best 18th century music.

Of the 18th century operas, those by Mozart were the chief sufferers. A classic example of mutilation was the production in 1801 of Mozart's *Zauberflöte* at the Paris Opéra. Under the title *Les mystères d'Isis*, the text and music were freely altered, music from *Don Juan*, *Figaro*, *La Clemenza di Tito* was inserted, as well as parts from Haydn's symphonies. The musical adaptor was Lachnith, who added recitatives of his own, and interfered with Mozart's orchestration. Reichardt saw and described this production in 1802,[1] and it was still being played in 1820 when Spohr was in Paris. The latter gave his views on the subject at some length[2]; "everything but the overture has been meddled with," wrote Spohr. Another of Mozart's operas treated in the same way at the Opéra was *Don Juan*, with "improvements and additions" by Kalkbrenner, in 1805; and again in 1828 the same opera was presented at the Odéon, the butcher on this occasion being Castil-Blaze.

[1] *Vertraute Briefe aus Paris*, I, p. 437.
[2] *Autob.*, II, pp. 109–10.

Mozart's operas fared no better in London, where the first of these works to be produced was *La Clemenza di Tito*, in 1806. *Don Giovanni* appeared in the guise of *The Libertine* in 1817 at Covent Garden, disarranged by Bishop, also *Figaro* (Covent Garden, 1828), *Così fan tutte* (*Tit for tat*, the English Opera House, 1828) and *The Seraglio* at Covent Garden in 1827. Of the latter production Hogarth wrote: "So many liberties were taken both with the drama and the music—so many retrenchments, interpolations, and changes of various kinds—that it could hardly be considered the same piece."[1] It was still running "languidly"' in January, 1828, when the *Harmonicon* complained that "too much of the original music is cut out, and too much that is new, put in."[2] Parke tells of how "Madame Vestris incurred the displeasure of the audience, by introducing into Mozart's opera (*Figaro*) that silly trash of a ballad *I've been roaming*."[3] Moscheles bemoaned that Mozart's *Seraglio* was given "with whole numbers cut out, and other popular English melodies substituted"[4]; Kramer, the conductor of the King's Household Band, was responsible for this adaptation. At a much later date, when Berlioz was in London, he saw at Her Majesty's Theatre "a performance of Mozart's *Figaro* that was trombonized, ophicleidized—in a word, *copper-bottomed*, like a ship of the line."[5]

The mania for adaptation was not so rampant in Germany, and Mozart's scores were probably treated with more respect in that country than anywhere else; but the few operas by that composer played in Italy appear to have been treated very freely. There was, however, a certain amount of tinkering with the scores of the classics even in German opera-houses. According to Berlioz, Gluck's scores were subjected to some touching up by Spontini, and later on by Meyerbeer, at Berlin. Schumann thought that he detected additions here and there to the music of Gluck's *Iphigenia in Aulis* when that opera was produced by Wagner at Dresden in 1847; he pronounced the additions "inadmissible," and commented: "Gluck would probably make use of a contrary process with Wagner's operas—he would cut out."[6] Wagner, in fact, subjected Gluck's scores to a great deal of adaptation, alteration and addition. He wrote connecting links and added recitatives of his own to *Iphigenia in Aulis*, endeavouring, as he said, "to make the interpolations of a strange composer as unnoticeable as possible."[7]

The few operas by Grétry that were revived in Paris were practically reorchestrated—and not altogether without good reason—by Adam, Berton, Auber and others. His *Guillaume Tell*, revived the year before Rossini's famous setting was produced, was "judiciously adapted," and numbers from other operas by the same composer were introduced, while "M. Berton, by adding accompaniments for wind instruments, particularly trombones, and by altering a few cadences which are obsolete, has given a freshness to compositions now between sixty and seventy years old that

---

[1] *Memoires*, II, p. 238.   [2] *Harm.*, Jan., 1828, p. 24.   [3] *Mem.*, II, p. 258.
[4] *Life of Moscheles*, I, p. 193.   [5] *Evenings*, p. 345.   [6] Schumann, I, p. 177.
[7] *My Life*, I, p. 409.

few people considered practicable."[1]   For a production at Covent Garden in 1842 of Grétry's *Richard Coeur de Lion*, the version arranged by Ad. Adam was used.   Contemporary operas were treated in much the same way by opera managers and their musical directors in France and England.   Weber's *Der Freischütz* was too tempting a bit to be overlooked in either capital; the "disfigured masterpiece," as Berlioz called it, which ran with such success at the Paris Odéon in 1824, was similarly disfigured at the same time in almost every theatre in London,[2] as Parke, Holmes, Hogarth and other contemporary witnesses have testified.   Operas in England had to end happily, and the course of the seventh fatal bullet was therefore diverted from the heroine to the villain.   Referring to the *finale* of the last act, the *Harmonicon* remarked: "All this is omitted in performance at the English Opera House, for the drama is there made to end happily, an unavoidable termination to an opera when Anglicised.   In the original, the seventh bullet which Rudolph shoots at the bird, recoils and enters the bosom of Agnes."[3]   Later on, Weber's *Abu Hassan* and *Preciosa* were likewise grabbed by English managers and made to suit the resources of their theatres and the taste of their audiences.

Rossini, himself an industrious adapter of his own early operas, could not prevent the London managers from making similar adaptations on their own account when there was any prospect of making a success with them. The *Barber of Seville* was severely mishandled by Bishop at Covent Garden Theatre in 1818.   This concoction was published under the following elaborate title: *The Overture and Music (complete) to the Comic Opera called the Barber of Seville, as performed at the Theatre Royal, Covent Garden, partly selected from Paesiello and Rossini's highly celebrated operas, Il Barbiere di Siviglia, partly composed, and the whole arranged, altered, and adapted to the English stage, by Henry R. Bishop.*   A review of the score includes the following: "The ingenious composer for Covent Garden, conforming to public opinion, has given us as much of the music as could be preserved in an English dress. The interstices he has filled, and very ably filled, with compositions of his own, or with selections from Paesiello.   Mr. Bishop has rejected Rossini's overture, and substituted one of his own."[4]

La Gazza Ladra was dished up as *Ninetta* in 1830 by the same hand, and in the same year *Cenerentola* appeared as *Cinderella* both at the King's Theatre and at Covent Garden, the adaptation of the latter having been made by Rophino Lacy, who "made copious addition from other works of the great composer, Rossini."[5]   At Drury Lane, *Hofer, the Tell of the Tyrol* was, of course, a mangled version of Rossini's *Guillaume Tell*, the music of which

---

[1] *Harm.*, July, 1828, p. 172.   At the first performance the public called for the composer (who had been dead for fifteen years), so a bust of Grétry was brought on to the stage.

[2] "The Freischütz is performing at all the minor Theatres, and in a most absurd, wretched manner at most of them" (*Harm.*, Oct., 1824, p. 192).   For a production at the Surrey Theatre, only the Bridal and the Huntsman's choruses were by Weber (Fitzball, *Thirty Years*, II, p. 178).

[3] *Harm.*, Sept., 1824, p. 172.   [4] *Quar. Mus. Mag.*, Vol. II, No. V, p. 74.

[5] Parke, II, p. 298.

"was selected and adapted with great ability to the English stage by Mr. Bishop."[1]   Bishop, indeed, seems to have been the arch-adapter of works which helpless foreign composers could do nothing to keep out of his clutches.   G. A. Sala described him as a "mutilater, patcher, and cobbler" of foreign operas.[2]

French composers were also made to contribute their share to the Londoner's insatiable appetite for adapted operas.   *The Night before the Wedding* at Covent Garden in 1829 was an adaptation of Boieldieu's *Les deux Nuits*, apropos of which Parke remarked: "The music is for the greatest part by Boieldieu, and the management of it has been ably performed by Mr. Bishop."[3]   Another of Bishop's adaptations was Boieldieu's *Jean de Paris*, which appeared in London at Covent Garden in 1829 as *John of Paris*; of 17 numbers in the opera, eight were by Boieldieu and nine were composed by Bishop.   Meyerbeer was made to contribute *Robert le Diable* in more than one version in 1832, and Auber's *Domino Noir* in some form or other was running in more than one London theatre in 1838.

Hogarth's list of the foreign operas adapted for the London theatres in the years 1827 to 1833[4] will give some idea of the extent of this traffic:

The Interrupted Sacrifice—Winter's *Unterbrochene Opferfest.*
The Turk—Rossini's *Turco in Italia.*
The Seraglio—Mozart's *Entführung aus dem Serail.*
The Freebooters—Paer's *Fuorusciti.*
Tit for Tat—Mozart's *Così fan Tutte.*
The Pirate of Genoa—Weigl's *Amor marinaso.*
Love in Wrinkles—A French piece by Fétis.
The Casket—A French piece, with music from Mozart's operas.
The Maid of Judah—Music from Rossini's *Semiramide.*
The Robber's Bride—Ries's *Die Räuberbraut.*
The Night before the Wedding—Boieldieu's *Les deux Nuits.*
Masaniello—Auber's opera.
The National Guard—Auber's *La Fiancée.*
Ninetta—Rossini's *La Gazza Ladra.*
Cinderella—Rossini's *Cenerentola.*
Hofer, the Tell of the Tyrol—Rossini's *Guillaume Tell.*
Don Giovanni—Mozart's opera, newly adapted.
The Vampire—Marschner's *Der Vampyr.*
Azor and Zemira—Spohr's *Zemire und Azor.*
The Emissary—Onslow's *Colporteur.*
The Love Charm—Auber's *Philtre.*
Fra Diavolo—Auber's opera.
Robert the Devil—Meyerbeer's opera.
The Alchymist—Music from Spohr's operas.

[1] Parke, II, p. 299.   [2] *Life and Adventures*, p. 21.   [3] Parke, II, p. 287.
[4] Hogarth, *Mem.*, p. 475.

During Alfred Bunn's management at Drury Lane from 1832 to 1839 a number of foreign operas by Auber, Marliani, Hérold, Mozart and Rossini were treated in the same way; these included *The Magic Flute, The Siege of Corinth, William Tell, Lestocq* and *Bronze Horse*.

Some of the above were really little more than *pasticcio* operas, loosely put together by Bishop, Rodwell, Tom Cooke, Lacy, and others, from any material that suited their purpose, with no idea but that of providing entertainment such as the audiences at most of the London theatres wanted. Fétis, indeed, classed them all under that heading: "*Pastiches,* composed of extracts from Italian operas with some English airs added, have for a long time been the only operas presented in England at the National Theatres" (i.e. Drury Lane and Covent Garden).[1] A typical "new opera" announced for production at Drury Lane in 1828, and entitled *Isidore di Merida* or *The Devil's Creek,* turned out to be founded on an old opera by Storace called *The Pirates* (1792), with additions by Braham, Cooke, Mercadante and Balducci, the whole put together by Cooke, who "has been occupied chiefly in augmenting the accompaniments to the original music, and in bringing to its aid instruments which either were not in the orchestra, or were in a most imperfect state, thirty years ago. This duty he has fulfilled with judgement."[2]

The whole system was bad and artistically dishonest; but it pleased, and the perpetrators of this sort of musical butchery made no effort to improve a taste which was content to remain at a deplorably low level: "The English musicians of that day could not shake off the propensity to introduce ballads, which they seemed to think were the only means of securing a favourable reception. They were tied and bound by the old-fashioned system, which could not designate anything as of an operatic character unless it had 'length' after 'length' of wearisome spoken twaddle introduced by way of helping the incidental music onward."[3]

Although the adaptation of operas included much more than merely interfering with the original score and the orchestration, in the case of oratorios and concert-music it was mainly adding to or readjusting the orchestration that occupied the arrangers.

The works subjected to this process were largely those of the few earlier 18th century composers whose music was still appreciated in the early part of last century, and of these by far the greater part consisted of Handel's oratorios, of which some twelve or more were still popular, and even growing in popularity.

There are signs that already in the last quarter of the 18th century it was being felt that some amplification of the instrumental parts of the oratorios was needed, and an important step was taken when Baron von Swieten commissioned Mozart to write additional parts to four of Handel's works for private performances in the hall of the Royal Library at Vienna, an apartment in which there was no organ.

[1] Fétis p. 251.   [2] *Harm.*, Jan., 1828, p. 24.   [3] *Mus. Recoll*, I, p. 303.

The use of a keyboard-instrument in the orchestra was dying out at that time, and the harmonic backing formerly supplied on one of these instruments by the player of the *basso continuo* had to be replaced by parts for the instruments of the orchestra.   The incentive to amplify Handel's orchestration was no doubt also due to some extent to the fact that the works were being sung by much larger choirs performing in larger halls, most of which had no organ.   Under these circumstances larger orchestras and fuller orchestration was called for, and this need became even more marked as the Musical Festivals in England and Germany increased in number and in scale during the first half of last century.

But the "additional accompaniments" written first by Mozart, then by Mosel, and after that by many others, did not end with merely supplying the essential harmony which in Handel's time was played on the harpsichord or organ.   Following Mozart's unfortunate lead, some of the parts which were superimposed on Handel's music were additional to the original conception, and displayed independence and individuality which went far beyond the former function of the keyboard-instrument.   The wood-wind parts, usually allotted by Handel to a pair of oboes, were laid out afresh for the standard four pairs of Beethoven's time; additional colour was added, generally that of clarinets, trombones, and a more free use of horns; the old trumpet parts were often modified so as to bring them within the range of players who were no longer trained to play in the high-lying *clarino* register; and the bass parts in big choruses were strengthened by the more weighty tones of serpents, bass-horns, ophicleides or double-bassoons. In fairness to the arrangers it may be said that they appeared to be quite unconscious of any lack of respect towards the great 18th century composer. The attitude of Mozart, Mendelssohn, and several English arrangers who bolstered up Handel's spare orchestration, was one of the greatest reverence, and quite free from any condescension.   They appeared to believe quite genuinely that they were only doing justice to the great man's music when they gave it the benefit of all the progress that had been made in orchestration since his day.   They felt that they were doing him a good service, and would have been horrified at the suggestion that they were acting in bad taste. The sense of historical style in music was not developed amongst the musicians of the early 19th century to the extent that it is now; they did not think of reconstructing the style of performance that had prevailed when Handel's works were written; they aimed rather at giving effective performances according to the standard and taste of their own time.   This idea of bringing the means of presentation up-to-date underlies a contemporary comment on Mosel's accompaniments to *Solomon*: "With respect to the accompaniments, they are always in strict conformity to the spirit and character of the original, and are exactly of that description which is suited to the *present state* of the art, and the wants of the time."[1]

The author of *Musical Recollections* had not the slightest doubt as to the

[1] *Harm.*, Aug., 1826, p. 171.

propriety of adding to Handel's orchestration: "Such accompaniments have blended and incorporated with the happiest success the sweetness, the tenderness, and the variety of Italian illustration with the strong and natural character of the original score, which Handel himself could not possibly have equally adorned, although it was his custom, by presiding at the organ, to fill up the harmonies according to his taste and tact, in the absence of these appliances which are now available by means of improved wind-instrumentation."[1]

Vincent Novello, who called his additions to Handel "corroborative accompaniments," wrote to Henry Phillips of the "profound veneration I feel for the memory of the most sublime of all composers," and explained how he had "made a point of not omitting or altering a single note of Handel's own score, but merely made such additions as would carry out and enforce the contrasts and orchestral effects which he *himself* intended. . . . I have carefully selected only such additional instruments to enrich my new edition of the orchestral score, as to the best of my judgement, I think that Handel would *himself* have chosen, if these instruments had been at his command when he first wrote the oratorios."[2]

Every one of these adders of parts was complacently sure that, had he been living in the 19th century, Handel would have done exactly what they were now doing to his music. It never occurred to them to question their own judgement, nor to admit the possibility that it might not have been exactly in accordance with Handel's views. And they were often encouraged and highly commended for their moderation and good taste in applying colour and volume where the composer had failed to do so: "Costa's sparing use of the brass in the few additional accompaniments is attended with the finest results: nothing can be more happy than the introduction of the ophicleide in the chorus 'But the waters'."[3] Perry's additions to *Samson*, "cautiously and tastefully added," were said to "reflect great credit upon his respect for the giant composer's conceptions, and are to be considered more as developments than intrusions."[4]

When a dramatic version of *Acis and Galatea* was presented at the Queen's Theatre in 1831, additional accompaniments were provided by Cipriani Potter, and this is how the *Harmonicon* justified the arrangement: "Had Handel lived within the last half century, he would doubtless have availed himself of the widely extended means of orchestral effects which are now at the command of the composer, but which were unknown in his time; and it is hardly fair towards his reputation to bring his music before the public in its original simplicity, not to say meagreness of score."[5] The same argument has been put forward over and over again since that time; it cropped up ominously in Monck Mason's prospectus for the opera season of 1832: "The very considerable improvements which have taken

[1] *Mus. Recoll.*, I, p. 16. [2] Phillips, *Mus. and Personal Recoll.*, I, pp. 315–16.
[3] *Illus. Lon. News*, Feb. 15, 1851. [4] *Ibid.*, Nov. 15, 1850.
[5] *Harm.*, March, 1831, p. 77.

place within the last fifty years in orchestral arrangements, particularly in the wind instrument department, it is to be hoped, will sufficiently justify the Director in adopting a system which has for its object only the addition of effect to the works of masters who lived when the modern improvements were unknown, and who, for a certainty, would have availed themselves of their powerful assistance had they then existed."

The following list is probably far from complete, but it is ample enough to give some idea of how many additional accompaniments to Handel's works were written up to about the middle of last century:

MOZART.   Messiah, Acis and Galatea, Alexander's Feast, Ode to St. Cecilia's Day.

MOSEL.   Samson, Belshazzar, Jephtha, Solomon, Israel in Egypt, Hercules, and two others.

MENDELSSOHN.   Acis and Galatea, Dettingen *Te Deum*, Israel in Egypt.

LINDPAINTER.   Judas Maccabaeus, Israel in Egypt.

CLASING (1779–1829).   Judas Maccabaeus, Joshua, Athalia, Utrecht *Te Deum*, 100th Psalm.

HILLER.   Theodora, Deborah.

SMART.   Dettingen *Te Deum*, Israel in Egypt, and probably others.

TAYLOR (Edward).   Israel in Egypt.

PERRY.   Judas Maccabaeus, Triumph of Time and Truth, Samson, Dettingen *Te Deum*, and others.

GREATOREX.   Many arias and separate movements.

KEARNS.   Scores used at Westminster Abbey, York and Birmingham Festivals, including Messiah and Israel in Egypt.

NOVELLO.   Judas Maccabaeus.

COSTA.   Samson, Judas Maccabaeus, Deborah, Israel in Egypt, Solomon, Saul.

RUGENHAGEN (Berlin).   Joseph.

The number of Handel's arias, overtures and other movements arranged by English musicians will never be known; most of the scores and parts have long since disappeared.   Contemporary programmes rarely mention an arranger's name, but occasionally they crop up in the musical journals. So we learn that a "movement from Handel's lessons, skilfully arranged by Mr. Greatorex for a full band," was played at the Ancient Concert in 1824,[1] that the overture to *Esther*, "with additional parts for a grand orchestra," was played at the Birmingham Festival in 1834, and that the same overture was given with "additional accompaniments" for wind instruments by Mr. Perry at the Three Choirs' Festival in 1842.

It is only fair to add that these additions to Handel's music were not always favourably received.   A correspondent of the *Quarterly Musical Magazine* in 1822 evidently felt uneasy as to the propriety of gilding the lily when he wrote: "That no improvement can be made upon Handel's

---

[1] *Harm.*, April, 1824, p. 74.

accompaniments I am far from denying, but that the additional accompaniments (even admitting them to be Mozart's) are generally improvements, I think will hardly be maintained.   They have a different stamp upon them, and alter, if they do not destroy, the effect which he intended.   If his music does not contain within itself the seeds of immortality, let it sink into obscurity and be forgotten.   It will acquire no additional fame by being tricked out in modern dress; but if any alteration or addition be made, it should be made sparingly, and with a strict attention to the style and intention of the composer."[1]

In 1828 Mozart's parts for *Messiah* were still "resisted" at the Ancient Concert, although a reviewer was of the opinion that "as a stronger light seems lately to have broken into the Hanover Square Rooms, we may hope that it will shortly illuminate the royal and noble directors on the subject of Handel's *Messiah*; particularly as we find that the most influential among those personages has sanctioned their use at the Festival now celebrating in the Cathedral which gives to his grace his archiepiscopal throne."[2]   The Royal and Noble directors of the Ancient Concert were evidently "illuminated" soon after the above was written, for we learn that in 1830 Mozart's parts were used at these concerts.   Hullah's brave effort in 1850 to discard the "beautiful accompaniments added by Mozart" was given no encouragement: "The effect of Handel's original instrumentation on Wednesday night was felt to be dull and monotonous."[3]

When Bach's works began to be revived, the same sort of problems that had arisen over the presentation of Handel's works about fifty years earlier had to be faced again, and they were dealt with much in the same way. That we don't hear of them so often as in the case of Handel's works is only because performances of Bach's larger works before the mid-century were comparatively few, even in Germany, and then they were not usually on the large scale of the more popular Handel oratorios.   Nevertheless, the problem of the *basso continuo* again presented itself, and was generally solved by writing additional accompaniments for performances where there was no organ on which the necessary harmonic background could be played. The additional parts for the earlier revivals were written by such as Mendelssohn, Moscheles and Hauptmann, and after the mid-century were done on a more comprehensive scale by Robert Franz.

The difficulty arising from obsolete instruments was encountered more often in Bach's scores than in those of Handel, and various makeshifts were freely employed.   Hauptmann tells of how he rewrote a *Gamba* part for the cor anglais, and at the same time added "some discreet inner parts" (*discrete Mittelstimmen*) for violas and 'cellos, because only the bass part was written out in the score.[4]   Mendelssohn also took some liberties with Bach's scores when difficulties cropped up; so, for example, in the instrumental

---

[1] *Quar. Mus. Mag.*, Vol. V, No. XV, p. 288.
[2] *Harm.*, Oct., 1828, p. 230.   This refers to the Archbishop of York.
[3] *Illus. Lon. News*, Dec. 21, 1850.   [4] *Briefe*, II, p. 42.

Suite No. 3, which was revived for the first time at the *Gewandhaus* in 1838, he found it necessary to modify the trumpet parts, and to give these instruments the support of a pair of clarinets.[1]   This readiness to rearrange Bach's parts was evidently caused, not only from a desire to amplify the lay-out of the orchestration, but also because the parts were often technically very difficult to play.   The trumpet parts seem to have been a sore stumbling block in the earlier revivals of Bach's works.   It appears that even Harper, who played Handel's trumpet parts so successfully and was reputed the best trumpeter in Europe, was unable to tackle the more exacting parts by Bach. Chorley wrote of the difficulties with which the players were faced: "The trumpet parts in his (Bach's) scores, again,—which now no Harper, Distin, or Arban, can manage, distancing every thing that the author of *Joshua* and the *Messiah* wrote for "the famous Mr. Snow," may be susceptible of this reason in interpretation of their present impossibility."[2]

We also hear of the disastrous attempt to perform parts of the B minor Mass at the Ancient Concert in 1838.   Regarding the trumpet part, a critic wrote: "This part of course Mr. Harper could not play, nor indeed could any body, with the instrument now in use in our orchestras."   Nor, it appears, did the other wind parts fare much better on the same occasion: "The passages for the horn were next to impracticable, and Mr. Denman was furnished with a fagotti part which appeared greatly incorrect. Of course the selection was slaughtered, the solo players retiring in dismay, and leaving Mr. Knyvett to play their parts on the organ."   When Grattan Cooke attempted to play a part for the oboe d'amore on the ordinary oboe, he "of course stopped at the very outset of his exertions."[3]   When Moscheles played a piano concerto by Bach for the first time in this country in 1837, it was provided with "new accompaniments given to the wind band," written by himself "with great taste and ready appreciation of the character of the music"[4]; and when a little later Bach's triple concerto was played by Thalberg, Benedict and Moscheles, "the orchestral accompaniments were re-scored for the occasion by Mr. Moscheles, and the wind instrument parts (the whole written in masterly keeping with the genius and character of the music) were entirely by Mr. Moscheles."[5]

Another composer whose music was subject to the "additional accompaniment" menace in this country was Purcell.   *King Arthur* had been revived from time to time, and in a presentation at the English Opera House in 1827 the music was thus roughly handled by Kearns: "Purcell's accompaniments, consisting of little else than stringed instruments, are much too quiet for modern ears; we require the excitement of trombones, horns and drums, with the luxuries of flutes, clarinets and bassoons, all of which have, we think wisely, been added on the present occasion.   To Mr. Kearns this task was assigned, who has executed it with taste and discretion."[6]   At the

[1] *Vorwort*, by Altmann, in Eulenberg's score.   [2] *Modern German Music*, II, p. 58.
[3] *Mus. World*, May 24, 1838, p. 67.   [4] *Ibid.*, March 24, 1837, p. 25.
[5] *Ibid.*, June 2, 1837, p. 187.   [6] *Harm.*, *Aug.*, 1827, p. 172.

Ancient Concert Greatorex was congratulated on the "complete success of his additions vocal and instrumental," to a scene from a piece called in the programme *Tyrannic Love*. Greatorex was also concerned with instrumental additions to a *Te Deum*,[1] and Edward Taylor was another who tried his hand at bringing *King Arthur* up to date.

A few other old works were sometimes revived with added instrumental support, notably Astorga's *Stabat Mater* and Pergolesi's setting of the same with instrumental parts by J. Adam Hiller. The latter was possibly the earliest writer of additional accompaniments; he died in 1804, and had exercised his hand on some of Handel's works at a time when they were not very well known in Germany, and before Mozart had made the additions which later provided the precedent for so many others. Amongst other older works treated in this way may be mentioned a *Te Deum* by Hasse, with accompaniments by Siegert of Breslau, and works by Palestrina and Marcello scored for a full orchestra by Greatorex for the Ancient Concert.

That a writer of additional accompaniments should in turn have his own music treated in the same way may perhaps be regarded as a judgment falling on the right head. It is odd to read that a *Te Deum* by Mozart with additional accompaniments by *Kapellmeister* Seyfried was performed at Vienna in 1828.

There can be no doubt that the practice of touching up the scores of both dead and living composers was quite common during the first half of last century, and that it was more freely exercised in this country than elsewhere. Ferdinand David wrote about the performance of the Choral Symphony by the London Philharmonic in 1841, and said that Moscheles had added an organ accompaniment to the choruses, and had entirely re-written some of the vocal parts.[2] Berlioz wrote: "That is the way they have in England. Neither Mozart, Rossini, Weber, nor Beethoven have been able to escape *reinstrumentation*. Their orchestra is not sufficiently spiced, and it is considered necessary to remedy this defect."[3] Although the censure may have been well deserved, it cannot be denied that Berlioz was rather apt to overstate his case; some of these "reinstrumentations" may well have been nothing more than the minor adjustments of the orchestration such as are often made in Beethoven's and Schubert's symphonies by many distinguished conductors of to-day.

Nevertheless, even in Germany, where a composer's intentions were more respected than anywhere else, conductors were not unready to make alterations in the scoring of the classics when they considered that they were able to produce a better effect. Schunemann[4] quotes Gassner (1844) for the statement that the scores of Gluck and Beethoven were often "improved" in Germany, and Wagner told of the havoc wrought in opera scores by conductors who made closes and interpolations "in other men's scores,"

---

[1] A full score of Purcell's *Te Deum and Jubilate in D*, with the additional accompaniments made by Boyce in 1755, was published by Novello in 1829.

[2] Eckardt, pp. 123–4.   [3] *Evenings*, p. 345.   [4] *Geschichte des Dirig.*, p. 299.

and were such masterhands at making cuts "solely with a view to the good of the work."[1]   In fact, in Germany, as elsewhere, most conductors allowed themselves a great deal of liberty in disregarding the intentions of the composer; to them the written score was by no means sacrosanct; with easy conscience and doubtful taste they supposed themselves quite well justified in amending or "improving" the works of any composer, great or small, dead or living, and rarely doubted their own competence to do so.

Alterations were sometimes brought about by executive difficulties in the parts, and it seems that a very easy and popular method of surmounting them was to have awkward passages in the string parts played by the leader alone.   The same remedy was often applied when the ensemble presented any difficulty.   In London at the Philharmonic concerts the few bars of introduction to the finale of Beethoven's first symphony were played as a solo by the leader in 1826, when a correspondent of the *Harmonicon*[2] referred to it as a "barbarous custom so universally adopted," and not until two years later did the Philharmonic venture to have the well-known scales played by all the first violins together.[3]   Apropos of this same introduction, Daniel Türk, the conductor at Halle, used to omit these few bars altogether because he thought that his audience would only laugh at these little scraps of ascending and lengthening scales.[4]

But, incredible as such breaches of taste may seem to us, we must remember that these things happened while Beethoven was still a living composer, a man whom anyone might meet in the streets of Vienna, before Time had placed on his head the halo of greatness, and had surrounded him with an aura of semi-divinity, infallibility and untouchableness.

The records of the writers of additional accompaniments, arrangers, adapters and "improvers" in the first half of last century are indeed black enough; but if we are too ready to deplore the bad taste, the lack of style-sense, and their apparent disregard of composers' most precious rights on the part of our grandfathers and great grandfathers, a glance at the records of the present century may act as a wholesome corrective to any who are pharisaically satisfied that we are not as they were.

If contemporary and recent music now escapes the hand of the arranger, it is obviously because of the immunity afforded by copyright laws which provide protection over a longer period, and which are international in scope.   But once the music emerges from that protective cover, the arranger and adapter is busy as ever before, and the use recently made of music by Wagner, Brahms, Tschaikowsky, Dvořák and Grieg, for example, demonstrates very clearly that nothing but protection by law has hitherto provided the safeguard against inartistic exploitation.

If we deplore the mangled pasticcio operas of the past, we should remember that in our own time we have had operas pieced together from music by Schubert, Chopin, Tschaikowsky and Grieg.   Our arrangers for

---

[1] *On Cond.*, pp. 7, 90, 100.
[2] *Harm.*, April, 1826, pp. 83, 84.
[3] *Ibid.*, April, 1828, p. 89.
[4] Leowe, p. 28.

the concert-room have also been industrious, and such combinations as
Handel-Harty, Handel-Elgar, Handel-Beecham, Rossini-Respighi, Grétry-
Mottl, Purcell-Holst, Mozart-Busoni, Weber-Berlioz-Weingartner, etc.,
etc., are by no means uncommon in our programmes.   Moreover, we have
bred another type of arranger who siezes on the keyboard-music of even
the 16th and 17th centuries and decks it out with all the resources and
showy effects of modern orchestration.

In the realm of ballet, the arrangers and adapters of the present century
have easily outdistanced those of the past.   The music of Purcell, Bach,
Handel, Beethoven, Chopin, Schumann, Grieg, and many others has been
ravaged to serve as ballet-music, and whole symphonies by Tschaikowsky,
Brahms, Beethoven and Berlioz have been forcibly united in unholy
matrimony with the posturing of ballet dancers.

The advent of music by wireless transmission has opened up a new front
for the arranger and adapter, who have not neglected their opportunities of
using music for purposes very different from those for which it was intended.
Scraps of symphonies torn out of their context and made to serve as incidental or background-music, bleed even more freely than the "bleeding
chunks" of opera in our concert-rooms, and the new art of cutting up music
into strips of given lengths has altogether outpaced the skill of the operators
apropos of whom Wagner wrote: "Herein shalt thou lie, whatsoever is too
long with thee shall be chopped off, and whatsoever is too short shall be
stretched."[1]

We have not yet got rid of additional accompaniments to Handel's
oratorios, and if we condemn Costa for strengthening the bass parts of the
choruses with his serpents and ophicleides, then we must also condemn the
organists who now do exactly the same thing with their pedal-organs.

This is not to condemn the arrangers and adapters of the present time,
nor to absolve those of the past; but merely to suggest that it is dangerous
to throw stones about as long as there is so much glass in our own house.

[1] *On Cond.*, p. 99.

XI

Rehearsal, Pitch, Arrangement of Orchestra.
Conclusion

A FEW threads remain to be gathered together in order to complete the story of the orchestra in the first half of last century. Perhaps the most important of these is that which concerns the preparatory work which usually precedes a public performance.

REHEARSAL

The playing of an orchestra depends quite as much on how, and how much it is rehearsed as upon the efficiency of the executants. It may be that an orchestra in which the quality of the players is not of the very best throughout may, if it is well and sufficiently rehearsed, give better perform-ances than one which contains only first-class players but is under-rehearsed. Good common-sense and practical experience lay behind Weber's reputed preference for "a willing and patient musician of ordinary ability, to the great artist who shirked rehearsals."[1]

Where the players were permanently and exclusively engaged, as in many court or subsidised theatres, the conditions for rehearsing were the most favourable, and adequate time for preparation was usually available; but at unsubsidised theatres run on a commercial basis the economic situa-tion only too often hampered the proper rehearsal of new works, and familiar operas were apt to be left to look after themselves. Generally speaking, it might be said that at the best German and the best Paris theatres the operas were well prepared; in Italy they were too quickly produced to be properly presented at the first performance, and in London they were only too often under-rehearsed.

At Berlin, Spontini, and after him Meyerbeer, could have just as many rehearsals as they required. The former's *Olimpia* (1821) was brought out there after 42 rehearsals, and according to *Kammermusiker* Hanemann, Spontini's rehearsals for one production might be as many as 80.[2] Weber had to be content with 16 rehearsals, of which four were with the orchestra, for his production of *Der Freischütz* at Berlin in 1821.

At the Dresden and Munich opera-houses the works appear to have been well rehearsed, even if the conductors at these places did not enjoy the opportunities for such thorough preparation as were allowed to Spontini

[1] Ella, p. 127. [2] Robert, p. 55.

at Berlin. But not everywhere in Germany were the conditions so favourable as in the capital cities. Lobe told of many an opera failing at its first performance in Germany, not because it was not a good opera, nor because the public lacked discrimination or good judgement, but only because the first representation was inadequate owing to insufficient rehearsal.[1] It was, he said, often only after a work had been played in public several times that the performance became good enough to reveal its quality, and that then only could a work be fairly judged and gain the appreciation that it merited.

At the Paris *Opéra* important new productions were given ample preparation; 28 full rehearsals for *Les Huguenots* in 1836, 29 for *Benvenuto Cellini*, and six months spent in preparing Halévy's *La Juive*,[2] suggest that time and money were not stinted when the occasion was sufficiently important. Meyerbeer's *Robert le Diable* was under preparation for nine months, but, according to Davison, the composer contributed about 25,000 francs from his own pocket towards the cost of these protracted rehearsals.[3]

What evidence there is, tends to show that in Italy the operas were produced very quickly, and that the music was rather sketchily rehearsed. Of Rossini's earlier days it was said that about twelve days generally sufficed for the production of a new opera,[4] and Hauptmann asserted that in Italy (1838), after the piano rehearsals, only two with the orchestra were considered enough.[5] Liszt had very much the same story to tell of Milan in 1837: "In this blessed land putting a serious opera on the stage is not at all a serious thing. A fortnight is generally time enough."[6]

In London, where time was always money, opera-production was done at top-speed; even the Italian Velutti "could not be reconciled to the more rapid preparations of the King's Theatre."[7] In 1823 a writer in the *Quarterly Musical Magazine* (probably a composer) contrasted the feverish haste of productions in London with the more leisurely methods of the continent: "What haste! What inaccuracy! What a scrambling to get to the end! Then what a shutting up of fiddle cases; what a pocketing of flutes and clarionets, and a running off in all directions! I have before mentioned the value of time to most of our practical men, and no one feels this so sensibly as the luckless wight who meets them for the purposes of rehearsal. The leader is in a hurry; the conductor is in a hurry; the singers, if they deign to attend, are in a very great hurry. In short, every one is in a hurry, but the poor author; who, in this general hurry, discovers the sad presage of the imperfect performance of his music and its probable failure.

"On the Continent, no pains are spared in rehearsals, and there compositions are repeated till the composer is satisfied that the effects intended by him will be produced. It is not unusual to hear that an opera, or symphony, has been rehearsed thirty or forty times; and it is related of Leo, that, intending to have his famous *"Miserere"* sung in Passion week, he ordered

[1] Lobe, *Cons. und Dis.*, p. 280.   [2] Castil-Blaze, *L'Acad. Imp.*, II, p. 355.
[3] *From Mend. to Wagner*, p. 412.   [4] Edwards, *Life of R.*, p. 133.
[5] *Briefe*, I, p. 244.   [6] Ramann, II, p. 279.   [7] Ebers, XXVII.

the rehearsals to commence on Ash Wednesday, and to be continued daily till the time of performance.

"How different is the case with us. At the theatre, an author must consider himself fortunate if he can have his opera tried over five or six times; with the band scarcely complete on any one occasion. . . . New music is frequently brought before the public after having been merely run through ONCE—and that, perhaps, so closely to the hour of performance, that the author has hardly time to correct any mistakes, which may have been discovered in the parts—nay, Sir, I have known new compositions which have been publicly performed, *without any rehearsal whatever*."[1] This was 120 years ago—and such things still happen in London.

Berlioz had some amusing things to say about the pace at which operas were produced in London: "London impresarios are truly the men to get the most out of time; it is through the English that the art of accelerated musical rehearsals has been brought to a degree of splendour unknown to other nations. I cannot pay a higher tribute of praise to the method they follow than to say that it is the very reverse of the one adopted in Paris. On our side of the British Channel, to learn and stage a five-act opera, ten months are required; on the other, ten days."[2] But Weber was not so badly treated in London when his *Oberon* was produced for the first time in 1826; he had altogether 16 rehearsals, starting on March 9, and the performance took place on April 12.

The production of opera, and especially of new works, with all its attendant complications, involved much more than orchestral rehearsing, and it was not until the preparations were well advanced that the orchestra began to take any part in the proceedings. A piano or a string quartet, or both, supplied the music until soloists, chorus, and dancers were becoming more or less familiar with their work, and all the elaborate paraphernalia of stage-production was shaking down into its place.

For purely orchestral music there can be no such rehearsing in advance, unless it be done by sections. Berlioz always pleaded for sectional rehearsals, and his works demanded such preliminary practice more urgently than those of most of his contemporaries; yet he was only rarely able to put his ideas on rehearsing into practice, and his pleading was largely theoretical. Like most of his theories, Berlioz's demands for rehearsals were little more than dreams of ideal conditions which he had little hope or chance of realising.

In the ordinary course the rehearsing of concert-pieces was done with a full orchestra, and usually with no more than one rehearsal for each concert.

Nowhere else were the symphonies so thoroughly practised as for the Paris Conservatoire concerts under Habeneck. An important work was not played in public until it had become familiar to all the musicians by means of continual repetition, an admirable method which no conductor has ever been able to improve on, and one which admits of no short-cuts. Beethoven's symphonies, in particular, were practised for months, or years

---

[1] *Quar. Mus. Mag.*, Vol. V, No. XX, pp. 433, 434.   [2] *Evenings*, p. 107.

if necessary, and Mendelssohn's *Midsummer Night's Dream* overture was given seven rehearsals, although the composer was quite satisfied with the playing after two.[1]   But this was exceptional, even in Paris, where ordinary concerts with scratch orchestras were not much better rehearsed than they were in London.

The rule at the Philharmonic concerts in London was one rehearsal for each concert,[2] a state of affairs which amazed Wagner when he came in 1855 to conduct the season's concerts.   "Benefit" and other odd concerts fared even worse in London.   Fétis wrote of these in 1829: "An orchestra, which has not been rehearsed, is got together in a hurry,"[3] and Moscheles told much the same story in 1822: "We have, however, rehearsed here in quite a different manner from what people usually do, for, generally speaking, there is no rehearsal at all, often one half of a band runs once through the music."   For his concert in 1833 Moscheles had "half a band, in consequence of the long rehearsal at the opera, and only a few over-tired players arrived, and hastily ran through the new piece."[4]   For Mad. Dulcken's concert in 1843, it was "next to impossible to get up a proper rehearsal, and in spite of all the pains and trouble taken by Mr. Dulcken, he could never collect more than half of the gentlemen of the orchestra for the purpose of rehearsing."[5]

Chorley's opinion was that English orchestral players were always at their worst during rehearsals: "That painful conviction, that nine-tenths of the orchestra feels itself employed in manufacturing music, which is so constantly forced upon the listener at English rehearsals, could never be entertained here for one single moment"; that was written anent a rehearsal at Brunswick under Mendelssohn.   But after a bad rehearsal the English players gave of their best at a public performance: "having been more than usually indifferent and insubordinate at a trial, the English orchestral player is compelled at a full performance to fulfil his duties with that extra measure of zeal and attention which the German musician finds it his pleasure to bring to bear upon all he does,—whether going through the flimsy and worn-out symphony to one of Bellini's *cavatinas*, or trying an intricate and not engaging slow movement by Lachner or Lindpaintner."[6]   It was apparently not until 1852 that the London players were given the novel experience of rehearsing a symphony several times.   This was done for the concerts of the New Philharmonic Society when Berlioz conducted the first season of that society in that year.   According to the *Musical World*, Berlioz had seven rehearsals for Beethoven's Choral symphony, but according to Wilhelm Ganz,[7] there were five rehearsals, "which for England at that time was a really great innovation."   Of course, the society that was so lavish with rehearsals endured for only a few years.

Orchestral concerts at Vienna in Beethoven's time were deplorably

[1] Eckardt, p. 46.   [2] Hueffer, p. 200.   [3] *Curiosités*, p. 263.
[4] Moscheles, *Life*, I, pp. 65, 290.   [5] *Mus. World*, June 22, 1843, p. 214.
[6] *Mus. and Manners*, I, p. 228.   [7] *Mem.*, p. 61.

under-rehearsed, and, according to Hanslick,[1] in the 'twenties and 'thirties the *Spirituel-Concerte* were given without rehearsal, and those of the *Gesellschaft der Musikfreunde* with only one; and both orchestras contained amateur string players. Not until Lachner (1832) and Nicolai (1841) came and started the Philharmonic concerts did the Viennese begin to learn what could be done with an adequately rehearsed and fully professional orchestra. Parish Alvars, the harpist, wrote from Vienna in 1845 saying that the Philharmonic orchestra there had from ten to twelve rehearsals for each concert; in the following year a correspondent of the *Musical World* said that this orchestra usually had from twelve to sixteen rehearsals—"hence the perfection of the band, which has been so much, and so justly, vaunted." The comment on this by the editor of the London paper was: "what wonder that the London Philharmonic, with its one rehearsal, should be so inferior to the continental orchestras."[2]

If orchestral concerts in Germany were not always rehearsed as well as might have been wished, it was because nearly all the orchestras were there primarily for the purpose of playing in the opera-houses; concert-playing was a side-line rather than the main purpose of their existence. Much depended on the conductor, and where an energetic and painstaking man was in charge, he could generally get sufficient time adequately to prepare the orchestra for concert performances. Mendelssohn could get time enough with the *Gewandhaus* orchestra to satisfy his requirements, and when Wagner prepared for a performance of the Choral Symphony at Dresden, he insisted on, and was able to secure rehearsals enough to carry out his project according to his own ideas. The *recitative* for 'cellos and basses at the beginning of the last movement had always been a hard nut to crack, and Wagner succeeded in getting it played with the requisite freedom of style and the expression he wanted only after twelve special rehearsals with these instruments alone.[3]

Berlioz found the German orchestras, on the whole, ready and willing to give him time enough to rehearse his works to his satisfaction, and some even offered him extra time when his exacting parts presented difficulties which demanded more practice than usually sufficed.

Smart often remarked on the orderliness of orchestral rehearsals in Germany, and added—"so different to our opera-house." But the Germans were always a well-disciplined people, and Smart's remarks were made in 1825, before Costa had introduced discipline into our orchestras.

PITCH

The advantage of a universal and standardised pitch is one of the blessings that musicians of the present day are apt to take for granted, and having known nothing else, probably do not fully appreciate.

During the first half of last century there was no standard pitch; it varied in each country, and there was no certainty that it would be the same

---

[1] Hanslick, p. 62.   [2] *Mus. World*, 1846, p. 166.   [3] *My Life*, I, p. 401.

even in the theatres or institutions of any one town or locality. The general tendency of a rising pitch was not checked until after the mid-century, when, following the lead of France in 1859, most countries gradually fell into line and adopted the pitch which is now practically standardised.

It is difficult for us now to realise what these chaotic variations of pitch must have meant to the players, singers and instrument-makers of the past. In this country the pitch was already high, and was still rising. An English singer who travelled in Italy in 1819 wrote as follows: "I have in my possession a tuning fork, which I carried with me within the last twelve months through all the principal cities of Italy, and I can aver that in Naples, Rome, Florence, Genoa, Milan, Turin, Bologna, etc., etc., the pitch was uniformly half a note at least below that adopted in the concerts of England; I beg leave also to mention that a clarinet player who some time since arrived here from Germany, and brought with him the instrument he had used for years, found himself unable to play upon it in concerts in England."[1]

Spohr told how in 1820, at a concert in the King's Theatre, London, it was found that the piano intended to be used for a Mozart piano concerto was pitched so high that none of the wind instruments could play with it. There had been no rehearsal, and at the performance only the string orchestra could be used to accompany the concerto. Spohr remarked that such a thing could have happened nowhere but in England.[2]

According to Smart,[3] "the Philharmonic fork was decided upon by Mrs. Billington and Mr. Braham for the vocalists, to which Sir George Smart, for the pianoforte, and Mr. Griesbach (oboe) for the wind instruments, consented." That was in 1813; in 1825 Smart found the pitch at one of the Vienna theatres and at the Paris *Opéra* both above the London Philharmonic pitch.

Busby wrote in 1825: "In London, scarcely two orchestras have their scales in precisely the same point of the great compass. St. Paul's organ, till of late years, was half a tone above the usual standard; the theatrical bands, and those of the Opera, the Philharmonic, and the concert of Ancient Music, differ from each other, and not infrequently perplex and distress the vocal performers."[4]

In 1838 the situation was no better: "The pitch has been rising for many years, and is higher in England than in most other countries. The organs abroad are more than a note (tone?) below the opera pitch in England, and some of the modern wind instruments half a tone above concert pitch. The Abbey organ is half a tone above the St. Pauls, and the Ancient Concert nearly half a tone above that in the Abbey."[5] At the Paris *Opéra*, the pitch rose steadily from a' = 427 in 1811, to 434 in 1829, and to 446 in 1858, while at the *Opéra Comique* it was lower, but nevertheless rising.[6] At St. Petersburg in 1840 the pitch was even higher; according to Adolphe

[1] *Quar. Mus. Mag.*, Vol. I, No. II, p. 152.   [2] Speyer, p. 53.
[3] *Journals*, p. 80 f.n.   [4] *Anecdotes*, II, p. 70.   [5] *Mus. World*, Feb., 1838, p. 125.
[6] Sachs, *History*, p. 390.

Adam, it was at that time nearly half a tone higher than in Paris.   Spohr complained in 1826 about the difficulty of bringing "all the instruments to the same pitch" at the Rhenish musical Festival at Düsseldorf.[1]   At musical festivals, for which players from many different places were usually assembled and where organs in churches sometimes had to be taken into account, these troubles must have been multiplied, and the conflicting claims of vocalists, string and wind players next to impossible to satisfy.

ARRANGEMENT OF ORCHESTRA

A full account of the various ways of placing the players in the orchestra is rendered practically impossible owing to the fact that there were just as many different arrangements as there were orchestras; only a few salient features need be noticed.

The plans fall into two classes, namely, those for theatres and those for concert-rooms.   The shape of the orchestra pit in a theatre always necessitates spreading out most of the players on either side of the conductor, while in a concert-room the players are generally spread out more or less in front of the conductor.

The usual arrangement in German theatres was to place the whole of the string orchestra on one side, and all the wind instruments on the other side. In 1825 Smart found the strings at Dresden all on the right, and the wind all on the left of the conductor.   That was Weber's arrangement when he reorganised the orchestra in 1817.   But at Stuttgart the strings were on the conductor's left and the wind on his right, with the 'cellos and basses behind him.   According to Berlioz[2] (1843) the strings in Germany were usually on the right and the wind on the left.   Gassner's plans[3] (1844) confirm this as a general plan, but show that in some places the positions were reversed.   Sterndale Bennett remarked on the division of the orchestra at Cassel in 1842 into strings on one side and wind on the other side of the conductor, with the double basses in the centre.[4]

Spontini, at Berlin, did not approve of this German way of separating the string and the wind bands, and arranged the string orchestra on both sides, with the heavy wind and drums on either flank, the first violins being on his left and the seconds on his right: "my left eye is for the first violins, and my right for the second violins."[5]   Spontini liked to have the oboes behind him, a fad of his which Wagner said owed its origin to a mere accident.   When he came to Dresden in 1844 to conduct his *Vestalin*, Spontini had the orchestra rearranged according to his accustomed plan, and this plan was approved and adopted with some slight modifications by Wagner, who had then just taken up his appointment at Dresden.   Even as late as the time when Wagner was writing *Mein Leben*, he said that some German orchestras still adhered to the old plan of placing the strings and

---

[1] *Autob.*, II, p. 162.   [2] *Mem.*, II, p. 13.   [3] *Dir. und Rip.*
[4] *Life*, p. 117.   [5] Wagner, *Prose Works*, III, p. 134.   *My Life*, I, p. 342.

wind on opposite sides of the conductor. Meyerbeer retained Spontini's arrangement at Berlin, and had the violins on either side of him.

A new arrangement of the orchestra at the *Königstädter* theatre in Berlin in 1827 shows a similar departure from the old German custom: "The leader (conductor), instead of being seated, as formerly, low in the centre, is raised and stationed with his back immediately to the pit. . . . the contrabasses are ranged round him like a rampart, the violins on both sides, with their faces to the stage, while the wind instruments, and those of a noisier character, are distributed in the two wings of the orchestra."[1] This would be similar to Spontini's plan, except that the violins faced the stage instead of looking towards the conductor.

Spontini's arrangement was no doubt the outcome of his experience in Paris, where the first and second violins generally sat on either side of the conductor, facing inwards. Kastner's plan in 1837[2] (no doubt that of the *Opéra*) was to have the first violins, violas, and wood-wind on one side, the second violins and brass instruments on the other, with the 'cellos and basses near the centre.

Franz Stöber's sketch of the orchestra at the *Kärntnerthor* theatre at Vienna in 1821 shows that the conductor stood in the centre nearest the stage; close around him were the 'cellos and basses, and the violins were seated in a single row nearest the auditorium facing the stage. On the conductor's right were the wood-wind and horns, and on his left the violas, a harp, and the heavier brass and drums behind them. The leader's desk was raised above the level of the others, and each was provided with a green-shaded lamp. The same arrangement was evidently kept for many years. A plan of the orchestra at the same theatre in the 'forties shows the strings grouped in the centre, round the conductor, with the wood-wind and horns on his extreme right, and the brass and drums on his left.[3]

A plan of the orchestra at *La Scala*, Milan, shows that in 1825 all the wind players were seated in pairs next to the stage, with all the strings between them and the auditorium[4] (see p. 474).

The arrangement at the *San Carlo* at Naples in 1818 is very similar to that at Milan in that the wind players face inwards and are placed between the stage and the string orchestra; the division of the lower stringed instruments into two groups, one at each side of the orchestra, was evidently an Italian custom which was extended to the violas, no doubt because the instruments so often played the bass part in the upper octave, and were given nothing of importance to play in the Italian orchestration of that time[5] (see p. 475).

The arrangements for placing concert-orchestras were quite as diverse as those in the theatres, and the widely different sizes and shapes of the platforms in concert-rooms gave plenty of scope for variety. Some platforms were deep, and some were shallow; some were flat, and others rose in tiers; some were rectangular, and others were semicircular; on

[1] *Harm.*, Oct., 1827, p. 211.   [2] *Cours*, p. 28.   [3] Schunemann, p. 315.
[4] *Harm.*, Aug., 1825, p. 140.   [5] *All. Mus. Z'tung*, July 15, 1818.

some there was an organ in the centre, and on others there was none. Only a few of the rooms were originally designed for musical performances, and in most cases a choir as well as an orchestra had to be accommodated.

The platform in the old *Gewandhaus* at Leipzig was slightly rounded at the back, and was practically flat; in the Munich *Odeon* it was semicircular

and rose in tiers; at Dresden the concerts were given on the stage of the old court theatre, which was temporarily built up in rising tiers. The large *Salle* at the Paris Conservatoire was built in the form of a theatre; for concerts, the stage was built up in rising tiers, and a large flat platform in front of the stage projected well into the auditorium. In the Hanover Square Rooms the platform was almost rectangular; an early picture shows it without an organ, and perfectly flat, but a later picture (1843) shows it with an organ in the centre and a few rising tiers. Performances in continental churches often required orchestra and choir to be scattered or widely separated in galleries.

In most places the choir and soloists were placed in front, facing the audience, with the conductor in the centre; the orchestra was generally behind the choir, rising by steps above it. At the Paris Conservatoire

Habeneck stood between two groups of choral singers, who would be obliged to turn their heads very considerably to see his beat; a group of male choristers were placed immediately in front of him, and to the left and right of these singers were the first and second violins; further back,

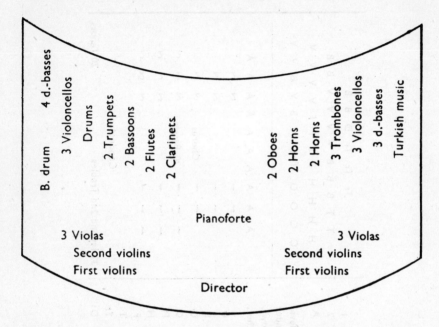

the violas stretched across the platform, and behind these the stage proper rose in four tiers, on which were placed the 'cellos and basses to the right, the wind to the left, and the heaviest brass and drums on the uppermost tier.[1] The plan of the Conservatoire orchestra appeared in the *Musical World* in 1840[2]; it corresponds fairly closely with Elwart's plan (see p. 476).

At the Munich *Odeon* the choir occupied the whole of the frontal flat platform, with the conductor in the centre and the singers on both sides of him; he faced the orchestra (but not the choir) which was arranged on the rising tiers. The violas, 'cellos and basses were immediately in front of him, the first violins to his left and the seconds to his right, with the wind instruments rising in the centre. At Dresden the arrangement was somewhat similar, but that both first and second violins were on the left, the wood-wind on the right, and the brass and drums on the uppermost tier.[3]

The arrangement with the choir on a low platform in front, and the orchestra rising behind was also chosen by Berlioz for a large-scale

[1] See the *Plan de l'Orchestre*, following p. 114 in Elwart's *Histoire*.
[2] March 26, 1840, p. 194.
[3] Schünemann, p. 308. No date is given, but it was probably before Wagner's time.

performance at Paris in 1844.[1]   In his *Instrumentation*,[2] Berlioz again recommended the plan of placing the choir in front on a low platform, the orchestra rising behind it with first and second violins on opposite sides, violas in the centre, 'cellos, basses and wood-wind on rising tiers, and the

[Orchestra seating plan diagram, with labels including: Conductor; Chorus; 20 Basses; 20 Tenors; 32 1st and 2nd Trebles]

REFERENCE

15 First violins, marked	1
15 Second ditto	2
10 Violas	A

These are on the floor or level of the stage. The remainder are on four straight rows, raised one above the other, viz.:

12 Violoncellos, marked	V
9 Double basses	B
2 Clarinets	C
2 Oboes	O
2 Flutes	Fl
4 Horns	H
4 Bassoons	F
2 Trumpets	T
3 Trombones	Tr
1 Drums	D

heaviest brass and drums at the back on the highest tier.   Berlioz, however, insisted that the choir should not face the audience, but should be turned diagonally towards the conductor in a fan-shaped formation.

Rowlandson's aquatint of the interior of Covent Garden theatre (1808) with an oratorio concert in progress, shows the choir in front of the orchestra, and the sketches of Weber conducting a concert at Covent Garden Theatre (1826) likewise suggest that the choir sat at the front of the platform,

---

[1] *Mem.*, II, p. 161.   [2] Page 254.

facing the audience. Several later contemporary pictures show that time-beating conductors in London usually faced the audience. No doubt it would have been considered impolite to turn one's back to the audience.

A noticeable feature of most of these plans is that the situation of the choir was the least favourable for seeing the beat of the conductor.

Another point which cannot escape notice in most of the old orchestral plans is the position of the leading 'cello and bass players. These two always played at the same desk, and were placed close to the conductor. This was no doubt a relic of the time when the leading 'cello and bass players sat on either side of the conductor at the piano, and played from his score or bass part. They were mainly or entirely responsible for accompanying the recitatives, and it was important that they should be near the centre of control. The rest of the lower strings were generally spread about the orchestra, rather than concentrated in one area. This, again, was a legacy of the days before orchestras were directed with a baton, when the ensemble depended largely upon every player hearing the bass part distinctly.

Fétis (1829) was very much struck with the peculiar situation of the basses in the London Philharmonic orchestra. They were, he said, placed in front of the orchestra, on a level below that of the violins. The effect, Fétis admitted, was not so disagreeable as he would have expected.[1] But Moscheles told how in 1833, when the Philharmonic moved to the Hanover Square Rooms, the orchestra was differently arranged: "the basses being separated and placed more in the background than hitherto."[2] At the Sacred Harmonic Society's concerts "all the bassi and violoncelli are in a row in front, the more acute violins immediately behind, while the wind instruments are ranged in equal progression."[3] The custom of placing the basses in front of the orchestra seems to have been peculiar to this country; in 1839 it was said that the basses of the Philharmonic orchestra were "invariably in front."[4] But when baton-conducting became the usual method of controlling orchestral playing in London, it was no longer necessary to rely so much on the prominence of the bass part in order to keep the ensemble intact, and in 1840 the Philharmonic took an important step when the whole orchestra in the Hanover Square Rooms was rearranged, and the violins were placed in front of the basses, and to the left and right of the conductor in the same way as was usual in Paris; the leading 'cello and bass players, however, still retained their central position on an "elevated platform" immediately behind the pianoforte. The new plan which was adopted for the season of 1840[5] is shown on p. 478.

When Costa became conductor in 1846 he considerably modified the above plan, and had the rising steps on the platform lowered so that the drums and trombones were no longer "perched up in the roof, to drown the stringed instruments, which were down in a valley."[6] From the same

[1] *Curiosités*, p. 186. [2] Moscheles, *Life*, I, p. 288. [3] Phillips, II, p. 5.
[4] *Mus. World*, May 2, 1839, p. 11. [5] *Ibid.*, Feb. 6, 1840, p. 83.
[6] *I. L. News*, May 21, 1846.

source we learn that "the Conductor faced his troops, instead of fronting the audience." The new arrangement was illustrated in the plan on p. 479, which shows how the basses were more widely distributed at the back of the orchestra, although the two leaders remained in the centre immediately behind the piano.

ORGAN

Trombones   Drums   Cymbals, etc.

Horns   Trumpets

Flutes   Oboes   Clarinets   Bassoons

Tenors

Violoncello and D. bass

(principals)

First violins · Ditto · Ditto · Leader and three violins

Basses · Ditto · Ditto

Basses · Ditto · Ditto

Second violins · Ditto · Ditto · Ditto

┌─────────────────────────┐
│   PIANOFORTE   │
└─────────────────────────┘

CONDUCTOR

Singers

Flight of steps   Front of the Orchestra   Flight of steps

This plan became more or less standardised by the middle of the century, and was generally adopted by concert orchestras in England during the second half of the century.

CONCLUSION

There must have been many people living in 1850 who had been old enough in 1800 to listen intelligently to an orchestra. Within their lifetime these people must have been able to record a growth in the size and treatment of orchestras that almost linked Mozart with Wagner; which included in its course the contributions of Beethoven, Weber, Rossini, Mendelssohn, Berlioz, Meyerbeer and Schumann; which saw the strings of the orchestra greatly increased in power, the introduction of more and much more efficient wind instruments, and the permanent addition of harps and sundry percussion instruments. They also saw the development and stabilisation of the orchestral baton-conductor.

The ears which in 1800 knew only the sounds of Haydn's and Mozart's orchestras, must have become inured by 1850 not only to an orchestral texture that had become much more complex and crowded, to more varied and richer colouring, but also to a great increase in sheer volume of sound. This cumulative growth must have been absorbed gradually by ears trained step by step to receive it, and which developed, so to speak, an enlarged capacity for hearing ever more instrumental matter and more volume of sound. The ears to which the sounds produced by the orchestras of Haydn and Mozart were ample and satisfying could not at once have adjusted their capacity to receive the sounds flung at them by Berlioz, Meyerbeer or Wagner; the process was graduated and eased by the intermediate training provided by the orchestration of Beethoven, Weber, Spontini, Rossini, and

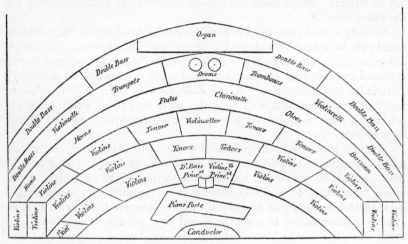

THE PHILHARMONIC ORCHESTRA IN 1846, AS ARRANGED BY COSTA

others who built up textures, colouring and volume compared with which those of the preceding generation tended to sound thin, and which in its turn also became thin by comparison as the work of the succeeding generation became ever more dense and voluminous.

The progress of this training can be traced in a series of protests against the growing sonority of the orchestra, each stage of which in turn was eventually accepted, and by simultaneous complaints about the lack of sonority and colour in the older scores, and by the efforts made to amplify them and bring them up to date.

We may perhaps detect something of this sort even towards the end of the 18th century when the Emperor Joseph II told Mozart that there were "too many notes" in the score of his *Entführung*, and in Grétry's remark that Mozart placed the statue in the orchestra and the pedestal on the stage; or when, referring to Cherubini's music, Napoleon said that he wanted a composer "who would make music, and not noise."

Then, when Beethoven gave his hearers still more notes to listen to, there were those who found the sounds too much for their ears, and set up the orchestral sounds made by Haydn and Mozart as a limit which should not be exceeded. Even Beethoven's first symphony was found rather too noisy for the ears of a critic who complained in a German musical periodical about "too much use of wind instruments, so that the music sounded more as if written for a military band than an orchestra."[1] As Beethoven's orchestral sonority grew, there were plenty of objections to its noisiness; Spohr, while complaining about the meagreness of Italian orchestration, could not endure the "unmeaning noise" in the *Finale* of Beethoven's fifth symphony, and regretted that, after the *Scherzo* was re-introduced in the last movement, the pleasant impression was so soon obliterated "by the returning noise."[2]

Nobody would now suspect that Schubert's handling of the orchestra could ever have been considered too heavy; but the *Allgemeine Musikalische Zeitung* in 1820 found that in *Die Zwillingsbrüder* "the music suffered from a confused overladen instrumentation," and again commented on Schubert's "overladen instrumentation" in *Die Zauberharfe*.[3] Even in 1843, after he had had a taste of Wagner's sonority, there was "too much brass" in Schubert's great C major symphony for the quiet-loving ears of Moritz Hauptmann.

Spontini made his orchestra sound too loud for some ears, and we are told that at the first performance of his *Olimpia* in Berlin, "some left the house, unable to endure the incessant thundering of the orchestra," while others "seemed to be perfectly satisfied at having their ears so stunned."[4] Edward Holmes censured Spontini for overloading his arias "with as thick a score of instruments as might be found in a sinfonia or overture," and asked why Julia in *Die Vestalin* should "be called upon to overpower four horns and three trombones."   From the same source we learn that "Weber is one of the moderns who has followed the noisy example, and it is a method which not only destroys the clearness of the parts, but robs the overture of its most striking peculiarity."[5] Another English critic also complained that Weber's orchestration in *Oberon* often overpowered the human voice: "He too frequently forgets, in the search after the philosophical and the sublime, the relative power of his agents—the voices, which in spite of all the science of the scientific, the hearts of a mixed audience pronounce to be the first and chiefest, is too much disregarded and often totally overpowered, to make way for the band, the wind instruments especially, and the noisy over the harmonious."[6]

When Rossini, in his more light-hearted manner, made the orchestra rattle and reverberate with the sounds of brass and drums to an extent which had hitherto been unknown in Italian scores, complaints about noisiness were showered upon him.   Bellini's *Norma* was calculated to "stun one with all kinds of noisy instruments, whilst half, or more, of the first act is accompanied by the same intolerable din."[7] Clementi is reported to have said that it required forty years' study to learn how to fill a score, and an

---

[1] *All. Mus. Zeit.*, 1800.   [2] *Autob.*, I, p. 214.   [3] Hellborn, I, pp. 175, 177.
[4] From *A Tour in Germany* . . . *in* 1820, 1821, 1822.   [5] *Rambles*, p. 258.
[6] *Q. M. Mag.*, Vol. VIII, No. XXIX, p. 100.   [7] *Harm.*, July, 1833, p. 160.

equally long time to learn how to empty one. Commenting on this in 1840, a writer remarked: "The noisy writers of the ultra-modern school acquire the ability to fill a score to a much greater plenitude than Clementi could ever have imagined in a far briefer term than the octogenarian theorist allows; but it would take a century's serious consideration to learn how to empty their scores, that may almost be called grosses; for, when the noise is abstracted the music is bankrupt, having no effects."[1] The last sentence was no doubt true then, as it is now; but one has a suspicion that these complainers about noise in the growing sonority of orchestral sounds were unable or unwilling to distinguish between volume and noise. They seemed to regard the two as being synonomous; loud orchestration to them was noisy orchestration. It can only be supposed that their capacity for hearing sound in greater volume than they were used to was unequal to the strain of taking in both the content of the music and the increased volume of sound at the same time. But the "ultra-modern" composers of 1840— presumably Meyerbeer, Berlioz, and possibly Wagner—were then only beginning to pile on the sound which was so promptly designated noise, and which was presently to grow still greater in volume, sonority, and—if they must call it so—in noisiness. Little did they know what was coming, and how much more "noise" was yet to be extracted from the orchestra.

In the meantime the scores of the earlier 18th century composers were being found unbearably thin, and "additional accompaniments for full orchestra" were superimposed on their skeleton structure in order to satisfy ears that had developed an appetite for greater sonority. And when these additional accompaniments in turn became too thin for the large-scale performances of Handel's works which were the rule at the English musical festivals, there was a call for still more fulness and volume. The following relates to Mozart's additional parts to *Acis and Galatea*: "Those by Mozart are too delicate for a force so large as the five hundred players and singers at Birmingham. Those by Signor Costa are enriching and supporting— nowhere intrusive, in nowise contradictory of the design, but completing it for performance on a scale of which its maker never dreamed."[2]

Then the hollow orchestration of Grétry, through which "you might drive a coach-and-four between the bass and the first-fiddle," had to be padded out with more sound.

Mozart's texture, which had formerly contained "too many notes," was now not full enough of notes: "There was a time when our amateurs accused Mozart of having corrupted the purity of music by the luxury of his accompaniments; scarcely the fourth part of a century has passed, and the scores of Mozart, abounding as they do with vigour and breathing inspiration, appear by comparison somewhat cold and naked."[3] Ten years later Mozart's orchestration was not exciting enough for ears now getting

[1] *Mus. World*, Dec. 17, 1840, p. 395.   [2] *Athenæum*, Sept. 4, 1858.
[3] *Harm.*, May, 1828, p. 119.

accustomed to the colour and sparkle of Rossini, Hérold and Donizetti: "his instrumentation has not the bright and popular character which our large houses demand, and of which the more modern operatic composers have made liberal use. Rossini, Hérold and Donizetti, in the scores of their arias, seem to have arrived at the summit of perfection; and there is no concealing the fact that Mozart is too quiet in his details to captivate the ear of the public in general."[1] The same periodical told its readers that Mozart's instrumentation was "perhaps *too* refined for uninformed ears. Spohr, and his contemporaries of the German school, have carried orchestral combinations to such an excess, that the voice is reduced to a mere cipher, one feeble instrument against a myriad."[2] Mozart's scores were too empty, and Spohr's were too full!

A contest between the human voice and the orchestra had by then been in progress for some time, and now seemed to be going in favour of the latter. The pedestal was coming into the orchestra to join the statue. Gyrowetz complained, in his old age, that the voices in opera were now overwhelmed by the strength of the orchestral accompaniment, and he regarded this, not as a sign of progress, but of retrogression.[3] In 1820 we hear, apropos of the Paris *Opéra*, of "the screaming of the singers and the noise of the orchestra."[4] The Paris correspondent of a London paper put his protest against the domination of the orchestra in semi-humorous form: "What passion animates the orchestra of the opera? Is it thunder or is it harmony? What rage urges on those bows, and riots with such immeasurable fury on this great drum? A combat is taking place between the singers and the orchestra, an unequal strife, in which the orchestra, the giant of a hundred arms, triumphs by frightening the public. In vain does Mlle. Sainville utter her loudest notes"—and so on. Then the writer relapses into a more serious vein: "To speak seriously, no time should be lost in curing these noisy habits of the orchestra. To execute with violence is not to execute either with passion or taste, . . . the duty of the accompaniments is to strengthen the expression, and not to usurp its place."[5] We learn that in the 'forties the singers at the *Opéra* often merely opened their mouths and let the orchestra do the rest, and that this was a "wise plan" adopted by several singers in order to avoid straining their voices. For nine years the great tenor Duprey bore up "against the overpowering loudness of M. Habeneck's orchestra."[6] And this was before they had fully learned what Berlioz and Wagner could do with an orchestra.

In 1828 Fétis wrote about the evolution of the orchestra; after tracing its growth from early in the 17th century, he asked if instrumentation could be carried any further? his answer was—No! Beethoven, Weber and Rossini had brought the art as far as it would go. What then, we would ask him, was there left for Berlioz, Meyerbeer and Wagner to do?

[1] *Mus. World*, March 15, 1838, p. 182.   [2] *Ibid.*, April 5, 1838, p. 226.
[3] *Autob.*, p. 123.   [4] *Quar. Mus. Mag.*, Vol. II, No. VIII, p 507.
[5] *Harm.*, Oct., 1824, p. 186.   [6] Hervey, p. 35.

As it transpired, there was quite a lot left for them to do. And when they added still more colour, volume and complexity to their orchestral scores, the taste which had been formed on Beethoven and Weber, and found great delight in Mendelssohn's smooth and very deft handling of the orchestra, quite naturally found this newer orchestration rather strong meat, and wondered why these younger composers must be eternally searching for original effects, and why they could not be content to re-employ the orchestral sounds that had served the older generation so well. In this spirit Spohr recorded his "special hatred of this eternal speculating upon extraordinary instrumental effects"[1] by Berlioz, and found Wagner's early orchestration "overcharged." These very words—overcharged and over-laden—occur again and again in the comments by adherents of the *Leipzig-Gewandhaus* school on the more opulent orchestral colour of the composers who discovered that there was more volume in the orchestra than ever Weber and Mendelssohn had extracted from it.

Hauptmann and Moscheles, both of whom expressed themselves in moderate language, use these and similar expressions when they touched on the orchestration of Berlioz and Wagner. Moscheles thought that the score of *Romeo and Juliet* was so "complicated" and the noise so "over-whelming" that he did not venture to give any judgment on the music. He listened "with pleasure to the simple opera *Doctor und Apotheker* by Dittersdorf," and forgot how Rossini in his *Tell*, and Meyerbeer in his *Roberto*, had "crammed us with their loaded instrumentation," and how Wagner had "gone beyond both."[2] *Lohengrin* contained "bright but transient effects," but it was "overloaded"; and when as an old man Moscheles listened to *Die Meistersänger*, he could not but sympathise with the singers who were struggling against "overwrought" orchestral effects.

Chorley (who thought that Wagner was "weak in musical gifts") said that *Rienzi* was "overcharged," that the orchestration of *Tannhäuser* was "singularly unpleasant" and "too preposterous to be overlooked." The sound was "strident, ill-balanced and wanting body," and there was a "heavy bass to support a squeaking treble poised high aloft." Chorley decided that Wagner could not produce the "full, brilliant, well-nourished sound" that was to be heard in Mendelssohn's orchestration.[3]

Davison protested against the "monstrous ferocity" of Verdi's instru-mentation, and thought that if this composer continued writing successfully "there will not be a voice in all Italy in ten years."

All that had hitherto been done with the orchestra was not all that could be done with it. When Beethoven, Weber, Spontini, Mendelssohn and a host of their contemporaries had finished with it, they had by no means exhausted its possibilities, and the wheel of progress would not stop turning. Still more volume of sound, more brilliance, more colour, and

[1] *Autob.*, II, p. 311. [2] Moscheles, *Life*, II, p. 243.
[3] *Modern German Music*, I, pp. 349, 365, 366.

more variety were issuing from it, and to those who were satisfied with what had been done with it, it seemed as if a monster had been unloosed whose power was getting beyond control.

That great composite instrument, made of human beings, wood, metal, reeds, gut and hide, which so many generations of musicians from far back in the 17th century had helped to bring to life, had only reached its adolescence when Haydn had finished with it and Beethoven had just begun to use it. By that time it had developed stamina enough to enable it to stand the more rapid and vigorous growth into full manhood that ensued during the first half of last century. During that period the body, at first little more than a skeleton, was covered with more flesh, and more blood flowed through its veins than at any other time in its long-drawn-out childhood of some two centuries. The half century between *The Creation* and *Lohengrin* gave to its composers the instrument for their use, and the use they made of it may be seen in the full scores they wrote, and can be heard almost daily in the orchestral music we hear at the present time. But while we are apt to think only in terms of composers and their works, we should not forget that they wrote their scores to be played by the orchestras which have been described in these pages, and that these orchestras consisted of individual players, many of whose names have also been recorded in these pages. Many of the works have lived on, and their composers' names are well remembered; but the original players of these works are all long since dead, and their names are forgotten. The question arises: Was it the composers who took the lead and made the orchestra the thing it has become, or were the orchestras the pioneers who gave the composers the advantage of a better medium for the expression of their music? or, put in another way: did the orchestra develop and improve as a consequence of the composers' progressive way of handling it, or did the composers develop their orchestration as a consequence of the progressive growth of orchestras?

The question cannot be answered with a plain affirmative in favour of either the first or the second of these propositions. The bulk of the composers undoubtedly took the orchestra as it was in their time and benefited by its improved and growing capacity; the better instrument was put into their hands, and they played upon it to their own advantage, but they did not initiate the progress or lead the way. There were a few, however, who wrote for better orchestras than they ever knew or heard; they asked from it what it could give only long after their time. They went so far ahead of their medium that they may be said to have created the demand for a better instrument, and the supply followed the demand only as a consequence of their lead.

When Beethoven wrote his earlier scores he asked for little more than the orchestras of that time could give him; but by the time he was writing his ninth symphony he was far ahead of the best that any existing orchestra could give him, and still further ahead of any that he ever heard in Vienna. Perhaps his deafness helped to drive him back on his imagination, away from the real to the unreal, opening out a prospect that existed in mind, but not in fact. When Schubert composed his early symphonies he wrote in a practical way for such orchestras as he had heard and had come into touch with; but when writing his great C major symphony he had advanced far ahead of what he could expect or get from any orchestra that he ever knew or heard, and with a sort of prophetic instinct put down in his score what should and could be, but what was not yet.

Berlioz, more impatient, more wilful and impulsive than either of the foregoing, plunged straight away into writing for an imaginary orchestra such as he had never heard, but which must eventually be, because he asked for nothing that was impossible. He dreamed and struggled and kicked against pricks all through his life, but, although he lived till 1869, the orchestra never quite caught up with him. Wagner, with untiring determination and boundless egoism, kept his demands always ahead of the capacity of the orchestras he knew in his early days, and with his unlimited will-power and disregard of the obstacles strewn in his path, eventually succeeded in dragging them up to the level that he demanded, and in the end lived long enough (1883) to realise what he had striven for. Meyerbeer went onward by more carefully calculated stages, asking much, and then still more from the orchestra, but always prudently avoiding any rash adventures that might lead him into difficulties or dangers. He was neither dreamer nor idealist, but a practical man who knew his business and kept a level head.

Other composers had been pressing onwards, but never outpaced the capacity of the orchestras of their time by more than a step or two. Weber, Spontini, Rossini and Mendelssohn, each in their totally different ways, were level-headed pioneers who sought out new orchestral paths, but took care to see that the ground was fairly firm under their feet before taking any step forward. Behind them trailed an army of followers who viewed the prospect with the comfortable assurance that the roughness of the path would be well trodden down for them by those who had ventured to take risks and go ahead.

But all of them, leaders as well as followers, could have done nothing if the players in the orchestras had not been able to respond to the demands of the composers, and (it should not be forgotten) if the makers of wind instruments had not been able to provide the improved instruments without which orchestration would have come almost to a standstill before the middle of last century. Can anyone grudge the mere mention in these pages of the names of so many of these players and makers? *They* deserve to share in fair measure the tribute due to the comparatively few composers who were the real pioneers, and who wrote for an orchestra which has not yet been mentioned in these pages. It is one that every composer knows, but can never locate; one which makes everything in the score sound exactly as the composer intended it to sound, even though his scoring is faulty or ill-balanced. This orchestra never plays out of tune and never makes mistakes; it never gets before or behind the conductor's beat, always hits off exactly the right *tempo*, never gets tired or impatient at rehearsals, and never asks for higher pay.   It always plays the right notes, even though the score or parts are incorrect, and every instrument the composer asks for is always forthcoming.   It is the perfect orchestra that never has been and never will be; it is that great orchestra which exists only in the composer's imagination.

Appendix
Orchestral Lists

DRESDEN, COURT MUSIC, 1805

(From *All. Mus. Zeitung*, 7 Jahrgang, 1805.)

Kapellmeister. Joseph Schuster, Franz Seydelmann, Fernando Paër.

Concertmeister. Christ. Babbi.

Violin. Uhlig, Kunze, Salomon, Dietsch, Scholze, Hunt jun., Dunkel, Schmiedel Limberg, Dietze, Wenzel, Camillo Babbi, Kühnel, von der Ahée, Schmiedel.

Viola. Frenzel, Jos. Schubert, Pohland, Rottmeyer.

'Cello. Callmus, Höckner, Franz Eisert, Jos. Eisert.

Bass. Franz Schubert, Ant. Schubert, Peschke, Petermann.

Flute. Götzel, Prinz, Ham.   *Oboe.* Besozzi, Dietze, Kummer.

Clarinet. Rothe sen. and jun.   *Bassoon.* Nessel, Schmidt, Kummer, Heffen.

Horn. Haudeck, Listing, Miecksch, Gladewitz.

(No trumpet, drum, or trombone players are named.)

DRESDEN, COURT MUSIC, 1817

(From Weber, *Ein Lebensbild*, II, p. 37.)

Kapellmeister. Franz Morlacchi.

Musikdirector der deutschen Oper. Karl Maria von Weber.

Concertmeister. Giovanni Battiste Polledro.

Violin. Karl Gottfried Dietsch, Joh. Gottlob Scholz, Franz Karl Hunt, Franz Dunkel, Anton Schmiedel, Joh. Gottlob Limberg, Ludwig Liez, August Wenzel, Joh. Fried. Castelli, Karl Kühnel, Karl Gotthelf v. der Ahée, Karl Sedelmeyer, Karl Schmidt, Karl Peschke, Karl Gottlob Taschenberg, Franz Morgenroth, Anton Haensel, Moritz Hauptmann, August Lind, Moritz Salomon.

Viola. Christ. Benjamin Frenzel, Jos. Schubert, Franz Pohlandt, Joh. Gottlieb Listing, Anton Rottmeyer.

'Cello. Karl Wilh. Höckner, Joh. Eisert, Joh. Fried. Dotzauer, Xaver Pischel, Fried. Aug. Kummer jun.

Bass. Anton Schubert, Karl Gottfried Kummer, Joh. Gottlob Peschke, Hein. Salomon, Jos. Besozzi.

Flute. Fried. Götzel, Joh. Fried. Prinz, Gotthelf Stendel, Christ. Fried. Gerhardt (one vacant place).

Oboe. Fried. Aug. Kummer sen., Karl Gustav Dietze, Christ. Lud. Taschenberg, Karl Hein. Scheibel, Karl Gotthelf Kummer.

Clarinet. Joh. Traugott Rothe, Gottlob Rothe, Christoph Gäbler, Joh. Gottlieb Lauterbach, Gottlieb Cotta.

Bassoon. Franz Schmidt, Hein. Aug. Kummer, Gottlob Peschl, Adolph Wilh. Bergk, Sebastian Kummer.

Horn. Karl Haudeck, Christian Gottlob Fischer, August Haase, Karl Gottlob Kretschmar, Karl Gottlob Listing jun., Ludwig Haase.

Trumpet. Joh. Georg Klemm, Karl Fried. Grimmer.

Copyists, instrument makers, organblowers, attendants, etc.

(No trombone players or drummers are named.)

487

DRESDEN, COURT MUSIC, 1842

(From Prölss, *Geschichte des Hoftheaters zu Dresden*, p. 489.)

Kapellmeister. Reissiger. (Wagner in 1843.)

Concertmeister. Lipinski, Franz Morgenroth.

Vice Concertmeister. Franz Schubert.

Violin. Castelli, Schmiedel, Pescke, Franz, Kühn, Lindt, Pohland, Koprasch, Richter, Mitscherling, Seiss, Winterstein, Pfeiffer, Müller.
Viola. Pohland, Horak, Beyer, Helbig.
'Cello. Dotzauer, Kummer, Schlick, F. Schubert.
Bass. Schubert, Besozzi, Schmerbitz, Tietz.
Flute. Stendel, Fürstenau, Pauli, Löwe.
Oboe. Kummer, Edel, Hiebendahl, Krätzschmar.
Clarinet. Kotte, Lauterbach sen., Dominik, Lauterbach jun.
Bassoon. Peschel, Suchanek, Kabisius.
Horn. Haase, Kretzschmar, Adam, Lewy, Muschke.
Trumpet. Kunze, Schrader, Schwarz, W. Queisser.
Trombone. Gottschalk, Rühlmann, Queissert.
Drums. Herfort.   *Harp.* Richter.

LONDON, THE KING'S THEATRE, 1818

(From the *Quar. Mus. Mag.*, Vol. I, No. II, p. 257.)

Leader. Weichsell.

First Violin. Griesbach, Condell, Simonett, Ireland, Gledhill, Littoff, Brown, Cardini, Earle.
Second Violin. Reeve, Collard, Chabran, Pilotti, Klose jun., Wm. Fletcher, Baker, Cooper, Davis.
Viola. Mountain, Ware, Klose sen., Davis.
'Cello. Lindley, Crouch, Brooks, Piel.
Bass. Dragonetti, Anfossi, Taylor, Jouve, Fletcher.
Flute. Ireland, Brandy.   *Oboe.* Griesbach, Cornish.
Clarinet. Willman, Mahon.   *Bassoon.* Holmes, Tully.
Horn. Messrs. Petrides.   *Trumpet.* Schmidt, Libe.
Trombone. Mariotti.   *Drums.* Platts.

LONDON, THE KING'S THEATRE, 1832

(From Anon., *Musical Recollections*, I, p. 240.)

Conductor. M. Costa.   *Leader.* Spagnoletti.

Violin. Mori, Dando, Watts, Murray, Nadaud, Pigott, Ella, Kearns, Wallis, Baker, Reeve, Bohrer, Tolbecque, Griesbach, Zerbini, Littolff, Anderson, Watkins, Thomas.
Viola. Moralt, Warre, Alsept, Daniels, Chubb, Nicks.
'Cello. Lindley, Rousselot, Hatton, Bohrer, Crouch, Brooks.
Bass. Dragonetti, Wilson, Howell, Anfossi, Flower, Taylor.
Flute. Nicholson, Card.   *Oboe.* Cooke, Barret.
Clarinet. Willman, Powell.   *Bassoon.* Baumann, Tully.
Horn. Platt, Rae, Calcott, Tully.   *Trumpet.* Harper, Irwin.
Trombone. Mariotti, Smithers sen. and jun.   *Drums.* Chipp.

LONDON, HER MAJESTY'S THEATRE, 1839

(From the *Musical World*, May 9, 1839, p. 23.)

Conductor. Maestro Costa.

Violin I. Mori, Tolbecque, Nadaud, Watts, Ella, Watkins, Griesbach, Thomas, Willy, Patey, Richards, Cramer, Dunford, Newsham.
Violin II. Reeve, Pigott, Wagstaff, Payton, Brown, Westrop, W. Blagrove, Hope, Jacobs, Webbe, Betts, Harper, Perry, Marshall.
Viola. Moralt, Hill, Alsept, Daniels, Kearns, Calkin, Glanville, Morriss.
'Cello. Lindley, Rousselot, Crouch, Hatton, Lucas, Phillips, Bonner, Lavenu.

Bass. Dragonetti, Anfossi, Howell, Wilson, Griffiths, Flowers, Vaudreland, Campanile.
Flute. Ribas, De Folly. *Oboe.* Barret, Wilton.
Clarinet. Willman, Bowley. *Bassoon.* Baumann, Tully.
Horns. Platt, Rousselot, Calcott, Rae.
Trumpet. Harper, Irwin, Laurent.
Trombones. Smithers, Smithers jun., Healey.
Ophicleide. Elliason. *Harp.* Neilson. *Drums.* Chipp.
Long drum. Horton. *Side drum.* Carter. *Triangle.* Calcott jun.

Nadaud conducts the ballet music; Tolbecque plays the solos; Mori, Lindley and Dragonetti are exempt from playing in the ballets.

LONDON, HER MAJESTY'S THEATRE, 1849
(From the *Musical World*, April 7, 1849, p. 212.)
Conductor. Balfe.

Violin I. Tolbecque (leader), Nadaud, Deloffre, Cooper, Collins, Michiels, Pluys, Shargood, Jacquin, Diechmann, Thillon, Dawson, Villani, Day.
Violin II. Oury (leader), Pigott, Collins, Hall, Pugni, Tallance, Stephen (also plays horn), Lawrence, Ganz jun.[1] Ridgway, Charles, Betts, Kreutzer, Love.
Viola. R. Hughes, Calkin, Ganz, Suppus, Rice, Boden, Jones, Morris, Ruckner.
'Cello. Piatti, Pilet, Collins, Ehrmann, Crouch, Gardner, Praeger, Piatti jun.[2]
Bass. Anglois, Percival, Bull, Russell, Giles, Pickaert, Waud, Winterbottom.
Flute. Rémusat, G. King. *Oboe.* Lavigne, Horton.
Clarinet. Billetta, Maycock. *Bassoon.* Tamplini, Koessel.
Horn. Steglich, Catchpole, Kreutzer, Callcott.
Trumpet. Zeiss, Davis. *Trombone.* Winterbottom, Giguet, Martin.
Ophicleide. Dayet. *Drums.* Ista. *Side drum.* Hughes jun.
Triangle. Callcott jun. *Long drum.* Hinckey. *Harp.* Thomas.

LONDON, COVENT GARDEN THEATRE, 1818
(From Northcott, *Life of Sir Henry R. Bishop*, p. 44.)

Violin. William Henry Kearns, 14s.; Thomas Burns (principal 2nd), 8s. 4d.; Joseph Young, 6s. 8d.; John Woodcock, 6s. 8d.; Joel Bowden, 6s. 8d.; Thomas Watkins, 6s. 8d.; James Bowden, 6s. 8d.; George Wells, 5s. 10d.; Robert Spencer (also to play viola when required), 5s. 10d.; John Rost (also trumpet, bugle horn, or trombone), 5s. 10d.; George Henry Neighbour (also viola), 5s. 10d.; Henry Nicholson (also pipe and tabor), 5s. 10d.
Viola. George Frederick Davis, 7s.; Matthew Simrock, 6s. 8d.
'Cello. Charles Woodarch, 10s.; J. C. H. Hoffmann, 5s. 10d.
Bass. Thomas Skillern (also viola), 5s. 10d.; James Sidebotham (also viola), 5s. 10d.
Flute. Joseph Birch, 9s. 2d.; *Oboe.* William Parke, 10s. 6d.; Samuel Underhill, 5s. 10d.
Clarinet. George Hopkins (also violin), 5s. 10d.
Bassoon. John Mackintosh, 14s.; Edmund Denman, 5s. 10d.
Horn. Frederick Shusler, 6s. 8d.; Cornelius Bryant, 5s. 10d.
Trumpet. Thomas Wallis, 9s. 2d., with additional 5s. per night when required to play the keyed bugle; John Polglaze, 5s. 10d.
Trombone. Samuel Pritchard (also bugle horn), 5s. *Drums.* Thomas Chipp (also harp, and piano tuner), 5s. 10d.; Bells, etc., William Goodwin, £1 a week.

LONDON, COVENT GARDEN THEATRE (R.I.O), 1847
From the *Musical World*, Feb. 6, 1847, p. 78.)
Conductor. Costa.

Violin I. Sainton (leader), H. Blagrove, Willy, A. Griesbach, Watkins, Case, Thirlwall, E. Thomas, Mellon, Patey, Zerbini, Browne, Goffrie, Hill.
Violin II. Ella, Newsham, W. Thomas, Payton, H. Westrop, H. Griesbach, J. Jay, Perry, Marshall, W. Blagrove, Betts, Kelly, Bort, Wilkins.

---

[1] Wilhelm Ganz. [2] Brother of the leading 'cello.

Viola. Moralt,[1] Hill, Alsept, Lyon, Glanville, Thomson, Hann, Westlake, Trust, R. Blagrove.
'Cello. Lindley, Lucas, Hatton, Lavenu, W. L. Phillips, Hancock, Hausmann, W. Loder, Goodban, Guest.
Bass. Anfossi, Howell, Casolani, Griffiths, C. Severn, Pratten, Campanile, Castell, Vaudrelan.
Flutes. Ribas, De Folly.   *Oboe.* Barret, Nicholson.
Clarinet. Lazarus, Boosé.   *Bassoon.* Baumann, Keating.
Horn. Platt, Jarrett, C. Harper, Rae.   *Trumpet.* T. Harper, Handley.
Trombone. Cioffi, Smithies, Healey.   *Ophicleide.* Prospère.
Drums. Chipp.   *Triangle.* Seymour.   *B. drum.* Horton.   *Harp.* E. Perry.
Military band. Coldstream Guards under Godfrey.
Leader of the Ballet. Alfred Mellon.

LONDON, DRURY LANE THEATRE, JULLIEN'S OPERA SEASON, 1847
(From the *Musical World*, Dec. 11, 1847, p. 798.)
Conductor. Berlioz

Sainton	Kreutzer	W. Loder	Sonnenberg
Tolbecque	Band	Chapman	Baumann
Nadaud	Eisenbaum	Howell	Larkin
Blagrove	Collins	Casolani	Platt
Mellon	C. Barrett	Anglois	C. Harper
Case	Hill	Rowland	Jarrett
Mori	Dabriol	Pratten	Hooper
V. Collins	G. Thompson	Castell	Koenig
T. Baker	Westrop	Alsept	W. Davis
Payton	Schmidt	Waud	Cioffi
Jay	Thompson	Winterbottom	Antoine
Jacquin	Trust	Richardson	Horton
Dawson	Piatti	De Folly	Prospère
Pluys	Rousselot	D. Godfrey	Hughes
Watkins	G. Collins	Barret	Baker
E. J. Kreutzer	Hausmann	Jennings	
Goffrie	Lavenu	Lazarus	

LONDON, PHILHARMONIC SOCIETY, 1837
(From the *Musical World*, March 3, 1837, p. 175.)
Leaders. F. Cramer, Mori, Weichsell, Loder of Bath.

Violin I. Wagstaff, Eliason, Thomas, Ella, A. Griesbach, Watkins, Dando, W. Cramer, Seymour, Gattie.
Violin II. Watts (principal), Mountain, Blagrove, Kearns, Tolbecque, Reeve, Pigott, Nicks, Rawlings, Anderson, Fleischer, A. Mackintosh, Litolff, Rooke.
Viola. Moralt (prin.), Lyon, Challoner, Joseph Calkin, Daniels, Ware, Dance, Abbott.
'Cello. Lindley (prin.), Crouch, Rousselot, Hatton, James Calkin, C. Lindley, Binfield, Lucas.
Bass. Dragonetti (prin.), Anfossi, Howell, Hill, Wilson, C. Smart.
Flute. Nicholson, Card.   *Piccolo.* Price.
Oboe. G. Cooke, Keating.   *Clarinet.* Willman, Powell.
Bassoon. Denman, Tully.   *Horn.* Platt, Kielbach, C. Tully, Rae.
Trumpet. Harper, Irwin.   *Trombone.* Albrecht, Smithies and son.
Ophicleide. Ponder.   *Drums.* Chipp.

LONDON, PHILHARMONIC SOCIETY, 1842
(From announcement for the season.)

Violin I. F. Cramer, Loder, T. Cooke, Blagrove, Eliason, Wagstaff, E. Thomas, Patey, Griesbach, Gattie, J. Banister, W. Cramer, N. Mori, Guymeyer, Payton, Thirlwall.
Violin II. Watts, Reeve, Dando, W. Thomas, Willy, Pigott, Kearns, Anderson, Watkins, Westrop, Hope, W. Blagrove, J. J. Calkin, J. Loder, Marshall, Mackintosh.

[1] Moralt died, and his place was taken by Hill. W. Thomas took Hill's place in the violas, and John Loder took Thomas's place as second violin.

Viola. Moralt, Hill, Challoner, Glanville, Calkin, Alsept, Sherrington, Abbott, S. Calkin, Daniels.
'Cello. R. Lindley, Lucas, Crouch, C. Lindley, Hatton, Banister, J. Calkin, Phillips.
Bass. Howell, Wilson, Flower, Severn, Schroeder, Casolani, Griffiths.
Flute. Ribas, Card, Price.   *Oboe.* Cooke, Keating.
Clarinet. Williams, Lazarus.   *Bassoon.* Baumann, J. Tully.
Horn. Platt, Rae, C. Tully, Kielbach.   *Trumpet.* Harper, Irwin.
Trombone. Smithies, Smithies jun., Albrecht.   *Drums.* Chipp.

LONDON, ORCHESTRA AT WEBER'S FUNERAL AT MOORFIELDS CHAPEL, 1826

(From *Quar. Mus. Mag.*, Vol. VIII, No. XXIX, p. 127.)

Conductor at the organ. Attwood.   *Leader.* Cramer.

Violin. Mori, Ella, Thomas.
Violin II. Betts, Kemis, Pigott, Davis.   *Viola.* Moralt, Daniels.
'Cello. Hatton, Hagart.   *Bass.* Woodham, C. Smart.
Flute. Birch, Birch jun.   *Clarinet.* Willman, Powell.
Bassoon. Godfrey, Mancor.   *Trumpet.* Harper, E. Harper.
Trombone. Mariotti, Smithies, Schoengen.   *Drums.* Chipp.

LONDON, ROYAL ACADEMY OF MUSIC, 6TH CONCERT AT THE HANOVER SQUARE ROOMS, 1826

(From the programme.)

Violin. *Cramer, *Spagnoletti, *Kiesewetter, *Mori, Watts, Wagstaff, Moralt, Mountain, *Oury, †*Ella, *Watkins, Bellon, Griesbach, Wodarch, Anderson, Simonet, Litolf, Nicks, Nadaud, Collard, †*Seymour, †*Mawkes, †Patey, †Blagrove, †Baker.
Viola. Ashley, Daniels, Ware, Dance, †Goodwin (librarian), †*Phipps, †*J. B. Taylor.
'Cello. *Lindley, Crouch, †*Lucas, W. Lindley jun., C. Lindley, Brooks.
Bass. Dragonetti, *Anfossi, *Taylor, †*Harrington, Bond, Wilson.
Flute. *Nicholson, †Price.   *Oboe.* Whitton, †*Cooke.
Clarinet. *Willman, Powell.   *Bassoon.* *Mackintosh, Tully, †Smith.
Horn. Puzzi, *Platt, Schunke, Kielbach, †*Daniels.
Trumpet. Harper, *Norton, Signori Gambati.
Trombone. Mariotti, *Smithies, *Schoengen.
Drums. †Pye.   *Piccolo.* Card.

* Professors employed in the Academy.
†* Sub-professors and Students.
† Students.

ANCIENT CONCERTS, 1839
(From the programme.)

Conductor. Mr. W. Knyvett.   *Leader.* Mr. F. Cramer.

Violins. Mr. Moralt, Mori, Rawlings, Wagstaff, Fleischer, Anderson, A. Griesbach, Smith, Mackintosh jun., Watkins, Cramer jun., Wood, Patey.
Violas. Kearns, Nicks, Glanvill, Samuel Calkin, Daniels, Abbott.
'Cellos. Lindley, Crouch, Charles Lindley, Lucas.
Double basses. Dragonetti, Anfossi, Flower, Smart, Howell.
Flutes. Card, F. Hill.   *Oboes.* Cooke, Keating.
Clarinets. Willman, Bowley.   *Corno Bassetto.* Willman.
Bassoons. Denman, J. Tully.
Horns. Platt, Rae, C. Tully, Kielbach.
Trumpets. Harper, John Irwin, Harper jun.
Trombones. Smithies, Smithies jun., Albrecht.
Ophicleide. Ponder.   *Drums.* Chipp.
Seven pupils of the Royal Academy of Music, violins and violas.
Secretary and Library. W. Greatorex.
Asst. Librarian and Copyist. Hedgley.
Music Porter. Field.

London, Subscription Evening Concerts at the Hanover Square Rooms and the London Tavern, 1842

(From the *Musical World*, Sept., 1842, p. 288.)

Conductor. G. F. Harris, director of the Professional Choral Society.

Violin. F. Cramer, Dando, Willy (leaders), E. Thomas, W. Cramer, A. Griesbach, Payton, Thirlwall, J. Banister, T. Baker, Dunsford, E. Perry, W. Blagrove, J. Jay, Marshall, C. W. Doyle, C. Betts, Watson, Presbury, Case, Newsham, C. Smith, T. Browne, Stevenson, Chipp, S. Jay, S. Smith, T. Westrop, Kelly, H. Griesbach.

Viola. Moralt, Hill, Kearns, Alsept, Glanville, S. Calkin, Holland, E. Westrop, D. Reeve.

'Cello. Lindley, Lucas, Crouch, W. L. Phillips, Hancock, Packer.

Bass. Howell, C. Severn, Casolani, Cubitt, Griffiths, Reinagle.

Flute. Carte, Schmidt.   *Oboe.* Barret, W. Keating.

Clarinet. Lazarus, McDonald.   *Bassoon.* Baumann, C. Keating.

Horn. Platt, C. Harper, Rae, Callcott.   *Trumpet.* Harper, T. Harper.

Trombone. Smithies, Mason, Albrecht.   *Serpent.* André.

Ophicleide. Ellison.   *Timpani.* Chipp.

Librarian. Hedgley.

London, Grand National Concerts at Her Majesty's Theatre, 1850

(From *The Athenæum*, Oct. 12, 1850.)

Conductor. Balfe.

Violin I. Molique (principal), Browne,* Cooper,* Dando,* Dawson,† Goffrie,* H. Griesbach,* Hartnagl,† Kreutzer,† Oury,† Patey,* Pigott,† Shargood,† Thirlwall,* Watkins,* Zerbini.*

Violin II. Willy* (principal), W. Blagrove,* Barnett,† Hall,† Hennen,† Jay,* Kelly,* J. Loder,* Marshall,* Ridgway,† Ridgway II,† Schmidt,† Tallance,† Thirlwall II,† Villani,† Watson.*

Viola. R. Hughes† (principal), R. Blagrove,* Boden,† Calkin,† Ganz,† Glanville,* Rice,† Trust,* Webb,* Westlake.*

'Cello. Piatti† (principal), Gardner,† Goodban,* Guest,* Hancock,* Hausmann,* W. Loder,* Lovell Phillips,* Rousellot, Thorley (Manchester).

Bass. Anglois† (principal), Casolani,* Castell,* Mount,* Müller (Darmstadt), Percival,† Pickaert,† Pratten,* Rowland,* Russell,† Severn.*

Harp. Ap Thomas,† H. J. Trust.*

Flute. Richardson, Briccialdi (Milan).   *Piccolo.* Rémusat.†

Oboe. Barret,* Nicholson.*   *Clarinet.* Franc (Brussels), Maycock.†

Bassoon. Baumann,* Larkin.*

Horn. Steglich,† Blangini, Calcott,† Calcott jun.†

Trumpet. Zeiss,† Davis.†   *Cornet.* Arban (Paris).

Trombone. Marin,† King,† Winterbottom.†   *Ophicleide.* Prospère.*

Drums. Chipp.*   *B. drum and cymbals.* Hinchey.†

Side drum. R. Hughes jun.†   *Triangle.* W. Ganz.†

* R.I.O. Covent Garden.   † Her Majesty's Theatre.

Paris, Napoleon's Chapelle-Musique, 1806

(From Castil-Blaze, *Chapelle-Musique des Rois de France*, p. 171.)

MM. Lesueur, *directeur.*   Rey, *maître de musique.*

Rigel, *organiste-pianiste-accompagnateur.*   Piccini, *Idem en second.*

(The names of vocalists are omitted.)

Premiers violons. R. Kreutzer, Grasset, Duret, Gasse, Guiges, Vacher.

Second violons. Baillot, Pradher, A. Kreutzer, Manceau, Cartier, Chol, Ertault.

Violes. Tariot, Bernard, Delézenne, Lefebvre.

Violoncelles. Baudiot, Boulanger, Charles, Levasseur.

Contre-basses. Hoffelmayer, Perne, Rifaut, Sorne.

Flutes. Schneitzhœffer, Tulou.   *Hautbois.* Vogt, Gebauer, Sallentin.

Clarinettes. Ch. Duvernoy, Dacosta, Solère, Lefebvre.

Cors. F. Duvernoy, Domnich, Collin, Othon.[1]

Bassoons. Ozi, Henry, Delcambre, Gebauer.

Harpe. Dalvimare.

[1] Othon Joseph Vandenbroeck.

PARIS, SOCIÉTÉ DES CONCERTS (CONSERVATOIRE CONCERTS), 1828
(From Elwart, *Histoire*, p. 101.)

Violin I. Habeneck (*chef d'orchestre*), Tilmant aîné (suppléant), Urhan, Battu, Aug. Tolbecque, Gras, Halma, Sauzay, Cuvillon, Colot, Girard, Seghers, Demouy, De Rivals, Clément.
Violin II. Clavel, Guérin, Saint-Laurent, Claudel, Millault, Philippe, Artôt, Manera, Lepoivre, Straw, Masset, Cherblanc, Javault, Dubreuil, Charles Tolbecque.
Viola. Amédée, Labadens, Nargeot, Seuriot, Lagrave, Baptiste Tolbecque, Maussant.
'Cello. Norblin, Vaslin, Huber, Chaft, Franchomme, Déjazet, Desnos, Rogé, Mercadier, Chevillard, Tilmant jume, Ch. Thomas.
Bass. Chénié, Michu, Gide, Niquet, Mathieu, Hémet, Perrin, Roll.
Flute. Tulou, Guillou, Hermel, Roger.
Oboe. Vogt, Brod, Veny.
Clarinet. Dacosta, Buteux, Boufil, Frion.
Bassoon. Henry, Dossion, Barizel, Rickmans.
Horns. Dauprat, Blangy, Mengal, Meifred.
Trumpets. Dauverné, Legros.
Trombones. Barbier, Benard, Devise.   *Ophicleide.* Pavart.
Drums. Schneitzboeffer.   *Harp.* Edmond Larivière.

PARIS, CHARLES X's CHAPELLE-MUSIQUE, 1830
(From Castil-Blaze, p. 224.)

Surintendans et Compositeurs de la Chapelle du Roi. MM. Lesueur, Cherubini.
Maîtres de Musique. Plantade, Valentino, en survivance.
(Vocalists and other officials are omitted.)
Premiers violons. Baillot, Marcou, Xavier, Kreubé, Libon, Habeneck, Vidal.
Second violons. A. Kreutzer, Spitz, Manceau, Cartier, Morena, Tilman(t), C. Habeneck.
Violes. Tariot, Quinebaux, Chol, Amédée.
Violoncelles. Baudiot, Boulanger, Charles, Berger, Norblin, Vaslin.
Contrebasses. Gélineck, Sorne, Lami, Rifaut.
Flutes. Tulou, Roger.   *Hautbois.* Vogt, Brod.
Clarinettes. Ch. Duvernoy, Dacosta.   *Bassoons.* Gebauer, Henry.
Cors. F. Duvernoy (solo), Mengal, Dauprat.
Trompettes. D. Bühl, Dauvernet.   *Timbales.* St.-Laurent.
Harpes. Naderman, Naderman jeune.
Pianistes accompagnateurs. Piccinni, Pradher.
(Organists, tuners, blowers, porters, etc., are omitted.)

PARIS, OPÉRA COMIQUE, 1839
(From *L'Indicateur*, No. 3, 1839.)

Conductor. Girard.   *2nd Cond.* Huny.   *3rd Cond.* Merlé.

Violin I. Javault (solo), Dancla aîné (solo), Croissilles, Dailly, Faucheux, Aumont, Dancla III, Letourneur.
Violin II. Demoux, Ducrotois, Larivierre, Debreuil, Franco Mendes, Gailhac, Tolosa, Morin.
Viola. Merlé, Josse, De Flamesnil, Nivert, Roubier.
'Cello. Mercadier, Thomas, Dancla II, Batteuchon, Sautreuil, Bruzzèse.
Bass. Toutain, Labro aîné, Abadie, Labro jeune, Guillaumot, Pickaert.
Flute. Leplus (solo), Leplanquai, Petitot.
Oboe. Léonard (solo), Lemerle, Delattre.
Clarinet. Hugot (solo), Rion, Mongé.
Bassoon. Blaise (solo), Henry, Magiatti.
1st Horn. Caillaut, Jacqmin, Henricet.
2nd Horn. Schneider, Nagel, Bonnfay.
Trumpet. Reitter (solo), Mongin, Stainborr.
Trombone. Carteret (alto), Buisson (alto et ténor), Marchal (ténor et basse), Marez (ditto).
Drums. Charles. *B. drum.* Meunch.   *Triangle and S. drum.* Planque.
Harp. Prumier père et fils.
(Attendants, tuners, and instrument makers.)

PARIS, OPÉRA, 1855

(From Castil-Blaze, L'Académie Impériale, II, p. 446.)

Chef d'orchestre. Girard.

Deuxième Chef d'orchestre. Battu.   *Troisième Chef d'orchestre.* Deldevez.

Premiers Violons. MM. Leudet, Claudel, Landormy, Saenger, Périer, Mainvielle, Altès jeune, Chéri, Gout, Ferrand, Deloigne.

Second Violons. Millault, Rochefort, Dubreuil, Venettoza, Philip, Ropicquet, Thibout, Tolbecque, Lebrun, Lamoureux, Lancien.

Violes. Viguier, Adam, Gard, Henricet, Fridrich, Millaut II, Givre, Bernard.

Violoncelles. Desmarets, Norblin, Marx I, Jouet, Marx II, Tilmant, Pilet, Dufour, Sauvaget, Guérot.

Violonars. Guillion, Sauzay, Gouffé, Pérot, Verrimst, Bordeau, Pasquet.

Flutes. Dorus, Altès aîné, Leplus.   *Hautbois.* Cras, Barthélemi, Corret.

Clarinettes. Leroi, Rose, Duprez.   *Bassoons.* Cokken, Divoir, Verroust, Villaufret.

Cors. Mohr, Rousselot, Duvernoy, Urbin, Halary.

Trompettes. Dubois I, Dubois II, Forestier, Hermans.

Trombones. Dieppo, Simon, Dantonnet, Lahou (ophicleide).

Harpistes. Dretzen, Gillette.   *Timbalier.* Prévost.

Timbalier-Tambour. Semet.   *Cymbalier.* Tardif.

Grosse Caisse. Cailloué.   *Triangle.* Hénon.   *Chef de la copie.* Leborne.

Bibliography

Adam, Ad. Souveniers d'un Musicien; Paris, 1868.
Ambros, A. W. Bunte Blätter; Leipzig, 1874.
Ambros-Bramberger. Das Konservatorium für Musik in Prag; 1911.
Andries, J. Aperçu théorique de tous les instruments de Musique; Ghent, 1856.
Anon. A Tour in Germany and some of the Southern Provinces of the Austrian Empire, in the years 1820, 1821, 1822; London, 1824.
„ Bemerkungen eines Reisenden über die zu Berlin vom 1787 bis 1788 gegebene Musiken; Halle, 1788.
, A Biographical Dictionary of Musicians; 2 vols., 2nd Ed., London, 1827.
, (An Amateur) Her Majesty's Theatre; London, 1838.
„ Le Conservatoire national de Musique et de Déclamation; Paris, 1928.
„ (Rev. J. E. Cox). Musical Recollections of the last half-century; 2 vols., London, 1872.
„ (Ed. Holmes). A Ramble among the Musicians of Germany; London, 1828.
„ (A professor of eminence). Tutor for the Royal Keyed Bugle; Purday, London.
„ (Einem teutschen Biedermann). Wahrheiten die Musik betreffend; Frankfort, 1779.

Bacher, O. Die Geschichte der Frankfurter Oper im 18 Jahrhundert; Frankfort, 1926.
Backofen, J. G. H. Anweisung zur Klarinette und dem Bassethorn; 2nd Ed., Leipzig, 1824.
Barrett, W. M. Balfe: his Life and Work; 2nd Ed., London, 1883.
Bechler-Rahm. Die Oboe; Leipzig, 1914.
Bellasis, E. Cherubini; London, 1874.
Bennett. See Sterndale Bennett.
Berlioz, H. Memoirs of Hector Berlioz; trans. Holmes, 2 vols., London, 1884.
„ Evenings in the orchestra; trans. Roche, London, 1929.
„ A Treatise upon Modern Instrumentation and Orchestration; trans. Clarke, London, 1858.
„ A critical study of Beethoven's nine Symphonies; trans. Evans, London.
Biberhofer, R. Theater an der Wien, 1801–1926; Vienna, 1926.
Boehm, T. An Essay on the construction of flutes; London, 1882.
Boigne, C. de. Petits Mémoirs de l'Opera; Paris, 1857.
Bunn, A. The Stage, both before and behind the curtain; 3 vols., London, 1840.
Burgh, A. Anecdotes of Music, historical and biographical, in a series of letters from a gentleman to his daughter; 3 vols., London, 1814.
Burney, C. The Present State of Music in France and Italy; 2nd Ed., London, 1773.
„ The Present State of Music in Germany, the Netherlands and United Provinces; 2nd Ed., London, 1775.
Busby, T. A Dictionary of Music; 4th Ed., London, 1813.
„ Concert-room and Orchestra anecdotes; 3 vols., London, 1825.

Cambiasi, P. La Scala 1778–1906; Milan, 1906.
Carse, A. Musical Wind Instruments, London, 1939.
„ The Orchestra in the 18th century; Cambridge, 1940.
Castil-Blaze. De l'Opéra en France; 2 vols., Paris, 1826.
„ Chapelle-Musique des Rois de France; Paris, 1832.
„ L'Académie Impérial de Musique; 2 vols., Paris, 1855.
Caussinus, V. Solfège-Méthode pour l'Ophicleide-basse; Paris, c. 1840.
„ Solfège-Méthode . . . de cornet à pistons; Paris, 1846.
Chamberlain, H. S. Richard Wagner, Munich, 1896.
Chorley, H. F. Music and Manners in France and Germany; London, 1841.
„ Modern German Music; London, 1854.
„ Thirty years' Musical Recollections; (E. Newman) London, 1926.

Cocks. Notes, historical and miscellaneous, concerning the Queen's Concert Rooms, Hanover Square; London, 1862.
Colomb, C. La Musique; Paris, 1878.
Conservatoire, Paris, see under Anon.
Cox, Rev. J. E. See under Anon.
Creuzburg, E. Die Gewandhaus-konzerte zu Leipzig; Leipzig, 1931.

Dandelot, A. La Société des Concerts du Conservatoire de 1828 à 1897; Paris, 1898.
Davison, H. From Mendelssohn to Wagner, being the memoirs of J. W. Davison, forty years critic of *The Times*; London, 1912.
Deldevez, E. M. E. L'art du Chef d'Orchestre; Paris, 1878.
Devrient, E. My recollections of Felix Mendelssohn-Bartholdy, and his letters to me; trans. Macfarren, London, 1869.
Dörffel, A. Geschichte der Gewandhausconcerte zu Leipzig; Leipzig, 1884.
Dorn, H. Aus meinem Leben; Berlin, 1870–75.

Ebers, J. Seven years of the King's Theatre; London, 1828.
Eckardt, J. Ferdinand David und die Familie Mendelssohn-Bartholdy; Leipzig, 1860.
Edwards, F. G. Musical Haunts in London; London, 1895.
Edwards, H. Sutherland. The Life of Rossini; London, 1869.
Ella, J. Musical Sketches; London, 1878.
Elwart, A. Histoire de la Société des Concerts du Conservatoire Impérial de Musique; Paris, 1860.
Encyclopædia Londinensis; Vol. XVI, London, 1819.
Erler, H. Robert Schumanns Leben; Berlin, 1887.

Farmer, H. G. Memoirs of the Royal Artillery Band; London, 1904.
   „ The Rise and Development of Military Music; London, 1912.
Fétis, F. J. Curiosités historique de la Musique; Paris, 1830.
   „ Biographie universelle des Musiciens; 2nd Ed., 8 vols., Paris, 1868.
Fisher, H. A. L. A History of Europe; London, 1836.
Fitzball. Thirty years of a dramatic author's life; 2 vols., London, 1859.
Fitzgibbon, H. Macaulay. The Story of the Flute; London, 1914.
Foster, M. B. History of the Philharmonic Society of London; London, 1912.
Fröhlich, F. J. Vollständige theoretisch-practisch Musiklehre; Bonn, 1811.
Fürstenau, M. Zur Geschichte der Musik und des Theaters am Hofe der Kurfürsten von Sachsen; Dresden, 1861.

Ganz, W. Memories of a Musician; London, 1913.
Gardiner, W. Sights in Italy with some account of the present state of Music in that country; London, 1847.
Garnier. Méthode pour l'Ophicléide; Paris.
Gassner, F. S. Partiturkenntniss, ein Leitfaden zum Selbstunterricht für angehende Tonsetzer; 2 vols., Carlsruhe, 1838.
   „ Dirigent und Ripienist; Carlsruhe, 1844.
   „ Universal-Lexikon der Tonkunst; Stuttgart, 1849.
Gerber, E. L. Lexikon der Tonkünstler; Leipzig, 1790–92.
Gevaert, F. A. Traité général d'Instrumentation; Ghent-Paris, 1863.
Gollmick, C. Autobiographie.
Grétry, A. E. M. Mémoirs ou Essais sur la Musique; 3 vols., Paris, 1826.
Grimm, F. M. Le petit Prophéte de Boehmischbroda; Paris, 1753.
Grove, G. Dictionary of Music and Musicians; 3rd Ed., London, 1927.
   „ Beethoven and his nine symphonies; London, 1896.
Gyrowetz, A. Biographie des Adelbert Gyrowetz; reprint, Leipzig.

Haas, R. Aufführungspraxis; Potsdam, 1931.
Hallé, C. Life and Letters of Sir Charles Hallé; London, 1896.
Hanslick, E. Geschichte des Concertwesens in Wien; Vienna, 1869.
Harper, T. Instructions for the Trumpet; London, 1836.
Harvey, C. The Theatres of Paris; Paris and London, 1846.
Hauptmann, M. Briefe von Moritz Hauptmann an Franz Hauser; Vols. I and II, Leipzig, 1871.
   „ Briefe von Moritz Hauptmann an Ludwig Spohr; III, Leipzig, 1876.

Hellborn, H. K. von. Life of Schubert; trans. Coleridge, 2 vols., London, 1869.
Hensel, S. The Mendelssohn Family; trans. Klingemann, 2 vols., London, 1882.
Hess, H. Galerie Musicale.
Hiller, F. Mendelssohn, Letters and Recollections; trans. Glehn, 2nd Ed., London, 1874.
„   Musikalisches und Persönliches; Leipzig, 1876.
Hogarth, G. The Philharmonic Society of London; London, 1862.
„   Memoirs of the Musical Drama; London, 1838.
Holmes, E. See under Anon.
Hueffer, F. Half a century of music in England; London, 1889.

Jahn, O. W. A. Mozart, 2 vols., Leipzig, 1867.
James. A word or two on the flute; London, 1826.
Joachim, J. Letters from and to Joseph Joachim; trans. Bickley, London, 1914.
Jullien, Ad. Weber à Paris en 1826; Paris, 1877.

Kalkbrenner, A. Wilhelm Wieprecht, sein Leben und Wirken; Berlin, 1882.
Kapp, J. Geschichte der Staatsoper in Berlin; Berlin, 1938.
„   Berlioz, Ein Biographie; Berlin, 1917.
Kastner, G. Traité général de l'Instrumentation; Paris, 1837; Supp. 1844.
„   Cours d'Instrumentation; Paris, 1837, and Supp.
„   Manuel général de Musique Militaire; Paris, 1848.
Keller, O. Die Operette in ihren geschichtlichen entwicklung; Leipzig, 1926.
Kelly, O. Reminiscences; 2 vols., London, 1826.
Kenney, C. L. A Memoir of M. W. Balfe; London, 1875.
Knight, C. London; London, 1841.
Kobald, K. Alt. Wiener Musikstätten; Vienna, 1919.
Koch, H. C. Musikalisches Lexikon; Frankfort, 1802.
Koch-Dommer. Musikalisches Lexikon; Heidelberg, 1865.
Köchel, L. Ritter von. Die Kaiserliche Hof-Musikkapelle in Wien; Vienna, 1869.
Kracauer, S. Offenbach and the Paris of his time; London, 1937.
Kralik, H. von. Die Wiener Philharmoniker; Vienna, 1938.
Krebs, C. Meister des Taktstocks; Berlin, 1919.
Kruse, G. R. Otto Nicolai, ein Künstlerleben; Berlin, 1911.
Kuhe, W. My musical Recollections; London, 1896.

Lajarte, T. de. Curiosités de l'Opéra; Paris, 1883.
Lampadius, W. A. Felix Mendelssohn; Leipzig, 1886.
Lange, F. Josef Lanner und Johann Strauss; Leipzig, 1919.
Lasalle, A. de. Les treize Salles de l'Opéra; Paris, 1875.
Lasalle et Thoinan. La Musique à Paris; Paris, 1863.
Lavignac-Laurencie. Encyclopédie de la Musique, II, Paris, 1927.
Lavoix fils, H. Histoire de l'Instrumentation; Paris, 1878.
Lobe, J. C. Consonanzen und Dissonanzen; Leipzig, 1868.
„   (Anon.) Musikalische Briefe; Leipzig, 1860.
Loewe, J. C. G. Selbstbiographie; Berlin, 1870.
Lumley, B. Reminiscences of the opera; London, 1864.
Lyson, D. Origin and progress of the Meetings of the Three Choirs; Gloucester, 1895.

Malliot, A. L. La Musique au Théâtre; Paris, 1863.
Mapleson, J. H. The Mapleson Memoirs, 2 vols., London, 1888.
Marpurg, F. W. Historisch-kritische Beyträge; Berlin, 1754–57.
Marx, A. B. Erinnerungen; Berlin, 1865.
Matthews, J. B. The Theatres of Paris; London, 1880.
Mee, J. H. The oldest Music Room in Europe; London, 1911.
Moscheles. Life of Moscheles; 2 vols., London, 1873.
„   Life of Beethoven (Schindler); 2 vols., London, 1841.
Moser, A. Joseph Joachim, ein Lebensbild; Berlin, 1898.
Mozart (Anderson). The letters of Mozart and his family; 3 vols., London, 1938.
Musical Association. Proceedings; London, from 1874.

Nemetz, A. Neueste Posaunenschule; Vienna.
Newman, E. The Life of Richard Wagner; 3 vols., London, 1933, 1937, 1945.
Newmarch, R. The Russian opera; London, 1914.

Nicholson, C. A School for the Flute; London, 1836.

✱ *Noblet.* Nouvelle Méthode de Bugle; Bonn.

Nohl, L. Briefe Beethovens; Stuttgart, 1865.

„ Neue Briefe Beethovens; Stuttgart, 1867.

Northcott, R. The Life of Sir Henry R. Bishop; London, 1920.

Novello, C. (by her daughter). Reminiscences; London, 1910.

Parke, W. T. Musical memoirs; 2 vols., London, 1830.

Phillips, H. Musical and Personal recollections during half a century; 2 vols., London, 1864.

Pierre, C. La Facture instrumentale à l'Exposition universelle de 1889; Paris, 1890.

„ Les Facteurs d'Instruments de Musique; Paris, 1893.

„ Le Magazin de Musique à l'usage des Fêtes Nationales et du Conservatoire; Paris, 1895.

Planché, J. R. The Recollections and Reflections of J. R. Planché; 2 vols., London, 1872.

Pohl, C. F. Mozart und Haydn in London; 2 vols., Vienna, 1867.

Pontécoulant, Le Comte de. Essai sur la Facture instrumentale (1857), Part II, Organographie; Paris, 1861.

Praeger, F. Wagner as I knew him; London, 1892.

Prölss, R. Geschichte des Hoftheaters zu Dresden; Dresden, 1878.

Quantz, J. J. Versuch einer Anweisung die Flöte traversière zu spielen; (1752), Reprint, Leipzig, 1906.

Raabe, P. Franz Liszt; Stuttgart, 1931.

Ramann, L. Franz Liszt; trans. Cowdrey, 2 vols., London, 1882.

Reichardt, J. F. Vertraute Briefe aus Paris; 3 vols., Hamburg, 1804.

„ Vertraute Briefe geschrieben auf einer Reise nach Wien; (1808), reprint, 2 vols., Munich, 1915.

Rellstab, J. K. F. Ueber die Bemerkungen einer Reisenden; Berlin, 1789.

Ries, F. Biographische Notizen über Ludwig van Beethoven; Coblenz, 1838.

Rivière, J. My musical life and recollections; London, 1893.

Robert, C. Spontini, ein biographische Skizze; Berlin, 1883.

Rockstro, R. S. The Flute; rev. ed., London, 1928.

Rousseau, J. J. Dictionnaire de Musique; 2 vols., Amsterdam, 1768.

Sachs, C. The History of Musical Instruments; New York, 1940.

Sala, G. A. A Journey due north; London, 1859.

„ The Life and Adventures of G. A. Sala; London, 1896.

Saxe Wyndham, H. The Annals of Covent Garden Theatre; 2 vols., London, 1906.

Schneider, L. Geschichte der Oper und des Königlichen Opernhauses in Berlin; Berlin, 1852.

Schindler, A. Life of Beethoven; trans. Moscheles, 2 vols., London, 1841.

„ Beethoven in Paris; Münster, 1842.

Schreiber, O. Orchester und Orchesterpraxis in Deutschland, 1780–1850; Berlin, 1938.

Schumann, see Erler.

Schumann, R. Music and Musicians; trans. Ritter, 2 vols., London, 1891.

Schünemann, G. Geschichte des Dirigierens; Leipzig, 1913.

Smart, G. (Cox and Cox). Leaves from the Journals of Sir George Smart; London, 1907.

Soubies, A. Le Théâtre Italien de 1801 à 1913; Paris, 1913.

Speyer, E. Wilhelm Speyer, der Liedercomponist, 1790–1878; Munich, 1925.

Spohr, L. Louis Spohr's Autobiography, trans., London, 1878.

Sterndale Bennett, J. R. The Life of Sterndale Bennett; Cambridge, 1907.

Thayer, A. W. Life of Beethoven; 3 vols., New York, 1921.

Tully. Tutor for the Keyed Bugle; London, c. 1828.

Ursprung, O. Münchens Musikalische Vergangenheit; Munich, 1927.

Wagner, R. Prose works; trans. Ashton Ellis, 6 vols., London, 1895.

„ My Life; 2 vols., London, 1911.

„ On Conducting; trans. Dannreuther, London, 1897.

„ Richard Wagner an Mathilde Wesendonk; Berlin, 1906.

Wasielewski, J. W. von. Aus ziebzig Jahren; Stuttgart, 1897.
Weber, Max von. C. M. von Weber, ein Lebensbild; 3 vols., Leipzig, 1864.
Weingartner, F. On Conducting; trans. Newman, London, 1906.
Wotton, T. S. Hector Berlioz; London, 1935.
Wroth, W. The London Pleasure Gardens of the 18th century; London, 1896.

Zenger, M. Geschichte der Münchener Oper; Munich, 1923.

Periodicals

Allgemeine Musikalische Zeitung, Leipzig, from 1799.
Almanach historique du Théâtre ou Calendrier historique et chronologique de tous les Spectacles,
    Paris, from 1751.
Apollonicon, London, 1832.
Athenæum, London.
Bath and Cheltenham Chronicle, 1845.
Berliner Musikzeitung. Neue Berliner Musikzeitung.
British Musician, 1894.
Das Orchester, Zeitschrift für Deutsche Musiker, Zeitz, 1849.
Gloucester Journal.
Harmonicon, London, 1823–33.
Illustrated London News, London, from 1842.
Illustrated Times, London.
L'Indicateur général des Théâtres de Paris, No. 3, Paris, 1839.
Mnemosyne, Leipzig, 1817.
Monthly Chronicle, London, 1839.
Morning Herald, London.
Musical World, London, from 1836.
Music and Letters, Vol. XXII, No. 1, 1941.
Neue Zeitschrift für Musik, Leipzig, from 1834.
Philobiblion, Jahrgang 8, 1935.
Pictorial Times, London, 1847.
Quarterly Musical Magazine, London, 1818–28.
Queen (The), London, Feb., 1862.
Revue Musicale, Paris, 1833.
Signale für die Musikalische Welt, Leipzig, 1843.
Tallis's Dramatic Magazine, London, 1851.
The News, London, 1815.
Times (The), London.

Index

(THE NAMES IN THE APPENDIX ARE NOT INDEXED)

ABEILLE, 143
Abenheim, 143
Adam, Ad., 3, 84, 193
Adamy, 156
Adapted operas, 456
Additional accompaniments, see Handel
Aerts, 280
Ahl, 153
Aiblinger, 5, 126, 127, 302
Alard, 6, 93
Albion Rooms, 160
Albrecht, 181, 215
Almenräder, 145, 400, 406
Alsept, 203, 213
Altès, 75
Amateurs in Viennese orchestras, 260, 261
Amédée, 69, 92, 93
America, orchestras in, 285–8
Amsterdam, pl. 18, 282
Ancient Concert, see London
Andersen bros., 278
Anderson, 333
André, 181
Andrei, 274
Andreoli, 270
Andries, 31, 36, 394
Anfossi, 166, 195, 208, 220
Angiolini, 274
Anglois, 186, 203, 236, 398
Anschütz, 203, 242
Antwerp, 281–2
Appold, 153
Arban, 101, 236, 420
Argyll Concert, 226
Argyll Rooms, see London
Arnull, 210
Arrangement of orchestra
  Opera, 472
  Concert, 473
Arrangements and adaptations, 453–465
Artôt, 280
Ashe, 173, 209, 210
Ashley, Gen. Chas., 197, 209
  J. James, 197
  John, 37, 197
  Richard, 171, 209
Assmayer, 252
Attwood, 206, 209, 218, 226
Auber, 1, 69, 72, 84, 426
Ayrton, 169, 170

BABBI, C., 118
  G., 117

Bach-Abel Concerts, 162
Bach, J. C., 87, 162
Bach, J. S., 2, 8, 137, 407, 429, 442, 461
  B Minor Mass, 462
  St. Matthew Passion, 8, 30, 348, 429
Bach, P. E., 108
Bachmann, C. L., 392
  G. C., 280
Backofen, 147, 153
Bahr, 186
Baillot, 67, 69, 73, 209
Baker, 236
Balance of strings and wind, 18, 19, 21, 29, 38
Baldicci, 237
Balfe, 1, 3, 37, 171, 185, 200, 204, 242
  as conductor, 186, 187, 188, 189, 389
  Bohemian Girl, 201
Bänder, 150, 151
Baneux, 86
Banister, J., 208, 213
  H. J., 213
Barbereau, 100
Barbier, 92
Barbier (Drum Major), 237
Barcelona, 284
Bargans, 111, 412
Barizel, 75, 92
Bärmann, C., 111
  H. J., 128, 130
Barnbeck, 150
Barnett, 1, 200
Barré, see Barret
Barret, 37, 86, pl. 10, 175, 195, 203, 218, 225, 236, 237
Barth, 278
Bartleman, 206
Bärwolf, 153
Bass clarinet, 31, 75, 406
Basset-horn, 32, 407
Bass-horn, 36, 43
Bassoon, 404, 405
Bath, 173, 243
Baton, 197, 297, 309, 312, 333–335
Baton-conductor, 136, 169, 213, 290–1, 295, 319
Baton in England, 317–340
  France, 309–317
Baton in Germany, 297–306
  Vienna, 306–9
Batteur de Mesure, 72, 293, 309, 312
Battu, 73, 92, 313, 376

Baudiot, 69
Bauer, 265
Bauler, 236
Baumann, 37, 102, 177, 195, 203, 214, 225, 229, 236, 237
Bayr, 254
Becke, 127
Becquié, 86
Becquire de Peyreville, 229
Beer, 111
Beerhalter, 143
Beethoven, 1, 9, 15, 59, 266
  As conductor, 307, 365–368
  Choral Sym., 42, 59, 93, 94, 97, 99, 125, 133, 135, 157n., 215, 226, 242, 261, 262, 263, 287, 294, 307, 351, 355, 367, 369, 370, 398
  Concertos, 93, 137, 254, 255, 442
  D.-bass parts, 395
  Fidelio, 37, 145, 190, 200, 255, 261, 306, 427
  Mass in D, 59
  Orchestration, 479
  Overtures, 92, 94, 205, 219, 281, 442
  Scores and parts, 427, 431, 437
  Symphonies, 2, 11, 92, 93, 94, 133, 135, 139, 153, 211, 276
  Sym. No. 1, 90, 133; No. 2, 90, 91, 133, 219; No. 3, 90, 91, 92, 98, 99, 133, 215, 216, 224, 251, 440; No. 4, 133, 226; No. 5, 91, 92, 129, 138, 222, 255, 364, 393, 395, 397, 440; No. 6, 95, 133, 213, 218, 255, 440; No. 7, 91, 113, 133, 281, 439
  Symphonies in Paris, 91, 92, 93, 94
  Wellington's Victory, 35
Belcke, 40 n., 111
Belgian Guides Band, 234, 281
Belgium, orchestras in, 279
Bellini, 1, 2, 426
Belloli, 270
Bellon, 101
Bénard, 77, 92
Benda, 108, 110
Bender, 237, 281
Benedict, 190, 194, 201, 202, 222, 242, 255, 271
  as conductor, 389
Benzon, 150
Berlin. Concert room in the opera, 12
  Court opera orchestra, 46, 108–115
  Königstadt theatre, 46, 109, 115
  Opernhaus, 109, pl. 4
  Schauspielhaus, 13, 109, pl. 4
  Theatres, 109
Berlioz, 1, 2, 4, 92, 101, 291
  as conductor, 313, 373–376
  at Berlin, 114
  at Darmstadt, 148
  at Dresden, 124–5
  at Frankfort, 145
  at Hanover, 149
  at Hechingen, 154

Berlioz, at Leipzig, 140
  at London, 203, 224
  at Mannheim, 153
  at Naples, 272
  at Prague, 266
  at Stuttgart, 143
  at Vienna, 255, 258
  at Weimar, 151
  Benvenuto Cellini, 30, 215
  Damnation de Faust, 94, 266
  in Italy, 268
  in Russia, 277
  Instrumentation, 334, 338, 373, 407, 446
  Overtures, 30, 92, 94
  Romeo and Juliet, 148
  Scores and parts, 427
  Sym. Fantastique, 30
Berner, 156
Berr, F., 83
Berton, 42, 72, 82
Berwald, 279
Beskowsky, 156
Besozzi, F., 119, 120
  H., 86
  J., 119
Bettlach, 265
Bianchi, 169
Bierey, 156
Biletta, 188
Binder, 260
Birch, 192, 193
Birmingham Festival, 60, 181
Bishop, 1, 164, 169, 190, 199, 200, 205, 206, 209, 228
  Aladdin, 199
  as arranger, 455
  as conductor, 218, 219, 222, 323, 388
Blaes, 280
Blagrove, H. G., 195, 201, 203, 208, 236
  R., 224
Blaise, 86
Blangini, 5, 127, 150
Blangy, 92
Blasius, 84, 313
Blatt, 265
Blühmel, 400, 414
Bochsa, 166, 167, 168, 170, 174
Böck, 128
Boehm, 128, 130, 400, 404, 406, pl. 23
Boehm flute, 75, 405
Böhm, 265
Böhm, J., 252
  L., 254
  (Brother of Joseph Böhm), 276
Bohrer, A., 110, 127, 149
  M., 111, 143
Boieldieu, 1, 2, 72, 84, 426
Boigne, Ch. de, 72, 74, 78, 333
Boimi, 283
Bombardon, see Tuba
Bonn, 283
Bontempo, 285
Boom, van, 283

Boosé, 188
Boracchi, 270
Borne, le, 447
Borzaga, 256
Bösecke, 148
Bosselet, 280
Botgorschek, 256
Bott, 150
Bottesini, 196, 224, 394
Boucher, 287
Bournemouth municipal orchestra, 247
Bovery, 281
Bowing, 96, 127, 201
Braham, 164, 229
Brandt, 128
Brass band on stage, 44, 45, 275, 421
Brass, extra, in operas, 44
Brass instruments, 38–45, 409–421
    addition of, 19
Braun, A., 40 n., 41
    C. A. P., 278
    W., 111, 279
Bree, van, 282
Bremen, 46, 157
Breslau, 46, 156
Briccialdi, 270
Brighton, 244
Brille, 406
British Army Quadrilles, 237
British Concerts, 226
Brod, 69, 75, 92, 93, 138
Brooks, 228
Brown, 192
Brunswick, court orchestra, 47, 148
Brussels
    Concerts, 281
    Conservatoire, 17, 281, 282
    Opera, 47, 279–280
Budapesth, 265
Buffet, 400
Bugles, valved, 420
Buhl, 69, 77, 83, 411 n.
Bull, 220
Bülow, 130, 151
Burgoin, 186
Busby, 79
Buteux, 75, 92, 93, 96

CALKIN, 204
Camus, 75, 83, 86
Campanoli, 132
Cannabich, 126, 144
Canthal, 155
Capeller, 128
Capo d'orchestra, 270, 271, 292
Carafa, 5
Carcani, 39
Card, 197, 208, 213, 225, 226
Carlsruhe, see Karlsruhe
Carnicer, 284
Carte, 173
Casati, 278

Case, 237
Casolani, 203, 236
Cassel, court orchestra, 12, 43, 150
Castil-Blaze, 39, 72, 73, 74, 105, 310
Catalani, 173
Catchpole, 187
Catel, 31, 72
Catrufo, 393, 445
Caussinus, 42
Cavallini, Em., 270
    Eug., 270
Cavos, 275, 276
Centroni, 174, 213, 215
Chabran, 100
Chaft, 93
Chalon, 86
Chamber orchestras, 20
Chef d'attaque, 73, 331
Chef d'orchestre, 69, 72, 73, 84
Chelard, 5, 75, 100, 127, 151, 331
Chemnitz, 47
Chénié, 74, 83, 92, 93, 398
Cherubini, 1, 2, 68, 72, 84, 90, 91, 92, 209,
    333, 426
Chevillard, 83, 92
Chiossi, 287
Chipp, T., 182, 193, 195, 197, 208, 215, 218,
    224, 237, 422
Chipp, H., 236
Chorley, 74, 80, 81, 96, 114, 123, 139, 145,
    149, 157, 183, 222, 258, 330, 350, 357,
    378, 385, 390, 469
Christiani, 283
Chwoy, 265
Cianchettini, 431
Ciebras, 237
Cimarosa, 4, 7
Cioffi, 195, 203, 236
City Amateur Concerts, 33, 226
Clarinet, 401–7
Clarinet d'amour, 407
Clarono, 32 (see Bass clarinet)
Clavicor, 238
Clement, 254, 264, 306
Clementi, 6, 209, 212
Clinton, 173, 187
Coburg, see Koburg
Coccia, 6, 167, 169, 170, 318, 331
Coche, 75
Cocks, 210
Cokken, 76, 83, 86, 93
Collins, G., 236
    J., 236
Collinet, 234, 235, 236
Cologne, 47, 157
Colosanti, 236
Colosseum (London), 229
Composer-conductor, 290, 303
Composers' output, 6
Composers plentiful, 3–6
Composers' rights, 449
Concert halls, 12, 160, 250
Concertmeister, 292, 295, 305

Concert orchestra, 12, 87, 204
Concertos, how conducted, 307, 324, 330
Concerts à la Valentino, 230
Concert spirituel, see Paris, Vienna
Conducting from violin part, 371, 446
Conducting technique, 337
Conductor, see Baton-conductor, Keyboard-conductor, *Kapellmeister*, *Maestro di Capella*, etc.
Conductor at the organ, 205, 297, 318, 327
  at the piano, 209, 213, 297, 318
Conductor versus Leader, 324, 326, 329, 332
Conservatoire concerts, see Paris, Société des Concerts
Conservatoire, see Paris
Conservatoires, 17
Contemporary music, 7–8
Contre basson, see double bassoon
Cooke, Grattan, 31, 175, 197, 208, 213, 224, 229, 330
Cooke, Tom, 190, 193, 199, 200, pl. 12, 201, 202, 205, 213, 222, 330
Copenhagen, 278
Copyists, 448, 451
Copyright, 448
Cor anglais, 30, 406
Cordella, 6
Corfu, 278
Cornet-à-pistons, 44, 77, 101, 200, 417, 419
Cornet de poste, 419
Cornette, V., 86
Cornetto, 40 n.
Cornopean, see *cornet-à-pistons*
Cossmann, 152
Costa, 87, 291, 477
  as conductor, 223, 323, 332, 382–387
  at the King's Theatre, 169, 171, 183, 184, 185, 186
  at Covent Garden, 81, 87, 185, 186, 194–196
  Phil. Soc., 220, 223
  Sacred Harm. Soc., 207
Court music, 15
Covent Garden theatre, see London
Cramer, C. F., 20
  F., 205, 209, 213, 215, 226, 318
  J. B., 6, 209, 318
  W., 184, 205, 206, 207, 226
Cras, 75
Cremont, 84, 313
Crotch, 5, 209, 218, 226, 322
Crouch, 209, 236
Crown and Anchor Tavern, 160
Crusell, 279
Crystal Palace orchestra, 247
Curoni, 274
Czerny, 6
Czerwenka, F. J., 252, 256
  T., 111
Czeyka, 254

Dacosta, 69, 75, 83, 92, 93
dall 'Occa, 398

Dalvimare, 68, 88
Dancla, 86, 87, 93, 101
Dando, 207, 213
Dantonnet, 77, 102, 236
Danzi, 126, 143, 152
Darmstadt court orchestra, 47, 146–148
Dattmar, 283
Dauprat, 69, 76, 92, 93
Daussoigne, 5
Dauverné, 69, 77, 92
David, Ferd., 116, 136, 138, 139, pl. 6, 141, 142, 218, 301, 394
Davison, 98, 222, 231, 332, 356, 375, 378
De Folly, 236
Delabarre, 236, 280
Delcambre, 75
Deldevez, 93, 313, 336, 447
Dell'Uomo, 186
Deloffre, 186, 236
Demange, 236
Demeur, 280
Demin, 278
De Munck, 236
Denman, 177, 192, 197, 214
De Prins, 236
Desmarets, 74
Dessau, 154
Devise, 92
Devrient, 113, 138, 348
Diabelli, 6
Dibdin, 164
Dickhuth, 153
Dieppo, 77, 93, 101
Diethe, 137
Dietze, 120
Discipline in orchestras, 141, 158, 183, 222–3, 346, 386
Disraeli, 147
Distin family, 236, 420–1
  Henry, 238, 409, 422
Divided string parts, 23
Divior, 76, 83
Doke, 35
Dominick, 120
Domnich, 67, 76
Donizetti, 1, 2, 7
Dont, J., 252
  V., 256
Döring, 145
Dorn, 110, 142, 345, 362
Dortmund, 48
Dortu, 236
Dorus, 75, 93, 101
Dossion, 76, 92
Dotzauer, 119, 124, 133, 150
Double-bass, 392–398
  bow, 395
  compass, 395
  in England, 394
  in France, 81, 393
  in Germany, 392
  in Italy, 27, 394
  simplified parts, 74, 397

Double bassoon, 34–38, 42, 406
Dozer, 156
Dragonetti, 28, 37, 74, 166, 167, 171–2, 181, 185, 195, 196, 200, 207, 209, 213, 217, 225, 226, 294 330, 394, 398
Drechsler, 259, 368
Dresden
   Concerts, 125
   Court orchestra, 48, 116–125, 487, 488
   Old opera house, 12, pl. 5, 116
   Theatres, 116–117
Dressler, 181
Dressler, R., 149, 256
Dreyschock, 141
Drouet, 197
Drums, see Timpani
Drury Lane theatre, see London
Dual control of orchestra, 219, 220, 222, 292, 295, 308, 324
Dublin, 243, 244
Dubois, 77, 420
Dufrêsne, 101
Dugnazzi, 278
Duhême, 236, 280
Duk, 265
Duport, 88, 110
Dupuy, 279
Duret, 90
Durst, 256
Düsseldorf, 107, 154, 155–6
Duvernoy, Chas., 67, 69, 86
   Fred., 67, 69, 73, 76, 77, 88

EBELL, 156
Ebers, 169
Eberwein, 151, 153
Eck, 276
Eckert, 264
Edel, 120
Edinburgh, 245
Edinburgh Festival, 61
Eiser, 265
Eisert, 119
Eisner, 120, 277
Eliason, 200, 201, 220, 230
Elie, 186
Ella, 81, 86, 97, 99, 178, 195, 204, 205, 208, 227, 323, 384, 394
Elsner, 278
Elwart, 88, 90, 91
Engelke, 237
English Opera House, see London
Erkel, 266
Ernst, 153
Esser, 256, 259
Étienne, 287
Exeter Hall, see London
Eybler, 252, 253

FANARI, 277
Farinelli, 6
Farmer, 318

Faubel, 128
Federici, 6, 169
Félix Meritis, 282–3, pl. 18
Ferlendis, 173
Ferling, 149
Ferrari, 4
Feska, 4, 150, 152
Festa, 271, 272
Festivals, 245
Festival orchestras, 43, 60–63, 66
Fétis, 21, 74, 91, 177, 182, 185, 193, 199, 217, 269, 281, 322
Fioravanti, 6
Fischer, 173, 175 n.
Flack, 40 n., 181
Fladt, 128
Flageolet, 235, 407
Flotow, 3
Flügelhorn, 419, 420
Flute, 401–407
Flûte d'amour, 407
Fodor, 282
Forbes, 225, 226, 326, 330
Forestier, 77, 101
Forster, 157
Fougas, 83
France, provincial orchestras, 103–106
Franchomme, 74, 83, 92
Francœur, 72, 445
Frankenhausen Festival, 61
Frankfort opera, 49, 144–146
Fränzl, 126, 129, 144
Freemason's Hall, 160, 162
Freudenthal, 149
Frey, 152
Friedlowsky, J., 252, 254
   A., 256
Frinta, 265
Frisch, 241
Fröhlich, 445
Funke, 278
Fürstenau, A. B., 120, 145, 153
   M., 120
Furtwängler, 141

GABRIELSKI, 111
Gade, 136
Galeotti, 274
Gallay, 76, 83, 93
Gallini, 162
Gambaro, 83
Gambati bros., 167, 180
Gandini, 274
Gang, 283
Ganz, A., 203
   L., 110
   M., 111
   W., 188, 203, 375
Garcia, 286
Garde Nationale, 237, 238
Gardiner, 272
Garies, 111
Garnier, 75

Garret, 417
Gasse, 90
Gassner, 24, 31, 36, 37, 127, 276, 392, 446
Gaveaux, 5
Gebauer, E. F., 86
    F. R., 69, 75
    F. X., 251, 252
Gebler, 254
Geissler, 262
Gélinek, 74, 393
Gellert, 265
Generali, 6
Genoa, 274
Gensse, 280
Gentlemen's Concerts, Manchester, 243
Gerber, 298, 299
German opera houses, 15
Gesellschaft der Musikfreunde, see Vienna
Gestewitz, 117
Gevaert, 32, 394
Gewandhaus, see Leipzig
Ghent, 281, 282
Ghirardini, 278
Gide, 5
Gilles, 83
Girard, 73, 81, 82, 84, 86, 87, 92, 93, 94,
    100, 313, 373, 376
Glanville, 184
Gläser, 116, 253, 259, 260, 278, 306, 308, 368
Glinka, 1, 275, 276
Gloucester Festival, 61, 181
Gluck, 7, 45, 113, 454
Gnecco, 6
Godard, Arabella, 236
Godfrey, Chas., 195, 208
    Sir Dan, 247
Goebel, 156
Goffrié, 208, 236
Gontershausen, von, 32
Goodwin, 193
Goss, 207
Gotha, 48, 153
Göttingen, 49
Gottschalk, 121
Götzel, 120
Gouffé, 93, 393, 398
Grand National Concerts, 242, 390, 492
Grasset, 82, 295, 313, 376
Gratz, 265
Graun, 7, 108
Greatorex, T., 205, 206, 226, 318
    W., 206
Grenser, C. A., 133, 135, 138
    F. A., 135, 137
    F. W., 135
Grétry, 309, 454
Griebel, 111
Griesbach, A., 184
    F., 173, 174, 207, 210
    W., 209
Grimmer, 121
Grua, von, 126
Grutsch, 256

Gugel, 277
Gugielmi, 4
Guhr, 145, 258, 302, 361
Guillou, 75, 92
Gürrlich, 110, 343
Guymeyer, 213
Gyrowetz, 4, 255, 257, 306

HAASE, 121
Haake, 136
Habeneck, 68, 69, 73, 80, 81, 85, 90, 91,
    92, 94, pl. 3, 201, 222, 291, 303, 313,
    314, 353
    as conductor, 310, 312, 369–373
Habeneck, Jos., 69, 85
Häffner, 279
Hague, the, 49, 283, 284
Hainl, 104, 105, 313, 376
Halary, 42, 76, 77, 400
Halévy, 1, 2, 72, 408, 416, 426
Hallé, 93, 236, 243, 244, 375
Hallé orchestra, 247
Halliday, 412
Hamburg, Stadttheater, 50, 154
Hampel, 120
Hancock, 236
Handel, additional accompaniments, 428,
    457–461, 481
    Com. Festival, 37
    Festival, 61
    Oratorios, etc., 7, 35, 39, 63, 201
    Scores, 428
Handley, 236
Hanemann, 345
Hann, 195
Hanover court orchestra, 50, 149
Hanover Square Rooms, see London
Hanslick, 262, 308, 354
Hanssens (family), 280, pl. 19, 281
Hardy, 236
Harp, 45, 398
Harper, Chas., 179, 195, 203, 215, 236
    T. sen., 113, 129, 138, 167, 168, 179–180,
    197, 204, 207, 208, 210, 215, 218, 225,
    226, 229, 410, 411, 417
    T. jun., 215, 224, 230, 236
Harrington, 173
Harrison, 206
Hasemann, 150
Hasse, 7, 116
Hatton, 229
Haudeck, 120, 121, 122
Hauptmann, 43, 119, 139, 140, 150, 151,
    304, 336, 427, 461
Hausmann, 203, 236
Haydn, 1, 2, 15, 68
    Creation, 35, 36, 58, 61, 62, 63
    Oratorios, 7
    Seasons, 1, 35
    Scores and parts, 429, 432, 436
    Symphonies, 7, 9, 11, 39, 88, 90, 92, 93,
    94, 133, 205, 211

Haydn-Salomon Concerts, 25, 162, 173, 176, 206
Hechingen, 50, 154
Heckel, 37, 145, 400
Heinemeyer, 149
Heinrich, 287
Heinze, 135, 137, 156
Hellmesberger, G., 252, 256, 263
  jun., 149
Henneberg, 253
Henning, 110
Henri, 69, 86, 92
Herbst, 254
Her Majesty's Theatre, see King's Theatre, under London
Hérold, 3, 72, 82, 84, 86, 87, 426
Hesse, 156
Hiebendahl, 120
Hill, Henry, sen., 209
  Henry, 195, 203, 213, 224, 236
Hill, U. C., 287
Hiller, 5, 98, 136, 138, 156, 303, 348, 364
Himmel, 109
Hindle, 254, 393, 398
Hinterholzer, 127
Hirschfeld, 279
Hochmann, 265
Hodges, 287
Hoffman, 144
Hofmann, 153
Hofner, 265
Hogarth, 321, 325, 358
Höllmayer, 253
Holt, 236
Holmes (bassoon), 176, 210
Holmes, Ed., 112, 127, 128, 129, 134, 145, 147, 151, 216, 253, 257, 259, 264, 265, 292, 392
Holz, 262
Hook, 164
Hope, 220
Hopkins, E., 192
  G., 192
Horák, 35
Horn, alto and tenor, 420
  hand, 39, 76, 409, 410
  valve, 76, 93, 121, 124, 416, 417
Horns, four, 38–39
Horn, C. E., 164, 287
Horncastle, 207
Horton, 187, 188
Howell, 200, 203, 213, 236
Hradetzky, 253, 256
Hughes, 193, 202, 236
  F., 237
Hughes, R., 188
  S., 236
Hugot, 73, 86
Hummel, 4, 118, 151, 331
Hunt, 119
Huny, 86
Hürth, 253, 256
Hutschenruyer, Hutschenruijter, 283

Hüttner, 265
Hyde, J., 179, 207, 410
  W., 179, 411

INTEN, von, 137
Ireland, 173, 210
Irwin, 180, 215
Isouard, 5, 35, 42
Ista, 186, 188
Italian music, 5, 11
Italian opera houses, 15, 267, 268
Italian orchestration, 268
Itjen, 236

JACOBSON, 283
Jadin, 5, 78
Janatka, 265
Jancourt, 76, 83, 86, 236
Jannusch, 264, 407
Jansa, 189, 252
Janssen, 86
Jarrett, 203, 214, 236
Javault, 85, 86
Jenkinson, 37, 182
Jennings, 236
Jennizeck, 156
Jepp, 181
Joachim, 141, 142, 149, 152, 231, 266, 360
Jommelli, 143
Jullien, 14, 38, 53, 77, 98, 195, 220, 236
  as conductor, 377–382
  in Paris, 101, 102, 313
  Opera in London, 203
  Promenade concerts in London, 192, 202, 230–241, 409, 420

KABASIUS, 121
Kalliwoda, 5, 265
Kallusch, 265
Kandler, 272, 273
Kapellmeister, 108, 289, 292, 296, 302, 303
Karlsruhe court orchestra, 50, 152
Kastner, 33, 35, 36, 313, 338, 393, 407, 446
Kearns, 192
Keat, 417
Keating, Chas., 236
  (oboe) 208, 237
Keil, 153, 265
Keller, C., 143, 150
Keller, 276
Kelly, 164
Kenn, 76
Ketenus, 236
Keyboard-conductor, 169, 292–4, 318, 319
Keyed brass instruments, 410
Keyed bugle, 44, 412–413
Khayll, 252, 256
Kiel, 149
Kielbach, 214
Kies, 35
Kiesewetter, 209, 213, 215
King's Theatre, see London

Kittl, 266
Kleine, 282, 283
Klemm, 121
Klengel, 133, 135
Klepsch, 265
Kletrinski, 307
Klindera, 265
Klosé, 400, 406
Knyvett, 205, 206, 226, 318, 327
Koburg, 50, 153, 157
Koch, 265
Koch (Lexikon), 24, 31, 36, 392
Koch (Vienna), 35
Koenig, 101, 203, 234, 236
    Ad., 236
Koessel, 186, 188
Köhler, H., 132
    (London), 417
    (double-bass), 398
Kohne, 266
Königsberg, 50, 157
Kopitus, 265
Kotte, 120
Kraft, 143, 256
Krähmer, 252, 256
Kramer, C., 181 n., 209, 210
Kranz, 143, 155
Krebs, 118, 255, 363
Kretzschmer, 120
Kreubé, 84, 313
Kreutzer, Aug., 68
    Carl, 188
    Conradin, 3, 255, 260, 261, 306, 307, 308, 368
    Rud., 6, 11, 67, 68, 69, 72, 73, 78, 88, 313, 376
Krommer, 11
Krüger, G., sen., 143
    G., jun., 144
Kuhe, 266
Kuhlau, 278
Kuhn, 92
Kummer family, 119, 120
Kunze, 121
Kunzen, 144, 278
Kurpinski, 278
Küss, 35

Labarre, 84, 87, 313
Labbaye, 76
Labitzky, 242
Labro, 87
Lachner, F., 5, 127, 130, 152, 255, 258, 262, 263, 303, 308, 362, 368
    I., 127, 152, 153, 368
    V., 192
Lachnith, 453
Lafont, 88
Lahou, 77
    J. F. J., 280, 283
Lahoussaye, 84, 313
Lajarte, de, 447
Lampadius, 349

Lamy, 74, 398
Landgraf, 137
Landoni, 274
Lang, 128
Lange, 135
Lannay, 262
Lanner, 251
La Scala, see Milan
Launer, 73
Laurent, C., 229
Laurent, jun., 236, 420
Lauterbach, 120
Lavelli, 278
Lavenu, 203, 236
Lavigna, 6, 270
Lavigne, 83, 102, 175, 186, 188, 218, 236
Lazarus, 176, 195, 203, 208, 214, 236, 237
Leader, see Violinist-leader
Leander bros., 206, 210
Lebrun, 32, 173
    J., 111
Le Cerf, 102
Lefèvre, 67, 73, 75, 88
Legrande, 127, 128
Legros, 77, 92
Leibrock, 149
Leicester Festival, 61
Leipzig, Conservatoire, 17
    Euterpe Soc., 142
    Gewandhaus concerts, 8, 12, 13, 36, 131, pl. 6
    Gewandhaus orchestra, 12, 18, 51, 131–141
    publishers, 426
    Stadttheater, 51, 131, 141–2
Lelong, 101
Leloup, 236
Léonard, 86
    H., 101
Leplus, 75, 86
Lerey, 236
Leroy, 75
Lesueur, 45, 67, 68, 72
Leudet, 73
Levasseur, 73, 74
Leveque, 149
Lewy, E. C., 253, 256, 416
    J. R., 121, 124, 143
    R., 253, 256
Liége, 279, 281, 282
Lincke, 156, 254, 256
Lindemann, 155
Lindley, R., 28, 166, 167, 168, 171–2, 185, 195, 196, 197, 207, 208, 209, 213, 225, 226, 258, 330
    W., 173
Lindpaintner, 5, 118, 126, 127, 143, 303
    as conductor, 361–2
Ling, 174, 207
Lipinski, 118, 123, 124, 125
Lisbon, 285
Liszt, 1, 152, 262

Liverpool, 243
  Festival, 61
  Philharmonic, 244
Lobe, 13, 98, 127, 151, 303, 350
Loder, 197, 205, 209, 225, 226, 287, 292, 330
Loffelmann, 265
Lohse, 156
London
  Ancient Concert, 53, 204
  Argyll Rooms, 12, 160, 206, 210, 211
  Covent Garden, 52, 160, 163, 189–198, 489
  Drury Lane, 53, 160, 163, 198–204, pl. 13, 490
  English Opera House, 160, pl. 8, 163, 229
  Exeter Hall, 160, 162, 207, 208, 233
  Hanover Square Rooms, 12, 18, 160, 161, 162, 205, 206, 210, 221
  King's Theatre (Her Majesty's), 33, 51, 160, 162, pl. 9, 164–189, 488–9
  New Philharmonic Soc., 224, 362, 373
  Opera theatres, 15, 160
  Oratorio Concerts, 52, 196–8
  Philharmonic Soc., 8, 13, 52, 141, 208–225, 319, 477, 479, 490
  Promenade Concerts, 14, 192, 202, 226, 228–241
  Royal Academy of Music, 17, 53, 170, 227, 491
  Sacred Harmonic Soc., 207
  St. James's Hall, 162, 210
  St. Martin's Hall, 160, 162
  Societa Armonica, 225
  Vocal Concert, 53, 206
  Willis's Rooms, 160, 206
London Orchestra, The, 243
Lortzing, 3, 254, 255
Lotter, 253
Löwe, 5, 113, 187
Lower Elbe Festival, 37
Lower Rhine Festival, 61
Lübeck, 284
Lubin, St., 116
Lucas, 184, 207, 213, 222
Luft, 277
Luigini, 105
Lumbye, 278
Lutgen, 189, 236
Lutz, 128
Lutz, Meyer, 242
Lyon, 166
Lyons, 105

MACFARLANE, 419
Macfarren, 192
Machaczek, 265
Mackintosh, 113, 166, 167, 176, 192, 207, 210, 214
Madrid, 284
Maestro al piano (cembalo), 82, 169, 270, 292
  di Capella, 169, 292

Maffai, 188
Magdeburg, 54
Mahon, J., 175, 210
  W., 175
Maître de Musique, 67, 68, 292
Makers of wind instruments, 400
Maldere, van, 87
Malik, 265
Manchester, 243, 244
  Festival, 62
  Philharmonic, 54, 243
Manera, 101, 313, 376
Mangold family, 147, 148
Mann, 283
Mannheim, 54, 152
Manns, 247
Mapleson, 188
Marcziczek, 265
Mariotti, 180, 181, 215
Marpurg, 289
Marschner, 3, 5, 118, 142, 149, 303, 362
Marshall, 213
Martin, 188
Martini, 68
Marzoli, 83
Matthäi, 132–3, 134, 135, 136, 141, 301
Mattuschek, 253
Matys, 265
Maurer, 149, 276, 277
Maycock, 188, 236
Mayence, 54, 157
Mayr, 4
Mayseder, 252, 256
Mazas, 209
McDonald, 237
Meartine, 237
Meerts, 280
Megelin, 119
Méhul, 1, 2, 84, 86, 94, 426
Meifred, 76, 83, 92, 93, 400
Meiningen, 54, 151
Mellon, 195, 203, 236, 243
Mendelssohn, 1, 9, 15, 86, 222, 272
  Antigone, 192
  as conductor, 300, 303, 323, 348–352
  at Berlin, 110, 113, 351
Mendelssohn, at Düsseldorf, 155
  at the Gewandhaus, 136–141
  Elijah, 207
  at London, 215, 217, 220
  Midsummer Night's Dream, 43, 114, 173, 219, 443
  Overtures, 94
  Reformation Symphony, 36, 37
  Scores and parts, 427, 441
  Symphonies, 2, 93, 135, 215, 230
Mengal, J., 69, 76, pl. 1, 83, 92, 93
  M. J., 282
Mercadante, 6, 284
Mercadier, 86
Merk, 252, 256
Merlé, 86
Messer, 146

Messurier, 102
Methfessel, 148, 155, 264
Metzger, 127
Meyerbeer, 1, 2, 9, 72, 110, 183, 185, 426
 as conductor, 115
Milan, Canobbiana, 271
 Conservatoire, 17
 La Scala, Frontispiece, 19, 55, 270, pl. 17, 271
Mildner, 264
Military band, 42, 65, 417–18
 on stage, 44
Modena, 274
Mohr, 76, 77
Molineuf, 282
Molique, 127, 143, 236, 254
Montag, 151
Montéclair, 394
Monzani, T., 173
 jun., 166, 173
Moralt, 127, 129, 130, 185, 195, 208, 313
Morgenroth, 119
Mori, 166, 171, 185, 197, 206, 209, 215, 219, 225, 226, 243, 318, 330
Morini, 277
Morlacchi, 117, 123
Morris, 184
Mosca, 6
Moscheles, 6, 13, 69, 122, 134, 151, 213, 222, 231, 243, 283, 292, 367
Moscow, 55, 277
Mosel, 308
Moser, 41
Möser, 110
Mountain, 209
Mozart, 2, 4, 7, 260
 Don Giovanni, 184, 200, 264, 265
 Figaro, 45, 443
 Les Mystères d'Ísis, 78, 79, 453
 Operas in London, 454
 Orchestration, 481
 Overtures, 92, 94
 Requiem, 33, 40
 Scores and parts, 429, 435, 437, 442
Mozart, Symphonies, 7, 9, 39, 84, 90, 92, 93, 94, 133, 205, 211, 239
 Zauberflöte, 78, 253
Mühlenbruck, 116
Müller, 236, 265
 A., 253
 A. E., 133, 151
 Aug., 147, 395
 C. G., 135
 F., 153
 G., 154
 Ivan, 83, 150, 400, 406
 W., 259, 264, 308, 398
Müller family (Brunswick), 148
Munich Conservatoire, 17
 Court orchestra, 55, 125–130
 Odeon concerts, 12, 13, 55, 130
 Theatres, 126

Musard, 14, 57, 77, 101, 102, 228, 229, 230, 241, 313, 321, 376
Mutilation of operas, 453

Nabich, 236
Nadaud, 171, 185, 186, 187, 203, 236
Nadermann, 69
Nägeli, 284
Naples, Conservatoire, 17
 San Carlo, 18, 55, 271
Napoleon I, 45, 67, 117, 122
 III, 69
Nasolini, 169
Nau, 40 n., 41
Naumann, 117
Neate, 213
Negri (cond.), 229, 230
 (flute), 271
Nehrlich, 111
Neithardt, 305
Neukirchner, 143, 144
Newcastle Festival, 62
New Philharmonic Soc., see London
New Rooms, Tottenham St., 205
New York, 285–288
 Philharmonic, 287
Nicholson, A., 214
 Chas., 113, 166, 167, 173, pl. 10, 184, 207, 210, 217, 225, 328
Nicolai, 3
 as conductor, 306, 308, 369
 at Berlin, 110, 115, 263
 at Vienna, 249, 251, 256, 258, 263
Nicolini, 6
Nidezki, 278
Nikisch, 141
Noisy conducting, 272, 297, 307, 322, 336–7
Norblin, 69, 74, 92
Norton, 287
Norway, 279
Norwich Festival, 62
Novello, V., 209
Nowak, F., 265
Nowak, J., 265
Nürnberg, 55, 157

Oboe, 401–7
Oboe d'amore, 407
Octobasse, 238, 396
Odéon, see Munich, Paris
Odessa, 278
Offenbach, 85, 313
Onslow, 4, 92, 385
Opéra, see Paris
Opéra Comique, see Paris
Ophicleide, 34, 37, 38, 42, 43, 181, 234–5, 413
Oratorio Concerts, see London
Order of instruments in score, 443
Orchestral players in Germany, 157
 in London, 227, 247
 in Paris, 101

Orchestral Union, The, 243
Orchestration, Text books, 445
  retouching, 463
Orlandi, 6
Oswald, 154
Oury, 187
Oxford, 55
Ozi, 67, 73, 75

Pace, 417
Pacini, 6
Pacque, 236
Paër, 4, 67, 82, 117
Paisiello, 67, 68
Palsa, 111
Panizza, 270
Pantheon, 162
Paquis, 102
Paris
  Athénée musival, 100
  Concert de la Loge Olympique, 87, 88
  Concert des Amateurs, 87, 100
  Concert orchestras, 87
  Concert spirituel, 18, 20, 84, 87, 90
  Conservatoire, 17, 42, 68, 72, 73, 89, 90
  Exercices des élèves, 89, 313
  Gymnase musicale, 100
  Odéon, 71
  Opéra, 15, 16, 18, 70, 71, 79
  Opéra Comique, 57, 70, 71, 84–87, 493
  Opéra orchestra, 21, 39, 56, 71–82, 494
  Philharmonic Soc., 101
  Promenade Concerts, 101–103
  Publishers, 426
  Royal orchestra, 56, 67, 492, 493
  Rue de Cléry Concerts, 12, 57, 88–89
  Salle (Conservatoire), 12, 91
  Société des Concerts, 8, 11, 13, 17, 36,
    57, 70, 89–100, 493
  Société de Sainte-Cécile, 101
  Théâtre Italien, 21, 57, 70, 71, 82–84, pl. 3
  Theatres, 15 n., 70, 84
  Union Musicale, 101
Paris, G. A., 297
Parke, J., 174, 228
  W. T., 165, 167, 173, 192, 193, 197, 203,
    209, 212, 228
Partition d'intelligence, 447
Parts, symphonies, etc., 430
Pasdeloup, 101
Paur, 265
Pavart, 92
Pavesi, 6
Payer, 282, 304
Payton, 220
Pechatschek, 143, 149, 152
Pelitti, 417
Pellicia, 274
Pensam, 213
Percival, 186, 417
Percussion instruments, 45, 64
Percy, 417
Périnet, 400

Perry, 207, 227, 331
Persius, 11, 73, 313, 376
Peschel, 121
Pestalozzi, 284
Petersen, 155
Petit, 86
Petracchi, 169
Petrides bros., 177–8, 210, 214
Petrie, 285
Petschacher, 256
Pfau, 137
Pfundt, 137, 138
Philharmonic Soc., see London, Paris,
  Vienna
Phillips, H., 197, 201, 327
  W. L., 220
Piatti, 186, 189, 196, 203, 224, 236
Piccini, 7
Piccolo, 30
Pierre, 36
Pilati, 229, 241
Pillet, 101, 186, 236
Piringer, 262
Pisendel, 116
Pitch, 105, 470–472
Pixis, 264, 265
Planché, 163
Plantade, 68
Platt, 179, 195, 197, 203, 204, 208, 214, 218,
  229, 236
Platts, 182
Pleyel, 6, 432
Pluys, 186, 203
Pohland, 119
Pohle, 137
Pohlenz, 132, 135
Polledro, 118, 122, 272
Ponder, 181, 197, 208
Portagello, 6
Potdevin, 283
Potter, Cipriani, 53, 222
Poussard, 77, 93
Powell, 214, 225, 226
Praeger, 141, 149
Prague, conservatoire, 17, 264, 266
  Opera, 57, 264
Pratten, 213, 236
Preissing, 153
Prell, 149
Preumayr (Preymeyer), 177, 279
Prévost, 77
Price, 193
Prinz, 120
Pritchard, 192
Proch, 256, 260, 263
Professional Concert, 162, 206, 210, 212,
  226
Programmes, 13, 92, 133, 137, 211, 215
Promenade Concerts, see London, Paris
Prospère, 102, 195, 203, 234, 235, 236
Public concerts, 14
Puccita, 6
Pugni, 5

Puppo, 271
Puzzi, 37, 84, 178, 210, 214, 218, 225

QUANTZ, 7, 116, 392
Queisser, C. T., 40 n., 134, 135, 142
    F. B., 121
    J. G., 121

RABBONI, 270
Radicati, 169
Rae, 179, 214
Raimondi, 6
Raoux, M. A., 83
Rastrelli, J., 117
    V., 117
Rauch, 129, 130
Raumer, von, 98
Rauzzini, 173
Reeve, C., 171, 185, 192
Reeve, W., 164
Regent's bugle, 413
Rehearsal, 99, 203, 220, 224, 262, 355, 466–
    470
Reicha, 4
Reichardt, 78, 88, 90, 108, 150, 257, 260
Reichert, 236
Reichmans, 76, 92
Reinecke, 141
Reinhardt, 143, 145
Reissiger, 5, 118, 123, 124, 125, 133, 303,
    362
Rémusat, 86, 102, 188, 236
Reuling, 256, 263
Rey, 67, 72
Ribas, 173, 184, 195, 213, 224, 225
Richardson, 203, 229, 235, 236, 237
Richter, 360
Riedl, 400, 416
Ries, F., 4, 11, 307, 319
    H., 110, 116
Riemann, 151
Rietz, 5, 116, 141, 142, 156, 303, 364
Riga, 157
Righini, 109, 297
Riotte, 253
Ritter, 111, 152
Rivière, 77, 101, 102, 313, 381
Roberts, 237
Rode, 6, 73
Rodwell, 190
Roeckel, 118
Rohde, 153
Rolla, 118, 122, 270
Romberg, And., 143, 153, 155
    Anton, 256
    B., 110, 343
    H., 276, 277
Rombergs, The, 4, 5
Romédan, 86
Ronzoni, 278
Rose, C., 75
    E., 150
Rosenkranz, 254

Röser, 253
Rossini, 1, 2, 7, 72, 82, 169
    as conductor, 331
    Orchestration, 480, 482
    Scores, 426
Rotta, 274
Rothe, G., 120
    J. T., 33, 120
Rotterdam, 283
Rousseau, 116, 310
Rousselot ('cello), 167, 203, 213
    J. F., 76, 77, 93
Rovelli, 127
Rowe, 237
Rowland, 236
Royal Academy of Music, see London
Royal Household Band, 41, 180, 181
Royal Surrey Gardens, 231, 233
Rückner, 135
Rudolstadt, 58, 153
Rühlmann, 121
Russel, 190
Russian bassoon, 36

SACHSE, 150, 152
Sacred Harmonic Soc., see London
Sainton, 195, 203, 223, 236
Salieri, 4, 252, 307, 368
Sallantin, 73, 75, 88
Salle Valentino, 100
Salomon, 209, 212
Sapienza, 276
Sauzaz, 92
Savary, 83, 400, 406
Sax, 32, 43, 44, 396, 400, pl. 22, 420
Saxhorn, 43, 420–1
Saxophone, 203, 238, 407–409
Schäfer, 132
Schaufler, 143, 144
Schall, 278
Schelbe, 146
Schindelmeisser, 116, 145
Schindler, 91, 93, 95, 100, 260, 308, 368, 372
Schira, 202
Schlicht, 132
Schlick, 153
Schloesser, 147
Schlottman, 83
Scappa, 167, 169
Schmidt, 237
    (double-bass), 398
    G., 145
    H., 111
    J., 144
    J. G., 179
Schmied, 120
Schmitbach, 135, 137, 150
Schnabel, 156, 157
Schneider, F., 5, 118, 154, 361, 427
    G. A., 110
Schneitzhoeffer, 77, 92, 93
Schoengen, 181
Schöllnast, 35

Scholz, 277
Schott, 36
Schrade, 149
Schreiber, 36
Schreuss, 236
Schroeder, 220, 395
Schroek, 111
Schubert, Franz, 1, 4, 9, 262, 307
    C Major Symphony, 10, 137, 441
    Orchestration, 480
    Scores and parts, 441
    Symphonies, 2, 442
    Unfinished Symphony, 9, 442
Schubert, Franz (Dresden), 118
    F. A., 118
    A., 119
    J., 119
Schulz, 132
Schumann, 1, 134, 137, 138
    as conductor, 363
    Genoveva, 142
    Scores and parts, 441
    Symphonies, 2, 137
Schunke, 214
    A., 111
    C., 111, 214
    E., 143, 144
    G., 143, 150, 214, 279
    M., 143, 150
Schuppanzigh, 251, 252, 256, 260, 261, 306, 368
Schuster, G., 117
Schuster (Vienna), 35
Schwarz, A. G., 111
    C. G., 111
Schwenke, 155
Scores and parts, 424
Scores, opera and oratorio, 425
    Symphonies, etc., 430
Scottish orchestra, 247
Scraub, 264
Sebastiani, 271
Sedlatzek, 37, 256
Seemann, 150
Seghers, 92, 101, 313, 376
Seidel, 110
Seidl, 354, 374
Seidler, 110
Seligmann, 85, 101
Sellner, 252, 256, 264, 400
Serpent, 34, 36, 37, 42
Serpentcleide, 237
Serwaczynski, 266
Seuriot, 93
Severn, 220
Seydelmann, 117
Seyfried, 118, 253, 255, 262, 306, 368
Seymour, 184
    C., 244
Sharfenberg, 287
Sharp, 175, 210
Shaw, 199
Sherrington, 209, 213

Shield, 164
Sieber, 41
Silva, 274
Sina, 91
Singelée, 280
Simon, 77, 101
Sivori, 236
Slama, 256
Slide, 410
Slide-trumpet, see Trumpet
Smart, G., 78, 86, 112, 116, 122, 129, 135, 143, 147, 149, 150, 157, 190, 197, 199, 206, 209, 213, 218, 222, 226, 255, 260, 265, 300, 311, 318, 330
    as conductor, 388
Smart, H., 199
Smithies (Smithers), 181, 195, 197, 208, 215, 236
Snel, 280
Societa Armonica, see London
Société des Concerts, see Paris
Solére, 86
Solo violin, 73
Solo players, 73, 86
Sommers, 236
Sonnenberg, 236
Sonnleithner, 251, 308
Sor, 5
Sorne, 74
Souallé, 236, 238, 409
Soussmann, 277
South America, 288
Spagnoletti, 165, 166, 167, 169, 171, 184, 209, 215, 226
Spain, orchestras in, 284
Sperati, 171
Speyer, 68
Spohr, F., 150, 254
Spohr, Louis, 1, 12, 69, 78, 82, 83, 86, 128, 129, 132, 154, 182, 185, 211, 219, 222, 427, 449
    as conductor, 298, 300, 341-2
    at Berlin, 112
    at Cassel, 150
    at Frankfort, 144
    at Gotha, 153
    at London, 209, 212, 215, 226
    at Vienna, 254
    Berg-geist, 141, 266
    in Italy, 268, 272, 273
    in Russia, 276
Spontini, 1, 2, 72, 82, 334
    as conductor, 299, 322, 344-348
    at Berlin, 110, 112
    Fernand Cortez, 112, 147
    Olimpie, 31, 42, 44, 45
    Orchestration, 480
    Scores, 426
Spring, 277
Stadler, 252, 256, 259
Stadtmusiker, 28, 40, 107, 132, 136
Stamitz, 87
Steglich, 135, 137, 188

Stegmayer, 115, 116, 142
Stehle, 35
Steinbach, 151
Stenberger, 236
Stern, 154
Sterndale Bennett, 134, 136, 141, 151, 213, 222, 224
Stiebelt, 276
St. James's Hall, see London
St. Martin's Hall, see London
Stöber, 35, 257, 473
Stobilini, 274
Stockhausen, 91
Stockholm, 279
Stölzel, 111, 157, 400, 414
Stopping (brass instruments), 409
Stowiczek, 265
Strassburg, 58
Strauss, Johann (elder), 103, 241, 251, 324
Streather, 237
Strebinger, 256
Strinasacchi, 278
Stringed, bowed instruments, 391
String orchestra, 22–28
    Proportionate strength of parts, 28
Stuntz, 126, 127, 129, 300
Stuttgart, 58, 142–144
Suchanek, 121
Sundelin, 445
Suppé, 253, 260
Surman, 207, 331
Sutor, 149, 300
Swingman, 181
Switzerland, 284
Swoboda, 266, 445

Taborsky, 265
Tadolini, 274
Täglichsbeck, 154
Taillez, 304
Tamplini, 186, 187, 188
Tariot, 69
Taubert, 110
Tausch, 111
Telemann, 7
Temmler, 134, 135
Tempi, 139, 351, 365
Teusch, 128
Théâtre Italien, see Paris
Thirlwall, 193, 220, 236
Thomas, 193, 213
Three Choirs Festival, 37, 62, 176
Thurner, 145, 150, 283
Tietz, 119
Tilmant, 69, 82, 83, 84, 92, 94, 100, 313, 376
Time-beating, 135, 293, 311
Timm, 287
Timpani, 64, 422
Titze, 262
Toeschi, 87
Tolbecque, A. J., 92, 93, 185, 186, 187, 188, 203, 220, 225, 236
    J. B., 69, 83, 92, 101, 102

Toutain, 86
Trento, 6
Tretbar, 149
Trickler, 119
Triébert, C. L., 75, 83, 86, 407
    F., 75, 400, 406
Trombone, 40, 410
Trumpet, 410, 412
    keyed, 411
    slide, 179, 410, 411
    stop, 409, 412
    valved, 417
Trust, 195, 203, 237
Tuba, 34, 42, 43, 420
Tuczek, 156, 259
Tully, C., 210, 214
    J., 177, 210, 214
Tulou, 67, 68, 69, 75, 83, 91, 92, 217
Turbry, 100
Turin, 272
Turkish music, 88, 127, 271
Turle, 207
Turrschmidt, 111, 255

Uhlig, 119
Uhlmann, 35, 252, 256, 400, 416
Umlauf, 255, 261, 306, 307, 367, 368
Uniform or livery, 68, 107
Urhan, 73, 74, 91, 92

Vaccai, 6
Vachon, 110
Valentino, 68, 69, 73, 312, 313, 376
Valve-system, 409, 414–418, 421
Vandenbroeck, 76, 445
Vanhal, 87
Vaslin, 69, 92
Vauxhall Gardens, 228
Venice, 58, 272
Vény, 93
Verdi, 1, 2
Verroust, A. C. J., 76
    S., 75, 83
Vertovsky, 277
Viccari, 209
Vidal, 100
Vienna
    Augarten, pl. 15, 260
    Conservatoire, 17
    Double-bassoon in Vienna, 34
    Gesellschaft der Musikfreunde, 10, 11, 17, 250, 260, 470
    Imperial Court orchestra, 35, 58, 251, 252–3
    Josephstädter Theater, 250, 259, 307
    Kärntnerthor Theater, 35, 59, 249, pl. 16, 255–259, 265
    Leopoldstädter Theater, 250, 259, 265
    Orchestras for concerts, 260
    Philharmonic concerts, 13, 251, 262–264, 470
    Publishers, 426
    Spirituel Concerte, 59, 96, 251, 261, 470

Vienna (*cont.*)
  Theater-an-de-Wien, 250, pl. 15, 253–255
  Theatres, 15, 249
  Tonkünstler-Societät, 250, 307
Villaufret, 76
Viola d'amore, 26
Viola players, 26
Violas in Italian orchestras, 27
Violin-conductor, 73, 82, 84, 85, 169, 313, 431, 446
Violinist-leader, 171, 292, 306, 318, 332, 387. See also *Concertmeister, Chef d'orchestre, Capo d'orchestra*
Viotti, 6, 209
Virtuoses d'élite, 73, 86
Vivier, 236
Vobaron, 101
Vocal Concert, see London
Vogel, 236
Vogler, Abbé, 33, 146, 279
Vogt, 67, 68, 69, 75, 83, 86, 92, 174, 175, 407
Volkert, 259

WACH, 134, 135, 398
Wagner
  as conductor, 352–361
  at Dresden, 118, 122, 123–125, 352
  at London, 224, 355–360
  Flying Dutchman, 115, 427
  Lohengrin, 1, 31, 32, 38, 152, 427
  On conducting, 11, 123, 353
  on the Paris orchestra, 94, 95
  Rienzi, 115, 123, 290, 427
  Scores, 427
Wagner, *Tannhäuser*, 31, 82, 123, 427
  Tristan, 152
Wagner, C. J., 146
Wagstaff, 184, 186, 197
Walch, 153
Wallace, 3, 201, 202, 287
Wallis, 192
Ward, 422
Ware, 166, 192, 193, 197
Warsaw, 278
Watts, 186
Weber, C. M. von, 1, 2, 9, 79, 268, 450
  as conductor, 299, 300, 302, pl. 21, 342–344
  at Berlin, 112
  at Breslau, 156
  at Copenhagen, 278
  at Dresden, 117, 118, 122
  at London, 190, 193, 197, 215, 216
  Euryanthe, 96, 123
  Freischütz, 30, 109, 112, 114, 122, 123, 197, 199, 204, 455
  Oberon, 136, 190, 192, 193, 199
  Overtures, 64, 92, 94, 96, 226
  Scores and parts, 427
Weber, Bern. A., 109, 110, 112, 297
  D., 264, 265, 337

Weber, G., 128, 298
  Ed. von, 157, 300
Wednesday Concerts, 242
Weichsell, 171, 209, 213
Weidinger, 256, 411
Weidl, 265
Weigl, J., sen., 252
  J., jun., 252, 255, 257, 306, 368
Weimar court orchestra, 59, 151
Weingartner, 353, 365, 371
Werner, 282
Wesetsky, 265
Wesley, 197
Westenholz, F., 111
  W. F., 111
Westrop, 184
Wexall, 278
White, 236
Widemann, 279
Wiedebein, 148
Wiele, 150
Wieniawski, 239
Wieprecht, 43, 110, 133, 142, 400
Willent, 76, 83, 177
Williams, 33, 167, 214
Willis's Rooms, see London
Willman, 32, 33, 37, 113, 128, 166, **167, 168**, pl. 11, 175–6, 197, 210, 214, **217**
Willy, 213, 229, 230, 236
Winter, 4, 126, 129, 169
Winterbottom, A., 236
  J., 236
  W., 188, 236
Wood, 32
Woodham, 193
Wood-wind instruments, 401–409
Wood-wind group, 28–38
Wolfram, 118
Wooley, 318
Worcester Festival, 246
Wranitsky, 255
Wuille, 236, 409
Wunderlich, 75
Würfel, 255
Würzburg, 157
Wylde, 54

YORK, 244
York Festival, 63

ZEDLACZEK, 253
Zehrfeld, 135
Zeiss, 186, 188, 280
Zelenka, F., 265
  J., 265
Zelter, 304
Zillmann, 121
Zingarelli, 6, 68
Zinkeisen, 149
Zouaves, 237
Zumsteeg, 143